The **SAT**
Big Book
of Questions

Reading, Writing & Language, and Math

SUMMIT
EDUCATIONAL
GROUP

Focusing on the Individual Student

The Eden Projects   Summit commits to planting a tree for every printed course book. Visit **edenprojects.org** to learn more.

Copyright Statement

The SAT Big Book of Questions, along with all Summit Educational Group Course Materials, is protected by copyright. Under no circumstances may any Summit materials be reproduced, distributed, published, or licensed by any means.

Summit Educational Group reserves the right to refuse to sell materials to any individual, school, district, or organization that fails to comply with our copyright policies.

Third party materials used to supplement Summit Course Materials are subject to copyright protection vested in their respective publishers. These materials are likewise not reproducible under any circumstances.

Ownership of Trademarks

Summit Educational Group is the owner of the trademarks "Summit Educational Group" and the pictured Summit logo, as well as other marks that the Company may seek to use and protect from time to time in the ordinary course of business.

SAT is a trademark of The College Board.

All other trademarks referenced are the property of their respective owners.

CONTENTS

MATH – PASSPORT TO ADVANCED MATH

MATH – ADDITIONAL TOPICS IN MATH

ANSWER EXPLANATIONS

Preface

Since 1988, when two Yale University graduates started Summit Educational Group, tens of thousands of students have benefited from Summit's innovative, comprehensive, and highly effective test preparation. You will, too.

Effective test preparation requires the identification of specific areas for improvement and thorough practice. The *SAT Big Book of Questions* provides the material for both. You'll assess your strength in different sections and specific question types. Along with our *SAT Course Books*, these are the most effective, innovative, and comprehensive preparation tools available.

The Reading chapter is divided by section (Information & Ideas and Rhetoric) and subject (Fiction, Great Global Conversation, Science, and Social Studies). At the end of this chapter are passages focused on Data Graphics.

The Writing & Language chapter begins with Section Quizzes (Standard English Conventions and Expression of Ideas). The rest of the chapter is divided by question types. At the end of this chapter are passages focused on Data Graphics.

The Math content is divided into four chapters (Problem-Solving & Data Analysis, Heart of Algebra, Passport to Advanced Math, and Additional Topics in Math). Each Math chapter begins with a Section Quiz. The rest of each Math chapter is divided by question types.

We are confident that you will not find more complete or effective SAT supplementary material anywhere.

We value your feedback and are always striving to improve our materials. Please write to us with comments, questions, or suggestions for future editions at:

      edits@mytutor.com

Good luck, and have fun!

Section Quizzes

The purpose of this book's Section Quizzes is to identify the specific areas (question types) you need to work on to improve your scores.

Section Quizzes are groups of question types within the College Board's categories for the Math and Writing & Language Tests. These categories are represented by subscores on official SAT score reports (with the exception of Additional Topics in Math).

SAT Test	Category	Sample Question Types
Math	Problem-Solving & Data Analysis	Percents, Proportions, Probability
	Heart of Algebra	Equations, Absolute Value, Slope
	Passport to Advanced Math	Functions, Quadratic Equations
	Additional Topics in Math	Triangles, Circles, Trigonometry
Writing & Language	Standard English Conventions	Pronouns, Fragments, Commas
	Expression of Ideas	Organization, Transitions, Wordiness

The College Board's score reports do not provide subscores for the Reading Test's question categories. Reading passages in this book are divided based on two categories of question types, as defined by the College Board: Information & Ideas and Rhetoric.

Within each category, there are specific question types that appear on the SAT.

Assessment

Use the Section Quizzes to assess your proficiency with specific question types. For example, the Heart of Algebra quiz has a few of each question type within that category. You can use this quiz to measure your proficiency with question types such as equations, absolute value, and slope. Based on your performance, you can determine which question types you should practice more. If you cannot solve most of the absolute value questions in your Heart of Algebra Section Quiz, you should prioritize working through the later quiz that focuses exclusively on absolute value questions.

Effective preparation for the SAT requires determining which question types you should practice. Official SAT score reports do not provide assessments for specific question types (with the exception of Command of Evidence). Test scores give very broad assessments, and subscores give somewhat more useful assessments of content areas, but a more specific assessment is needed to customize your prep. This book's Section Quizzes bridge the gap between official subscores and specific question types so you can focus on what you need most to reach your highest potential on the test.

Review & Reflect

Following each set of Section Quizzes or Question Type Quizzes is a page for you to review and reflect on your performance. Use these pages to take notes on your experience of working through the previous quizzes.

Being aware of your own thought processes and skills is an important step toward improvement.

Consider and note the following:

❑ With which questions did you feel **confident**?

❑ With which questions did you **struggle**?

❑ Were you **surprised** by any of the questions?

❑ Did you have to **guess** on any questions?

❑ Did any of the questions take you a **long time** to answer?

❑ Did you spot any **tricks** or "attractors" in the questions?

❑ Did you make any careless **mistakes** or misread any questions?

❑ Do you feel that there are **underlying skills** you need to learn or strengthen before you can confidently answer some of the questions?

❑ Any other notes?

Math Reference

On official SATs, the formulas and rules below appear at the beginning of every Math section.

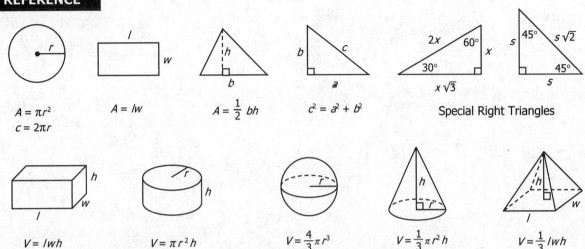

REFERENCE

$A = \pi r^2$
$c = 2\pi r$

$A = lw$

$A = \frac{1}{2} bh$

$c^2 = a^2 + b^2$

Special Right Triangles

$V = lwh$

$V = \pi r^2 h$

$V = \frac{4}{3}\pi r^3$

$V = \frac{1}{3}\pi r^2 h$

$V = \frac{1}{3}lwh$

The number of degrees of arc in a circle is 360.
The number of radians of arc in a circle is 2π.
The sum of the measures in degrees of the angles of a triangle is 180.

Math Grid-Ins

Grid-in questions are just like the multiple-choice questions without the multiple answer choices. Instead of providing answer choices, these questions require you to grid an answer into a set of ovals.

Mixed numbers must be gridded as improper fractions or decimals. Decimals must be gridded to the highest degree of accuracy possible. In other words, an answer of 0.6666... should be gridded as .666 or .667 or 2/3. .66 or .67 will be marked wrong. Some grid-in questions may have more than one correct answer; you need to grid in only one of the correct answers.

Calculators

On official SATs, one of the two Math sections does not allow usage of a calculator.

In this book, questions that do not allow usage of a calculator are noted with this symbol: 🖩

Reading

- ☐ **Information & Ideas**
  - ○ Fiction
  - ○ Great Global Conversation
  - ○ Science
  - ○ Social Studies

- ☐ **Rhetoric**
  - ○ Fiction
  - ○ Great Global Conversation
  - ○ Science
  - ○ Social Studies

- ☐ **Data Graphics**

Information & Ideas – Fiction – Passage 1

This passage is adapted from "The Overcoat" by Nikolai Gogol.

It would be difficult to find another man who lived so entirely for his duties. It is not enough to say that Akakiy laboured with zeal: no, he laboured with love. In his copying, he found a varied and agreeable
5 employment. Enjoyment was written on his face: some letters were even favourites with him; and when he encountered these, he smiled, winked, and worked with his lips, till it seemed as though each letter might be read in his face, as his pen traced it. If
10 his pay had been in proportion to his zeal, he would, perhaps, to his great surprise, have been made even a councillor of state. But he worked, as his companions, the wits, put it, like a horse in a mill.

Moreover, it is impossible to say that no
15 attention was paid to him. One director being a kindly man, and desirous of rewarding him for his long service, ordered him to be given something more important than mere copying. So he was ordered to make a report of an already concluded
20 affair to another department: the duty consisting simply in changing the heading and altering a few words from the first to the third person. This caused him so much toil that he broke into a perspiration, rubbed his forehead, and finally said, "No, give me
25 rather something to copy." After that they let him copy on forever.

Outside this copying, it appeared that nothing existed for him. He gave no thought to his clothes: his undress uniform was not green, but a sort of
30 rusty-meal colour. The collar was low, so that his neck, in spite of the fact that it was not long, seemed inordinately so as it emerged from it, like the necks of those plaster cats which wag their heads, and are carried about upon the heads of scores of image
35 sellers. And something was always sticking to his uniform, either a bit of hay or some trifle. Moreover, he had a peculiar knack, as he walked along the street, of arriving beneath a window just as all sorts of rubbish were being flung out of it: hence he
40 always bore about on his hat scraps of melon rinds and other such articles. Never once in his life did he give heed to what was going on every day in the street; while it is well known that his young brother officials train the range of their glances till they can
45 see when any one's trouser straps come undone upon the opposite sidewalk, which always brings a malicious smile to their faces. But Akakiy Akakievitch saw in all things the clean, even strokes of his written lines; and only when a horse thrust his
50 nose, from some unknown quarter, over his shoulder, and sent a whole gust of wind down his neck from his nostrils, did he observe that he was not in the middle of a page, but in the middle of the street.

Even at the hour when the grey St. Petersburg
55 sky had quite dispersed, and all the official world had eaten or dined, each as he could, in accordance with the salary he received and his own fancy; when all were resting from the departmental jar of pens, running to and fro from their own and other people's
60 indispensable occupations, and from all the work that an uneasy man makes willingly for himself, rather than what is necessary; when officials hasten to dedicate to pleasure the time which is left to them, one bolder than the rest going to the theatre; another,
65 into the street looking under all the bonnets; another wasting his evening in compliments to some pretty girl, the star of a small official circle; another—and this is the common case of all—visiting his comrades on the fourth or third floor, in two small rooms with
70 an ante-room or kitchen, and some pretensions to fashion, such as a lamp or some other trifle which has cost many a sacrifice of dinner or pleasure trip; in a word, at the hour when all officials disperse among the contracted quarters of their friends, to play whist,
75 as they sip their tea from glasses with a kopek's worth of sugar, smoke long pipes, relate at times some bits of gossip which a Russian man can never, under any circumstances, refrain from, and, when there is nothing else to talk of, repeat eternal
80 anecdotes about the commandant to whom they had sent word that the tails of the horses on the Falconet Monument had been cut off, when all strive to divert themselves, Akakiy Akakievitch indulged in no kind of diversion. No one could ever say that he had seen
85 him at any kind of evening party. Having written to his heart's content, he lay down to sleep, smiling at the thought of the coming day—of what God might send him to copy on the morrow.

Thus flowed on the peaceful life of the man,
90 who, with a salary of four hundred rubles, understood how to be content with his lot; and thus it would have continued to flow on, perhaps, to extreme old age, were it not that there are various ills strewn along the path of life for titular councillors as well as for
95 private, actual, court, and every other species of councillor, even for those who never give any advice or take any themselves.

1

Which choice best summarizes the passage?

A) A man is extremely devoted to his work and abstains from most everything else.

B) A man is distracted by his work when he would rather engage in more entertaining activities.

C) A man who gets no joy out of life wonders why he is so unlike the people around him.

D) A man refuses a promotion because he is waiting for other opportunities.

2

As used in line 12, "councillor" means

A) lawyer.

B) psychologist.

C) political figure.

D) advocate.

3

According to the passage, which of the following best describes Akakiy?

A) overpaid

B) appreciated

C) discontent

D) unenthusiastic

4

Which choice provides the best evidence for the answer to the previous question?

A) Lines 9-10 ("If...zeal")

B) Lines 2-4 ("It...love")

C) Lines 14-15 ("Moreover...him")

D) Line 5 ("Enjoyment...face")

5

According to lines 15-18, Akakiy's boss

A) gave him a new job because he wasn't good at copying.

B) wanted to give him a harder job.

C) thought he worked too hard.

D) wanted to promote him because he had done the same job well for many years.

6

What does the author suggest when he states that "Akakiy Akakievitch saw in all things the clean, even strokes of his written lines" (lines 47-49)?

A) He was always thinking about his work.

B) He compared everything to literature.

C) He had a problem with his eyesight.

D) He was anxious about getting his work done.

7

What choice provides the best evidence for the answer to the previous question?

A) Lines 22-24 (This...forehead")

B) Lines 24-25 ("No...forever")

C) Lines 27-28 ("Outside...him")

D) Lines 41-43 ("Never...street")

8

As used in line 32, "inordinately" most nearly means

A) disproportionately.

B) extraneously.

C) inexplicably.

D) unoriginally.

9

It is implied in the last paragraph that

A) Akakiy lived the rest of his life in peace.

B) Akakiy earned a salary of four hundred rubles.

C) all councillors have misfortunes.

D) Akakiy will experience hardships.

10

The main idea of the fourth paragraph (lines 54-88) is that

A) Akakiy does not need anything other than his work to make him happy.

B) Akakiy's peers enjoyed life more than he did.

C) there are many ways that workers spend their leisure time.

D) Akakiy should do more than just work.

Information & Ideas – Fiction – Passage 2

This passage is adapted from "Caline" by Kate Chopin.

The sun was just far enough in the west to send inviting shadows. In the centre of a small field, and in the shade of a haystack which was there, a girl lay sleeping. She had slept long and soundly, when
5   something awoke her as suddenly as if it had been a blow. She opened her eyes and stared a moment up in the cloudless sky. She yawned and stretched her long brown legs and arms, lazily. Then she arose, never minding the bits of straw that clung to her black hair,
10 to her red bodice, and the blue cotonade skirt that did not reach her naked ankles.

The log cabin in which she dwelt with her parents was just outside the enclosure in which she had been sleeping. Beyond was a small clearing that
15 did duty as a cotton field. All else was dense wood, except the long stretch that curved round the brow of the hill, and in which glittered the steel rails of the Texas and Pacific road.

When Caline emerged from the shadow she saw
20 a long train of passenger coaches standing in view, where they must have stopped abruptly. It was that sudden stopping which had awakened her; for such a thing had not happened before within her recollection, and she looked stupid, at first, with
25 astonishment. There seemed to be something wrong with the engine; and some of the passengers who dismounted went forward to investigate the trouble. Others came strolling along in the direction of the cabin, where Caline stood under an old gnarled
30 mulberry tree, staring. Her father had halted his mule at the end of the cotton row, and stood staring also, leaning upon his plow.

There were ladies in the party. They walked awkwardly in their high-heeled boots over the rough,
35 uneven ground, and held up their skirts mincingly. They twirled parasols over their shoulders, and laughed immoderately at the funny things which their masculine companions were saying. They tried to talk to Caline, but could not understand the French
40 patois with which she answered them. One of the men—a pleasant-faced youngster—drew a sketch book from his pocket and began to make a picture of the girl. She stayed motionless, her hands behind her, and her wide eyes fixed earnestly upon him. Before
45 he had finished there was a summons from the train; and all went scampering hurriedly away. The engine screeched, it sent a few lazy puffs into the still air, and in another moment or two had vanished, bearing its human cargo with it.
50 Caline could not feel the same after that. She looked with new and strange interest upon the trains of cars that passed so swiftly back and forth across her vision, each day; and wondered whence these people came, and whither they were going.
55 One day she walked miles down the track to talk with the old flagman, who stayed down there by the big water tank. Yes, he knew. Those people came from the great cities in the north, and were going to the city in the south. He knew all about the city; it
60 was a grand place. He had lived there once. His sister lived there now; and she would be glad enough to have so fine a girl as Caline to help her cook and scrub, and tend the babies. And he thought Caline might earn as much as five dollars a month, in the
65 city.

So she went; in a new cotonade, and her Sunday shoes; with a sacredly guarded scrawl that the flagman sent to his sister.

The woman lived in a tiny, stuccoed house, with
70 green blinds, and three wooden steps leading down to the banquette. There seemed to be hundreds like it along the street. Over the house tops loomed the tall masts of ships, and the hum of the French market could be heard on a still morning.
75 Caline was at first bewildered. She had to readjust all her preconceptions to fit the reality of it. The flagman's sister was a kind and gentle task-mistress. At the end of a week or two she wanted to know how the girl liked it all. Caline liked it very
80 well, for it was pleasant, on Sunday afternoons, to stroll with the children under the great, solemn sugar sheds; or to sit upon the compressed cotton bales, watching the stately steamers, the graceful boats, and noisy little tugs that plied the waters of the
85 Mississippi. And it filled her with agreeable excitement to go to the French market, where the handsome Gascon butchers were eager to present their compliments and little Sunday bouquets to the pretty Acadian girl; and to throw fistfuls of lagniappe
90 into her basket.

When the woman asked her again after another week if she were still pleased, she was not so sure. And again when she questioned Caline the girl turned away, and went to sit behind the big, yellow cistern,
95 to cry unobserved. For she knew now that it was not the great city and its crowds of people she had so eagerly sought; but the pleasant-faced boy, who had made her picture that day under the mulberry tree.

1

When Caline's employer asks how Caline likes living in the city, which words best characterize her initial response?

A) Neutral and cautious
B) Confused and concerned
C) Uncertain and revelatory
D) Positive and confident

2

Which choice provides the best evidence for the answer to the previous question?

A) Lines 66-68 ("So she went… to his sister.")
B) Lines 75-76 ("She had to… reality of it.")
C) Lines 79-85 ("Caline liked… Mississippi.")
D) Lines 95-98 ("For she … mulberry tree.")

3

Which of the following is the best description of events in the passage?

A) Caline is intrigued by the trains, seeks information about their destinations, and accepts an invitation to live with a relative.
B) Caline becomes interested in the big city, goes looking for a job, and finds fulfilment in her new position.
C) Caline has an unusual experience, follows her interest to the big city, and realizes she made an incorrect assumption.
D) Caline is alarmed by a large event, grapples with the decision to move, and decides she's better off away from home.

4

Which is the most effective way to describe Caline compared to the ladies that get off the train?

A) She is unrefined, and the women appear sophisticated.
B) She is uneducated, and the women are learned.
C) She is hopeful, and the women seem jaded.
D) She is fanciful, and the women are practical.

5

What effect does the arrival of the train passengers have on Caline?

A) She's startled by their arrival and avoids them.
B) She's interested in them and engages with them.
C) She's concerned that they will disrupt her day-to-day life.
D) She avoids speaking with them because of a language barrier.

6

What is the main idea of the last paragraph?

A) The city is a lonely place for women, especially women from the country.
B) Caline will never be reunited with the boy she sought.
C) Caline made a mistake in chasing the feeling left by a fleeting encounter.
D) Caline's employer has purposefully made Caline feel foolish.

7

Based on the fourth paragraph (lines 33-49), the boy and Caline appear to relate to one another in which way?

A) The boy sees Caline as an object of artistic study, while their exchange deeply affects Caline.
B) The boy observes Caline in a technical way, while his actions mildly concern Caline.
C) The boy considers Caline to be lower class, while the boy's behavior leads Caline to believe he's wealthy.
D) The boy notices Caline, but doesn't pay her any attention, while he becomes an object of obsession for Caline.

8

Based on the passage, what does Caline's family do to make money?

A) They farm cotton.
B) They raise animals.
C) They work on the train lines.
D) They are housekeepers.

9

In the passage, what is the meaning of the word "stupid" in line 24?

A) Disorderly
B) Unintelligent
C) Startled
D) Simple

10

Based on the passage, a "cotonade", as mentioned in line 66, is most likely what?

A) A life plan
B) An item of clothing
C) A bundle of cotton
D) A train car

Information & Ideas – Fiction – Passage 3

This passage is adapted from "His Smile" by Susan Glaspell.

She couldn't get on the train that would take her back to that house to which Howie would never come again. Once more it all seemed slipping from her. There must be something. As a frightened child runs
5　for home, she turned to that place where—for at least a moment—it was as if Howie were there.

She went to the telegraph office and wired the company that sent out "The Cross of Diamonds," asking where that film could be seen. She was
10　excited when she had decided to do this. It lifted her out of the nothingness. From this meager thing her great need could in a way create the feeling that she was going to meet Howie. Once more she would see him do that thing which was so like him as to bring
15　him back into life. Why should she turn from it? What were all the other things compared with this thing? This was one little flash of life in a world that had ceased to be alive.

So again that night, in the clothes he had most
20　liked, she went for that poor little meeting with her husband—so pitifully little, and yet so tremendous because it was all she would ever have. Again she sat in a big, noisy place with many jostling, laughing people—and waited to see Howie. She forgot that the
25　place had ugly red walls and sickly green lights; she could somehow separate herself from harsh voices and smells—for she was here to meet Howie!

The picture had begun. She had to wait until almost half of it had passed before her moment came.
30　The story was a tawdry, meaningless thing about the adventures of two men who had stolen a diamond cross—a strange world into which to come to find Howie. Chance had caught him into it—he was one of the people passing along a street which was being
35　taken for the picture. His moment was prolonged by his stopping to do the kind of thing Howie would do, and now it was as if that one moment was the only thing saved out of Howie's life. They who made the picture had apparently seen that the moment was
40　worth keeping—they left it as a part of the stream of life that was going by while the detective of their story waited for the men for whom he had laid a trap. The story itself had little relation to real things—yet chance made it this vehicle for keeping something of
45　the reality that had been Howie—a disclosing moment captured unawares.

She had known she ought to stop following the picture around, she had even told herself this would be the last time she would come to see it—but to feel
50　it wouldn't any longer be there to be seen—that even this glimpse of Howie would go out—go out as life goes out! She sat up straight and cleared her throat.

She would have to leave. She must get air. But she looked to see where they were. Not far now. She
55　might miss Howie! With both hands she took hold of the sides of the seat. She was not going to fall forward! Not suffocating. Not until after she had seen him.

Now. The detective has left the hotel—he is
60　walking along the street. He comes to the cigar-store door, and there steps in to watch. And there comes the dog! Along comes the little dog—pawing at his muzzle. He stops in distress in front of the cigar-store. People pass and pay no attention to the dog—
65　there on the sidewalk. And then—in the darkened theater her hands go out, for the door has opened—and she sees her husband! Howie. There. Moving as he always moved! She fights back the tears that would blur him. That dear familiar way he moves! It
70　is almost as if she could step up and meet him, and they could walk away together. He starts to go the other way. Then he sees the dog. He goes up to him; he is speaking to him, wanting to know what is the matter. She can fairly hear the warmth and kindness
75　of his voice as he speaks to the little dog. He feels of the muzzle—finds it too tight; he lets it out a notch. Dear Howie. Of course he would do that. No one else had cared, but he would care. Then he speaks to the dog—pats him—tells him he is all right now. Then
80　Howie turns away. But the dog thinks he will go with this nice person! Howie laughs and tells him he can't come. A little girl has come across the street. Howie tells her to keep the dog from following him. Then again he turns to go. But just before he passes from
85　sight the child calls something to him, and he looks back over his shoulder and smiles. She sees again the smile that has been the heart of her life. Then he passes from sight.

She never left her seat at once, as if moving
90　would break a spell. For a little while after she had seen it, his smile would stay with her. Then it would fade, as things fade in the motion pictures. Somehow she didn't really have it. That was why she had to keep coming—constantly reaching out for something
95　that was not hers to keep.

When her moment had gone, she rose and walked down the aisle. It was very hard to go away tonight. Only for an instant Howie's smile had brought her into life. It was gone now. It had passed.

1

Based on the passage, the narrator's attitude toward her husband can best be described as

A) indifferent and distant.
B) extremely attached and devoted.
C) reluctantly loving.
D) overly obsessive.

2

According to the passage, what happened to the woman's husband?

A) He left her.
B) He is away on a trip.
C) He is missing.
D) He passed away.

3

Which choice provides the best evidence for the answer to the previous question?

A) Lines 1-3 ("She couldn't... come again")
B) Lines 5-6 ("she turned to... were there")
C) Lines 13-15 ("Once more... into life")
D) Lines 19-21 ("So again... her husband")

4

As used in line 27, "meet" most nearly means

A) date.
B) see.
C) encounter.
D) join.

5

The statement in line 33, "chance had caught him into it" refers to

A) a once-in-a-lifetime chance to star in a movie.
B) being included in the movie by accident.
C) a chance to be a hired extra in a movie.
D) being caught in a robbery.

6

According to the sixth paragraph, what kind of man was Howie?

A) Kind and compassionate
B) Gentle but standoffish
C) Playful and nosy
D) Cheerful but private

7

It can be logically inferred from the passage that the woman keeps going to see "The Cross of Diamonds" because

A) she wants to support her husband's career.
B) she greatly enjoys the whole film.
C) she can't let go of her husband.
D) she meets her husband there.

8

Which choice provides the best evidence for the answer to the previous question?

A) Lines 22-24 ("Again she... see Howie")
B) Lines 43-46 ("The story... unawares")
C) Lines 86-87 ("She sees... her life")
D) Lines 93-95 ("That was... to keep")

9

As used in line 51, "go out" most nearly means

A) exit.
B) date.
C) cease.
D) snuff.

10

The questions the narrator asks in lines 15-17 suggest that

A) she recognizes some people would criticize her behavior.
B) she does not know what she'll do to stay busy.
C) Howie does not want her to see the movie.
D) she and Howie may end their marriage.

Information & Ideas – Fiction – Passage 4

This passage is adapted from "Round the Red Lamp"
by Sir Arthur Conan Doyle.

My first interview with Dr. James Winter was
under dramatic circumstances. It occurred at two in
the morning in the bedroom of an old country house.
I kicked him twice on the white waistcoat and
5 knocked off his gold spectacles, while he with the aid
of a female accomplice stifled my angry cries in a
flannel petticoat and thrust me into a warm bath.
From this time onwards the epochs of my life were
the periodical assaults which Dr. Winter made upon
10 me. He vaccinated me; he cut me for an abscess; he
blistered me for mumps. It was a world of peace and
he the one dark cloud that threatened. But at last there
came a time of real illness—a time when I lay for
months together inside my wickerwork-basket bed,
15 and then it was that I learned that that hard face could
relax, that those country-made creaking boots could
steal very gently to a bedside, and that that rough
voice could thin into a whisper when it spoke to a
sick child.

20 And now the child is himself a medical man, and
yet Dr. Winter is the same as ever. I can see no
change since first I can remember him, save that
perhaps the brindled hair is a trifle whiter, and the
huge shoulders a little more bowed. That big back of
25 his has curved itself over sick beds until it has set in
that shape. His face is of a walnut brown. It looks
smooth at a little distance, but as you approach him
you see that it is shot with innumerable fine wrinkles
like a last year's apple.

30 But it was only when I had myself become a
medical man that I was able to appreciate how
entirely he is a survival of a past generation. Fifty
years have brought him little and deprived him of
less. Vaccination was well within the teaching of his
35 youth, though I think he has a secret preference for
inoculation. Bleeding he would practice freely but for
public opinion. Chloroform he regards as a dangerous
innovation, and he always clicks with his tongue
when it is mentioned. He has even been known to
40 refer to the stethoscope as "a new-fangled French
toy." He carries one in his hat out of deference to the
expectations of his patients. He is so very much
behind the day that occasionally, as things move
round in their usual circle, he finds himself, to his
45 bewilderment, in the front of the fashion. Dietetic
treatment, for example, had been much in vogue in
his youth, and he has more practical knowledge of it
than any one whom I have met. Massage, too, was
familiar to him when it was new to our generation.

50 We made him president of our branch of the
British Medical Association, but he resigned after the
first meeting. "The young men are too much for me,"

he said. "I don't understand what they are talking
about." Yet his patients do very well. He has the
55 healing touch—that magnetic thing which defies
explanation or analysis, but which is a very evident
fact nonetheless. His mere presence leaves the patient
with more hopefulness and vitality. The sight of
disease affects him as dust does a careful housewife.
60 It makes him angry and impatient. "Tut, tut, this will
never do!" he cries, as he takes over a new case. He
would shoo Death out of the room as though he were
an intrusive hen. But when the intruder refuses to be
dislodged, when the blood moves more slowly and
65 the eyes grow dimmer, then it is that Dr. Winter is of
more avail than all the drugs in his surgery. Dying
folk cling to his hand as if the presence of his bulk
and vigour gives them more courage to face the
change; and that kindly, windbeaten face has been the
70 last earthly impression which many a sufferer has
carried into the unknown.

When Dr. Patterson and I—both of us young,
energetic, and up-to-date—settled in the district, we
were most cordially received by the old doctor, who
75 would have been only too happy to be relieved of
some of his patients. Very shortly afterwards the
epidemic of influenza broke out, and we were all
worked to death. One morning I met Patterson on my
round, and found him looking rather pale and fagged
80 out. He made the same remark about me. I was, in
fact, feeling far from well, and I lay upon the sofa all
the afternoon with a splitting headache and pains in
every joint. As evening closed in, I could no longer
disguise the fact that the scourge was upon me, and I
85 felt that I should have medical advice without delay.
It was of Patterson, naturally, that I thought, but
somehow the idea of him had suddenly become
repugnant to me. I thought of his cold, critical
attitude, of his endless questions, of his tests and his
90 tappings. I wanted something more soothing—
something more genial.

"Mrs. Hudson," said I to my housekeeper, would
you kindly run along to old Dr. Winter and tell him
that I should be obliged to him if he would step
95 round?"

She was back with an answer presently. "Dr.
Winter will come round in an hour or so, sir; but he
has just been called in to attend Dr. Patterson."

1

Based on the passage, when does the narrator first encounter Dr. James Winter?

A) When the narrator becomes a doctor and is trained by Dr. Winter
B) When Dr. Winter becomes the president of the British Medical Association
C) When the narrator is sick and stuck in bed for several months
D) In the middle of the night, when the narrator is a small child

2

Which of the following does the narrator use to describe the physical appearance of Dr. Winter?

A) A healing touch
B) A piece of aged fruit
C) A disruptive bird
D) A cautious homemaker

3

Overall, how does the passage characterize Dr. Winter's skills as a doctor?

A) Old-fashioned but effective
B) Outdated and problematic
C) Modern and comprehensive
D) Ineffectual but soothing

4

How does the narrator's opinion of Dr. Winter change from the beginning of the passage?

A) As an adult, the narrator is concerned for the doctor, and, when he was a small child, he had fond feelings for him.
B) As a medical professional, the narrator depends on the doctor, and, as a patient, the narrator will only seek treatment from him.
C) As a child, the narrator understood that the doctor cared for him, and, as a grown man, he realizes the doctor is generally surly.
D) As a young child, the narrator feared the doctor, and, as an adult, the narrator respects his success.

5

For what reason does the narrator decide not to request Dr. Patterson for medical treatment?

A) He discovers that Dr. Patterson is ill and can't see him.
B) He doesn't consider Dr. Patterson to be knowledgeable enough to treat his ailment.
C) He is disinterested in Dr. Patterson's technical manner.
D) He generally prefers Dr. Winter whenever possible.

6

Which of the following statements best summarizes the main idea of the passage as a whole?

A) A doctor can be highly trained, but there is more to being a doctor than medical knowledge.
B) Every doctor is different, having his or her own strengths and weaknesses.
C) It's crucial for medical professionals to be aware of and able to use innovative treatments.
D) Older doctors are more likely to misunderstand their patients.

7

What does the last paragraph imply about Dr. Winter?

A) He is an ineffective but busy clinician.
B) His services are preferred by other doctors.
C) He is in high demand in the winter.
D) Mrs. Hudson does not find him helpful.

8

When the narrator describes Dr. Winter calling a stethoscope "a new-fangled French toy," what can you infer about Dr. Winter's opinion of this medical device?

A) He finds it to be a useful new tool.
B) He thinks it is too difficult to use.
C) He feels that it will be fun to use.
D) He deems it unnecessary.

9

In the context of the passage, "scourge" (line 84) most nearly means

A) cleanser.
B) blessing.
C) whip.
D) affliction.

10

In the context of the first paragraph, what is the best synonym for "epochs" (line 8)?

A) Periods
B) Troubles
C) Ailments
D) Struggles

Information & Ideas – Fiction – Passage 5

This passage is adapted from "Martand" by N. Sahgal.

There was a crowd as usual outside Martand's clinic next morning, looking torpidly, dully at me as I walked through. Flies, dust, heavy, hopeless heat. Another day of learning to love it, I thought, and
5 another minute till I open that door to Martand.

He was sitting at his desk, his sleeves rolled up, his feet in slippers, his stethoscope still around his neck. He had forgotten to take it off, like he sometimes forgot to eat, and continually forgot the
10 huge dishevelment around him. He asked his assistant to bring some coffee. "Sorry the cup isn't very elegant," he said when it came.

He was always saying things like that. Sorry, when he repaid a debt, about handing me grubby-
15 looking change or a tattered note. Sorry that we could not see the hills from his window—there were none to see. There was only a grim growing mass of humanity, almost machine-like in its menacing immobility as it waited. I couldn't see these people as
20 individuals any more. It was it. Waiting for cholera shots, for rations, for clothes, for space, for air, for life, for hope, as if it could do nothing, nothing for itself. A monster robot seeking succor, devouring the pitifully little we had.
25 "Do you think the kingdom of heaven is a germ-free place?" asked Martand, giving me his smile over his coffee cup.

I put mine noisily down, spilling coffee. I felt a rush of hysteria and horror at all the sights and smells
30 of suffering interminably around us. How could he stay so untarnished at the heart of them?

"Who cares? It's here in this mess we have to live. Oh Martand, I can't bear to stay or to go away. I can't bear anything anymore."
35 "You must," he warned, no longer smiling. "There's a very long road ahead of us yet. Don't lose your nerve now." He meant the refugee crisis, as well as the time span left to him and me to find our way to each other on the dangerous, joyful, heart-breaking
40 road we were travelling together. He got up to go into the dispensary and carry on his work, and I remembered why I had come.

"I found these peaches in the bazaar. There hasn't been any good fruit for such a long time, I had
45 to bring them for you. I'm taking some home for us, too."

"Then take these with you. I'll come and eat them at your house. I'll come to dinner," he said.

"No, don't. Naresh won't like it. He was very
50 irritable last night."

"Was he? Why?"

There was that untouched innocence about Martand, a purity without which I could no longer

live. That was why I couldn't give him up, however
55 long we had to wait for this to work out. There was so little time to talk about personal problems, and when we were alone together we did not talk.

At the door to the dispensary Martand turned around to say, "Let me speak to Naresh about us." It
60 is not the first time he had urged this.

"No!" I cried.

"He is too good a man to deceive."

"Don't you know anything about human nature?" Panic made me shrill.
65 "All right, all right," said Martand softly, "I must go now, my love. Take care, won't you, as you drive home. It's a bad day today. Some of my staff are giving trouble and refusing to work. And thank you for the peaches."
70 I left his share on the table. For my cheap ideas of safety—my safety—I would deprive myself of the sight of him and the sound of his voice this evening. Safety in a mad world did not make much sense, and I was not made for living a double life. My endurance
75 was wearing thin. One of these days I would throw myself on Naresh's mercy and tell him. One of these days, but not today.

At home I washed the peaches and put them on the dining table. When I came back into the dining
80 room with plates and cutlery, Naresh was standing there staring at them.

"You're home early," I said and I knew in a flash it was time—at once—to tell him about Martand.

Naresh was waiting, a queer stricken look on his
85 face of half-knowing, fearing, unbelieving, and the tension grew intolerable. I went up to him and he put his arms around me.

"Then you hadn't heard," he said. "That's why I came—to tell you—"
90 I looked up at him, all my terrors realized.

"Martand was stabbed," he said, "less than half an hour ago. Not by a refugee, but one of his own assistants. They sent for me immediately. I was with him when he died."
95 Naresh sobbed while I stood holding him, deadly calm, as if I had known this would happen. I still had my sight and hearing, but that was all. Nothing could move me anymore.

"We'll go away," he wept, "we'll go away."
100 Yes, I thought, to a place where there was enough of everything and charity could be a virtue, not a crime. We would go where my child could be born in safety, and where a man would not be murdered for loving mankind. As we clung together,
105 I knew we had both changed invisibly beyond recall. Naresh, mourning Martand, had found his faith in goodness again, while I, surely as I breathed, knew that everywhere within hand's reach was evil.

1

Martand, referring to Naresh, states "He is too good a man to deceive" (line 62). About what were they deceiving Naresh?

A) The size of the refugee problem.

B) The lack of good fruit in the bazaar.

C) Martand's love for Naresh's wife.

D) Martand's personal safety at the clinic.

2

Why does the narrator mention the peaches from the bazaar when speaking to Martand?

A) To contrast her standard of living with that of the refugees served by the clinic

B) To show the scarcity of fruit in the area

C) To demonstrate her generosity in offering fruit to a stranger

D) To emphasize how much she cares about Martand and provide a reason for her visit

3

What is the main topic of this passage?

A) The size of the refugee problem

B) The scarcity of medical assistance for the refugees

C) The love the narrator shared with Martand, despite being married to Naresh

D) The death of Martand

4

What can you infer from the narrator's statement, "I still had my sight and my hearing, but that was all" (lines 96-97)?

A) She was worried about her health.

B) She was in shock from hearing the news about Martand.

C) She could not taste the peaches.

D) Her dismay and sadness had robbed her of all her senses.

5

The word "succor" (line 23) most nearly means

A) fruit.

B) medical aid.

C) support.

D) foolishness.

6

Why does the narrator say that she is leading a "double life" (line 74)?

A) She was living in a nice home compared with the refugee camp she visited.

B) She is married to Naresh but loves Martand.

C) She could shop for fresh fruit at the bazaar while the refugees begged for food.

D) She had the option of moving to a safer place while the refugees were trapped.

7

How did the author foretell the death of Martand?

A) By describing the refugees as "a grim growing mass of humanity" (line 17-18)

B) By having the narrator refer to her "cheap ideas of safety" (lines 70-71)

C) By noting the "dangerous" road (lines 39-40) that the narrator and Martand are traveling

D) By having Martand state, "Some of my staff are giving trouble" (lines 67-68)

8

It can be inferred that Naresh viewed Martand as

A) a good man whom he respected.

B) a rival for his wife's love.

C) his brother.

D) an employee.

9

Which choice provides the best evidence for the answer to the previous question?

A) Lines 52-54 ("There was… live.")

B) Lines 75-76 ("One of… tell him.")

C) Lines 84-86 ("Naresh… grew intolerable.")

D) Lines 106-107 ("Naresh… again.")

10

As used in line 40, the word "road" most nearly means

A) street.

B) existence.

C) lifestyle.

D) lane.

Notes and Reflections

Information & Ideas — Great Global Conversation — Passage 1

This passage is adapted from "Narrative of the Life of Frederick Douglass" by Frederick Douglass.

I was born in Tuckahoe, near Hillsborough, and about twelve miles from Easton, in Talbot county, Maryland. I have no accurate knowledge of my age, never having seen any authentic record containing it.
5   By far the larger part of the slaves know as little of their ages as horses know of theirs, and it is the wish of most masters within my knowledge to keep their slaves thus ignorant. I do not remember to have ever met a slave who could tell of his birthday. They
10 seldom come nearer to it than planting-time, harvest-time, cherry-time, spring-time, or fall-time. A want of information concerning my own was a source of unhappiness to me even during childhood. The white children could tell their ages. I could not tell why I
15 ought to be deprived of the same privilege. I was not allowed to make any inquiries of my master concerning it. He deemed all such inquiries on the part of a slave improper and impertinent, and evidence of a restless spirit. The nearest estimate I
20 can give makes me now between twenty-seven and twenty-eight years of age. I come to this, from hearing my master say, some time during 1835, I was about seventeen years old.

My mother was named Harriet Bailey. She was
25 the daughter of Isaac and Betsey Bailey, both colored, and quite dark. My mother was of a darker complexion than either my grandmother or grandfather.

My father was a white man. He was admitted to
30 be such by all I ever heard speak of my parentage. The opinion was also whispered that my master was my father; but of the correctness of this opinion, I know nothing; the means of knowing was withheld from me. My mother and I were separated when I
35 was but an infant—before I knew her as my mother. It is a common custom, in the part of Maryland from which I ran away, to part children from their mothers at a very early age. Frequently, before the child has reached its twelfth month, its mother is taken from it,
40 and hired out on some farm a considerable distance off, and the child is placed under the care of an old woman, too old for field labor. For what this separation is done, I do not know, unless it be to hinder the development of the child's affection
45 toward its mother, and to blunt and destroy the natural affection of the mother for the child. This is the inevitable result.

I never saw my mother, to know her as such, more than four or five times in my life; and each of
50 these times was very short in duration, and at night.

She was hired by a Mr. Stewart, who lived about twelve miles from my home. She made her journeys to see me in the night, travelling the whole distance on foot, after the performance of her day's work. She
55 was a field hand, and a whipping is the penalty of not being in the field at sunrise, unless a slave has special permission from his or her master to the contrary—a permission which they seldom get, and one that gives to him that gives it the proud name of being a kind
60 master. I do not recollect of ever seeing my mother by the light of day. She was with me in the night. She would lie down with me, and get me to sleep, but long before I waked she was gone. Very little communication ever took place between us. Death
65 soon ended what little we could have while she lived, and with it her hardships and suffering. She died when I was about seven years old, on one of my master's farms, near Lee's Mill. I was not allowed to be present during her illness, at her death, or burial.
70 She was gone long before I knew anything about it. Never having enjoyed, to any considerable extent, her soothing presence, her tender and watchful care, I received the tidings of her death with much the same emotions I should have probably felt at the death of a
75 stranger.

Called thus suddenly away, she left me without the slightest intimation of who my father was. The whisper that my master was my father, may or may not be true; and, true or false, it is of but little
80 consequence to my purpose whilst the fact remains, in all its glaring odiousness, that slaveholders have ordained, and by law established, that the children of slave women shall in all cases follow the condition of their mothers; and this is done too obviously to
85 administer to their own lusts, and make a gratification of their wicked desires profitable as well as pleasurable; for by this cunning arrangement, the slaveholder, in cases not a few, sustains to his slaves the double relation of master and father.

1

The author indicates that he does not know his precise age because

A) he was not white.

B) he never saw his birth certificate.

C) it was illegal for slaves to know their birthdate.

D) most masters preferred that their slaves not have this information.

2

Which choice provides the best evidence for the answer to the previous question?

A) Lines 13-14 (The white… ages.)
B) Lines 3-4 (I have no… containing it.)
C) Lines 15-17 (I was not… concerning it.)
D) Lines 6-8 (it is the wish… thus ignorant)

3

The central theme of the passage is the

A) author's reflection on age and parentage issues faced by slaves.
B) cruelty of separating slave children from their mothers at an early age.
C) misery of the author's childhood.
D) author's wish to know who his father was.

4

The information in the fourth paragraph (lines 48-75) explains

A) why slave children were separated from their mothers at a young age.
B) the deep love the author's mother had for him, despite being separated.
C) why the author has only a few memories of his mother.
D) the author's intense sadness over the death of his mother.

5

The author implies that his mother never visited during the day because

A) she was too busy working in the fields.
B) she would have been whipped if she had come during the day.
C) slaves were not allowed to travel during the day.
D) she preferred seeing him at night when she could put him to sleep.

6

The author suggests slave children were separated from mothers at a young age because

A) female slaves had to return to the fields to work as soon as possible.
B) the children needed to learn to live without their mothers.
C) it was less expensive to have older women care for slave children
D) it was needed to break the mother-child bond.

7

Which choice provides the best evidence for the answer to the previous question?

A) Lines 29-30 ("He was… my parentage.")
B) Lines 34-35 ("My mother… my mother")
C) Lines 38-42 ("Frequently… field labor.")
D) Lines 42-46 ("For what… the child")

8

As used in line 77, "intimation" most nearly means

A) suggestion.
B) frightfulness.
C) simulation.
D) question.

9

As used in line 45, "blunt" most nearly means

A) strengthen.
B) weaken.
C) sharpen.
D) decry.

10

The narrator suggests his life as a slave child, as compared to that of other slave children, was

A) more difficult because he didn't know his own age.
B) better because his mother visited him.
C) similar because he barely knew his mother and didn't know his father at all.
D) harder because his grandparents were both slaves.

Information & Ideas – Great Global Conversation – Passage 2

Passage 1 is adapted from "Social Contract" by Jean Jacques Rousseau. Passage 2 is adapted from "Rights and Involved Duties of Mankind Considered" by Mary Wollstonecraft.

Passage 1

The most ancient of all societies, and the only one that is natural, is the family: and even so the children remain attached to the father only so long as they need him for their preservation. As soon as this
5 need ceases, the natural bond is dissolved. The children, released from the obedience they owed to the father, and the father, released from the care he owed his children, return equally to independence. If they remain united, they continue so no longer
10 naturally, but voluntarily; and the family itself is then maintained only by convention. The family then may be called the first model of political societies: the ruler corresponds to the father, and the people to the children; and all, being born free and equal, alienate
15 their liberty only for their own advantage.

Since no man has a natural authority over his fellow, and force creates no right, we must conclude that conventions form the basis of all legitimate authority among men. Now, a man who becomes the
20 slave of another does not give himself; he sells himself, at the least for his subsistence: but for what does a people sell itself? A king is so far from furnishing his subjects with their subsistence that he gets his own only from them; and kings do not live
25 on nothing. Do subjects then give their persons on condition that the king takes their goods also? I fail to see what they have left to preserve.

It will be said that the despot assures his subjects civil tranquility. Granted; but what do they gain, if
30 the wars his ambition brings down upon them and the vexations conduct of his ministers press harder on them than their own dissensions would have done? What do they gain, if the very tranquility they enjoy is one of their miseries? Tranquility is found also in
35 dungeons; but is that enough to make them desirable places to live in? The Greeks imprisoned in the cave of the Cyclops lived there very tranquilly, while they were awaiting their turn to be devoured. To say that a man gives himself gratuitously, is to say what is
40 absurd and inconceivable.

To renounce liberty is to renounce being a man, to surrender the rights of humanity and even its duties. For him who renounces everything no indemnity is possible. Such a renunciation is
45 incompatible with man's nature; to remove all liberty from his will is to remove all morality from his acts. Finally, it is an empty and contradictory convention that sets up, on the one side, absolute authority, and, on the other, unlimited obedience. Is it not clear that
50 we can be under no obligation to a person from whom we have the right to exact everything? It will always be equally foolish for a man to say to a man or to a people: "I make with you a convention wholly at your expense and wholly to my advantage; I shall
55 keep it as long as I like, and you will keep it as long as I like."

Passage 2

Reared on a false hypothesis, Rousseau's arguments in favor of a state of nature are plausible, but unsound. To assert that a state of nature is
60 preferable to civilization, in all its possible perfection, is to criticize supreme wisdom. And the paradoxical exclamation that God has made all things right and that error has been introduced by the creature, whom he formed, knowing what he formed,
65 is as unphilosophical as impious.

When that wise Being who created us and placed us here saw the fair idea, he willed, by allowing it to be so, that the passions should unfold our reason, because he could see that present evil would produce
70 future good. Could the helpless creature whom he called from nothing break loose from his providence, and boldly learn to know good by practicing evil, without his permission? No. But if there were to be rational creatures produced, allowed to rise in
75 excellence by the exercise of powers implanted for that purpose; if benevolence itself thought fit to call into existence a creature above the brutes, who could think and improve himself, why should that inestimable gift, for a gift it was, if man was so
80 created as to have a capacity to rise above the state in which sensation produced brutal ease, be called, in direct terms, a curse? A curse it might be reckoned, if the whole of our existence were bounded by our continuance in this world; for why should the
85 gracious fountain of life give us passions, and the power of reflecting, only to embitter our days and inspire us with mistaken notions of dignity? Why should he lead us from love of ourselves to the sublime emotions which the discovery of his wisdom
90 and goodness excites, if these feelings were not set in motion to improve our nature, of which they make a part, and render us capable of enjoying a more godlike portion of happiness? Firmly persuaded that no evil exists in the world that God did not design to
95 take place, I build my belief on the perfection of God.

Rousseau exerts himself to prove that all was right originally: and I, that all will be right.

But, true to his first position, next to a state of nature, Rousseau celebrates barbarism. It is pestilent

100 prose which renders the progress of civilization a
curse. It warps the understanding, till men of
sensibility doubt whether the expansion of intellect
produces a greater portion of happiness or misery.
But the nature of the poison points out the antidote;

105 and had Rousseau mounted one step higher in his
investigation, or could his eye have pierced through
the foggy atmosphere, which he almost disdained to
breathe, his active mind would have darted forward
to contemplate the perfection of man in the

110 establishment of true civilization, instead of taking
his ferocious flight back to the night of sensual
ignorance.

1

The central idea in Passage 1 is

A) the defense of the argument that the family
unit is integral to society.

B) the argument that civic tranquility is a
desired benefit for societies.

C) the assertion that liberty is a primary right of
individuals in society.

D) the existence of a king prevents a society
from reaching its ideal state.

2

Rousseau suggests that the family unit

A) should be celebrated for the natural bonds it
creates.

B) is not necessary for the provision of
children's needs.

C) encourages children to stay with their
families upon reaching adulthood.

D) is a useful example for analyzing modes of
governance.

3

Which choice provides the best evidence for the
answer to the previous question?

A) Lines 4-5 ("As soon as… is dissolved")

B) Lines 5-8 ("The children… independence.")

C) Lines 8-11 ("If they… by convention.")

D) Lines 11-15 ("The family… advantage.")

4

In line 23, the term "subsistence" most nearly
means

A) basic needs.

B) rights.

C) privileges.

D) honor.

5

In the example of the cave of the Cyclops (lines
36-37), Rousseau

A) praises leaders who provide civil tranquility
for their subjects.

B) illustrates the inadequacy of civil tranquility
as a substitute for liberty.

C) compares modern society to Greek
civilizations.

D) admires the tranquility of the Greek
prisoners in the cave.

6

Wollstonecraft's main premise is that

A) happiness comes from a belief in God.

B) civilization, as opposed to nature, was
ordained by God to be a benefit to humanity.

C) mankind has been cursed since the
beginning of the world.

D) no evil exists in the world.

7

Wollstonecraft bases her argument on

A) her faith in a perfect Creator.

B) Rousseau's ideals of family and nature.

C) Greek philosophy.

D) the conflict between good and evil.

8

Wollstonecraft implies that the natural state of mankind is

A) capable of enjoying a godlike happiness.
B) progressing towards ignorance.
C) best expressed by the family unit.
D) close to barbaric.

9

Wollstonecraft's analysis of Rousseau's beliefs suggests that

A) she philosophically disagrees with him.
B) she accepts his basic premise.
C) she admires his conclusions.
D) she is angry at his portrayal of humanity.

10

Whereas Rousseau argues that humanity needs to return to its original state to move closer to perfection, Wollstonecraft

A) believes that humanity cannot move closer to perfection.
B) asserts that mankind will eventually reach perfection through progress.
C) claims that humanity has already reached a state of perfection.
D) declares that only God has reached perfection.

11

According to the information in the passages, both Rousseau and Wollstonecraft

A) share the view that liberty is a basic human right.
B) explore the nature of humanity and the impact of civilization on its development.
C) consider the role of God in the history of humanity.
D) agree on the importance of civil tranquility as the basis for human happiness.

Information & Ideas – Great Global Conversation – Passage 3

Passage 1 is adapted from "Walden" by Henry David Thoreau. Passage 2 is adapted from "Letters on a Regicide Peace" by Edmund Burke.

Passage 1

I see young men, my townsmen, whose misfortune it is to have inherited farms, houses, barns, cattle, and farming tools; for these are more easily acquired than got rid of. Better if they had been born in the open
5 pasture and suckled by a wolf, that they might have seen with clearer eyes what field they were called to labor in. Who made them serfs of the soil? Why should they eat their sixty acres, when man is condemned to eat only his peck of dirt? Why should
10 they begin digging their graves as soon as they are born? They have got to live a man's life, pushing all these things before them, and get on as well as they can. How many a poor immortal soul have I met well nigh crushed and smothered under its load, creeping
15 down the road of life, pushing before it a barn seventy-five feet by forty, its Augean stables never cleansed, and one hundred acres of land, tillage, mowing, pasture, and wood-lot! The portionless, who struggle with no such unnecessary inherited
20 encumbrances, find it labor enough to subdue and cultivate a few cubic feet of flesh.

But men labor under a mistake. The better part of the man is soon plowed into the soil for compost. By a seeming fate, commonly called necessity, they are
25 employed, laying up treasures which moth and rust will corrupt and thieves break through and steal. It is a fool's life, as they will find when they get to the end of it, if not before. Most men, even in this comparatively free country, through mere ignorance
30 and mistake, are so occupied with the factitious cares and superfluously coarse labors of life that its finer fruits cannot be plucked by them. Their fingers, from excessive toil, are too clumsy and tremble too much for that. Actually, the laboring man has not leisure for
35 a true integrity day by day; he cannot afford to sustain the manliest relations to men; his labor would be depreciated in the market. He has no time to be anything but a machine. How can he remember well his ignorance—which his growth requires—who has
40 so often to use his knowledge? We should feed and clothe him gratuitously sometimes, and recruit him with our cordials, before we judge of him. The finest qualities of our nature, like the bloom on fruits, can be preserved only by the most delicate handling. Yet
45 we do not treat ourselves nor one another thus tenderly.

Passage 2

Let government protect and encourage industry, secure property, repress violence, and discountenance fraud, it is all that they have to do. In other respects,
50 the less they meddle in these affairs the better; the rest is in the hands of our Master and theirs.

The vigorous and laborious class of life has lately got, from the good manners of the humanity of this day, the name of the "labouring poor." We have
55 heard many plans for the relief of the "labouring poor." This puling jargon is not as innocent as it is foolish. In meddling with great affairs, weakness is never innoxious. Hitherto the name of poor (in the sense in which it is used to excite compassion) has
60 not been used for those who can, but for those who cannot, labour—for the sick and infirm, for orphan infancy, for languishing and decrepit age.

But when we affect to pity, as poor, those who must labour, or the world cannot exist, we are trifling
65 with the condition of mankind. It is the common doom of man that he must eat his bread by the sweat of his brow, that is, by the sweat of his body, or the sweat of his mind. If this toil was inflicted as a curse, it is—as might be expected from the curses of the
70 Father of all blessings—tempered with many alleviations, many comforts. Every attempt to fly from it, and to refuse the very terms of our existence, becomes much more truly a curse; and heavier pains and penalties fall upon those who would elude the
75 tasks which are put upon them by the great Master Workman of the world, who, in his dealings with his creatures, sympathizes with their weakness, and speaking of a creation wrought by mere will out of nothing, speaks of six days of labor and one of rest.
80 I do not call a healthy young man, cheerful in his mind, and vigorous in his arms, I cannot call such a man poor. I cannot pity my kind as a kind, merely because they are men. This affected pity only tends to dissatisfy them with their condition, and to teach
85 them to seek resources where no resources are to be found, in something else than their own industry, and frugality, and sobriety. Whatever may be the intention (which, because I do not know, I cannot dispute) of those who would discontent mankind by
90 this strange pity, they act towards us, in the consequences, as if they were our worst enemies.

1

According to the author of Passage 1, a life of farming is

A) a necessary evil.
B) a trap set up by the government.
C) a fortunate inherited situation.
D) an obstacle to man's greater pursuits.

2

Which choice provides the best evidence for the answer to the previous question?

A) Lines 1-3 ("I see… farming tools.")
B) Lines 28-32 ("Most men… by them.")
C) Lines 37-38 ("He has… a machine.")
D) Lines 42-44 ("The finest… handling.")

3

What can be inferred from the rhetorical questions in the first paragraph of Passage 1?

A) The author disagrees with some commonly accepted practices surrounding labor.
B) The author is demanding better conditions for people working on farms.
C) The author does not understand why people would accept an unpleasant job.
D) The author is confused about the circumstances farm workers tolerate.

4

In Passage 1, the fruits that Thoreau says need to be handled gently are

A) berries that require careful handling.
B) the finest qualities of our nature.
C) factitious cares and superfluously coarse labors of life.
D) fate, which is commonly called necessity.

5

In the first paragraph of Passage 2, Burke suggests the role of government is to aid and protect

A) business and property.
B) the working poor.
C) the sick and elderly.
D) religious organizations.

6

The central idea of the third paragraph of Passage 2 (lines 63-79) is that

A) having to work for a living is a curse.
B) God provides rewards for those who work hard.
C) hard work is necessary and has its consolations.
D) God tells us to work six days and rest on the seventh.

7

Which choice provides the best evidence for the answer to the previous question?

A) Lines 57-58 ("In meddling… innoxious")
B) Lines 63-65 ("But… mankind.")
C) Lines 68-71 ("If this toil… comforts.")
D) Lines 73-76 ("heavier… world")

8

Unlike Passage 1, Passage 2 discusses labor in terms of

A) government and poverty.
B) human ignorance and drudgery.
C) laziness and industriousness.
D) inheritance and family.

9

How does the author of Passage 1's opinion of the working man differ from that of the author of Passage 2?

A) The author of Passage 1 believes that workers have manufactured their own situation, while the author of Passage 2 blames the government.
B) The author of Passage 1 considers the laborer robbed of certain aspects of life, while the author of Passage 2 doesn't share his concerns.
C) The author of Passage 1 thinks more should be done to support laborers, while the author of Passage 2 considers this notion foolish.
D) The author of Passage 1 harbors excessive empathy for workers, while the author of Passage 2 expresses scorn for them.

10

What does Thoreau consider the result of inheriting a farm and the accompanying accoutrements?

A) A life of unrewarded hard work
B) A modest fortune worth maintaining
C) An unliftable curse upon the recipient's entire family
D) A back-breaking provisionary job

11

What is the main idea of Passage 2?

A) Workers do not deserve sympathy because each worker's situation is unique and can't be classified with a broad statement.
B) The government's classification of workers has caused a rift between how others view workers and how workers view themselves.
C) Hard work encourages young men to improve their station in life.
D) The labeling of able-bodied workers as poor is inaccurate and can be damaging to the worker's view of themselves.

12

As it is used in line 59, "excite" most nearly means

A) galvanize.
B) thrill.
C) elicit.
D) explain.

Information & Ideas – Great Global Conversation – Passage 4

Passage 1 is adapted from John F. Kennedy's "We Choose to Go to the Moon" speech in 1962. Passage 2 is adapted from Ronald Reagan's address to the nation in 1986 following the Challenger Disaster, the explosion of a manned space shuttle.

Passage 1

No man can fully grasp how far and how fast we
have come, but condense, if you will, the 50,000
years of man's recorded history in a time span of but
a half-century. Stated in these terms, we know very
5 little about the first 40 years, except at the end of
them advanced man had learned to use the skins of
animals to cover them. Then about 10 years ago,
under this standard, man emerged from his caves to
construct other kinds of shelter. Only five years ago
10 man learned to write and use a cart with wheels.
Christianity began less than two years ago. The
printing press came this year, and then less than two
months ago, during this whole 50-year span of human
history, the steam engine provided a new source of
15 power. Newton explored the meaning of gravity. Last
month electric lights and telephones and automobiles
and airplanes became available. Only last week did
we develop penicillin and television and nuclear
power, and now if America's new spacecraft
20 succeeds in reaching Venus, we will have literally
reached the stars before midnight tonight.

This is a breathtaking pace, and such a pace
cannot help but create new ills as it dispels old, new
ignorance, new problems, new dangers. Surely the
25 opening vistas of space promise high costs and
hardships, as well as high reward.

So it is not surprising that some would have us
stay where we are a little longer to rest, to wait. But
this city of Houston, this state of Texas, this country
30 of the United States was not built by those who
waited and rested and wished to look behind them.
This country was conquered by those who moved
forward—and so will space.

William Bradford, speaking in 1630 of the
35 founding of the Plymouth Bay Colony, said that all
great and honorable actions are accompanied with
great difficulties, and both must be enterprised and
overcome with answerable courage.

If this capsule history of our progress teaches us
40 anything, it is that man, in his quest for knowledge
and progress, is determined and cannot be deterred.
Those who came before us made certain that this
country rode the first waves of the industrial
revolution, the first waves of modern invention, and
45 the first wave of nuclear power, and this generation

does not intend to founder in the backwash of the
coming age of space. We mean to be a part of it—we
mean to lead it.

Passage 2

Ladies and Gentlemen, I'd planned to speak to
50 you tonight to report on the state of the Union, but
the events of earlier today have led me to change
those plans. Today is a day for mourning and
remembering. Nancy and I are pained to the core by
the tragedy of the shuttle Challenger. We know we
55 share this pain with all of the people of our country.
This is truly a national loss.

For the families of the seven, we cannot bear, as
you do, the full impact of this tragedy. But we feel
the loss, and we're thinking about you so very much.
60 Your loved ones were daring and brave, and they had
that special grace, that special spirit that says, "Give
me a challenge and I'll meet it with joy." They had a
hunger to explore the universe and discover its truths.
They wished to serve, and they did. They served all
65 of us.

We've grown used to wonders in this century.
It's hard to dazzle us. But for twenty-five years the
United States space program has been doing just that.
We've grown used to the idea of space, and perhaps
70 we forget that we've only just begun. We're still
pioneers. They, the members of the Challenger crew,
were pioneers.

And I want to say something to the
schoolchildren of America who were watching the
75 live coverage of the shuttle's takeoff. I know it is
hard to understand, but sometimes painful things like
this happen. It's all part of the process of exploration
and discovery. It's all part of taking a chance and
expanding man's horizons. The future doesn't belong
80 to the fainthearted; it belongs to the brave. The
Challenger crew was pulling us into the future, and
we'll continue to follow them.

I've always had great faith in and respect for our
space program, and what happened today does
85 nothing to diminish it. We don't hide our space
program. We don't keep secrets and cover things up.
We do it all up front and in public. That's the way
freedom is, and we wouldn't change it for a minute.
We'll continue our quest in space. There will be more
90 shuttle flights and more shuttle crews and, yes, more
volunteers, more civilians, more teachers in space.
Nothing ends here; our hopes and our journeys
continue. I want to add that I wish I could talk to
every man and woman who works for NASA or who
95 worked on this mission and tell them: "Your
dedication and professionalism have moved and

impressed us for decades. And we know of your anguish. We share it."

There's a coincidence today. On this day 390 years ago, the great explorer Sir Francis Drake died aboard ship off the coast of Panama. In his lifetime the great frontiers were the oceans, and a historian later said, "He lived by the sea, died on it, and was buried in it." Well, today we can say of the Challenger crew: Their dedication was, like Drake's, complete.

1

The main idea of the last paragraph in Passage 1 is that

A) our ancestors were successful in becoming leaders of the Industrial Revolution.

B) the quest for knowledge and progress is never-ending.

C) as our ancestors were pioneers, we must pioneer the coming age.

D) despite its costs, we must lead the age of space.

2

The author of Passage 1 indicates that

A) the pace at which progress is moving creates new problems.

B) we have to wait a little more before we explore space.

C) the last 50 years were the most significant in the recorded history of man.

D) on the day the author is making the speech, the spacecraft will reach Venus.

3

Which choice provides the best evidence for the answer to the previous question?

A) Lines 11-15 ("The printing… power.")

B) Lines 17-21 ("Only… tonight.")

C) Lines 22-24 ("This… dangers.")

D) Lines 34-38 ("William…courage.")

4

It is implied from the third paragraph of Passage 1 (lines 27-33) that

A) the author would like to wait a little while before continuing the space program.

B) the author sees the foundation of the United States as an example for how to approach the space program.

C) the author sees the age of space as another era such as the Industrial Revolution.

D) Texas does not support the space program.

5

As used in line 106 of Passage 2, the word "complete" most nearly means

A) finished.

B) necessary.

C) essential.

D) absolute.

6

Which of the following statements best expresses the main idea of paragraph 5 in Passage 2 (lines 83-98)?

A) The US will openly continue the space program.

B) The employees of NASA are dedicated and impressive.

C) The Challenger crew was brave and dedicated, and they were leading us into the future.

D) Tragedies happen during times of exploration and discovery.

7

In the fourth paragraph of Passage 2 (lines 73-82), the author implies that

A) people who don't want to explore space are fainthearted.

B) the paragraph's message is only meant for schoolchildren.

C) the Challenger crew's bravery guides us to continue the space program.

D) countries without freedom keep secrets.

8

The author of Passage 1 and the author of Passage 2 would most likely DISAGREE on which of the following?

A) We should continue our endeavors to explore space.

B) Difficulties and dangers come with exploration and discovery.

C) Historical figures provide us guidance and inspiration as we begin to explore space.

D) Progress is inevitable.

9

Whereas the author in Passage 1 compares the space program to conquering new land, the author of Passage 2 compares the space program to

A) exploring a new land.

B) sailing in Panama.

C) racing.

D) taking a journey.

10

As used in line 37 of Passage 1, the word "enterprised" most nearly means

A) created.

B) undertaken.

C) purchased.

D) gathered.

Information & Ideas – Great Global Conversation – Passage 5

Passage 1 is adapted from Malala Yousafzai's Nobel lecture. Passage 2 is adapted from "The Purpose of Education" by Martin Luther King, Jr.

Passage 1

Education is one of the blessings of life—and one of its necessities. That has been my experience during the 17 years of my life. In my paradise home, Swat, I always loved learning and discovering new
5 things. I remember when my friends and I would decorate our hands with henna on special occasions. And instead of drawing flowers and patterns we would paint our hands with mathematical formulas and equations.
10 We had a thirst for education, we had a thirst for education because our future was right there in that classroom. We would sit and learn and read together. We loved to wear neat and tidy school uniforms and we would sit there with big dreams in our eyes.
15 But things did not remain the same. When I was in Swat, which was a place of tourism and beauty, suddenly changed into a place of terrorism. I was just ten that more than 400 schools were destroyed. Women were flogged. People were killed. And our
20 beautiful dreams turned into nightmares. Education went from being a right to being a crime. Girls were stopped from going to school.

When my world suddenly changed, my priorities changed, too. I had two options. One was to remain
25 silent and wait to be killed. And the second was to speak up and then be killed. I chose the second one. I decided to speak up.

Sometimes people like to ask me why should girls go to school, why is it important for them. But I
30 think the more important question is why shouldn't they, why shouldn't they have this right to go to school.

Dear sisters and brothers, today, in half of the world, we see rapid progress and development.
35 However, there are many countries where millions still suffer from the very old problems of war, poverty, and injustice. We are living in the modern age and we believe that nothing is impossible. We have reached the moon 45 years ago and maybe will
40 soon land on Mars. Then, in this 21st century, we must be able to give every child quality education.

Dear sisters and brothers, dear fellow children, we must work… not wait. Not just the politicians and the world leaders, we all need to contribute. Me. You.
45 We. It is our duty. Let us become the first generation to decide to be the last, let us become the first generation that decides to be the last that sees empty classrooms, lost childhoods, and wasted potentials. Let this be the last time that a girl or a boy spends
50 their childhood in a factory. Let this be the last time that a girl is forced into early child marriage. Let this be the last time that a child loses life in war. Let this be the last time that we see a child out of school. Let this end with us.

Passage 2

55 As I engage in the so-called "bull sessions" around and about the school, I too often find that most college men have a misconception of the purpose of education. Most of the "brethren" think that education should equip them with the proper
60 instruments of exploitation so that they can forever trample over the masses. Still others think that education should furnish them with noble ends rather than means to an end.

It seems to me that education has a two-fold
65 function to perform in the life of man and in society: the one is utility and the other is culture. Education must enable a man to become more efficient, to achieve with increasing facility the legitimate goals of his life.
70 Education must also train one for quick, resolute and effective thinking. To think incisively and to think for one's self is very difficult. We are prone to let our mental life become invaded by legions of half-truths, prejudices, and propaganda. At this point, I
75 often wonder whether or not education is fulfilling its purpose. A great majority of the so-called educated people do not think logically and scientifically. Even the press, the classroom, the platform, and the pulpit in many instances do not give us objective and
80 unbiased truths. To save man from the morass of propaganda, in my opinion, is one of the chief aims of education. Education must enable one to sift and weigh evidence, to discern the true from the false, the real from the unreal, and the facts from the fiction.
85 The function of education, therefore, is to teach one to think intensively and to think critically. But education which stops with efficiency may prove the greatest menace to society. The most dangerous criminal may be the man gifted with reason, but with
90 no morals.

The late Eugene Talmadge, in my opinion, possessed one of the better minds of Georgia, or even America. Moreover, he wore the Phi Beta Kappa key. By all measuring rods, Mr. Talmadge could think
95 critically and intensively; yet he contends that I am an inferior being. Are those the types of men we call educated?

We must remember that intelligence is not enough. Intelligence plus character—that is the goal
100 of true education. The complete education gives one not only power of concentration, but worthy objectives upon which to concentrate. The broad education will, therefore, transmit to one not only the accumulated knowledge of the race but also the
105 accumulated experience of social living.
If we are not careful, our colleges will produce a group of close-minded, unscientific, illogical propagandists, consumed with immoral acts. Be careful, "brethren!" Be careful, teachers!

1

According to Passage 1, the world is divided into

A) places with education and places without it.

B) developed places and places struggling with war, poverty, and injustice.

C) places with tourism and places with terrorism.

D) places with freedom of speech and places where speaking up puts you in danger.

2

Which choice provides the best evidence for the answer to the previous question?

A) Lines 15-17 ("When … terrorism.")

B) Lines 20-21 ("Education… crime.")

C) Lines 24-26 ("I had… killed.")

D) Lines 33-37 "(Dear… injustice.")

3

In Passage 1, lines 28-32 argue the point that

A) education is a privilege and not a right.

B) some people still do not believe girls should go to school.

C) education is a right for everybody.

D) people are asking the wrong questions about school.

4

Which of the following statements best expresses the main idea of Passage 1?

A) The women in Swat should have the right to education again.

B) It is time for people to stand up for all children to have the right to a safe education.

C) It is not fair that half the world still struggles with war and injustice when we are living in the modern age.

D) We must rebuild the schools in Swat to enable children there to return to school.

5

In line 73, the word "legions" most closely means

A) a group of soldiers.

B) a multitude.

C) lies.

D) a small number.

6

In Passage 2, the example of Eugene Talmadge emphasizes the point that

A) thinking critically and intensively is the purpose of education.

B) having a better mind means that you are better educated.

C) education is more than intelligence.

D) education taught Eugene Talmadge to think logically and weigh evidence.

7

The author of Passage 2 would most likely agree with which of the following statements?

A) Education has never fulfilled its purpose or potential.

B) The accumulated knowledge of our race is the most important part of education.

C) Properly educated men are impervious to propaganda.

D) A truly educated man is not only knowledgeable but ethical.

8

In passage 2, the mention of "bull sessions" displays that

A) the author's colleagues have meaningful discussions concerning the proper reasons for education.

B) the author finds fault with the discussions of education he finds among college men.

C) the author agrees with the "brethren" about the importance of education.

D) education should furnish students with noble ends rather than means to an end.

9

Whereas the author of Passage 1 sees education as a right, the author of Passage 2 argues that education is

A) a necessity for a moral society.

B) a means to achieve one's goals.

C) primarily a way to train a person to think logically.

D) a means to measure intelligence.

10

In contrast to Passage 1, Passage 2 focuses on

A) the right to education.

B) how best to improve "bull sessions."

C) the education of college men.

D) how to teach for a thoughtful and moral society.

Notes and Reflections

Information & Ideas – Science – Passage 1

This passage is adapted from an article about the use of certain metals for everyday items.

"All that glitters is not gold." This oft-quoted proverb is usually used to describe situations that turn out to be quite different from their initial appearances—not necessarily to comment on the
5 properties of literal gold itself. However, it is true that many of the metallic items we encounter in our daily lives are not indeed what they may seem, or at least, are not made of the namesake materials which we liberally use to describe them. More likely than
10 not, the "tin" can you're drinking out of is made from aluminum, the "lead" in your pencil is actually graphite, and the shiny "copper" penny in your wallet is more than 97% zinc. While all of these products did, at one time in their history, contain the tin, lead,
15 and copper we still refer to them as possessing, they have since come to be made using cheaper or less dangerous metals.

The same could be said for the "silverware" on your dining room table—except for very special
20 occasions, few households these days rely on utensils made of pure silver, instead opting for cheaper and more durable stainless steel alternatives. However, despite the many benefits of owning and using stainless steel forks, knives, and spoons, there is one
25 significant reason why true, made-of-silver silverware may be a preferable choice: it is likely to be cleaner. In fact, silver is a natural antiseptic, and the healthful benefits of eating with pure silverware have been reducing diners' risk of infection for
30 centuries.

Silver—along with brass and copper—is one of several metals to exhibit the *oligodynamic effect*, a process wherein silver ions infiltrate bacterial and fungal cells, inhibiting their spread. Although the
35 exact cellular processes behind the oligodynamic effect are still being studied, scientists believe that, after breaking down the cell membrane, positively-charged silver ions bond with a targeted cell's proteins (including its DNA) to form new compounds
40 called silver sulfides. These sulfides then precipitate—or filter—out of the protein, thereby deactivating it. Once enough of a pathogen's critical proteins are damaged in this way, the cell can no longer function, and dies. Some studies have shown
45 that, when cooking pots coated in a mixture of silver and copper were exposed to water contaminated with small doses of *E. coli* and *Salmonella*, the metals had completely expunged the bacteria within eight to twelve hours.
50 Although the oligodynamic effect of silver was first described in the late 19th century by Swiss scientist Carl Nägeli, silver compounds have been

used in medicine for their antiseptic properties since antiquity. Over two thousand years ago, the ancient
55 Greek physician Hippocrates advocated the benefits of using silver in wound dressings. The first gynecological surgeries, performed in the 1840s by J. Marion Sims, were sutured with thin silver wire—a stunning improvement over the natural silk threads
60 previously used, which frequently caused surgical sites to become infected. Bandages lined with silver foil were still in common usage at hospitals through the end of World War II, though the expense of sourcing the material during wartime led to the
65 development of other sterilization methods for bandages. These new forms of antimicrobial dressings have since become the standard in the medicine cabinets of today.

Unlike other heavy metals used in medicinal
70 practice throughout history—such as mercury, once ubiquitous in oral thermometers, and lead, a folk-remedy for wart removal—silver is very low in toxicity for humans, and therefore continues to be used. You might be surprised to discover just how
75 much of modern medicine relies on the oligodynamic effect of silver! Many patients with second- or third-degree burns are treated with a topical cream containing silver sulfadiazine compounds to prevent infection at the burn site. Infants who contract
80 conjunctivitis (commonly known as pink eye) are given diluted solutions of silver nitrate in their eye drops to lessen inflammation and prevent further contamination. And, if you've had an implant of any kind, the sterile, silver parts of your cardiac device,
85 prosthetic bones, or even your tooth fillings are there to keep your body healthy and bacteria-free--though, you may need to be careful about setting off a metal detector at the airport.

Often, those who come from a background of
90 privilege are said to have been fed with a proverbial "silver spoon." While it is doubtful that the origin of this saying intended for us to take the oligodynamic effect into account, one could say that the opportunity to eat from a self-disinfecting utensil is a gleaming
95 privilege indeed!

1

According to the passage, silver's antiseptic qualities were recognized by all of the following except

A) J. Marion Sims.
B) Carl Nägeli.
C) Albert Schweitzer.
D) Hippocrates.

2

The word "standard," as it is used in line 67, most likely means

A) exception.
B) norm.
C) quality.
D) tradition.

3

In lines 69-74 the author indicates that silver differs from mercury and lead in that it

A) has not been used throughout history.
B) is more toxic for humans.
C) is more expensive to use.
D) is less toxic for humans.

4

It can be logically inferred from the passage that "These new forms of antimicrobial dressings have since become the standard in the medicine cabinets of today" (lines 66-68) because

A) silver compounds' antiseptic properties are rarely used in modern life.
B) silver compounds' antiseptic properties are widely used in modern life.
C) silver compounds' antiseptic properties have declined over time.
D) silver compounds' antiseptic properties have improved over time.

5

What is a main idea of the third paragraph (lines 31-49)?

A) The antibacterial properties of some metals are effective but not fully understood.
B) The oligodynamic effect should be utilized in more kitchen tools.
C) Cultural traditions are based on a deep knowledge of scientific properties.
D) The oligodynamic effect is limited to impacting only a small variety of bacteria.

6

The passage asserts that modern medicine relies on silver's oligodynamic effect for all of the following except

A) hip replacement components.
B) bandages lined with silver foil.
C) eye drops for babies.
D) topical burn cream.

7

As used in line 71, "ubiquitous" most nearly means

A) rare.
B) preferred.
C) harmful.
D) universal.

8

The passage primarily focuses on

A) the benefits of various metals.
B) the history of mercury and lead in medical practice.
C) the true composition of metal items in daily use.
D) the benefits and uses of silver.

9

According to the author, silver's oligodynamic effect

A) increases a diner's risk of infection.
B) promotes bacterial contamination when coating cooking pots.
C) reduces infection in animals.
D) is a mainstay of modern medicine.

10

Which choice provides the best evidence for the answer to the previous question?

A) Lines 54-56 ("Over two… wound dressings")
B) Lines 61-66 ("Bandages… for bandages.")
C) Lines 74-76 ("You might… effect of silver")
D) Lines 89-91 ("Often, those… 'silver spoon'")

Information & Ideas – Science – Passage 2

This passage is adapted from an article about the influence of agriculture on plant genetics.

Through genetic variation and natural selection, species can adapt and change over generations. Evolution is a natural phenomenon that can take millions of years for its subtle influence to take
5 noticeable effect. Through carefully controlled, selective breeding, however, we can see species change in a much briefer span of time.

Corn is perhaps the greatest success story in human-guided evolution. In the archaeological
10 record, corn suddenly appeared about 9,000 years ago. In the modern world, corn is the source for nearly one-quarter of all human nutrition across the globe, but its origin had long been a mystery. Recently, geneticists were able to trace the ancestor
15 of corn to an unlikely source: a wild grass known as teosinte. This grass grows in bushy clusters of thin stalks that end in clusters of seeds. These are not the large, yellow cobs with hundreds of plump, sweet kernels, but single rows of less than a dozen stacked
20 seeds. The teosinte seeds are small, green, hard, and triangular. It's easy to understand how archaeologists never made the connection between this wild grass and modern cultivated corn. In fact, teosinte was once classified as more closely related to rice than to
25 corn.

The connection between corn and teosinte was first made in the 1930s, when a graduate student at Cornell University discovered that corn and teosinte have identical chromosomes. Through breeding corn-
30 teosinte hybrids, he showed they were the same species. With further testing of genetic inheritance, he concluded that corn and teosinte, although exhibiting very different features, only differed in four or five genes. He even showed that teosinte
35 seeds would pop when heated, similar to corn kernels.

More recently, geneticists have mapped the genetic material of a 5,000-year-old corncob to determine which genes distinguish modern corn from
40 teosinte. This fossil is smaller than the ears of corn we find in today's markets. At less than an inch long and an eighth of an inch wide, it's an important stepping stone between modern corn and its ancient ancestor. Scientists found the 5,000-year-old corn
45 already showed the modern form of the "tga1" gene, which is responsible for the hardness of the seed casing. Based on this, scientists know one of the first traits to change in teosinte was its seeds evolved to be softer, making them easier to eat, like the plump,
50 juicy kernels in modern corn.

Based on the genetic and archaeological evidence, a story of corn's evolution emerges. About 9,000 years ago, migratory settlements of people in Central America were harvesting wild teosinte and
55 beginning to cultivate the most ideal specimens. These people carefully scrutinized the grass seeds, prioritizing those with the softest casing and using these seeds for new crops. Each season, they continued to reserve the best seeds for the next
60 planting. Over generations, their selective breeding of teosinte led to crops that looked more distinct from the wild grass and more ideal for consumption. The change in seed casing was one of the first and most significant changes. Another change, directly caused
65 by mankind's intervention, was the change of how the seeds clung to the stalk. Rather than a single stack of seeds that easily broke apart, there were multiple rows of seeds that clung to the stalk. This change would not likely have occurred naturally, because it
70 is in the plant's best interest for the seeds to fall off easily, thus allowing the organism to better proliferate. For agriculture, however, it was ideal to have large groups of seeds that remained intact, thus minimizing loss. In a relatively short time, teosinte
75 was coaxed into a new form. Selective breeding led to changes in a few genes, which had dramatic effects. Over the following millennia, many more minor adaptations were developed, including changes in starch production, kernel size and shape, and pest
80 resistance.

1

Based on information provided in the passage, modern corn is similar to teosinte in

A) color.
B) shape.
C) chromosomes.
D) size.

2

According to the passage, the "tga1" gene is responsible for

A) the number of chromosomes.
B) the softness of the seed cover.
C) the color of kernels.
D) the taste of teosinte.

3

As used in line 72, "proliferate" most nearly means

A) gather energy.
B) reproduce.
C) die off.
D) grow.

4

The evolution of corn from teosinte was primarily due to

A) careful breeding done by agricultural societies.
B) genetic manipulation performed in laboratories.
C) a series of natural disasters over several millennia.
D) changes in the seed casing caused by alterations in climate.

5

Which choice provides the best evidence for the answer to the previous question?

A) Lines 37-40 ("More recently... teosinte.")
B) Lines 44-47 ("Scientists... the seed casing.")
C) Lines 56-58 ("These people... new crops.")
D) Lines 66-68 ("Rather than... to the stalk.")

6

One advantage of the teosinte plant over the modern corn plant is that teosinte

A) makes better popcorn.
B) is easier to harvest.
C) plants produce more starch.
D) seeds break apart more easily.

7

Selective breeding of food crops such as corn and teosinte began

A) 5000 years ago with the tgal gene discovery.
B) in the 1930s at Cornell University.
C) when mapping of the human genome was completed.
D) 9000 years ago in Central America.

8

As used in line 37, "mapped" most nearly means

A) carefully drawn.
B) perfectly copied.
C) fully documented.
D) naturally grown.

9

Which choice best supports the idea that the evolution of modern corn could not have occurred without human intervention?

A) Lines 47-50 ("scientists... modern corn.")
B) Lines 60-62 ("Over... for consumption.")
C) Lines 69-72 ("it is... to better proliferate.")
D) Lines 75-77 ("Selective... effects.")

10

What is a main idea of the third paragraph (lines 26-36)?

A) Corn and teosinte both pop when exposed to enough heat.
B) Cross-breeding corn and teosinte showed their genetic similarity.
C) Not all genetic differences manifest in recognizable ways.
D) Ancient people created the first corn-teosinte hybrids.

Information & Ideas – Science – Passage 3

This passage is adapted from an article about the spread of regional foods that are now common worldwide.

Contact with pre-Columbian populations in the Americas has long been a matter of research and controversy. Circumstantial evidence indicates that language and art were almost certainly shared across
5 the Pacific Ocean well before 1500 C.E. A new study of DNA from 1,245 varieties of sweet potato suggests that Polynesians traveled to South America and began to spread the sweet potato westward no later than 1200 C.E.; such work adds new details to the
10 intertwined histories of humans and plants.

Examining the historical paths agricultural products have traveled is a common way for scientists to track the migrations of people. Europeans brought the sweet potato, a versatile and
15 nutritious crop native only to the Americas, with them as they colonized the Pacific region, but there is also evidence that the plant was already there when they arrived. One Polynesian word for the sweet potato—*kuumala*—is thought to be based on the
20 words *kumara* and *cumal*, which refer to the plant in Quencha, a native Andean language. Furthermore, archeologists have found remnants of sweet potato plants at Polynesian sites dating to before 1100 C.E. The spread of the sweet potato across Polynesia and
25 Oceania raises many questions: Did the plant reach the region before it was introduced by Europeans? If so, who brought it? Where and when did it arrive? And how did the sweet potato achieve such rich and complicated genetic variety?

30 Until recently, researchers investigating the spread of the sweet potato had to rely on the genetic profiles of modern day varieties for clues. Studies searching these specimens for genetic markers that would indicate early movement of the plant across
35 the Pacific instead revealed a complex and clouded history; none was able to demonstrate where in the region the plant was first introduced or how it spread.

A new study by a team of French researchers used stable markers common to both modern and
40 herbarium samples of sweet potato DNA to resolve this puzzle. The team sampled preserved specimens that had been brought back by early European explorers of the region such as James Cook; by comparing these herbarium samples to modern
45 varieties of sweet potato, the team was able to identify complementary sets of genetic markers—chloroplast and nuclear micro-satellites—that allowed them to track the initial spread of the plant across the Pacific. They noted two distinct shifts in
50 the distribution of genetic variation over the genetic

history of the region's sweet potatoes. These temporal shifts indicated that the plant's natural evolution had been altered by recombination with other distinct sweet potato gene pools. The sweet
55 potato had arrived in Oceania and Polynesia in three separate waves, the first of which had to have occurred hundreds of years before two later reintroductions.

The paper, recently published in the
60 "Proceedings of the National Academy of Sciences," finally reveals the course the sweet potato traveled. A variety native to the Ecuadoran and Peruvian Andes was likely first retrieved by Polynesian explorers and planted in eastern Polynesia around 1100 C.E. This
65 Andean sweet potato adapted well to its new island environment and spread across the region, eventually reaching as far as New Zealand. Two other distinct varieties of the sweet potato, native to other parts of the Americas, were subsequently carried to the region
70 by Spanish and Portuguese colonizers, and these were interbred with the original to create an explosion of new varieties with obscured genetic origins.

"There's been many kinds of evidence, linguistic
75 and archeological, for the connection between these two peoples," said Caroline Rouiller, the evolutionary biologist who led the French study, referring to the interaction of native Polynesians and South Americans, "but the sweet potato is the most
80 compelling."

1

The passage suggests that the sweet potato was first brought to Polynesia by

A) Spanish and Portuguese colonists.
B) Polynesians who voyaged to South America.
C) Explorers including James Cook.
D) Natives from the Andean Mountains.

2

Which choice provides the best evidence for the answer to the previous question?

A) Lines 14-16 ("Europeans... the Pacific region")
B) Lines 32-36 ("Studies... clouded history")
C) Lines 54-58 ("The sweet potato... later reintroductions.")
D) Lines 61-64 ("A variety... 1100 C.E.")

3

The most important difference between the experiment described in the fourth paragraph (lines 38-58) and previous studies of Polynesian sweet potatoes was that previous researchers

A) only analyzed DNA from specimens collected after European colonization.

B) were unaware of the history of Spanish and Portuguese exploration in the region.

C) had difficulty growing sweet potatoes from Polynesia in a cooler climate.

D) relied only on linguistic and archeological evidence.

4

The author refers to which of the following as recent evidence of pre-Columbian contact between Polynesians and South Americans?

A) Natives of Polynesia and South America use similar words to refer to the sweet potato.

B) Evidence of sweet potato plants in Polynesia dating to before 1100 C.E.

C) The collection of sweet potato specimens by early European explorers of Polynesia

D) The widespread cultivation of sweet potatoes in Spain and Portugal

5

It can be reasonably inferred from the passage that the variety mentioned in the second paragraph (lines 28-29) was caused by

A) the reintroduction of the sweet potato by Spanish and Portuguese colonists.

B) the mixing of varieties as different groups shared multiple types of sweet potatoes.

C) the presence of chloroplasts and nuclear micro-satellites.

D) genetic engineering by French scientists.

6

The passage is primarily concerned with

A) the colonization of Polynesia and Oceania.

B) modern shipping routes for sweet potatoes and other produce.

C) representations of the sweet potato in Polynesian and South American art.

D) the origins of the different varieties of sweet potato found in the Pacific region.

7

The scientists discussed in the passage chose to study the sweet potato in order to better understand

A) the history of early contact between native Polynesians and South Americans.

B) how food-producing plants adapt to new environments.

C) the political consequences of European colonization in the Pacific region.

D) genetic differences between the inhabitants of neighboring Polynesian Islands

8

As used in lines 40 and 44, "herbarium samples" are

A) genetic markers common to several related organisms.

B) plant specimens that have been preserved.

C) DNA that has recently been extracted from living plants.

D) a group of plants that share a common ancestry.

9

According to scientific studies, South American sweet potato varieties were likely first brought home by Polynesian explorers

A) around 1100 C.E.

B) around 1200 C.E.

C) around 1500 C.E.

D) after sweet potatoes were brought from South America by James Cook.

10

According to the studies cited in the passage, the sweet potato originated in

A) Polynesia.

B) Oceania.

C) South America.

D) Europe.

Information & Ideas – Science – Passage 4

This passage is adapted from an article about Middle-Eastern architecture.

Humans have always been captivated by great heights. From the natural majesty of the sequoia tree growing over 300 feet tall, to East Asia's holy tiered tower pagodas, to the intimidating sight of a castle's
5 defensive turrets, we are awed by structures looming high above us. As soon as man learned to stack stones, we sought to reach loftier heights. This obsession with reaching the heavens is perhaps best captured in the story of Babel, the ambitious tower
10 which sought to reach the realm of God and which ended in catastrophe. For as we aim to climb ever higher, we contend with the ever greater risk of plummeting disastrously back to earth. The awe of towers, primarily seen today in modern skyscrapers,
15 is accompanied by the fearful and exhilarating anticipation of their falling, a risk we carefully and stubbornly strive to overcome.

As of 2018, the tallest building on the planet is the Burj Khalifa, Dubai's astonishingly high
20 skyscraper. At a height of 2,717 feet, more than 1,000 feet taller than Taipei 101, the previous titleholder, the Burj Khalifa must contend with incredible pressures to remain upright. Since the creation of the world's first skyscraper, Chicago's 10-story Home
25 Insurance Building erected in 1885, architects have known the primary stressor that threatens these tall buildings is not the vertical pull of gravity but the horizontal push of wind. This can be easily demonstrated on a smaller scale: imagine a wood
30 stick driven a couple inches into the ground; as long as the stick is sufficiently rigid, it is in little danger of collapsing, but a sudden breeze may quickly knock it over. A marvel of engineering, the Burj Khalifa's design is focused primarily on finding ways to
35 contend with stress from winds, or "wind loading."

In heavy winds, you may notice trees, street signs and even streetlight poles swaying. Imagine this force multiplied on the scale of a super-tall skyscraper. How, then, do architects and engineers
40 develop buildings that can withstand such pressures? The most important phenomena with which a skyscraper must contend are vortices—swirling currents of air—forming as the wind blows by. When wind strikes a building, it first pushes against the
45 structure, but then must get around it. The wind moves around the sides of the building in whirlpools. You may have seen a similar effect on water as it flows around large stones in a stream. These vortices of wind create suction, pulling at the building on one
50 side while the wind also pushes on another side. These vortices exert pressure on one side and then the other, rocking the building from side to side, a force

which can push a building over. When tall buildings are close together, the turbulence of wind among the
55 buildings will break up these vortices, so they don't grow stronger. However, when a building stands alone at great heights, as the Burj Khalifa does, it cannot rely on others to assist in combatting the winds.

60 The Burj Khalifa stands like a lightning bolt from the lavish urban sprawl of Dubai. The spire climbs to a sharp point in staggered rises, seeming to shift from side to side as it reaches ever upward. This unique, uneven design is not only stylistic; it's one of
65 several ways the building is designed to "confuse the wind." Burj Khalifa is designed as a series of stalks terminating at various heights. This inconsistency breaks up the wind, preventing the creation of massive, destructive vortices. In a sense, it acts as a
70 collection of buildings. Furthermore, the edges are rounded and the spires are organized in a triangular layout, which helps wind move fluidly around the structure. Even with all of its brilliant design features, the Burj Khalifa is not immune to the wind's forces.
75 At its highest levels, it slowly sways about 6 feet from side to side.

Confusing the wind is not the only way skyscrapers contend with wind. The Taipei 101 tower lets something else carry the burden. Near the top of
80 the building, between the 87th and 91st floors, is suspended an enormous pendulum. A golden orb, 18 feet across and weighing 728 tons, swings gently from 4 cables. As wind pushes in one direction, the orb swings the opposite way. Termed a "tuned mass
85 damper," the swaying ball helps stabilize the structure and is useful against not only wind but also other vibratory forces, such as earthquakes.

As innovations in engineering and material sciences allow us to build ever higher, one may
90 wonder if there is any limit. Long the topic of science fiction, space elevators—towers that reach 22,000 miles in height to extend beyond geostationary orbit and deliver cargo to outer space—may prove to be tangible reality. At the most extreme, architects have
95 imagined the Analemma Tower, a building that would dangle from an asteroid circling 31,000 miles above the Earth, reaching down to only 3 miles above the planet's surface and drifting over major cities. Looking ahead, we can anticipate being regularly
100 wowed by the greater and greater heights we'll reach.

1

The Baj Khalifa's unique approach to resisting the power of the wind utilizes

A) a smooth skin that helps the wind flow past.
B) energy harnessed from lightning bolts.
C) sections of different heights on all sides.
D) skyscrapers nearby to break up the wind.

2

The author states that many skyscrapers

A) cause wind problems for the buildings around them.
B) are designed to lean into the wind.
C) use counterweights to help resist the wind.
D) rely on neighboring buildings to break up the wind currents.

3

The passage primarily focuses on

A) structural techniques for building skyscrapers.
B) the beauty and design of the Baj Khalifa.
C) how skyscrapers resist the wind.
D) the locations of the world's tallest skyscrapers.

4

Wind is a problem for skyscrapers because

A) the wind is stronger high up and pushes the top of the building.
B) while the wind pushes the building from one side, the currents formed when the wind passes by pull it in the same direction.
C) winds can come from various directions which makes the building unstable.
D) the wind pushing against the building combines with suction to make the building rock back and forth.

5

As used in line 5, the word "looming" means

A) weaving together.
B) threatening.
C) standing.
D) appearing.

6

It can be inferred that the author believes that

A) the problems created by wind on skyscrapers have been totally overcome.
B) the Baj Khalifa utilizes the best wind stabilization strategies thus far developed.
C) the dangers posed to skyscrapers by the wind will limit how tall humans can build.
D) engineers will continue to develop ever more effective methods of countering the dangers posed by wind on skyscrapers.

7

The Taipei 101 tower's "golden orb" serves as

A) a traditional decoration.
B) a damper on earthquakes and wind forces.
C) a pendulum to keep accurate time.
D) a stabilizer against the force of gravity.

8

The main idea of the passage is that

A) there are a variety of ways that engineers combat the force of the wind on skyscrapers.
B) humans feel compelled to build tall structures even though they are dangerous and difficult to build.
C) skyscrapers will continue being built taller as construction techniques and materials improve.
D) wind is the greatest challenge for engineers to overcome.

9

Which choice provides the best evidence for the answer to the previous question?

A) lines 1-2 ("Humans have… heights")
B) lines 23-28 ("Since the creation… wind")
C) lines 33-35 ("A marvel… 'wind loading'")
D) lines 77-78 ("Confusing… with wind")

10

As used in line 44, the word "strikes" means

A) assaults.
B) protests.
C) misses.
D) docks.

Information & Ideas – Science – Passage 5

This passage is adapted from an article about early ventures in space exploration.

Will humans ever make that great leap and travel beyond our solar system? As unlikely as it sounds, we actually already have. Voyager 1, a car-sized space probe that launched in 1977, left the solar
5   system in 2012, crossing over a threshold known as the "heliosphere," a protective bubble of particles and magnetic fields created by the sun. Voyager 2, launched in the same year, just recently entered interstellar space as well, and unlike its predecessor,
10   it still has working instruments that will be able to send back data about this unexplored region. Both of these probes were originally designed to explore the gas giants of our solar system, and together they made groundbreaking discoveries about Jupiter,
15   Saturn, Uranus, Neptune, as well as many of their moons, rings, and magnetic fields. As if this weren't enough, the two Voyagers have continued working for over forty years, and now serve as the farthest-flung time capsules humanity has ever devised. This
20   is because the probes each carry precious cargo: a 12-inch, gold-plated copper phonograph disc that tells a piece of humanity's story.

These "Golden Records" were designed to be a message to extraterrestrial life. If it sounds to you
25   like a difficult task to pack all of humanity into one small disc, you would be right! This monumental challenge was presented to astronomer Carl Sagan, who assembled a team of scientists, artists, and engineers. Their task was to create a record that
30   would stand the test of time, present information easily, and give other worlds a taste of humankind. In answer to the challenge of durability, the materials used to construct the records were carefully chosen to last for millennia and encased in a protective
35   aluminum jacket with a cartridge and a needle. So that aliens would know how to use the device, a diagram was engraved into the record showing how to play it, as well as images of human beings and our location in relation to nearby stellar landmarks.
40   Scientists carefully considered each aspect of the record's creation, but most difficult of all was what to actually put on the recording.

Timothy Ferris, a music journalist who helped Carl Sagan in his task, said their goals were to "cast a
45   wide net. Let's try to get music from all over the planet. And secondly: Let's make a good record." To that end, Ferris and his colleagues gathered as many records as they could from around the world and listened obsessively over the few months they had to
50   put their interstellar playlist together. Ultimately, the records mostly contained music, including opera, classical, rock 'n' roll, blues, and field recordings from several different cultures. In addition, there were greetings in dozens of languages, messages
55   from prominent leaders, and a history of Earth in sounds and pictures encoded into the records' grooves. Interestingly, for years this unique collection was unavailable to Earth ears; the record couldn't be produced commercially because of
60   copyright issues. In 2017, however, Voyager enthusiasts banded together and raised money to finally publish the music found on those golden discs.

Despite all the work the producers of the Voyagers' discs put into the project, it is uncertain
65   whether the probes will ever be discovered by aliens. While Voyager 2 is one of the fastest objects ever made by humanity, now moving at the healthy clip of 34,191 miles per hour, this speed is tiny compared to the enormous scales of distance in outer space. While
70   both Voyagers have technically emerged into interstellar space, some scientists consider the edge of the solar system to be the Oort Cloud, a collection of distant, small objects that are still influenced by the sun's gravity. This cloud is estimated to extend
75   out to around 100,000 AU from the sun (1 AU is the distance between the sun and Earth), which means the Voyagers will not pass through it for another 30,000 years. It will take at least 40,000 years before either of the two probes pass anywhere near another
80   star, but the nuclear batteries that power them will fail in only a few years, at which point we will no longer hear from them. In other words, it is unlikely that the messages encoded in the golden discs will ever reach their intended ears.
85   While aliens may never receive our golden discs, the Voyager probes are an expression of humanity's desire to explore. They will continue to fly through space for millions of years, serving as a legacy of our search for knowledge and as a time capsule of the
90   music, history, and voices we thought important at the time of their launch. In creating this time capsule, scientists and artists were tasked with defining humanity, our values and our culture. In doing so, the creators chose to emphasize our diversity,
95   connectedness, and desire to reach across the stars.

1

The word "monumental" in line 26 most nearly means

A) impossible.

B) enlarged.

C) significant.

D) modest.

SUMMIT
EDUCATIONAL
GROUP

2

According to the passage, the Voyagers will stop transmitting data to Earth when

A) they leave our solar system.
B) they pass through the Oort Cloud.
C) their batteries fail.
D) their heat shields melt.

3

It can be logically inferred from the passage that

A) the author supports additional exploration of outer space.
B) the author questions the individuals selected to produce the discs.
C) the author feels the content of the discs should have been publicly released sooner.
D) the author appreciates the Voyagers and their unique cargo.

4

As it is used in line 88, the word "legacy" most nearly means

A) enduring proof.
B) financial compensation.
C) a suggestion.
D) a leftover.

5

According to the passage, Voyagers 1 and 2 are different in that

A) they were launched in different years.
B) they have different goal destinations.
C) only one carries a "Golden Record."
D) only one is still transmitting data.

6

Which choice provides the best evidence for the answer to the previous question?

A) lines 3-7 ("Voyager 1… by the sun.")
B) lines 7-11 ("Voyager 2… region.")
C) lines 11-16 ("Both… magnetic fields.")
D) lines 16-19 ("As if… ever devised.")

7

Which of the following best describes the contents of the golden discs?

A) Diverse music, greetings in numerous languages, messages from American leaders, American history
B) Diverse music, greetings in numerous languages, messages from prominent leaders, world history
C) Contemporary music, greetings in several languages, messages from prominent leaders, world history
D) Contemporary music, greetings in numerous languages, messages from American leaders, world history

8

According to the passage, one of the most challenging aspects of creating the "Golden Records" was

A) determining the materials used to construct them.
B) finalizing the diagrams engraved on each.
C) designing the protective jacket.
D) narrowing down their contents.

9

Which choice provides the best evidence for the answer to the previous question?

A) Lines 29-31 ("Their task… humankind.")
B) Lines 31-35 ("In answer… needle."
C) Lines 40-42 ("Scientists… recording.")
D) Lines 57-60 ("for years… issues.")

10

Which of the following statements best summarizes the final paragraph?

A) The Voyagers represent humanity's attempt to reach the end of the universe.
B) The Voyagers and their discs show a futile attempt to explore the universe.
C) The Voyagers and their discs are a worthwhile endeavor and a positive representation of mankind.
D) The Voyagers and their discs represent mankind's intellectual prowess.

Information & Ideas – Science – Passage 6

This passage is adapted from an article about the winners of an international science fair.

It was the early days of the United States Civil War. In the months before the Battle of Shiloh, the Union army had taken control of much of Tennessee. Albert Sidney Johnston, the Confederate general, was
5 forced to gather his troops in northern Mississippi, where he planned a counterattack against two legions of Union troops, both tens of thousands strong, which were planning to rendezvous at Corinth, a railroad center of strategic importance. Johnston struck at the
10 army of Ulysses S. Grant before the second force, led by General Don Carlos Buell, would arrive. However, heavy rains and muddy roads slowed Johnston's advance. When he launched the surprise attack, on the dawn of April 6, Buell's troops were
15 already narrowing in. Throughout the day, the Union soldiers were battered by the Confederates and were pushed back toward the Tennessee River. The Confederates' advantage, however, faltered as Buell's supply of soldiers arrived. General Johnston
20 was mortally wounded in the battle, and the Union forces grew to greater numbers than that of the Confederates. Such setbacks led to the Confederates' defeat the following day, as the Union army pushed them back.
25 The Battle of Shiloh resulted in more than 16,000 wounded soldiers. Neither side, regardless of ultimate victory or defeat, was prepared for such bloodshed. The Union and Confederate armies both lacked adequate numbers of trained medics to treat
30 the injured. Soldiers waited for days while their wounds worsened. Surely, many died tragically from injuries that may have been treatable. Others fell prey to minor injuries that grew into deadly infections. Miraculously, however, some of the wounded
35 soldiers survived, and many of these lucky combatants exhibited a bizarre phenomenon: their injuries glowed.

As the sun set on the field of the Battle of Shiloh, troops scoured the land for wounded comrades. Some
40 of these soldiers were unusually easy to find, because parts of their bodies were casting faint blue lights in the darkness. Even more surprisingly, as was discovered after the soldiers were treated by doctors, the wounded soldiers with glowing blue spots had a
45 significantly higher survival rate. The glowing wounds were less susceptible to infection. At the time, the marvel was attributed to divine grace, as the phenomenon was called "Angel's Glow." Recently, a young scientist investigated this strange element of
50 the Battle of Shiloh to determine whether the tales of

Angel's Glow are true and to explain the link between the strange light and the rate of survival.

In 2001, 17-year-old Bill Martin heard about Angel's Glow while he was on a trip to the battlefield
55 of Shiloh with his family. Curious about the story, he inquired with his mother, who he was sure would have some insights. A microbiologist at the USDA Agricultural Research Service, his mother had experience studying luminescent bacteria. Bill may
60 have been surprised, however, when she didn't offer a definitive answer but instead encouraged him to create his own experiment to find the answer.

Bill, along with friend Jon Curtis, began by researching the bioluminescent bacterium
65 *Photorhabdus luminescens*, which they assumed was the source of the glow. This bacterium lives within the guts of nematodes, parasitic worms that burrow into the blood vessels of insect larvae. Upon finding insect larvae, usually within soil or on the surface of
70 plants, nematodes release *P. luminescens* bacteria. This kills that insect, as well as any troublesome microorganisms, allowing the nematode to feed in peace. The nematode also ingests the bacteria again so it can continue to be used. Scientists believe the *P.*
75 *luminescens* bacteria serves another beneficial purpose: its glow attracts more insects, allowing the nematode to easily feed again. Bill and Jon determined that *P. luminescens* was a likely cause of the Angel's Glow because its ability to kill
80 microorganisms would have protected the soldiers from infectious bacteria or pathogens. However, their experiments showed that *P. luminescens* cannot survive at the warm temperatures present in the human body. This seemed to disprove their theory,
85 until they did further research on the environmental conditions of the Battle of Shiloh. In the spring in Tennessee, the nights are cool. Also, there had been days of cold rain that further dropped temperatures. Furthermore, when sick or losing blood, the soldier's
90 bodies would have been colder than normal. Altogether, several factors could have worked together to create a hospitable environment within the soldier's wounds. While not as charming as the idea of angels, the nematodes and their bacteria were
95 saviors for many of the Union and Confederate troops. And with their research, Bill and Jon won first place in the 2001 Intel International Science and Engineering Fair.

1

After the Battle of Shiloh, Confederate troops were aided in finding some of their wounded soldiers by

A) their easily recognizable uniforms.
B) their particular location south of the Tennessee River.
C) their glowing wounds.
D) specially-trained dogs.

2

According to the passage, Angel's Glow was caused by

A) glowing nematodes.
B) *P. luminescens* bacteria.
C) divine grace.
D) deadly pathogens.

3

Based on the passage, the source of Angel's Glow was discovered by

A) high school students.
B) a U.S. Department of Agriculture biologist.
C) Civil War doctors.
D) General Don Carlos Buell.

4

According to the passage, the growth of Angel's Glow was aided by

A) treatment by battlefield medics.
B) the administration of antibiotics.
C) bright sunlight on the battlefield.
D) cool weather conditions.

5

Which choice provides the best evidence for the answer to the previous question?

A) Lines 34-37 ("Miraculously… glowed")
B) Lines 66-68 ("This bacterium… larvae")
C) Lines 81-84 ("their experiments… body.")
D) Lines 87-88 ("there had… temperatures")

6

As used in line 92, "hospitable" most nearly means

A) favorably receptive.
B) pleasantly courteous.
C) clinically medical.
D) amiably congenial.

7

Many of the wounded from the Battle of Shiloh succumbed to their wounds because of

A) the abundance of trained medics.
B) having to wait days for medical treatment.
C) the spread of *P. luminescens* bacteria.
D) the treatment of infections.

8

Based on the passage, nematodes helped wounded soldiers heal by

A) feeding on the soldiers' blood.
B) destroying insect larvae that would otherwise have killed them.
C) releasing bacteria that prevented infection.
D) producing Angel's Glow that enabled them to be found more quickly by other insects.

9

As used in line 75, "beneficial" most nearly means

A) profitable.
B) benign.
C) unhealthy.
D) advantageous.

10

As used in line 13, "advance" most nearly means

A) pay.
B) complexity.
C) progress.
D) privilege.

Information & Ideas – Science – Passage 7

This passage is adapted from an article about paleontological research into insects.

The dragonflies we know today seem more "flies" than "dragons." 300 million years ago, they were monstrous. Imagine these insects with wingspans two and a half feet across. They were the
5 size of modern crows and may have been fierce predators. Fossil records have preserved the legacy of these flying terrors, but scientists are still seeking a definitive explanation for how insects grew to such massive size. The likely condition allowing giant
10 prehistoric bugs is a surplus of oxygen. During the Carboniferous period, from 359 to 299 million years ago, much of Earth's surface was covered in swampy forests. The extraordinary levels of vegetation increased atmospheric oxygen, which was 50 percent
15 higher than modern levels. This oxygen-rich environment set the stage for drastic changes in some species, as seen in the dragon-like dragonflies, though scientists differ on what they believe is the causal link.
20   Not all insects grow larger in high-oxygen environments. During the Carboniferous period, for example, cockroaches were smaller in size than their modern counterparts. Unfortunately, the largest cockroaches to ever exist are those we have today. At
25 Arizona State University in Tempe, John VandenBrooks is leading research into how ancient oxygen levels would have influenced the evolution of insect species. The work was painstaking, as dragonflies are notoriously difficult to rear. For
30 nearly half a year, their supply of 225 young dragonflies had to be hand-fed worms and guppies daily. His team also raised cockroaches, beetles, grasshoppers, meal worms, and other insects, totaling twelve species, in conditions of varying oxygen
35 concentration. Ten types of the studied insects grew smaller in low oxygen, but the response to high oxygen was more varied. Dragonflies grew bigger in an oxygen-rich state, known as "hyperoxia." Cockroaches, however, remained the same size and
40 grew more slowly, taking about twice as long to reach maturity. VandenBrooks was surprised by this, as he had expected the increase in oxygen to speed up development of larvae. His team investigated by studying the insects' tracheal tubes, hollow structures
45 within insects' bodies that allow them to breathe. They discovered that insects reared in hyperoxic conditions had smaller tracheal tubes. "As you become a larger insect, more of your body is taken up by tracheal tubes," VandenBrooks explains.
50 "Eventually you reach a limit to how big you can be. The more oxygen that is available, the smaller that system needs to be and the bigger you can grow." This explains the increased size of dragonflies, but it doesn't account for why cockroaches did not grow
55 larger.
    At Plymouth University in the United Kingdom, Wilco Verberk and colleague David Bilton have also researched the connection between oxygen levels and insect growth. According to their study, the increased
60 size of insects may have been a reaction in defense against hyperoxia rather than an attempt to take advantage of it. Hoping to avoid the challenge of raising dragonflies in the lab, Verberk studied stonefly larvae because, like dragonflies, they live in
65 water before becoming terrestrial adults. When there are higher concentrations of oxygen in the atmosphere, there is also more oxygen present in water. As juveniles growing in water, stoneflies are very sensitive to fluctuations in oxygen levels.
70 Whereas adult stoneflies can regulate oxygen absorption by closing their valve-like spiracles, the larvae absorb oxygen through their skin. In large quantities, oxygen becomes poisonous. Even we humans, who depend on oxygen for every breath,
75 will experience problems with vision, nausea, and convulsions when exposed to excessive oxygen levels. In the hyperoxia of the Carboniferous period, some insects may have adapted by growing larger. As the insects grew, they lowered the risk of oxygen
80 toxicity because they would absorb lower amounts relative to their size. It's simple math, explains Verberk: "If you grow larger, your surface area decreases relative to your volume." This theory also explains why these larger insects no longer flourish.
85 "If oxygen actively drove increases in body mass to avoid toxicity, lower levels would not be immediately fatal, although in time, they will probably diminish performance of the larger insects."
    With enough understanding of the link between
90 insects and oxygen levels, scientists may gain new insights into different ancient eras. By studying the fossil records, changes in insects can reveal atmospheric conditions, unlocking one clue to the puzzle of what the world was like millions of years
95 ago.

1

VandenBrooks and Verberk both studied oxygen levels and why they led to dragonflies growing large. Their greatest disagreement is

A) VandenBrooks considers high oxygen levels to be an advantage that allowed extreme growth, while Verberk considers them to be a problem that dragonflies overcame by growing large.

B) VandenBrooks considers it critical to use dragonflies in the study, while Verberk replaced dragonflies with stoneflies.

C) VandenBrooks determined that high oxygen levels led to faster growth of dragonfly larvae, while Verberk states that high oxygen levels in water kill the larvae.

D) VandenBrooks believes his work will prove most important to controlling insect populations while Verberk believes it should be used to study changing atmospheric conditions.

2

It can be inferred that cockroaches are currently the largest ever because

A) dragonflies are no longer large enough to eat them.

B) oxygen levels are lower than in the past, so their larvae grow faster and bigger.

C) cockroaches have relatively large tracheal tubes, which allow them to grow larger.

D) cockroaches have relatively small tracheal tubes, which allow them to grow larger.

3

The passage focuses primarily on

A) the different methods used by the two teams of scientists.

B) the fate of the dragonfly's evolutionary development.

C) the effects of oxygen levels on the size of certain insects.

D) whether hyperoxia caused dragonflies to grow larger or smaller.

4

According to the studies described in the passage, most insects raised in low oxygen conditions

A) had smaller tracheal tubes.

B) consistently grew smaller.

C) grew larger, but some developed more slowly.

D) used spiracles to absorb water through their skin.

5

An unexpected finding made by VandenBrooks was

A) cockroach larvae developed more slowly in high oxygen.

B) it was not necessary to cultivate the hard-to-raise dragonflies to solve the problem.

C) oxygen becomes poisonous in high quantities.

D) even with high oxygen rates, there is a limit to the maximum size of an insect.

6

The author uses the word "painstaking" in line 28 to suggest that

A) it is painful to hand-feed dragonflies.

B) the work had to be done in an extremely careful, methodical manner.

C) it was disappointing when dragonflies died due to errors in feeding protocols.

D) VandenBrooks was overly fastidious about how his dragonflies were fed.

7

As used in line 29, "rear" most nearly means

A) end.

B) control.

C) back.

D) raise.

SUMMIT
EDUCATIONAL
GROUP

8

How do VandenBrooks and Verberk disagree on the primary adaptive mechanism changing insect size due to oxygen level increases?

A) VandenBrooks believes that increased tracheal tube size was most important in determining size, while Verberk thinks that larval spiracles were able to utilize increased oxygen to promote growth.

B) VandenBrooks believes that greater food availability during the Carboniferous period led to increased size, while Verberk believes that larval spiracles were able to utilize increased oxygen to promote growth.

C) VandenBrooks believes that slower larval development allows for greater size of the adult, while Verberk believes that slower larval development leads to smaller adults.

D) VandenBrooks considers the changing size of the tracheal tubes most important, while Verberk thinks the larvae grow larger so that there is less exposure to oxygen in relation to its mass.

9

Verberk believes that the insects of the Carboniferous Period grew larger by adapting to

A) have the larvae close their spiracles when necessary.

B) spend their larval stage in water before moving onto land for their adult lives.

C) change the ratio of their larval skin to their body size.

D) growing larger tracheal tubes.

10

Which choice provides the best evidence for the previous question?

A) Lines 37-38 ("Dragonflies… 'hyperoxia.'")

B) Lines 46-47 ("They discovered… tubes.")

C) Lines 65-68 ("When there are… water.")

D) Lines 78-81 ("As the insects… size.")

Information & Ideas – Science – Passage 8

Passage 1 is adapted from an article about the hypothesis that life on Earth began either at the bottoms or coasts of oceans. Passage 2 is adapted from an article about analyses of meteorites.

Passage 1

By replicating geological and chemical conditions similar to those that would have been present on an early Earth, a research team led by John Sutherland at the University of Manchester was for
5 the first time able to synthesize a ribonucleotide, one of only several basic building blocks of RNA. Mounting evidence in recent years has served to solidify the RNA World Hypothesis, a theory that suggests that RNA, also known as ribonucleic acid,
10 the smaller cousin to DNA, is responsible for the origin of life on Earth. It was not until Sutherland's 2009 experiment that there was any evidence that the basic components of RNA could be spontaneously produced through a series of chemical reactions that
15 were once abundant on a prebiotic Earth.
     RNA has long been a great candidate as the originator of life. Not only is RNA essential to the replication of DNA, but it is an integral component of transcription and translation, the cellular processes
20 through which proteins and many enzymes are decoded from DNA and then synthesized. Enzymes are molecules that speed up critical chemical reactions in biological systems, and they are absolutely crucial for sustaining all forms of life on
25 Earth. Finding a method to produce them from just the base materials of an early Earth is essential for understanding how life began.
     The first convincing evidence for the RNA World Hypothesis came in the 1980s from the
30 discovery of ribozymes, enzymes that are made entirely of RNA. Sidney Altman and Thomas Cech, who would both go on to win the Nobel Prize in Chemistry in 1989, were the first to discover this unusual class of molecules. The ribosome, a structure
35 found in all living cells, is perhaps the most prolific and famous of all ribozymes since it is the molecular complex that is responsible for the assembly of all proteins in the cell.
     But why even focus on RNA? If DNA contains
40 the code for life, why couldn't it alone have originated life as we know it? As it turns out, RNA carries the same basic type of information that DNA does, since it is composed of almost the same material, but unlike DNA, it is single-stranded,
45 simpler, and can replicate on its own. Just months before Sutherland's big discovery, Tracey Lincoln and Gerald Joyce at the Scripps Institute were able to

demonstrate that RNA could replicate itself in the absence of any other biomolecules, through using
50 only a soup of ribonucleotides and RNA-based enzymes (ribozymes). Not only could the RNA replicate as a self-sustaining molecular system, but sometimes different versions of the RNA enzymes would combine, forming mutant recombinant forms,
55 demonstrating that RNA had the potential to evolve. According to Joyce, "What we've found could be relevant to how life begins, at the key moment when Darwinian evolution starts."

Passage 2

It may sound like the plot of a sci-fi movie, but
60 there is strong evidence to suggest that life could have originated in outer space. The Murchison meteorite, a stony chondrite that fell to Earth in Australia in the late 1960s, contains a variety of life-sustaining organic compounds. Most notably, the
65 meteorite contained a complex mixture of at least 70 amino acids, the building blocks of proteins. These amino acids were found in a variety of geometric configurations that do not exist on Earth, strongly suggesting the molecules originated in space and
70 were not picked up from the Earth where the rock was found. The meteorite also contained nitrogenous bases (uracil and xanthine) that are commonly found in the nucleotides that make up DNA and RNA. A team lead by Zita Martins in 2008 compared samples
75 from the meteorite to those found on Earth, comparing the Carbon isotope ratios of the bases. The significant difference in radioactive isotope composition strongly suggests that the Murchison nucleotide bases are of extraterrestrial origin.
80   Given the rising evidence for meteorites carrying the components for nucleotides and proteins, it seems more likely that the basic ingredients for life came from outside of our world. It's not just the Murchison meteorite: there are several other examples of rocks
85 that contain organic molecules that were created in space, such as the Tagish Lake meteorite found in British Columbia in 2000.
     It has long been suggested that RNA and DNA are too large, too complicated, and too difficult to
90 have been randomly constructed from the basic ingredients of an early Earth. While the conditions of space seem at first more hostile to life, the sheer vastness of the universe presents many more opportunities for random and unlikely events to
95 occur. A 2017 study published in the Journal of Chemical Physics by a research team at the University of Sherbrooke was able to show that many of the building blocks necessary for life could be

created on icy films subjected to harsh radiation and
100   vacuum (extremely low pressure) conditions, such as
those found outside our planet. Professor Charles
Cockell, an astrobiologist at the University of
Edinburgh, summarized the study nicely: "What
these experiments show is that even at the extremely
105   low temperatures of interplanetary or interstellar
space, you can get chemical reactions occurring that
lead to more complex organic compounds." While
the evidence is not definitive, the possibility that
organic molecules were first introduced to our planet
110   from extraterrestrial origins is certainly viable.

1

In the context of the passage, the word
"prebiotic" most nearly means

A)   bacterial.
B)   before life existed on Earth.
C)   robot-like.
D)   before Earth existed.

2

It can be logically inferred from information in
the passage that enzymes are "crucial for
sustaining all forms of life on Earth" (lines 24-
25) because

A)   they are a type of molecule providing
     necessary nutrition for organisms.
B)   they are one of the raw ingredients needed
     for respiration in biological systems.
C)   they help chemical reactions occur at a rapid
     rate.
D)   they are one of the key structural
     components ensuring cell walls are rigid.

3

Which of the following is a similarity between
RNA and DNA?

A)   Number of strands
B)   Complexity
C)   Type of information transmitted
D)   Ability to self-replicate

4

Passage 1 and 2 differ in their discussion of
which of the following topics?

A)   Presence of organic compounds in early life
B)   The source of the origin of life on Earth
C)   The self-replication of RNA
D)   The information carried by DNA

5

Which of the following is provided as evidence
that RNA can evolve?

A)   The combination of different versions of
     DNA, creating new mutant forms
B)   Replication of ribosomes throughout the cell
C)   The presence of new varieties created by
     joining together different types of RNA
D)   The acceleration of reactions due to the
     activity of enzymes

6

According to the author of Passage 2, the theory
that the amino acids found on the meteorite
originated in outer space is most directly a
response to

A)   the mixture of proteins found in the amino
     acids.
B)   the ages of the amino acids.
C)   the sizes of the amino acids.
D)   the shapes of the amino acids.

7

Which of the following best paraphrases the
statement in the second sentence of the final
paragraph in Passage 2 (lines 91-95)?

A)   The vastness of space allows for the
     possibility that life has originated elsewhere.
B)   The universe has many lifeforms in it.
C)   Space is hostile to the creation of new life
     forms, and it is impossible for organisms to
     ever survive there.
D)   The basic ingredients of RNA and DNA
     were found on early Earth.

8

Which of the following statements best expresses the main idea of Passage 2?

A) There are definitely multiple life forms in the universe.

B) DNA and RNA are too large and complex to be transported by meteorites.

C) Evidence suggests the building blocks of life could not have originated in outer space.

D) It is possible that organic compounds formed in space before arriving at Earth.

9

Which choice best supports the idea that RNA could not have originated on Earth?

A) Lines 17-21 ("Not only… then synthesized.")

B) Lines 51-55 ("Not only… to evolve.")

C) Lines 64-66 ("the meteorite… of proteins.")

D) Lines 91-95 ("While the conditions… to occur.")

10

As used in line 26, "base" most nearly means

A) elementary.

B) simplified.

C) immoral.

D) safe.

Information & Ideas – Science – Passage 9

Passage 1 is adapted from an article about scientists' attempts to recreate and explain mysterious phenomena recorded throughout history. Passage 2 is adapted from an article about theories regarding the phenomenon of "ball lightning."

Passage 1

For as far back as we have records of lightning bolts striking down from the heavens, we also have accounts of a much odder phenomenon: floating orbs of electricity known as "ball lightning." The
5 characteristics differ from one sighting to the next. In some cases, balls of lightning are said to float through walls and drift about aimlessly. In others, they seem to navigate with some intelligence. Some are said to be dangerous, melting panes of glass and
10 killing people when touched, but others are seemingly innocuous. They range in size from a ping pong ball to a beach ball, glow as bright as a light bulb, and appear in a wide variety of colors. They typically appear during or after lightning storms,
15 though not always. Theories on the cause of ball lightning range from clouds of plasma to miniature black holes to alien life forms, but the simplest explanation, and therefore the most likely, is that ball lightning is the result of common chemical reactions
20 occurring within balls of airborne dust.

John Abrahamson, a professor of Chemical and Process Engineering at the University of Canterbury, proposes that ball lightning is caused by silicon particles burning in the air. This theory would explain
25 why ball lightning often coincides with normal lightning. When a lightning bolt strikes the ground, the intense energy causes silicon that is naturally present in the soil to combine with carbon and oxygen. The result is silicon vapor. This vapor cools
30 and condenses into a ball of fine dust. As the silicon is combined with atmospheric oxygen, chemical energy is released as light and heat. The process could also occur with materials other than silicon, as other metal oxide nanoparticles would also produce
35 the required energy. Also, other sources of electric discharge could cause the reaction. For example, a power cable or a geological fault line may provide enough energy to create ball lightning, according to Abrahamson's theory. Other scientists have
40 attempted to put his idea into practice. In Brazil, researchers Gerson Paiva and Antônio Pavão produced small fireballs by applying high-voltage arcs of electricity to silicon substrate. In Israel, Vladimir Dikhtyar and Eli Jerby have created similar
45 fireballs by burning through solid pieces of silicon and aluminum with microwave beams.

Passage 2

Ball lightning has been witnessed by approximately 5% of the world's population. This is similar to the number of people who have personally
50 witnessed a lightning bolt strike earth. Therefore, we can assume the occurrence of ball lightning is fairly common, and thus it must be caused by common circumstances. How, then, can we explain these spheres of energy, which apparently have the ability
55 to suddenly materialize anywhere and pass through glass windows, in a way that accounts for their prevalence? Although most sightings occur outside, ball lightning has been sighted appearing indoors, and on one occasion, in early 1963, the phenomenon
60 was witnessed within an airliner, passing down the aisle from the pilot's cabin. While theories abound, most cannot account for such occurrences.

In 1955, Russian physicist Pyotr Kapitsa theorized that ball lightning is an electrodeless
65 discharge from ultra-high frequency radio waves. Peter H. Handel, a physicist at the University of Missouri, further refined Kapitsa's ideas in his Maser-Soliton theory. Handel describes ball lightning as a stable mass of plasma created by microwave
70 radiation. In the occurrence of a lightning strike, charges are dispersed in the earth and water molecules in the atmosphere are brought to a higher, excited state. Within a wide open area or a conducting cavity, the molecules cannot consume the
75 energy, and so a localized electrical field, or soliton, is generated. A large volume of energized atmosphere, several cubic kilometers in size, generates sufficient microwave radiation to create a discharge of plasma. The atmosphere itself serves as
80 a maser, a low-energy laser. Such atmospheric masers have been observed on other planets, such as Mars, Venus, and Jupiter. The phenomenon has not been duplicated in laboratory settings, however.

Handel's theory is supported by the observation
85 that ball lightning rarely, if ever, occurs on high points that attract lightning strikes. It would seem these would be ideal locations for ball lightning, but Handel argues ball lightning doesn't occur in these places because they have relatively small, focused
90 field pulses. A much larger field pulse is required to generate the maser effect.

A hole to this Maser-Soliton theory, however, is its inability to account for the ways in which ball lightning does not exhibit the characteristics of
95 plasma. Wouldn't a hot ball of plasma rise upward, similar to a hot-air balloon? Ball lightning travels parallel to the ground, so either it is not plasma or some further explanation is needed.

1

Passage 1 suggests that the simplest explanation for the natural creation of ball lightning is that it results from

A) discharge from ultra-frequency radio waves.

B) stable masses of plasma created by microwaves.

C) common chemical reaction within balls of dust.

D) alien life forms with technology we cannot yet understand.

2

Professor Abrahamson attributes the formation of ball lightning to

A) the burning of silicon dust.

B) lightning striking a pane of glass.

C) burning through solid aluminum with microwave beams.

D) the interaction of a plasma mass with microwave radiation.

3

According to Passage 2, ball lightning may be caused by

A) lightning strikes.

B) volcanic eruptions.

C) a power cable.

D) a geological fault line.

4

As used in line 11, "innocuous" most nearly means

A) harmful.

B) pleasant.

C) restorative.

D) safe.

5

According to Passage 2, ball lightning travels

A) at the speed of light.

B) downward from mountain-top lightning strikes.

C) along the direction of the ground.

D) between microwave towers.

6

According to Passage 2, when ball lightning meets a pane of glass

A) the glass melts.

B) the glass shatters.

C) it passes through the glass.

D) it electrifies the glass.

7

The author of Passage 2 states that lightning balls

A) can only occur in small enclosed areas.

B) are an unstable form of plasma.

C) are formed from silicon vapor.

D) have never been duplicated in a lab setting.

8

As used in line 92, "hole" most nearly means

A) emptiness.

B) flaw.

C) space.

D) shack.

9

Passages 1 and 2 agree that ball lightning

A) appears in many different colors.

B) is a real form of energy.

C) is based on silicon.

D) has been observed on other planets.

10

Both passages agree that

A) ball lightning is formed by applying energy to some form of matter.

B) plasma forms the heart of all ball lightning.

C) ball lightning may be caused by small black holes.

D) ball lightning will only arise in the presence of a localized electrical field.

Information & Ideas – Science – Passage 10

Approximately 14,500 years ago, Earth left a frigid two and a half million-year Ice Age. Just 1600 years later, the climate suddenly snapped back. In the northern hemisphere, temperatures plummeted, reaching conditions similar to those found at the peak of the last Ice Age. This abrupt climate change event is known as the Younger Dryas (YD), and its end some 1500 years later was even more abrupt than its onset. The mysterious cause of the severe cold snap has remained a topic of debate among scientists.

Passage 1 is adapted from an article summarizing a recent study regarding the effects of a possible asteroid collision. Passage 2 is adapted from an article summarizing recent research on the Younger Dryas.

Passage 1

In a 2014 paper published in the *Journal of Geology*, an international team of researchers reported their findings from a survey of sediment samples taken from 32 sites across the world. The
5   group focused on the distribution and presence of nanodiamonds in the geological layer corresponding to the YD period. Using electron microscopy, the team studied various molecular arrangements of the nanodiamonds present in the samples, but of
10   particular note were the hexagonal and cubic configurations.

Nanodiamonds of all types are impossible to produce by natural means; they require some combination of extreme heat (above 3400°C),
15   extreme pressure, and anoxic (low oxygen) conditions. Lasers or other techniques can be used to attain the conditions needed, but even with them, the hexagonal and cubic forms abundant in the YD samples are impossible to produce. Only sediment
20   found at the Cretaceous-Tertiary Boundary, a period known for a mass extinction that is widely believed to have been caused by an asteroid collision, shows the same type of nanodiamond deposition. The team also found elevated levels of osmium, iridium, and
25   melted glass in the YD samples. Taken together, the evidence strongly supports the possibility of an impact of extraterrestrial origin that occurred roughly 12,900 years ago. This devastating event is likely what precipitated the dramatic YD climate shift of
30   the same period.

Prof. James Kennett of the University of California Santa Barbara, a co-author on the 2014 article, went on to publish two more papers in 2018 substantiating the cosmic impact theory. This time,
35   the team found unusually elevated levels of platinum, another element indicative of cosmic impact, in the sediment studied. The timing of the platinum spikes was perfectly aligned with the start of the YD cooling. Astonishingly, the new study also uncovered
40   a widespread mixture of soot, ammonium, nitrate, and other chemicals in the YD layer of core samples taken from northern ice sheets. This chemical signature is highly specific to regions affected by wildfires, and so Kennett and his team concluded that
45   the YD was characterized by massive wildfires that blazed over 10% of the surface of the Earth. The fires, likely caused by a catastrophic meteor collision, would have created enormous amounts of ash and smoke, which would have blocked out much of the
50   sun, triggering the abrupt cooling period.

Passage 2

The second Greenland ice sheet project (GISP2) was a US funded project that was completed in 1993, producing the deepest ice core samples for the time. The core samples have been extremely valuable in
55   providing a geological record of past atmospheric conditions and temperatures. They have been used to track past climate variations, including the Younger Dryas event, which has been linked to the disappearance of the prehistoric Clovis people.
60   A 2017 review of the data by James Baldini and his team of geologists at the University of Durham, UK, has substantiated a theory that the Laacher See volcano eruption in Germany may have spurred the YD cooling period. The volcano eruption was not just
65   massive (it ended up producing a 50-square-mile lake that now rests at the top of the dome-like crater formed), but it released unusually high amounts of sulfur-rich compounds into the atmosphere. Baldini's team was able to identify a corresponding sulfur
70   spike of volcanic origin in the GISP2 ice cores that arose during the beginning of the YD climate shift. They further showed how the combination of such a high magnitude volcano along with the sulfur-rich conditions during a deglaciation period could have
75   led to world-wide shifts in oceanic currents, triggering abrupt climate shifts around the north Atlantic.

While much recent research has proposed that a large impact event is what initiated the chain of
80   events leading up to the YD event, the impact hypothesis is still extremely controversial. Many research teams have found that the chemical signatures linked to a cosmic impact are much more widespread in geological sampling, and are not
85   specific to the YD boundary layer. The Laacher See eruption hypothesis could present a viable alternative for explaining the unusual cooling of the Younger Dryas, but future research still needs to be conducted to further justify the theory.

1

As it is used in line 29, the word "dramatic" most nearly means

A) theatrical.
B) impressive.
C) extreme.
D) vivid.

2

Passage 1 indicates that the production of nanodiamonds requires a condition of

A) low pressure.
B) low sulfur.
C) low temperature.
D) low oxygen.

3

As used in line 29, "precipitated" most nearly means

A) extracted.
B) rained.
C) solidified.
D) triggered.

4

The main focus of the second paragraph of Passage 1 (lines 12-30) is

A) the evidence for a possible cosmic impact.
B) the change created by the Younger Dryas climate shift.
C) the process used by an international team of researchers to collect sediment samples.
D) the impact of platinum on the climate.

5

The author of Passage 2 cites which of the following as a cause of climate shifts in the north Atlantic?

A) Sulfur-rich conditions during a glaciation period
B) Changes in ocean currents
C) Lower volcanic activity
D) Electron microscopy

6

Additional research showed that platinum spikes can be seen after large volcanic eruptions across the world. This would significantly strengthen which of the following passage's perspectives?

A) Passage 1
B) Passage 2
C) Both passages
D) Neither passage

7

The passages primarily focus on

A) researchers with competing views on climate change.
B) nanodiamond production.
C) potential causes for a cooling period.
D) evidence for volcanic eruptions.

8

Which choice best supports the idea that air pollutants contribute to the cooling of the climate?

A) Lines 19-23 ("Only… deposition.")
B) Lines 46-50 ("The fires… cooling period.")
C) Lines 64-68 ("The volcano… atmosphere.")
D) Lines 81-85 ("Many research… layer.")

9

Based on information in Passage 2, it can be inferred that oceanic currents

A) are the source of sulfur in the atmosphere.
B) are altered by asteroid collisions.
C) typically provide warmth to climates in the northern hemisphere.
D) are powered by energy from active volcanoes.

10

The authors of both passages would most likely agree with which of the following?

A) The cause of the Younger Dryas cooling is not yet fully understood.

B) Cooling during the Younger Dryas period was caused by an increase of particles in the atmosphere.

C) Heating from volcanic activity finally brought an end to the Younger Dryas period.

D) The concentration of nanodiamonds leads to shifts in oceanic currents.

Notes and Reflections

Information & Ideas – Social Studies – Passage 1

This passage is adapted from "A Mathematician's Apology" by G. H. Hardy.

I propose to put forward an apology for mathematics; and I may be told that it needs none, since there are now few studies more generally recognized, for good reasons or bad, as profitable and
5 praiseworthy. This may be true: indeed it is probable, since the sensational triumphs of Einstein, that stellar astronomy and atomic physics are the only sciences which stand higher in popular estimation. A mathematician need not now consider himself on the
10 defensive. He does not have to meet the sort of opposition described by Bradley in the admirable defense of metaphysics which forms the introduction to *Appearance and Reality*.

A metaphysician, says Bradley, will be told that
15 'metaphysical knowledge is wholly impossible', or that 'even if possible to a certain degree, it is practically no knowledge worth the name'. 'The same problems,' he will hear, 'the same disputes, the same sheer failure. Why not abandon it and come
20 out? Is there nothing else worth your labor?' There is no one so stupid as to use this sort of language about mathematics. The mass of mathematical truth is obvious and imposing; its practical applications, the bridges and steam-engines and dynamos, obtrude
25 themselves on the dullest imagination. The public does not need to be convinced that there is something in mathematics.

All this is in its way very comforting to mathematicians, but it is hardly possible for a
30 genuine mathematician to be content with it. Any genuine mathematician must feel that it is not on these crude achievements that the real case for mathematics rests, that the popular reputation of mathematics is based largely on ignorance and
35 confusion, and there is room for a more rational defense. At any rate, I am disposed to try to make one. It should be a simpler task than Bradley's difficult apology.

I shall ask, then, why is it really worthwhile to
40 make a serious study of mathematics? What is the proper justification of a mathematician's life? And my answers will be, for the most part, such as are expected from a mathematician: I think that it is worthwhile, that there is ample justification. But I
45 should say at once that my defense of mathematics will be a defense of myself, and that my apology is bound to be to some extent egotistical. I should not think it worthwhile to apologize for my subject if I regarded myself as one of its failures. Some egotism
50 of this sort is inevitable, and I do not feel that it really needs justification. Good work is not done by 'humble' men. It is one of the first duties of a professor, for example, in any subject, to exaggerate a little both the importance of his subject and his own
55 importance in it. A man who is always asking 'Is what I do worthwhile?' and 'Am I the right person to do it?' will always be ineffective himself and a discouragement to others. He must shut his eyes a little and think a little more of his subject and himself
60 than they deserve. This is not too difficult: it is harder not to make his subject and himself ridiculous by shutting his eyes too tightly.

A man who sets out to justify his existence and his activities has to distinguish two different
65 questions. The first is whether the work which he does is worth doing; and the second is why he does it, whatever its value may be. The first question is often very difficult, and the answer very discouraging, but most people will find the second easy enough even
70 then. Their answers, if they are honest, will usually take one or other of two forms; and the second form is a merely a humbler variation of the first, which is the only answer we need consider seriously.

We have of course to take account of the
75 differences in value between different activities. I would rather be a novelist or a painter than a statesman of similar rank; and there are many roads to fame which most of us would reject as actively pernicious. Yet it is seldom that such differences of
80 value will turn the scale in a man's choice of a career, which will almost always be dictated by the limitations of his natural abilities. Poetry is more valuable than cricket, but Bradman would be a fool if he sacrificed his cricket in order to write second-rate
85 minor poetry (and I suppose that it is unlikely that he could do better). If the cricket were a little less supreme, and the poetry better, then the choice might be more difficult: I do not know whether I would rather have been Victor Trumper or Rupert Brooke. It
90 is fortunate that such dilemmas are so seldom.

I may add that they are particularly unlikely to present themselves to a mathematician. It is usual to exaggerate rather grossly the differences between the mental processes of mathematicians and other people,
95 but it is undeniable that a gift for mathematics is one of the most specialized talents, and that mathematicians as a class are not particularly distinguished for general ability or versatility. If a man is in any sense a real mathematician, then it is a
100 hundred to one that his mathematics will be far better than anything else he can do, and that he would be silly if he surrendered any decent opportunity of exercising his one talent in order to do undistinguished work in other fields. Such a sacrifice
105 could be justified only by economic necessity or age.

1

The passage indicates that physics, compared to mathematics, is

A) more revered overall.
B) more popular among students.
C) more widely studied than math.
D) in greater need of an apology.

2

The passage states the public does not need to be persuaded of the value of math because

A) it is a respected topic due to its opacity.
B) it is widely used in economic transactions.
C) most people encounter math-based objects in their daily lives.
D) they learn about the value of math while studying it in school.

3

Which choice provide the best evidence for the answer to the previous question?

A) Lines 22-25 ("The mass… imagination.")
B) Lines 30-36 ("Any… defense.")
C) Lines 52-55 ("It is… in it.")
D) Lines 92-98 ("It is… or versatility.")

4

It is implied in the third paragraph (lines 28-38) that

A) math is the only genuine area of study.
B) Bradley's mission is easier than what G.H. Hardy is setting out to accomplish.
C) the value of math is obvious to all people.
D) mathematicians feel their subject is misunderstood by the general public.

5

When the author says, "shutting his eyes too tightly" (line 62), he most nearly means

A) avoiding criticism from others about the importance of mathematics.
B) ignoring doubts about the value of one's work and oneself.
C) shielding oneself from the egos of others.
D) staying humble no matter how valuable others perceive mathematics to be.

6

The main idea of the sixth paragraph (lines 74-90) is that

A) personal abilities should drive one's choice of career.
B) trying to become famous is not a valuable use of time.
C) the arts are more important than sports.
D) careers are most often chosen based on how much value they provide to society.

7

According to the author, one of the only justifiable reasons for a mathematician to work in a different field instead is

A) a desire to be a poet.
B) the popularity of cricket.
C) financial hardship.
D) family tradition.

8

As used in line 93, "grossly" most nearly means

A) easily.
B) disgustingly.
C) shockingly.
D) drastically.

9

As it is used in the last paragraph, the word "exercising" (line 103) most nearly means

A) utilizing
B) training.
C) working.
D) removing.

10

The main idea of the passage is that

A) math is a valuable science studied by those who are not suited to any other profession.
B) the only people who enjoy math are mathematicians, who should pursue other careers.
C) the reason students are forced to study math is because a few mathematicians are obsessed with their valueless science.
D) math is respected because mathematicians are more talented than other professions.

**Information & Ideas – Social Studies –
Passage 2**

This passage is adapted from an article about
impostor syndrome.

Veteran teacher Chantrisse Holliman likes to tell
the story of one of her former students, whom she
calls "Jarvis" for the sake of anonymity. According to
Holliman, Jarvis was an exceptional scholar, one of
5   the best students she ever had. As a junior, he had the
second highest GPA in his entire school of over
2,000 students, as well as impressive ACT and SAT
scores. He also worked hard in various clubs and
sports. Despite this, when Holliman asked Jarvis
10 about his collegiate ambitions, he responded in total
seriousness, "What if I don't get into college?" While
the rest of us might scoff at Jarvis's humility,
Holliman reports that this was a common feeling for
him. She explains that he would often brush off
15 compliments and identify students who he viewed as
smarter or more capable than himself. Even more
disturbingly, Holliman says that these feelings of
inadequacy are widespread amongst the highest-
achieving students in her school. For many of these
20 students, as well as people at all levels of
achievement, "impostor syndrome" can be
devastating.

First identified by psychologists Suzanne Imes,
PhD, and Pauline Rose Clance, PhD, in the 1970s,
25 impostor syndrome is when high-achieving people
believe that they are frauds. They often see their
successes as due to luck rather than ability, and
constantly fear being revealed as fakes. When first
described, impostor syndrome was believed to mostly
30 affect women and minorities, who at that time faced
many significant obstacles in employment and
academic success. Frederick Hives, an African-
American PhD student, explains that "I was taught I
would need to 'work twice as hard to be half as
35 good.' While this instills a goal-oriented approach
within me, it also keeps me feeling as though my
efforts will never be enough." A 2013 study by
researchers at the University of Texas at Austin
found that Asian-American students were even more
40 likely to experience these impostor feelings than
African-American and Latino students. Perceived
difference from the "norm" can often heighten
impostor feelings.

As the study of impostor syndrome has
45 developed, it has become clear that anyone, not just
women or people from minority groups, can be
affected. Indeed, a 2011 study from the International
Journal of Behavioral Science found that about 70
percent of people have struggled with impostor
50 syndrome before. It appears to be closely linked to

perfectionism, in which people feel the need to
perform every task perfectly and without help.
According to Imes, one major cause of such
perfectionism is pressure to succeed, whether from
55 parents and families or from society at large.
Specifically, "parents who send mixed messages—
alternating between over-praise and criticism—can
increase the risk of future fraudulent feelings."
Essentially, many people with impostor syndrome get
60 caught in a feedback loop wherein they experience a
great deal of anxiety when completing a task and are
afraid to ask for help. When they succeed and are
praised, they justify the isolation and self-torture they
put themselves through, and they do it all over again.
65 The truth is, however, that they need not repeat this
cycle forever.

Despite the pervasive nature of impostor
syndrome, there are steps that people can take to
combat its corrosive effects on self-confidence. One
70 major step is to recognize and utilize the assistance
that is available. When perfectionists reach out to
mentors and other resources to ask for help, they
realize that they are not in this alone. It is also
important for those suffering from impostor
75 syndrome to recognize and appreciate their existing
accomplishments. They are often so focused on the
next challenge that they are blind to what they have
already achieved. A student like Jarvis would do well
to be proud of all the goals he has already met, and
80 understand that he reached those heights through
effort, determination, and the support of his teachers,
friends, and family. Finally, it is important for people
who feel like frauds to recognize that nobody is
perfect, that everyone makes mistakes, and that
85 everyone needs help. This requires a shift in thinking,
and an openness and honesty about impostor feelings.
Ultimately, anyone can overcome feelings of being a
fraud, but it takes self-reflection, effort, and a
willingness to open up to supportive friends and
90 family.

We now live in a world in which everyone's
accomplishments and successes are on public display
on social media accounts, and this often serves to
heighten impostor feelings. Rarely do we see people
95 post about the struggles that went into getting good
grades, or how they had to get extra help in order to
design that award-winning science fair project. If
everyone took the opportunity to share their
challenges and insecurities, perhaps more people
100 would realize that feeling like an impostor is not
unusual, and that it is in fact counterproductive. Until
we as a society face this issue with more honesty,
then it will likely persist. Despite this, any individual
suffering from impostor syndrome has the capacity to
105 defy those feelings and recognize their own self-
worth.

1

The passage indicates that a symptom of impostor syndrome is

A) fear of being identified as successful.
B) viewing personal failures as a matter of luck.
C) being skeptical of personal achievements.
D) fearing that one's best is always improving.

2

The passage strongly suggests that

A) social media tends to promote impostor syndrome.
B) Asian-American students are less likely to suffer from impostor syndrome than Latino Students.
C) less than 50% of students suffer from impostor syndrome.
D) frequently asking for help is a major cause of impostor syndrome.

3

Which choice provides the best evidence for the answer to the previous question?

A) Lines 44-47 ("As the study… be affected.")
B) Lines 37-43 ("A 2013 study… feelings")
C) Lines 91-94 ("We now live… feelings.")
D) Lines 50-52 ("It appears… without help.")

4

As used in line 67, "pervasive" most nearly means

A) calming.
B) widespread.
C) convincing.
D) bullying.

5

According to the passage, which of the following steps can help an individual overcome impostor syndrome?

A) Stopping relying on support systems
B) Reflecting on what could have been achieved
C) Striving to repeat what was done before
D) Acknowledging and directly addressing feelings

6

According to the passage, impostor syndrome is most prevalent among

A) college students.
B) engineering majors.
C) poor students.
D) high-achieving students.

7

As used in line 41, "perceived" most nearly means

A) sensed.
B) feared.
C) unseen.
D) overheard.

8

It can reasonable be inferred from the passage that people who experience impostor syndrome

A) were exceptionally lucky and do not deserve the success they have experienced.
B) become trapped in a cycle of self-judgment from which they cannot escape.
C) affects all people, to various degrees of intensity.
D) are particularly successful and motivated, in spite of their doubts.

9

Which choice provides the best evidence for the answer to the previous question?

A) Lines 23-26 ("First identified… are frauds.")
B) Lines 26-28 ("They often see… as fakes.")
C) Lines 47-50 ("a 2011 study… before.")
D) Lines 59-62 ("many people… ask for help.")

10

What is a main idea of the fourth paragraph (lines 67-90)?

A) Impostor syndrome is often caused by an attitude of perfectionism.
B) There are several methods for preventing the continuation of impostor syndrome.
C) By comparing one's accomplishments to others', impostor syndrome is worsened.
D) Parents mixing praise with criticism can cause impostor syndrome for their children.

Information & Ideas – Social Studies – Passage 3

This passage is adapted from an article about oxytocin, a molecule popularly known as the "love hormone."

Across centuries and cultures, people have sought to unravel the mystery of love through various mediums such as art and literature. An often overlooked lens of analysis is that of scientists,
5   specifically endocrinologists. The scientific tale of love began in the early 1900s with the discovery of a chemical, excreted from the posterior pituitary gland, which promotes labor contractions, lactation, and antidiuretic activity and lowers blood pressure. In
10   1906, Sir Henry Dale named this chemical oxytocin, meaning "swift birth" in Greek, as it stimulated uterine contractions in a pregnant cat. Almost seven decades later, scientific studies revealed that the oxytocin produced by neurons of the hypothalamus, a
15   component of the brain, sends signals to other areas of the brain. Excited, scientists then started to explore oxytocin's potential implementation in regulating behavior.

In 1979, Pederson and Prange at the University
20   of North Carolina in Chapel Hill administered oxytocin to a group of virgin rats. Rather than continue their indifference towards unfamiliar pups, the virgin rats exhibited classic maternal behaviors such as grooming the pups and returning lost ones to
25   their nests. It was not until the effects of oxytocin on bonding was studied that the chemical adopted its tagline as the "love hormone." Prairie voles form monogamous relationships in which they prefer spending time with their partner, grooming one
30   another, and nesting together. When scientists inhibited oxytocin in prairie voles, they would act similarly to montane voles who do not prefer short or long-term partnership. In 2003, a study demonstrated increased levels of oxytocin in both humans and dogs
35   after petting sessions of five to twenty-four minutes.

So, is oxytocin the secret ingredient in mythological love potions? Sue Carter, a neuroscientist at Indiana University, states that "almost everybody who's tried to look at an effect of
40   oxytocin on anything like social behavior has found something." The issue with labeling oxytocin as the love hormone is that would assume oxytocin's mechanism is always the same regardless of circumstance. Scientists have not yet mapped where,
45   when, and how much oxytocin is typically released, and they cannot account for the exact order of events from its release to effect. Currently, the development of neuroscience relies on studying the different circuits in the brain and providing an understanding

50   of the overlap and interactions of these circuits. Without comprehending oxytocin's circuit, or if it is a component of another circuit, scientists cannot accurately study its effects on human behavior.

Furthermore, several studies showcase the role of
55   oxytocin in not just romance but also social bonding, mood, and even wound-healing. In 2009, scientists administered intranasal oxytocin to participants who would later look at images of neutral faces. When compared to the group of participants who did not
60   receive any form of oxytocin, they viewed the neutral faces as more trustworthy. The study's scientists theorized that oxytocin may reduce the fear of betrayal. Not only has oxytocin been shown to increase trust, but it has also demonstrated an impact
65   on generosity. Wittig's team in 2014 studied wild chimpanzees and measured their levels of oxytocin after sharing food or engaging in cooperative activities—such as grooming—with non-kin chimpanzees. Unsurprisingly, the monitored
70   chimpanzees had higher levels of oxytocin comparable to those of nursing mothers sharing with their own pups. In animal models of depression, oxytocin produces an antidepressant effect, though its exact biological mechanism remains undetermined.
75   Marazziti and colleagues tested the theory of oxytocin's role in modulating inflammation by decreased cytokines, proteins that signal a response from the immune system. They hypothesized that increased oxytocin levels in blood plasma would then
80   increase the rate of wound-healing. Studying heterosexual couples just after they interact with each other, Marazziti's team concluded inflammation in response to a wound decreased because of elevated oxytocin levels in the body.

85   But, oxytocin has also been associated with unfavorable effects. When a low-dose of the hormone is administered to young prairie voles, their social bonding as adults improved. Higher doses of oxytocin, however, interfered with their adult
90   behavior and resulted in decreased bonding. Scientists theorize that oxytocin may activate other receptors, not just their own. As much as oxytocin has been shown to improve trust and generosity, one puff of the chemical can increase a person's
95   aggression when trying to defend against strangers. In a 2014 controlled study, oxytocin actually promoted dishonesty when the outcome of an event favored an individual's group rather than just the individual. Moreover, oxytocin's effects in atypical
100   brains have not been studied thoroughly. Patients with borderline personality disorder, a psychiatric condition, demonstrate lowered trust and cooperation with a single dose of oxytocin.

Uncovering the mystery behind oxytocin
105   requires an interdisciplinary collaboration between

basic and clinical researchers, especially to decipher and map its biological-to-behavioral mechanism. Without such a team-up, it will be difficult to rebrand oxytocin. As Guastella explains, "The problem we've
110 got ourselves into is that we're trying to look for a simple answer: oxytocin is known to affect circuits in different ways, and it's not going to affect everyone in the same way." Science, just like love, is rarely simple and to understand either requires a multitude
115 of varied levels of analyses.

1

A central idea of the passage is that

A) humans and animals react the same way to social situations.

B) mental disorders are caused by chemical imbalances.

C) chemicals influence biological processes and behaviors.

D) traditional medicine practices are based on an intuitive understanding of biology.

2

Which choice provide the best evidence for the answer to the previous question?

A) Lines 5-9 ("The scientific… pressure.")

B) Lines 27-30 ("Prairie voles… together.")

C) Lines 41-44 ("The issue… circumstance.")

D) Lines 69-72 ("the monitored… own pups.")

3

As used in line 17, "potential" most nearly means

A) possible.

B) powerful.

C) dormant.

D) capable.

4

It can be inferred from information in the passage that scientists

A) are more confused than ever about how emotions are created.

B) cannot regulate the behavior of chimpanzees.

C) have discovered the recipe for love potions.

D) do not fully understand oxytocin's effect on the body.

5

As used in line 76, "modulating" most nearly means

A) alternating.

B) tuning.

C) switching.

D) adjusting.

6

According to the passage, patients with borderline personality disorder responded to a single dose of oxytocin by

A) displaying enhanced maternal instincts.

B) demonstrating the opposite effects seen in most patients.

C) showing reduced fear of betrayal.

D) having a reduction in the inflammation of wounds.

7

It can be inferred from this passage that oxytocin

A) should be tested more comprehensively to anticipate possible side effects.

B) inhibits excessive aggression in lab animals.

C) should be prescribed to patients diagnosed with atypical brains.

D) has major use as an antidepressant.

8

According to the passage, why have scientists been unable to accurately study how oxytocin impacts behavior?

A) Most studies of oxytocin have been conducted on rodents.

B) It is impossible to create a single definition for love that applies to everyone.

C) Scientists have not been able to fully understand the brain circuits associated with oxytocin.

D) Many universities ban the study of chemicals that affect humans' social behavior.

9

Which choice provide the best evidence for the answer to the previous question?

A) Lines 21-25 ("Rather than… their nests.")

B) Lines 44-47 ("Scientists have… to effect.")

C) Lines 96-99 ("oxytocin… individual.")

D) Lines 113-115 ("Science… analyses.")

**Information & Ideas – Social Studies –
Passage 4**

This passage is adapted from an article about the
history of the Sequoia National Park.

In the spring of 1852, hunter Augustus T. Dowd
chased a bear in the Sierra Nevada but caught,
instead, a glimpse of a giant sequoia in the "North
Grove" section of what is now Calaveras Big Trees
5 State Park. Dowd, in this first widely documented
sighting of one of the world's largest trees, was
stunned. Even the men at the mining camp he
returned to didn't believe his tale until they saw the
tree themselves. Once they did, however, "The
10 Mammoth Tree" or "The Discovery Tree," as
Dowd's find was dubbed, became a popular local
spectacle whose appeal spread around the world with
varying results.

Whole groves of sequoia, some even larger than
15 the tree Dowd first spotted, were discovered in the
following years, though these trees were already well
known to local Native American tribes. The
Yosemite tribe, for example, called the giant trees
Wawona, an onomatopoeia of the Northern Spotted
20 Owl's call. The tribe believed this owl was the
animal guardian of the forest, just as the sequoias
presided over the surrounding plant world. With the
largest *Sequoiadendron gianteum* recorded at over
300 feet tall, more than 26 feet in diameter, and an
25 estimated 3,200 years old, the Yosemite designation
of guardian was fitting.

But the revered sequoias were no match for 19th-
century Western colonial man and his "conquer all"
mentality. These massive trees provided the
30 speculators of the time, mostly gold miners, with
multiple avenues of commercial opportunity. Word
spread eastward, drawing a new influx of people as
California's gold rush waned. Roads were
constructed so crowds could visit these amazing
35 redwoods. Local commerce mushroomed to
accommodate the crowds. And one year after Dowd's
discovery, "The Discovery Tree," which had
withstood centuries of storms and forest fires, was
felled.
40 Felling the giant took five men 22 days using
axes and saws. Once the rings were exposed, the
tree's age was estimated at 1,300 years. The
remaining stump was so large it was used as a dance
floor for parties hosted by the hotel built on the site.
45 The enormous trunk, now prone, was turned into a
bowling alley. Other sequoias also became
attractions, perhaps the most widely-known the
"Wawona Tree" located in Yosemite National Park.
The base of that massive tree was bored through in

50 1881 to form a passage for horse-drawn
stagecoaches.

The zeitgeist of the 19th century was unbounded
optimism and an enthusiastic pursuit of technological
advances which produced railroads, bridges, and
55 skyscrapers. The corresponding desire to document
man's prowess motivated the felling of another giant
sequoia in 1891, the "Mark Twain Tree." Slabs of its
16-foot diameter trunk were sent to New York's
American Museum of Natural History and to the
60 British Museum of Natural History in London. Some
abroad believed the massive slice was a hoax. A 30-
foot tall section of still another giant was hollowed
out to form a one-of-a-kind, two-story home
exhibited at the 1893 Chicago World's Fair.
65 Like many other trees in the Sierra Nevada
forests, the giant sequoias were logged from the
1880s to the 1920s, in spite of limited commercial
returns. After the 1906 San Francisco earthquake, in
particular, lumber was desperately needed to rebuild
70 the area. Yet the great quantity of wood these trees
offered proved less than optimal—while highly
resistant to decay, the wood was fibrous and brittle,
unsuitable for construction. When felled, the huge
trees would often shatter, wasting much of the wood.
75 It is estimated that only 50 percent of felled trees
actually made it from grove to mill. The wood from
these stalwart guardians of the forest was instead
relegated to make shingles, fence posts, even
matchsticks.
80 The first call to conserve these magnificent trees
was drowned out in the dominant "manifest destiny"
mindset of the time, which elevated exploration and
territorial expansion, claiming it was man's God-
given role to understand and control the physical
85 world around him. As early as the felling of The
Discovery Tree, area residents expressed their
concerns in local newspapers. But it took time,
diminishing financial returns, and a shift toward
conservation in the national mindset for such efforts
90 to gain momentum.

Yellowstone was established in 1872 as the first
national park in the United States. In 1890, Sequoia
National Park followed. John Muir, the Scottish-
American naturalist who is often referred to as
95 "Father of the National Parks," was a vocal
proponent of preserving the western forests,
particularly in the Sierra Nevada. Although he died in
1914, Muir's efforts, and those of others, would
finally protect what remained of the original grove
100 discovered by Augustus Dowd: Calaveras Big Trees
State Park was established in 1931.

1

According to the passage, Augustus Dowd's 1852 discovery soon resulted in

A) population decline in the Sierra Nevada.
B) expanded transportation infrastructure.
C) widespread conservation efforts.
D) a decline in local commerce.

2

In the context of the passage, "limited commercial returns" (line 67-68) most nearly means

A) large profits.
B) little demand.
C) local demand.
D) minimal profits.

3

The passage primarily focuses on

A) the commercial usage of the redwoods.
B) the disparate views Native Americans and speculators had of the redwoods.
C) man's changing response to the redwoods.
D) redwood conservation efforts.

4

Which of the following most closely paraphrases the statement in lines 87-90?

A) Passing years and changing political viewpoints aided conservation efforts.
B) Recently, people have changed their views, which has led to renewed interest in using redwood trees for lumber.
C) The lack of profits, combined with passing years, slowed redwood conservation.
D) As years passed, profits shrank, the reigning philosophy shifted, and conservation efforts gained support.

5

According to the passage, harvested redwoods were used as

A) bowling pins.
B) road-paving materials.
C) a tunnel.
D) a three-story home.

6

It can be logically inferred from the passage that

A) conservation efforts always emerge in time.
B) speculators equated the redwoods' massive size with great profits.
C) the 19th-century mindset was exemplary.
D) the redwoods never should have been harvested.

7

Which choice provide the best evidence for the answer to the previous question?

A) Lines 7-9 ("Even … tree themselves.")
B) Lines 29-31 ("These … opportunity.")
C) Lines 33-35 ("Roads were… redwoods.")
D) Lines 42-44 ("The remaining … the site.")

8

The word "zeitgeist" in line 52 most nearly means

A) tradition.
B) mood.
C) comedy.
D) consequence.

9

The main focus of the final two paragraphs is

A) redwood history.
B) redwood conservation.
C) naturalist John Muir.
D) Calaveras Big Trees State Park.

10

Which of the following best parallels the difference between 19th-century speculators and naturalist John Muir?

A) Conservation vs. exploitation
B) Admiration vs. exploitation
C) Exploitation vs. conservation
D) Preservation vs. admiration

**Information & Ideas – Social Studies –
Passage 5**

This passage is adapted from an article about the
history of "gold rushes".

With his pithy insight, Mark Twain wrote: "A
mine is a hole in the ground, owned by a liar."
History has proven him true, as the promise of wealth
from gold mines has been undercut, all too often, by
5 deceit and manipulation. For as long as we have
coveted gold, there have been those who would take
advantage of that greed for the precious ore.

In the latter half of the 1800s, the American
West was the land of gold. Hoping to strike a vein
10 and find sudden wealth, people migrated toward the
Pacific coast in such numbers the era was known as
the Gold Rush. In the mountains and hills of Arizona,
California, and Oregon were hidden troves of raw
treasure that attracted hundreds of thousands of
15 prospectors. It was a lawless space in the early years.
California was not incorporated into the United States
and was under the legal control of the military. Thus,
there were no mechanisms to enforce rights to land.
For anyone who could find gold in those open spaces,
20 it was free for the taking. Informally, miners adopted
a code of "staking claims" to avoid conflict. It was
generally understood a prospector had the rights to a
property for as long as the property was being
actively mined. In the first few years, prospectors
25 hunted out sites where the gold was easiest to
procure. Indeed, the spark that ignited the Gold Rush
was a nugget of gold found among some onion bulbs,
and more nuggets were found on the ground nearby
without any digging required. After the surface-level
30 gold was exhausted, more work was required to find
the veins of gold hidden within the ground. Mining
operations began, and prospectors invested great
amounts of labor and funding into the purchase of
land, mining equipment, and workers who were
35 willing to endure the grueling task of excavating
earth. With so much investment, there was great risk.
After all, a mine may lead to nothing more valuable
than dirt.

Whenever there is wealth to be made, there is
40 also the con man, the hustler, the swindler, the
scammer who promises access to everything you
don't have and runs away with everything you once
did. In the time of the Gold Rush, the deception
involved "salting" mines. The scheme began with a
45 worthless mine. This may be either a mine that has
been stripped of all its gold or one that never

produced any. Such mines could be purchased easily
and cheaply, because they were little more than holes
in the ground. With such a mine acquired, a con man
50 might "salt" the area by scattering bits of gold.
However, this would likely seem suspicious. The
more cunning would load a shotgun shell with gold
particles and fire it against the walls of the mine,
creating the illusion the rocks were naturally rich
55 with the ore. They might be outwitted by a savvy
prospector who wishes to blast away the outer layer
of rock and see if there is gold in deeper layers. This
could be countered by packing some gold into the
dynamite sticks, thereby salting the rock with more
60 gold particles even as it blew away the outer layers.
Even prospectors who brought geologists to test
claims might be fooled, as some geologists were in
league with the con men and made fake analyses.
Indeed, whole communities would band together to
65 fool prospectors into buying worthless mines, as the
funds would support the local communities.

More recently, in the 1990s, the largest gold
mining scam in history took place. The story began
when a small mining company, Bre-X, acquired
70 property rights to some riverside land in the jungles
of Borneo. Michael de Guzman, a mining prospector,
had promoted the portion of land as a jackpot of gold.
To prove the claim's worth, he provided several core
samples, sections of ground layers that were drilled
75 up, which showed an abundance of gold waiting to be
excavated. Initial estimates were at 136,000 pounds
of gold, but within a few years estimates skyrocketed
to more than 13,000,000 pounds. As news of the site
spread, gaining fame as the largest potential gold
80 mine in the world, Bre-X's worth multiplied, too. The
company's stocks, which were worth about $0.30
each, rose in price to about $250, bringing billions of
dollars in value to the company. As excitement over
the mining site and the company's growth spread,
85 there was only one issue left: getting the gold. This,
however, is where Bre-X ran into troubles. The gold
wasn't there; Guzman's core samples had been
"salted," initially using shavings from his own golden
wedding ring. The potential riches were so great, the
90 government of Indonesia decided it was too much for
a single company as small as Bre-X, so a more
established mining firm was brought in to share the
mining operation. To their surprise, this new
company found there was no gold at the site. By this
95 time, incredible sums of money had been spent and
lost and many investors were left feeling like fools.

1

Which two ways does the author discuss as methods of "salting" a mine?

A) Taking bits of gold and scattering them around a mine and using a weapon to embed gold into the walls of a mine

B) Putting gold into dynamite sticks and exploding the sticks in a mine and selling a mine without allowing a buyer to inspect it

C) Convincing a whole community to be dishonest to prospective buyers and inflating the value of a mine with faulty calculations

D) Spreading chunks of gold around the floor of a cave and shooting gold out of the cave's surfaces

2

How did the geologists in paragraph three (lines 39-66) contribute to the misinformation given to prospectors interested in purchasing a mine?

A) They would produce false reports to exaggerate the amount of gold that had been found.

B) They would place gold in places where it would be easy for the prospectors to find.

C) They would lie for extravagant personal financial gain.

D) They would give incorrect, encouraging information to help support the people living in the area.

3

How did the mine in Borneo owned by Bre-X end up with an extremely inflated value?

A) The gold in the mine was thought to be genuine but was actually pyrite, also known as fool's gold.

B) When an additional company was brought in to help Bre-X with the mine, the merger upped the mine's merit.

C) The company's owner tricked investors into excessively funding the mine's excavation.

D) A prospector provided false evidence and made empty claims about the mine's worth.

4

Which choice provides the best evidence for the answer to the previous question?

A) Lines 76-78 ("Initial estimates… pounds.")

B) Lines 83-85 ("As excitement… the gold.")

C) Lines 86-89 ("The gold… wedding ring.")

D) Lines 89-93 ("The potential … operation.")

5

The best summary of the last paragraph is

A) Guzman promoted a mine to numerous companies, suspicions about his claims rose with the mine's estimated value, and another company was brought in to verify his assertions.

B) Guzman falsified information about a mine, estimates of the mine's value rose, and Guzman's lies were eventually exposed.

C) Bre-X started mining in Borneo and found gold, the amount of gold found was inflated to attract investments, and the money raised was eventually lost.

D) Bre-X encouraged Guzman to tout the value of a mine in Borneo, Guzman did as instructed, and was eventually fined for having knowingly given incorrect information.

6

In what way does the more modern salting scandal discussed in the last paragraph differ from the salting incidents in the 1800s?

A) The modern scandal relates to technology, while the incidents in the 1800s were interpersonal.

B) The modern scandal relates to finances, while the incidents in the 1800s related to territorial claims.

C) The incidents in the 1800s involved spreading small amounts of gold, while the modern scandal did not.

D) The incidents in the 1800s were widespread, while the modern scandal was more isolated.

7

The fact that California was not incorporated into the United States in the second half of the 1800s had which of the following effects on the Gold Rush?

A) There were no agencies in place to deal with land ownership, so people were generally allowed to mine anywhere they wanted.

B) The military was ineffective as a ruling agency, which allowed prospectors to take advantage of people new to the area.

C) California was considered its own country, so people moving into the area set up their own rules and regulations around mining.

D) The area had its own governing body, conflicting with that of the United States, so anyone moving to the area to mine had to deal with both governments.

8

Which of the following sentences best summarizes the main idea of the passage?

A) Much time and energy has been spent on trickery in mining, time that would have been better spent mining than deceiving.

B) Many miners from the time of the California Gold Rush to modern times have used dishonest methods to gain wealth.

C) Salting mines has been the primary way most miners have earned an income for as long as mining has existed.

D) The Gold Rush was a prime example of the enterprising spirit present in the early years of the United States.

9

The third paragraph's primary focus is on

A) explaining mine salting methods.

B) conveying common tactics used by con men.

C) detailing ways to excavate gold mines.

D) how geologists participated in mining scams.

10

In the first sentence of the passage, what does the Mark Twain quote, "A mine is a hole in the ground, owned by a liar," imply about miners?

A) Miners are incapable of telling the truth.

B) Miners do not know how to correctly assess the value of the items they procure.

C) Items that are mined may not have the value ascribed to them by miners.

D) Items that are mined are not worth anything, despite what miners might say.

11

As it is used in line 13, "troves" most likely means

A) minerals.

B) chests.

C) wellsprings.

D) sinkholes.

Notes and Reflections

Rhetoric – Fiction – Passage 1

This passage is adapted from "The Old Man at the Bridge" by Ernest Hemingway.

An old man with steel rimmed spectacles and very dusty clothes sat by the side of the road. There was a pontoon bridge across the river and carts, trucks, and men, women and children were crossing
5 it. The mule-drawn carts staggered up the steep bank from the bridge with soldiers helping push against the spokes of the wheels. The trucks ground up and away, heading out of it all, and the peasants plodded along in the ankle-deep dust. But the old man sat
10 there without moving. He was too tired to go any farther.

It was my business to cross the bridge, explore the bridgehead beyond, and find out to what point the enemy had advanced. I did this and returned over the
15 bridge. There were not so many carts now and very few people on foot, but the old man was still there.

"Where do you come from?" I asked him. "From San Carlos," he said, and smiled. That was his native town and so it gave him pleasure to mention it and he
20 smiled. "I was taking care of animals," he explained.

"Oh," I said, not quite understanding.

"Yes," he said, "I stayed, you see, taking care of animals. I was the last one to leave the town of San Carlos."

25 He did not look like a shepherd nor a herdsman, and I looked at his black dusty clothes and his gray dusty face and his steel rimmed spectacles and said, "What animals were they?"

"Various animals," he said, and shook his head.
30 "I had to leave them."

I was watching the bridge and the African-looking country of the Ebro Delta and wondering how long now it would be before we would see the enemy, and listening all the while for the first noises
35 that would signal that ever mysterious event called contact, and the old man still sat there.

"What animals were they?" I asked.

"There were three animals altogether," he explained. "There were two goats and a cat and then
40 there were four pairs of pigeons."

"And you had to leave them?" I asked.

"Yes. Because of the artillery. The captain told me to go because of the artillery."

"And you have no family?" I asked, watching the
45 far end of the bridge where a few last carts were hurrying down the slope of the bank.

"No," he said, "only the animals I stated. The cat, of course, will be all right. A cat can look out for itself, but I cannot think what will become of the
50 others."

"What politics have you?" I asked.

"I am without politics," he said. "I am seventy-six years old. I have come twelve kilometers now and I think now I can go no further."

55 "This is not a good place to stop," I said. "If you can make it, there are trucks up the road where it forks for Tortosa."

"I will wait a while," he said, "and then I will go. Where do the trucks go?"

60 "Towards Barcelona," I told him.

"I know no one in that direction," he said, "but thank you very much. Thank you again very much."

He looked at me very blankly and tiredly, and then said, having to share his worry with someone,
65 "The cat will be all right, I am sure. There is no need to be unquiet about the cat. But the others. Now what do you think about the others?"

"Why they'll probably come through it all right."

"You think so?"

70 "Why not," I said, watching the far bank where now there were no carts.

"But what will they do under the artillery when I was told to leave because of the artillery?"

"Did you leave the dove cage unlocked?" I
75 asked.

"Yes."

"Then they'll fly."

"Yes, certainly they'll fly. But the others. It's better not to think about the others," he said.

80 "If you are rested, I would go," I urged. "Get up and try to walk now."

"Thank you," he said and got to his feet, swayed from side to side, and then sat down backwards in the dust. "I was taking care of animals," he said dully,
85 but no longer to me. "I was only taking care of animals."

There was nothing to do about him. It was Easter Sunday and the Fascists were advancing toward the Ebro. It was a gray overcast day with a low ceiling so
90 their planes were not up. That and the fact that cats know how to look after themselves was all the good luck that old man would ever have.

1

Over the course of the passage, the primary focus shifts from

A) descriptions of people near a warzone to the narrator's inner thoughts.

B) the physical setting of the scene to an exchange between strangers.

C) different characters' personality traits to the development of a lasting relationship.

D) the narrator's experiences in war to observations made by other characters.

2

The repetition of "taking care of animals" throughout the passage primarily serves to

A) convey the old man's state of mind.

B) emphasize the heartlessness of the narrator.

C) cast doubt on the old man's story.

D) compare the effects of war on humans and nature.

3

The narrator's use of the words "staggered" (line 5) and "plodded" (line 8) have mainly which effect?

A) They create a sense of doubt that the enemy troops will be able to cross such difficult territory.

B) They emphasize the struggle of the refugees to flee the area.

C) They compare the relative youth of the narrator to the age of the old man.

D) They reflect the narrator's frustration with the politics of the war.

4

The main impression created by the narrator's description of the old man in lines 25-27 is that he is

A) unemployed.

B) hopeful.

C) crestfallen.

D) ill.

5

The narrator refers to "luck" (line 92) to suggest that

A) animals are more capable of adapting to change than humans are.

B) rain will be coming soon, which will bring some relief to the thirsty refugees.

C) the old man will likely be killed.

D) the narrator's army will probably be victorious in the next battle.

6

The passage is written from the point of view of a

A) military scout preparing for an upcoming conflict.

B) refugee attempting to rescue his fellow citizens from danger.

C) young man comforting his ailing grandfather during a time of need.

D) soldier feeling conflicted about his sympathy for citizens of an enemy nation.

7

The eighth paragraph (lines 31-36) primarily serves to

A) describe the difference between the narrator's native land and the current setting.

B) identify a problem that the old man is attempting to resolve.

C) suggest that the war has ended and the combatants are waiting for the orders to retreat.

D) reinforce the narrator's anxiousness to move and contrast it with the old man's immobility.

Rhetoric – Fiction – Passage 2

This passage is adapted from "About Barbers" by Mark Twain.

All things change except barbers, the ways of barbers, and the surroundings of barbers. These never change. What one experiences in a barber's shop the first time he enters one is what he always experiences
5   in barbers' shops afterward till the end of his days. I got shaved this morning as usual. A man approached the door from Jones Street as I approached it from Main—a thing that always happens. I hurried up, but it was of no use; he entered the door one little step
10 ahead of me, and I followed in on his heels and saw him take the only vacant chair, the one presided over by the best barber. It always happens so. I sat down, hoping that I might fall heir to the chair belonging to the better of the remaining two barbers, for he had
15 already begun combing his man's hair, while his comrade was not yet quite done rubbing up and oiling his customer's locks. I watched the probabilities with strong interest. When I saw that No. 2 was gaining on No. 1 my interest grew to solicitude. When No. 1
20 stopped a moment to make change on a bath ticket for a new-comer, and lost ground in the race, my solicitude rose to anxiety. When No. 1 caught up again, and both he and his comrade were pulling the towels away and brushing the powder from their
25 customers' cheeks, and it was about an even thing which one would say "Next!" first, my very breath stood still with the suspense. But when at the culminating moment No. 1 stopped to pass a comb a couple of times through his customer's eyebrows, I
30 saw that he had lost the race by a single instant, and I rose indignant and quitted the shop, to keep from falling into the hands of No. 2; for I have none of that enviable firmness that enables a man to look calmly into the eyes of a waiting barber and tell him he will
35 wait for his fellow-barber's chair.

I stayed out fifteen minutes, and then went back, hoping for better luck. Of course all the chairs were occupied now, and four men sat waiting, silent, unsociable, distraught, and looking bored, as men
40 always do who are waiting their turn in a barber's shop. I sat down in one of the iron-armed compartments of an old sofa, and put in the time for a while reading the framed advertisements of all sorts of quack nostrums for dyeing and coloring the hair.
45 At last my turn came. A voice said "Next!" and I surrendered to No. 2, of course. It always happens so. I said meekly that I was in a hurry, and it affected him as strongly as if he had never heard it. He shoved up my head, and put a napkin under it. He explored
50 my hair with his claws and suggested that it needed trimming. I said I did not want it trimmed. He explored again and said it was pretty long for the

present style—better have a little taken off; it needed it behind especially. I said I had had it cut only a
55 week before. He yearned over it reflectively a moment, and then asked with a disparaging manner, who cut it? I came back at him promptly with a "You did!" I had him there. Then he fell to stirring up his lather and regarding himself in the glass, stopping
60 now and then to get close and examine his chin critically or inspect a pimple. He put down his razor and brushed his hair with elaborate care, plastering an inverted arch of it down on his forehead, accomplishing an accurate "Part" behind, and
65 brushing the two wings forward over his ears with nice exactness. In the meantime the lather was drying on my face.

Now he began to shave, digging his fingers into my countenance to stretch the skin and bundling and
70 tumbling my head this way and that as convenience in shaving demanded. As long as he was on the tough sides of my face I did not suffer; but when he began to rake, and rip, and tug at my chin, the tears came. He now made a handle of my nose, to assist him
75 shaving the corners of my upper lip, and it was by this bit of circumstantial evidence that I discovered that a part of his duties in the shop was to clean the kerosene-lamps.

About this time I was amusing myself trying to
80 guess where he would be most likely to cut me this time, but he got ahead of me, and sliced me on the end of the chin before I had got my mind made up. He immediately sharpened his razor—he might have done it before. Next he poked bay rum into the cut
85 place with his towel, then choked the wound with powdered starch, then soaked it with bay rum again, and would have gone on soaking and powdering it forevermore, no doubt, if I had not rebelled and begged off. He powdered my whole face now,
90 straightened me up, and began to plow my hair thoughtfully with his hands. Then he suggested a shampoo, and said my hair needed it badly, very badly. I observed that I shampooed it myself very thoroughly in the bath yesterday. I "had him" again.
95 He next recommended some of "Smith's Hair Glorifier," and offered to sell me a bottle. I declined. He praised the new perfume, "Jones's Delight of the Toilet," and proposed to sell me some of that. I declined again.
100 He returned to business, sprinkled me all over, legs and all, greased my hair in defiance of my protest against it, and then combed my scant eyebrows and defiled them with pomade, till I heard the whistles blow for noon, and knew I was five
105 minutes too late for the train. Then he snatched away the towel, brushed it lightly about my face, passed his comb through my eyebrows once more, and gaily sang out "Next!"

1

The description of the barber in the last paragraph, lines 105-108 ("Then he snatched… sang out 'Next!'"), serves what purpose?

A) To show the severe delight the barber takes in vexing the narrator

B) To illustrate the contrast in the barber's experience to that of the narrator

C) To give additional details about the barber's day-to-day work

D) To bring to light the barber's complete and hostile disregard for the narrator

2

What is the author's likely purpose in including the names of the products the barber is trying to sell the narrator in lines 95-98?

A) Identifying these items gives additional information on the time period and setting.

B) Naming the products gives legitimacy to the barber's claims.

C) This specificity is meant to impress the reader with the narrator's attention to detail.

D) Including these details adds humor to the already comical situation.

3

Which answer choice best describes the progression of the first paragraph?

A) The story shifts from a personal narrative to a third person recounting of the events taking place in a barber shop.

B) The narrator describes an increasingly stressful interaction with a barber.

C) The narrative shifts from general discussion of visiting a barber shop to a specific situation the narrator experiences on the same topic.

D) The paragraph shifts from a specific trip to the barber's to a detailed description of a barber performing a shave.

4

How does the repetition of the word "Next!" contribute to the scene created in the passage?

A) By giving the reader a touchstone to keep track of time in the passage

B) By further contributing to the increasing panic experienced by the narrator

C) By breaking the narrator's thought process at inopportune moments

D) By illustrating the sentiment expressed in the first paragraph

5

In the first paragraph, what effect do the words "gaining," "stood still," and "lost ground" have on the activity taking place at the barber shop?

A) They dramatize a tense rivalry between the two barbers.

B) They add tension to an otherwise mundane series of occurrences.

C) They depict the movements taken by the patrons at the shop.

D) They further explain the conflicting emotions of the narrator.

6

In paragraph four (lines 68-78), what do the words "digging," "rake" and "rip" convey about the interaction between the barber and the narrator?

A) A typical experience one will go through during a haircut

B) How roughly the barber is physically treating the narrator

C) The severe pain the narrator is experiencing

D) How little the narrator understands what the barber is doing

7

Which words best characterize the narrator's overall perspective on going to a barber shop?

A) Ebullient and enraptured
B) Perturbed and excited
C) Anxious and eager
D) Fraught and complicated

8

With which of the following statements would the narrator most likely agree?

A) Visiting a barber shop can be a multifaceted experience.
B) People should avoid going to barber shops.
C) Most barbers are ill tempered.
D) Each visit to the barber shop is different.

Rhetoric – Fiction – Passage 3

This passage is adapted from "A Thousand Years of Good Prayers" by Yiyung Li.

In the evenings, when his daughter comes home, Mr. Shi has the supper ready. He took a cooking class after his wife died, a few years ago, and ever since has studied the culinary art with the same fervor with
5 which he studied mathematics and physics when he was a college student. "Every man is born with more talents than he knows how to use," he says at dinner. "I would've never imagined taking up cooking, but here I am, better than I imagined."
10 "Yes, very impressive," his daughter says.
"And likewise"—Mr. Shi takes a quick glance at his daughter—"life provides more happiness than we ever know. We have to train ourselves to look for it."
His daughter does not reply. Despite the pride he
15 takes in his cooking and her praises for it, she eats little and eats out of duty. It worries him that she is not putting enough enthusiasm into life as she should be. Of course, she has her reasons, newly divorced after seven years of marriage. His ex-son-in-law went
20 back to Beijing permanently after the divorce. Mr. Shi does not know what led the boat of their marriage to run into a hidden rock, but whatever the reason is, it must not be her fault. She is made for a good wife, soft-voiced and kindhearted, dutiful and beautiful, a
25 younger version of her mother. When his daughter called to inform him of the divorce, Mr. Shi imagined her in inconsolable pain, and asked to come to America, to help her recover. She refused, and he started calling daily and pleading, spending a good
30 solid month of his pension on the long-distance bill. She finally agreed when he announced that his wish for his seventy-fifth birthday was to take a look at America. A lie it was, but the lie turned out to be a good reason. America is worth taking a look at; more
35 than that, America makes him a new person, a rocket scientist, a good conversationalist, a loving father, a happy man.
After dinner, Mr. Shi's daughter either retreats to her bedroom to read or drives away and comes home
40 at late hours. Mr. Shi asks to go out with her, to accompany her to the movies he imagines that she watches alone, but she refuses in a polite but firm manner. It is certainly not healthy for a woman, especially a contemplative woman like his daughter,
45 to spend too much time alone. He starts to talk more to tackle her solitude, asking questions about the part of her life he is not witnessing. How was her work of the day? he asks. Fine, she says tiredly. Not discouraged, he asks about her colleagues, whether
50 there are more females than males, how old they are, and, if they are married, whether they have children. He asks what she eats for lunch and whether she eats

alone, what kind of computer she uses, and what books she reads. He asks about her old school
55 friends, people he believes she is out of contact with because of the shame of the divorce. He asks about her plan for the future, hoping she understands the urgency of her situation. Women in their marriageable twenties and early thirties are like
60 lychees that have been picked from the tree; each passing day makes them less fresh and less desirable, and only too soon will they lose their value, and have to be gotten rid of at a sale price.
Mr. Shi knows enough not to mention the price.
65 Still, he cannot help but lecture on the fruitfulness of life. The more he talks, the more he is moved by his own patience. His daughter, however, does not improve. She eats less and becomes quieter each day. When he finally points out that she is not enjoying
70 her life as she should, she says, "How do you get this conclusion? I'm enjoying my life alright."
"But that's a lie. A happy person will never be so quiet!"
She looks up from the bowl of rice. "Baba, you
75 used to be very quiet, remember? Were you unhappy then?"
Mr. Shi, not prepared for such directness from his daughter, is unable to reply. He waits for her to apologize and change the topic, as people with good
80 manners do when they realize they are embarrassing others with their questions, but she does not let him go. Her eyes behind her glasses, wide open and unrelenting, remind him of her in her younger years. When she was four or five, she went after him every
85 possible moment, asking questions and demanding answers. The eyes remind him of her mother too; at one time in their marriage, she gazed at him with this questioning look, waiting for an answer he did not have for her.
90 He sighs. "Of course I've always been happy."
"There you go, Baba. We can be quiet and happy, can't we?"
"Why not talk about your happiness with me?" Mr. Shi says. "Tell me more about your work."
95 "You didn't talk much about your work either, remember? Even when I asked."
"A rocket scientist, you know how it was. My work was confidential."
"You didn't talk much about anything."
100 Mr. Shi opens his mouth but finds no words coming. After a long moment, he says, "I talk more now. I'm improving, no?"
"Sure," his daughter says.
"That's what you need to do. Talk more," Mr.
105 Shi says. "And start now."
His daughter, however, is less enthusiastic. She finishes her meal quickly in her usual silence and leaves the apartment before he finishes his.

1

The main purpose of the passage is

A) to illustrate the insurmountable problems that arise between a father and daughter as they discuss her divorce.

B) to examine and analyze a daughter's disrespectful attitude towards her father.

C) to show a strained relationship between a father and daughter, though they are actually quite similar.

D) to explain, from a father's point of view, why divorce is an undesirable option for older women.

2

The main purpose of the last sentence in the passage is to

A) portray the daughter's lonely lifestyle.

B) condemn the father for his treatment of his daughter.

C) convey how thoroughly the father has ruined his relationship with his daughter.

D) show that the daughter does not plan to take her father's advice.

3

Which answer choice best describes the order of events in the passage?

A) Mr. Shi's daughter gets divorced; her father comes to visit her in America; their relationship is strained by the father's intrusiveness.

B) Mr. Shi visits his daughter in America; he gives his daughter unwanted advice; his daughter asks him to leave her apartment.

C) Mr. Shi takes a cooking class; he travels to America to take care of his daughter; he then counsels her on her divorce.

D) Mr. Shi's daughter isolates herself after a divorce; Mr. Shi tries to coax her into socializing; his daughter takes his advice.

.4

What does the fourth paragraph (lines 14-37) highlight about Mr. Shi?

A) The crowded thoughts and judgements of Mr. Shi show his concern.

B) The sparse and simple sentences underline Mr. Shi's level of disinterest.

C) The complicated and flowery language parallels Mr. Shi's jumbled thoughts.

D) The incessant questions paint a picture of Mr. Shi's irritating manner.

5

What does the comparison of the daughter's marriage to a boat crashing into a rock (lines 21-22) convey about the daughter's divorce?

A) The turbulent and violent nature of the daughter's marriage

B) How the marriage was perceived as previously peaceful by the father

C) The father's thorough understanding of the nature of the divorce

D) The irreversible damage the daughter has suffered from the divorce

6

How does the dialogue change from the first conversation between the characters (lines 6-14) and the second (lines 69-105)?

A) The first conversation is respectful, while the second is confrontational.

B) The first conversation is conversational, while the second is hostile.

C) The first conversation is forceful, while the second is conciliatory.

D) The first conversation is peaceful, while the second is furtive.

7

How does the point of view in the passage contribute to the tension in the passage?

A) The daughter's thoughts are given throughout, so the reader understands the anger she has for her father.

B) The father's thoughts are given throughout, so the reader understands how the father is editing what he says and his mounting concern.

C) The father's observations are given throughout, so the reader can see that he is behaving rationally towards his daughter.

D) The narrator is detached from both main characters, so the reader can only gather information through the characters' actions and words.

8

Based on the passage, Mr. Shi would most likely agree with which of the following statements?

A) Children will learn more from what you do than what you say.

B) Children tend to live up to the expectations set for them.

C) Parents shouldn't interfere with their adult children's lives.

D) Parents should be respected and their advice should be followed.

Rhetoric – Fiction – Passage 4

This passage is adapted from "Wants" by Grace Paley.

I saw my ex-husband in the street. I was sitting on the steps of the new library.

Hello, my life, I said. We had once been married for twenty-seven years, so I felt justified.

5 He said, What? What life? No life of mine.

I said, O.K. I don't argue when there's real disagreement. I got up and went into the library to see how much I owed them.

The librarian said $32 even and you've owed it
10 for eighteen years. I didn't deny anything. Because I don't understand how time passes. I have had those books. I have often thought of them. The library is only two blocks away.

My ex-husband followed me to the Books
15 Returned desk. He interrupted the librarian, who had more to tell. In many ways, he said, as I look back, I attribute the dissolution of our marriage to the fact that you never invited the Bertrams to dinner.

That's possible, I said. But really, if you
20 remember: first, my father was sick that Friday, then the children were born, then I had those Tuesday-night meetings, then the war began. Then we didn't seem to know them anymore. But you're right. I should have had them to dinner.

25 I gave the librarian a check for $32. Immediately she trusted me, put my past behind her, wiped the record clean, which is just what most other municipal and/or state bureaucracies will not do.

I checked out the two Edith Wharton books I had
30 just returned because I'd read them so long ago and they are more apropos now than ever. They were *The House of Mirth* and *The Children*, which is about how life in the United States in New York changed in twenty-seven years fifty years ago.

35 A nice thing I do remember is breakfast, my ex-husband said. I was surprised. All we ever had was coffee. Then I remembered there was a hole in the back of the kitchen closet which opened into the apartment next door. There, they always ate sugar-
40 cured smoked bacon. It gave us a very grand feeling about breakfast, but we never got stuffed and sluggish.

That was when we were poor, I said.

When were we ever rich? he asked.

45 Oh, as time went on, as our responsibilities increased, we didn't go in need. You took adequate financial care, I reminded him. The children went to camp four weeks a year and in decent ponchos with sleeping bags and boots, just like everyone else. They
50 looked very nice. Our place was warm in winter, and we had nice red pillows and things.

I wanted a sailboat, he said. But you didn't want anything.

Don't be bitter, I said. It's never too late.
55 No, he said with a great deal of bitterness. I may get a sailboat. As a matter of fact I have money down on an eighteen-foot two-rigger. I'm doing well this year and can look forward to better. But as for you, it's too late. You'll always want nothing.

60 He had had a habit throughout the twenty-seven years of making a narrow remark which, like a plumber's snake, could work its way through the ear down the throat, half-way to my heart. He would then disappear, leaving me choking with equipment. What
65 I mean is, I sat down on the library steps and he went away.

I looked through *The House of Mirth*, but lost interest. I felt extremely accused. Now, it's true, I'm short of requests and absolute requirements. But I do
70 want *something*. I want, for instance, to be a different person. I want to be the woman who brings these two books back in two weeks. I want to be the effective citizen who changes the school system and addresses the Board of Estimate on the troubles of this dear
75 urban center.

I *had* promised my children to end the war before they grew up.

I wanted to have been married forever to one person, my ex-husband or my present one. Either has
80 enough character for a whole life, which as it turns out is really not such a long time. You couldn't exhaust either man's qualities or get under the rock of his reasons in one short life.

Just this morning I looked out the window to
85 watch the street for a while and saw that the little sycamores the city had dreamily planted a couple of years before the kids were born had come that day to the prime of their lives.

Well! I decided to bring those two books back to
90 the library. Which proves that when a person or an event comes along to jolt or appraise me I *can* take some appropriate action, although I am better known for my hospitable remarks.

1

What is the main purpose of lines 84-88 ("Just this morning… of their lives.")?

A) To serve as a metaphor for the behavior of the narrator's children

B) To show the narrator's longing for a past she can no longer remember

C) To contrast the lack of growth within the narrator over a long period

D) To provide a concrete illustration of time passing and significant change

2

What is the function of the list of events in lines 19-23 ("But really… know them anymore.")?

A) It shows how the narrator is seeking sympathy.

B) It summarizes events and mirrors the way life passes quickly.

C) It provides valid excuses for the misstep in their marriage.

D) It gives background information to an otherwise confusing situation.

3

How does the presence of the librarian affect the confrontation between the narrator and her ex-husband?

A) It provides tension to contrast a comfortable situation.

B) It is a further illustration of the faults of the narrator.

C) It makes the ex-husband self-conscious and terse.

D) It supplies a contrast between absolution and lingering resentment.

4

Which two elements are most prominent in the passage?

A) ornate details and vibrant description.

B) muddled storytelling and poetic word choice.

C) direct dialogue and sporadic introspection.

D) internal conflict and authorial intrusion.

5

What is the effect of the comparison of the ex-husband's remarks to a plumber's snake (lines 60-63)?

A) It further explains how his actions destroyed their relationship.

B) It illustrates the hurtful and intrusive nature of his words.

C) It parallels his actions to those of a devious serpent.

D) It shows how he wasn't emotionally supportive in their marriage.

6

How do the two references to "war," lines 22 and 76, contribute to the passage as a whole?

A) They give a broader context to a specific situation.

B) They highlight the combative nature of the narrator's relationships.

C) They provide a time frame for the events in the passage.

D) They are unnecessary details that don't add pertinent information.

7

Which of the following is the best description of the point of view from which this passage is told?

A) That of an adult woman navigating a difficult chance meeting

B) That of a mature woman grappling with crippling challenges

C) That of a young woman struggling through a new marriage

D) That of an elderly woman looking back on her life with regret

8

Based on the passage, the narrator would most likely agree with which of the following statements?

A) People change rapidly over time.

B) People are ultimately capable of change.

C) Marriage isn't worth the effort it requires.

D) Children can make marriage difficult.

Rhetoric – Fiction – Passage 5

This passage is adapted from "A Summing Up" by Virginia Woolf.

Since it had grown hot and crowded indoors, since there could be no danger on a night like this of damp, since the Chinese lanterns seemed hung red and green fruit in the depths of an enchanted forest,
5 Mr. Bertram Pritchard led Mrs. Latham into the garden.

The open air and the sense of being out of doors bewildered Sasha Latham, the tall, handsome, rather indolent looking lady, whose majesty of presence
10 was so great that people never credited her with feeling perfectly inadequate and gauche when she had to say something at a party. But so it was; and she was glad that she was with Bertram, who could be trusted, even out of doors, to talk without
15 stopping. Written down what he said would be incredible—not only was each thing he said in itself insignificant, but there was no connection between the different remarks. Indeed, if one had taken a pencil and written down his very words—and one
20 night of his talk would have filled a whole book—no one could doubt, reading them, that the poor man was intellectually deficient. This was far from the case, for Mr. Pritchard was an esteemed civil servant; but what was even stranger was that he was almost
25 invariably liked. There was a sound in his voice, some accent of emphasis, some luster in the incongruity of his ideas, some emanation from his round, chubby brown face and robin redbreast's figure, which existed and flourished and made itself
30 felt independently of his words, indeed, often in opposition to them. Thus Sasha Latham would be thinking while he chattered on about his tour in Devonshire, about inns and landladies, about Eddie and Freddie, about cows and night travelling, about
35 cream and stars, about continental railways and Bradshaw, catching cod, catching cold, influenza, rheumatism and Keats—she was thinking of him in the abstract as a person whose existence was good, creating him as he spoke in the guise that was
40 different from what he said, and was certainly the true Bertram Pritchard, even though one could not prove it. How could one prove that he was a loyal friend and very sympathetic and—but here, as so often happened, talking to Bertram Pritchard, she
45 forgot his existence, and began to think of something else.

It was the night she thought of, taking a look up into the sky. It was the country she smelt suddenly, the somber stillness of fields under the stars, but here,
50 in Mrs. Dalloway's back garden, in Westminster, the beauty, country born and bred as she was, thrilled her because of the contrast presumably; there the smell of hay in the air and behind her the rooms full of people. She walked with Bertram; she walked rather like a
55 stag, with a little give of the ankles, fanning herself, majestic, silent, with all her senses roused, her ears pricked, snuffing the air.

This, she thought, is the greatest of marvels; the supreme achievement of the human race. She thought
60 of the dry, thick, well-built house stored with valuables, humming with people coming close to each other, going away from each other, exchanging their views, stimulating each other. And when they came to the end of the garden (it was in fact
65 extremely small), and she and Bertram sat down on deck chairs, she looked at the house veneratingly, enthusiastically, as if a golden shaft ran through her. Shy though she was and almost incapable when suddenly presented to someone of saying anything,
70 fundamentally humble, she cherished a profound admiration for other people. To be them would be marvelous, but she was condemned to be herself and could only in this silent enthusiastic way, sitting outside in a garden, applaud the society of humanity
75 from which she was excluded. Tags of poetry in praise of them rose to her lips; they were adorable and good, above all courageous, triumphers over night and nature.

By some malice of fate she was unable to join,
80 but she could sit and praise while Bertram chattered on. Suddenly Bertram, who was restless physically, wanted to explore the grounds, and, jumping on to a heap of bricks he peered over the garden wall. Sasha peered over too. There was London again; the vast
85 inattentive impersonal world; motor omnibuses; affairs; lights before public houses; and yawning policemen.

Having satisfied his curiosity, and replenished, by a moment's silence, his bubbling fountains of talk,
90 Bertram invited Mr. and Mrs. Somebody to sit with them, pulling up two more chairs. There they sat again, looking at the same house, the same tree, the same barrel; only having looked over the wall and had a glimpse of London going its ways
95 unconcernedly, Sasha could no longer spray over the world that cloud of gold. Bertram talked and the somebodies—for the life of her she could not remember if they were called Wallace or Freeman— answered, and all their words passed through a thin
100 haze of gold and fell into prosaic daylight. She looked at the dry, thick Queen Anne House; she did her best to remember what she had read at school about the Isle of Thorney and men in coracles, oysters, and wild duck and mists, but it seemed to her
105 a logical affair of drains and carpenters, and this party—nothing but people in evening dress.

Then she asked herself, which view is the true one? She could see the house half lit up, half unlit.

1

The author uses the description of Bertram's conversational style in lines 15-22 primarily to:

(A) illustrate Bertram's lack of intelligence.
(B) poke fun at Bertram's incoherence.
(C) explain a contradiction in Bertram's personality
(D) address Bertram's flaws frankly.

2

What is the main purpose of the first paragraph?

(A) To provide an explanation for the characters going outdoors
(B) To characterize Bertram and Sasha in terms of their environment
(C) To flood the reader with detail that is crucial to the passage
(D) To provide details that set the scene for the rest of the passage

3

Which of the following best describes the order of events in the passage?

(A) Sasha and Bertram go outside, walk around the garden, take a look at the cityscape over the garden wall, then sit with a couple with whiom Bertram chats.
(B) Sasha and Bertram are outside, take a long walk around the garden, admire the countryside, then talk with a couple whom they both enjoy.
(C) Sasha and Bertram escape the heat of the house, sit together through the afternoon, stroll through a field, then meet an unfamiliar couple and get to know them.
(D) Sasha and Bertram are sitting in a large house, leave to take in the view of the city, walk around, then daydream while a couple is attempting to talk with them.

4

What is the effect of calling the couple "Mr. and Mrs. Somebody" (line 90)?

(A) It personifies the apathy Bertram feels for the couple.
(B) It dehumanizes the other guests in the garden.
(C) It exposes Sasha's indifference to the world around her.
(D) It reiterates the sameness Sasha is experiencing.

5

Which of the following best describes Sasha's overall mood in the passage?

(A) Introspective
(B) Bewildered
(C) Bored
(D) Delighted

6

Which of the following best describes the point of view from which the passage is told?

(A) That of a woman severely troubled by the repetition in her life
(B) That of a social and affluent man
(C) That of a narrator outside of the story with access to one of the character's thoughts
(D) That of a narrator outside of the passage with access to all characters' thoughts

7

How does the author use the setting to contribute to the passage?

(A) It highlights the limited space to which the characters have access.
(B) It draws a clear contrast between the country and the city.
(C) It shows the suffocating nature of the area on Sasha.
(D) It further elevates the melancholy mood of the passage.

Notes and Reflections

Rhetoric – Great Global Conversation – Passage 1

This passage is adapted from president Dwight D. Eisenhower's 1953 speech "Atoms for Peace".

I feel impelled to speak today in a language that in a sense is new, one which I, who have spent so much of my life in the military profession, would have preferred never to use. That new language is the
5 language of atomic warfare.

The atomic age has moved forward at such a pace that every citizen of the world should have some comprehension, at least in comparative terms, of the extent of this development, of the utmost significance
10 to every one of us. Clearly, if the peoples of the world are to conduct an intelligent search for peace, they must be armed with the significant facts of today's existence.

On 16 July 1945, the United States set off the
15 world's biggest atomic explosion. Since that date in 1945, the United States of America has conducted forty-two test explosions. Atomic bombs are more than twenty-five times as powerful as the weapons with which the atomic age dawned, while hydrogen
20 weapons are in the ranges of millions of tons of TNT equivalent. Today, the United States stockpile of atomic weapons, which, of course, increases daily, exceeds by many times the total equivalent of the total of all bombs and all shells that came from every
25 plane and every gun in every theatre of war in all the years of the Second World War. A single air group, whether afloat or land based, can now deliver to any reachable target a destructive cargo exceeding in power all the bombs that fell on Britain in all the
30 Second World War. In size and variety, the development of atomic weapons has been no less remarkable. The development has been such that atomic weapons have virtually achieved conventional status within our armed services. In the United States,
35 the Army, the Navy, the Air Force, and the Marine Corps are all capable of putting this weapon to military use.

But the dread secret and the fearful engines of atomic might are not ours alone. In the first place, the
40 secret is possessed by our friends and allies, the United Kingdom and Canada, whose scientific genius made a tremendous contribution to our original discoveries and the designs of atomic bombs. The secret is also known by the Soviet Union. The Soviet
45 Union has informed us that, over recent years, it has devoted extensive resources to atomic weapons. During this period the Soviet Union has exploded a series of atomic devices, including at least one involving thermo-nuclear reactions.
50 If at one time the United States possessed what might have been called a monopoly of atomic power,

that monopoly ceased to exist several years ago. Therefore, although our earlier start has permitted us to accumulate what is today a great quantitative
55 advantage, the atomic realities of today comprehend two facts of even greater significance. First, the knowledge now possessed by several nations will eventually be shared by others, possibly all others. Second, even a vast superiority in numbers of
60 weapons, and a consequent capability of devastating retaliation, is no preventive, of itself, against the fearful material damage and toll of human lives that would be inflicted by surprise aggression.

The free world, at least dimly aware of these
65 facts, has naturally embarked on a large program of warning and defense systems. That program will be accelerated and extended. But let no one think that the expenditure of vast sums for weapons and systems of defense can guarantee absolute safety for
70 the cities and citizens of any nation. The awful arithmetic of the atomic bomb doesn't permit of any such easy solution. Even against the most powerful defense, an aggressor in possession of the effective minimum number of atomic bombs for a surprise
75 attack could probably place a sufficient number of his bombs on the chosen targets to cause hideous damage.

Should such an atomic attack be launched against the United States, our reactions would be
80 swift and resolute. But for me to say that the defense capabilities of the United States are such that they could inflict terrible losses upon an aggressor, for me to say that the retaliation capabilities of the United States are so great that such an aggressor's land
85 would be laid waste, all this, while fact, is not the true expression of the purpose and the hopes of the United States.

My country wants to be constructive, not destructive. It wants agreements, not wars, among
90 nations. It wants itself to live in freedom and in the confidence that the peoples of every other nation enjoy equally the right of choosing their own way of life.

So my country's purpose is to help us to move
95 out of the dark chamber of horrors into the light, to find a way by which the minds of men, the hopes of men, the souls of men everywhere, can move forward towards peace and happiness and well-being.

In this quest, I know that we must not lack
100 patience. I know that in a world divided, such as ours today, salvation cannot be attained by one dramatic act. I know that many steps will have to be taken over many months before the world can look at itself one day and truly realize that a new climate of mutually
105 peaceful confidence is abroad in the world. But I know, above all else, that we must start to take these steps now.

1

The speaker's main purpose in the passage is to

A) consider alternate explanations for an observation.

B) advocate for a particular response to a situation.

C) express judgment for a person's actions.

D) describe a series of recent events.

2

The fifth paragraph (lines 50-63) mainly serves to

A) list the steps necessary for the speaker to correct a mistake.

B) identify problems that the speaker attempts to address.

C) explain the speaker's discovery of a new technology.

D) establish issues that the passage then resolves.

3

The repetition of "all" in the third paragraph (lines 14-37) has the main effect of

A) mocking the overdramatic claims of the author's opponents.

B) encouraging cooperation with the author's objective.

C) emphasizing the power of the modern U.S. military.

D) presenting a belief as though it is universally held.

4

Which choice best supports the speaker's claim that nuclear weaponry is a threat to the United States?

A) "In the first place... the designs of atomic bombs." (lines 39-43)

B) "Even against the most powerful defense... to cause hideous damage." (lines 72-77)

C) "But for me to say... and the hopes of the United States." (lines 80-87)

D) "So my country's purpose... towards peace and happiness and well-being." (lines 94-98)

5

Which choice best describes the overall structure of the passage?

A) A list of several ways in which a nation has dealt with hardship over multiple generations

B) A detailed presentation of a complicated situation and a personal response

C) A careful analysis of a technology's impact on modern life

D) A definitive answer to a series of related questions

6

Over the course of the passage, the speaker's attitude shifts from

A) disdain for the hardships of war to appreciation of the technological advancements it may bring.

B) fear that a technology will be misused for war to confidence in military strength.

C) criticism of a government's actions to doubt about its improvement.

D) caution about international conflict to hope about its prevention.

7

The use of the words "awful" (line 70) and "hideous" (line 76) mainly have which effect?

A) They emphasize the impossibility of solving a complicated problem.

B) They reinforce the author's characterization of a situation as dire.

C) They dramatize the destruction that has been caused in past wars.

D) They criticize an opinion commonly held among the public.

Rhetoric – Great Global Conversation – Passage 2

This passage is adapted from president Franklin Delano Roosevelt's 1933 speech "On the Bank Crisis".

I want to talk for a few minutes with the people of the United States about banking—with the comparatively few who understand the mechanics of banking but more particularly with the overwhelming
5 majority who use banks for the making of deposits and the drawing of checks. I want to tell you what has been done in the last few days, why it was done, and what the next steps are going to be.

First of all let me state the simple fact that when
10 you deposit money in a bank the bank does not put the money into a safe deposit vault. It invests your money in many different forms of credit-bonds, commercial paper, mortgages and many other kinds of loans. In other words, the bank puts your money to
15 work to keep the wheels of industry and of agriculture turning around. A comparatively small part of the money you put into the bank is kept in currency—an amount which in normal times is wholly sufficient to cover the cash needs of the
20 average citizen. In other words the total amount of all the currency in the country is only a small fraction of the total deposits in all of the banks.

What, then, happened during the last few days of February and the first few days of March? Because of
25 undermined confidence on the part of the public, there was a general rush by a large portion of our population to turn bank deposits into currency or gold. A rush so great that the soundest banks could not get enough currency to meet the demand. The
30 reason for this was that on the spur of the moment it was, of course, impossible to sell perfectly sound assets of a bank and convert them into cash except at panic prices far below their real value.

By the afternoon of March 3 scarcely a bank in
35 the country was open to do business. Proclamations temporarily closing them in whole or in part had been issued by the Governors in almost all the states.

It was then that I issued the proclamation providing for the nation-wide bank holiday, and this
40 was the first step in the Government's reconstruction of our financial and economic fabric. The second step was the legislation promptly and patriotically passed by the Congress confirming my proclamation and broadening my powers so that it became possible in
45 view of the requirement of time to extend the holiday and lift the ban of that holiday gradually. This law also gave authority to develop a program of rehabilitation of our banking facilities. I want to tell our citizens in every part of the Nation that the
50 national Congress—Republicans and Democrats alike—showed by this action a devotion to public welfare and a realization of the emergency and the necessity for speed that it is difficult to match in our history.

55 The third stage has been the series of regulations permitting the banks to continue their functions to take care of the distribution of food and household necessities and the payment of payrolls.

It is possible that when the banks resume a very
60 few people who have not recovered from their fear may again begin withdrawals. Let me make it clear that the banks will take care of all needs—and it is my belief that hoarding during the past week has become an exceedingly unfashionable pastime. It
65 needs no prophet to tell you that when the people find that they can get their money—that they can get it when they want it for all legitimate purposes—the phantom of fear will soon be laid. People will again be glad to have their money where it will be safely
70 taken care of and where they can use it conveniently at any time. I can assure you that it is safer to keep your money in a reopened bank than under the mattress.

The success of our whole great national program
75 depends, of course, upon the cooperation of the public—on its intelligent support and use of a reliable system.

I hope you can see from this elemental recital of what your government is doing that there is nothing
80 complex, or radical in the process.

We had a bad banking situation. Some of our bankers had shown themselves either incompetent or dishonest in their handling of the people's funds. They had used the money entrusted to them in
85 speculations and unwise loans. This was of course not true in the vast majority of our banks but it was true in enough of them to shock the people for a time into a sense of insecurity and to put them into a frame of mind where they did not differentiate, but seemed
90 to assume that the acts of a comparative few had tainted them all. It was the Government's job to straighten out this situation and do it as quickly as possible—and the job is being performed.

There is an element in the readjustment of our
95 financial system more important than currency, more important than gold, and that is the confidence of the people. Confidence and courage are the essentials of success in carrying out our plan. You people must have faith; you must not be stampeded by rumors or
100 guesses. Let us unite in banishing fear. We have provided the machinery to restore our financial system; it is up to you to support and make it work.

It is your problem no less than it is mine. Together we cannot fail.

1

The main purpose of the passage is to

A) describe the events of a national banking crisis.

B) urge people to take all of their money out of banks.

C) encourage people to trust and have confidence in the banks.

D) compare and contrast the many trustworthy bankers with the few untrustworthy ones.

2

How does the word "hoarding" in line 63 affect the tone of the passage?

A) It shows approval for those who will withdraw a lot of money once the banks reopen.

B) It portrays those who take out money from the banks as acting unreasonably.

C) It displays the hatred of those who still do not trust the banks.

D) It highlights the trustworthy nature of the banks.

3

The purpose of the second paragraph (lines 9-21) is to

A) inform the audience about common banking practices.

B) describe the events of the banking crisis.

C) persuade banks to keep more currency in reserve.

D) chastise the audience for their actions during the banking crisis.

4

During the course of the passage, the central focus shifts from

A) the events of the banking crisis to banking practices.

B) the events of the banking crisis to the past confidence in the financial system.

C) the currency in banks to the undermined confidence of banks.

D) how banking works to what the speaker is doing to address the banking crisis.

5

Which of the following statements would the author most likely agree with?

A) Most bankers cannot be trusted.

B) The people are to blame for the banking crisis.

C) The audience must figure out how to solve the banking crisis by themselves.

D) The banking crisis would not have been as extreme if the public trusted the banking system throughout the event.

6

Which choice provides the best evidence for the answer to the previous question?

A) Lines 24-28 "Because… gold."

B) Lines 74-77 "The success… system."

C) Lines 100- 102 "We…work."

D) Lines 81-83 "We…funds."

7

The author includes the last paragraph to

A) reassure the audience that he is doing everything he can.

B) chastise the audience for not doing their work.

C) emphasize the actions of both the author and the audience and urge the audience to support the work that the author has done.

D) predict a promising future.

Rhetoric – Great Global Conversation – Passage 3

This passage is adapted from John F. Kennedy's speech to the American Newspaper Publishers' Association in 1961.

The very word "secrecy" is repugnant in a free and open society; and we are as a people inherently and historically opposed to secret societies, to secret oaths and to secret proceedings. We decided long ago
5 that the dangers of excessive and unwarranted concealment of pertinent facts far outweighed the dangers which are cited to justify it. Even today, there is little value in opposing the threat of a closed society by imitating its arbitrary restrictions. Even
10 today, there is little value in insuring the survival of our nation if our traditions do not survive with it. And there is very grave danger that an announced need for increased security will be seized upon by those anxious to expand its meaning to the very limits of
15 official censorship and concealment. That I do not intend to permit to the extent that it is in my control. And no official of my administration, whether his rank is high or low, civilian or military, should interpret my words here tonight as an excuse to
20 censor the news, to stifle dissent, to cover up our mistakes or to withhold from the press and the public the facts they deserve to know.

But I do ask every publisher, every editor, and every newsman in the nation to reexamine his own
25 standards, and to recognize the nature of our country's peril. In time of war, the government and the press have customarily joined in an effort based largely on self-discipline, to prevent unauthorized disclosures to the enemy. In time of "clear and
30 present danger," the courts have held that even the privileged rights of the First Amendment must yield to the public's need for national security.

For the facts of the matter are that this nation's foes have openly boasted of acquiring through our
35 newspapers information they would otherwise hire agents to acquire through theft, bribery or espionage; that details of this nation's covert preparations to counter the enemy's covert operations have been available to every newspaper reader, friend and foe
40 alike; that the size, the strength, the location and the nature of our forces and weapons, and our plans and strategy for their use, have all been pinpointed in the press and other news media to a degree sufficient to satisfy any foreign power; and that, in at least in one
45 case, the publication of details concerning a secret mechanism whereby satellites were followed required its alteration at the expense of considerable time and money.

The newspapers which printed these stories were
50 loyal, patriotic, responsible and well-meaning. Had we been engaged in open warfare, they undoubtedly would not have published such items. But in the absence of open warfare, they recognized only the tests of journalism and not the tests of national
55 security. And my question tonight is whether additional tests should not now be adopted.

The question is for you alone to answer. No public official should answer it for you. No governmental plan should impose its restraints
60 against your will. But I would be failing in my duty to the nation, in considering all of the responsibilities that we now bear and all of the means at hand to meet those responsibilities, if I did not commend this problem to your attention, and urge its thoughtful
65 consideration.

On many earlier occasions, I have said—and your newspapers have constantly said—that these are times that appeal to every citizen's sense of sacrifice and self-discipline. They call out to every citizen to
70 weigh his rights and comforts against his obligations to the common good. I cannot now believe that those citizens who serve in the newspaper business consider themselves exempt from that appeal.

I have no intention of establishing a new Office
75 of War Information to govern the flow of news. I am not suggesting any new forms of censorship or any new types of security classifications. I have no easy answer to the dilemma that I have posed, and would not seek to impose it if I had one. But I am asking the
80 members of the newspaper profession and the industry in this country to reexamine their own responsibilities, to consider the degree and the nature of the present danger, and to heed the duty of self-restraint which that danger imposes upon us all.

85 Every newspaper now asks itself, with respect to every story: "Is it news?" All I suggest is that you add the question: "Is it in the interest of the national security?" And I hope that every group in America—unions and businessmen and public officials at every
90 level—will ask the same question of their endeavors, and subject their actions to the same exacting tests.

1

The purpose of Kennedy's speech to the American Newspaper Publishers' Association is to

A) impose harsher restrictions on what publishers may communicate to the public.

B) convince publishers to balance freedoms with concerns for national security.

C) argue for repeal of the right to freedom of expression.

D) accuse publishers of treason.

2

Which statement provides the best description of a technique the speaker uses throughout the passage to advance his main point?

A) The author shares personal anecdotes and attempts to convince others to behave as he did in similar situations.

B) The author describes how problems were solved in the past and applies those solutions to a modern situation.

C) The author explains actions he won't take and expresses hope for what others will do.

D) The author takes credit for recent successes and blames others for problems.

3

Which choice best supports the speaker's argument that citizens have an obligation to consider the common good?

A) "The very… proceedings." (lines 1-4)

B) "Even today… with it." (lines 7-11)

C) "And no… to know." (lines 17-22)

D) "In time… national security." (lines 29-32)

4

In context, the intended effect of the speaker's use of "we" in lines 2, 4, and 62 is to

A) allow the audience to experience situations from the author's perspective.

B) specify a group in a unique situation.

C) establish a sense of mutual understanding.

D) split the audience into two opposing groups.

5

The first paragraph mainly serves to

A) provide context for the following statements and anticipate the audience's reactions.

B) chronicle the historical events that have led to the author's current discussion.

C) define a term that will be further analyzed throughout the passage.

D) describe the differences between two different government policies.

6

The speaker's consideration of publishers' rights and responsibilities can best be characterized as

A) an earnest request to prioritize public safety over the advancement of one's career.

B) an opinionated historical overview of the relationship between government and the press.

C) a frustrated condemnation of the actions of a few members of an influential group.

D) a philosophical examination of a person's duty to his or her fellow citizens.

7

According to information in the passage, the speaker would most likely agree with which of the following?

A) The country's enemies are getting important information that should be kept secret.

B) Secrecy, secret oaths, and secret societies are an unavoidable part of human society.

C) Government should censor the news and control what gets communicated.

D) The information in newspapers should not be inherently trusted.

8

Kennedy contrasts "tests of journalism" with "tests of national security" (lines 54-55) in order to

A) argue for government censorship of news.

B) provide information for the country's enemies.

C) ask the audience to censor itself with regards to information related to national security.

D) appeal to citizens' sense of sacrifice and self-discipline.

SUMMIT
EDUCATIONAL
GROUP

Rhetoric – Great Global Conversation – Passage 4

Passage 1 is adapted from "Democracy in America" by Alexis De Tocqueville. Passage 2 is adapted from president Theodore Roosevelt's message to Congress in 1901. During Roosevelt's presidency, corporate trusts monopolized industries, such as oil and railroads. Working together, corporations spread their influence to prevent other businesses from competing and to drastically raise prices for consumers.

Passage 1

It is acknowledged that when a workman is engaged every day upon the same detail, the whole commodity is produced with greater ease, promptitude, and economy. It is likewise
5   acknowledged that the cost of the production of manufactured goods is diminished by the extent of the establishment in which they are made, and by the amount of capital employed or of credit. When a workman is unceasingly and exclusively engaged in
10 the fabrication of one thing, he ultimately does his work with singular dexterity; but at the same time he loses the general faculty of applying his mind to the direction of the work. He every day becomes more adroit and less industrious; so that it may be said of
15 him, that in proportion as the workman improves the man is degraded. What can be expected of a man who has spent twenty years of his life in making heads for pins? And to what can that mighty human intelligence, which has so often stirred the world, be
20 applied in him, except it be to investigate the best method of making pins' heads? When a workman has spent a considerable portion of his existence in this manner, his thoughts are forever set upon the object of his daily toil; his body has contracted certain fixed
25 habits, which it can never shake off: in a word, he no longer belongs to himself, but to the calling which he has chosen.

Whereas the workman concentrates his faculties more and more upon the study of a single detail, the
30 master surveys a more extensive whole, and the mind of the latter is enlarged in proportion as that of the former is narrowed. In a short time, the one will require nothing but physical strength without intelligence; the other stands in need of science, and
35 almost of genius, to insure success. This man resembles more and more the administrator of a vast empire—that man, a brute. The master and the workman have then here no similarity, and their differences increase every day. They are only
40 connected as the two rings at the extremities of a long chain. The one is continually, closely, and necessarily dependent upon the other, and seems as much born to

obey as that other is to command. What is this but aristocracy?
45 But this kind of aristocracy by no means resembles those kinds which preceded it. The territorial aristocracy of former ages was either bound by law, or thought itself bound by usage, to come to the relief of its serving-men, and to succor their
50 distresses. But the manufacturing aristocracy of our age first impoverishes and debases the men who serve it, and then abandons them to be supported by the charity of the public. This is a natural consequence of what has been said before. Between
55 the workmen and the master there are frequent relations, but no real partnership.

Passage 2

There is a widespread conviction in the minds of the American people that the great corporations known as trusts are in certain of their features and
60 tendencies hurtful to the general welfare. This springs from no spirit of envy or uncharitableness, nor lack of pride in the great industrial achievements that have placed this country at the head of the nations struggling for commercial supremacy. It does not rest
65 upon a lack of intelligent appreciation of the necessity of meeting changing and changed conditions of trade with new methods, nor upon ignorance of the fact that combination of capital in the effort to accomplish great things is necessary
70 when the world's progress demands that great things be done. It is based upon sincere conviction that combination and concentration should be, not prohibited, but supervised and within reasonable limits controlled; and in my judgment this conviction
75 is right.

It is no limitation upon property rights or freedom of contract to require that when men receive from Government the privilege of doing business under corporate form, which frees them from
80 individual responsibility, and enables them to call into their enterprises the capital of the public, they shall do so upon absolutely truthful representations as to the value of the property in which the capital is to be invested.
85 Corporations engaged in interstate commerce should be regulated if they are found to exercise a license working to the public injury. It should be as much the aim of those who seek for social-betterment to rid the business world of crimes of cunning as to
90 rid the entire body politic of crimes of violence. Great corporations exist only because they are created and safeguarded by our institutions; and it is therefore our right and our duty to see that they work in harmony with these institutions.
95

1

De Tocqueville's purpose in the first paragraph of Passage 1 is to

A) extol the benefits of mass production of goods.

B) illustrate the daily life of workmen in the mass production of goods.

C) compare workmen in a factory to artisans in a studio.

D) examine the impact of mass production on the laborers who do the work.

2

In lines 28-44, de Tocqueville argues that

A) the workman is without intelligence while the master is a genius.

B) the master expands his mind while the workman's faculties are dulled.

C) the master is cruel while the workman is loyal.

D) the workman gains physical strength while the master lacks physical strength.

3

De Tocqueville employs the image of rings on a chain (lines 39-41) in order to

A) illustrate the dependence of the workman on the master.

B) equate a workman's position with a slave's.

C) demonstrate the interdependence between the workman and the master.

D) depict the cruelty of the master towards the workman.

4

De Tocqueville's purpose in paragraph 3 (lines 45-56) is to argue that

A) the new aristocracy offers a fairer outcome for those who serve than did the old aristocracy.

B) the old aristocracy provided care for those who served while the new aristocracy has relinquished this responsibility.

C) the old aristocracy debased the men who served while the new aristocracy offers means for growth.

D) the old aristocracy was bound by law while the new aristocracy is shaped by ideas.

5

De Tocqueville uses the term "brute" in line 37 in order to

A) portray the workman as cruel.

B) display his disdain for the workman.

C) compare the workman to an animal without the ability to reason.

D) emphasize the decline of the workman's intellect when engaged in mass production.

6

Roosevelt presents his message to Congress in order to

A) call for the elimination of trusts.

B) promote the growth of trusts.

C) discourage interstate commerce.

D) argue for the regulation of corporations.

7

Roosevelt's analysis of the general public's point of view about corporations demonstrates his belief that

A) individuals are envious of corporate power and wealth.

B) average citizens understand the need for reasonable supervision.

C) the general public doesn't have an intellectual appreciation for the intricacies of trade.

D) average citizens are ignorant of the value of capitalism.

8

Roosevelt structures his message by

A) acknowledging public opinion, presenting his own belief, then recommending reform.

B) disagreeing with public opinion, denouncing corporations, then demanding reform.

C) convicting public opinion, praising corporations, then encouraging reform.

D) addressing the failures of corporations, condemning public opinion, then legislating against corporations.

9

De Tocqueville and Roosevelt share a similar point of view in that both are concerned about

A) the negative economic impact of mass production of goods.

B) the loss of individualism with the rise of international corporations.

C) the social dangers inherent in the rise of manufacturing and industry.

D) the diminished role of artisans with the rise of manufacturing.

10

Whereas de Tocqueville's purpose is to address the plight of the workman in a manufacturing society, Roosevelt's purpose is to focus more on

A) the impact of corporations on society as a whole.

B) the economic principles of corporate industry.

C) corporations' refusal to accept limits on their power.

D) the failure of Congress to take action against corporations.

Rhetoric – Great Global Conversation – Passage 5

Passage 1 is adapted from "The Perils of Indifference" by Elie Wiesel. Passage 2 is adapted from "The Strenuous Life" by Theodore Roosevelt.

Passage 1

We are on the threshold of a new century, a new millennium. What will the legacy of this vanishing century be? How will it be remembered in the new millennium? Surely it will be judged, and judged
5 severely, in both moral and metaphysical terms. These failures have cast a dark shadow over humanity: two World Wars, countless civil wars, the senseless chain of assassinations, bloodbaths in Cambodia and Nigeria, India and Pakistan, Ireland
10 and Rwanda, Eritrea and Ethiopia, Sarajevo and Kosovo, the inhumanity in the gulag and the tragedy of Hiroshima. And, on a different level, of course, Auschwitz and Treblinka. So much violence, so much indifference.
15 What is indifference? Etymologically, the word means "no difference." A strange and unnatural state in which the lines blur between light and darkness, dusk and dawn, crime and punishment, cruelty and compassion, good and evil. What are its courses and
20 inescapable consequences? Is it necessary at times to practice it simply to keep one's sanity, live normally, enjoy a fine meal and a glass of wine, as the world around us experiences harrowing upheavals?
Of course, indifference can be tempting—more
25 than that, seductive. It is so much easier to look away from victims. It is so much easier to avoid such rude interruptions to our work, our dreams, our hopes. It is, after all, awkward, troublesome, to be involved in another person's pain and despair. Yet, for the person
30 who is indifferent, his or her neighbors are of no consequence. And, therefore, their lives are meaningless. Their hidden or even visible anguish is of no interest. Indifference reduces the other to an abstraction.
35 In a way, to be indifferent to that suffering is what makes the human being inhuman. Indifference, after all, is more dangerous than anger and hatred. Anger can at times be creative. One writes a great poem, a great symphony, one does something special
40 for the sake of humanity because one is angry at the injustice that one witnesses. But indifference is never creative. Even hatred at times may elicit a response. You fight it. You denounce it. You disarm it. Indifference elicits no response. Indifference is not a
45 response.
Indifference is not a beginning, it is an end. And, therefore, indifference is always the friend of the enemy, for it benefits the aggressor—never his victim, whose pain is magnified when he or she feels
50 forgotten. The political prisoner in his cell, the hungry children, the homeless refugees—not to respond to their plight, not to relieve their solitude by offering them a spark of hope is to exile them from human memory. And in denying their humanity we
55 betray our own.
Indifference, then, is not only a sin, it is a punishment. And this is one of the most important lessons of this outgoing century's wide-ranging experiments in good and evil.

Passage 2

60 I wish to preach, not the doctrine of ignoble ease, but the doctrine of the strenuous life. The life of toil and effort, of labor and strife; to preach that highest form of success which comes, not to the man who desires mere easy peace, but to the man who does not
65 shrink from danger, from hardship or from bitter toil, and who out of these wins the splendid ultimate triumph. We do not admire the man of timid peace. We admire the man who embodies victorious effort; the man who never wrongs his neighbor, who is
70 prompt to help a friend, but who has those virile qualities necessary to win in the stern strife of actual life. It is hard to fail, but it is worse never to have tried to succeed. In this life we get nothing save by effort.
75 A man can be freed from the necessity of work only by the fact that he or his fathers before him have worked to good purpose. If the freedom thus purchased is used aright, and the man still does actual work, though of a different kind, whether as a writer
80 or a general, whether in the field of politics or in the field of exploration and adventure, he shows he deserves his good fortune. But if he treats this period of freedom from the need of actual labor as a period, not of preparation, but of mere enjoyment, even
85 though perhaps not of vicious enjoyment, he shows that he is simply a cumberer of the earth's surface, and he surely unfits himself to hold his own with his fellows if the need to do so should again arise. A mere life of ease is not in the end a very satisfactory
90 life, and, above all, it is a life which ultimately unfits those who follow it for serious work in the world.
As it is with the individual, so it is with the nation. It is a base untruth to say that happy is the nation that has no history. Thrice happy is the nation
95 that has a glorious history. Far better it is to dare mighty things, to win glorious triumphs, even though checkered by failure, than to take rank with those poor spirits who neither enjoy much nor suffer much,

because they live in the gray twilight that knows not
100 victory nor defeat.

If in 1861 the men who loved the Union had
believed that peace was the end of all things, and war
and strife the worst of all things, and had acted up to
their belief, we would have saved hundreds of
105 thousands of lives, we would have saved hundreds of
millions of dollars. Moreover, besides saving all the
blood and treasure we then lavished, we would have
prevented the heartbreak of many women, the
dissolution of many homes, and we would have
110 spared the country those months of gloom and shame
when it seemed as if our armies marched only to
defeat. We could have avoided all this suffering
simply by shrinking from strife. And if we had thus
avoided it, we would have shown that we were
115 weaklings, and that we were unfit to stand among the
great nations of the earth. Thank God for the iron in
the blood of our fathers, the men who upheld the
wisdom of Lincoln, and bore sword or rifle in the
armies of Grant! Let us, the children of the men who
120 proved themselves equal to the mighty days, let us,
the children of the men who carried the great Civil
War to a triumphant conclusion, praise the God of
our fathers that the ignoble counsels of peace were
rejected; that the suffering and loss, the blackness of
125 sorrow and despair, were unflinchingly faced, and the
years of strife endured; for in the end the slave was
freed, the Union restored, and the mighty American
republic placed once more as a helmeted queen
among nations.

1

The purpose of paragraph 1 in Passage 1 is to

A) introduce an essay on the violence of the 20th century.

B) suggest that humanity is on the cusp of change in the new millennium.

C) consider the impact of two world wars on world history.

D) open a discussion on the dangers of indifference to suffering and violence.

2

Wiesel repeatedly uses the word "indifference" throughout Passage 1 to describe

A) the difficulty of caring about the fate of others.

B) the etymological significance of its background.

C) the blurring of lines between good and evil.

D) the tendency of humanity to attach little importance to suffering.

3

The author's overall tone in Passage 1 can best be described as

A) philosophical examination.

B) historical analysis.

C) angry denunciation.

D) sorrowful reflection.

4

Based on his arguments in paragraphs 2 and 3 of Passage 1, Wiesel sees indifference as

A) having no value.

B) occasionally attractive.

C) a necessary evil.

D) morally neutral.

5

The overall purpose of the argument in Passage 1 is to

A) question the value of indifference.

B) define indifference and examine its negative impact on individuals and humanity.

C) compare and contrast the consequences of violence and indifference.

D) call for the punishment of indifference by society.

6

In his essay on the strenuous life, Roosevelt

A) emphasizes the moral importance of taking action.

B) recommends an active life of labor and success.

C) considers the impact of toil and labor on a man's life.

D) reflects on the necessity of balancing work with leisure.

7

Roosevelt structures his argument by

A) questioning an ideal, contemplating its effects, and acknowledging a counterargument.

B) introducing a concept, acknowledging a counterargument, and referencing history as evidence for his assertion.

C) considering the historical background of a philosophy, arguing for change, and recommending a course of action.

D) comparing two competing ideals, accepting the benefits of both, and judging which is to be preferred.

8

The point of view from which Passage 2 is told is best described as

A) a president urging his people to take action for a good cause.

B) a minister urging his people to consider the virtues of taking action.

C) an activist persuading others to follow his cause.

D) an American proud of his country's past as a nation of individuals who fought for the good of humanity.

9

Which of the following is an argument which both writers would likely accept?

A) Violence and suffering in times of war should be avoided whenever possible.

B) Wars are fought to ensure peace and times of ease for members of a nation.

C) Despite the violence and suffering caused by wars, evil must be faced, not ignored.

D) The United States should be proud of its history of fighting for freedoms.

10

The purposes of Wiesel's argument and Roosevelt's argument differ in that

A) Wiesel looks back at history to warn against indifference in the coming century, while Roosevelt looks back at history to express pride in his nation.

B) Wiesel considers the consequences of individual action while Roosevelt considers the consequences of national action.

C) Wiesel is condemning worldwide suffering while Roosevelt focuses on the suffering of slaves.

D) Wiesel is urging nations around the world to act against indifference while Roosevelt is urging Americans to take action.

Notes and Reflections

Rhetoric – Science – Passage 1

This passage is adapted from an article about experiments concerning rubisco, a common enzyme in plants.

At least two and a half billion years ago, ocean algae took an evolutionary step that would change life on Earth. Fueled by the energy from sunlight, the algae converted water and carbon dioxide into a
5 sugar, which would provide the algae with needed energy. There was an unnecessary byproduct that resulted from the reaction: oxygen. The process wasn't perfect, but it was effective enough. Known as photosynthesis, this chemical reaction is the
10 foundational source of energy in most of Earth's food chains. Yet, while it has brought an abundance of life, it has also brought death and decay across the world. Even so, scientists aim to make the process more efficient.
15 As the first species of photosynthetic algae prospered in early Earth's oceans, the sugar-hungry organisms produced great amounts of oxygen. At this time, Earth's atmosphere consisted of much less oxygen and much more methane than it does today.
20 The sudden introduction of oxygen caused atmospheric methane—a powerful greenhouse gas— to oxidize and convert to carbon dioxide, a gas with a weaker greenhouse effect. This brought about a reduction in the retention of solar radiation, leading
25 to a harsh ice age that persisted for hundreds of millions of years. Toxic levels of atmospheric oxygen and frigid temperatures killed much of the life on Earth. Furthermore, oxygen changed the very Earth itself, degrading iron-laden land into rust. And yet,
30 despite all the trouble it brought, photosynthesis is the reason we now have food to eat and air to breathe. Considering the process's vital importance and its very potent global impact, it may be surprising to learn that photosynthesis is, as
35 biochemist Sabeeha Merchant of the University of California, Los Angeles, puts it, "an engineering failure."

Photosynthesis is much more complex than simply mixing water and carbon dioxide. First,
40 carbon dioxide must diffuse into the plant, entering through tiny pores called stomata. Once inside the cell, the gas will enter into the chloroplasts of plant cells, where it will mix with the hydrogen-rich carbon molecules, initiating a set of metabolic reactions
45 known as the Calvin Cycle. A key first step of this cycle is performed by the enzyme ribulose biphosphate carboxylase/oxygenase, referred to as rubisco. Rubisco's job is to attach carbon dioxide to the sugar ribulose biphosphate and then clip this
50 molecular chain into two pieces of phosphoglycerate, which are further phosphorylated into two molecules

of biphosphoglycerate. Most of these molecules are then recycled to create more ribulose biphosphate to keep the whole cycle going, but one of every six
55 molecules of biphosphoglycerate is used to make glucose, a food for the plant.

Rubisco's importance is indicated by its abundance—it's the most common enzyme on the planet. But rubisco is also abundant because it is
60 inefficient. Whereas enzymes typically process thousands of molecules per second, rubisco can process about three. Because plants depend on photosynthesis, which depends on rubisco, they compensate by stocking up large amounts of the
65 dawdling enzyme.

Rubisco's most frustrating characteristic is not its slowness but its lack of discernment. While rubisco is supposed to bind to carbon dioxide, it cannot differentiate between certain molecules.
70 About 20 percent of the time, rubisco accidentally binds to oxygen, which it then attaches to ribulose biphosphate to create phosphoglycolate, rather than the desired phosphoglycerate. To make matters worse, phosphoglycolate is a toxic acid that inhibits
75 the process of photosynthesis and requires the plant to invest even more energy into recycling the useless byproduct. Even the recycling of phosphoglycolate is an issue, as it can produce ammonia and hydrogen peroxide, which are toxic to plant cells. Furthermore,
80 about 25 percent of the carbon in phosphoglycolate is converted back into carbon dioxide, where the whole process started, thereby rendering the metabolic cycle entirely ineffectual! In the end, rubisco's unfortunate mistakes are so prevalent they cause crops such as
85 wheat and rice to lose 20 to 50 percent of their potential growth.

Recently, molecular biologists have been searching for ways to address rubisco's problems. Unfortunately, they cannot improve the enzyme
90 itself. Rubisco is stubbornly set in its ways, and billions of years of evolution have been built into its specific mechanisms, faulty as they are. One solution is to create environments where rubisco has access to much more carbon dioxide than to oxygen. Plants
95 may be genetically altered to isolate rubisco in compartments of the plant that are exposed to much higher concentrations of carbon dioxide, thereby decreasing the odds of rubisco acting on oxygen. Another solution is to adapt plants to process
100 phosphoglycolate more efficiently. Biologists have found a way to create shorter pathways through compartments in plant cells, resulting in plants with up to 40% more overall growth. This doesn't prevent rubisco's mistakes but makes it easier for plants to
105 clean up the mess.

When the ability of photosynthesis was first developed, the effect was deeply felt across Earth.

Similarly, if scientists can improve the process's efficiency, there may be an immense impact on our
110 society. Plants may be hardier, allowing them to grow in a greater variety of regions. More critically, the output of crops could be improved drastically, which would aid in combatting hunger across the world.

1

The main purpose of the passage is to

A) describe an experiment that has led to further questions in plant biology.

B) assert that the majority of people must make an effort to be less wasteful.

C) inform the reader about the history behind a prevalent technology.

D) describe efforts by scientists to resolve a problem.

2

How does the author develop her arguments about the effects of photosynthesis and effectiveness of rubisco?

A) The author explains how rubisco is similar to more commonly known enzymes.

B) The author uses analogies to examine particular topics and ideas.

C) The author uses numbers to support technical descriptions.

D) The author introduces common beliefs and then challenges them.

3

The author uses an exclamation point in line 83 to express a tone of

A) astonishment.

B) exasperation.

C) fury.

D) joy.

4

Which statement would the author most likely agree with?

A) Tampering with biological processes is too dangerous because it may lead to unforeseen problems.

B) A deeper understanding of our natural world may provide opportunities to improve it.

C) Technological progress should not have an effect on Earth's environment.

D) Evolution guarantees that biological processes are as efficient as possible.

5

Which choice best supports the author's claim that making photosynthesis more efficient will help solve the problem of hunger?

A) "As the… of oxygen" (lines 15-17)

B) "Whereas … about three." (lines 60-62)

C) "rubisco's unfortunate… potential growth" (lines 83-86)

D) "When the… across Earth." (lines 106-107)

6

The use of the words "toxic" (line 26) and "frigid" (line 27) have the main effect of

A) emphasizing the extent of the negative impact of photosynthesis.

B) comparing the efficiency of rubisco to that of other enzymes.

C) highlighting the benefits of modern technologies.

D) criticizing the impact of scientific progress.

7

The third paragraph (lines 38-56) mainly serves to

A) emphasize the fact that further research into biological processes is necessary.

B) introduce a theory that the rest of the passage will attempt to explain.

C) introduce a problem that will be expanded upon in later paragraphs.

D) explain a topic that will be the basis for later discussion.

Rhetoric – Science – Passage 2

This passage is adapted from an article about how industries influenced modern computing.

IBM's name is historically tied to the birth of computing. In the 1920s, the company began using its iconic "computer cards," pieces of stock paper about a quarter the size of a standard sheet of paper
5 and marked with small, rectangular holes along 80 columns. In those early days, these simple cards essentially served as hard drives. The cards stored data that could be read by computing machines capable of interpreting the columns of punched holes
10 In a sense, they operated like the toy musical boxes that produce melodies by plucking tuned metal teeth with pins on rotating cylinders; the cylinder is something like a data file that can be read by the musical box, just as IBM's paper cards are read by
15 special tabulators in early computers.

This system may seem primitive compared to modern computing technologies, but punch cards are still being used—and for critically important calculations. In the United States, many voting
20 districts continue to use this century-old design, which has repeatedly led to criticism due to the inaccuracy of some punch-card systems. The U.S. government has been using similar systems since 1890. Ten years prior, the U.S. Census Bureau began
25 its decennial assessment of the population, an endeavor that took eight long years to complete. Seeking a more efficient process of compiling and processing census data, engineer Herman Hollerith invented an electromechanical device that quickly
30 read census forms. He formed the Tabulating Machine Company in 1889, and the next year his company processed the census. With his invention, the task was completed within a single year. In that time, the data for nearly 63 million citizens was
35 processed and millions of dollars were saved. Eventually, Hollerith's company became IBM, whose punch card system would eventually lead to further innovations—giant, vacuum-tube-operated calculators, elegantly integrated circuits,
40 magnetically-encoded data on disks, up to the modern use of electric cell grids in solid state drives. Future technologies may include data storage on DNA, holograms, or quantum particles. As these technologies push steadily onward, it is important to
45 acknowledge the origins of data storage.

Weaving is a tedious process. While we all rely on the protection and warmth provided by fabric, and many of us greatly value the artistic expression of clothing fashion, we rarely consider the work
50 required to create even the simplest cloths. Basic weaving involves a loom with a series of strings, known as the warp, of which some are lifted so

another string, the weft, can run between them. To create patterns, specific strings in the warp must be
55 lifted in certain orders. Prior to the 19th century, luxury fabrics with elaborate patterns like brocades were time-consuming and complex to make. The drawloom, one of the more efficient tools for this process, required two people to operate. One person
60 performed the weaving while an assistant carefully hand-selected the strings to lift. The assistant had to follow complex instructions exactly to create the correct patterns. Mistakes were common, and the process was very slow.

65 Joseph Jacquard came from a family of weavers. Understanding the complexity of managing a loom, he devised a method for partially automating the process. He built a loom with series of hooks that could raise the strings of the warp. The hooks were
70 connected to levers that determined where they moved up or remained lowered. A paper card was pressed against the levers. Where holes were punched, the levers poked through, and these hooks would move up. With this system, a series of paper
75 sheets could perform the job of the weaver's assistant. These sheets were less prone to errors and worked immediately. In effect, complex textile patterns could be programmed into paper sheets, similar to how a data file is stored on a computer
80 drive. To say this invention revolutionized the world would be no exaggeration. Not only did Jacquard's loom bring profound changes to the textile industry, but it also inspired modern computing. In 1837, the brilliant mathematician Charles Babbage envisioned
85 an "analytical engine" modeled on Jacquard's loom design. Babbage's vision was purely conceptual—he never constructed the device—but it served as the inspiration for Hollerith's computational machines. Ada Lovelace, the famous mathematician and writer,
90 noted: "We may say most aptly that the Analytical Engine weaves algebraical patterns just as the Jacquard-loom weaves flowers and leaves."

SUMMIT
EDUCATIONAL
GROUP

1

The main purpose of the passage is to

A) argue that the origins of computer hardware technology are widely misunderstood.

B) discuss research that addresses an ongoing problem.

C) describe a series of advancements to a technology.

D) chronicle the origins of a modern technology.

2

The author describes Jacquard's invention with a tone of

A) respectful admiration.

B) smug ambivalence.

C) annoyed criticism.

D) puzzled curiosity.

3

Over the course of the passage, the main shift in focus is from

A) a description of the early stages of a technology to a prediction of its irrelevance.

B) a series of accomplishments to an account of how they have been improved upon.

C) a development of a modern technology to the origins of that technology.

D) a historical anecdote to how that event is remembered in different ways.

4

The author uses "we" in the third paragraph (lines 46-64) in order to

A) create a negative tone that reflects the tediousness of textile work.

B) assume a common mindset to which the reader can relate.

C) reinforce a sense of mutual respect among a group of people.

D) reflect the comradery among the people in a profession.

5

The reference to toy music boxes in the first paragraph serves to

A) provide a simple, commonly known example to illustrate something more complex.

B) suggest a hypothesis about scientific advancement being rooted in art.

C) emphasize the distinction between practical and theoretical technologies.

D) stress the relationship between musical theory and computer science.

6

The author most likely includes the quotation in the final sentence of the passage in order to

A) suggest a contrast between the use of computers and the traditional use of problem-solving skills.

B) connect Jacquard's invention to the earlier description of early computers.

C) point out a flaw in Jacquard's design that has recently been improved.

D) imply that modern innovations draw their inspiration from nature.

7

The author uses the words "specific," "carefully," and "exactly" to characterize the process of weaving as

A) outdated.

B) obnoxious.

C) meticulous.

D) comfortable.

8

Based on the passage, the author would most likely agree with which statement?

A) Too many advancements go unacknowledged and unappreciated until they are rediscovered many years later.

B) Machines inspired by modern technology should be considered as works of art.

C) Practical solutions to everyday problems can lead to major innovations.

D) All great ideas require several generations to be fully realized.

Rhetoric – Science – Passage 3

This passage is adapted from an article about theoretical research into energy production.

Research into energy efficiency focuses on EROEI (energy returned on energy invested), a ratio that measures how much energy needs to be spent to acquire additional consumable energy. Consider a
5   farm where wheat is grown: if it takes one bushel of wheat to sustain enough people to produce a new bushel of wheat, the energy returned is exactly equal to the energy invested, and the EROEI is 1:1. If the farm becomes more efficient and the same initial
10 bushel of wheat yields two new bushels, then the EROEI would be 2:1. On the other hand, if it takes two bushels of wheat just to produce one new bushel (an EROEI of 1:2), then the people who grow and eat the wheat are on their way to starvation. With a
15 higher EROEI, more usable energy is gained; in turn, this extra energy can be sold for a profit or used in some way to advance the quality of life.

The objective of many industries is not only, you know, to not starve but also to maximize the
20 ratio of energy returned to energy invested. If you express EROEI as a fraction, the ideal scenario would have a denominator of zero and the largest possible value in the numerator. The result of such a ratio would be infinite energy. While there have been
25 fantasies about "zero-point" energy sources— technology that would provide endless energy without additional fuel spent—our experience and understanding of physics rule out such notions as impossible. Physicists have fantasized about the
30 efficiency of devices such as an engine powered by a magical imp that can *somehow* sort atoms. In the real world, we must consider the advantages and disadvantages of more practical sources.

While it is difficult to calculate EROEI precisely
35 (it is easy to overlook some of the costs associated with acquiring energy), analysts do agree on how the EROEI for a particular source varies over time. In the 1930s, oil in the United States had an EROEI of about 100:1. In other words, it cost only one gallon
40 of gasoline to produce one hundred gallons of gasoline; the remaining ninety- nine could be used to power cars and airplanes, grow food, research new technology, and so forth. By the 1970s, domestic oil's EROEI had fallen to roughly 30:1. Today that
45 figure is closer to 10:1. How can EROEI decrease if the substance itself isn't losing its efficacy? As finite energy sources like oil are used up, they become harder to extract, requiring more energy to be spent for the same return. As we use up limited resources
50 like oil, coal, and natural gas—which account for

about eighty percent of global energy consumption today—we are heading toward the undesirable scenario in which it takes two bushels of wheat just to produce one new one.

55 One possible solution to this looming energy crisis is cold fusion. Like the "hot" fusion that powers stars like our Sun, cold fusion is a source of energy derived from the glue that holds atoms together. The idea behind the technology is based on
60 Einstein's famous equation for mass-energy equivalence. You see, the total mass of an atom is actually *less* than the sum of its parts: the "missing" mass has been converted to the energy that binds the parts of the atom together. If we can add enough
65 energy to break the atom apart, we can then put all those tiny pieces back together in a more stable arrangement. If the new arrangement requires less energy to hold the atom together, that unneeded energy is released. Einstein's equation also states
70 that a comparatively small amount of mass will yield a large amount of energy. In one potential form of cold fusion, in which nickel is converted to copper (and free energy), the mass of a mere three nickel coins could power a typical suburban American
75 home for an entire year.

Of course, this process only has potential if the energy needed to create the necessary reaction—and to obtain the materials that supply the reaction—is less than the energy that is released. In fact, not only
80 can the cold fusion process supply more energy than is required to sustain it, cold fusion's EROEI is tens of thousands of times greater than that of a non-renewable energy source such as coal. And in spite of cold fusion being a nuclear process like nuclear
85 fission (which fuels nuclear power plants today), the dangers and drawbacks that are commonly associated with nuclear power—meltdowns and radiation, for example—do not apply to cold fusion. In short, while cold fusion is not an endless source
90 of energy, its remarkably high EROEI makes it an attractive candidate to help tackle not-too-distant energy problems. It is not quite zero-point energy, but it's quite close.

So, why don't we all use cold-fusion reactors to
95 power our civilizations? There is one minor hiccup to the use of cold fusion technology: it may not actually work. There are anecdotes of scientists claiming they have achieved cold fusion, but many of these claims have been unsubstantiated,
100 questionable, or downright lies. The technology is viewed with hope and skepticism. Until we get definitive proof of cold-fusion as a legitimate and practical energy source, we will have to rely on less productive but more dependable alternatives.

SUMMIT
EDUCATIONAL
GROUP

1

The author's main purpose in the passage is to

A) describe two experiments with contradictory results and propose an explanation for this contradiction.

B) explore how innovations have influenced a profession over time.

C) criticize the lack of efficiency in an industry.

D) outline considerations in an area of study.

2

The author includes the phrase "you know" (line 19) most likely to

A) imply that a mathematical relationship requires careful consideration.

B) cast doubt on the accuracy of a commonly accepted idea.

C) acknowledge the obviousness of a statement.

D) emphasize the dullness of an area of research.

3

Information in the passage indicates that the purpose of italicizing the word "somehow" in line 31 is to

A) call attention to a detail that will be explained further in the passage.

B) reinforce the need to understand physics to make further advancements.

C) indicate that an understanding has been kept secret by scientists.

D) imply an idea is not based on realistic mechanics.

4

The italicizing of "less" in line 62 functions mainly to

A) emphasize the obviousness of a fundamental principle.

B) highlight the disappointment of a failed technology.

C) suggest the preceding information is surprising.

D) express frustration at an attempt to improve efficiency.

5

Which statement provides the best description of a technique the author uses throughout the passage to advance her main point?

A) The author uses personification to strengthen the emotional impact of her arguments.

B) The author anticipates the reader's assumptions and then counters them.

C) The author supports each of her central ideas with mathematical facts.

D) The author illustrates her claims with anecdotes from history.

6

Which choice best supports the conclusion that energy production is limited by physical properties?

A) "While there have been fantasies... such notions as impossible." (lines 24-29)

B) "With a higher EROEI... the quality of life." (lines 14-17)

C) "In one potential form... an entire year." (lines 71-75)

D) "In fact, not only can... such as coal." (lines 79-83)

7

The passage is written from the point of view of

A) a scholar recounting how a scientific understanding has influenced human culture throughout history.

B) an expert providing a simple overview of a hypothetical technology within a field of study.

C) an amateur enthusiast describing what makes an area of research so interesting.

D) an investor speculating on the long-term profitability of a growing industry.

8

What is the most likely intended effect of the question in lines 45-46?

A) It indicates there is an apparent logical issue in the earlier information.

B) It suggests a problem stated earlier in the passage cannot be resolved.

C) It stresses the difficulty in convincing others to adopt new ideas.

D) It points out a flaw in an experiment's setup.

9

Which of the following best reinforces the conclusion that cold fusion would be a superior alternative to fossil fuels?

A) It proves Einstein's famous equation.

B) It has a very high EROEI ratio.

C) It can produce more wheat than it consumes.

D) It can convert nickel to copper.

10

The author refers to "nuclear fission" (lines 83-88) in order to

A) emphasize the potential benefits of using cold fusion technology.

B) demonstrate the effects of nuclear power on wheat production.

C) argue for the construction of new nuclear power plants.

D) show that nuclear power plants have a high EROEI.

Rhetoric – Science – Passage 4

Passage 1 is adapted from an article about the wave heating theory explanation for the sun's heating. Passage 2 is adapted from an article summarizing recent research and theories regarding magnetic reconnection.

Passage 1

The fuel that powers our Solar System is almost entirely generated in the dense ball of plasma that sits in the sun's core. It is only at incredibly hot and pressurized conditions that positively charged
5 hydrogen ions can collide, fusing together to create a massive amount of energy. The core is hypothesized to reach temperatures well over 15 million Kelvin to sustain the fusion reactions that power it. The energy produced then journeys through multiple layers of the
10 sun, cooling all along the way. By the time it finally reaches the sun's visible surface, where it is ejected into space, the average temperature has chilled down to a brisk 6000 Kelvin. But remarkably, the corona, stretching thousands of kilometers further outward,
15 mysteriously blazes at temperatures that regularly top one million degrees Kelvin.

The coronal heating question has long challenged scientists, but one of its first proposed solutions has offered great promise. The wave
20 heating theory, which originated in 1949, suggests that magneto-acoustic and Alfvén waves carry energy directly from the sun's core to its corona. These waves are very similar to sound and low frequency radio waves, but instead of traveling through air, they
25 move through the hot plasma of the sun, generating distinctive wave patterns. Once they reach the upper atmosphere, the waves transform into shockwaves and lose their energy to heat, thereby contributing to the corona's high temperature.
30 In 2011, a research team led by Marcel Goosens announced exciting new evidence to finally substantiate the theory. For the first time, Alfvén waves had been detected at amplitudes and energies high enough to warm the corona. The waves detected
35 could do more than just heat the corona; they may be responsible for generating the strong solar winds characteristic of the upper solar atmosphere. More recently in 2017, a research team led by Samuel Grant presented astonishing evidence of Alfvén
40 waves forming a shock front in the sun's atmosphere, resulting in temperature increases of up to 5% in their localized regions. Unfortunately, Alfvén waves have been notoriously difficult to track because of their extremely dynamic spectroscopic signatures, but
45 mounting evidence continues to substantiate this warming mechanism.

Passage 2

Perhaps the most baffling part of our sun is its outermost atmosphere, a region called the corona. The principles of thermodynamics tell us that as
50 energy is produced, it will disperse across an open system, gradually cooling over time. And yet the corona regularly hits temperatures well over a million degrees Kelvin, 200 times the temperature of the surface below!
55 The so-called "coronal heating problem" has puzzled scientists for decades until recently. In July 2013, NASA launched its Interface Region Imaging Spectrograph (IRIS) into Earth's orbit. The satellite's primary mission is to glean further understanding into
60 the mechanisms behind coronal heating. IRIS observes the sun's pattern of ultraviolet light emissions, specifically in the region between the surface of the sun and the corona. In 2014, researchers led by Paolo Testa published their
65 conclusions from the first-year IRIS data. They identified evidence of tiny solar flares, known as nanoflares.

Solar flares have been observed as early as the 19th century, and their origin is linked to the sun's
70 magnetic field and a physical phenomenon known as magnetic reconnection. Magnetic reconnection refers to the crossing of magnetic field lines, causing them to break apart and reconnect with fields moving in the opposite direction. As this happens, magnetic
75 energy is transformed into bursts of thermal energy, resulting in solar flares. The flares certainly could contribute substantial heat to the corona, but the ones that had been observed up until IRIS's launch were not numerous enough to account for the corona's
80 high temperature. While large solar flares are easily observable because they have relatively long durations, shorter bursts of energy that result from smaller flares have been undetectable until now. According to Testa, "Because IRIS can resolve the
85 transition region ten times better than previous instruments, we were able to see hot material rushing up and down magnetic fields in the low corona. This is compatible with models from the University of Oslo, in which magnetic reconnection sets off heat
90 bombs in the corona."

Could these nanoflares account for the heat discrepancy? More recent evidence continues to corroborate the theory, including a 2017 publication in the Nature Astronomy Journal. Using data
95 collected from the FOXSI-2 (the Focusing Optics X-ray Solar Imager), researchers described their detection of extremely high energy "hard X-rays," a type of emission unique to solar flares. The FOXSI's imager was able to localize the solar region where the
100 hard X-rays originated, but it was not able to detect

any large solar flares in those locations, strongly suggesting that nanoflares were hard at work behind the scenes. Steve Christe, one of the authors on the study, summarized the conclusion nicely, "There's
105 basically no other way for these X-rays to be produced, except by plasma at around 10 million degrees Celsius. This points to these small energy releases happening all the time, and if they exist, they should be contributing to coronal heating."

1

The purpose of the first paragraph in Passage 1 is to

A) present evidence for a theory.
B) introduce an apparent contradiction.
C) refute prior theories.
D) suggest a new theory.

2

The author of Passage 1 structures his argument by

A) providing evidence for a new theory, offering details of the theory, and explaining the evidence.
B) proposing a new theory, documenting evidence for the theory, and refuting past theories.
C) introducing a problem, suggesting a possible solution, and providing evidence for the new theory.
D) questioning a past theory, suggesting a new theory, and providing evidence for the new theory.

3

The author of Passage 1 is most likely

A) a scientific journalist critiquing a new theory.
B) a researcher giving evidence for his/her new theory.
C) a scientist suggesting a new theory to peers.
D) a science writer explaining a new theory.

4

In Passage 2, the author argues that

A) nanoflares may be an explanation for the heretofore unexplained heat of the sun's corona.
B) thermodynamics may be an explanation for the heretofore unexplained heat of the sun's corona.
C) nanoflares may be an explanation for the heretofore unexplained heat of the sun's core.
D) heat discrepancy theory may be an explanation for the heretofore unexplained heat of the sun's corona.

5

The main purpose of paragraph 3 in Passage 2 (lines 68-90) is to

A) argue that nanoflares can explain the heat of the sun's corona.
B) explain the relationship between solar flares and magnetic reconnection.
C) reject the wave heating theory proposed in Passage 1.
D) offer new evidence for the role of nanoflares.

6

The author of Passage 2 uses the word "corroborate" (line 93) in order to

A) prove the existence of nanoflares.
B) challenge the existence of nanoflares.
C) indicate evidence for the existence of nanoflares.
D) offer personal support for the existence of nanoflares.

7

Both authors state that

A) the heat of the sun's corona is cooler than that of the sun's surface.

B) the heat of the sun's corona has not yet been fully explained.

C) magneto-acoustic waves may account for the heat of the sun's corona.

D) the discovery of nanoflares has solved a long-standing mystery about the heat of the sun's corona.

8

Whereas the author of Passage 1 argues that magneto-acoustic and Alfven waves contribute to the corona's high temperatures, the author of Passage 2 argues that

A) the Interface Region Imaging Spectograph (IRIS) contributes to the corona's high temperatures.

B) nanoflares may explain the corona's high temperatures.

C) hard X-rays within the sun's core contribute to the corona's high temperatures.

D) magnetic reconnection explains the corona's high temperatures.

Rhetoric – Science – Passage 5

This passage is adapted from an article about the search for life on other planets.

Here on Earth, we have certain ideas about what constitutes life, and most of us would feel confident in identifying what is alive and what is not. It is still common to reference the Aristotelian definition of
5 living beings as those that metabolize (consume nutrients and eliminate waste) and sexually reproduce. However, this does not describe a marine microbe that uses "wires" to draw electrons directly from rocks, nor organisms that "splinter" directly
10 from a parent, nor organisms that can lie dormant for centuries in a crystalline state. None of these examples are hypothetical or extraterrestrial; they are all organisms discovered on Earth in recent decades. Stranger still, abundant life has been found on Earth
15 in the most inhospitable places, such as deep at the bottom of the ocean, or underneath glaciers, or even far underground. The challenges in defining and limiting life's parameters on Earth demonstrate that it is an almost impossible task to know what life on
20 other planets will look like, but scientists have some ideas about the possibilities and limitations of alien life.

If you're looking for life on other planets, the most obvious start is to focus on conditions similar to
25 our own. Currently, the search for extraterrestrial life is still based on substances that are crucial to life on Earth: liquid water and carbon. Water is important because, as a solvent, it allows organisms to transfer important materials for creating energy across its cell
30 membranes. Due to these constraints, when scientists study exoplanets—worlds outside of our solar system—they often try to determine whether they exist within the "habitable zone" of their suns, the distance at which liquid water can potentially exist.
35 Any farther from its star, and the exoplanet's water would be locked up in ice, any closer and the water would evaporate. Earth exists within our sun's habitable zone, but so does Mars, which is why scientists still believe that life might exist there.
40 Samples taken by the Curiosity rover in 2013 established the likelihood that liquid water once existed on Mars, and more recent observations have demonstrated that it still flows on Mars, at least under the surface. Despite our proximity to Mars, the jury is
45 still out on whether it hosts life or not, demonstrating how difficult this search will be when extended to planets much farther away. Furthermore, the search for liquid water is not limited to the "habitable zone." Europa, a moon of Jupiter, exists far outside this
50 region but it is covered in a vast, deep ocean of water that is heated by gravitational forces. Thus, we may find Earth-like conditions in places entirely unlike Earth.

To further complicate matters, some scientists
55 contend that a focus on liquid water or carbon will blind us to the other possibilities of life. Just because those elements are necessary for life on Earth, they say, does not mean that there are not other ways for life to thrive. Instead of water, alien organisms might
60 use other solvents like ammonia or methane, which exist as a liquid at much lower temperatures than water. Likewise, silicon could take the place of carbon as a building block of life, since it can also create bonds with multiple atoms in order to form
65 complex molecules. Silicon is also one of the most common elements in the universe. For these reasons, life could take on many forms and make use of a variety of elements, so it may be shortsighted to only look for life as it exists on Earth. In other words,
70 many of the constraints we have defined for life may not be constraints at all.

As a result of the many factors that can influence the evolution of life (chemical availability, proximity to the sun, strength of gravity, etc.), the possibilities
75 for extraterrestrial life are seemingly endless, although before we imagine a *Star Trek*-ian future, there may be reason to temper our expectations. Physicist Brian Cox believes that there is almost a "chemical inevitability" for life on other planets, but
80 he also cautions that complex or intelligent life may be unlikely. This is because complex life on Earth depends on eukaryotes, cells containing organelles, which first arose when one primitive cell absorbed another. This event was so incredibly unlikely that
85 Cox calls it an "evolutionary bottleneck," so improbable that it may have happened only once in the universe. Because of this, life may be abundant throughout the universe, but in all likelihood it would mostly be single-celled slime.
90 Because the only life scientists have to study is that which exists on Earth, their ability to predict what it might look like elsewhere is severely limited. That said, life on Earth is so incredibly diverse, resilient, and resistant to definition that it may well
95 serve as a model for the range of forms of life on other planets. Suffice it to say that the study of extraterrestrial life is still in its infancy, and a universe of possibilities awaits for humankind to explore.

1

The author's main purpose in the passage is to

A) present different considerations for theories on life's various forms.

B) provide a historical overview of the development of a technology.

C) advocate for a particular definition of what constitutes life.

D) inform the reader about a recent, surprising discovery.

2

Which choice best describes the overall structure of the passage?

A) A detailed depiction of different forms of life across the universe and considerations of how they affect biological research on Earth.

B) An overview of familiar knowledge and application of that knowledge to everyday situations.

C) A careful analysis of the habitability of Mars and comparisons to other planets.

D) An introduction to a field of study and descriptions of its complexities.

3

Which of the following, if true, would disprove Cox's theory, as stated in the passage?

A) Improvements in telescopes have led to the discovery of more planets that may be hospitable to life.

B) Life can be commonly found in a wide variety of environments in many other parts of the universe.

C) Complex, multicellular life will develop commonly in a wide variety of situations.

D) Evidence for basic forms of life has been found on meteorites.

4

Based on the passage, the author would most likely say the search for life on other planets is

A) multi-faceted.

B) impractical.

C) shortsighted.

D) inevitable.

5

Which statement provides the best description of a technique the author uses throughout the passage to advance her points?

A) The author introduces a theory that has been proven entirely incorrect and then proposes an alternative theory.

B) The author proposes several ways to view a situation and then argues one view is superior.

C) The author uses direct quotes from scientists to challenge commonly held opinions.

D) The author presumes the reader's thoughts and offers a counterpoint.

6

In the first paragraph, the author uses quotation marks around "wires" and "splinter" to suggest

A) these are not technical terms but are used to provide a general understanding.

B) these are direct quotes from a well-established scientist.

C) these are theories that are not necessarily true.

D) these words are common slang terms.

7

The third paragraph (lines 54-71) mainly serves to

A) establish the reasons why it is impossible for an endeavor to succeed.

B) identify an error in a calculation that has not been resolved.

C) introduce factors that complicate an undertaking.

D) question the overall importance of a field of study.

Rhetoric – Science – Passage 6

This passage is adapted from an article about speculative investment in sciences.

In modern times, when long-distance connections between people are the cornerstones of personal and commercial relationships, the ability to instantly know what is happening in a far-away
5 location is invaluable. It is for this reason that speculators should consider investing some research time, and perhaps some money, in the application of "quantum entanglement." At the cutting edge of particle physics research, the phenomenon of
10 entanglement is as potentially revolutionary for industries as it is confusing; even particle physicists, who are undeniably intelligent folks, struggle with comprehending it. And yet, some basic understanding is useful for those who want to capitalize on
15 emerging markets. As you surely know, there is vast potential for new commercial opportunities to arise from the implementation of physics, just as the creation of the steam engine, electric motor, or radio brought sudden wealth to investors in their times.
20 With that in mind, let's attempt to understand what quantum entanglement is so we can speculate on how it may be utilized and whether it is worth investment.

In 1927, Werner Heisenberg threw a wrench in the gears of particle physics theory. With his
25 "uncertainty principle," he stated that an object's position and momentum cannot both be accurately measured. In other words, if you know where something is, you cannot know where it is headed, and vice versa. Physicists had been noticing odd
30 results in experiments with particles, and Heisenberg and Neils Bohr worked together to develop a cohesive explanation: the behavior of particles is completely unpredictable. We can know the probability of different outcomes of a particle, but
35 that's all. The physical state of any subatomic object can be likened to something like a coin toss. Heisenberg characterized the state of a particle as a "probability wave function," a mathematical statement that represents all the different potential
40 states of the particle, just as the flipped coin's ultimate fate is undetermined until it finally lands. But as soon as the particle's position or momentum is detected by an instrument, the elements of chance disappear. Most importantly, measuring the particle
45 requires interfering with it, making it impossible to accurately measure any other quantity. At this point, you're likely already confused. Rest assured, our crash course in particle physics is almost finished.

Quite curiously, when two particles
50 spontaneously form from the same source of energy, such as an electron and a positron pair, they will share the same wave function. The two particles are said to be "entangled." Quantum mechanics, which describes the physics of particles, is largely based on
55 balance, and in this spirit, the states of entangled particles are always opposites to one another. If one moves up, the other must move down, and so on.

In 1935, Albert Einstein, Boris Podolsky, and Nathan Rosen proposed a tricky paradox. The basic
60 idea went something like this: an entangled positron-electron pair go off in opposite directions and are detected at two different sites, separated by a great distance. Lab 1 first detects the electron's momentum and records it as "spin up." Since the electron and the
65 positron are entangled, the wave function for the positron must have simultaneously collapsed, and so it will always be measured as "spin down" at the detection site at Lab 2. In fact, the detection at Lab 1 has already affected the detection that will happen at
70 Lab 2. Einstein termed this phenomenon "spooky action at a distance," the instantaneous communication from the electron to the positron.

To demonstrate the phenomenon, imagine we have two friends: Mary and Kate. Mary buys a pair of
75 shoes and she mails one of these shoes to Kate. If Kate opens her package and has a shoe that fits her left foot, then, well, the shoe Mary kept must be for a right foot. Not too "spooky" yet, right? But things get odder with particle physics. Imagine a shoe that is not
80 left or right, but is both at the same time—a shoe that only takes a definite shape when you try it on. When Kate gets her shoe, if she puts it on her left foot, then Mary's shoe will suddenly turn into a right-foot shoe, and vice versa. To make things even weirder,
85 imagine Mary sends a bunch of clothes to Kate, and the two friends agree they'll only try on one piece of clothing and they'll do it at the same time. They keep it a secret, so neither knows what the other will try on. Then, when Kate chooses to put on a left-handed
90 glove, Mary puts on a right-handed glove. Whatever Kate chooses, it determines what Mary will choose. The effect is almost like mind control, or perhaps like prophecy. It might be explained if Kate calls Mary and tells her what she chose to wear, but the effect is
95 instant. In fact, that is one of the most troubling aspects of quantum entanglement: the communication between entangled particles is faster than the speed of light, which should be impossible. To Einstein, who knew the speed of light was an upper limit to which
100 all matter was restricted, this type of data transfer was scientific heresy.

Currently, this heresy is being analyzed for two purposes: understanding and commerce. Physicists are developing new experiments to analyze the
105 relationship between entangled particles. Is there a limit to the distance between entangled particles? Is the communication between them actually instantaneous or just very, very quick? Through what

mechanism do the particles communicate so quickly
110 if they are so far apart? Uncovering the answers to
such questions may reshape our understanding of the
universe. Also, physicists are developing ways to
utilize entangled particles for new, profitable
technologies. Instant communication could vastly
115 improve computing speeds. Also, because entangled
particles have no physical connection, their
communication cannot be intercepted, which is
valuable for messages that must be kept secret. Such
technologies could be incredibly valuable. As history
120 has shown, when we know more, we are capable of
pursuing new opportunities, and this often means
there is money to be made.

1

The main purpose of this passage is to

A) show how today's research on quantum
mechanics relies on the creativity of early
20th century scientists.

B) question multiple aspects of Heisenberg's
"uncertainty principle."

C) prove Einstein's "theory of relativity" in the
context of data from new experiments.

D) explain the phenomenon of "entanglement"
and consider its potential profitability.

2

The first paragraph primarily serves to

A) emphasize the idea that further research into
the field of particle physics is necessary.

B) introduce a controversy that the rest of the
passage will attempt to resolve.

C) illustrate the difficulty of studying a field of
science that is still developing.

D) establish the importance of the passage's
topic.

3

The passage is written from the point of view of

A) a journalist investigating the sources of
investments into cutting-edge physics
research.

B) a knowledgeable scientist explaining how
funding could revolutionize a field of study.

C) a historian exploring different theories for
the origins of particle physics discoveries.

D) an industry expert considering the potential
of funding research on a phenomenon.

4

Over the course of the passage, the main focus
shifts from

A) a brief biography to an analysis of how a
person's accomplishments continues to
impact modern society.

B) a historical overview of a theory to an
anticipation of future application.

C) a list of personal accomplishments to a
description of future goals.

D) an example of a modern innovation to a
discussion of its benefits.

5

The author uses the word "well" in line 77 to
suggest

A) "entanglement" is too complicated to put
into words.

B) the following information should be
obvious.

C) the situation is unfair to one person.

D) the narrator is annoyed by the topic.

6

Which statement provides the best description of
a technique the author uses throughout the
passage to advance her main point?

A) The author introduces conflicting ideas and
attempts to convince the reader which
viewpoint is superior.

B) The author uses personal anecdotes and
historical stories to dramatize information.

C) The author proposes questions and then uses
data from modern research to answer them.

D) The author illustrates her main points with
relatable analogous situations.

Rhetoric – Science – Passage 7

This passage is adapted from an article about recent experiments into bioelectricity.

Some great ideas take a long time to gain support. In 1876, when the telephone was first invented, corporate investors joked it was "hardly more than a toy." For decades, people mocked and
5 threw garbage at the visionaries who first used umbrellas. The first electric car was made in 1828 and then promptly ignored. So perhaps it's little surprise it took more than two hundred years for the idea of biological fuel cells to catch on.
10 In the late 1700s, the Italian scientist Luigi Galvani conducted an experiment which resembled that of the infamous Doctor Frankenstein and which changed our perception of life. There is debate over the initial discovery, but each experimental setup is
15 equally disturbingly morbid. Some believe Galvani and his wife had been studying static electricity using an odd, macabre material: frog skin. By chance, they touched one of the frogs' corpses with a metal scalpel, resulting in a static shock that made the body
20 eerily twitch. Others believe the shock was caused by Galvani's electric generators and capacitors he kept in his laboratory. No matter the cause, the phenomenon gave him insight into the function of muscular movement and created a new scientific
25 interest in the connection between life and electricity. Surely, Galvani figured, if muscles are operated through electricity, animals' bodies must generate electricity to power their muscles.

It was over a century later before scientists began
30 using organisms as generators of electricity. In 1911, British botanist Michael C. Potter showed that electrical voltage is produced during the fermentation of baker's yeast upon glucose. Unfortunately, he could not explain how or why digestion resulted in
35 electric current, and the discovery was largely ignored.

Another century later, scientists have shown renewed interest in revisiting the potential in generation of electricity through biological processes.
40 In essence, the goal is to create batteries powered by microbial life. Every electric battery has three core parts: an anode, a cathode, and electrolyte (a solution of positive and negative ions). Chemical reactions in the battery cause negatively charged electrons to flow
45 from the anode to the cathode through the electrolytic solution. As negative charge builds up at the cathode, it becomes increasingly more difficult to send more electrons to it. The electrolytic solution is meant to solve this problem: it introduces inert positive and
50 negative ions to the system to redistribute charge between the two sides of the battery, allowing the continued flow of electrons from anode to cathode to

continue. Devices that plug into this circuit are powered by the flow of electric current by these
55 traveling electrons. The battery will continue to work as long as the anode continues to have electrons to donate. In the process, batteries create an electric potential, a difference in potential energy per unit charge between the two electrodes, the anode and the
60 cathode.

In a biological fuel cell, a bacterium breaks down organic waste into carbon dioxide, a process that results in excess electrons that can be transferred to the anode, increasing the supply of electrons for the
65 battery. It turns out that a variety of bacteria can harness electric potential at the anode as energy to fuel their own growth. In general, as the electrical potential at the anode increases, so does the bacteria's metabolic rate, making the anode an attractive home
70 for a variety of bacterial species. Once the bacteria move in, the cells will grow, divide, and colonize the anode surface just as if they were in an agar-rich Petri dish, forming what is known as a "biofilm," a community of bacteria clinging to the anode. These
75 bacteria form a conductive matrix of material composed of extracellular proteins, sugars, and bacterial cells. This sticky mixture is what the colony uses to adhere to any surface. As a conductive mesh of material, the matrix also promotes the flow of
80 electrons produced by the bacteria into the anode, providing a steady supply of electrons to fuel the battery.

There is an enormous variety of bacterial species that can be used for microbial fuel cells, each one
85 potentially specializing in extracting electrons from a different waste product. According to Bruce Rittmann, the director of the University of Arizona's Biodesign Institute, "There is a lot of biomass out there that we look at simply as energy stored in the
90 wrong place. We can take this waste, keeping it in its normal liquid form, but allowing the bacteria to convert the energy value to our society's most useful form, electricity. They get food while we get electricity." The potential to tap into living organisms
95 as a source of renewable energy is enormous. With the right bacteria, we can convert industrial or consumer waste into useful energy.

This technology is still developing. In the future, we may have specialized microbial fuel cells
100 generating electricity from a broad array of otherwise useless waste products. Industries would be revolutionized and new industries would be formed for the procurement of waste and implementation of these fuel cells. Eventually, this technology could
105 reshape much of our lives. Until then, it is the subject of speculation, as it has been for centuries.

1

The main purpose of the passage is to

A) make the case that living things should not be exploited for scientific advancement.

B) share the recent progress and future potential of technology relating to a discovery.

C) describe an experiment that apparently contradicts a widely held belief.

D) discuss various explanations for a historical event.

2

The author uses the word "visionaries" (line 5) to emphasize

A) the impact of being able to communicate with people you cannot see.

B) the lack of foresight of unsuccessful scientists.

C) the brilliance of an underappreciated idea.

D) the potential profits available from new technologies.

3

The author's use of the words "macabre" (line 17) and "eerily" (line 20) in the second paragraph functions mainly to

A) establish the narrator's negative opinion of Rittman's experiment.

B) reflect the narrator's sinister attitude toward outdated science.

C) evoke the narrator's sense of disgust for Galvani's research.

D) reveal the narrator's love for a classic work of fiction.

4

Which finding, if accurate, would undermine the author's argument in the second to last paragraph?

A) Some industries have already developed systems for repurposing waste products.

B) A single type of bacteria cannot be used to process every type of waste product.

C) The need for energy sources will only increase over time.

D) Bacteria are too fragile to be used in many applications.

5

What statement provides the best description of a technique the author uses to advance her point in the first paragraph?

A) The author illustrates the irony of great inventions being initially under-appreciated and suggests the same situation applies to the subject of biological fuel cells.

B) The author proposes an idea and criticizes opponents of the idea by showing how these opponents have been wrong in the past.

C) The author describes a well-known modern phenomenon and considers various explanations for its occurrence.

D) The author lists a series of sequential events and hints at what event they will lead to next.

6

Which choice best describes the overall structure of the passage?

A) An overview of how to profit from scientific discoveries, a presentation of a hypothesis about energy production, and a detailed description of a business opportunity.

B) An introduction to a phenomenon and description of its discovery, and information regarding its modern application.

C) An overview of modern research in a scientific area and a list of several potential uses for its discoveries.

D) A description of personal experiences and an analysis of how these events led to a series of discoveries.

7

The last paragraph mainly serves to

A) consider the potential of future advancements for a technology.

B) acknowledge a counterpoint to the author's central argument.

C) introduce a controversy that the author hopes to resolve.

D) summarize a series of historical events.

Rhetoric – Science – Passage 8

This passage is adapted from an article about recent research into nanorobotics.

A close look at the ATP synthase enzyme reveals what appears to be a complex machine. A pair of rotating gears spins about a central axle. One gear is powered by an electric motor, the other is powered
5   by sugar. Together, they work as a generator to create more sugar, the main form of energy for life on Earth. All of this complexity is packed into an unbelievably small size: ten thousand times smaller than the thickness of a sheet of paper. From an
10 engineering standpoint, ATP synthase is a marvel of efficiency. Such natural machines serve as inspiration to chemists who seek to operate in the molecular realm, where sizes are measured in nanometers. By observing the mechanisms of molecular wonders
15 such as ATP synthase, chemists can devise new machines. Once the subject of pure science fiction, "nanobots" are a modern reality.

On the macro scale, we have robots that have revolutionized manufacturing. Assembly lines are
20 largely automated with machines that construct complex products such as automobiles. Such automation has revolutionized industries, allowing work to be done with greater speed and accuracy. Robots have such precision, they are even used in
25 some surgeries, as a machine can operate with more exactness than any human is capable of. Machines operating at the nano scale have other potential benefits: they can perform chemical operations that are entirely beyond the scope of human labor.
30 Whereas large-scale robots improve our traditional work, nanobots allow us to achieve new tasks that would otherwise be impossible.

At the University of Manchester, scientists have created a robot composed of only 150 atoms of
35 hydrogen, oxygen, nitrogen, and carbon. These are so small, a billion of the machines would be less than one-billionth the size of a grain of rice. Powered by chemical reactions, each robot is designed to manipulate individual molecules. By manipulating
40 the solutions the robots are in, scientists can control the robots and make them perform specific tasks. Based on foundational chemical properties, the robots' work is exact. Professor David Leigh, a lead researcher at the University of Manchester, explains
45 these nanomachines: "Our robot is literally a molecular robot constructed of atoms, just like you can build a very simple robot out of Lego bricks. The robot then responds to a series of simple commands that are programmed with chemical inputs by a
50 scientist. It is similar to the way robots are used on a car assembly line. Those robots pick up a panel and position it so that it can be riveted in the correct way

to build the bodywork of a car. So, just like the robot in the factory, our molecular version can be
55 programmed to position and rivet components in different ways to build different products, just on a much smaller scale at a molecular level… Our aim is to design and make the smallest machines possible. This is just the start, but we anticipate that within 10
60 to 20 years molecular robots will begin to be used to build molecules and materials on assembly lines in molecular factories." Such "factories" could be used to mass-produce molecules that are currently difficult to procure, such as particular pharmaceuticals. Some
65 forward-looking chemists imagine we'll eventually be able to install such factories inside our bodies, allowing us to create medication on demand and administer it from within. These tiny machines could determine need for medications before symptoms are
70 outwardly apparent, allowing for treatment of illnesses before our senses could even detect them.

At Pennsylvania State University, researchers have used recent discoveries regarding enzymes to create new types of nanobots. Previously, it was
75 believed that enzymes passively drift about the cytoplasm of cells and much of their reactions are based purely on chance, but recent discoveries proved enzymes propel themselves toward reactants. Ayusman Sen, a principal researcher at Pennsylvania
80 State University, used this property of enzymes to create machines that convert chemical energy into motion. Sen explains: "If we take enzymes and anchor them to a surface so they cannot move, and we give them their reactant, they end up pumping the
85 fluid surrounding them. So they act as miniature fluid pumps that can be used for a variety of applications." He and his fellow researchers designed nanobots that neutralize organophosphates, a class of dangerous nerve agents. Exposure to organophosphates, which
90 may occur during warfare or due to terrorist acts, can lead to neurological damage and, in severe cases, death. Sen and his team secured molecules of organophosphorus acid anhydrolase, which destroys organophosphates, to a gel that contained an antidote
95 to the harmful nerve agent. Their system is remarkably effective, fueled by the organophosphate reactant that it combats. According to Sen, "The enzyme actively pumps in the organosphosphate compound and destroys it, and at the same time
100 pumps out an antidote," Sen says. Such machines may eventually be standard protective equipment for soldiers and emergency medical technicians.

Future development of nanorobotics depends on the refinement of a few efficient, widely applicable
105 mechanisms. Similar to the way large robots are built on a foundation of common parts, such as hydraulic levers and rotating motors, nanomachines need such standardized components.

1

The author's main purpose in the passage is to

A) summarize research into the function and structure of enzymes.

B) provide an overview of recent discoveries made in biology.

C) describe advancements made in a specific field of science.

D) predict future applications of a new technology.

2

Which choice best describes the overall structure of the passage?

A) A description of a natural substance, an analogous man-made creation, and new technology that blends the two.

B) An analysis of a natural process and an overview of how scientists have failed to replicate it.

C) A presentation of a problem, an explanation of its origin, and a list of potential solutions.

D) A comparison between two technologies and an argument about which is superior.

3

Throughout the passage, the author provides insight into nanobots research mainly by

A) highlighting features of nanobots and explaining the historical influences behind each of their developments.

B) presenting problems and explaining how specific experiments have solved them.

C) describing personal experiences and using them to explain fundamental concepts.

D) using relatable references to explain and portray ideas.

4

In the third paragraph (lines 33-71), the author uses the words "individual," "specific," and "exact" to emphasize

A) how challenging it is to control biological processes.

B) the tedious nature of biology research.

C) how easy it is to ruin an experiment.

D) the precision of nanomachines.

5

Which of the following would Leigh most likely agree with?

A) Enzymes cannot be used in nanorobots because their actions are based on chance.

B) Machines can never replace the artistry inherent in human labor.

C) There is great potential for more advancement with robotics.

D) Nanobots are the fastest way to assemble rare molecules.

6

Which of the following best supports the conclusion that nanobots will allow us to accomplish tasks that are unachievable by traditional human labor?

A) "Assembly... automobiles." (lines 19-21)

B) "By manipulating... tasks." (lines 39-41)

C) "These tiny... detect them." (lines 68-71)

D) "Previously, it ... reactants" (lines 74-78)

7

The author includes the analogy of robotic automobile manufacturing primarily

A) to make it easier to understand nano manufacturing processes that cannot be seen.

B) to describe how nanobots will eventually replace automobile assembly lines.

C) to argue that robots are robbing people of traditional work opportunities.

D) to explore the use of nanobots in industrial assembly lines.

Rhetoric – Science – Passage 9

Passage 1 is adapted from an article about the "quantum tunneling" explanation for olfaction, the sense of smell. Passage 2 is adapted from an article summarizing various theories regarding olfaction.

Passage 1

At first glance, quantum tunneling seems outlandish, even impossible, but we must remember that nothing is intuitive at the subatomic level. In the tiny world of the electron, matter behaves very
5 differently than how we think of it classically. Electrons exhibit wave-like properties, and their location is mapped by a probability equation known as the Schrödinger wave equation. This means that at *very* small distances an electron has a chance of
10 moving anywhere in its local vicinity, and the odds of it being found at a location steadily drop the further away that location is. Even if the electron encounters a physical barrier that it does not have the energy to overcome, at these very small distances, there is a
15 chance the electron will tunnel through to the other side. When an electron tunnels however, it must have the same energy going into the process that it did leaving. Any energy gained must be donated back to other particles in the environment.
20 Luca Turin, the most prominent proponent of the vibrational theory of olfaction, claims that quantum tunneling is at work in one of the most basic ways we interact with the environment: our sense of smell. Just like the electron traveling through an
25 insurmountable barrier, olfactory receptors work the same way. In addition to an odorant molecule binding site, every smell receptor has an electron donor and acceptor site, which are at different energy levels separated by a short distance across the receptor. If
30 an odorant attaches to the binding site and can vibrate at a resonant frequency corresponding to the energy difference between the sites, then an electron will be able to tunnel from the higher energy donor site to the lower energy acceptor site. As the electron
35 tunnels, it donates the energy it gains to the odorant molecule, causing the odorant to vibrate. The electron is not being generous here; in order to tunnel, the electron must experience no net energy change. Once the electron arrives at the second site, the receptor
40 becomes activated, triggering nerve signals to the brain. Each receptor is tuned to a specific resonant frequency in this way.

While the shape theory of olfaction is more popular, there is growing evidence that the
45 vibrational hypothesis offers explanations where the shape theory fails. Firstly, there are a wide variety of molecules that are drastically different in shape but have the same smell. Turin observed this as well; the only other compound that has the same "rotten egg"
50 smell as a sulfur hydride is boron hydride. The molecules have nothing in common except for the vibrational frequency of their bonds; their resonant frequencies are both just around 2600 cm^{-1}. Even more fascinating is that common fruit flies, which
55 have olfactory receptors with drastically different shapes than ours, find the scents identical too. In 2017, Turin trained flies to avoid the molecule mercaptoethanol, which contains sulfur-hydrogen bonds. Surprisingly, the same flies responded to
60 decaborane, a much larger compound containing boron hydride, in the same avoidant way, suggesting that decaborane smelled the same to them.

The team also tested a version of mercaptoethanol where the hydrogens on the sulfur
65 were replaced with deuterium, an isotope of hydrogen. Deuterium has the same shape as standard hydrogen (known as protium), but the sulfur-deuterium bond's resonant frequency is different than the sulfur-protium bond's frequency. When trained to
70 avoid regular mercaptoethanol, the flies did not avoid the deuterium version of the molecule in the same way. Many other researchers have found similar results: isotopomers (otherwise identical molecules with equal isotopic ratios where the deuteriums have
75 just been moved into different locations) have consistently been shown to smell differently across a wide range of species, such as mice and bees. The different vibrations in the bonds must be triggering odor discernment in these animals.

Passage 2

80 In 1991, Linda Buck and Richard Axel, who would both go on to win the 2004 Nobel Prize in Medicine and Physiology, were the first to identify that olfactory receptors in mice were made up of G-protein coupled receptors (GPCRs). Olfactory
85 receptors constitute the largest subfamily of GPCRs; in humans, around 350 have been identified. GPCRs are large proteins found anchored in the cell membrane, weaving in and out of the cell. They are involved in detecting molecules outside the cell, and
90 once activated, they change conformation, initiating a cascade of intracellular reactions, known as signal transduction pathways, that culminate in the cell's response to the initial stimulus.

In the case of olfactory GPCRs, the molecule
95 detected is the odorant, which attaches to the receptor and activates it. Various molecules bind to GPCRs, such as hormones, neurotransmitters, odorants, and even light-sensitive molecules. These binding

molecules are known as ligands. Currently, all well-
100 understood GPCRs have a high specificity for their
ligands, in particular for their shape and for the weak
surface interactions between the ligand and the
receptor. Since GPCRs already act this way, it makes
sense that olfactory receptors largely function the
105 same way. They are activated by odorants that,
generally speaking, "fit" into the shape of the
receptor, much like a lock and key.

The only widely accepted alternative to this
theory of olfaction is the exotic vibrational theory.
110 While research into vibrational theory has largely
focused on isotopomers (much of which was
debunked by Eric Block et al. in 2015), the theory
still fails to explain why some generic stereoisomers
of compounds smell so differently. Stereoisomers are
115 molecules with the same atomic makeup and same
bonds, but they differ in their three-dimensional
spatial orientations. Since they have the same bonds,
they have the same resonance frequencies, and yet
the two stereoisomers of carvone, for example, have
120 drastically different scents: one smells like caraway
and the other is downright minty. Because the
molecules only differ in shape and would fit
differently into three-dimensional receptors, their
shapes must be inherent to how they can be
125 distinguished.

1

In paragraph 1 of Passage 1, the author uses the
word "intuitive" (line 3) to suggest

A) the importance of intuition in scientific
    research.
B) the negative consequences of intuition in
    scientific research.
C) that concepts at the subatomic level are not
    easily perceived.
D) that concepts at the subatomic level can be
    easily perceived.

2

The purpose of paragraph 2 in Passage 1 (lines
20-42) is to explain

A) the similarities between the way electrons
    and olfactory receptors act.
B) the differences between the way electrons
    and olfactory receptors act.
C) the similarities between the vibrational
    theory of olfaction and the shape theory of
    olfaction.
D) the differences between the vibrational
    theory of olfaction and the shape theory of
    olfaction.

3

The primary argument in Passage 1 is that

A) the shape theory of olfaction lacks sufficient
    evidence.
B) the vibrational theory of olfaction solves
    problems encountered in the shape theory of
    olfaction.
C) both shape theory and vibrational theory
    have substantial evidence.
D) neither shape theory nor vibrational theory
    has sufficient evidence.

4

Which of the following best summarizes the
overall structure of Passage 1?

A) Begins with information, broadens to
    introduce a theory, provides evidence for
    that theory, then concludes with a positive
    assessment of the theory
B) Introduces a theory, provides a
    counterargument to the theory, presents
    evidence for both the theory and its
    counterargument, then concludes that both
    theories are valid
C) Critiques a prior theory, introduces a new
    theory, provides evidence for the new
    theory, and concludes with a positive
    assessment of the theory
D) Provides background on a concept, develops
    a theory based on the concept,
    acknowledges a counter-argument to the
    theory, and concludes that more evidence is
    needed

5

The author of Passage 2 is most likely

A) a scientist defending his/her research.
B) a researcher seeking to disprove a theory.
C) a writer for a popular culture magazine.
D) an expert in the field, explaining two theories.

6

The author of Passage 2's use of the word "exotic" in line 109 suggests that vibrational theory is

A) not scientifically valid.
B) a foreign concept.
C) an exciting and promising new idea.
D) absurd.

7

The authors of both passages agree that

A) the shape theory of olfaction is outdated.
B) the vibrational theory of olfaction needs further evidence.
C) both shape theory and vibrational theory are prominent theories in the study of olfaction.
D) both shape theory and vibrational theory have been recently discredited.

8

In their arguments, both authors

A) recommend further research for his/her preferred theory.
B) cite specific examples of flaws in the opposing theory and offer examples of solutions to these flaws in his/her preferred theory.
C) suggest that a new theory is needed to resolve flaws in both the vibrational theory and the shape theory.
D) acknowledge the flaws in his/her preferred theory and suggest solutions to these flaws.

Rhetoric – Science – Passage 10

This passage is adapted from an article summarizing techniques used in modern astrophysics and astrometry (the measurement of celestial bodies).

Every method used in the search for exoplanets has both advantages and disadvantages, and by combining them we obtain the best results. All methods currently used are indirect: radial velocity
5 (RV) surveys are based on Doppler shift measurements; the transit photometry method detects variations in brightness as a planet passes in front of its star; the method of astrometry measures the wobble of a star caused by any planet orbiting that
10 star; and the microlensing technique relies on Einstein's general theory of relativity. Direct detection and imaging of exoplanets is exceedingly difficult to perform, because the brightness of light from a star and of reflected light from a planet differ
15 greatly. Exoplanets are obscured in the stellar light of their own stars.

As an exoplanet orbits a distant star, it is periodically moving towards and away from an observer on Earth. Using the Doppler effect (the
20 wavelength of light from objects is shifted when the object moves toward or away from the observer) it is possible to detect the presence of a planet orbiting a distant star, not by direct observation of the Doppler effect in the very faint reflected light from a planet,
25 but by observing the wobble of its star. The gravitational attraction of the planet pulls the star in a circular path. In this way, by recording the period and amplitude of the oscillation, the mass and orbital radius of the exoplanet can be determined. Only
30 planets having orbital planes close to our line of sight are detectable, but the method of Doppler spectrometry is very sensitive.

Unlike the RV method, transit photometry records variations in the brightness of the star. As an
35 exoplanet crosses in front of our view of a star, a dip in the observed brightness can be detected. However, observations of exoplanet transits are complicated by the low signal, which can be difficult to detect amid the noise of background stellar variability, variations
40 of brightness across the disk, starspot modulation, and limb darkening. In addition, ground-based observations are affected by turbulence in the Earth's atmosphere, which produces scintillation of the stars. This apparent glinting of stars can be mistaken for the
45 obstruction of a passing exoplanet. Instruments installed on board CoRoT and Kepler alleviate many of these problems.

Astrometry, involving ground-based or, eventually, space-based interferometers, which can
50 detect the wobble of stars produced by orbiting planets, has the potential to provide the most accurate measurements of planetary masses. The installation of space-based interferometers would allow us to detect Earth-like planets near a star. For more distant
55 planets, the method of microlensing can be employed, whereby variations in brightness are observed when light from a star bends as it passes near a massive object located between the distant source and the observer. If the star has a planet,
60 characteristic patterns appear on the light curve from which the star-planet mass ratio can be determined. The microlensing technique provides an opportunity to find stars with multiple planetary systems, and is most advantageous for finding very distant planets
65 too faint to be discovered by other techniques; it provides, therefore, a powerful tool to assess the amount and distribution of planetary systems in the Galaxy.

1

The purpose of the first paragraph is to

A) defend the transit photometry method as the best means of searching for exoplanets.

B) explain the use of radial velocity (RV) surveys in the search for exoplanets.

C) define the meaning of exoplanets.

D) present an overview of methods used in the search for exoplanets.

2

The author uses the term "indirect" in line 4 to

A) summarize the current state of techniques with a shared characteristic.

B) suggest that current techniques are ineffective.

C) note that current techniques can be unreliable.

D) criticize the scientific community for avoiding direct detection methods.

3

Which of the following best describes the overall structure of the passage?

A) Introduces a concept, critiques current techniques, and proposes a new technique

B) Presents an overview of techniques, lists the pros and cons of two techniques, and concludes with the potential advantages of two techniques

C) Defines a scientific dilemma, considers the pros and cons of solutions to the dilemma, and recommends the best solution

D) Examines the history of a scientific dilemma, reviews past solutions, and suggests a new solution

4

The author's main argument in the fourth paragraph (lines 48-68) is that

A) microlensing offers more potential than astrometry in the search for exoplanets.

B) neither microlensing nor astrometry has much potential in the search for exoplanets.

C) astrometry offers more potential than microlensing in the search for exoplanets.

D) both microlensing and astrometry have strong potential in the search for exoplanets.

5

The central purpose of the passage is to

A) criticize current methods used in the search for exoplanets.

B) persuade scientists to focus on a specific method in the search for exoplanets.

C) examine the pros and cons of various methods used in the search for exoplanets.

D) consider the importance of the search for exoplanets.

6

The author uses the term "obscured" in line 15 in order to express

A) the vagueness of results in current methods used to search for exoplanets.

B) the darkness of the matter surrounding exoplanets.

C) the reality that exoplanets are usually hidden from sight.

D) the difficulties experienced in trying to understand the properties of exoplanets.

7

The author of the passage writes from the standpoint of

A) optimism for the future of the search for exoplanets.

B) discouragement over the challenges faced in the search for exoplanets.

C) doubt that current methods will prove fruitful in the search for exoplanets.

D) fascination with the recent developments in the search for exoplanets.

8

The author's voice is one of

A) excited exploration.

B) critical analysis.

C) pessimistic prediction.

D) academic curiosity.

Notes and Reflections

Rhetoric – Social Studies – Passage 1

This passage is adapted from an article about "Molyneux's Problem."

In 1689, scientist and politician William Molyneux wrote a letter to philosopher John Locke in which he posed his now infamous problem. Molyneux questioned whether a man who was born
5   blind and who had learned to discern a globe and a cube by touch only would be able to distinguish between the two objects by sight only, if he was suddenly able to see. Locke had, prior to receiving Molyneux's question, published an extract theorizing
10 that certain concepts can be acquired with just one sense whereas others require more than one sense to be understood. For example, a blind man can never comprehend ideas pertaining to color, as it takes only vision to understand the concept of color. Ideas such
15 as space and motion, however, require a combination of senses. Perhaps inspired by Locke's theories, Molyneux sent this problem to Locke, who never replied.

Many years later, in 1693, when the men began a
20 correspondence, Molyneux altered his ingenious problem and presented it to Locke once more. Enthusiastically, Locke published Molyneux's problem, with a sphere substituted for the globe, in his new publication, "An Essay Concerning Human
25 Understanding," thereby making the question accessible to a wider audience. Notable philosophers such as George Berkley, Gottfried Leibniz, Voltaire, Diderot, Adam Smith, and William James considered the puzzling question as well. Philosophers and
30 scientists wrestled with this conundrum for decades, to no avail. The relationship of space to sight and touch generated a polarizing debate: are sight and touch innately connected to create the idea of space, or, as Locke believed, is the relationship between the
35 two senses learned through experience. According to Locke, the blind man "would not be able with certainty to say which was the sphere, which the cube, whilst he only saw them though he could unerringly name them by his touch." The solution to
40 Molyneux's problem, sought via theories, experiments, and educational discourse, evaded even the brightest minds for at least three centuries.

The Nature Neuroscience Journal, however, recently proposed a viable answer to Molyneux's
45 problem, and it supports Locke's stance! Modern researchers established that a blind man's brain cannot immediately understand visual information but he can, over time, learn how to process it. They reached this conclusion by studying five subjects,
50 four boys and one girl ranging in age from eight to seventeen, who were born blind in rural northern India. Almost all of them had cataracts and one had a corneal disorder. From birth, all the subjects could perceive light, and two of them could even
55 distinguish the direction of light. Most importantly, however, none of them could see objects. After the subjects received operations for their medical conditions, courtesy of a local group, they each demonstrated vision measuring at 20/160 or better.
60 At this visual acuity level, the subjects would be able to distinguish objects.

Within two days of their operations, the subjects were tested using twenty small objects, similar to Lego blocks, placed on a table where they could be
65 seen but not touched. The subjects were then instructed to match those blocks with identical blocks placed under the table where they could not be seen, but could be felt. The matching rate of the subjects was barely better than the rate of random chance.
70 However, by touch or sight alone, subjects could match identical objects at a rate of about 100%. Over the course of one week with the same exercise, one subject became proficient in cross-sense matching and within three months, all subjects could match a
75 seen object by touch at an average rate of above 80%.

The experiment upheld Locke's answer to Molyneux's problem only to an extent, as the subjects' brains learned how to process visual information with time and exposure. Looking beyond
80 the immediate benefit of solving Molyneux's problem, senior author and MIT professor of vision and computational neuroscience Pawah Sinha notes that the results from the study "strengthen the case that cross-modal learning is possible despite years of
85 deprivation" as the brain is able to adapt from early childhood up to even adulthood. Unexpectedly, Molyneux's problem significantly contributed to the argument for making visual treatment available to all, regardless of age.

1

The author considers Molyneux's Problem to be

A) an entertaining, if silly, exercise for philosophers and scientists.

B) crucially important to the understanding of visual problems.

C) a superficial question that was pondered considerably before its time.

D) a challenging topic for abstract debate that has recently proven useful.

2

In line 30, the author uses the word "conundrum" to suggest

A) an argument.

B) a confusing puzzle.

C) a group of scholars.

D) a crucial question.

3

The purpose of the last paragraph is

A) to complete the essay by restating the information in the first paragraph.

B) to show that modern science can answer questions philosophers struggled with for centuries.

C) to illustrate that solving abstract questions can have practical value.

D) to demonstrate that debating ideas without evidence is a waste of time.

4

The author chose the word "viable" (line 44) to characterize the answer proposed by The Nature Neuroscience Journal because

A) it describes the liveliness of the debate.

B) it suggests that the study will grow.

C) it emphasizes the practical application of the problem.

D) it contrasts with the assertion that the debate cannot be resolved.

5

The third paragraph (lines 43-61) serves to

A) shift from past, abstract argument to a modern, practical solution.

B) vindicate John Locke.

C) provide an example of a successful experiment.

D) illustrate how we gather information from our senses.

6

The author wrote this in the style of

A) a personal memoir.

B) a legal brief.

C) an informational essay.

D) a persuasive essay.

7

The author would most likely agree that

A) Molyneux wasted everybody's time with his problem.

B) Molyneux's problem did not lead to the successful experiment.

C) pondering abstract questions is a valuable endeavor.

D) blind people cannot distinguish object shapes.

8

Which choice provides the best evidence for the answer to the previous question?

A) Lines 8-12 ("Locke had… to be understood")

B) Lines 29-31 ("Philosophers and scientists… to no avail")

C) Lines 62-65 ("Within two days… but not touched")

D) Lines 86-89 ("Unexpectedly… regardless of age")

Rhetoric – Social Studies – Passage 2

This passage is adapted from an article about traditional ingredients used in the perfume industry.

Ambergris has its origins in mystery. Its impression on the senses is indescribable and the story of its creation is not fully known. The enigmatic substance is born in the dark depths of the oceans,
5 formed in the vast guts of sperm whales. It is rare, it is incredibly expensive, and it is very, very smelly.

Perhaps so little is understood of ambergris because we know so little of its creators: the sperm whales. Most of our familiarity with these creatures
10 comes from the briefest glimpses. Atop the waves, we spy gray flukes or the crest of a bulbous head spurting mist before drawing a long breath and slipping back below. They rise into our world for an instant and then descend back into another beneath
15 the waves. The ocean depths are not our realm and so we can only guess at what transpires with the sperm whales as they dive nearly 4,000 feet below the surface. Certainly they are often preoccupied with eating. In order to maintain their massive size—bulls
20 may weigh as much as 100,000 pounds—they must consume thousands of pounds of food per day. While they are known to eat crabs, octopuses, rays, sharks, and a variety of fish, sperm whales have a diet that primarily consists of squid. This includes such
25 monstrous prey as the giant and colossal squids. In a survey of sperm whale stomach contents, cetologists found only a few fish among the remains of tens of thousands of squid. Mostly comprised of soft tissues, squid are digested quickly, except for a single organ:
30 the beak. A pair of scissor-like jaws, the squid's beak is so hard it cannot be digested by the whale. With this fact lies the incredible origin to ambergris.

Within the guts of a sperm whale, a single day's worth of feeding may result in thousands of
35 undigested squid beaks. The sperm whale's guts are similar to those of cows in that they have multiple stomachs. The food passes between the whale's four stomachs as it is digested, and the numerous squid beaks merge into a dense, chitinous mass. The
40 process is unsustainable, as the stomachs are eventually packed full of beaks. As part of the sperm whale's normal feeding cycle, they must vomit every few days to expel the amassed indigestible material. It is commonly believed this regurgitation is the
45 source of ambergris, but the rarity of ambergris is proof that a less common process is responsible for its creation. No, ambergris is not expelled from a whale's mouth. Instead, the substance is created when squid beaks travel through all of a whale's
50 stomachs and into the intestines. Here is where our knowledge of the development of ambergris is limited to speculation. It seems that some squid beaks

become lodged or snagged, causing irritation in the whale intestines, which produce a lubricant to ease
55 the beak's passing. This may be likened to the way oysters will coat grit and other irritants in pearl. Like pearls, this occurrence seems to be rare. Only about 1 in 100 sperm whales may be able to secrete the waxy lubricant. Once a beak is finally passed, it seems the
60 beak is coated in a thick layer of the substance that becomes ambergris.

On seashores, nuggets of ambergris appear as pale, inconspicuous stones. By this point, they may have spent years at sea, floating atop the waves.
65 During this time, they have been hardened by sunlight and beaten by waves. Originating as a tar-like mass, they shrink, get lighter and smoother, and develop an outer rind. Washed ashore, they resemble chunks of pumice or dried clay. Their surface may
70 have a sheen or a chalky texture. Inside, there are specks of squid beaks like dark seeds. Although its appearance might be mistaken for any unremarkable rock, one trait distinguishes ambergris as extraordinary: the smell.
75 "Unique" is the most common description, a label of last resorts when the author is at a loss for words. Attempts at capturing the experience are often poetic. One researcher cited "tobacco, the wood in old churches, sandalwood, the smell of the tide, fresh
80 earth, and fresh seaweed in the sun." An article appearing in the New York Times noted "the blending of new–mown hay, the damp woodsy fragrance of a fern–copse, and the faintest possible perfume of the violet." An experienced ambergris
85 hunter recounted "My brain swims. All at once, I smell: old cow dung; the lumps of wet, rotting wood that I have kicked along the beach; tobacco, drying seaweed… And, beneath it all, something indescribably elemental. It is a mixture of the low
90 and the high. The unavoidable and the unobtainable." Ambergris's odor is complex, elusive, and captivating.

Famously, ambergris is renowned as an essential ingredient in many perfumes. Affordably small
95 chunks of it are also melted into drinks or grated over food. In different cultures, the rare substance is used as medicine, fragrance, seasoning, or a symbol of wealth. Certainly some of its famed reputation comes from its mystery, both in its shadowy origins and
100 puzzling aroma. There have been attempts to synthesize the fragrance, but similar to the situation in the market for synthetic pearls or artificial diamonds, people prefer the real thing.

1

The main purpose of the passage is to

A) compare numerous theories and assess their accuracy.

B) explore the history of research into a phenomenon.

C) inform the reader about an unusual substance.

D) encourage the reader to search for ambergris.

2

The repetition of "seems" in the third paragraph (lines 33-61) has the main effect of

A) suggesting that the information is incorrect and another, unknown process must lead to the formation of ambergris.

B) reinforcing the author's claim that the origin of ambergris is not entirely known.

C) creating analogies that allow the reader to personally relate to unusual situations.

D) establishing comparisons between multiple theories.

3

Over the course of the passage, the main shift in focus is from

A) a potential explanation for the origins of ambergris to examples of the substance's qualities and uses.

B) a description of a mystery to an account of how its solution would impact various professions.

C) a personal account of an experience to a series of similar experiences by other people.

D) a summary of historical research to an analysis of modern discoveries.

4

In the fifth paragraph (lines 75-92), the author uses multiple quotations in order to

A) build credibility for the author's personal experiences by showing that others have had the same experience.

B) emphasize the author's point about the distinctiveness of ambergris's fragrance.

C) present differing explanations for an unresolved problem.

D) explain how ambergris is created.

5

Which of the following would the author most likely agree with?

A) Synthetic products are inferior to ones created from natural sources.

B) The lives of sperm whales will always remain a mystery.

C) Considering its simple origins, ambergris is too expensive.

D) People are attracted to things that are rare and mysterious.

6

If true, which finding would most undermine the theory described in the third paragraph (lines 33-61)?

A) Along the centers of squids are hard, feather-shaped structures called "pens," which are also hard to digest.

B) Whale digestive systems do not create a lubricant that could become ambergris.

C) The creation of manmade pearls often utilizes natural processes.

D) Some whales have more than four stomachs.

7

The first paragraph primarily serves to

A) introduce a controversy that will be considered from various angles.

B) identify a topic the passage will further explain.

C) assert the value of studying ocean life.

D) present a theory in an ongoing debate.

SUMMIT
EDUCATIONAL
GROUP

Rhetoric – Social Studies – Passage 3

This passage is adapted from an article about the history of the Eiffel Tower.

Imagine a small, mahogany wood box with complicated brass dials and rollers aside a thin slot. With a few twists of the dials, a brand-new hundred-dollar bill emerges from the slot. This contraption,
5 the "Rumanian money box," uses a piece of radium to create perfect copies of these bills, though the machine requires six hours of chemical processing for each bill. After a short wait and a crank of the dials, another hundred-dollar bill will be cloned and
10 will roll out from the box. The process will continue indefinitely, promising $400 daily. Surely such a box would be worth a great deal. How much would you pay for the device? In the 1920s, Victor Lustig sold these Rumanian money boxes for $25,000—a smart
15 investment if you collect the bills for more than 2 months to generate profits. There was one issue, however. The boxes only contained two bills. Lustig would print the first bill as a demonstration the device worked. 6 hours later, the new owner of the
20 box would get another bill, proving the value of their purchase. However, no more bills would roll out, no matter how much the dials were twisted. By then, Lustig would be gone with his $25,000. Once, when arrested for fraud, Lustig offered one of these boxes
25 to the arresting sheriff in exchange for freedom and an additional $10,000. It was enough to tempt the sheriff, who released Lustig and paid him the extra money. Later, the sheriff was arrested for using counterfeit bills. You see, even the hundred-dollar
30 bills in the box were fakes. This elaborate trick proves the age-old saying: when something seems too good to be true, it is.

According to Victor Lustig, he was a lion tamer, a death-defying bicycle rider, a royal count, a
35 Broadway musical producer, a stock market investor, and a realtor. In total, he had 47 false identities and carried dozen of fake passports, as well as numerous disguises to masquerade as a rabbi, priest, porter, or bellhop. Surely, one of these had to be the actual
40 Lustig, right? In reality, he was nothing more than a con man. In fact, he may be the greatest scam artist to have ever lived. He fooled bankers, detectives, gamblers, businessmen, and even the notorious gangster Al Capone.
45 Lustig's most famous con began in 1925, when an article in a Paris newspaper described the poor condition of the Eiffel Tower. Decades after it had been built, the architectural landmark was decaying and would require extensive, expensive repair. The
50 article noted it might be cheaper to scrap the entire tower than to attempt patching its rust damage. Readers may have feared the loss of the iconic Eiffel Tower or lamented the necessary costs to preserve it. Lustig, however, saw money to be made.
55 The scheme began with a new identity. Lustig created counterfeit government stationary claiming he was the Deputy Director General of the Ministère de Postes et Télégraphes. With this title, he contacted five well-established scrap iron dealers in France.
60 "Because of engineering faults, costly repairs, and political problems I cannot discuss," he told them, "the tearing down of the Eiffel Tower has become mandatory." He started a bidding war for the 7000 tons of scrap metal, reminding the businessmen the
65 Tower had been originally constructed for the 1889 World Fair as a temporary fixture. As so often occurred, Lustig's confidence and charm were enough to overcome any doubts. Within a few days, he had taken the bid money, including an additional
70 bribe, from scrapper André Poisson and had left the country. When he found out he had been deceived, Poisson was so embarrassed he never reported the crime, lest his reputation be ruined. Half a year later, realizing he had escaped any consequences from his
75 crime, Lustig returned to Paris and performed the scam a second time!

Finally, in 1935, Lustig was caught by U.S. authorities and arrested for multiple counts of counterfeiting. Never one to disappoint, Lustig had
80 one more trick up his sleeve. While incarcerated at the Federal Detention Headquarters in New York, Lustig escaped from his third-floor cell. The prison was believed to be escape-proof, but Lustig had somehow vanished on the day he was scheduled to
85 stand trial. Apparently, he had made a rope of bedsheets to climb down from his window. On his way down, he pretended to be a window washer. Would you have suspected a man suspended from the outer wall of a prison, casually wiping the windows?
90 Although Victor Lustig's criminal profession is impressive, he is hardly a role model. A peaceful and productive society depends on trust and integrity, so while we may be amazed by his schemes, we must also resist the temptation of similarly robbing gullible
95 strangers. If there is one aspect of Lustig's life and character that can serve as an inspiring example, it is this: confidence can get you nearly anything. With enough self-assuredness, you can convince people of the impossible, such as a magic money-making box,
100 or the absurd, such as a prison paying for professionals to wash the windows of inmates' cells.

1

The main purpose of the passage is to

A) make the case that people have become too dependent on charity.

B) discuss theories on why people have a tendency to believe lies.

C) provide an account of how the Eiffel Tower was constructed.

D) relate entertaining anecdotes that serve a lesson.

2

The point of view from which the passage is told is best described as that of

A) an engineer providing simple explanations of complicated devices to non-experts.

B) a journalist warning about a series of recent local crimes.

C) a researcher explaining social phenomena to fellow scholars.

D) a historian sharing an amusing biography.

3

In context, what is the main effect of the author's use of the word "surely" in lines 11 and 39?

A) It establishes a critical tone that reflects the author's negative view of Lustig.

B) It creates a sense of confidence in the author's theories about Lustig's life.

C) It highlights the logic of those people who were fooled by Lustig.

D) It emphasizes the certainty of an obvious fact.

4

Which statement provides the best description of a technique the author uses throughout the passage to advance his points?

A) The author uses basic math to emphasize the reasonableness of his arguments.

B) The author offers rhetorical questions and follows them with thorough answers.

C) The author presents challenging situations and considers how he would react.

D) The author asks the reader to personally relate to the scenarios described.

5

In describing the exploits of Victor Lustig, the author's tone is

A) impressed.

B) disgusted.

C) ashamed.

D) envious.

6

What is the purpose of the second paragraph (lines 33-44)?

A) To show the breadth and depth of Lustig's deceptions beyond the earlier examples

B) To show that Lustig was a master of disguise

C) To reveal that Lustig was a con man

D) To present a list of Lustig's victims

7

The author uses an exclamation point in the last sentence of the fourth paragraph (lines 55-76) to express

A) astonishment.

B) despair.

C) anger.

D) guilt.

Rhetoric – Social Studies – Passage 4

This passage is adapted from an article about the history of American football.

November 12, 1892, was no ordinary day. While the Allegheny Athletic Association (AAA) football team defeated the Pittsburgh Athletic Club (PAC), the match birthed a new era in the world of sports.
5 The game was mainly of local interest, but the fact that one of the AAA players, William (Pudge) Heffelfinger, was paid in cash would prove pivotal in sports history. As a result, American professional football, a sport that now grosses 14 billion dollars a
10 year and is followed by tens of millions worldwide, was born.

Relatively new in 1892, American football derived from two long-enjoyed sports—soccer and rugby. The first college football game was reportedly
15 played in 1869, between Rutgers and Princeton, but it wasn't until Yale rugby player Walter Camp pioneered new rules for the game in the 1880s that American football, as we know it now, began to emerge.
20 Athletic club football teams were widespread in the 1880s, engendering heated competition. In their attempts to attract the best talent, some clubs created "jobs" for star players, while others "awarded" their players fancy trophies or expensive watches. Yet
25 another popular practice of the time was to pay "double expenses" to each player. The Amateur Athletic Union challenged these practices, which were only thinly veiled compensation for athletes who were supposed to be amateurs. But clubs merely
30 devised more creative forms of benefits.

The sporting scene evolved leading up to that significant November 12 AAA-PAC game. The Allegheny and Pittsburgh teams were fierce rivals and had ended their first contest of the year in a 6-6
35 tie. When AAA argued that William Kirschner, PAC's top player, was a professional, PAC vehemently denied it. In the midst of this controversy, both teams aggressively explored ways they could bolster their lineups before their second
40 match. Both teams traveled to watch the impressive Chicago Athletic Association team, a precursor to today's scouting trips.

The AAA recruited Ben "Sport" Donnelly and Ed Malley, both of whom would play for AAA on
45 November 12 for their usual double expenses. But with Kirschner injured, the PAC decided to sweeten the deal it offered. Focusing on Heffelfinger, a three-time All-American guard while at Yale, and Knowlton "Snake" Ames, the PAC offered each man
50 $250 to play against the AAA on November 12, according to the October 30, 1892, issue of *The Pittsburgh Press*. Ames refused the deal, unwilling to endanger his amateur status. Heffelfinger, though, held out for a better offer. In the end, he would join
55 Donnelly and Malley to play for the AAA after quietly being offered $500.

The Allegheny and Pittsburgh teams gathered at Recreation Park in Pittsburgh that November day, but play did not begin immediately. Instead, the PAC
60 coach had his team leave the field after recognizing the three Chicago players—in particular Heffelfinger, who was considered the best of that time—in AAA uniforms. Supporters of both teams had bet heavily on the game's outcome, and the contest was now
65 unfairly stacked in the AAA's favor. Kickoff was delayed, bickering commenced, and the game was only begun when both teams agreed to play it as an exhibition, all bets off. The talented Heffelfinger did, in fact, score the sole touchdown, then worth four
70 points, after forcing a fumble and running 25 yards to score.

The immediate aftermath of the game was messy. AAA fans, excited for their team's win, were frustrated when they could not realize their financial
75 winnings. PAC fans were livid that the AAA team had brought in ringers. Further, Pittsburgh charged Allegheny with paying Heffelfinger cash to play, a blatant violation of the day's amateur rules. Heffelfinger kept mum on the subject, and AAA
80 manager O.D. Thompson admitted nothing, simply replying he had done "what the Pittsburghs tried to do. Only we were successful where they failed." While later documentation showed the AAA netted $621 on the game even after paying Heffelfinger, no
85 clear proof of the violation was then evident, so little could be done. But a new precedent was set, and within four years every AAA player would be paid, making Allegheny the country's first professional football team.
90 Sixty-eight years after that historic game, the Pro Football Hall of Fame acquired an old page from the Allegheny Athletic Association's expense ledger. The page, dated November 12, 1892, displayed the following line item: "Game performance bonus to W.
95 Heffelfinger for playing (cash) $500." The truth was finally clear. William "Pudge" Heffelfinger was the first professional American football player. The November 12, 1892, AAA-PAC game opened the door to the professional sport. And football as we
100 know it today was born.

1

How does the use of "birthed" (line 4) and "born" (line 11) help establish the focus of the passage?

A) They suggest the passage will examine something new that came into being.

B) They are used because it's the beginning of the passage.

C) They suggest that the passage will focus on the excitement of professional football.

D) They are used to indicate the passage will consider the conclusion of an era.

2

The third paragraph (lines 20-30) primarily serves to

A) describe early methods of professional compensation.

B) describe early cash salaries.

C) describe early methods of amateur compensation.

D) persuade the reader that football should have remained an amateur sport.

3

Over the course of the fourth paragraph (lines 31-42), the author's focus shifts from

A) AAA-PAC similarities to AAA-PAC differences.

B) AAA-PAC differences to AAA-PAC similarities.

C) amateur football to professional football.

D) controversy in Pittsburgh to controversy in Chicago.

4

Which of the following statements would the author most likely agree with?

A) The evolution of amateur football into professional football was a mistake.

B) November 12, 1892, is a significant date in the world of professional sports.

C) Betting on sporting events is wrong.

D) November 12, 1892, is an obscure date in the world of professional sports.

5

How does "pivotal" (line 7) help the reader to anticipate the contents of the passage?

A) The passage will justify a particular point of view.

B) The passage will focus on a series of events.

C) The passage will describe how things changed following the significant event.

D) The passage will focus exclusively on long-term outcomes of the event.

6

One of the main purposes of the final paragraph is to

A) question if Heffelfinger was the first professional American football player.

B) deny that Heffelfinger was the first professional American football player.

C) conclusively prove Heffelfinger was the first amateur American football player.

D) conclusively prove Heffelfinger was the first professional American football player.

7

Which order best describes the progression of the passage?

A) game day, compensation and clubs, early days, the new precedent

B) early days, compensation and clubs, game day, the new precedent

C) game day, early days, compensation and clubs, the new precedent

D) early days, game day, the new precedent, compensation and clubs

8

The author argues "a new precedent was set" (lines 86) because

A) Heffelfinger admitted to receiving payment to play.

B) AAA's cash payment to Heffelfinger eventually became the norm.

C) American amateur, club football would fade and eventually disappear.

D) AAA's cash payment to Heffelfinger could not be proven.

Rhetoric – Social Studies – Passage 5

This passage is adapted from an article about intrusive thoughts.

We've all experienced the occasional rogue thought, the kind that flits into your mind unbidden and makes you wonder where it came from or simply dismiss it out of hand. It could take the form of an
5 inappropriate comment you have to suppress, a flash of emotion you hadn't expected, or a sudden, inexplicable desire to do something you know you shouldn't. When you're sitting quietly in class and suddenly get the urge to shout out, it's easy to
10 attribute that impulse to boredom and dismiss it. But when you're looking down from an observation point atop a tall building and something in your brain suddenly seems to be telling you to jump, that can be a little harder to brush off as something as innocent
15 as a bored mind.

If you've ever felt that unexpected, irrational urge to jump, rest assured that you're not alone. The phenomenon is common enough to go by many names. Edgar Allan Poe used it as a basis for his
20 1845 story "The Imp of the Perverse," in which he describes a sense "far more terrible than any genius or any demon of a tale, and yet it is but a thought … it is merely the idea of what would be our sensations during the sweeping precipitancy of a fall from such
25 a height." The story's title was ultimately adopted as one name for the experience. The French, meanwhile, call that impulse "l'appel du vide," or "the call of the void," endowing it with a seductive, siren-like quality. In modern psychological parlance, it's
30 known alternately as the "high place phenomenon" or as an "intrusive thought." Scary though it may seem, the experience under any name is neither uncommon nor dangerous.

Miami University professor April Smith has
35 studied intrusive thoughts extensively. She has found that, far from signaling an inclination to self-harm, "an urge to jump affirms the urge to live." Smith explains we may be misinterpreting a series of self-protecting thoughts after they have flashed by in
40 quick succession, identifying an urge in retrospect that was never actually there to begin with. Smith's research suggests that when a person looks out over the edge of a cliff or rooftop, the brain sends an "alarm signal" telling him to be careful. Naturally, he
45 takes a step back from the edge in response, at which point his rational mind catches up with his actions and begins to overanalyze them. The person would not have stood so close to the edge in the first place if it was unsafe, so the mind questions the motive (why
50 take a step back when there was no real danger?), concludes that there must have been a real threat, and connects the dots to determine that the person himself is the source: he must in fact have been contemplating jumping off the edge.

55 This sense of uncertainty or mistrust toward one's own mind can certainly be unnerving, but it would be a mistake to fret over intrusive thoughts that occur only occasionally. Concordia University researcher Shiu Wong, a specialist in behavior and
60 anxiety disorders, does not believe such thoughts are inherently harmful. Wong clarifies, however, that it is important to address them effectively. Deliberate efforts to banish them can require sustained attention that actually makes them more likely to occur, and
65 attempts to control them through ritualistic behaviors are fruitless. The latter can also indicate an anxiety disorder such as OCD, which should be treated by a medical professional.

Simply experiencing intrusive thoughts from
70 time to time, though, is quite normal. As a matter of fact, research shows conclusively that people who have occasional intrusive thoughts are in good company with over 90% of the "clinically normal" (those who have not been diagnosed with a mental
75 illness). "I'm as convinced as it's possible to be that the real figure is 100 per cent," says clinical psychologist Paul Salkovskis, a researcher and professor at the University of Bath. Salkovskis posits that such thoughts may be a byproduct of the same
80 evolutionary processes that gave us problem-solving skills and the subconscious. If Salkovskis is correct, the intrusive thoughts are actually an indicator that the brain is functioning as it should be, working continuously behind the scenes to weigh the options
85 and prepare for the worst. This constant brainstorming is generally successful but if (or more accurately, when) the occasional bad idea surfaces, our better judgement acts as a safety net and prevents us from acting on it.

90 It can certainly be alarming to be ambushed by an intrusive thought, and it can lead one to wonder what it might mean. It's easy to fear that hearing the call of the void is an indicator of some deep dark other side hidden even to yourself. But unless you
95 experience a persistent onslaught of such thoughts, or find them increasingly difficult to resist, they are nothing to worry about. Intrusive thoughts, the high place phenomenon, the imp of the perverse… no matter the nomenclature, the experience is normal
100 and part of what makes you human—just like the better judgement that keeps you safe.

1

The author's central purpose in the passage is to

A) argue the process of developing memories is widely misunderstood.

B) examine the connection between psychology and art.

C) inform the reader about the results of an experiment.

D) explore the underlying causes of an experience.

2

Over the course of the passage, the main focus shifts from

A) an explanation of a phenomenon to a consideration of its harmfulness.

B) an account of a personal experience to several possible explanations.

C) a description of a historical event to an explanation of similar events.

D) a summary of a fictional story to an analysis of its origins.

3

Which choice supports the conclusion that intrusive thoughts are typically not dangerous?

A) "We've all experienced… dismiss it out of hand." (lines 1-4)

B) "Smith's research suggests… telling him to be careful." (lines 41-44)

C) "This sense of uncertainty… occur only occasionally." (lines 55-58)

D) "Deliberate efforts… ritualistic behaviors are fruitless." (lines 62-66)

4

The author's tone toward the reader is best described as one of

A) appreciation.

B) reassurance.

C) criticism.

D) concern.

5

The first paragraph mainly serves to

A) describe a common experience to which the reader can relate.

B) introduce the results of an experiment that will be explained.

C) share a personal experience from the author.

D) explain the reason why an event occurs.

6

The primary purpose of the second paragraph (lines 16-33) is to

A) help the reader understand the mechanics of a complicated phenomenon.

B) ask the reader to consider an experience from another person's point of view.

C) provide an overview of how a phenomenon has been described.

D) compare the accuracy of several explanations.

7

The author's use of the phrase "in fact" (line 53) has mainly which effect?

A) It stresses the distinction between how scientists and artists portray mental illness.

B) It indicates the author will support the information with experimental data.

C) It supports the point that the brain believes a false scenario is true.

D) It asserts that the following statement is accurate.

8

In lines 74-75, what is the purpose of the information in parentheses?

A) It provides an analogy to help understand an idea.

B) It presents a potential source for the origin of a term.

C) It clarifies the meaning of an expression.

D) It offers an alternate explanation.

9

How does the author develop her argument about intrusive thoughts?

A) The author describes common scenarios and then refers to various sources to further describe and explain them.

B) The author describes one person's experiences and then analyzes the influences that contributed to it.

C) The author assumes her views are shared by the reader and criticizes multiple counterarguments

D) The author presents puzzling situations and shows how scientists have created experiments to find explanations.

Notes and Reflections

Data Graphics – Passage 1

Although snow-covered terrain may seem inhospitable, snow can be nurturing. It provides insulation and is a source of water.

5 A recent study analyzed how snow cover can affect the soil temperature of forests, which can in turn affect tree growth. Starting on December 1, 2000, three flat plots of land, each measuring 10 meters by 20 meters, were established at an ecological research site in a forest in northern New 10 England. For all three plots, the types of vegetation present were the same. The distribution, size, and counts of vegetation present were the same. Three mature sugar maple trees (*Acer saccharum*) were present on each plot.

15 Over the course of a 12-year period, Plot 2 was shoveled for any snow regularly between December 1 and January 30 of each winter. Plot 3 was shoveled regularly throughout the entire winter (December 1 through May 1) each year of the study. Plot 1 was 20 never shoveled during the experiment.

During May of each year, increment core samples from all of the sugar maple trees were extracted to find the radius of the tree, which was then used to calculate basal area increment (BAI), a 25 measure of a tree's growth. From the months of December through March, ground penetrating radar was used daily to measure the depth of soil freeze (in centimeters) surrounding the sugar maple tree on the three plots. Soil depth freeze is the depth into the soil 30 at which the soil remains frozen.

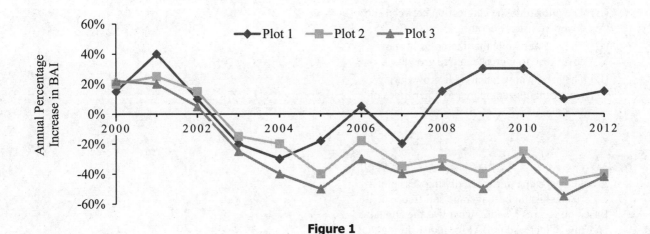

Figure 1

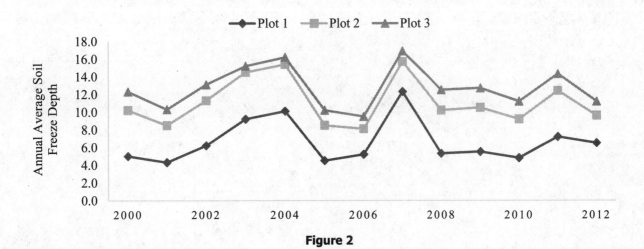

Figure 2

1

According to figure 1, between which of the following pairs of years did all three plots experience a percentage decrease in BAI?

(A) 2001-2002
(B) 2004-2005
(C) 2005-2006
(D) 2008-2009

2

How do the figures support the author's point that snow cover affects tree growth?

(A) They reveal the depth to which soil will freeze in different areas.
(B) They illustrate the connection between snow cover and freeze depth.
(C) They demonstrate that increases in snow cover lead to increase in tree growth.
(D) They show how much trees grow during winter months compared to other times of year.

3

A cold frost came unexpectedly the year plot 1 experienced its highest average soil freeze depth. Based on figures 1 and 2, what was the annual percentage increase in BAI for plot 1 during that year?

(A) –40%
(B) –20%
(C) 5%
(D) 15%

Data Graphics – Passage 2

Contact with pre-Columbian populations in the Americas has long been a matter of research and controversy. Circumstantial evidence indicates that language and art were almost certainly shared across
5 the Pacific Ocean well before 1500 C.E. A new study of DNA from 1,245 varieties of sweet potato suggests that Polynesians traveled to South America and began to spread the sweet potato westward no later than 1200 C.E.; such work adds new details to the
10 intertwined histories of humans and plants.

Examining the historical paths agricultural products have traveled is a common way for scientists to track the migrations of people. Europeans brought the sweet potato, a versatile and
15 nutritious crop native only to the Americas, with them as they colonized the Pacific region, but there is also evidence the plant was already there when they arrived. One Polynesian word for the sweet potato—*kuumala*—is thought to be based on the words
20 *kumara* and *cumal*, which refer to the plant in Quencha, a native language from the Andes in South America. Furthermore, archeologists have found remnants of sweet potato plants at Polynesian sites dating to before 1100 C.E. The spread of the sweet
25 potato across Polynesia and Oceania raises many questions: Did the plant reach the region before it was introduced by Europeans? If so, who brought it? Where and when did it arrive? And how did it achieve such complicated genetic variety?

30 A new study by a team of French researchers used stable markers common to both modern and herbarium samples of sweet potato DNA to resolve this puzzle. The team sampled preserved specimens and was able to identify complementary sets of
35 genetic markers—chloroplast and nuclear micro-satellites—to track the initial spread of the plant across the Pacific. They noted two distinct shifts in the distribution of genetic variation over the history of the region's sweet potatoes. These shifts indicated
40 the sweet potato had arrived in Polynesia in three waves, the first of which had to have occurred hundreds of years before two later reintroductions.

The study reveals the course the sweet potato traveled. A variety native to the Ecuadoran and
45 Peruvian Andes was likely first retrieved by Polynesian explorers and planted in eastern Polynesia around 1100 C.E. This Andean sweet potato adapted well to its new island environment and spread across the region. Two other varieties of sweet potato,
50 native to other parts of the Americas, were subsequently carried to the region by Spanish and Portuguese colonizers, and these were interbred with the original to create new varieties with obscured genetic origins.

55 "There's been many kinds of evidence, linguistic and archeological, for the connection between these two peoples," said Caroline Rouiller, the biologist who led the study, referring to the interaction of native Polynesians and South Americans, "but the
60 sweet potato is the most compelling."

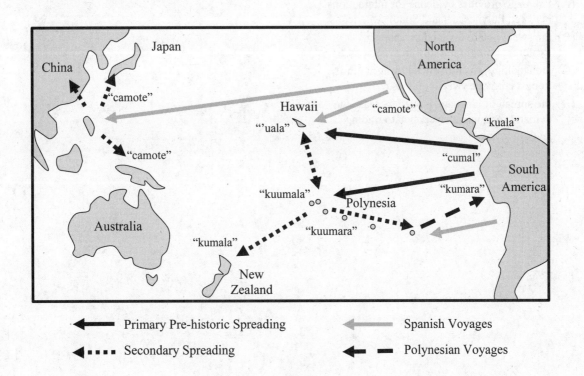

⬅━━ Primary Pre-historic Spreading   ⬅━━ Spanish Voyages

◄••••• Secondary Spreading   ◄━ ━ Polynesian Voyages

1

Which claim about the spread of the sweet potato is supported by the map?

(A) Sweet potatoes are only native to South America.

(B) The variety of sweet potato found in Japan originated in North America.

(C) The sweet potato was brought to Australia before it reached China.

(D) Polynesian explorers transported the sweet potato directly from South America to New Zealand.

2

According to the map, the population of which of the following regions initially received sweet potatoes from Spanish explorers?

(A) Hawaii

(B) East Asia

(C) South America

(D) New Zealand

3

Information presented on the map most strongly supports Rouiller's view that

(A) language provides evidence for interactions between Polynesians and South Americans.

(B) the sweet potato evolved as Spanish explorers brought it to different regions.

(C) archaeology was influenced by agriculture to best cultivate sweet potatoes.

(D) the spread of language helped increase the demand for ancient sweet potato trading.

Data Graphics – Passage 3

Machines should make our lives better. A washing machine does the laundry for us. A car or train or bus can help us move around more quickly. Microwaves and vacuum cleaners and ATMs and so
5 many other machines are used to do the hard work for us so we can enjoy the rest of our lives more. We see the conveniences of automation in our homes every day, but the greatest effect has been felt in the factories.

10 With innovations and advancements in machines that help us manufacture, our factories have become much more productive. From the invention of the cotton gin to the modern robotic assembly line, it takes fewer workers to create more goods. While this
15 type of progress is a welcome convenience in our homes, it can be an issue in some labor industries. When each laborer is able to produce more with machines, fewer laborers are needed to meet the production needs. A whole team of workers may be
20 replaced by a single machine operator. If the machine becomes fully automated, not even the operator is needed. Thus, as productivity has increased over the recent generations, the number of people employed in factories has steadily decreased. There is concern,
25 certainly, that this trend will lead to levels of joblessness that will drag down our economies and societies. Another concern, beyond the unemployment caused by automation, is the compensation for those who are still employed.

30 Between 1975 and 2010, the productivity of the average U.S. worker increased by 100%. This improvement is primarily due to advancements in machines. However, while each worker is capable of creating twice as much, wages have not risen at the
35 same level. In fact, when adjusted for inflation, average hourly wages have fallen by 7% during those 35 years. This discouraging figure does not capture the entirety of the situation, because workers are compensated in ways besides wages. Using the
40 Consumer Price Index (CPI) estimation of inflation, the total compensation of workers increased by 30%

over this period. Using another measure of consumer prices, the Personal Consumption Expenditures (PCE) index, the number rises to 56%. These values
45 still show an approximately 2- or 3-fold increase in productivity compared to compensation, but the difference is less drastic. It is impossible to perfectly quantify how much the expense of living has increased, because the world in 2010 is so different
50 from that in 1975, and different surveys and formulas paint very different pictures of how prices have shifted. Still, no matter how we gather and interpret the data, the base result is the same: workers are getting paid less to produce more.

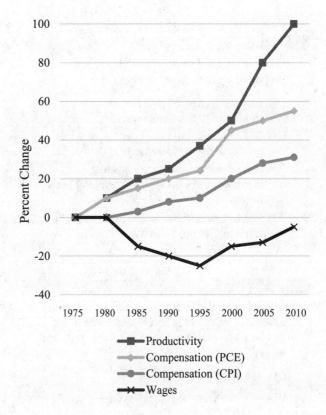

1

Which additional information, if included in the figure, would be most helpful for evaluating the passage's claim in lines 22-24 ("Thus, as productivity… decreased.")?

(A) Number of factory positions held each year from 1975-2010

(B) Prices for factory-created products from 1975-2010

(C) Annual rates of inflation in the U.S. economy from 1975-2010

(D) Lists of industries that have seen the highest increases in factory automation from 1975-2010

2

Which of the following statements is best supported by the figure?

(A) Increasing wages leads to greater productivity from workers.

(B) Total compensation has decreased while productivity has increased.

(C) Increasing productivity leads to unemployment because of shrinking labor needs.

(D) Worker compensation has not risen at the same rate as productivity.

3

According to the figure, which of the following timespans showed the greatest increase in the gap between percent change in productivity and wages?

(A) 1985-1990

(B) 1995-2000

(C) 2000-2005

(D) 2005-2010

Data Graphics – Passage 4

Every method used in the search for exoplanets has advantages and disadvantages. All methods currently used are indirect: radial velocity (RV) surveys are based on Doppler shift measurements; the
5 transit photometry method detects variations in brightness as a planet passes in front of its star; the method of astrometry measures the wobble of a star caused by orbiting planets; and the microlensing technique relies on Einstein's general theory of
10 relativity. Direct detection and imaging of exoplanets is exceedingly difficult because the brightness of light from a star and of reflected light from a planet differ greatly.

As an exoplanet orbits a distant star, it is
15 periodically moving towards and away from an observer on Earth. Using the Doppler effect (the wavelength of light from objects is shifted when the object moves toward or away from the observer) it is possible to detect the presence of a planet orbiting a
20 distant star, not by direct observation of the Doppler effect in the very faint reflected light from a planet, but by observing the wobble of its star. The gravitational attraction of the planet pulls the star in a circular path. In this way, by recording the period and
25 amplitude of the oscillation, the mass and orbital radius of the exoplanet can be determined.

Unlike the RV method, transit photometry records variations in the brightness of the star. As an exoplanet crosses in front of our view of a star, a dip
30 in the observed brightness can be detected. Ground-based observations are affected by turbulence in the Earth's atmosphere, which produces scintillation of the stars. This apparent glinting of stars can be mistaken for the obstruction of a passing exoplanet.
35 Launched in 2009, the Kepler space telescope used this method to detect thousands of exoplanets until its mechanical systems failed in 2013. In February 2014, astronomers pioneered a new technique called "verification by multiplicity," to detect planets in
40 multiple-planet systems. In early 2016, scientists revived the Kepler mission by utilizing solar winds to stabilize the telescope, allowing Kepler to search for more exoplanets.

For more distant planets, microlensing can be
45 employed, whereby variations in brightness are observed when light from a star bends as it passes near a massive object located between the distant source and the observer. If the star has a planet, characteristic patterns appear on the light curve from
50 which the star-planet mass ratio can be determined. The microlensing technique provides an opportunity to find stars with multiple planetary systems, and is most advantageous for finding very distant planets too faint to be discovered by other techniques.

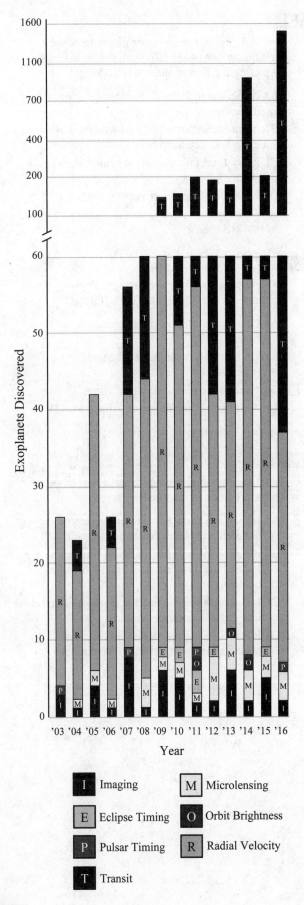

SUMMIT
EDUCATIONAL
GROUP

1

Based on the figure and information from the passage, which of the following can be inferred regarding the Kepler space telescope?

(A) Its revival in 2016 led to many exoplanet discoveries.

(B) It introduced an entirely new method of exoplanet detection.

(C) Its systems failed before it could discover any exoplanets.

(D) It uses the Doppler effect to detect exoplanets.

2

Which statement from the passage is best supported by data presented in the figure?

(A) "Direct detection… differ greatly." (lines 10-13)

(B) "In this way… can be determined." (lines 24-26)

(C) "Unlike the RV… the star." (lines 27-28)

(D) "For more… the observer." (lines 44-48)

3

What purpose does the figure serve in relation to the information in the passage?

(A) It indicates the relative effectiveness of different exoplanet detection methods.

(B) It places the information about Einstein's general theory of relativity into a broader context.

(C) It demonstrates the decline in usage of direct imaging for exoplanet detection.

(D) It criticizes the practicality of the "verification by multiplicity" technique.

Notes and Reflections

SUMMIT
EDUCATIONAL
GROUP

Writing & Language

❑ Section Quizzes

- ○ Standard English Conventions
- ○ Expression of Ideas

❑ Standard English Conventions

- ○ Pronouns
- ○ Subject-Verb Agreement
- ○ Comparisons
- ○ Idioms
- ○ Diction
- ○ Fragments
- ○ Run-Ons

- ○ Parallelism
- ○ Modifiers
- ○ Verb Tense
- ○ Semicolons & Colons
- ○ Commas
- ○ Apostrophes

❑ Expression of Ideas

- ○ Main Idea
- ○ Addition & Deletion
- ○ Organization

- ○ Transitions
- ○ Wordiness
- ○ Style

❑ Data Graphics

Standard English Conventions 1

Galen's four humors impacted the field of medicine for over a millennium and a half. This concept spread across the globe over many eras, impacting the Roman Empire, the medieval period, and the Renaissance. In the eighteenth century, the humors loose their standing as the foundation of the medical field, but they still form the basis of many folk medical practices throughout the world.

Galen was a Greek physician under the Roman Empire in the second century CE. As a student of medicine in the ancient world, a lot of Galen's ideas were owed to his predecessor, Hippocrates, whom is credited with introducing the theory of humors. Galen promoted this theory and expanded upon it.

Galen's primary interest was in human 4 anatomy, however, his research was hampered by Roman law, which prohibited human dissection. Galen practiced dissection on dead and living animals to gain a better understanding of anatomy. He promoted Hippocratic teachings, and he defended his practices of venesection and bloodletting despite their controversies in Rome. Though controversial in his time, Galen's teachings and practices had a vast impact long after he died.

1
A) NO CHANGE
B) lose there
C) lost their
D) lost there

2
A) NO CHANGE
B) Galen's lot of ideas were owed
C) Galen owed a lot of his ideas
D) owing a lot of Galen's ideas

3
A) NO CHANGE
B) whom's
C) who is
D) whose

4
A) NO CHANGE
B) anatomy, however;
C) anatomy, however—
D) anatomy; however,

While Galen contributed to the medical field in many ways, he is most associated with the idea of the four humors. The theory of the [5] humors was based on the foundation that there are four bodily fluids which must be kept in balance: blood, phlegm, yellow bile, and black bile. Blood was associated with agitation and dysentery, yellow bile with anger, black bile with depression, and phlegm with swelling and pneumonia. If any one of these humors amassed dominance in a person, the imbalance would result in symptoms of disease and would also explain aspects of their personality. Finding a balance in the humors depended on each person's age and [6] body, as well, as other factors such as the current season. In addition, each humor was tied to heat, cold, wetness, or dryness. [7] Patients treatments' involved ingesting or applying to their bodies certain treatments to get the proper amount of warmth and moisture, as well as the correct balance of the four elements for each specific situation.

Galen's influence can be found throughout the world over many centuries. The idea of these humors is evident in the classical Arabic medical text Kit¬āb al-Malakī, which the Islamic doctor al-Majūsī created. The Arabic word denoting health, Misáj, finds its roots in the word that means "to mix" because of Galen's belief that any imbalance would result in sickness.

5
A) NO CHANGE
B) humors, was based
C) humors were based
D) humors, were based

6
A) NO CHANGE
B) body as well, as
C) body, as well as,
D) body, as well as

7
A) NO CHANGE
B) Patients treatment's
C) Patients' treatments
D) Patient's treatments

Centuries later, Galen's impact was apparent in Elizabethan England. People managed their diet, clothing, activities, and hygiene in an attempt to balance their humors. For example, because masculinity was tied to the dry and hot humors, Elizabethans believed bathing was more harmful to men **8** then women. We can also see that Shakespeare, as well as Chaucer and other famous **9** writers utilizes the idea of these humors for characterization, including physical appearance, motivations, and behavior. Until the seventeenth century, the medical field in the UK relied on a humors-based system called Constitutional Imbalance, which was the basis for the medicine practiced by the Royal College of Physicians.

Galen's practices travelled across the Atlantic Ocean, as well. Until the nineteenth century, medicine in the United States used the same practices **10** as the Royal College of Physicians. In some areas of Central America, there is still a saying: "An orange in the morning is medicine, in the middle of the day it makes you sick, in the evening it kills you." This odd advice is based on the idea that oranges are "cold" foods and mornings are typically **11** cold, it is believed that eating cold food at other times will cause shock to your body.

Galen's humors dominated medical practices for sixteen hundred years, and their influence expanded further than treatments for illnesses. While Galen's theory no longer directly influences modern medicine and science, it still has some impact on medicine and culture worldwide.

8
A) NO CHANGE
B) than women
C) than to women
D) then to women

9
A) NO CHANGE
B) writers, utilizes
C) writers utilize
D) writers, utilize

10
A) NO CHANGE
B) than the Royal College of Physicians
C) as for the Royal College of Physicians
D) as did the Royal College of Physicians

11
A) NO CHANGE
B) cold, it is believed, that
C) cold. It is believed that
D) cold, it is believed. That

Standard English Conventions 2

The 17th century was a golden time for the newly created Dutch Republic. Amsterdam, the largest of the new nation's cities, **1** was the more prosperous city in Western Europe, due largely to its role in international trade. One of the most coveted imports **2** being the tulip's bulb, which came from Turkey in 1593 when a sultan sent stems and roots of the flower. The Dutch were captivated by this never-before-seen bloom. The beauty and novelty of the flowers made them important status symbols, valued highly in the Dutch Republic and across Europe. In fact, they were so valued that tulip bulbs reshaped the nation's entire economy.

The bulb market grew increasingly sophisticated, as tulips' many varieties were classified according to color and rarity, and multicolored varieties were commanding higher prices than **3** any variety being traded. The multicolored Rosen were characterized by white streaks on a red or pink background. Violetten featured white streaks on purple or lilac background. **4** Flame-like streaks of white or yellow marked the Bizarden. It is now known that this effect is due to the bulbs being infected with a rare and benign virus, known as the "tulip breaking virus" because it "breaks" the one petal color into two or more. The most valuable among these was known as Semper Augustus.

1
A) NO CHANGE
B) were the more
C) was the most
D) were the most

2
A) NO CHANGE
B) having been
C) were
D) was

3
A) NO CHANGE
B) any other variety being traded was
C) was trading any variety
D) being traded by any other variety

4
Which choice is most consistent with the style of the other examples provided in the paragraph?
A) NO CHANGE
B) Marking the Bizarden were white or yellow flame-like streaks.
C) The Bizarden was marked with white or yellow flame-like streaks.
D) The Bizarden's flame-like streaks marked it white or yellow.

By 1633, tulips began to be used as actual money. From 1634 to 1637, tulip prices soared from one guilder per bulb to over sixty guilders. At the height of the craze, in 1637, a single bulb of Semper Augustus was worth an amazing 10,000 guilders, ten times a craftsman's annual income and enough to support a family for several years. The tulip mania generated several amusing anecdotes, including one in which a hapless sailor ate one of [5] the rare treasured bulbs, thinking it was an onion. The cost of a single bulb [6] might of fed the entire crew of his ship for a year. Supposedly, the sailor was then arrested and jailed for his mistake. Thousands of ordinary Dutch citizens, from bankers and tradesmen to lowly carpenters and bricklayers, got involved in the market, thinking they would make their fortunes. Many traded their land, life savings, and whatever else they could liquidate, for the bulbs. There were some successful traders, analogous to day traders of the 1990s' Dot-Com bubble, [7] that could make the equivalent of over $60,000 a month in current US dollars.

The collapse of the tulip market began in Haarlem when some buyers apparently refused to show up at a routine bulb auction. This may have been because buyers were losing confidence in the market, or it may have been because Haarlem was then experiencing an outbreak of bubonic plague. The pessimism brought by the plague may actually have been responsible for the culture of fatalistic risk-taking that allowed the market to skyrocket; fearing they were likely to [8] die. People may have been more willing to bet all they had on an uncertain investment.

5
A) NO CHANGE
B) the, rare, treasured, bulbs
C) the rare, treasured bulbs,
D) the rare, treasured bulbs

6
A) NO CHANGE
B) mite of
C) might have
D) mite have

7
A) NO CHANGE
B) which
C) whom
D) who

8
A) NO CHANGE
B) die, and people
C) die, people
D) die people

In the winter of 1636-37, sellers overwhelmed the market and buyers disappeared. Prices dropped to a hundredth of their previous value. The government attempted to stem the collapse by offering to honor contracts at 10% of their value, causing the market to plunge even lower. For nearly 50 years before it crumbled, the tulip market **9** had had an unprecedented effect on European economics, particularly that of the Dutch Republic. The collapse of the tulip market signaled the end of the Dutch Golden Age, throwing the country into an economic depression. It also led to a Dutch suspicion of speculative investment that would persist for a very long time.

This story bears a strong resemblance to the stock market craze in America that led to the Crash of 1929. In the **10** 20's, investors were all too eager to get in on the action, but, inevitably, this market bubble "popped." In the 21st century, journalists have compared the "tulip mania" **11** of the failure of the dot-com bubble and the subprime mortgage crisis. In 2013, Nout Wellink, the former president of the Dutch Central Bank, described Bitcoin as "worse than the tulip mania," adding, "at least then you got a tulip; now you get nothing." The story of Dutch Tulip Mania remains a classic cautionary tale about irrational expectations and foolhardy speculation.

9
A) NO CHANGE
B) have had
C) has had
D) has

10
A) NO CHANGE
B) 20s', investor's
C) '20s, investors
D) 20s investors,

11
A) NO CHANGE
B) between
C) on
D) to

SUMMIT
EDUCATIONAL
GROUP

Standard English Conventions 3

We don't need to look very hard to see what happens when man-made structures are abandoned. In many of our own communities, there are **1** many old, unused buildings where neglect and the absence of routine maintenance have caused them to become overgrown with weeds and vines and led them to become the home to various kinds of local animal life. Nature returns to reclaim the spaces people have cleared with surprising speed, often within a few decades. Now imagine what nature could do to the remnants of an ancient civilization located in the tropics, a region of aggressive plant growth, after several hundred **2** years? The ancient Mayan civilization buried beneath the rainforests of Guatemala offers the perfect example.

The zenith of Mayan power lasted from approximately 600-800 C.E. By the time the Spanish conquistadors came to the Americas in the sixteenth century, they were not confronted by a single, unified Empire but rather by numerous Mayan statelets that were easy for the Spanish to individually conquer. As war and disease were spread by the Spanish conquistadors, the great cities of the Maya were emptied. The vastness of the Guatemalan jungle crept back to bury the remnants of that civilization with **3** its dense greenery. By the nineteenth century, knowledge of the achievements of the Mayan people **4** are nearly lost to all but the local population.

1
A) NO CHANGE
B) many, old, unused buildings,
C) many old unused buildings,
D) many old unused buildings

2
A) NO CHANGE
B) years; the
C) years, the
D) years the

3
A) NO CHANGE
B) it's
C) their
D) they're

4
A) NO CHANGE
B) were
C) was
D) is

The outside world may well have forgotten it [5] all together if not for the curiosity of a few brave explorers. From 1839-1841, a [6] former American Ambassador, John Lloyd Stephens, hacked his way through the jungles of the Yucatan peninsula. Guided only by the vague accounts of the conquistadors and local legends, [7] exploring by Stephens of the region's mysterious structures. It was arduous, dangerous work to push through the dense jungle foliage and avoid the many deadly creatures that lurked within. The scientific expeditions that followed Stephens hardly had it better than he did. Archaeologists and their teams would methodically criss-cross the uneven terrain, mapping out pyramids and temples and making occasional exploratory digs. In this manner, many large cities and settlements were discovered, but many more were missed.

Now, thanks to LiDAR technology, rather than inefficiently exploring random parts of the jungle hoping to stumble across potential archaeological sites, scientists are [8] capable to mapping the land from the sky. Slow-flying airplanes can deploy millions of canopy-penetrating laser beams that bounce back a detailed mapping of the contours of the ground below, revealing what has been hidden for centuries.

5
A) NO CHANGE
B) all too gether
C) alt together
D) altogether

6
A) NO CHANGE
B) former, American, Ambassador, John Lloyd Stephens,
C) former, American Ambassador, John Lloyd Stephens
D) former American Ambassador John Lloyd Stephens,

7
A) NO CHANGE
B) exploration of the region's mysterious structures by Stephens
C) the region's mysterious structures were explored by Stephens
D) Stephens explored the region's mysterious structures

8
A) NO CHANGE
B) capability to
C) capable with
D) capable of

So far, LiDAR surveys have provided a fresh perspective on the world of the [9] Maya, revealing it to be a complex culture with a high degree of societal organization. The scans have uncovered over 60,000 new structures, including previously unknown settlements that sprawl for miles around city centers. This has led scientists to re-evaluate their estimates about the size of the Mayan [10] population, they now believe to have been as high as 11 million people at its apogee. In some areas near major cities like Tikal, population densities likely rose to hundreds of people per square mile.

LiDAR technology has forever changed the practice of archaeology in Central America and is allowing researchers to rewrite the history of a civilization we thought we knew. The more we learn about these incredible indigenous people, the more impressive the scale and diversity of Mayan achievement becomes. In the past, research into the Mayans was constantly hampered at the very first [11] step; knowing where to dig. As archaeologists are increasingly able to pull up LiDAR maps on their laptops and "fly" over a virtual representation of the surrounding landscape with a click of the mouse, they are being given the roadmap for years of future exploration and discovery.

9
A) NO CHANGE
B) Maya; revealing
C) Maya. Revealing
D) Maya reveals

10
A) NO CHANGE
B) population;
C) population, this
D) population, which

11
A) NO CHANGE
B) step:
C) step,
D) step, thus

Standard English Conventions 4

Individualism and autonomy, rights we may consider essential to freedom, **1** <u>are</u> at the center of modern life. For many, the idea of **2** <u>loosing your self</u> or losing control over one's actions is nightmarish. Nothing embodies how this might occur better than mind control, so it's hardly surprising that storylines including mind control are often found at the heart of popular entertainment. The classic story of the Manchurian Candidate, where hypnosis is used to get the protagonist to unknowingly commit **3** <u>crimes,</u> just one of many books and films that allow us to watch as the consequences of people losing their individualism and autonomy play out at a safe distance.

But what many readers and moviegoers don't realize is that there is an example of mind control in the natural world. If they were to venture deep into the tropical rainforests of South America, they would not find monsters or hypnotists but a mind-controlling parasitic fungus—*Ophiocordyceps unilateralis*. **4** <u>Perfectly adapted to snatching the bodies of living things, we're lucky this fungus</u> has evolved to only seek out one specific host: carpenter ants.

1
A) NO CHANGE
B) being
C) have
D) is

2
A) NO CHANGE
D) losing your self
C) losing yourself
D) losing oneself

3
A) NO CHANGE
B) crimes. It's
C) crimes, is
D) crimes, being

4
A) NO CHANGE
B) Perfectly adapted to snatching the bodies of living things, this fungus that we're lucky
C) We're lucky this fungus, perfectly adapted to snatching the bodies of living things,
D) This fungus, we're lucky it's perfectly adapted to snatching the bodies of living things,

Known as the zombie-ant fungus, its mind-control process starts when a spore floats down from a fungal growth on plants above and attaches to an ant's exoskeleton, where [5] it uses pressure and enzymes to eventually break through and infect the host. Over the course of a week or so, *O. unilateralis* spreads through the ant's body, growing in strength, until it's capable of manipulating the [6] insect's behaviors so the ant acts for the fungus's benefit rather than its own. Once the fungus has control, it takes the ant's body for a walk to find the place with the right conditions to complete its life cycle.

How precisely *O. unilateralis* accomplishes this is of particular interest to researchers. As Kelly Weinersmith from Rice University notes, "[the] manipulation of ants by Ophiocordyceps is so exquisitely precise that it is perhaps surprising that the fungus doesn't invade the brain of its host." David Hughes, an entomologist at Pennsylvania State [7] University agrees, believing the fungus exerts more direct control over the ant's muscles, controlling them as a puppeteer controls a marionette doll. Once an infection is underway, he says, the neurons in the ant's body—the ones that give its brain control over [8] its muscles, start to die. Hughes suspects that when the fungus takes over, it effectively cuts the ant's limbs off from its brain and inserts itself in place, releasing chemicals that force the muscles there to contract. In this way, the ant ends its life as a captive in the vehicle of its own body. Its brain is still in the driver's seat, but the fungus has the wheel.

5
A) NO CHANGE
B) one
C) some
D) the spore

6
A) NO CHANGE
B) insects' behaviors
C) insects' behaviors'
D) insects behaviors'

7
A) NO CHANGE
B) University agrees
C) University, agrees
D) University, agrees,

8
A) NO CHANGE
B) it's muscles,
C) its muscles—
D) it's muscles—

Once the fungus has control, it usually has its host climb up a nearby plant stem, stopping the ant at a height of 25 centimeters above the forest floor, always on the northern side of the plant, in an environment with 94–95% humidity and temperatures **9** among 68° and 86° F. The fungus then forces the ant to permanently lock its mandibles around a leaf vein. *O. unilateralis* then continues to grow within the ant's soft tissue, draining its host of nutrients. Eventually, it will send a long stalk through the ant's head. This stalk grows into a bulbous capsule of spores that will be released upon another unsuspecting ant, beginning the cycle over again. Perhaps the most sinister part of this process is **10** that an infected ant typically climbs a leaf that overhangs its colony's foraging trails, the fungal spores rain down onto its sisters below. It's not unusual for there to be up to 30 diseased ants per square meter in infected areas, allowing *O. unilateralis* to easily wipe out entire colonies.

Recently, scientists have begun to look at the medicinal potential of *O. unilateralis* in humans. Within the fungus, certain molecules have been discovered that doctors hope will lead to advances in modifying autoimmune responses, inhibiting tumor growth, and **11** control blood sugar and cholesterol levels. Such research is not without peril. It would be a touching story of redemption if a devastating parasite like the zombie-ant fungus could be used to do some good. However, any avid reader or moviegoer knows the common plot of scientists naively meddling with the forces of nature and thus bringing unintended, terrifying consequences.

9
A) NO CHANGE
B) with
C) to
D) between

10
A) NO CHANGE
B) that,
C) since
D) that, since

11
Which of the following choices provides another example that is most similar to the structure of the previous examples in the sentence?

A) NO CHANGE
B) blood sugar and cholesterol levels control
C) control of blood sugar and cholesterol levels
D) controlling blood sugar and cholesterol levels

Notes and Reflections

Expression of Ideas 1

The period of the Middle ages known as the "Dark Ages" was called so because of a lack of cultural and intellectual achievements. [1] Some historians argue against the negative implications of the name. During this time, a general knowledge of the classics was lost and Latin Literature was deemed unimportant. This was so in Europe, but not for Islamic countries. Arab scientific study, specifically the study of medicine, flourished between the 8th and 16th centuries. [2] Despite this, some historians of science refer to the period from the 8th to the 16th centuries as the "Islamic Golden Age."

1

The author is considering whether to delete the underlined sentence. Should it be kept or deleted from the paragraph?

A) Kept, because it explains the connection between the fall of European society and the rise of Islamic culture.

B) Kept, because it provides information necessary for understanding a key term in the passage.

C) Deleted, because it adds information that distracts from the paragraph's description of a historical period.

D) Deleted, because it isn't relevant to the paragraph's focus on ancient technologies.

2

A) NO CHANGE

B) Nonetheless,

C) Likewise,

D) In fact,

[3] Islam emerged in the 7th century and quickly became a major world power, conquering the old Egyptian, Persian, Roman, and Near Eastern Empires. These nation's cultures influenced Islam. It drew from the rich traditions of Greece, Rome, Judaism, Christianity, and the Near East, becoming the center of a scientific, philosophic, and artistic culture. The Islamic world expanded rapidly until it eventually encompassed Spain, Sicily, and North Africa, and surrounded Byzantium in Egypt, Palestine, and Syria. As it expanded, the Islamic world maintained the Arabic language while building upon the legacies of Greek and Roman scholars. [4] This work required a great deal of translation by talented linguists.

[3]

Which choice most effectively combines the underlined sentences?

A) Influenced by the cultures of the old Egyptian, Persian, Roman, and Near Eastern Empires, conquered by Islam, which emerged in the 7th century and quickly became a major world power.

B) Influenced by the cultures of the old Egyptian, Persian, Roman, and Near Eastern Empires, Islam conquered these nations, then emerged in the 7th century, and quickly became a major world power.

C) Emerging in the 7th century, the old Egyptian, Persian, Roman, and Near Eastern Empires were conquered by Islam, which quickly became a major world power and was influenced by these cultures.

D) Emerging in the 7th century, Islam quickly became a major world power, conquering the old Egyptian, Persian, Roman, and Near Eastern Empires, and was influenced by these cultures.

[4]

Which of the following choices best introduces readers to the rest of the passage?

A) NO CHANGE

B) The scientists of ancient Greece and Rome were surprisingly insightful, considering the limited technology available to them.

C) Islamic scholars recognized history's knowledge could be built upon and should not be forgotten.

D) Much of the scholarly progress of ancient civilizations was lost due to political upheaval, warfare, and the passage of time.

It is due to the Arabs that many ancient Greek and Roman texts were preserved. This is especially **5** <u>spot-on</u> in the area of medicine. Islamic scholars created an organized system for the Greco-Roman medical knowledge they collected. They wrote everything they learned in encyclopedias and summaries. **6** Thus, the advance of medicine was built on a foundation of Islamic traditions and these Arabic translations.

5

Which of the following choices best maintains the tone of the passage?

A) NO CHANGE
B) on the money
C) legit
D) true

6

At this point, the author is considering adding the following sentence:

> "Later, Western doctors learned about Greek medicine, even the works of Hippocrates and Galen, through these Arabic texts."

Should the author make this addition here?

A) Yes, because it provides necessary clarification of the sequence of events mentioned in the passage.
B) Yes, because it supports the main idea of the paragraph and leads to the following sentence.
C) No, because it presents a claim that is countered later in the passage.
D) No, because it adds irrelevant information that distracts from the focus of the paragraph.

The places where learning thrived were Baghdad, Damascus, Cairo, and later Cordoba, Spain. Scholarly institutions and schools developed in these cities and were staffed with the highest caliber scholars who were dedicated to gathering information and developing new schools of thought. Learning and faith were integrated; dogma and science were studied side-by-side. **7** For some religions, a knowledge of mathematics is integral to the understanding of certain relationships and ideas. Like most scholars of the time, Islamic scientists wrote on vast and diverse **8** fields of study. Among these were physiology, medicine, ophthalmology, embryology, psychology, philosophy, law, and theology. These scholars, who worked in many fields, were known as polymaths and had a profound impact on a broad array of knowledge that is still relied on today.

7

Which of the following provides a detail that best reinforces the idea in the preceding sentence?

A) NO CHANGE
B) Scholars were not only knowledgeable in the field of medicine.
C) Meanwhile, Europe seemed to forget many of its medical advancements.
D) Next to religious mosques, there were academic hospitals, libraries, and observatories.

8

Which choice most effectively combines the sentences at the underlined portion?

A) fields of study, for example,
B) fields of study, including
C) fields of study were
D) fields, and studying

Al-Razi and Ibn al Nafis were particularly influential Arabic polymaths. Al-Razi, who lived from 865 to 925 C.E., made incredibly significant discoveries. For example, he [9] distinguished pediatrics as a separate field of medicine. Al-Razi was also a pioneer in the fields of ophthalmology, immunology, and allergy. He seems to be the first person to discover that a fever is part of the body's defense mechanism against infection. Ibn al Nafis, born in Damascus in 1213, wrote the first description of pulmonary blood circulation. To these two Arabic scientists, and many more, we owe much of our medical knowledge.

In the 15th century, European nations began to rise again and colonize the world. This, combined with the Crusades, Mongol invasions, natural disasters, loss of international trade, the capitulations of the Ottoman Empire to Western interests, and the rise of European imperialism, led to a decline of the Islamic world. [10] Many Arab nations were impoverished and their cultural influence diminished. [11] The sciences are typically not supported in societies that are not affluent. Struggling societies focus more on survival than advancement. Scientific inquiry requires extra resources and the luxury of time to pursue non-vital interests. Without these, the Islamic nations lost their positions as pioneers in the sciences. While European nations rose through the Renaissance and the Enlightenment periods, the Islamic nations experienced an era akin to their own Dark Ages.

9

The author wants to include a specific example to support the previous sentence. Which of the following best accomplishes the author's goal?

A) NO CHANGE
B) wrote more than 200 scientific books and articles.
C) and wrote books on distinguishing diseases.
D) explored how eyes react to light.

10

The author wants to emphasize the contrast between European and Islamic nations in the 15th century. Which of the following best accomplishes the author's goal?

A) NO CHANGE
B) Europe was entering the Renaissance period, which boasted some of the greatest thinkers in human history.
C) In both European and Arab nations, the state of scientific progress is closely tied to economic strength.
D) As the prosperity of Arab nations faltered, their scientific progress was carried on by strengthening European nations.

11

A) Struggling societies, which focus more on survival than advancement, so the sciences are typically not supported.
B) The sciences are typically not supported in struggling societies, which focus more on survival than advancement.
C) Focusing more on survival than advancement, the sciences are typically not supported in struggling societies.
D) Struggling societies that typically do not support sciences and focus more on survival than advancement.

Expression of Ideas 2

On October 7th, 1955, a hundred or so audience members gathered for a poetry reading, and none of them had any idea that they were about to witness literary history. The setting was a rundown, makeshift space called the Six Gallery in a former garage in San Francisco. One of the poets that read that night was 29-year-old Allen Ginsberg, and his poem *Howl* **1** would eventually be sold to over a million readers.

The '50s were a time of traditionalism in America. This was the generation of the nuclear family living comfortably in the suburban home. There was great economic progress, **2** so there was also a sense of restrictive conformity. The nation as a whole was thriving, but many people felt stifled, marginalized, and suppressed. Beneath the coating of idealism, there were many who wanted social recognition but who were seen as disruptive or unseemly to the cultural majority.

1

Which choice would best connect to the next paragraph and introduce readers to the rest of the passage?

A) NO CHANGE
B) would be the start of a literary career for Ginsberg
C) was about to challenge and change the culture of America
D) was based on the lives of his own friends and family

2

A) NO CHANGE
B) because
C) but
D) or

SUMMIT
EDUCATIONAL
GROUP

[1] With *Howl*, Ginsburg became the voice for many factions of a disaffected population, including poets, artists, jazz musicians, and political radicals, as well as drug addicts and psychiatric patients. [2] He personally knew many people that fit these descriptions, and he had seen many of them being judged, suffering, and not being supported by mainstream culture. [3] Meanwhile, the rise of industries during the second World War had carried over to an era of increased production and successful commerce. [4] As he wrote in the poem's opening: "I saw the best minds of my generation destroyed by madness". [5] He wanted everyone to **3** recognizably acknowledge issues like mental illness, which many people ignored because these topics were simply unpleasant. [6] By highlighting these issues, he hoped to inspire awareness and acceptance for people whose lives did not fit the traditional mold of '50s culture in America. **4**

3
A) NO CHANGE
B) acknowledge recognition of
C) have an acknowledgement of recognizing
D) acknowledge

4
For the sake of creating the most logical and cohesive paragraph, sentence 3 should be:

A) placed where it is now.
B) placed before sentence 1.
C) placed after sentence 5.
D) DELETED from the passage.

5 The success of *Howl* can be attributed to a variety of factors. The timing was perfect for such an intense support of non-mainstream culture. **6** For example, Ginsberg was not only a talented artist but also an expert promoter. Ginsberg was actually the organizer of the Six Gallery poetry event. His former career was in advertising and marketing, and these skills proved useful in promoting events like this. Also, the right people happened to be in the right spot at the right time. Both Jack Kerouac and Lawrence Ferlinghetti were in the audience at Six Gallery. The former would become an icon of the Beat Generation. The latter immediately saw the potential in the poem, and would, upon its completion, become its publisher through his San Francisco company, City Lights Books. All of these elements contributed to the poem's widespread and resounding effect.

5

Which of the following choices best introduces the main idea of this paragraph?

A) NO CHANGE
B) The key to artistic success is anticipating what the public will be thinking in the near future.
C) The presentation of art is as important as the art itself.
D) Ginsberg was not the only person in his time creating countercultural art.

6

A) NO CHANGE
B) Nonetheless,
C) Furthermore,
D) Consequently,

The reading at the Six Gallery is sometimes referred to as the beginning of the Beat Generation, a cultural movement focused on anti-materialism, Eastern religion, and less restriction of recreational drugs and sexuality. In many ways, the Beats were the precursors of the 1960s' hippies. **7** *Howl* would challenge censorship laws, promote ideas about the destructive forces of conformity and capitalism, and inspire myriad other social and cultural changes. The boundaries of art would be redefined as Ginsberg became the most recognizable poet since Walt Whitman, **8** whose free verse works inspired the style of *Howl*.

7

At this point, the author is considering adding the following sentence:

> "It is very difficult to define a generation or date its origin."

Should the author make this addition here?

A) Yes, because it explains why certain information cannot be included in the passage.

B) Yes, because it transitions from the preceding sentence to the focus of the rest of the paragraph.

C) No, because it introduces details that contradict the main idea of the passage.

D) No, because it is not relevant to the focus of the paragraph.

8

The author is considering deleting the underlined portion (and adjusting punctuation as needed). Given that the information is accurate, should the author remove the underlined portion from the paragraph?

A) Yes, because the information is irrelevant to the main focus of the paragraph.

B) Yes, because the information contradicts an earlier statement about Ginsberg's artistic style.

C) No, because the information clarifies a term that is used later in the passage.

D) No, because the information is necessary for explaining the popularity of Ginsberg's poetry.

It is noteworthy that Ginsberg's *Howl* was not a construction of fantasy but [9] a truthfully real account of people in his life. The poem relates the stories of many of Ginsberg's friends and acquaintances, including Neil Cassady, Kerouac, William S. Burroughs, and Peter Orlovsky. *Howl* is dedicated to Carl Solomon, who Ginsberg met in a mental institution. The poem also expresses his guilt and sympathy for his mother, who was schizophrenic and had undergone a lobotomy. The content was faithful to real life, though it covered elements of life that many people wished to ignore.

[1] Anticipating some backlash, Ferlinghetti did not print the poem in the US because he correctly anticipated legal problems. [10] [2] The trial boosted the fame of *Howl* and of Ginsberg. [3] In 1957, customs officials [11] nabbed 520 copies of the poem imported from its London printer, and the San Francisco police arrested Ferlinghetti on obscenity charges. [4] However, the legal charges against the printer were dropped in court and the poem was allowed to be published. [5] Ginsberg used this celebrity to promote a variety of countercultural causes: opposing the Viet Nam War, easing anti-homosexuality statutes, and recognizing oppressed minorities. [6] From its humble origins, *Howl*'s message resonated across the country, and *Howl* became the most important poem of the late 20th century and one of the most influential of all time.

9

A) NO CHANGE
B) a really truthful account
C) a real, true account
D) an account

10

To make the paragraph most logical, sentence 2 should be placed:

A) where it is now.
B) before sentence 1.
C) after sentence 3.
D) after sentence 4.

11

A) NO CHANGE
B) seized
C) pinched
D) grasped

Expression of Ideas 3

For about half of the world's population, rice is part of the daily calorie intake, making rice a staple of the world diet. However, while white rice might make a person feel full, it contains little to no nutritional value. [1] Chronic lack of nutrition in foods currently leaves large populations malnourished. Searching for a way to address this problem, scientists have found, and are additionally looking for, ways to genetically modify rice so they can keep this dietary necessity as part of many meals but increase its nutritional value. Genetically modified rice, with a [2] similar taste and texture to that of regular white rice, but with more nutrients, may be a solution to many people's incomplete diets.

1

Which of the following provides information that is most relevant to the focus at this point of the passage?

A) NO CHANGE
B) Typically, rice is paired with other foods to make it more palatable.
C) To prevent malnutrition, many people supplement their diets with necessary vitamins.
D) In other parts of the world, grains such as wheat and corn are major components to most meals.

2

A) NO CHANGE
B) simulated
C) copycat
D) mimic

3 People who do not consume enough vitamins, like vitamin A or zinc, can suffer from anemia, a condition in which the body does not produce enough healthy red blood cells, and have problems with brain development. Additionally, a weakened immune system from nutritional deficiency can lead to higher susceptibility to infectious diseases, like measles or malaria. According to the World Health Organization, 45% of deaths of children under the age of five can be linked to malnutrition. **4** Programs have been created to provide children with vitamin supplements, but given the widespread nature of this problem, humanitarians and scientists continue to seek additional solutions.

3

Which of the following, if added here, would best introduce the main idea of the paragraph and explain why this topic is important?

A) Genetic modification is one possible solution to several of mankind's most persistent problems.

B) In spite of the many advancements of modern pharmaceutical technologies, people around the world suffer from chronic conditions.

C) Malnutrition is a serious issue that must be addressed because it affects about half a billion people across the globe.

D) Although they are important to cultures, some traditional foods are not healthy as regular diets.

4

If the author were to delete the preceding sentence, the paragraph would primarily lose:

A) a statement that establishes the main focus of the paragraph.

B) a description of how scientists have dealt with malnutrition in the past.

C) a clarification about why malnutrition affects certain populations.

D) a detail emphasizing the severity of a problem.

In 1982, the journey to formulating a more nutritious rice began. It was seventeen years before the project yielded a usable product: golden rice. By adding the genes of daffodil plants and bacteria to the genes of the rice, scientists created grains containing beta-carotene, which, when consumed, is stored in the body or converted to vitamin A. **5** This addition also gives the rice its distinctive yellow, or golden, hue. Biofortification, the process of enhancing food to fight nutrient and vitamin insufficiencies, goes beyond this one project. Food companies add vitamins and minerals to sugary breakfast cereals to make these foods more nutritionally supportive for children, **6** and golden rice is altered to provide similar benefits. Such enhancements to foods ensure proper diets aren't reserved to only the most health-conscious.

5

The author is considering adding the following sentence to the passage:

"The body is able to identify the amount of vitamin A a person needs and only convert the appropriate amount of beta-carotene to vitamin A through intracellular metabolization."

Should the author make this addition here?

A) Yes, because it creates an effective transition from the creation of golden rice to its production and sales.

B) Yes, because it helps explain why golden rice is limited in treating malnutrition.

C) No, because it is irrelevant to the paragraph's focus on the economic factors tied to the problem of malnutrition and its potential solutions.

D) No, because it includes unnecessary details that do not strengthen the main idea of the paragraph.

6

If the author were to delete the underlined portion (adjusting punctuation as needed), the paragraph would primarily lose:

A) an introduction to ideas that are expanded upon later in the passage.

B) a suggestion that more companies should promote healthy habits.

C) an explanation of how industries can impact the cultural practices of societies.

D) a clarification of how preceding details relate to the main focus of the paragraph.

[1] The widespread issue of malnutrition involves several needed nutrients. [2] The changes made to golden rice, **7** in particular, currently only solve the issue of vitamin A deficiency. [3] For example, rice can be altered to increase iron and zinc consumption, but this cannot be combined with the addition of beta carotene. [4] The solution may be a blend of rice varieties. [5] However, rice farmers may be reluctant to grow multiple crops, which adds complexity and labor to their work. [6] Current solutions are imperfect, but scientists are striving to make more progress. **8** [7] Other modifications to rice have likewise only solved one problem at a time.

7

A) NO CHANGE
B) overall
C) however
D) for example

8

To make the paragraph most logical, sentence 7 should be placed:

A) where it is now.
B) after sentence 2.
C) after sentence 4.
D) after sentence 5.

A major **9** limiting obstruction to the success of golden rice has been the controversy around genetically modified foods. Some organizations claim that an expensive, biofortified crop like golden rice may worsen the issue of poverty, the underlying cause of much malnutrition. Also, many skeptics argue that GMOs are unnatural and that we don't know whether genetically modifying our foods will have future consequences for our health or the environment around us. **10** Considering the potential benefits of genetic modification, can we use this technology to solve problems besides malnutrition? Today, golden rice is being used in breeding programs in places like southeast Asia, but its use is limited. **11**

9

A) NO CHANGE
B) limit and obstruction
C) obstructing limit
D) obstruction

10

The author wants to pose a question that summarizes the preceding ideas in the paragraph. Which choice best accomplishes the author's goal?

A) NO CHANGE
B) Is progress through genetic modification worth the risk of creating other problems?
C) Should companies that invest in new technologies consider their social impact as well as profits?
D) If golden rice cannot solve the problem of malnutrition, can it have other positive uses?

11

The author wants the final sentence to restate the main idea of the passage. Which of the following choices best accomplishes this goal?

A) Although it isn't a perfect solution, golden rice is one step toward preventing the widespread problem of malnutrition.
B) Malnutrition has always been a problem, and there is no way to put an end to it without discovering new technologies.
C) New technologies always come with risks, so we must maintain traditional practices that are well known and trustworthy.
D) More advanced societies have a responsibility to aid those that are struggling and that have less resources or technologies.

Expression of Ideas 4

Almost all animals on Earth have ways in which they try to keep cool: some seek the shade, some minimize physical activity during the day, others cover themselves in mud, but humans turn to technology. Primitive air-conditioning systems have existed since ancient times. However, in most cases, **1** these were too costly and inefficient for all but the wealthiest people. For instance, in second-century China, an inventor created a room-sized, hand-powered, rotary fan for the Han Emperor. In the West, affluent Roman patricians took advantage of the empire's **2** remarkably impressive aqueduct system to circulate cool water through the walls of their homes. One of Rome's most decadent emperors, Elagabalus, took it a step further in the third century, building a mountain of snow—imported from the mountains via donkey trains—in the garden next to his villa to keep cool during the summer. These efforts **3** flaunt the vital importance of comfort, which is sought at any cost.

1

Which version of the underlined portion of the sentence provides the most relevant information for this paragraph?

A) NO CHANGE
B) these were even more effective than some modern technologies.
C) these were only needed in particular climates.
D) these were dismissed by people who simply accepted that warm temperatures were a fact of life.

2

A) NO CHANGE
B) impressively remarkable
C) remarked as impressive
D) impressive

3

A) NO CHANGE
B) exhibit
C) brandish
D) demonstrate

4 For example, in the 19th century American South, people turned to architecture to combat heat. In a time before electricity, by utilizing unique structural design features, they succeeded in **5** shrinking the interior temperatures of homes by as much as 10 to 15 degrees compared to outside. Homes built in the latter 19th century had high ceilings, averaging 12 to 14 feet—since heat rises, much of it was above head height. These homes were also oriented to take advantage of the sun in winter and the cooling shade of trees in summer.

6 Additionally, the walls tended to be 4 to 6 inches thick due to the substantial insulation within them. At night, when shutters and windows were opened, the homes were able to capture the cooler air which was let in and maintain it more efficiently once the windows and shutters were closed again for the day in the morning.

4

Which choice, if added here, would provide the most effective transition from the previous paragraph?

A) All of the ancient cooling technologies continue to be used to this day.

B) Many cultures have made more practical decisions about the way they stay cool.

C) Some of Rome's greatest advancements were lost during the nation's decline in the 5th century.

D) A change of just a few degrees in temperature can make all the difference.

5

A) NO CHANGE
B) curtailing
C) reducing
D) dipping

6

A) NO CHANGE
B) Particularly,
C) Therefore,
D) Nevertheless,

[1] This began to change in the early 1900s. [2] It was at this time Nikola Tesla developed alternating current motors, which in turn made possible the invention of oscillating fans. [3] By 1902, a 25-year-old engineer from New York named Willis Carrier had also invented the first modern air-conditioning system, which sent air through water-cooled coils. [4] However, his early designs were only for industrial settings. **7** [5] It wasn't until 1922 that Carrier introduced a smaller version of his air conditioning technology to the public. **8**

7

If the author were to delete the preceding sentence, the paragraph would primarily lose:

A) a description of the many complications in adapting products for different consumer markets.

B) information clarifying the effect of Carrier's invention and connecting to the following sentence.

C) a statement that establishes the focus of the rest of the passage.

D) a detail emphasizing the environmental impact of air conditioning.

8

The author is considering adding the following sentence to the passage:

"Unfortunately, even the innovations in home building in the American South were still relatively limited to the wealthy."

If the author were to add this sentence to the passage, it should logically be placed:

A) before sentence 1.

B) after sentence 1.

C) after sentence 3.

D) after sentence 4.

Today, 80% of American households have some form of air conditioning, and it has grown from a luxury to a necessity. This technology has contributed in many ways to the quality of life in America and the industrialized world.

9 For example, thanks to climate control, heat-related deaths of infants and of the elderly have declined.

10 [1] Due to all the good that air conditioning has done, it has come at a price. [2] For years, many air conditioners relied on stable, nonflammable, moderately toxic gases or liquids called chlorofluorocarbons (CFCs) as refrigerants to produce their cooling effect. [3] More recently, CFCs were found to produce a "super-greenhouse effect" and to deplete the Earth's ozone layer. **11** [4] Thus the use of air conditioning helped create a vicious cycle. [5] It significantly contributed to rising global temperatures that humans naturally responded to by seeking more air conditioning. [6] Luckily, CFCs have been increasingly regulated since 1987 and less harmful and more energy-efficient alternatives are largely used today.

9
A) NO CHANGE
B) Similarly,
C) In spite of this,
D) On the other hand,

10
A) NO CHANGE
B) According to
C) In spite of
D) Instead of

11
To make the paragraph most logical, sentence 4 should be placed:

A) where it is now.
B) before sentence 1.
C) after sentence 1.
D) after sentence 6.

Notes and Reflections

Standard English Conventions – Pronouns 1

If it weren't for a friendly wager and a sack of flour, Reuelt Colt Gridley might have remained an unknown shopkeeper, one of many lost to the pages of history. However, in 1864, he made a fateful decision to run as the Democratic candidate for mayor in Austin, Nevada. Gridley accepted the bet proposed by his opponent, Republican candidate, Dr. H.S. Herrick: **1** whomever lost the race would carry a 50-pound sack of flour for more than a mile while a marching band played a tune of the winner's choice.

Gridley lost the race and accepted his fate graciously. He carried the designated flour sack decorated with red, white, and blue ribbons. **2** He and his son, who followed carrying an American flag, marched from Austin to the next town, Clinton. Along the way, Gridley attracted a crowd, and what started out as a loss turned into something he could never have imagined. When he arrived at the saloon where his parade was to end, Gridley realized **3** they didn't know what to do with the bag of flour. Nobody wanted **4** those, so someone suggested it be auctioned off for charity. Since the Civil War was coming to a close, the proceeds would go to the U.S. Sanitary Commission, an organization that aided wounded Union soldiers.

1
A) NO CHANGE
B) whoever
C) whatever
D) whatsoever

2
A) NO CHANGE
B) Him and his son, who
C) He and his son, whom
D) Him and his son, who

3
A) NO CHANGE
B) it
C) he
D) who

4
A) NO CHANGE
B) them
C) they
D) it

Although many parts of the country were suffering the effects of the war, the pockets of Nevada's residents were full due to the success of silver mines. **5** <u>They</u> had money to spare, especially if it was going to a good cause. In the saloon that day, **6** <u>it was</u> happy to bid on anything—even a sack of flour. They provoked one another to bid higher and higher. Finally, **7** <u>it was</u> a local millman who made the highest bid of more than two hundred dollars.

5
A) NO CHANGE
B) It
C) He
D) The people

6
A) NO CHANGE
B) it is
C) the miners were
D) OMIT

7
A) NO CHANGE
B) they were
C) is
D) OMIT

Samuel Clemens, better known as Mark Twain, immortalized the story of Gridley's sack of flour in his book *Roughing It*. He was a contemporary of Gridley and 8 its rumored they may have even gone to the same school. According to 9 him when the millman was asked where he'd like the flour delivered, he stated, "Nowhere—sell it again!" This cycle was repeated that day over and over, until $5,000 (about $75,000 today) had been collected.

The story doesn't stop there for Gridley. The failed politician, 10 which lost the mayorship but became locally famous because of that loss, was asked to come to the surrounding towns with his legendary sack of flour. Gridley went on to auction the sack of flour throughout the other wealthy mining areas of the west, including California. His last stop was in St. Louis, where the flour was finally used to make little cakes. 11 This was even sold for $1 each, which was the last of the funds the sack of flour generated for the Commission. In total, that one 50 lb. bag of flour raised close to $275,000 (about $4 million today) for the needs of the wounded Union soldiers.

8
A) NO CHANGE
B) it's
C) it
D) is

9
A) NO CHANGE
B) him,
C) Clemens
D) Clemens,

10
A) NO CHANGE
B) that
C) who
D) whose

11
A) NO CHANGE
B) That was
C) It was
D) These were

Standard English Conventions – Pronouns 2

Petra, the legendary Rose Red City, was forgotten. The ancient site had been neglected for thousands of years. [1] They were lost somewhere in modern day Jordan. Tucked into a desert valley within a range of mountains, [2] it's long hidden by the area's geographical features and mostly unknown to the world. The local Bedouin tribe knew of the city's history, but they had kept the path to Petra a secret and made an effort to dissuade or deceive each greedy treasure-hunter in order to protect [3] it from looting. Jean Louis Burckhardt was the first outsider to see Petra in more than 600 years. [4] They were closed off to Europeans, until Burckhardt laid his eyes on it once again on August 22, 1812.

1
A) NO CHANGE
B) They're
C) Its
D) It was

2
A) NO CHANGE
B) they were
C) the city of Petra was
D) DELETE

3
A) NO CHANGE
B) them
C) theirs
D) the city

4
A) NO CHANGE
B) Their
C) It was
D) Its

At [5] it's height, Petra was the center of the Nabataean kingdom. This once-nomadic Arab tribe had managed to amass vast wealth in the caravan trade, mostly dealing in frankincense and myrrh. Burckhardt, however, was not interested in wealth. Like many other young men of his [6] time, who wanted to explore the wonders of the world. However, his dedication surpassed that of many of his peers.

During Burckhardt's travels, he heard about Dr. Seetzen, who had set out from Egypt into Arabia in search of the lost city of Petra, but had been murdered. Burckhardt became enamored with this mystery and obsessed with finding [7] it. Burckhardt settled down in Syria, converted to Islam, and took the name Sheikh Ibrahim bin Abdullah. He gained access to areas and information, access that an outsider would be excluded from, because he was disguised by [8] this false identity. He traveled around the region of Syria, searching for information on Petra. Finally, he heard from local people about ruins near the supposed tomb of Aaron.

5

A) NO CHANGE
B) its
C) Petra's
D) a

6

A) NO CHANGE
B) time, whom
C) time, they
D) time, Burckhardt

7

A) NO CHANGE
B) that
C) them
D) the lost city

8

A) NO CHANGE
B) it
C) them
D) him

Burckhardt hired a guide to lead him to Aaron's tomb. Along the way to this site, [9] himself and his guide went straight through the ruins of Petra. Burckhardt was stunned when he finally saw the ruins of Petra. What took Burckhardt's breath away as he came out of the dark canyon were the soaring buildings of Petra that are carved directly into sandstone. The most famous of these is Al-Khazneh, or "The Treasury." The name is misleading, as [10] it is actually a tomb. It is twice as high as Mount Rushmore and boasts intricate carvings. Burckhardt discovered hundreds of buildings like [11] those before he was forced to leave. He was caught up in the splendor of majestic temples, which rose up in the midst of a desolate valley. However, the guide grew suspicious at Burckhardt's acute interest in the ruins. Burckhardt could not hide his wonder, and his disguise finally failed him. His guide recognized him as exactly the kind of person his tribe had been protecting these ruins from. "I see now clearly that you are an infidel!" his guide exclaimed, and Burckhardt was forced to return home before he could fully explore the city of Petra.

9
A) NO CHANGE
B) him
C) his
D) he

10
A) NO CHANGE
B) its
C) they're
D) there

11
A) NO CHANGE
B) this
C) them
D) theirs

Standard English Conventions – Pronouns 3

Two hundred years after the Salem Witch Trials, New England farmers became convinced that their relatives were rising from their graves to feed on **1 them**. To combat this supernatural menace, bodies were dug up and examined for evidence of vampiric activity. While **2 these investigations** began in the 1700s, most occurred in the late 1800s, in what became known as the Great New England Vampire Panic.

The fear of vampires almost always occurred in the midst of tuberculosis outbreaks. Tuberculosis, then known as consumption, was a disease that progressed in such a way that it seemed like the life and blood were being drained from the victim. With no readily available treatment for the disease, and the population of many communities already decimated by the casualties of the Civil War, people were desperate for answers about what was happening to **3 there** friends and family. A particularly appealing theory was disseminated throughout New England: vampires are roaming among the public, and **4 its** feeding on the flesh and blood of their still living loved ones.

1
A) NO CHANGE
B) those
C) it
D) the living citizens

2
A) NO CHANGE
B) these
C) they
D) this

3
A) NO CHANGE
B) they're
C) their
D) its

4
A) NO CHANGE
B) it's
C) their
D) they're

Each community dealt with [5] their vampire infestation differently. In many cases, only family and neighbors of the suspected vampire got involved, but in others, town fathers, clergymen, and even doctors would assist in the proceedings. In Maine and Massachusetts, bodies were simply flipped over. In places like Vermont and Rhode Island, however, they would often remove the corpse's heart and burn it. The infected person would breathe in the smoke and might even have been told to eat the ashes, which was believed to cure [6] their condition and restore health.

Word of these rituals spread. Local and foreign journalists commented on the phenomenon, wondering how people of modern times, some of whom lived fewer than twenty miles away from the summer homes of the scions of the Industrial Revolution, could believe in vampires. Theories ranged from the locals playing a practical joke on the rest of the world to [7] themselves having addled minds due to inbreeding.

5
A) NO CHANGE
B) they're
C) its
D) it's

6
A) NO CHANGE
B) they're
C) its
D) his or her

7
A) NO CHANGE
B) theirselves
C) them
D) they're

From a modern perspective, removed from these events by over a hundred years, the cause of this behavior seems clearer. When one finds **8** <u>themselves</u> in dire situations and has no guidance from rational authorities, **9** <u>one resorts</u> to alternative explanations and solutions. The New Englanders of the late 1800s were far less religious than their ancestors and were not properly educated in modern medicine. The tuberculosis bacterium was discovered in 1882 by a Prussian physician using a new staining method; unfortunately, it was some time before residents of rural areas heard about that discovery. Without scientific understanding or organized worship, people turned to folklore and superstition to help them face hardship and situations they could not understand. Faced with a rapidly dwindling population and no effective way of combatting **10** <u>it</u>, the people performed exhumations. The rituals offered evidence that the people in charge were doing everything they could to save **11** <u>it</u>. Fortunately, in this case, unlike the more famous witch trials, only the dead were disturbed, and in the 1940s, drug treatments for tuberculosis became available.

8
A) NO CHANGE
B) themself
C) oneself
D) them

9
A) NO CHANGE
B) one resort
C) you resort
D) your resorts

10
A) NO CHANGE
B) them
C) one
D) that situation

11
A) NO CHANGE
B) them
C) one
D) their peers

Notes and Reflections

Standard English Conventions – Subject-Verb Agreement 1

Maria Elena Gonzalez, internationally recognized for her innovative blend of architecture and sculpture, was born in Cuba in 1957. Just four years prior **1** <u>were</u> the onset of the Cuban Revolution. A Catholic by birth, Gonzalez's early life was influenced by that faith, but Castro's revolution and push toward an atheistic state were disruptive forces that quashed this religious influence. As an adult, Gonzalez's rediscovered faith, as well as her art, from small prints to large-scale displays, **2** <u>were</u> deeply reflective of those sensibilities.

Gonzalez left Cuba at the age of 11. Although left behind, her childhood homeland and faith **3** <u>is an influence</u> that colored her consciousness. As a young artist, she began exploring the idea of memory. Her 1990 work *Untitled*, for example, resembled a diptych, a two-paneled altarpiece or ancient writing tablet. On one of **4** <u>the panels were</u> a cloudy reflection of the other, just as memories are a muted reflection of the original person, place or event. Later exhibitions, such as *Mnemonic Architecture*, first installed at the Bronx Museum of Art, were based on memories of a childhood home. The life-size floor plan was recreated in a skewed, impressionistic manner to reflect the changes in perspective that the passing of years brings.

1
A) NO CHANGE
B) are
C) was
D) is

2
A) NO CHANGE
B) are
C) was
D) is

3
A) NO CHANGE
B) was an influence
C) were influences
D) influenced

4
A) NO CHANGE
B) the panels was
C) the panel were
D) the panel was

As Gonzalez continued to develop her craft, further exploring the relationship of memory to art, she held her first solo exhibition in New York in 1991, gaining additional exposure within the art community. The prestigious Rome Prize from the American Academy in Rome, as well as numerous grants, **5** <u>were</u> awarded to Gonzalez. It was during that fellowship in Rome that she would rediscover her childhood faith, indelibly marking her works to come.

Italy's most populous city and home of Vatican City, the center of Roman Catholicism, Rome would be the site of both a rekindling of Gonzalez's Catholic faith and a launching of new artistic ideas. **6** <u>In this site,</u> the Sistine Chapel, St. Peter's Basilica, and Vatican Museums, which house religious artifacts. For Gonzalez, the sight of relics, such as a saint's bone, lock of hair, or possession, and reliquaries, the often jewel-encrusted containers that held **7** <u>it, was</u> an inspiring confluence of religion and design.

5
A) NO CHANGE
B) was
C) had
D) DELETE

6
A) NO CHANGE
B) In this, site
C) In this site is
D) In this site are

7
A) NO CHANGE
· B) it, were
C) them, was
D) them, were

Renaissance paintings depicting St. Catherine and St. Lawrence **8** were certainly influential to Gonzalez. The spiked wheel and gridiron used to torture and kill **9** them makes an appearance in her New York exhibition entitled *The Project*, where sections of a spiked wheel are embossed on paper and sketched in graphite, and a gridiron emerges as both a barred window and a stark floor sculpture. Gonzalez's *Internal DupliCity* installation a few years later at Knoedler & Company presented a different iteration of a similar theme. There, a set of nine blood-red scale models of Roman structures—burial vaults, Renaissance villas, and agrarian sheds— **10** appearing on white pedestals, each model encased in a frosted Plexiglas box. While the boxes are not bejeweled and the contents lack clarifying details, the reference to reliquaries is unmistakable.

A Guggenheim Fellow in 2006, Gonzalez has continued to create works of unique design. An artist, sculptor, and teacher who constantly **11** pushes, the boundaries of what art is and how we create and interact with it, Maria Elena Gonzalez continues to make a unique contribution to the world by allowing her personal journey and rediscovered faith to so poignantly inform her art.

8
A) NO CHANGE
B) were influentially certain
C) was certainly influential
D) was influentially certain

9
A) NO CHANGE
B) them make
C) him makes
D) him make

10
A) NO CHANGE
B) appears
C) appear
D) DELETE

11
A) NO CHANGE
B) push, the boundaries
C) pushes the boundaries
D) push the boundaries

Standard English Conventions – Subject-Verb Agreement 2

Alan Finkel has been involved in public art for many years. One of his pieces, called *View for the Catenary Curve*, the first of a Public Arts Fund series of works, **1** being a modified water tower created to operate as a viewing station for the iconic Brooklyn Bridge. Created in the early 1980s, this public art installation was part of a project to bring art to ignored portions of the five boroughs' waterfronts. Finkel may not be a household name, but he has worked steadily in the arts and **2** have been frequently part of exhibitions in New York's Museum of Modern Art.

In Japan, Finkel has been part of the Haizuka Earthworks Project (HEP), which was formed due to the construction of a dam. A group including local citizens, Japanese artists, and foreign artists **3** having been assembled to contribute to the project. The building of a new dam may not sound like an opportunity to create art, but that has been one of the goals of HEP. Part of the agreement made in building the dam was that the leaders of the project would inform citizens of each phase of the construction, as well as hear suggestions from local people on how to best provide for a region in flux. Dams frequently cause widespread ecological damage. HEP was formed to use an artistic approach to combat negative outcomes to the environment and culture.

1
A) NO CHANGE
B) been
C) are
D) is

2
A) NO CHANGE
B) is
C) are
D) were

3
A) NO CHANGE
B) have been
C) were
D) DELETE

The proposal for the dam was made in 1965 as a result of frequent flooding of a part of the Gonokawa River, located about 40 miles from Hiroshima. The construction of the dam and the resulting effect on the Gonokawa River **4** were certain to greatly change the landscape and the agricultural practices in the area. The lake created by the dam would displace enormous quantities of water, putting parts of three towns, Mirasaka, Kisa and Soryo, underwater and causing many people to relocate. In addition to the relocation of people, the top layer of soil in agricultural portions of the region would be transported so citizens could continue growing rice in this fertile dirt. There **5** has been, for this reason, many people who opposed the building of the dam. However, the threat of more flooding, a failing local economy, and a declining population made the construction of the dam crucial.

The goals of the HEP organization, such as nature preservation, community revitalization, artist colony formation, and workshop creation, **6** which sounds lofty. Projects have ranged from growing a small amount of moss to building bridges. Often in Japan, such care has not been taken to preserve culture and the environment in the name of progress. The landscape in the country is scarred by damaged mountains and improperly-cared-for forests. HEP is an example of the country moving toward a greater consideration for conservation and public approval.

4
A) NO CHANGE
B) was
C) has
D) have

5
A) NO CHANGE
B) have
C) were
D) was

6
A) NO CHANGE
B) which sound
C) sounds
D) sound

Completed projects by HEP, most consisting of the creation of parks, **7** <u>includes</u> some fascinating multi-use spaces. One of these spaces, constructed to help secure the river banks, also **8** <u>has</u> an open air stage. Another, the Natkatsukuni Mid-Earth Park, contains a variety of trees and plants. A small series of parks is clustered around the largest bridge in the area and is designed to allow people to listen to nature: they are even named after various animals, like *Otter's Ear*.

In Soryo, Finkel has contributed to the landscape by creating *Wind Mirage*, a large outdoor sculpture. He's not interested in nostalgia but in maintaining place: allowing citizens to remain active and proud of their region. Finkel, as well as the other participants in HEP, is aware of the mental damage that locals will incur in addition to the physical impact on the area. With this in mind, the legacy of local plants, stories, buildings, and **9** <u>traditions has been</u> preserved and documented. The building of the dam and of its accompanying parks and art installations **10** <u>have had</u> a lasting impact, much of it negative, but Finkel, along with the rest of HEP, **11** <u>were</u> still working hard to ease the transition. The actions HEP continues to take could be considered as healing, and the dam could be considered as the wound.

7
A) NO CHANGE
B) include
C) including
D) that include

8
A) NO CHANGE
B) have
C) having
D) have had

9
A) NO CHANGE
B) traditions have been
C) tradition have been
D) tradition

10
A) NO CHANGE
B) has had
C) have
D) DELETE

11
A) NO CHANGE
B) are
C) have
D) is

Notes and Reflections

Standard English Conventions – Comparisons 1

It might surprise most people to find out that the city of Cincinnati, Ohio, is named after a Roman leader who lived 2,500 years ago. Although Lucius Quinctius Cincinnatus lived long before America was even thought of as a possibility, he upheld many ideals that the United States was founded upon. Early Americans, who held a common knowledge of classical history and literature, even compared the noble character of George Washington to **1** that of the ancient Roman leader, giving the former the nickname of "the American Cincinnatus." When given the choice between power and principle, they both chose the path **2** most honorable. These men resisted becoming attached to the rewards of their positions, and this integrity defined their reputations as great leaders more than any **3** characteristic.

In the time of 458 B.C., Cincinnatus had retired to a quiet life on his four-acre farm after serving as a consul for the legal term of one year. He had performed so well as a counselor that his peers encouraged him to serve another term, but he refused to do so because it was against Roman law. That year, when Rome was attacked, the ruling senate decided Cincinnatus would make a better commander in chief **4** than anyone. Our modern martial law is similar **5** to Rome, which allowed for the temporary appointment of a dictator during times of

1
A) NO CHANGE
B) the leader of ancient Rome
C) the ancient Roman leader
D) each other

2
A) NO CHANGE
B) mostly
C) more
D) as

3
A) NO CHANGE
B) other characteristic
C) others
D) OMIT

4
A) NO CHANGE
B) then anyone
C) than anyone else
D) then anyone else

5
A) NO CHANGE
B) to Rome's
C) with Rome
D) with Roman

military emergency. Whoever was appointed would serve for a limited term of six months and have absolute authority during that time. The senators were confident Cincinnatus would not take advantage of his role. There was great risk in giving one citizen such power. Later dictators, such as Julius Caesar, who abused his role by appointing himself dictator for life, proved to have more corruptible characters than **6** Cincinnatus.

At first, Cincinnatus was reluctant to leave his simple life and accept the role of dictator. However, spurred by patriotism, he agreed to respond to this call to serve his homeland. He was revered by people throughout the Roman empire and earned an esteemed reputation comparable to **7** a savior or master. Within 15 days, the Roman army claimed victory over its enemies and peace returned. Immediately following Rome's victory, on day sixteen of his reign, he resigned and returned to his small farm, grateful to have been of service. He showed no reluctance in giving up this office and seemed happy to have shed the weight of such responsibility. For Cincinnatus, it was more important to preserve the integrity of Rome's laws than **8** preserving power.

6
A) NO CHANGE
B) did Cincinnatus
C) that
D) him

7
A) NO CHANGE
B) a savior or a master
C) a savior's or master's
D) saviors or masters

8
A) NO CHANGE
B) to power
C) power's
D) to preserve his own power

In a story resembling <u>9 of Cincinnatus</u>, Washington spent his days before the American Revolutionary War running his plantation at Mount Vernon. When the war commenced in April of 1775, Washington was unanimously elected as commander in chief of the army. In the chaos of the Revolution, when Americans were looking for direction, Washington, like Cincinnatus, could have taken control as a dictator. Rather, when the war was over in 1783, he readily resigned from his post and returned to his farm. Today, Washington is remembered more as a defender of democracy than <u>10 as a commander</u>.

In an age when we seem to be surrounded by corruption, Cincinnatus and Washington serve as reminders of venerable leaders. When given the choice between authority or integrity, they both chose the path <u>11 least likely</u> to compromise the political values of their nations.

9
A) NO CHANGE
B) that Cincinnatus
C) that of Cincinnatus
D) of that Cincinnatus

10
A) NO CHANGE
B) of a commander
C) of commander
D) a commander

11
A) NO CHANGE
B) lesser likely
C) less likely
D) least like

Standard English Conventions – Comparisons 2

Paul Cezanne is one of the most esteemed artists in history, though that opinion is more commonly held by critics, art historians, and other **1** artists than the public at large. It's a shame that Cezanne, though he has been so influential, has not achieved a reputation as beloved and widespread with the general public **2** as that of many other Impressionists and Post Impressionists. His paintings are **3** less accessibly than those of artists such as Van Gogh and Monet. They lack the eye-popping color and excitement of Van Gogh's landscapes, the soft prettiness of Monet's *Waterlilies*, or the sensuous exoticism of Gauguin's scenes of the tropics.

Cezanne painted still life, portraits, and landscapes, but his artistic obsession was with the structure of objects, whether a mountain, an apple, or the human face and body. Between the subject matter and the act of painting itself, the latter was **4** the more important to him. He was more concerned with the method and application of paint—the mechanics of the art—than **5** classical artists of his time. His breaking up of forms into multiple points of view led to the development of Cubism and other forms of abstraction. However, this revolutionary approach was not easily understood or accepted at the time.

1
A) NO CHANGE
B) artists then the public
C) artists than by the public
D) artists then by the public

2
A) NO CHANGE
B) as that
C) as
D) than

3
A) NO CHANGE
B) less accessible
C) least accessibly
D) least accessible

4
A) NO CHANGE
B) the most important
C) most important
D) more importantly

5
A) NO CHANGE
B) that of classical artists of his time
C) were classical artists of his time
D) classical artists' of his time

Cezanne was a difficult man in his personal life, as well. Of his aloofness, tendency to hold grudges, and violent temper, the aloofness was **6** most influential in driving away his few friends and relationships. The most long lasting and productive relationship of his life was with a woman named Hortense Fiquet, who was his model, muse, and long-suffering companion, and eventually his wife. He was initially attracted by the sharp geometry of her face and body, which he painted over and over. At least 29 paintings of her survive. He approached her more as an inanimate object than **7** a living human being, recording her as a collection of shapes: triangles, ovals and oblongs. This is obvious in the lack of personality she displays; indeed, she seems stern and unhappy in many of the portraits. This may have something to do with the long and grueling sessions without moving a muscle. He greatly admired her for her ability to hold a pose for a length of time longer than **8** that which most people would be capable of, and he would work on a single painting over the course of months or even years. This was true of his non-portraits as well: the fruit in his still life setups often rotted, requiring the substitution of fake fruit.

6
A) NO CHANGE
B) mostly influentially
C) most influentially
D) more influential

7
A) NO CHANGE
B) living human beings
C) as a living human being
D) as living human beings

8
A) NO CHANGE
B) most
C) most people
D) capable

The couple's relationship was **9** as colder than most: he insisted on his freedom to paint and they lived apart for much of the time. Eventually, after 17 years together and the birth of a son, Cezanne married Hortense. This was more to ensure an inheritance for his beloved son, Paul, than **10** showing his affection for Hortense. Indeed, he publically announced his lack of feelings for her, and left her for good later that year, 1887.

Though his personal relationships were strained, Cezanne's art created many favorable bonds. Success came later to Cezanne than **11** most artists. It wasn't until he was in his mid-fifties that he was able to survive solely on the income from his paintings. And over a century later, his fame is still slowly growing and his work continues to inspire. His influence has been acknowledged by many of the superstars of 20th century art. "He was like the father of us all," said Picasso. A recent exhibit was based on the premise that no artist had a bigger influence on art of the 20th century than Paul Cézanne. Among the many artists who acknowledge his influence are Mondrian, Braque, Giacometti, and Marsden Hartley. As Matisse commented, "Cézanne, you see, is a sort of God of painting."

9
A) NO CHANGE
B) more colder
C) coldest
D) colder

10
A) NO CHANGE
B) his affection showing
C) to show his affection
D) a show of his affection

11
A) NO CHANGE
B) it does to most artists
C) more artists
D) artists

Notes and Reflections

Standard English Conventions – Idioms 1

Our addiction to coffee can be traced back centuries into mankind's stimulant-seeking past. A common legend of the discovery **1** in coffee is that of Kaldi, an Ethiopian goat-herder who noticed that his flock, upon nibbling on the red fruits of a particular tree, grew so spirited that they began prancing and frolicking. **2** <u>Curiosity about</u> what made his goats dance so energetically, Kaldi ate some of the berries, and soon he was also dancing. The coffee berries gave him a rush of caffeine, a powerful stimulant. Kaldi's passion for coffee quickly spread **3** <u>on</u> the local monasteries, where monks began roasting and brewing coffee beans so they could stay awake throughout long days of prayer. By the 16th century, the culture of coffee had spread across Yemen, Egypt, Turkey, and throughout the Near East. Coffee became so vital to these societies that, in some areas, a woman could divorce her husband **4** <u>for</u> the grounds of not providing her with enough of the beverage.

1
A) NO CHANGE
B) of
C) with
D) about

2
A) NO CHANGE
B) Curiosity to
C) Curious about
D) Curious to

3
A) NO CHANGE
B) for
C) to
D) DELETE

4
A) NO CHANGE
B) with
C) about
D) on

The first recording of a coffee shop was in Constantinople – now known as Istanbul. As brewers devised new methods **5** <u>with preparing</u> the drink to fully extract its flavor, coffee shops grew in popularity. These were places where people could meet to discuss ideas and exchange views. The invigorating effect of coffee was so encouraging of thought and discussion that coffee shops were commonly **6** <u>known for</u> "schools for the wise." From the beginning, coffee shops were centers for political dialogue, and they were often closed down by governments that worried **7** <u>for</u> unrest and opposing ideologies would spread. More commonly, however, coffee shops were peaceful places where people gathered to gossip, tell stories, read, and relax. Coffee had gained popularity in Europe by the 17th century. European explorers had returned with stories and samples of the beverage.

In time, coffee houses were seen throughout European cities. Here, as in the Near East, coffee houses were common places for the exchange of ideas. In England, these shops were called "penny universities," because for the price of a single penny anyone could enter and join in intellectual conversation. As these shops became gathering areas for academics and thinkers, they also became the **8** <u>subjective controversy</u>.

5
A) NO CHANGE
B) to preparing
C) of preparing
D) in preparation

6
A) NO CHANGE
B) known as
C) known to
D) known

7
A) NO CHANGE
B) to
C) about
D) DELETE

8
A) NO CHANGE
B) subject in controversy
C) subject of controversy
D) subject on controversy

At several points in history, coffee houses became the targets of leaders who felt their authority threatened. In the late 1500s, Catholic officials were trying to put an end **9** to the spread of coffee-drinking in Europe. Since the drink originated from the Islamic world, which the Catholic Church opposed, it was deemed "Satanic." However, Pope Clement VIII decided to sample the beverage before condemning it. The Pope must have enjoyed his first cup: instead of banning coffee, he gave the drink his blessing. In 1685, King Charles II attempted to rid England of its thousands of coffee houses. Despite the king's concerns, the people of England were unwilling to give **10** of their cafés, and the attempt to close England's coffeehouses failed in just a few days. The fears of coffee fueling rebellious ideas proved true in early America. In Boston, the Green Dragon was a famous coffeehouse, and the host to patriots who first planned the revolution against Great Britain. At a time when the British imposed severe taxes on tea, coffee was often the drink of choice and became a symbol of rebellion and American patriotism.

Throughout its contentious history, coffee has remained a vital part of human culture. Willing to brave controversy and combat **11** to defense of their beloved bean, coffee-drinkers have proudly and bravely supported the energizing beverage. For some, the rich flavor and the jolt it can offer in the morning (or any time of day!) is just too good to give up.

9
A) NO CHANGE
B) too
C) with
D) in

10
A) NO CHANGE
B) off
C) up
D) with

11
A) NO CHANGE
B) of
C) with
D) in

SUMMIT
EDUCATIONAL
GROUP

Standard English Conventions – Idioms 2

Over 150 years after the theory of evolution revolutionized modern thought, Charles Darwin is a household name. In fact, Darwin is so strongly linked to his theory of natural selection and evolution **1** as the concept is often called "Darwinism." While Darwin's name and fame continue to grow with time, other scientists of his time have been forgotten to history. Charles Darwin was not the only scientist in the mid-nineteenth century working **2** for a theory of evolution. Like Darwin, Alfred Russel Wallace was a British naturalist researching evolution in the 1850s, and he is one of the reasons why Darwin is a figure famous to us today.

Alfred Russel Wallace was born in 1823. He earned an elementary education at a grammar school, but received no schooling after the age of fifteen. After grammar school, he worked with his brother on engineering and surveying projects for six years. Most of this work was outdoors where he became interested **3** in the plants and animals that crossed his path. Wallace took a position **4** is an English teacher in 1844 but continued to develop his passion for the outdoors through reading. He read accounts of expeditions and voyages by Humboldt and Darwin. In 1848, Wallace **5** set up on an adventure himself. He traveled to the Amazon and explored the region for four years. Despite a fire destroying most of his notes, Wallace published a book on his experience in the Amazon in 1853.

1
A) NO CHANGE
B) than
C) that
D) so

2
A) NO CHANGE
B) in
C) on
D) to

3
A) NO CHANGE
B) as
C) to
D) for

4
A) NO CHANGE
B) to
C) as
D) about

5
A) NO CHANGE
B) set out
C) left out
D) left over

Wallace continued to explore, travelling to the Malay Archipelago where he conducted research and formed his ideas on evolution. During this eight year expedition, Wallace investigated the immense diversity of the region's flora and fauna. He collected over 100,000 specimens of insects, birds, and animals, which he **6** gave up British museums. On this expedition, Wallace recognized that evolution was a characteristic of all living things, and in 1855, he published a piece about the gradual process in which new species are introduced in regions inhabited by similar species.

A couple of years later, when he was confined indoors due **7** with a fever, Wallace realized animals have the ability **8** adapt to their environment. He reasoned that the animals who survive pass **9** out beneficial characteristics to their offspring. In a matter of weeks, he wrote an essay about his theory and sent it to Charles Darwin. Wallace also requested Darwin to send it to Sir Charles Lyell, a prominent geologist.

6
A) NO CHANGE
B) gave in
C) gave out
D) gave to

7
A) NO CHANGE
B) for
C) to
D) from

8
A) NO CHANGE
B) of adapt of
C) with adapting
D) to adapt to

9
A) NO CHANGE
B) on
C) with
D) from

SUMMIT
EDUCATIONAL
GROUP

By this time, Darwin had been working on this topic for twenty years, but this letter impelled him to hasten his work. After Darwin sought advice **10** for Lyell and Joseph Hooker, a botanist, he wrote an abstract concerning his own theory. Darwin's and Wallace's ideas were combined in a joint paper, which Lyell and Hooker presented in July of 1858 at the Linean Society in London. Just over a year after this presentation, Darwin published a book on his theory, titled "The Origin of Species." Wallace's article the year before had provoked Darwin to publish his research.

While it would seem natural for a rivalry to form between Wallace and Darwin, the two scientists often gave credit to each other. Wallace continued his career through addresses and articles in which he insisted Darwin had the honor of discovering the theory. In response, Darwin stated how he felt ashamed to take the credit.

Alfred Russel Wallace is an inspiring figure in history, both because of his scientific advancement and as a result **11** from his willingness to credit and elevate others in his field. Although Darwin is the scientist to whom natural selection is accredited, it is important to recognize that he was not the only scientist working towards the theory. Many other scientists, such as Wallace, also contributed to the way we understand evolution and how it impacts our world.

10
A) NO CHANGE
B) from
C) to
D) as

11
A) NO CHANGE
B) for
C) of
D) with

SUMMIT
EDUCATIONAL
GROUP

Notes and Reflections

Standard English Conventions – Diction 1

"Victory attained by violence is tantamount to a defeat, for it is momentary." These are the words of Mahatma Gandhi, the man who led the charge for India's independence from British rule through peace in protests. Almost twenty years after Ghandi's death, Cesar Chavez, leader of the National Farmworkers Association (NFA), used Gandhi's nonviolent approach to fight for the **1** rights of grape workers in California.

The Delano Grape Boycott began on September 8th, 1965, when a group of workers walked out of their farm jobs to demand that their employers **2** ensure fare wages and better treatment. This group of mostly Filipino men contacted Cesar Chavez to help them in their effort. Chavez was in charge of the predominantly Latino NFA, and his union agreed to join the grape workers' strike. This unification was key to the strike; if the groups didn't work together, Mexican American workers would be brought **3** into break the strike. Of Mexican American **4** decent and a farm worker himself, Chavez insisted the strike remain non-violent, putting into action the practices of Gandhi and Martin Luther King Jr., men he studied and admired. Chavez, in addition to requesting peaceful action, felt that persistence would be the farm workers' greatest asset. He was not willing to give up, and he expected other protesters to fight for as long as it took. The striking workers were already poor, but they were willing to risk further poverty for their cause.

1
A) NO CHANGE
B) rites
C) writes
D) wrights

2
A) NO CHANGE
B) ensure fair
C) insure fair
D) insure fare

3
A) NO CHANGE
B) into brake
C) in to break
D) in to brake

4
A) NO CHANGE
B) dissent
C) descent
D) docent

SUMMIT
EDUCATIONAL
GROUP

Perseverance did prove to be a powerful tool, but not without drawbacks. Two and a half years into the strike, some workers were understandably **5** <u>losing patience</u>. These workers wanted to use violence against the employers who had mistreated them for so long, but Chavez remained committed to **6** <u>peace and lead</u> a 300-mile march to draw attention to the strike. This march started with just seventy workers and ended with thousands of supporters. Chavez also ran other campaigns, protests, and marches for the cause. While the workers remained non-violent, their opponents did not. The strikers were abused and threatened by grape growers and community leaders. Still, Chavez stayed the course.

Chavez was instrumental in spreading the word to the American people not to buy Delano grapes, and the movement to boycott grapes extended across and beyond the borders of the United States. Not **7** <u>a lot have</u> people could afford to take such a broad action as going on strike, but individuals could easily avoid buying table grapes to show solidarity with the workers. Chavez understood that the culmination of all actions, great and small, would ultimately lead to victory.

5
A) NO CHANGE
B) loosing patience
C) losing patients
D) loosing patients

6
A) NO CHANGE
B) piece and lead
C) piece and led
D) peace and led

7
A) NO CHANGE
B) a lot of
C) alot of
D) allot of

Three years into the boycott, Chavez began a hunger strike. The water-only fast lasted twenty-five days, during which Chavez lost 35 pounds. At this point, there was some disagreement among his previous supporters. Not everyone involved in the strike agreed with this fast: [8] sum felled it was a powerful symbol while others didn't understand the purpose of his actions. Chavez described the fast as the purification of his body, [9] mined, and soul. "The fast," he explained, "is also a heartfelt prayer for purification and strengthening for all those who work beside me in the farm worker movement." He ended the fast at an event attended by thousands of people at the Forty Acres Complex, the headquarters of the strike. With this fast, Chavez was mirroring methods employed by Gandhi, who often used fasting as a form of political protest. While it's hard to measure the [10] effect, the number of people in attendance at its cessation certainly tell a tale of success.

The entire strike lasted for five years. By this time, a lot of the workers had lost all of their worldly possessions to remain on strike. Going without pay for such a long period of time had to be [11] specially challenging for impoverished workers, but their hard work did pay off. Grape Growers signed a contract in 1970, giving workers better wages and more benefits. This protest stimulated the labor movement and inspired minorities to demand better working conditions for many decades.

8
A) NO CHANGE
B) some felled
C) some felt
D) sum felt

9
A) NO CHANGE
B) mind, and soul
C) mind, and sole
D) mined, and sole

10
A) NO CHANGE
B) affect, the number
C) effect, the amount
D) affect, the amount

11
A) NO CHANGE
B) specific
C) especially
D) special

Standard English Conventions – Diction 2

On the surface, food and science can appear to be two entirely separate disciplines. Studying and problem solving are not frequently connected to cuisine, nor are cooking and eating associated with the scientific method. Nevertheless, not only is there a significant overlap **1** between the principals of science and the joy of food, but also that overlap is continually being expanded. As our understanding of the chemistry of cuisine deepens, **2** there is fewer distinction between chemists and chefs.

What is the kitchen, if not a laboratory? Both are places **3** where being too careless can result in disaster. What is a recipe, if not a list of materials and procedures for a culinary experiment to be carried out? Science has long played a main role in the preparation of food, from hard boiling eggs to baking bread. But in most cases, the scientific phenomena were simply observed without being fully understood. Cheese makers, for example, were practicing their craft long before they understood the science behind their art. If they had access to modern scientific understanding, they **4** would of seen how bacteria, enzymes, and acids work together to transform milk into countless varieties of cheese.

1
A) NO CHANGE
B) between the principles
C) among the principles
D) among the principals

2
A) NO CHANGE
B) their is less
C) there is less
D) their is fewer

3
A) NO CHANGE
B) were being too
C) where being to
D) were being to

4
A) NO CHANGE
B) would of scene
C) would have seen
D) would have scene

Only recently have some chefs sought to comprehend more fully the specific scientific properties behind the physical and chemical transformations of ingredients. This quest for delectable understanding, known as molecular gastronomy, has been driven by a strong sense of curiosity and of boundless potential. Hungarian physicist Nicholas Kurti, one of the pioneers in the field, once asked, "Is it not quite amazing that today we know more about the temperature distribution in the atmosphere of the planet Venus than that in the center of our soufflé?" Kurti's question—and the motivation behind it—**5** spored an increased interest in the field. Considering the possibilities for new flavors and experiences, experimental chefs will no longer **6** accept anything less than bold, odd, or surprising.

Over the last few decades, molecular gastronomy has been used both to better understand existing ingredients and to create new foods. Hervé This, a pioneer of molecular gastronomy, is both a physical chemist and a renowned culinary professor and experimenter. His obsession with the science of food began with his own soufflé crisis: when trying to perfect a recipe, he was frustrated by the instruction to add eggs two at a time, rather than all at once. He wondered if the recommendation **7** maybe baste more on tradition than science.

5
A) NO CHANGE
B) spared
C) sparred
D) spurred

6
A) NO CHANGE
B) except anything less than
C) accept anything fewer than
D) except anything fewer than

7
A) NO CHANGE
B) maybe based
C) may be baste
D) may be based

As a scientist, This sought to understand the chemical processes of creating foods. It inspired him to join forces with Nicholas Kurti and apply molecular gastronomy to undertake an evaluation of the countless French sauces. **8** Through there investigation, This discovered that all of these sauces belong to a limited number of groups based on the type of "complex disperse system" used to prepare the sauce. With this understanding, This and other chefs are able to **9** devise knew methods of creating innovative sauces that retain characteristics of the classics. At the most extreme, This imagines constructing foods from their most basic components. Imagine a recipe involving a series of chemicals and compounds in exact measurements, precisely calibrated to be perfectly delicious.

Other advancements push beyond the classics and into entirely foreign territory. Molecular gastronomy has afforded a number of innovative techniques. One such technique is spherification, which relies on a simple gelling reaction **10** between small amounts of calcium chloride, alginate (found in brown seaweed), and a liquid to create edible, flavorful beads of everything from apple juice to liquid olives. Another technique, flavor juxtaposition, uses an understanding of the molecules responsible for flavors to create striking pairings, such as caramelized cauliflower and cocoa. In this way, science enables chefs to be adventurous and unique while **11** ensuring new flavors will compliment one another.

8
A) NO CHANGE
B) Threw their
C) Through their
D) Threw there

9
A) NO CHANGE
B) devise new
C) device knew
D) device new

10
A) NO CHANGE
B) between small numbers
C) among small amounts
D) among small numbers

11
A) NO CHANGE
B) insuring new flavors will compliment
C) ensuring new flavors will complement
D) insuring new flavors will complement

Notes and Reflections

Standard English Conventions – Fragments 1

In the industrial sector on the outskirts of Jaipur, India, **1** where summer heat swelters to an average of nearly 100° Fahrenheit and peaks at temperatures significantly higher. Here, cooling the environment is not a luxury but a necessity. In this area, one **2** building, in particular, which uses cooling methods that are surprisingly simple and effective, if not especially innovative. The Pearl Academy of Fashion employs traditional architectural features, namely "jaali" and "baoli," to efficiently beat the heat.

3 Jaali, a traditional type of latticework composed of ornamental patterns. The decorative designs of jaali are based on geometry or elements of calligraphy, but this aspect of jaali is more about artistry than practicality. The function of jaali is to serve as a filter providing partial shade from sunlight, as well as some protection from wind. In **4** effect, they are ornate window shades, but on the Pearl Academy they work on a much larger scale, covering the whole exterior of

1
A) NO CHANGE
B) when
C) if
D) DELETE

2
A) NO CHANGE
B) building, which, in particular,
C) building, which,
D) building, in particular,

3
A) NO CHANGE
B) Jaali, which is
C) Jaali, being
D) Jaali is

4
A) NO CHANGE
B) effect, they are,
C) effect, are
D) effect,

the building. The architectural firm Morphogenesis, which designed the Pearl Academy, calculated the optimal setup for the jaali covering. The shades **5** placed 4 feet from the external walls, providing ideal light diffusion and heat absorption. Altogether, the use of jaali allows the building to stay cool while also honoring regional architectural traditions.

In addition to the use of jaali, a special pool of water **6** that cools the Pearl Academy of Fashion. Dating back to the 2nd century, baoli, or "stepwells," **7** are a traditional feature of Indian architecture. Many people, when picturing a well, will imagine a cylinder reaching down into the earth with a pulley for pulling buckets of water up from below. A stepwell is a much more impressive and useful structure. As the name suggests, a stepwell is a trench with a series of steps descending below ground level and a pool of water at its base. They may sink as far as 10 stories below the surface to allow access to the water table. In a climate that is arid through most of the year but has a few weeks of intense monsoon **8** rains. Stepwells allow access to subterranean water levels that can widely fluctuate. During the late dry season, when water is scarce, people may have to descend to the very lowest levels

5
A) NO CHANGE
B) that were placed
C) were placed
D) DELETE

6
A) NO CHANGE
B) to cool
C) cooling
D) cools

7
A) NO CHANGE
B) a traditional feature
C) traditionally feature
D) are traditionally featured

8
A) NO CHANGE
B) rains; stepwells
C) rains: stepwells
D) rains, stepwells

of the stepwell for water. On the other hand, during the monsoon season, 9 when the waters may be only a step or two lower than the surface. No matter the time of year, people could access the stores of water, though it might require climbing quite a few steps. Another benefit of baoli was their cooling effects. As the open pool of water evaporated, it altered the climate in the immediate vicinity. Near the baoli, 10 temperatures would be cooler. For this reason, palaces and gardens utilized baoli as sources of water and milder weather. Over the centuries, baoli became increasingly elaborate accomplishments of architecture, engineering, and art. It is fitting, then, that the Pearl Academy of Fashion would incorporate one into its design. The Pearl Academy's stepwell is only a few meters deep, but this is enough to cool the building's interior.

In the hottest days of summer, the Pearl Academy of Fashion is 20 degrees cooler inside than it is outside. This incredible difference is entirely due to passive cooling technologies based on ancient methods. 11 Architect Manit Rastogi, who designed the Pearl Academy. He marvels at the cleverness of ancient architects. The effectiveness of Rastogi's traditional designs serves as an inspiration to other architects. Passive cooling methods can save long-term building management expenses and reduce the environmental impact of construction and upkeep.

9
A) NO CHANGE
B) since
C) so
D) DELETE

10
A) NO CHANGE
B) where temperatures would be cooler
C) if temperatures would be cooler
D) cooler temperatures

11
A) NO CHANGE
B) Designed by architect Manit Rastogi,
C) It was architect Manit Rastogi who designed
D) Manit Rastogi, who was the architect who designed

SUMMIT
EDUCATIONAL
GROUP

Standard English Conventions – Fragments 2

Technically capable of self-pollination, avocados are challenging to cultivate. The flowers of an avocado tree have both pollen and stigma; however, these flowers are unique because they switch between male and female. Commonly, an avocado flower will first open in the morning, as the temperature warms, with a functional stigma, which is used to collect pollen. The **1** flowers, which close after several hours and then reopen the next day, in the afternoon, now functionally male, spreading pollen. This schedule **2** known for a "Type A" flowering sequence. Trees with a "Type B" sequence **3** following the opposite schedule, with flowers dispersing pollen in the morning and collecting pollen in the afternoon. On each avocado tree, all flowers are synchronized. In other words, the flowers on an avocado tree will not be a mix of male and female at the same time. It may happen that the pollen released by an avocado flower one day will still be around to pollinate the same flower on the next day, but the odds of that are very low. The flowers of an avocado tree sprout in bunches of 2 to 3 hundred and may number a million in total. This might seem excessive, but out of every thousand flowers, only a few **4** that will produce fruit.

1
A) NO CHANGE
B) flowers that
C) flowers,
D) flowers

2
A) NO CHANGE
B) known to be
C) known as
D) is known as

3
A) NO CHANGE
B) that follow
C) follows
D) follow

4
A) NO CHANGE
B) producing
C) producers of
D) DELETE

WRITING & LANGUAGE 215

The Haas avocado is a particularly desirable cultivar. You may recognize these plump fruits from the grocery market. **5** Their bumpy, dark skin and grow soft around their stem when ripe. Haas are especially popular because they are fatty, flavorful, and pleasantly soft when ripe. The difficulty with this cultivar, however, is they are all Type A. In an orchard of only Haas avocado trees, pollination is unlikely because all flowers will be either male or female at once. **6** Leading to the question: how are markets so full of Haas avocados if these fruits are so notoriously difficult to produce?

Though it may seem counterintuitive, **7** it is in the avocado trees' best interest to discourage self-pollination. It could be very simple for flowers to pollinate themselves, eliminating the logistical complications of pollination among multiple trees or across spans of time. However, self-pollination, like inbreeding, leads to problems due to lack of genetic variation. Genetic diversity through cross-pollination brings hardiness to species, so plants such as the avocado have developed traits that encourage this.

5
A) NO CHANGE
B) There
C) They have
D) They've

6
A) NO CHANGE
B) This leads
C) Leads
D) A lead

7
A) NO CHANGE
B) is in
C) in
D) DELETE

SUMMIT
EDUCATIONAL
GROUP

Ironically, while evolution has tried to encourage genetic diversity, most Haas avocado trees are clones. In order to ensure that the fruits all have the same desirable traits, new avocado trees **8** that are grown through "grafting." When a tree grown from an avocado seed sprouts into a small tree, it is trimmed down to its trunk, and small branches from a mature tree are implanted onto it. While the seed's sprout will grow into the root system, the new tree's branches and fruit will all be genetically identical to its donor tree. Nearly all of California's Haas trees are clones of a single ancestor.

To improve pollination, thus leading to increased fruit generation, **9** growers will plant a few Type B avocado trees among their orchards of Haas trees, which are Type A. These few Type B cultivars will serve as pollinators. In the mornings when the Type A flowers are functionally female, the Type B flowers will be functionally male.

The next logistical problem is how to get a relatively small number of Type B trees to pollinate a much larger number of Type A trees. The primary vehicle for avocado pollination is the honey bee. Apiarists, who raise the **10** bees to provide hives to the owners of avocado orchards. Unfortunately, bees seem to be ineffective pollinators of avocados. Many avocado growers must resort to the arduous process of hand-pollinating. **11** Involved in the use of a special brush to collect the pollen from Type B flowers and then "paint" that pollen inside the Type A flowers.

8
A) NO CHANGE
B) that have
C) that
D) are

9
A) NO CHANGE
B) growers who plant
C) growers planting
D) planted by growers

10
A) NO CHANGE
B) bees and provide
C) bees, providing
D) bees, provide

11
A) NO CHANGE
B) Involved in using
C) This involves using
D) Use of this involving

Notes and Reflections

Standard English Conventions – Run-Ons 1

Many people believe the electric car to be a modern
1 invention, in fact, the history of the electric vehicle begins
even before that of the gasoline-powered cars that are
beginning to look distinctly old-fashioned in the modern era of
hybrid gas-electric vehicles. In the early 1800s, inventors and
tinkerers in Europe and North America were already
experimenting with battery power for cars. British inventor
Robert Anderson built the first electric carriage in the
2 1830s, more practical versions emerged in France and
England in the second half of the 19th century. The first
electric car to find success in the United States actually hit the
market over 100 years ago.

The majority of Americans living in the late 1800s were
still using horses for transportation, but as the 19th century
rolled into the next, more people were beginning to turn to the
newly available personal motor vehicles. Consumers had three
options for power at the time: steam, gas, or electricity. Steam
had the attraction of an established **3** reputation, having been
in use for large-scale operations like factories and locomotives
since the late 1700s, but it also had several flaws that made it
impractical for private use. For one thing, steam engines
required as much as 45 minutes to start **4** up, they simply
weren't worthwhile for anyone wanting to run some quick

1
A) NO CHANGE
B) invention, in fact
C) invention in fact,
D) invention. In fact,

2
A) NO CHANGE
B) 1830s
C) 1830s;
D) 1830s; while

3
A) NO CHANGE
B) reputation. Having been
C) reputation, it had been
D) reputation, had it been

4
A) NO CHANGE
B) up, so they
C) up,
D) up

errands. They were ill-equipped for long-distance <u>5 travel, because</u> they needed to be refilled frequently. Gasoline-powered cars, meanwhile, had the distance problem sorted, but they still weren't a viable option for many potential customers due to the physical strength required to operate them. It was all too easy to sustain an injury while attempting to start a gas car using the hand crank, and the gear shifts were equally difficult to manage.

For the right customer, electric cars provided an attractive alternative to their gas- and steam-powered <u>6 counterparts, they</u> were easy to start up and free of the odors, pollutants and noise associated with gasoline cars and the hassles that accompanied steam power. They quickly earned popularity among city-dwellers, who were glad of an easy way to get around <u>7 town,</u> among women, who could operate electric cars independently without recruiting help to start them. More U.S. automakers began to develop their own versions to meet the <u>8 demand, and as</u> electricity became more widely available in American homes, the electric car outpaced its gas-powered competitors to reach the height of its popularity.

5
A) NO CHANGE
B) travel, too, because
C) travel, too,
D) travel,

6
A) NO CHANGE
B) counterparts. They
C) counterparts they
D) counterparts

7
A) NO CHANGE
B) town, and
C) town;
D) town

8
A) NO CHANGE
B) demand, as
C) demand as
D) demand;

Electricity as a power source for personal vehicles was not without its flaws, however. [9] They were great for quick jaunts across town, electric cars couldn't compete with gasoline when it came to speed and range. Taking note of the popularity electric cars were enjoying in urban areas, many major players in the industry sought to eliminate these problems. Automobile mogul Henry Ford teamed up with the inventor Thomas Edison in an effort to improve upon the electric design, [10] which Edison believed to have better potential. Ford and Edison hoped to address the range problems of electric power at an affordable price, and Edison did succeed in producing a battery that would allow an electric car to travel 100 miles—a dramatic improvement—but it came at a cost. Edison's battery was too heavy, fragile, and expensive to be commercially viable.

It was ultimately Henry Ford's own Model T that put an end to the electric car's heyday. Ford had adapted the assembly line into a highly efficient production method that saw Model Ts rolling off the line every 3 minutes. This allowed Ford to undercut his [11] competitors, made the Model T appreciably more affordable than any other automobile on the market—particularly electric cars, which were now more expensive than gasoline-powered vehicles by over $1,000 (closer to $26,000 in today's money). The substantial benefits previously exclusive to electric power now belonged to gasoline, as did the future of the industry.

9
A) NO CHANGE
B) Great, they were
C) They were great, though,
D) Though they were great

10
A) NO CHANGE
B) that Edison believed to
C) Edison believed
D) they were believed by Edison to

11
A) NO CHANGE
B) competitors. Which made
C) competitors; which made
D) competitors, which made

Standard English Conventions – Run-Ons 2

[1] <u>Helium is</u> an element best known for making party balloons float, is currently in short supply, and the effects of this shortage will reach far beyond your birthday celebration. The world uses 6.2 billion cubic feet of helium each year. It is the second most prominent element in the world, accounting for 23 percent of the mass of the universe, but large quantities of helium in the atmosphere float off into space, making it more challenging to collect.

Helium has extremely high and low boiling [2] <u>points, in helium, these have</u> a wider range than that of any other known substance. This quality makes helium useful in [3] <u>cryogenics is the</u> scientific study of materials at radically low temperatures. Helium isn't poisonous or flammable. Additionally, helium is inert, meaning it doesn't react with other elements; this makes helium highly stable. Helium is crucial in making microchips, running MRIs, operating scuba tanks, cooling nuclear reactors, and completing certain types of welding, as well as accomplishing many other scientific and production tasks. The magnets used in MRIs need to be soaked in liquid helium to work properly. In the past, helium has also been affordable. In fact, it was more expensive to recycle than to purchase [4] <u>more, this</u> low cost is another reason the element has been crucial in everything from space

1
A) NO CHANGE
B) Helium:
C) Helium;
D) Helium,

2
A) NO CHANGE
B) points, they are
C) points, it has
D) points,

3
A) NO CHANGE
B) cryogenics the
C) cryogenics. The
D) cryogenics, the

4
A) NO CHANGE
B) more;
C) more,
D) more this

exploration to military operations. **5** If the Large Hadron

Collider, an enormous innovative particle collider located on

the border of France and Switzerland, depends on helium.

    Why the shortage? While helium is highly abundant, it is

too expensive to collect out of the air, so it is predominantly

collected as a byproduct of natural gas **6** production, in

addition to how easily helium is lost in our atmosphere,

overuse is a major factor in the shortage of helium. Its use in

balloons is a generous contributor to the problem. The

problem is a permanent one: we are unable to produce more

helium once we have used up the supply on earth.

    In 1925, the United States government created a large

storage facility, which for many years was the largest reserve

of helium in the U.S. Due to the large quantities of natural gas

found there, the area containing the facility, the Texas

Panhandle, **7** it is considered the helium capital of the United

States, or even the world. The United States produces 75

percent of the world's helium, and a large portion of that

supply comes from **8** Amarillo, Texas, in fact, there are only

about 14 plants on earth that refine helium, and seven are in

the U.S. However, in 1996, the government decided to sell off

its stockpile and privatize the helium program, greatly

5
A) NO CHANGE
B) While
C) Even
D) Since

6
A) NO CHANGE
B) production, in addition,
C) production. In addition,
D) production. In addition

7
A) NO CHANGE
B) it
C) is
D) DELETE

8
A) NO CHANGE
B) Amarillo, Texas, in fact;
C) Amarillo, Texas; in fact,
D) Amarillo, Texas,

reducing the size of the supply. This move was designed to help pay off the large debt the government incurred by creating this [9] reserve. Unfortunately, private producers of helium aren't numerous or interested in producing as much helium as the government had hoped. The United States helium reserve may only last until 2020. The shortage is causing a spike in the price of helium. Over the past decade, the price increased by over 250 [10] percent, prices are set by the federal government and have increased as the supply of helium decreases. Without helium, scientific and production facilities would have to alter or halt production. Hospitals may need to limit the use of MRIs, which are crucial diagnostic and monitoring tools for patients.

There are some current programs working to curb the issue. Many labs recycle helium, and new helium plants will be opening in Russia and Qatar in the coming years. There are also efforts to get the United States to stop selling off its helium reserve. Moreover, helium is still being [11] discovered in Tanzania, for the first time, researchers found a helium gas field in 2016. This discovery points to the possibility of other such discoveries. However, given that helium is a non-renewable resource, more needs to be done. Alternatives to helium need to be researched and conservation of helium needs to be prioritized.

9
A) NO CHANGE
B) reserve, unfortunately,
C) reserve,
D) reserve

10
A) NO CHANGE
B) percent, prices,
C) percent. Prices,
D) percent. Prices are

11
A) NO CHANGE
B) discovered,
C) discovered;
D) discovered, for example,

Notes and Reflections

Standard English Conventions – Parallelism 1

Most college students feel insecure from time to time. The college years are a time full of not only encountering new people and experiences but also **1** to overcome challenges. However, you may not suspect that one of the most famous and well-regarded writers of the twentieth century dealt with the same fears and worries that most of us do, and there is a record of her struggles printed many years after her life had ended. Flannery O'Connor's journal shows she had at least as much insecurity **2** as most typical students. These entries stand in stark contrast to the strong, brilliant, award-winning writer she became.

Flannery O'Connor is best known for her fiction, short stories, **3** as well as novels. Her work was often set in the American South, where she was born and lived for most of her life. Her stories deal with consistent themes: poverty, alienation, religion, and **4** exercise free will. These reflect her Roman Catholic upbringing in Georgia. She went to college in

1
A) NO CHANGE
B) challenges overcome
C) she overcame challenges
D) overcoming challenges

2
A) NO CHANGE
B) as typically most students
C) as do most typical students
D) than most typical students do

3
A) NO CHANGE
B) as well as writing novels
C) and novels
D) and writing novels

4
A) NO CHANGE
B) the exercise of free will
C) to exercise free will
D) of free will

SUMMIT
EDUCATIONAL
GROUP

Georgia and then attended the Iowa Writers' Workshop, a well-known institution for blossoming authors. O'Connor is regarded as both a seminal artist in American literature and **5** defining voice of the Southern Gothic style.

However, O'Connor passed away at just thirty-nine years old, so her volume of work is slim. Fans have wished for more stories to enjoy. Writers have wanted more prose to study. **6** This scarcity of material has led to the publication of her college journal. She kept a journal for a mere forty days as a sophomore at what was then called Georgia State College for Women. From December 1943 to February 1944, O'Connor recorded her thoughts in a journal labeled, "Higher Mathematics," presumably to keep others from opening the volume. In it, **7** revealing of her anxiety, her lack of confidence, and her desire for social acceptance. She takes note of entertaining her classmates: "I achieved a nice success in Eng. 360 by making a rather humorous remark and then not laughing at it while the others did. I must try to do it again." She notes that this minor event built her up, just as many of us need building up in our younger years.

5
A) NO CHANGE
B) she was a defining voice
C) for her defining the voice
D) a defining voice

6
At this point, the author wants to include another example that is consistent with the style of the other examples provided. Which choice best accomplishes that author's goal?

A) Having more popular books to sell would please publishers.
B) More popular books to sell have been desired by publishers.
C) Publishers have desired more popular books to sell.
D) More popular books have been desired by publishers to sell.

7
Which of the following choices best establishes the stylistic pattern seen in the rest of the sentence?

A) NO CHANGE
B) her anxiety is revealed
C) she reveals her anxiety
D) anxious revelation

SUMMIT
EDUCATIONAL
GROUP

In her journal, O'Connor not only worries about the acceptance of her peers but also **8** her intellectual abilities are doubted. She was anxious about being seen as "just a brainy kid" rather than as a clever individual who had refinement, culture, and **9** having artistic potential. Her difficulties continued during her education at the Iowa Writers' Workshop. One of her professors, Paul Engle, wrote that Flannery was shy about having her stories read. When it was her turn to have one of her stories presented in the workshop, Engle would read it aloud anonymously. O'Connor, despite her eventual literary greatness, walked through these earlier years with as much anxiety and concern as typical awkward young adults have. Expected? Perhaps, though seeing these words in print highlights the sameness of the human experience.

Despite these setbacks, O'Connor went on to achieve publishing success. By comparing her adult accomplishments to her **10** eighteen-year-old musings, her personal story arc is highlighted. Once a young woman full of doubts and in need of confidence boosting, she became a writer at a time when women were not necessarily encouraged to write. Later in her life, when asked by a young student why she writes, O'Connor famously answered, "Because I'm good at it," an answer that could leave no doubt as to how far she had come. Certainly, the older and more accomplished O'Connor entertained fewer worries than **11** her college journal.

8
A) NO CHANGE
B) intellectual abilities are doubted by her
C) doubted are her intellectual abilities
D) doubts her intellectual abilities

9
Which of the following choices best continues the pattern of descriptions established in the sentence?
A) NO CHANGE
B) potentially artistic
C) artistic potential
D) her potential as an artist

10
Which of the following choices best continues the stylistic pattern established in the previous example in the sentence?
A) NO CHANGE
B) musings as an eighteen-year-old
C) old musings from eighteen years
D) old as eighteen years musings

11
A) NO CHANGE
B) did she whom we see in her college journal
C) whom we see in her college journal
D) in her college journal

Standard English Conventions – Parallelism 2

What do you see when you imagine a barn? In most people's minds, there is a similar image: an old, tall building made of wood, filled with hay and farm animals, **1** and its paint is vibrant red. Why are barns usually red instead of any other color? There are some who believe it to be simply a style trend followed by leagues of farmers. There are others who believe the red color would help cows find their way back to the farm (which is not true because cows are colorblind to red). **2** Perhaps farmers chose rusty-colored hues to mimic the color of brick, a material considered a sign of wealth. However, the actual reason is more complex, practical, and tied to fundamental processes of the universe.

Why paint a barn? Ideally, farmers could build their barns solely of bare wood. Certainly this would be less expensive than buying the vast amounts of paint needed to coat an entire barn. However, the expense of leaving wood unprotected is greater, in the long run, than **3** protective paint. That's because wood, though it is a strong and versatile construction material, is prone to deterioration from the elements of nature. Moisture can cause wood to swell, warp, splinter, and **4** mold growth. Insects and other creatures can infest and destroy unprotected wood. The solution to these threats is paint, which can seal away moisture and guard from damage.

1
A) NO CHANGE
B) and painted vibrant red
C) as well as its paint is vibrant red
D) as well as vibrant red paint

2
Which choice is most consistent with the style of the other examples provided in the paragraph?
A) NO CHANGE
B) It's believed
C) Still others believe
D) It is believed by others that

3
A) NO CHANGE
B) that of protective paint
C) that protective paint
D) paint protection

4
A) NO CHANGE
B) growth of mold
C) growing mold
D) grow mold

How was paint invented? Until the 18th century, before barns were commonly painted, builders had to consider sun exposure, temperature, water drainage, [5] seasonal, moisture, ventilation to determine how to keep barns dry. In the late 1700s, farmers began creating their own paint coating made out of milk from cows, linseed oil from the flax plant, [6] as well as sand from crushed limestone. This basic paint was enough to seal moisture away, which helped preserve the wood, but it wasn't enough to deter the spread of mold and fungi.

[7] Eventually, someone stumbled onto an answer: ferric oxide, or iron rust. When mixed into paint, a powder of iron rust would kill mold and fungi. Other materials can be used as mildewcides and fungicides, but iron rust had one clear advantage: it's very common. The reason for its abundance is found in the life cycles of stars.

What is it about stars that leads to so much iron? Stars are formed from a balance of pressure. The inward pull of gravity is countered by the outward force of energy from nuclear fusion reactions. Stars begin as balls of hydrogen. In the core of young stars are intense pressure and temperatures in the tens of millions of degrees Celsius. This is the setting for nuclear fusion, a reaction in which the nuclei of atoms are

---

5

A) NO CHANGE
B) seasonal, moisture, and ventilation
C) seasonal moisture, and ventilation,
D) seasonal moisture, and ventilation

6

A) NO CHANGE
B) as well as limestone crushed into sand
C) and sand from crushed limestone
D) and limestone crushed into sand

7

The author wants to begin this paragraph in such a way that it will maintain the pattern of the other paragraphs in the passage. Which choice best accomplishes the author's goal?

A) Eventually, the problem of mold and fungi was solved.
B) How was the problem of mold and fungi solved?
C) Farmers solved the mold and fungi problem.
D) How the mold and fungi problem was eventually solved.

combined, resulting in the release of energy. Hydrogen atoms are joined to form helium atoms. [8] Carbon is created from helium fusion. Carbon is used to make oxygen. The process continues, creating heavier and heavier elements. If the star is large enough, this process progresses until the core reaches temperatures above one billion degrees Celsius and begins fusing iron. This is where the whole process grinds to a halt. The amount of energy needed to fuse iron is greater than [9] the release of a reaction's energy amount. When a star begins making iron, its core grows weaker. Suddenly, the power of gravity on the outer layers is greater than the outward energy from the core, so the outer layers collapse. The core continues to make more iron, unable to produce enough energy to make any heavier elements, until it collapses and then explodes in a supernova. This explosion spreads elements, including a great deal of iron, across the universe. In this fashion, the life cycle of a star leads to the abundance of iron – and iron rust – on Earth.

What does this have to do with barns? Iron rust provided farmers with a solution to their problems with wood degradation. This rust was not only simple to procure but also [10] ground into powder easily and mixed into liquid paint. When mixed with homemade paint, the result was a paint that was simple to produce, affordable, and [11] protected from both moisture and mold. The color resulting from the mixture of iron rust was a deep, vibrant red, the iconic color of barns.

8

Which of the following choices best maintains the stylistic pattern in the previous and following sentences?

A) NO CHANGE
B) Fusion of helium creates carbon.
C) Helium creates carbon.
D) Helium is fused to create carbon.

9

A) NO CHANGE
B) that of the energy released by the reaction
C) the reaction releasing an amount of energy
D) the reaction's release of energy

10

A) NO CHANGE
B) ground easily and mixed into powder and liquid paint
C) easy to grind into powder and mix into liquid paint
D) powder ground into and liquid paint mixed into easily

11

A) NO CHANGE
B) protect from
C) from which protected
D) to be protected from

Notes and Reflections

Standard English Conventions – Modifiers 1

Wassily Kandinsky was born in Russia in 1866 to a wealthy family. **[1]** When, as a child, he traveled around Europe, playing piano and cello. He didn't take up painting seriously until he turned thirty. **[2]** Before pursuing this art, several academic subjects, including law, were his key interests. In Munich, Kandinsky became an art student in a private school run by Anton Azbe, a Slovenian realist painter. Later, he enrolled in the Munich Academy to further his art education. He graduated in 1900, at the turn of the century.

This background led Kandinsky to start off painting in a realistic style, though he became influenced by impressionism, pointillism, and expressionism. **[3]** Kandinsky's effect, early on in his artistic career, by Monet, who caused him to grapple with the concept of abstraction. **[4]** Continuing to paint, his work became more abstract, eventually morphing into the style he is ultimately known for: bold, unreal paintings, crowded with circles, lines, and other geometric forms. He's commonly called the world's first true abstract artist.

1
A) NO CHANGE
B) As a child
C) As children
D) A child

2
A) NO CHANGE
B) Before pursuing art, his key interests were several academic subjects, including law.
C) His key interests were several academic subjects, including law before pursuing this art.
D) His key interests, before he pursued this art, were several academic subjects, including law.

3
A) NO CHANGE
B) Early on in his artistic career, Monet's effect on Kandinsky,
C) Monet's effect on Kandinsky early on in his artistic career,
D) Early on in his artistic career, Kandinsky was affected by Monet,

4
A) NO CHANGE
B) Continually painting,
C) As he continued to paint,
D) Painting and continuing,

But how did Kandinsky develop this style and what was he trying to convey? [5] A young age, Kandinsky had an unusual relationship with color; he would hear noises associated with colors as he mixed paints as a child. Later in life, while watching a performance of the opera *Lohengrin* in Moscow, [6] there were colors and lines he saw. He had a similar experience during a concert performed by Schoenberg, [7] with whom Kandinsky eventually struck up a friendship. These sense-bending experiences may mean Kandinsky had synaesthesia, a condition in which the senses confuse and combine. In a person with this condition, when one sense is activated, another unrelated sense is also activated, so a person may "taste purple" or "hear red."

It's difficult to retroactively prove Kandinsky's synaesthesia, but much more research has been done on the condition since his time. Affecting approximately one in every 2,000 people, synaesthesia is found more commonly in women than men. There are different types, involving different combinations of senses, two of the most common being colors associated with letters or numbers and colors associated with sounds. The condition is typically harmless. Though it can be classified as a neural disorder, synaesthesia brings sensations that are often even enjoyed by people who experience them.

5
A) NO CHANGE
B) From a young age,
C) From its youth,
D) Young,

6
A) NO CHANGE
B) colors and lines were seen there
C) the sight of colors and lines
D) he saw colors and lines

7
A) NO CHANGE
B) a friendship whom with Kandinsky eventually struck up.
C) Kandinsky eventually struck up a friendship with him.
D) an eventual friendship Kandinsky struck up.

Many people in creative professions have synaesthesia or are said to have had synaesthesia before it was identified as a neurological difference. Beethoven, 8 the connection of musical keys with color, may have had synaesthesia. Authors Nabokov and Baudelaire both experienced this blurring of senses; Baudelaire wrote about feeling a merger of sensations and emotions. An influential artist who painted just before Kandinsky's time, 9 sounds were also tied to hues by van Gogh. Since people with synaesthesia experience senses in a unique way, it's perhaps not surprising that many of them end up in creative professions like Kandinsky.

10 An experience of a composition of music, Kandinsky saw colors. He associated the sound of a cello with deep blue. He began merging artistic forms to express how he experienced the senses. He created a book of connected poems and woodcuts and wrote plays that brought together words, music, color, and sound. In his book "Concerning Spirituality in Art," Kandinsky wrote about his associations between colors and emotions, which also adds credibility to the idea that he was a synaesthete.

11 Combining the visual, auditory, and literary, Kandinsky was attempting to create an unspoken language with his art. He may or may not have had synaesthesia, but he combined the products of the senses in new and unusual ways, leaving the world a new form of art to ponder for generations.

8
A) NO CHANGE
B) connected, with musical keys, color
C) musical keys connected with color
D) connecting musical keys with color

9
A) NO CHANGE
B) sounds tied by van Gogh to hues also
C) van Gogh also tied sounds to hues
D) tying sounds to hues by van Gogh

10
A) NO CHANGE
B) A composition of music when experienced,
C) When experiencing a composition of music,
D) When a composition of music is experienced,

11
A) NO CHANGE
B) The visual, auditory, and literary combined,
C) A combination of the visual, auditory, and literary
D) Visual and auditory combining with literary,

Standard English Conventions – Modifiers 2

What is more American than baseball, hot dogs, and apple pie? Each of these items embodies a quintessential element of American culture. But another, architectural, symbol of American life has proven even more iconic: the American front porch. Although its popularity has waxed and waned through the years, [1] the front porch's enduring symbol of America is currently enjoying a resurgence. What are the origins of this American icon, and what is its future?

While the concept of a porch has existed since prehistoric times, e.g. taking shelter under an overhanging rock ledge, the word "porch" can be traced to the Greek "portico" or the Latin "porticus." These words referenced the covered entrance to a building which was often defined by columns, or an extended, covered walkway sometimes enclosed by walls. In the Middle Ages, the porch form appeared in European cathedrals as vestibules, [2] the enclosed entrances where people could congregate before services. Through the Renaissance, loggias began to appear more frequently in countries like Italy, [3] outdoor spaces where they provided sheltered for public buildings.

Motivated by warmer climates, [4] West Africa was common in such regions as porch builders. In the American colonies, porches began to appear with greater frequency in

---

1

A) NO CHANGE
B) America is currently enjoying a resurgence of the front porch's enduring symbol
C) the front porch, the enduring symbol of America, is currently enjoying a resurgence
D) the resurgence of an enduring symbol of America is currently enjoyed by the front porch

2

A) NO CHANGE
B) people could congregate before services in these enclosed entrances
C) services before which people could congregate in the enclosed entrances
D) congregate people in the enclosed entrances before services

3

A) NO CHANGE
B) sheltered provided where there were outdoor spaces for public buildings
C) public buildings with outdoor spaces to provide shelter
D) where they provided sheltered outdoor spaces for public buildings

4

A) NO CHANGE
B) porches were more commonly built in regions such as West Africa
C) people in regions such as West Africa commonly built porches
D) building porches was more common in regions such as West Africa

SUMMIT
EDUCATIONAL
GROUP

the 1800s, largely in the South. Familiar with wide porches designed to take advantage of ocean breezes in the Caribbean, [5] homes built by Southern traders had porches built on. Not surprisingly, the large plantation homes of the South began to incorporate similar designs. George Washington owned a home featuring a two-story roofed gallery, resembling an Italian piazza, that ran the full width of the house.

But porches were no longer just for the wealthy. Slaves from western Africa built whole communities of shotgun houses across the southern states. One room wide and two or three rooms deep, [6] building these narrow houses was inexpensive and several could be situated on a single plot of land. Because their close proximity limited air circulation and sunlight on the sides, each structure was designed with a small front porch. These groupings of shotgun houses played a large role in the development of the iconic status of the American front porch, which reached its zenith between the mid-1800s and mid-1900s. Not just a physical structure, [7] the American front porch represented a transition between the public and private. Although its architectural details might vary, the front porch promoted family unity and encouraged a larger sense of community. While children played in the yard, parents could look on from the porch and relax in comfort. [8] Television sets gathered in front of families before they gathered around the porch.

5
A) NO CHANGE
B) porches were built onto homes by Southern traders
C) building homes with porches by Southern traders
D) Southern traders had porches built on their homes

6
A) NO CHANGE
B) builders made these narrow houses inexpensively
C) these narrow houses were inexpensive to build
D) inexpensive building of these houses was narrow

7
A) NO CHANGE
B) a transition between the public and private represented the American front porch
C) between the public and private transition represented the American front porch
D) a representation of the American front porch transitioned between the public and private

8
A) NO CHANGE
B) Gathered in front of television sets before, families,
C) Families, before gathering in front of television sets,
D) Before families gathered in front of television sets,

Following World War II, the popularity of these structures declined. [9] Owning an increasing number of cars, traffic noise and exhaust fumes made time on a front porch less appealing. With the advent of television and air conditioning, the family no longer needed to seek diversion or more comfortable temperatures outside. It seemed like late-twentieth century Americans neither had the time nor the inclination to gather on their porches, even if they had one.

But the American front porch is not dead yet; in fact, it has been experiencing an early twenty-first century revival. A surprising phenomenon is now resurrecting this icon, with a twist. Started in 2007 in Ithaca, New York, and now appearing in hundreds of cities across the United States, [10] the front porch is used as a stage for Porchfests. These events are tremendously popular annual music events which bring together local communities and area musicians. This exciting retrofit both affirms the legacy of promoting community and answers twenty-first century culture. Because of its adaptability, [11] the American front porch will surely endure into the future.

9
A) NO CHANGE
B) Bringing an increase in car ownership,
C) Brought by the increased ownership of cars,
D) Increasing the ownership of cars,

10
A) NO CHANGE
B) using the front porch as a stage is the idea behind Porchfests
C) the idea behind Porchfests is using the front porch as a stage
D) Porchfests are using the front porch as a stage

11
A) NO CHANGE
B) America will surely endure into the future with its front porch
C) the future will show the American front porch enduring
D) enduring into the future will be done by the American front porch

Notes and Reflections

Standard English Conventions – Verb Tense 1

If you're a frequent grocery shopper in the United States, you know it's as easy to get an orange in July as it is in January, though, for most of the country, growing season for oranges **1** didn't stretch beyond winter. Yes, it is satisfying to enjoy an orange in the middle of summer, but where do these out-of-season oranges come from?

Currently, the United States **2** importing over a third of its produce. Much of this food comes from Canada and Latin America, though some products can come from as far away as Vietnam or New Zealand. Different hemispheres **3** had had different seasons as well, so winter in Canada is summer in Argentina. Therefore, a product can easily be grown in the sunny southern half of the world while there **4** is frost and snow in the much of the United States. A large quantity of our produce production has shifted to Mexico, where labor is cheaper and the climate is warmer than in most of the United States. Many growers who started off in the United States have moved their operations to Mexico for these reasons. Often, an avocado on your dinner table has already made a long journey from the southern region of Mexico to your local supermarket.

1
A) NO CHANGE
B) doesn't
C) hasn't
D) hadn't

2
A) NO CHANGE
B) imported
C) imports
D) had imported

3
A) NO CHANGE
B) have had
C) had
D) have

4
A) NO CHANGE
B) was
C) are
D) were

As the United States becomes a more diverse country, tastes become increasingly diverse as well. Take the previously mentioned avocado. How did the avocado become such a popular staple of the American diet? As Mexicans migrated to the U.S., they **5** have brought their love of avocados with them. Naturally, immigrants want to import flavors from home. As tastes have shifted, so has demand for these products, for home and commercial use. Thirty years ago, you may not have been able to try tacos or tandoori chicken in the suburbs of the United States, but now there are many Mexican and Indian restaurants in both urban and suburban areas, and the variety **6** had been ever-expanding. As our country becomes more cosmopolitan, so do our food preferences.

Without modern transportation technologies, it **7** would not have been possible to grow produce many miles away and keep it fresh until it lands in American stores. Now, with advanced shipping and storing technology, people have the ability to transport large quantities of whatever food they desire. Also, as air travel and roads **8** expand, it's simply easier to get products from one place to another. Horticultural advances have also been made such that the potential to grow a wider variety fruits and vegetables in different environments has expanded.

5
A) NO CHANGE
B) had brought
C) brought
D) bring

6
A) NO CHANGE
B) has been
C) was
D) would be

7
A) NO CHANGE
B) will not have been
C) would not be
D) has not been

8
A) NO CHANGE
B) had expanded
C) will expand
D) expanding

As with most advancements, this shift is not without its drawbacks. Transporting produce hundreds, and sometimes thousands, of miles [9] wasn't good for the environment. An apple traveling from New Zealand to Los Angeles, for example, has made a trip of over six thousand miles. With time, fruit [10] will lose nutritional value and flavor. Anyone who has eaten a fresh-picked strawberry and a berry from the same batch a week later can vouch for this difference. Furthermore, given how far food frequently travels, producers concern themselves with longevity more than with taste or nutrition. This can lead to products with little flavor but a long shelf life, like a bland, watery tomato purchased in the dead of winter.

Consumers in the United States are unlikely to request a change in these conditions. As a country, we're used to being able to buy seasonal produce year-round, and it seems unlikely that most Americans would be willing to forgo this privilege. Yet, given the environmental impact of transporting food long distances and the sacrifice of quality for durability, perhaps it's time for us to examine our habits and return to a more natural cycle of production and consumption. After all, if we [11] had to wait until fall to bite into a crisp, juicy apple, doesn't that make the fruit all the sweeter?

9
A) NO CHANGE
B) hadn't been
C) not being
D) isn't

10
A) NO CHANGE
B) has lost
C) had lost
D) lost

11
A) NO CHANGE
B) had had
C) have had
D) have

SUMMIT
EDUCATIONAL
GROUP

Standard English Conventions – Verb Tense 2

Growing populations relying on the finite amounts of food, water, fuels, and minerals that the Earth can offer must eventually seek resources elsewhere. For much of human history, we have imagined what wealth lies among the stars. By the time of the Kennedy era, when space travel became scientific fact, scientists and investors **1** have dreams of harvesting resources in outer space for generations. Now, scientists are certain the future **2** involved the human colonization of other worlds or drifting among resource-rich asteroids, as new industries of mining, processing, and shipping **3** become available. To achieve this, most experts agree the migration process cannot be reliant on what people can take with them from Earth. It would be far less expensive and technically challenging to use the rich harvests that already **4** lied in space. This is what makes asteroids so vital to the endeavor.

Science fiction writers have long theorized what space exploration would look like. Now, real scientists are hoping to bridge the technological gap between ambitions and ability. In 2010, President Barack Obama pushed for NASA's efforts in the 21st century to be directed towards landing on an asteroid

1
A) NO CHANGE
B) had
C) have had
D) had had

2
A) NO CHANGE
B) has involved
C) had involved
D) will involve

3
A) NO CHANGE
B) became
C) becomes
D) had become

4
A) NO CHANGE
B) laid
C) lie
D) lay

by 2025. He identified this achievement as an important first step towards creating sustainable industries in space. In that same speech, Obama **5** <u>stressed</u> the vital need to find partners in the private sector to further these endeavors. The private sector has responded, and multiple companies have expressed the shared belief that humans **6** <u>spread</u> across the solar system. Multiple companies hope to position themselves in a way to profit from the eventuality. It's no coincidence that Grant Bonin, Chief Technology Office of DSI, likes to call the roughly 18,000 asteroids near Earth, "giant piles of money."

Still, nobody in the burgeoning space industry is sure what asteroid mining will look like or what will drive profits in these new markets. DSI envisions a swarm of small low-cost spacecraft going out and mining many near-Earth asteroids. These craft **7** <u>harvested</u> small amounts of raw material and aggregate them at a central depot. "It is like honey bees going out to a lot of different flowers and flying [resources] back to the hive," says Bonin.

From the depot, the company would then sell whatever raw material makes the most economic sense. That might be water-derived propellant (which would also fuel DSI's "swarm"), but it also might be metals such as iron and nickel. These depots can supply resources for further space expeditions, while also **8** <u>to deliver</u> valuable materials to Earth.

5
A) NO CHANGE
B) will stress
C) stresses
D) stress

6
A) NO CHANGE
B) have spread
C) had spread
D) will spread

7
A) NO CHANGE
B) will harvest
C) will have harvested
D) have harvested

8
A) NO CHANGE
B) delivered
C) had delivered
D) delivering

The company Planetary Resources is betting that water [9] being the first major market for space mining. A depot could provide water as a fuel source, like an orbital gas station. One argument goes that there [10] are already gas station customers in space: rocket components floating as space junk. If you could retrieve and refuel them, you could reuse these abandoned rocket parts. Such ventures would be worth much more than the necessary investment.

The 1967 Outer Space Treaty (OST) says that nations can use but can't appropriate either the moon or other celestial bodies. However, the treaty is silent on a private company harvesting space resources. So, whether space miners will be legally entitled to possess what they dig up [11] will be a vital question which remains to be answered. That private companies are essential to the next step of the human odyssey seems certain. It therefore seems the international community needs to act to ensure these entrepreneurs are entitled to the fruits of their labor.

9
A) NO CHANGE
B) has been
C) will be
D) was

10
A) NO CHANGE
B) were
C) is
D) was

11
A) NO CHANGE
B) being
C) was
D) is

Notes and Reflections

Standard English Conventions – Commas 1

The "First Lady of Jazz," Ella Fitzgerald was a uniquely talented woman who rose from humble beginnings to become one of America's most influential twentieth-century singers. Born in 1917 in Newport **1** News, Virginia, Ella, experienced instability and poverty as a child. Her parents separated soon after her birth, and she and her mother moved to Yonkers, New York. When Ella was only 15, her mother died and Ella went to live with an aunt in Harlem. That provided little more stability, and Ella began skipping school and was eventually sent to reform school. By age 16, Ella was living on the **2** streets, her dream of becoming an entertainer seemingly unrealizable.

Her big **3** break however came in 1934 when Ella entered an amateur contest held at Harlem's Apollo Theater. Originally planning to dance, she was intimidated by the impressive act preceding hers **4** and decided, at the last minute, to sing instead. Young Ella stunned the audience with

1
A) NO CHANGE
B) News Virginia, Ella
C) News, Virginia, Ella
D) News Virginia Ella

2
A) NO CHANGE
B) streets, her dream,
C) streets her dream,
D) streets her dream

3
A) NO CHANGE
B) break, however came
C) break, however, came
D) break, however, came,

4
A) NO CHANGE
B) and, decided at the last minute,
C) and decided, at the last minute
D) and decided at the last minute,

her amazing voice and won first place, a grand prize of $25. Soon after, Ella joined <u>5 drummer Chick Webb's, band,</u> as a singer, a move that would prove pivotal in her music career. Becoming a regular act at Harlem's famous Savoy club, Ella went on to co-write and record her first number one hit in 1938, "A-Tisket, A-Tasket," also performing and recording with the popular Benny Goodman Orchestra. When Chick Webb died in 1939, Ella took over leadership of the <u>6 band which was</u> renamed Ella Fitzgerald and Her Famous Orchestra. Thus began a musical career that would span nearly six decades.

What made Ella Fitzgerald such an enduring songstress? Her silvery tone and absolute pitch were certainly remarkable. Velvety, agile, and ageless, Ella's voice was well suited to <u>7 the evolving American Jazz music scene</u>. She could croon a simple ballad, her notes pure and sweet, and, for the next number, belt out powerful vocals to a <u>8 boisterous playful, big-band piece</u>. She possessed absolute pitch, more commonly referred to as perfect pitch. This rare ability, found in maybe one in 10,000, allows a person to instinctively identify a desired tone. In Ella's case, musicians could accurately tune to her voice without needing the usual reference notes. This unusual ability enabled her to maintain perfect pitch as she navigated the most intricate and demanding of vocal passages.

5
A) NO CHANGE
B) drummer, Chick Webb's, band,
C) drummer, Chick Webb's, band
D) drummer Chick Webb's band

6
A) NO CHANGE
B) band, which was
C) band, which was,
D) band, which, was,

7
A) NO CHANGE
B) the evolving American, Jazz music, scene
C) the evolving American, Jazz, music scene
D) the, evolving, American, Jazz, music, scene

8
A) NO CHANGE
B) boisterous, playful, big-band, piece
C) boisterous, playful big-band piece
D) boisterous playful big-band piece

Ella's impeccable [9] timing, and sense of rhythm also, set her apart as popular music in America transitioned from jazz to swing to bebop. While as a teen she had [10] imitated, popular, singer, Connee Boswell, Ella began to study the music of jazz trumpeter Dizzy Gillespie and jazz saxophonist Lester Young, perfecting a technique known as skat singing. This form of vocal improvisation leaves behind the words, notes, and rhythms of a typical music score and instead ad libs, using the voice in an instrumental, often playful, way. Louis Armstrong was the first musician to popularize skat singing in his 1926 recording of "Heebie Jeebies," but Ella became known as the "First Lady of Scat" as her unparalleled vocal technique and brilliant improvisation amazed audiences and fellow musicians alike. Few singers can claim such a lengthy or significant career: Ella Fitzgerald [11] performed, for nearly 60 years and remains one of the most prolific jazz recording artists, with more than 200 albums recorded under multiple labels, 14 Grammys earned, and 40 million records sold. This remarkable woman's legacy is as inspiring as her talent was legendary.

9
A) NO CHANGE
B) timing, and sense of rhythm, also
C) timing, and sense, of rhythm also,
D) timing, and sense of rhythm also

10
A) NO CHANGE
B) imitated, popular, singer Connee Boswell,
C) imitated, popular singer Connee Boswell,
D) imitated popular singer Connee Boswell,

11
A) NO CHANGE
B) performed for, nearly 60, years
C) performed for nearly 60 years,
D) performed for nearly 60 years

Standard English Conventions – Commas 2

Many of <u>the ancient, world's, great, wonders,</u> are swathed in mystery, which today can lead to rampant speculation. Consider the great pyramids of Giza, Stonehenge, or the giant heads of the Easter Islands. All of these impressive works of engineering have been studied **2** <u>obsessively, they serve</u> as reminders of the brilliance of our ancestors. Sometimes this brilliance has been difficult for scientists to explain; as a result, past ingenuity has led to supernatural or far-fetched theories about the creation and purpose of these structures.

The Nazca Lines of Peru are no exception to this tendency for wild speculation. Created around 2,000 years ago, the Nazca Lines are a group of geoglyphs: large line drawings that have been etched into the ground on the arid Pampa Colorada in southern Peru. They stretch over an area of about 190 square miles and were largely created by the Nazca people, while some were the work of the earlier Paracas culture. The figures fall under three different categories: **3** <u>straight, lines, geometric, designs,</u> and pictorial representations. There are more than 800 straight lines etched along the plain, some as long as 30 miles. Some 300 geometric designs are also scattered throughout the region, including shapes like triangles, rectangles, **4** <u>and trapezoids, as well as,</u> spirals, arrows, zig-zags, and wavy lines. Perhaps most intriguing are

1
A) NO CHANGE
B) the ancient world's, great wonders,
C) the ancient world's great wonders,
D) the ancient world's great wonders

2
A) NO CHANGE
B) obsessively, they serve,
C) obsessively—they serve—
D) obsessively—they serve

3
A) NO CHANGE
B) straight, lines, geometric, designs
C) straight lines, geometric designs,
D) straight lines geometric designs

4
A) NO CHANGE
B) and, trapezoids, as well as,
C) and trapezoids, as well as
D) and trapezoids, as well, as

the 70 representations of plants and animals, some of which are up to 1,200 feet long and include images of spiders, hummingbirds, cacti, monkeys, dogs, and a variety of other things. Many of these images are difficult to decipher from the ground and are best viewed from the [5] air, that has led many to question how the Nazca people could have created them.

Were they created with the help of aliens or people from the future? How did ancient people manage to construct such enormous, intricate designs, especially when they couldn't see them from above? As the Nazca Lines have been further [6] studied—as, with most other wonders of the ancient world, it has become clearer how and why they were constructed. However, there is still room for wonder, as the accomplishments of these ancient engineers produced intriguing monuments that have stood the test of time for millennia.

In the modern age, the first person to encounter the Nazca Lines was [7] Peruvian archaeologist Toribio Mejia Xesspe, who stumbled upon them while traversing an arid coastal area of Peru in 1927. As commercial flight became more widespread in the [8] 1930s further, explorers, researchers, and tourists were able to admire the massive geometric figures from the sky above. Throughout the decades in which they have been studied, there have been multiple theories about the purpose of the lines. What is known is that the Nazca

5
A) NO CHANGE
B) air
C) air,
D) air, which

6
A) NO CHANGE
B) studied—as
C) studied, as,
D) studied, as

7
A) NO CHANGE
B) Peruvian archaeologist, Toribio Mejia Xesspe
C) Peruvian archaeologist, Toribio Mejia Xesspe,
D) Peruvian, archaeologist, Toribio Mejia Xesspe,

8
A) NO CHANGE
B) 1930s, further explorers, researchers,
C) 1930s further explorers, researchers,
D) 1930s further explorers researchers

people somehow removed the top 12 to 15 inches of rock on the desert floor in order to reveal lighter sand below to form their designs. As to their purpose, researchers have debated this question for years. American historian Paul Kosok proposed that the geoglyphs might have an astronomical and calendrical purpose, like 9 Stonehenge, and a German archaeologist Maria Reiche agreed. She also believed that some of the geoglyphs, like the constellations of 10 Greek, and Roman mythology— corresponded to groups of stars in the sky.

The current theory is that the geoglyphs were related to water, a key commodity in the desert. The Nazca Lines did not serve a practical 11 purpose, like aqueducts did but may have been used as part of a ritual to the gods in an effort to bring forth water. Debate is still ongoing to further decipher why the ancient Nazca people expended so much effort to construct these massive figures.

9
A) NO CHANGE
B) Stonehenge, and, a German archaeologist, Maria Reiche,
C) Stonehenge, and a German archaeologist, Maria Reiche,
D) Stonehenge and, a German archaeologist, Maria Reiche,

10
A) NO CHANGE
B) Greek and Roman mythology—
C) Greek, and Roman mythology,
D) Greek and Roman mythology,

11
A) NO CHANGE
B) purpose like aqueducts did but
C) purpose, like aqueducts did; but
D) purpose, like aqueducts did: but

Standard English Conventions – Commas 3

Artemisia Gentileschi is not a name that immediately comes to mind when thinking of great 17th century painters, yet she **1** was; in her time, one of the most sought-after artists in Europe. She was commissioned by royalty and the very wealthy, such as Charles I of England and the Medicis, to produce powerful and masterly works, mainly of biblical and mythological subjects.

Becoming an artist was an incredibly difficult task for women in Gentileschi's era. The vast majority of women became **2** wives, mothers, or they entered a convent. In addition, there were overwhelming restrictions on their ability to make legal decisions or purchases. Gentileschi had the advantage of having a father who was a well-known artist. Orazio Gentileschi recognized his daughter's talent and apprenticed her to **3** famed older painter, Agostino Tassi.

Unfortunately, Tassi's influence was far from positive. He sexually assaulted the young Artemisia, promised to marry her, and then reneged on his promise. This led to a famous trial, during which Artemisia was tortured using thumbscrews as a means of proving her claims. She ultimately won the trial, and Tassi was sentenced to be exiled from **4** Rome. However the sentence was never carried out. Her scars from this experience lasted a lifetime and were apparent in much of the work she subsequently produced.

1
A) NO CHANGE
B) was, in her time,
C) was, in her time;
D) was, in her time

2
A) NO CHANGE
B) wives, and mothers, or
C) wives and mothers, or,
D) wives and mothers, or

3
A) NO CHANGE
B) famed older painter
C) famed, older painter,
D) famed, older, painter,

4
A) NO CHANGE
B) Rome, however, the sentence
C) Rome—however, the sentence
D) Rome—however—the sentence

She made dozens of paintings of women of courage overcoming great odds. Victims, warriors, and martyrs were her chosen subjects. Following in the footsteps of the great Baroque painter Caravaggio, perhaps the most influential artist of 17th century Italy, she adopted his use of **5** dramatic lighting, effects powerful, compositions, and vibrant color. She was recognized for her **6** talent and pursued by some of the greatest collectors of the time. Additionally, she achieved the highest honor possible for an artist, that of being inducted into the Accademia del Disegno. Upon receiving this **7** honor, she attained a unique level of independence, which allowed her to travel on her own and sign contracts, among other benefits. She proceeded to separate from her husband, travel freely, live in Naples and London, and support her two daughters, who both went on to become painters as well.

Artemisia was a feminist long before the term was invented. She had to fight throughout her life for equal pay and recognition. She took great pride in her accomplishments and spoke of herself to patrons proudly: "You will find the spirit of Caesar in this soul of a woman." As she told her friend **8** Galileo, the great scientist, "I have seen myself honored by the great kings and rulers of Europe," pronouncing that her paintings would endure as "evidence of my fame."

5
A) NO CHANGE
B) dramatic, lighting, effects, powerful, compositions,
C) dramatic lighting effects, powerful compositions,
D) dramatic lighting, effects powerful compositions,

6
A) NO CHANGE
B) talent, and pursued
C) talent and pursued,
D) talent, and, pursued,

7
A) NO CHANGE
B) honor she attained,
C) honor, she attained,
D) honor, she, attained,

8
A) NO CHANGE
B) Galileo the great scientist,
C) Galileo, the great scientist
D) Galileo the great scientist

SUMMIT EDUCATIONAL GROUP

Despite all of these successes, her name was omitted from most art history texts until her work was rediscovered in the early 20th century. Even then, her work was often misattributed and the focus was on **9** her personal story, rather, than her talent. In recent times, thanks largely to the work of feminist scholars, her work has received the acclaim it deserves. In the 1970s, an article by art historian Linda Nochlin, titled *Why Have There Been No Great Women Artists?*, analyzed that question. Nochlin's article prompted scholars to make an attempt to "integrate women artists into the history of art and culture."

Her life and work have recently been used as a basis for various forms of popular culture. Susan Vreeland published *The Passion of Artemisia*, a novel loosely based on Artemisia's life, in 2002. The film *Artemisia* (1997), by **10** Agnès Merlet, tells her, story and there have been many other interpretations of her life. She is also part of Judy Chicago's feminist installation *The Dinner Party* (1979).

The influence of her work on many artists who came after her has now been fully recognized. Her paintings share wall space at the Uffizi gallery with her **11** muse Caravaggio, as well, as at many other major museums throughout the world, and her works are a part of every survey of Western art. She stands as a proud example of what women can accomplish, even against seemingly insurmountable odds.

9
A) NO CHANGE
B) her personal story rather,
C) her, personal story, rather
D) her personal story rather

10
A) NO CHANGE
B) Agnès Merlet, tells her story,
C) Agnès Merlet tells her story,
D) Agnès Merlet, tells, her story

11
A) NO CHANGE
B) muse Caravaggio as well
C) muse, Caravaggio, as well
D) muse, Caravaggio, as well,

Notes and Reflections

Standard English Conventions – Semicolons & Colons 1

Is coffee healthy, or not? Over the past few decades, there have been many scientific studies contradicting each other on the **1** topic, coffee has been shown to reverse the effects of liver damage, increase the risk of miscarriage, raise blood pressure, and lower the risk of stroke. The issue may not necessarily have arisen due to the science itself. Scientists are under constant pressure to publish new findings in order to win **2** funding; leaving little to no incentive for studies double-checking previously produced results.

When the experiments of published studies are replicated, their results can be tested and verified, or they can be **3** discredited, however; of the $30 billion that the federal government spends and $20 billion that universities and private foundations spend on scientific studies, almost none of that money is designated for research replication by the original researchers or other scientists working independently. In order to duplicate the experiments, scientists would need to put in the same amount of time and money. Meanwhile, they would have to forego any of the same **4** perks, such as: eligibility for academic or financial recognition. But, without research replication, the empirical nature of science is threatened, hindering the durability and power of scientific knowledge.

1
A) NO CHANGE
B) topic
C) topic; while
D) topic;

2
A) NO CHANGE
B) funding, it's
C) funding,
D) funding

3
A) NO CHANGE
B) discredited, however:
C) discredited; however,
D) discredited, however,

4
A) NO CHANGE
B) perks: such as,
C) perks:
D) perks;

Given the increasing trend of inadequate replication, scientific communities are facing an alarming dilemma. In the past few years, some studies have been touted as ground-breaking, garnering thousands of citations and shaping scientific **5** literature; yet they are debunked through replication years after their original publication. This environment—affecting scientific investigations across the **6** spectrum; serves as a breeding ground for false facts. The growing evidence for a concerning lack of research replication has even been given a **7** name: replication crisis.

Typically, researchers blame the development of this crisis on the aforementioned publishing culture of science; this publishing industry rewards new discoveries and brushes off necessary, yet mundane, replication studies. Journals leave little to no room for studies that cover already-published findings. Scientists want to be **8** published and journals want to publish exciting new research rather than repeated studies.

5
A) NO CHANGE
B) literature;
C) literature,
D) literature

6
A) NO CHANGE
B) spectrum;
C) spectrum,
D) spectrum—

7
A) NO CHANGE
B) name; replication
C) name, replication
D) name "replication

8
A) NO CHANGE
B) published, and,
C) published: and
D) published;

Perhaps a more obvious cause of the replication crisis is the failure to incentivize researchers to replicate other scientists' work. Without a routine for replication, established by a monetary and incentive structure, there is always room for the replication crisis to [9] exist; researchers need: reasons aside from serving the greater good of the scientific process, to spend a great deal of time and money re-testing their own studies and those of others. Without the incentive to gain tenure or a publication, especially in high-profile journals, scientists have very little to achieve with replication work. They may even have to face a social loss, as not all researchers would want to hear that one of their groundbreaking findings was not, in fact, true.

When investing so much into scientific studies, it seems completely reasonable to incorporate a part of that investment into research [10] replication; if new findings can be validated, then perhaps we would not have a sea of false facts plaguing our scientific communities. Psychologist and Executive Director of the Center for Open [11] Science, Brian Nosek, argues that, "one or two percent of research budgets devoted to replication might be enough to really balance the efforts, the dollars, going to novelty, new areas of research, versus replications." Perhaps then we can truly resolve the important, infamous debate: what are coffee's effects on health?

9

A) NO CHANGE
B) exist; researchers need reasons,
C) exist; researchers need reasons
D) exist, researchers need reasons,

10

A) NO CHANGE
B) replication,
C) replication
D) replication?

11

A) NO CHANGE
B) Science, Brian Nosek argues, that
C) Science: Brian Nosek argues that
D) Science, Brian Nosek, argues:

Standard English Conventions – Semicolons & Colons 2

When an important institution is struggling financially, the business sector often steps in to rescue it. Companies have used their capital **1** to support: political movements, health care, and even prisons. Professional sports arenas have been funded **2** by corporations known for beverages, shaving equipment, insurance, petroleum, telephone service, and airlines. Public parks are sponsored **3** by a variety of companies: vehicle manufacturers, credit card companies, and railroad businesses. There are benefits, certainly, to having such institutions **4** supported, however, these investments are not only done out of the kindness of corporate hearts. Rather than altruism, the funding is often an effort to improve public perception of brand names or to allow marketing in areas

1
A) NO CHANGE
B) to: support
C) to support,
D) to support

2
A) NO CHANGE
B) by: corporations known for
C) by corporations known for:
D) by corporations known for;

3
A) NO CHANGE
B) by a variety of companies;
C) by a variety of companies
D) by a variety of; companies,

4
A) NO CHANGE
B) supported, however
C) supported; however,
D) supported—however—

where it would otherwise be prevented. The morality of the situation can **5** be blurry, for what we gain from these sponsorships, we must also make up for in some sacrifices. A fundamental element of our right to privacy, some argue, is the right to not be advertised to. There can be great value in being free from media that attempt to manipulate our purchasing decisions. You may have no objections to advertisements or products tied to positive investments, such as charities and medical research. The conditions are harder to **6** support, though; when the education system is involved.

There is a sacredness inherent to schools. The realm of education, unlike areas meant purely for **7** diversion; should always be kept free from external influence. Schools serve a higher purpose than determining what brand of soda we drink or the car we'll drive. They are institutions of pure knowledge designed to build students into productive citizens. A core virtue of schools is that **8** they are unbiased; the learnings in ideal classrooms do not steer students toward certain choices or ideologies. As such, schools are places where young people can be free from outside pressures. In this protected environment, people can discover their true selves, rather than being unnaturally shaped.

5
A) NO CHANGE
B) be: blurry
C) be blurry
D) be blurry—

6
A) NO CHANGE
B) support, though:
C) support, though,
D) support, though

7
A) NO CHANGE
B) diversion:
C) diversion,
D) diversion

8
A) NO CHANGE
B) they are unbiased,
C) they are: unbiased,
D) they are: unbiased

As populations have migrated away from urban areas and less tax revenue is directed to education, schools must sacrifice quality of instruction and resources if they cannot increase budgets. Administrators don't want to see teachers laid off or new equipment avoided. On the other side **9** are: corporations that see the marketing potential of schools. Companies have purchased textbooks with their logo on the cover. Others have offered to pay teacher salaries if they could install television sets that continually play commercials. Some people see these as win-win situations; others are troubled by a violation of the integrity of students' education.

According to the influential economist Milton Friedman, corporations have a responsibility to purely focus on profits. Such greedy priorities can lead to morally unsupportable **10** decisions. For example; according to Friedman's views, there is no incentive to fix a faulty vehicle airbag if the cost of the repairs is greater than the lawsuits for injured passengers. Such an outlook leads to dangerously toxic products, illegal financial transactions, and low-quality manufacturing. This practice is opposed by business ethicists who argue businesses are responsible for the well-being and upbringing of citizens.

Fortunately, some corporations are invested in a good education system because they view students as upcoming **11** employees: in order to ensure future advantages over foreign competitors, companies have funded education that will foster smarter, more talented employees.

9
A) NO CHANGE
B) are;
C) are,
D) are

10
A) NO CHANGE
B) decisions. For example:
C) decisions; for example,
D) decisions; for example

11
A) NO CHANGE
B) employees; in order,
C) employees, in order
D) employees in order

Notes and Reflections

Standard English Conventions – Apostrophes 1

The discovery of DNA, which contains the blueprint for life, is usually attributed to biologist James Watson and physicist Francis Crick. The famous image of these **1** scientists model, made of beads, cardboard, and wire, has become a symbol of their pioneering genius. As with many **2** stories of mankinds' historic discoveries', there is much more to the tale than only a couple of clever scientists.

Watson and Crick were aware of the importance of their discovery. They were not modest about their own work, declaring that they had "found the secret of life." However, as is too often the case, the shine of history's spotlight illuminates a few while excluding many. Just as **3** Edison's invention's regarding lightbulbs occlude the brilliance of other scientists—Alessandro Volta, Humphry Davy, and Warren de la Rue, to name a few—Watson and Crick have long enjoyed the fame of this major scientific event, though there are many other scientists **4** who's contributions deserve some recognition.

1
A) NO CHANGE
B) scientists'
C) scientist's
D) scientists's

2
A) NO CHANGE
B) story's of mankind's historic discoveries
C) stories' of mankinds' historic discoveries
D) stories of mankind's historic discoveries

3
A) NO CHANGE
B) Edisons' inventions'
C) Edison's inventions
D) Edisons' inventions

4
A) NO CHANGE
B) whos'
C) whose
D) whom's

More than 75 years before **5** Watson and Cricks' groundbreaking research, chemist Friedrich Miescher identified "nuclein" inside white blood cells. He had been studying the blood and pus left on **6** his surgical bandage's and extracted this substance, which was unlike the proteins he had expected. Nuclein was later renamed "nucleic acid," and then "deoxyribonucleic acid," or the more common name of "DNA." Unfortunately, although Miescher's discoveries are well known, his name faded into obscurity.

Half a century later, biochemist Phoebus Levene used his extensive studies on yeast to infer a model of the DNA molecule. Levene identified **7** DNA's components – guanine, adenine, thymine, cytosine, and deoxyribose – and proposed a structure. Though his tetranucleotide model was overly simplistic, **8** it's structure was accurate enough to allow scientists to gain a much clearer understanding of DNA.

5
A) NO CHANGE
B) Watson and Crick's
C) Watsons and Cricks
D) Watson's and Crick

6
A) NO CHANGE
B) his surgical bandages'
C) his' surgical bandage's
D) his surgical bandages

7
A) NO CHANGE
B) DNAs' component's
C) D'N'A's components
D) D'N'A's' components

8
A) NO CHANGE
B) it's'
C) its'
D) its

Later, it was physical chemist Rosalind Elsie Franklin, along with Raymond Gosling and Maurice Wilkins, who discovered the structure of the DNA molecule. Franklin used a form of x-ray scanning to analyze the shape of DNA. Her research revealed some of DNA's features, namely its helix structure. With these discoveries made, scientists began racing to be the first to discover the full model of DNA.

With cardboard cutouts representing the chemical [9] components and the multiple molecules' bonds', Watson and Crick shifted the pieces around in the hope of putting together the DNA puzzle. However, the solution came from another scientist: chemist Jerry Donohue, with whom they shared an office. Before their breakthrough, Watson and Crick were working with a hypothesis based on an incorrect chemical form. Donohue overheard them and identified [10] they're error's. This led Watson and Crick to discard their original hypothesis. It was only then that they hit upon the correct theory.

In 1962, Watson, Crick, and Wilkins were awarded the Nobel Prize in Physiology or Medicine. Since then, there have been [11] debate's over whose most deserving of the credit for the discovery. Watson believed that Rosalind Franklin should have received an award, though she was deceased at the time the award was given.

9
A) NO CHANGE
B) component's and the multiple molecule's bond's
C) component's and the multiple molecules' bonds
D) components and the multiple molecules' bonds

10
A) NO CHANGE
B) their error's
C) their errors'
D) their errors

11
A) NO CHANGE
B) debates' over whose
C) debate's over who's
D) debates over who's

Standard English Conventions – Apostrophes 2

You get up early and check your package delivery app, which **1** show's your deliveries to make throughout the morning. You drive to the distribution center, pack your trunk with small packages, then use the app to direct you to different homes, dropping off **2** customers' orders. Returning home for lunch, you check your odd jobs app and see that your services have been requested by a couple of homeowners in your town, so you head out to make some minor repairs to cabinets and doors. On your last job, several miles from **3** you're home, its close to rush hour, so you check your ridesharing app to pick up some passengers and cash in on the higher rates offered at these times. After dinner, you work on a client's requests for wooden sculptures and cutting boards you sell online. After a long day working for the "gig economy," you turn in for the night. For most **4** workers who've taken part in the gig economy, this account might be a little exaggerated, but not unfamiliar. The new ways people find work in our society present many opportunities, and there are mixed feelings about whether this is good for our future.

1
A) NO CHANGE
B) shows your deliveries
C) show's your delivery's
D) shows your delivery's

2
A) NO CHANGE
B) customers' orders'
C) customer's order's
D) customer's orders

3
A) NO CHANGE
B) you're home, it's
C) your home, its
D) your home, it's

4
A) NO CHANGE
B) worker's who've
C) workers' who've
D) worker's whove

First, it's important to define the gig economy, since it can take on so many different forms. The term [5] takes' its name from each piece of work being compared to an individual "gig" that a worker is hired to complete. Workers are paid for each "gig" completed, rather than being paid an hourly rate. This is no new phenomenon—since the time of the "cottage industry" of the [6] 1800's, workers have toiled on their own to create items or perform services that were paid for piecemeal. The difference today is that much of this work is facilitated by phone apps and websites, many of which are controlled by algorithms. This has led to the term "platform economy" to describe the multiple electronic platforms used to distribute these gigs. [7] It's sometime's described as the "sharing economy." With the ubiquity of smartphones, it has become easier for people to both request and take part in the gig economy, but is that a good or a bad thing?

The gig economy has drawn both praise and skepticism over the past decade, and [8] it's remains unclear whether it is beneficial to workers. Optimists point to the flexibility of

5
A) NO CHANGE
B) take's its
C) takes it's
D) takes its

6
A) NO CHANGE
B) 1800's, worker's
C) 1800's, workers'
D) 1800s, workers

7
A) NO CHANGE
B) It's sometimes
C) Its sometime's
D) Its sometimes

8
A) NO CHANGE
B) its remain's
C) its remains
D) it remains

work and the options that workers have. Workers can fit many jobs within their differing lifestyles. Many of the gig [9] economys workers' don't subsist solely on gig work, but use it to gain supplemental income outside of their main job. At the same time, critics warn people about relying on gig work. For one, the income is inconsistent and not guaranteed. While one day there'll be plenty of rides to pick up and packages to deliver, the next might offer nothing. Also, workers in the gig economy have fewer protections and typically pay for their health insurance out of pocket. Still, many workers may still find gig work necessary to make ends meet, and so are willing to take the risks with the benefits.

These issues have generated controversy and conversation amongst pundits, [10] workers-rights groups, corporations, and the general public. Recent reporting has called into question whether the gig economy is such a big deal after all. A recent report from the Bureau of Labor Statistics, examining the impact of "nontraditional work" since 2005, claimed the old-fashioned job still reigns supreme. This report indicated that bigger factors influencing American workers included outsourcing and the rise of temporary work, both of which limit [11] Americans options' for full-time employment. While the gig economy may be highly visible, it may not have as widespread an effect as many believed. At the end of the day, it comes down to individuals to choose if the gig economy can benefit them, or if they'll stick with the traditional job market.

9
A) NO CHANGE
B) economy's workers don't
C) economys worker's don't
D) economys worker's dont

10
A) NO CHANGE
B) workers-right's groups
C) workers'-rights groups
D) workers-rights' group's

11
A) NO CHANGE
B) Americans option's
C) American's options
D) Americans' options

Notes and Reflections

Expression of Ideas – Main Idea 1

When asked which sea creature is the fiercest ocean predator, most would suggest the shark. Hollywood's portrayal of this menacing creature, **1** <u>which is endangered due to overfishing of its prey</u>, as well as news coverage of occasional shark attacks, would certainly support the idea. Yet a far more fearsome predator hunts among coral reefs and in the shallow waters off tropical islands: the mantis shrimp. **2** <u>Not actual shrimp but stomatopod crustaceans</u>, mantis shrimp have been perfecting their predatory skills in the world's oceans for nearly 400 million years.

While mantis shrimp resemble a lobster, they are more aptly compared to a military tank: not only are they heavily armored, but also they **3** <u>wield devastating weaponry</u>. Once they spot their prey, they capture it with what scientists term their "raptorial appendages." Unlike lobsters' claws, these lightning-fast limbs end in either lethal pointed spines, for some mantis shrimp, or powerful hammers called dactyl clubs, for others. Species with spiny appendages harpoon their prey, **4** <u>a different function than that of lobster claws</u>. Those with dactyl clubs mount split-second, violent attacks so fast and

---

1

Which of the following best reinforces the preceding idea in the sentence?

A) NO CHANGE
B) weighing as much as two tons
C) with its intimidating body and myriad jagged teeth
D) one of hundreds of shark species

2

Which of the following choices best introduces readers to the rest of the passage?

A) NO CHANGE
B) Standing humbly at the top of its food chain,
C) Capable of seeing colors far beyond human perception
D) Looking much like rainbow-colored lobsters

3

Which of the following choices gives another detail that best supports the main point the author is making in this paragraph?

A) NO CHANGE
B) hide within underwater hollows
C) are only a few inches in length
D) often choose to mate for life

4

A) NO CHANGE
B) hunting down prey like a true predator
C) maintaining their position in the ocean's food chain
D) impaling and retrieving their victims in the blink of an eye

forceful that they create tiny bubbles, which then collapse and create temperatures of thousands of degrees Celsius, propelling further energy into the target. This phenomenon, known in hydrodynamics as "cavitation," **5 can even destroy boat propellers and turbine blades.** It is harnessed by the canny mantis shrimp to crack victims' hard shells. Whether they have spines or clubs, mantis shrimp **6 still resemble lobsters more than any other commonly known ocean creature.**

7 Like other crustaceans, mantis shrimp have compound eyes. In a compound eye, there are hundreds of separate facets, each operating as a distinct unit within the eye. But mantis shrimp eyes, which are on mobile stalks and can move independently, are like three eyes in one: all three parts of each eye look at the same point in space, much like both human eyes focus on the same spot, but the mantis shrimp uses the top and bottom sections of its eyes to gauge distance to objects and the middle part, or "midband," to see ultraviolet light. The mantis shrimp's compound eyes make them especially cunning and nearly impossible to hide from. These eyes allow the mantis shrimp to locate prey by seeing their body heat. By observing ultraviolet light, mantis shrimp can detect prey that would otherwise be invisible. **8 Many ocean creatures depend on their camouflage.**

5

Which version of the underlined portion of the sentence provides the most relevant information for this paragraph?

A) NO CHANGE
B) creates brief bursts of light
C) can also occur within plants
D) is used to cleanse surgical tools

6

The author wants a logical conclusion to the paragraph and an effective transition to the next paragraph. Which choice best accomplishes these goals?

A) NO CHANGE
B) have several features, including their appendages, that make them talented predators.
C) have been shaped by the pressures of competition and survival.
D) must still satisfy their needs for food, safety, and procreation.

7

Which of the following, if added here, would best introduce this paragraph and transition from the previous paragraph?

A) There are even more ways in which mantis shrimp resemble sharks.
B) Physicists aren't the only scientists researching traits of mantis shrimp.
C) Mantis shrimps' raptorial arms aren't the only factor that make them such a formidable hunter.
D) While some traits make the mantis shrimp uniquely menacing, it also has relatively mundane qualities.

8

Which of the following choices most effectively summarizes the preceding ideas in the paragraph?

A) NO CHANGE
B) They ambush prey from burrows.
C) Sharks can sense electrical pulses from their prey's muscles.
D) This ability makes them very effective hunters.

When is a predator too good at killing? Mantis shrimp not only prey on fish, octopus, and crabs, they also can easily kill each other. And herein lies a problem: when mantis shrimp encounter one another, how do they know if one hopes to eat the other or if mating is intended? Those unique compound eyes again come into play. Mantis shrimp are colorful to the human eye, but they display additional patterns in ultraviolet, polarized light that is only visible to other mantis shrimp. These complicated displays clarify intention, letting mantis shrimp determine whether others are threats. [9] Their raptorial appendages are impressively dangerous.

[10] Specimens of the fierce mantis shrimp, like some sharks, can be studied in captivity, but beware—their raptorial appendages can easily crack glass tanks and either club or pierce both tank mates and unwary humans. Scientists use special shatter-proof enclosures to contain mantis shrimp and study this creature's amazing anatomy. Insight into the mantis shrimp's dactyl club, in particular, has inspired the development of ultra-strong composite materials that could be helpful in the aerospace and automotive fields or even as body armor. The mantis shrimp, [11] with its bullet-fast strikes and radar-like vision, has a lot to teach us.

9

Which of the following reiterates information that is most relevant to the focus of this point of the passage?

A) NO CHANGE
B) Such caution is necessary for creatures as dangerous as mantis shrimp.
C) One species, the peacock mantis shrimp, is particularly colorful.
D) For many animals, the males and females exhibit different coloration.

10

Given that each choice is accurate, which would best introduce the paragraph?

A) Research of mantis shrimp has great potential, as well as complications.
B) Though commonly known as mantis shrimp, these predators are referred to as "stomatopod crustaceans" by researchers.
C) In the time since shrimp first appeared, the ancestors of mantis shrimp have followed a unique evolutionary route.
D) Most mantis shrimp live in shallow, tropical waters, but they may be found in other environments.

11

The authors wants the final sentence to include details that relate the main idea of the passage. Which of the following choices best accomplishes this goal?

A) NO CHANGE
B) including more than 400 distinct species
C) much like the great white shark
D) unfortunately for researchers of biology and physics

Expression of Ideas – Main Idea 2

It's well-known that prices rise as the years go by. Your great-grandparents would have **1** recognized that marketing in the '60s was more straightforward than that in the '70s and later. This sort of price increase is the hallmark of a healthy economy. It may surprise you to learn, then, that the bottle of Coca-Cola your great-great grandparents could have bought for 5 cents in 1886 would still have cost your grandparents just 5 cents a full 70 years later. While the rest of the world was **2** informed about wars, the Great Depression, and the vagaries of supply and demand, the price of a bottle of Coke remained fixed at 5 cents. What accounts for this abnormal stability in price point? **3** Although the Coca-Cola recipe remains a secret, the company's history is well known.

Coca-Cola made its official debut in 1886 and for the next 13 years it was sold exclusively at soda fountains. In 1899, two lawyers approached Asa Candler, the President of the Coca-Cola Company, with a proposition: they wanted to buy the rights to bottle Coca-Cola. Bottled drinks were a new phenomenon. It seems that Candler didn't see much future in this new fashion, and perhaps he was also too busy to spend much time on the finer details of this negotiation. Whatever the reason, he agreed to sell the bottling rights if the buyers would commit to purchasing all the syrup for their sodas from Coca-Cola, but he didn't stipulate an expiration date in the contract! **4** Coca-Cola had locked in a price for the syrup and was bound to honor it, with no end in sight.

1

The author wants to include a specific example to build on the main idea of the paragraph and connect to the following sentence. Which of the following best accomplishes the author's goal?

A) NO CHANGE
B) paid 24 cents in the '60s for a can of soup that costs more than four times that today
C) noticed many economic changes over generations
D) been able to purchase numerous products for much cheaper prices than what we know currently

2

The author wants to emphasize the contrast between Coca-Cola's price and the world around it. Which choice best accomplishes the author's goal?

(A) NO CHANGE
(B) constantly troubled by
(C) deeply altered by
(D) enduring

3

Which of the following choices most effectively introduces readers to the rest of the passage?

(A) NO CHANGE
(B) Eventually, everything changes.
(C) Some stories are too odd and complicated to fully explain.
(D) It all started with a business deal done wrong.

4

Which choice would best build on the main idea of this paragraph and connect to the next paragraph?

(A) NO CHANGE
(B) Eventually, the contract had to be renegotiated for the sake of profits.
(C) Candler led the company until 1916.
(D) Soon after, soda fountains lost their popularity across the nation.

5 Coca-Cola needed a way to adapt to changing markets. The company made little profit from the sale of syrup, and they were unable to change the price and charge more to the bottlers. Profits fell. Candler and Coca-Cola had only one course of action: if they could not increase prices, they would increase the number of sales. They would turn the tables on the bottlers.

6 Coca-Cola attempted several marketing campaigns, with varying effectiveness. Coca-Cola could still generate profit if they sold a large amount of syrup, and the best way to promote sales would be to keep a low price for bottles of coke. The Coca-Cola Company couldn't actually print the price on the bottles—that was up to vendors to do themselves. They could affect consumer expectations, though. Coca-Cola set about advertising the 5-cent price on a massive scale. Stores couldn't very well get away with charging a customer 10 or even 6 cents for a coke if that customer had just walked by a sign saying "Drink Coca-Cola, 5 cents" on their way into the store! Now it was the bottlers and retailers who were locked into a price point and forced to hustle to raise profits.

The bottling contract was eventually renegotiated in 1921, but by that time, **7** the first World War had ended. Vending machines at the time could only process single-coin transactions; making change was simply too complicated. Coca-Cola vending machines **8** were a major marketing investment. Even if the company were to convert the machines to accept a different denomination, their options were limited.

5

Which of the following best introduces the main idea of this paragraph?

(A) NO CHANGE
(B) Alfred Marshall, the famed economist, pioneered the idea of supply and demand.
(C) Before the 1890s, glass bottles were individually made by glass blowers.
(D) Coca-Cola was advertised as not just a beverage but a health tonic.

6

Which of the following provides the best introduction to the paragraph's main idea?

A) NO CHANGE
B) Due to legal and social changes, Coca-Cola's syrup recipe changed.
C) Candler had a clever idea to make the most of his bad deal.
D) Technological advances have widespread effects.

7

Which of the following best introduces the focus of the rest of the paragraph?

A) NO CHANGE
B) social trends had changed.
C) another obstacle had sprung up to prevent price adjustments
D) U.S. foreign policies were altered by shifts in political views

8

Which of the following choices best supports the information in the previous sentence?

A) NO CHANGE
B) were seen commonly in most cities and large towns
C) were only equipped to accept a nickel
D) used simple mechanisms to simplify the task of repairs

Matching the amount of the next highest value coin, the dime, meant doubling the price. 9 Beyond that, the next highest value coin would be the quarter. Over the next 30 years, Coca-Cola executives tried everything they could think of to fix their vending machine problem. They approached the U.S. Treasury Department to request that a 7.5-cent coin be added to the country's currency. When this plea fell on deaf ears, they appealed to President Eisenhower 10 (who served two terms). They even tested a scheme in which they purposely included one empty bottle for every eight full ones so that an occasional unlucky customer would have to pay twice to get a coke.

Eventually, the cost of the ingredients rose until the 5-cent price tag couldn't be sustained. Although inflation won in the end, the nickel price lasted over 70 years. That incautious business decision Candler made in 1899 meant the company had to scramble to recoup its losses, but it may have been for the best. Coca-Cola's growth into the massive and ubiquitous organization we all know today 11 seems to have been destined from the company's beginning.

9

The author wants to emphasize the complications Coca-Cola faced due to vending machines. Which of the following choices most effectively accomplishes the author's goal?

A) NO CHANGE
B) Foreign denominations of coin would not be usable at all in these vending machines.
C) That was the smallest increase the machines were capable of, but it would be unacceptable to buyers.
D) Such a dramatic price increase may take decades under typical economic inflation.

10

Which of the following true statements, if added here, would provide the most relevant information to this portion of the passage?

A) NO CHANGE
B) who promoted proper budgeting by government
C) who did not intervene to help the struggling company
D) who oversaw a period of economic prosperity

11

The authors wants the final sentence to restate the main idea of the passage. Which of the following choices best accomplishes this goal?

A) NO CHANGE
B) contrasts its humble origins of dealing syrup to soda fountains
C) serves as an inspiring example for small business owners
D) is thanks to those desperate efforts to sell as many cokes as possible

Notes and Reflections

Expression of Ideas – Organization 1

[1] Dances that were previously celebratory were now being used as a means of survival. [2] When Africans were brought as slaves to the West Indies in the 1500s, they brought their dancing traditions with them. **1** [3] <u>As they crossed the Atlantic Ocean, slaves were brought on deck by their captors. [4] There, they danced as a form of exercise because their captors had a vested interest in keeping them healthy.</u> [5] The performances were also meant to entertain the crew, another humiliating aspect of the proceedings. [6] This unfortunate start was the first step in African dance styles moving towards the United States. **2**

1

Which choice most effectively combines the underlined sentences?

A) There, as they crossed the Atlantic Ocean, where they were brought on deck because their captors had a vested interest in keeping them healthy, they danced as a form of exercise.

B) Their captors had a vested interest in keeping them healthy, crossing the Atlantic Ocean, and they danced as a form of exercise because they were brought on deck.

C) As they crossed the Atlantic Ocean, their captors, who had a vested interest in keeping slaves healthy, brought them on deck to dance as a form of exercise.

D) Slaves danced as a form of exercise as they crossed the Atlantic Ocean on the deck where they were brought by their captors who had a vested interest in keeping them healthy.

2

To make the paragraph most logical and cohesive, sentence 1 should be placed

A) where it is now.

B) after sentence 4.

C) after sentence 5.

D) after sentence 6.

SUMMIT
EDUCATIONAL
GROUP

[1] For example, instruments and songs were traded and combined, and new styles developed as Irish jigs met traditional African dances. [2] Once West African slaves arrived in the Caribbean, they lived alongside Irish indentured servants. **3** [3] <u>These Irish were sent off as indentured servants and they were often women and children.</u> [4] <u>After their husbands and fathers went to war against Spain, this tragedy occurred.</u> [5] Living together for over a century, West Africans and Irish started to merge musical traditions. [6] The origins of tap can be found in this fusion. **4**

3

A) Often women and children, these Irish were sent off as indentured servants after their husbands and fathers went to war against Spain.

B) After their husbands and fathers went to war against Spain, these Irish were often women and children and were sent off as indentured servants.

C) Sent off as indentured servants were these Irish, often women and children, their husbands and fathers going to war against Spain.

D) These Irish were sent off as indentured servants, which occurred after their husbands and fathers, them often being women and children, went to war against Spain.

4

To make the paragraph most logical and cohesive, sentence 1 should be placed

A) where it is now.
B) after sentence 2.
C) after sentence 4.
D) after sentence 5.

5 [1] <u>Eventually, many Africans were transported to the United States. [2] In urban areas in the 1800s, African Americans and Irish immigrants continued to come together.</u> [3] Here, African dances were performed, and these dances included using the body to create sound by dragging the feet or slapping the hands. [4] Irish performances also included rhythmic footwork, a hallmark of tap. [5] One such place was the Five Points district of Manhattan, where free black people and Irish immigrants lived in close quarters. [6] In poor neighborhoods, these dances would be performed in informal settings, like the street or in dance halls. **6**

[1] Since tap dancing developed informally, copying was key to mastering the form. [2] As such, performers would mimic other dancers to practice and then put their own twist on borrowed moves. [3] This organic transferal of the form, with dancers continually copying and trying to improve on each other's performances, lead to "challenge" dancing. [4] In this style, two dancers take the stage and perform in a call-and-response to one another. [5] Each dancer's moves are meant to respond to their opponent in a kind of dialogue. **7**

5

Which choice most effectively combines the underlined sentences?

A) Irish immigrants in the 1800s in urban areas with many Africans who were eventually transported to the United States continued to come together.

B) Eventually transported to the United States, urban areas in the 1800s were where many Africans were and Irish immigrants continued to come together.

C) In the 1800s, many Africans were eventually transported to the United States, where they came together with Irish immigrants in urban areas.

D) Many Africans in the 1800s continued to come together with Irish immigrants in urban areas and were eventually transported to the United States.

6

For the sake of creating the most logical and cohesive paragraph, sentence 5 should be

A) placed where it is now.
B) placed before sentence 1.
C) placed after sentence 2.
D) DELETED from the passage.

7

To make the paragraph most logical, sentence 2 should be placed

A) where it is now.
B) before sentence 1.
C) after sentence 3.
D) after sentence 5.

[1] Some of these performers were Irish, further cementing the combination of both cultures' dance styles. [2] In the 1800s, tap was a popular component of minstrel shows, where the "jigging" style of tap was put on display. [3] Minstrel shows were variety shows, often performed by white performers in blackface. [4] After the Civil War, black dancers also began performing in minstrel shows, bringing new steps to the form. **8** [5] Minstrel shows eventually fell out of fashion because they were rife with racial stereotypes. [6] This shift marks how there was seen a continual change in public attitudes toward racism after the Civil War. **9**

8

To make the paragraph most logical, sentence 1 should be placed

A) where it is now.
B) after sentence 2.
C) after sentence 3.
D) after sentence 6.

9

A) Public attitudes toward racism, such as the racial stereotypes that minstrel shows, which eventually fell out of fashion, were rife with, continued to change after the Civil War.

B) The shift of minstrel shows eventually falling out of fashion marks how public attitudes toward racism continued to change after the Civil War because racial stereotypes were things with which the minstrel shows were rife.

C) Rife with racial stereotypes, minstrel shows after the Civil War when public attitudes toward racism continued to change eventually fell out of fashion.

D) After the Civil War, as public attitudes toward racism continued to change, minstrel shows eventually fell out of fashion because they were rife with racial stereotypes.

[1] Today, tap is still alive. [2] This attention has led to The United States establishing a National Tap Dance Day, and yearly tap conferences have been organized. [3] It experienced a revival in the 1980s and 1990s with several Broadway shows, like 42nd Street, as well as a merger with hip hop music of the time. [4] Additionally, a recent revival of step dancing, similar to tap in the creation of sound with the body, has aided in giving attention to the art form. **10** [5] <u>Tap dancing continues to develop and grow. [6] It is a form with a long and troubled, though treasured, history</u>. **11**

10

A) Though its history is treasured, its history is long and troubled, and tap dancing continues to develop and grow.

B) Continuing to develop and grow, and being treasured, a long and troubled history is had by tap dancing.

C) Tap dancing, a form with a long and troubled history, continues to develop and grow, though it is treasured.

D) Though it is a form with a long and troubled history, tap dancing is treasured and continues to develop and grow.

11

To make the paragraph most logical, sentence 2 should be placed

A) where it is now.

B) before sentence 1.

C) after sentence 4.

D) after sentence 6.

Expression of Ideas – Organization 2

[1] Few would imagine that the paint-by-numbers kits we remember from grade school were inspired by one of the greatest artists of all time. [2] And yet, what may seem to us like child's play truly did originate in the workshop of the master artist Leonardo da Vinci. **1** [3] <u>Da Vinci would distribute numbered patterns to his apprentices. [4] He was a celebrated painter and inventor, and these patterns served as guidelines for the coloring of their underpaintings.</u> [5] So how was the legendary genius's invention handed down from 15th century neophyte painters to the amateurs of today? [6] That was the work of another type of genius: marketing genius. **2**

1

Which choice most effectively combines the underlined sentences?

A) A celebrated painter and inventor, da Vinci would distribute numbered patterns as guidelines to his apprentices for the coloring of their underpaintings.

B) Numbered patterns distributed by Da Vinci, a celebrated painter and inventor, to his apprentices, and these patterns served as guidelines for the coloring of their underpaintings.

C) For the coloring of their underpaintings, da Vinci's apprentices were distributed by celebrated painter and inventor da Vinci numbered patterns that served as guidelines.

D) Da Vinci's apprentices, to whom were distributed numbered patterns by him, a celebrated painter and inventor, were served guidelines for the coloring of their underpaintings.

2

For the sake of creating the most logical and cohesive paragraph, sentence 2 should be

A) placed where it is now.
B) placed before sentence 1.
C) placed after sentence 5.
D) DELETED from the passage.

[1] Palmer Paint Co employee Dan Robbins created the first paint-by-numbers kit, called the Craft Master, in 1950, having realized that da Vinci's pedagogical method could be used to make artists of amateurs. **3** [2] Palmer theorized the average un-trained American could, with a reasonable expectation of success, pick up a brush and paint for fun. [3] If his theory were accurate, his market would no longer be limited to professionals. [4] An artist himself, Robbins created a prototype and brought it to Palmer Paint Co founder Max Klein. [5] More importantly for his company, this product would also increase the demand for Palmer Paint Co paint. [6] Klein didn't think the prototype, titled "Abstract No. 1," had enough mass appeal to sell well, but he recognized the merit of the idea and encouraged Robbins to improve upon his design. **4**

3

A) Palmer's market would no longer be limited to professionals, he theorized, if a reasonable success could be had by the average un-trained American if they could pick up a brush and paint for fun.

B) The average un-trained American, with a reasonable expectation of success, could pick up a brush and paint for fun, as theorized by Palmer, whose market, if his theory were accurate, would no longer be limited to professionals.

C) If, as Palmer theorized, the average un-trained American could pick up a brush and paint for fun with a reasonable expectation of success, the market would no longer be limited to professionals.

D) Palmer, whose theory was that the average un-trained American could pick up a brush and paint for fun with a reasonable expectation of success, his market no longer limited to professionals any longer if his theory were accurate.

4

To make the paragraph most logical, sentence 5 should be placed

A) where it is now.
B) before sentence 1.
C) after sentence 1.
D) after sentence 3.

[1] Robbins soon found that perfecting the paint kit was more complicated than he'd imagined. [2] The landscapes and portraits he subsequently developed checked all the right boxes. [3] The end result would have to be something the amateur painter could handle, but not on his or her own, and something he or she would be proud to have completed. **5** [4] He had originally proposed an abstract depiction of fruit on a table because it was simple and modern. [5] However, the proper mix of impressive and manageable wasn't offered by his proposal. [6] Finally Robbins had six designs that Klein approved, and the Craft Master paint-by-numbers kit was born. **6**

5

A) An abstract depiction of fruit on a table that didn't offer the proper mix of impressive and manageable but was simple and modern was his original proposal.

B) Because it was simple and modern, his original proposal had been an abstract depiction of fruit, but it didn't offer the proper mix of impressive and manageable.

C) Offered originally by his proposal was not the proper mix of impressive and manageable but, an abstract depiction of fruit on a table, it was simple and modern.

D) He had originally proposed, because it was simple and modern, however it didn't offer the proper mix of impressive and manageable, a depiction of fruit on a table that was also abstract.

6

For the sake of creating the most logical and cohesive paragraph, sentence 2 should be

A) placed where it is now.
B) placed before sentence 1.
C) placed after sentence 5.
D) DELETED from the passage.

[1] The Craft Master's debut was disappointing because retailers didn't share Robbins's vision and were hesitant to place orders. [2] To make matters worse, when large-scale store chain Kresge finally did bite, the Craft Master paint kits got their big chance—and promptly blew it. [3] With no buyers, it seemed the product would be a flop. [4] A mixup during packaging had swapped the paints meant for "The Fishermen" with those intended for "The Bullfighter" kit, with predictably outrageous results. **7** [5] Customers went to Kresge to ask for refunds, and Kresge cut the money-losing product line from its stores. [6] The customers had correctly assumed the bulls they had painted green were not actually supposed to be painted this color. **8**

7

A) Customers who had painted the bulls green and asked for refunds from Kresge had correctly assumed the bulls were not actually supposed to be painted green, and so Kresge cut from its stores the money-losing product line.

B) Kresge cut the money-losing product line from their stores when customers asked for refunds because, as they had correctly assumed, the bulls were not actually supposed to be painted green.

C) The bulls that customers, who had painted them green, were not supposed to painted that color, was assumed by customers who asked for refunds from Kresge, which cut the money-losing product line from their stores.

D) The bulls, which had been painted green by customers but were correctly assumed by customers to not be supposed to do so, were the reason why customers went for refunds to Kresge, and the money-losing product line was cut the from their stores.

8

To make the paragraph most logical, sentence 2 should be placed

A) where it is now.
B) before sentence 1.
C) after sentence 3.
D) after sentence 4.

[1] The Palmer Paint Co now had not only paint but whole paint kits it needed to sell, but Klein soon came up with a plan to fix the problem. **9** [2] He had a no-risk proposition with which he approached the owners of Macy's. [3] Klein asked them to let Palmer, within the Macy's stores, demonstrate the kits. [4] The request was made on the condition that any unsold product would be taken back by his company. [5] Klein hoped that those 200 sales would be enough to spark a trend. [6] His plan couldn't have come off better: the tide of fake customers rushing in to get their (free) paint kits caught the attention of other shoppers, and soon the kits were flying off the shelves. [7] He then made sure there wouldn't be any unsold kits: he hired sales representatives and gave them $500 (enough for 200 kits) to distribute to friends and family for paint kits! **10**

Clearly Klein and Robbins had been right; "A beautiful oil painting the first time you try," as the tagline went, appealed to the general public, no matter what critics and artists might think of it. The massive popularity of the Craft Master kits, bought with a $500 ploy, ultimately brought in over $20 million in sales and catapulted Dan Robbins to new career heights. **11** Today, Robbins is the most exhibited artist ever. And yet, he is still less well-known than da Vinci. Millions of amateur artists have painted in his designs and displayed them proudly on their walls.

9

A) He approached the owners of Macy's with a no-risk proposition he had, which requested that they, his company buying back any unsold product being the condition, let Palmer demonstrate the kits within the Macy's stores.

B) He approached the owners of Macy's with a no-risk proposition: they would let Palmer demonstrate the kits in stores, on the condition that his company would take back any unsold product.

C) On the condition that any unsold product would be taken back by his company, the owners of Macy's were approached by him to let Palmer demonstrate the kits in their stores, which was a no-risk proposition requested by Klein.

D) Palmer demonstrating the kits in the Macy's stores was the no-risk proposition to the store owners requested by Klein, the condition on which being that any unsold product would be taken back by his company.

10

To make the paragraph most logical, sentence 7 should be placed

A) where it is now.
B) before sentence 1.
C) after sentence 4.
D) after sentence 5.

11

A) Today, though he is still less well-known than da Vinci, Robbins is the most exhibited artist ever.

B) The most exhibited artist ever being, today, Robbins, da Vinci is still more well-known.

C) Da Vinci is more well-known than Robbins, who, yet, is the most exhibited artist ever, today.

D) Though Robbins today, still being the most exhibited artist ever, he is, compared to da Vinci, less well-known.

Notes and Reflections

Expression of Ideas – Addition & Deletion 1

In one of the first accounts of encountering the famous dodo, the dodo was referred to as "Dodaars," likely its original name, which is Dutch for "fat butt." Another possibility for the bird's original name is the Portugese word "doudo," which means "fool." **1** Although the dodo bird has not existed for over 300 years, its image is still a symbol of awkwardness and stupidity, as well as humanity's responsibility for preservation of nature. Our current knowledge of the dodo is based on a few remains of fossilized dodo skeletons, as well as illustrations and descriptions of the birds by 17th century explorers. Because the dodo, or *Raphus cucullatus*, is a relatively modern species, natural records exist as subfossils with preserved organic material. **2** Based on this information, we have an image of the dodo having an unusually large, turkey-like body, a vulture-like head, and small wings. Over time, this image has evolved into one that is cartoonish and foolish. In reality, the dodo was not a fool but was simply carefree due to a leisurely life with ample nourishment and without danger. **3**

1

If the author were to delete the preceding sentence, the paragraph would primarily lose

A) a description of one of humanity's first encounters with the dodo.

B) details supporting the dodo's lasting symbolism.

C) an explanation of the dodo's physical traits.

D) clarification that the dodo's extinction is significant because it was influenced by people.

2

The author is considering whether to delete the preceding sentence. Should it be kept or deleted from the paragraph?

A) Kept, because it provides information about the species and genus of the dodo.

B) Kept, because it suggests that some dodo may still be living.

C) Deleted, because it isn't relevant to the focus on ecosystems.

D) Deleted, because it doesn't add necessary information to what is already stated in the paragraph.

3

If the author were to delete the phrase "due to a leisurely life with ample nourishment and without danger" from the sentence, the passage would primarily lose

A) clarifications about the length of time dodo thrived without the worry of predators.

B) a suggestion that the extinction of the dodo was inevitable.

C) a summary of ideas described throughout the paragraph.

D) an introduction to ideas expanded upon later in the passage.

[1] The dodo's vulnerability can be attributed to the fact that it only existed in one place in the world: Mauritius, a small island in the Indian Ocean. [2] Because the island is so remote, life evolved in unique ways there. [3] **4** Mauritius was home to a wide array of flora and fauna that only existed there, including the once numerous dodo, which evolved from a type of pigeon that first settled on Mauritius four million years ago. [4] **5** Accordingly, it evolved to be mostly defenseless, with stubby legs and ineffective wings.

4

The author is considering deleting the following phrase from the sentence (and adjusting punctuation as needed):

"which evolved from a type of pigeon that first settled on Mauritius 4 million years ago"

Given the phrase is accurate, should the author remove it from the paragraph?

A) Yes, because the information is irrelevant to the focus of the paragraph.

B) Yes, because the information is previously stated by information in the paragraph.

C) No, because the information clarifies how dodo evaded predators for so long.

D) No, because the information explains why the dodo's extinction occurred so rapidly.

5

At this point, the author is considering adding the following sentence:

On this island, the dodo bird never experienced any threats from predators.

Should the author make this addition here?

A) Yes, because it clarifies a claim made earlier in the paragraph.

B) Yes, because it effectively sets up the sentence that follows in the paragraph.

C) No, because it includes information that is irrelevant to the main focus of the paragraph.

D) No, because it unnecessarily repeats information from earlier in the passage.

[5] The dodo also had small clutches, possibly laying only one egg at a time, because there had been no dangers against preserving the bird's population. **6**

[1] The common image of the unintelligent dodo is likely due to its unawareness of predator threats. [2] **7** Based on journals and records, when explorers first came to Mauritius,

---

6

The author is considering adding the following sentence to the passage:

> "Altogether, the dodo had these many characteristics, which made it an especially vulnerable species, because it had only known the safety of its native, secluded home."

If the author were to add this sentence to the passage, it should logically be placed

A) after sentence 2.
B) after sentence 3.
C) after sentence 4.
D) after sentence 5.

7

The author is considering adding the following sentence to the passage:

> "The iconic depiction of the dopey dodo was made popular from its prominent role in the well-known story 'Alice's Adventures in Wonderland'."

Should the author make this addition here?

A) Yes, because it helps explain why the dodo bird was so vulnerable to changes in its ecosystem.
B) Yes, because it creates an effective transition from the history of ecological research to the discussion of popular culture's effect on wildlife conservation.
C) No, because it offers information that is repeated later in the passage.
D) No, because it is irrelevant to the main focus of the paragraph.

the dodo showed no fear of humans and would calmly allow people to approach them. [3] This lack of self-protection allowed people to hunt them easily, <u>8</u> <u>simply walking up and grabbing the large birds</u>. [4] However, despite the dodo's size and the ease of hunting them, the dodo were not a great source of food because their meat was mostly tough and fatty. [5] The extinction of the dodo was not directly caused by humans, but rather by the introduction of predatory pigs and monkeys to the island of Mauritius. [6] The ecosystems of Mauritius were quickly and permanently disrupted by these changes. 9

8

If the author were to delete the underlined portion (adjusting punctuation as needed), the paragraph would primarily lose

A) a description of the dodo's natural behaviors.

B) details that support previous information.

C) a suggestion that humans were not to blame for the dodo's extinction.

D) clarification of the origins of the records that remain of the dodo.

9

The author is considering adding the following sentence to the passage:

> "These animals destroyed the dodo's habitat and preyed on the dodo's eggs."

If the author were to add this sentence to the passage, it should logically be placed

A) after sentence 1.

B) after sentence 2.

C) after sentence 4.

D) after sentence 5.

In natural ecosystems, change brings further changes. When the dodo went extinct, several other species struggled. The broad-billed parrot 10 went extinct shortly after the end of the dodo. There is also the tambalacoque tree, native to Mauritius, which relied on dodo because the birds would eat fruit from the tree and the undigested seeds would then grow. The dodo would also eat stones, known as "gizzard stones," to help digest its food. 11 Fortunately, this tree has managed to survive without the aid of the dodo, though only a few hundred of the trees live today.

Humanity's role in the fate of the dodo has brought an important lesson: nature can be surprisingly fragile. Our zeal for expansion and exploration must be coupled with a recognition of our responsibility toward preservation.

10

The author is considering adding the following phrase to the sentence (adjusting punctuation as needed):

> "a species that depended on eating the undigested palm seeds left in dodo droppings"

Should the author make this addition here?

A) Yes, because it emphasizes the ease with which the dodo population was eliminated.

B) Yes, because it provides specific information explaining how the loss of the dodo caused other changes.

C) No, because it adds information that directly contradicts the main idea of the paragraph.

D) No, because it implies that all environmental changes are unpreventable.

11

The author is considering whether to delete the preceding sentence. Should it be kept or deleted from the paragraph?

A) Kept, because it implies that the extinction of a single species may have effects beyond what we can perceive.

B) Kept, because it explains an important connection between the dodo and the tambalacoque tree.

C) Deleted, because it doesn't provide information that is relevant to the paragraph's focus on ecological research in the 17th century.

D) Deleted, because it is irrelevant to the discussion of how one part of an ecosystem can affect other parts.

Expression of Ideas – Addition & Deletion 2

In school, we are provided with the knowledge that Earth is round, that it orbits the sun, and that the moon controls the ocean's tides. **1** Ancient Greeks over two millennia ago recognized that the earth is round. Pythagoras first posited this idea in 500 BCE, and Aristotle used the horizon to confirm that theory in the fourth century BCE. **2**

1

At this point, the author is considering adding the following sentence:

"Throughout history, however, scholars have relied on their own observations to derive this information."

Should the author make this addition here?

A) Yes, because it transitions from the preceding sentence to the rest of the paragraph.

B) Yes, because it gives a specific example that supports the main idea of the paragraph.

C) No, because it presents a claim that is countered later in the passage.

D) No, because it adds irrelevant information that distracts from the focus of the paragraph.

2

At this point, the author is considering adding the following sentence:

"About a hundred years after Aristotle, Eratosthenes calculated Earth's circumference."

Should the author make this addition here?

A) Yes, because it provides a detail that contrasts the main claim of the paragraph.

B) Yes, because it effectively sets up the focus of the rest of the passage.

C) No, because it introduces irrelevant information that distracts from the focus of the passage.

D) No, because it includes information that contradicts the main idea of the passage.

Eratosthenes founded the field of geography. His calculation of Earth's circumference was fueled by his interest in Earth's characteristics. He wanted to make a map of the planet, but before accomplishing this, he needed to know its size. He wanted precision, which required accurate measurements and a perfect instrument: mathematics. In his quest to map the Earth, he would need to find a few clues to guide him and some clever calculations. [3] Eratosthenes was a learned man, studied in poetry, music, astronomy, and mathematics, and in 240 BCE, Ptolemy III appointed him to be the chief librarian of the library of Alexandria.

News came to Eratosthenes about a well in Syene, Egypt. [4] The sun completely illuminated the bottom of this well at noon on the summer solstice; there were no shadows, which indicated the sun was directly overhead. This was not the case in Alexandria. In fact, when Eratosthenes stuck a stick in the ground in Alexandria at noon on the summer solstice, he found the stick cast a shadow which made an angle of about one fiftieth of a circle. Using degrees to measure angles had not yet been adopted from the Babylonians. [5] Eratosthenes correctly assumed sun rays ran parallel when they hit Earth, and he understood this could reveal the circumference of the Earth through proportions.

3

The author is considering deleting the underlined sentence. Should the sentence be kept or deleted?

A) Kept, because it elaborates on a key term that is used in the passage.

B) Kept, because it adds an important detail that supports the main idea of the paragraph.

C) Deleted, because it distracts from the paragraph's discussion by adding irrelevant information.

D) Deleted, because it repeats details stated earlier in the paragraph.

4

At this point, the author is considering adding the following sentence:

> "In modern day, it is known as Aswan."

Should the author make this addition here?

A) Yes, because it provides necessary contextual information.

B) Yes, because it puts in perspective how much can change with time.

C) No, because it is not relevant to the focus of the paragraph.

D) No, because it interrupts the discussion of the history of Greek mathematics.

5

If the author were to delete the preceding sentence, the passage would primarily lose

A) a clarification about how much time has passed since geometry was invented.

B) a clarification about a particular detail of Eratosthenes' calculation.

C) a detail emphasizing the ingenuity of modern mathematicians.

D) details emphasizing the many advancements that led to our current understanding of geometry.

Eratosthenes reasoned he could calculate Earth's circumference if he knew the distance between Alexandria and Syene. Accurately measuring distance at that time was not easy. Distances between cities were measured by the time it took a caravan to travel between cities, [6] but this was not reliable due to variances in the speeds and wandering paths of camels. Another unit of measurement were stadia, units of distance between 500 and 600 feet, which was the distance covered in ancient Greek footraces. [7] Eratosthenes hired a man to walk with even footsteps between Alexandria and Syene to get an accurate distance. This man found that Alexandra is about 5,000 stadia away from Syene.

6

The author is considering whether to delete the underlined phrase from the sentence (and adjust punctuation as needed). Should it be kept or deleted from the paragraph?

A) Kept, because it suggests that no measurement of the Earth's circumference can be accurate.

B) Kept, because it provides information supporting an earlier claim in the paragraph.

C) Deleted, because it doesn't provide information that is relevant to the paragraph's focus on transportation technologies.

D) Deleted, because it doesn't state which other cities Eratosthenes could have used to make his calculations.

7

The author is considering deleting the preceding sentence. Given that the sentence is accurate, should the author remove it from the paragraph?

A) Yes, because the information is already suggested by information provided in the previous paragraph.

B) Yes, because the information is irrelevant to the main focus of the paragraph.

C) No, because the information clarifies what motivated Eratosthenes' work.

D) No, because the information clarifies a term that is used later in the passage.

[1] **8** Based on his measurement that the stick cast a shadow of one fiftieth of a circle, Eratosthenes figured the distance of 5,000 stadia distance between Syene and Alexandria could be multiplied by 50 to get the circumference of the Earth. [2] Accordingly, he estimated this distance is approximately 250,000 stadia. [3] Using an estimate of between 500 and 600 feet, however, his calculation would be between 24,000 and 29,000 miles. [4] **9** The circumference of the Earth known through modern technology is 24,900 miles. [5] This measurement lies well within the range of possibilities from Eratosthenes' estimate. **10**

8

If the author were to delete the phrase "Based on his measurement that the stick cast a shadow of one fiftieth of a circle" from the sentence (and adjust punctuation as need), the passage would primarily lose

A) a detail casting doubt on the accuracy of Eratosthenes' maps.

B) a clarification about how Eratosthenes arrived at his calculation.

C) a clarification about how much time it took Eratosthenes to make his calculation.

D) a detail emphasizing the intricacy of map-making.

9

The author is considering deleting the underlined sentence. Should the sentence be kept or deleted?

A) Kept, because it shows that measurements always have some inaccuracy.

B) Kept, because it provides a transition between the preceding and following sentences.

C) Deleted, because it does not account for different units of measurement.

D) Deleted, because it interrupts the paragraph's description of the history of map creation.

10

The author is considering adding the following sentence to the paragraph

"Modern scholars are not certain of the exact length of a stadium, so it is not possible to know how precise Eratosthenes' calculation was."

The paragraph would be most logical if the sentence were placed:

A) after sentence 1.

B) after sentence 2.

C) after sentence 4.

D) after sentence 5.

Recognizing the importance of Eratosthenes' calculations, later Greek scholars and scientists throughout history have attempted to repeat or refine them. **11** For example, Posidonius tried to measure the circumference based on light from the star Caponus with the measurement between the cities of Alexandria and Rhodes. However, he did not have a correct distance between the two cities and calculated a much smaller circumference. Later scientists, using new technologies, continued to build on Eratosthenes' work, but it took many centuries before they could make measurements with much more accuracy.

Modern technology allows us to analyze the Earth through lenses unimaginable to ancient people. Nevertheless, Eratosthenes serves as a reminder to modern students and scholars alike that it is possible to procure amazing insights about the world through astute observation, deduction, and some simple math.

11

If the author were to delete the preceding sentence, the paragraph would primarily lose

A) clarification that Eratosthenes was the only person to ever calculate the Earth's circumference.

B) a description of the many obstacles that mathematicians face.

C) a description of an event that reveals how the legacy of Eratosthenes was passed through the generations to present day.

D) a statement that establishes the focus of the paragraph.

Notes and Reflections

Expression of Ideas – Transitions 1

Artificial intelligence, commonly known as AI, is often heralded as the future of humanity, while also being depicted as the central context of dystopian science fiction films. [1] Likewise, artificial intelligence is not just reserved for our cinematic imaginations. We now have it in our homes. AI has existed in research laboratories since computer scientists at the 1956 Dartmouth Conferences first investigated the concept. These pioneers wanted to create complex machines that could act with human intelligence, a state of computer advancement named "General AI." [2] Undoubtedly, such visions for artificial intelligence have been polarizing: some view AI as the greatest step forward for mankind and others as a foolish, hopeless pursuit.

[3] Until 2012, both of these perspectives were supported by evidence. The increased accessibility of graphics processing units (GPUs), specialized electronic circuits that make parallel processing faster and cheaper, opened the door for unlimited storage and mass data collection. [4] On the contrary, GPUs did not open the door to "General AI;" instead, they progressed the pursuit towards "Narrow AI," which describes technologies that can perform specific tasks as well as, or sometimes even better than, humans. This is achieved through the developing practice of machine learning: the use of algorithms to sort through data and learn from them in order to make increasingly accurate predictions. Prior to machine learning, software engineers code a system to follow

1

A) NO CHANGE
B) Therefore,
C) However,
D) In particular,

2

A) NO CHANGE
D) Particularly,
C) Similarly,
D) In fact,

3

Which choice, if added here, would provide the most effective transition from the previous paragraph?

A) How many companies are currently investing in General AI research?
B) Are there other opinions on scientists' attempt to create General AI?
C) Which of these two views on AI is most likely accurate?
D) Why is AI research important in the modern world?

4

A) NO CHANGE
B) Indeed,
C) Overall,
D) Despite this,

a specific set of instructions in order to complete tasks. The engineers use data and algorithms to continually train [5] the AI system. Most importantly, the AI system is also able to build on its initial set of instructions by creating its own connections and learning from them.

As forward as it was for its time, machine learning did not immediately pave the way for [6] Narrow AI. Machine learning did progressed the field of computer vision. Computers could be trained to "see," though the ability had limits. Computer vision still required traditional coding, such as edge detection filters, to determine the beginning and ending of objects. [7] Then, if the object was not in an ideal state, such as a stop sign in foggy weather causing obscured visibility, traditional coding would fail to accurately recognize the object.

Another algorithmic approach enhanced by machine learning was Artificial Neural Networks, which derived its name from the interconnected neurons sustaining our brains. A human brain is composed of neurons that communicate with physically neighboring neurons, whereas artificial neural networks utilize a systematic hierarchy of data propagation. [8] Instead of analyzing a stop sign by its edges, shape, and letters, these artificial neural networks would divide the image of a stop sign and individually examine its shape, color, letters, size, and motion, or lack thereof. Only then would the network, using the information from the individual modes of

[5]

Which choice most effectively combines the sentences at the underlined portion?

A) it, most importantly,

B) the AI system, the one that, and it is most important,

C) the AI system, which, most importantly,

D) the AI system, but, most importantly, despite this,

[6]

Which choice most effectively combines the sentences at the underlined portion?

A) NO CHANGE

B) Narrow AI, and so did

C) Narrow AI, which it

D) Narrow AI; rather, it

[7]

A) NO CHANGE

B) Though,

C) For example,

D) Likewise,

[8]

A) NO CHANGE

B) Because of

C) Despite

D) In the same manner,

analyses, conclude if the image was of a stop sign. The determination, however, would not be a simple yes or no.

9 At any rate, the system outputs a probability vector, which is a quantitative educated guess; it could be 80% confident the image is of a stop sign, 10% confident it's a speed limit sign, and 10% confident it's actually a picture of a kite in a small tree. Using its hierarchy, the neural network is told whether it is correct or not. In order to build its accuracy, the artificial neural network needs more practice, which means analyzing and recognizing thousands of images until the inputs are precise regardless of original image quality. Only then, when it has achieved a near-perfect accuracy rate, can the network undoubtedly know what a stop sign looks like.

10 Although this task may seem simple, and its method of achievement may seem mundane, but this process of deep learning for image recognition can be applied to incredibly challenging jobs, such as identifying cancer in blood or tumors in MRI scans. **11** On the other hand, the ability of machines to recognize images is a strong assurance for the future of artificial intelligence. In the movies, the presence of AI is always presented in a distant future society, but with machine learning, that future may not be as far away as we think, though it may still be polarizing.

9
A) NO CHANGE
B) Instead,
C) On the other hand,
D) Nonetheless,

10
A) NO CHANGE
B) Because
C) If
D) DELETE the underlined portion and capitalize the next word.

11
A) NO CHANGE
B) By contrast,
C) And yet,
D) Furthermore,

Expression of Ideas – Transitions 2

The universe is cold. **1** <u>Particularly,</u> there are spots where matter aggregates and gravity's force brings intense heat, such as within stars or the cores of some planets. **2** <u>Therefore,</u> the majority of space is frigid. When astrobiologists consider the possibility of life existing beyond Earth, their search primarily focuses on environments where humanity thrives, places with comfortably warm climates. Yet some focus must be given to environments where we cannot survive but other forms of life do manage to live.

On our own planet, life is found in the most extreme environments. Far to the south, in regions of the Arctic that are hostile to most species, life is thriving. Evolution has brought adaptation and hardiness. At frigid arctic temperatures, the water in cells of most lifeforms freezes, causing cells to burst. How, **3** <u>regardless,</u> can any life persist in these environmental conditions?

Nearly four hundred miles from the South Pole, on the West Antarctic Ice Sheet, a group of hardy scientists found life where it seemed impossible: within Lake Mercer. Normally, a lake would seem an obvious place to find living things, since this is where we would expect to encounter fish, frogs, birds, insects, and all manner of bacterial life. **4** <u>On the other hand,</u> Lake Mercer is not a typical lake at all. The water in Lake

1
A) NO CHANGE
B) In fact,
C) Granted,
D) Overall,

2
A) NO CHANGE
B) Despite this,
C) Additionally,
D) Furthermore,

3
A) NO CHANGE
B) likewise,
C) then,
D) however,

4
A) NO CHANGE
B) For example,
C) In addition,
D) Afterward,

Mercer is below freezing temperatures, only remaining liquid because of the quantity of [5] salt. Furthermore, Lake Mercer is more than a kilometer below ground. Scientists had to drill through 3,500 feet of solid ice to get samples of water from Lake Mercer, which lies buried beneath a glacier. In the samples retrieved from Lake Mercer, scientists found an abundance of bacteria. Per milliliter of water, there were approximately 10,000 bacterial cells, only about 1% of the quantity found in typical open-ocean water, but enough to suggest there may also be more advanced lifeforms within Lake Mercer that could prey on these bacteria. Even in subfreezing temperatures and with absolutely no sunlight, life finds a way to adapt and persist. The discovery has some scientists hopeful that similar life may exist on other planets. [6] Admittedly, Mars is a likely candidate. On that planet, evidence suggests the presence of underground saltwater lakes where lifeforms may also exist.

[7] As some scientists believe, organisms must be built differently. One reason that many psychrophiles can thrive in cold conditions is [8] because of, these organisms have a high amount of polyunsaturated fats stored in their cell membranes. Psychrophiles use polyunsaturated fats because they remain pliable in cold temperatures. In contrast, in freezing temperatures, our phospholipids in our cell membranes

5
Which choice most effectively combines the sentences at the underlined portion?
A) salt, and the lake is
B) salt, it is therefore
C) salt, additionally
D) salt, which is

6
A) NO CHANGE
B) Previously,
C) Although,
D) In particular,

7
Which choice provides the most effective transition from the previous paragraph?
A) NO CHANGE
B) If all goes according to plan,
C) In order to survive in such cold climates,
D) To continue scientific research,

8
A) NO CHANGE
B) that,
C) because that,
D) DELETE the underlined portion

become stiff. This hampers the movement of crucial proteins and can restrict the passing of oxygen and glucose. **9** <u>To illustrate this,</u> consider how chilled margarine can spread across bread much more easily than chilled butter because margarine has much more polyunsaturated fat. In fact, psychrophilic organisms are so flexible they may fall apart at the temperatures in which humans are most comfortable.

10 <u>Because</u> some scientists respectfully marvel at the resilience of psychrophiles, others see them as a nuisance. Many industries, particularly those involving groceries and medication, rely on refrigeration to protect their products from spoilage. Most organisms cannot thrive in the cool temperatures of a refrigerator, and even fewer can survive the deep cold of a **11** <u>freezer. For food preservation, these technologies are useful because of this fact about most organisms' survivability.</u> Conversely, those lifeforms that are more than comfortable in such environments bring the threat of spoilage. For this reason, it is important for us to discover how these organisms live so we can ensure that, in some situations, they do not.

9
A) NO CHANGE
B) Just imagine,
C) Furthermore,
D) And yet,

10
A) NO CHANGE
B) Whereas
C) However,
D) On one hand,

11
Which choice most effectively combines the sentences at the underlined portion?

A) freezer, which is why these technologies are useful for food preservation.
B) freezer, both of these being technologies for food preparation that for this reason are useful.
C) freezer, the survivability of these organisms making, for food preservation, these technologies useful.
D) freezer, this fact is because these technologies are useful for the preservation of food.

Notes and Reflections

Expression of Ideas – Wordiness 1

There are certainly **1** benefits and advantages to recycling. Your empty plastic bottles can spend a thousand years in a landfill before they **2** fully, entirely decompose, or they can be repurposed quickly for use in other plastic items. It takes more than a hundred years for your aluminum cans to decay, glass takes a million years, and styrofoam cannot ever biodegrade. Recycling returns these valuable materials back into the production cycle.

An illustrative case is that of the American automobile. By weight, the automobile is the most recycled product, but this wasn't always **3** a true fact. Until the 1970s, vehicle disposal was a growing problem. When your car stopped running properly and you could no longer repair it, there was **4** no good method that existed for your getting rid of it. In New York City in 1969, about 70,000 vehicles were left stranded in the streets and alleys. As the paint chipped, metal rusted, and windows shattered, these vehicles became local eyesores. Across the country, tens of millions of cars were abandoned in back yards, roadsides, and waterways.

1
A) NO CHANGE
B) advantageous benefits
C) beneficial advantages
D) benefits

2
A) NO CHANGE
B) fully decompose entirely
C) fully decompose in entirety
D) decompose fully

3
A) NO CHANGE
B) a truth, in fact
C) truly factual
D) true

4
A) NO CHANGE
B) no method in which you could get rid of it that was a good method
C) no good method to get rid of it
D) none of it

Finally, 5 it eventually occurred in the 1960s, some junkyard owners in Texas invented an automobile shredder, which could scrap cars into useful materials. 6 Currently, each year these shredders are used to recycle up to 14 million cars annually. The materials from these cars supply 15% of America's raw steel. However, the worldwide recycling industry is more complicated and often not as profitable.

China is the world leader in recycling. American businesses benefit from the export of these recyclable products, and Chinese industries benefit from access to materials that are cheaper than alternative sources, such as forestation or mining, 7 which are more expensive. To illustrate, more than a third of all copper in Chinese electronics comes from recycling. As the primary recycler, China can greatly influence the industry.

Many cities have facilities dedicated to the sorting and preparation of recyclable materials so they can be shipped to China and other nations to be recycled. There are standards for purity in order to reuse certain materials. For example, it may be difficult or even impossible to reuse a cardboard pizza box if it has been soaked in grease. Even worse, the wrong materials can contaminate large batches of recyclable material, rendering it all worthless. This problem becomes more 8 likely to probably occur when people accidentally place unrecyclable materials or plain garbage in their recycling bins.

5

A) NO CHANGE
B) on the eventuality of occurring in the 1960s
C) in the 1960s
D) 1960s

6

A) NO CHANGE
B) Currently,
C) Each year,
D) Yearly,

7

A) NO CHANGE
B) the more expensive
C) more expensive
D) DELETE the underlined portion and adjust punctuation as needed.

8

A) NO CHANGE
B) probable of occurring
C) likely
D) probably

A processing plant is tasked with sifting through the bins and sorting the material into pure groups, but the work is **9** imperfect and flawed.

The inherent flaw in recyclable material processing became a major problem when China upped its standards: the country will not accept waste papers, plastics, or metals unless they are 99.5% pure. This near-perfect requirement is far beyond the capability of most processing plants. Much of the recycling in the United States is "single stream," meaning all sorts of waste products can be thrown together in the same bins. This increases the risk of contamination. Also, **10** a small number of some few recycling programs require people to wash out their bottles and cans, sort their plastics and papers according to types, or place different materials into different bins. These low requirements make the process very easy for people to submit their recyclable goods, which has aided contributions, but they also prevent processing plants from reaching high enough levels of material purity.

With processing plants unable to reach China's standards, recyclables cannot be shipped out of the country. This **11** leads to bringing about a surplus of domestic recyclables, which reduces the value of materials. Thus, much of America's recyclable waste is getting diverted back to where we didn't want it: the trash heap.

9
A) NO CHANGE
B) with imperfections and flaws
C) imperfectly flawed
D) not without flaws

10
A) NO CHANGE
B) a small number of
C) numbering a few
D) a few in number

11
A) NO CHANGE
B) brings to leading
C) brings
D) leads

Expression of Ideas – Wordiness 2

According to a story (probably apocryphal) recorded by the artist and art historian Giorgio Vasari, the elder Cimabue, one of the great masters of Byzantine painting, met the Florentine artist Giotto Bondone when Giotto was a young shepherd **1** watching an observation of his flock. Vasari says that Cimabue (1240-1300), while walking through the fields, was stunned by the extraordinary drawings of ewes that the young Giotto had made with chalk on rocks. The older artist asked his name, and soon the young Giotto (1266-1337) was apprenticed to Cimabue. In another account, **2** during the time when Cimabue was absent from the workshop, Giotto painted a remarkably realistic fly on one of his paintings. When Cimabue **3** returned back to the place of his workshop, he **4** tried attempts several times repeatedly to brush the fly

1
A) NO CHANGE
B) observing a watch of
C) observing and watching
D) observing

2
A) NO CHANGE
B) the time during
C) when
D) during

3
A) NO CHANGE
B) came back to his workshop
C) returned back to the place
D) returned

4
A) NO CHANGE
B) repeatedly tried several attempts
C) attempted several times
D) repeated

off. Vasari also relates that the Pope sent a messenger to Giotto, asking him to send a drawing to demonstrate his skill. Giotto drew a circle so [5] perfect in its flawlessness that it seemed as though it must have been drawn using a compass, but it was done entirely by hand. The Pope was duly impressed and gave him a commission.

Giotto went on to surpass his master. In fact, Giotto Bondone became one of history's most influential painters [6] of all time to ever live. Many critics consider him the first genius of European painting and a key figure in the transition from the Middle Ages to the Renaissance, along with other geniuses such as Galileo, Petrarch, and Dante.

The Italian Renaissance (usually dated from the 15th to the 16th centuries) is notable for the increased interest in Ancient Greek and Roman ideas and aesthetic concerns [7] that rose in fashion during this time. After centuries in which the Church ruled completely over the lives of the populace, a new spirit of humanism took hold and changed the course of history.

Religion was still an important part of the lives and beliefs of most people, but there was growing resistance to the acceptance of all of the Church's practices. This change in outlook eventually led to the occurrence [8] of the Protestant Reformation after some amount of time. The 14th century was a time of great change, today known as Late Gothic or Proto

5
A) NO CHANGE
B) perfectly flawed
C) flawlessly perfect
D) flawless

6
A) NO CHANGE
B) living of all time ever
C) ever to live in all time
D) DELETE the underlined portion.

7
A) NO CHANGE
B) during this time's fashion
C) this time
D) DELETE the underlined portion

8
A) NO CHANGE
B) after some time
C) of the Protestant Reformation
D) DELETE the underlined portion

Renaissance. Giotto was instrumental in connecting the ideas and visual schemes of the medieval world with the Renaissance, which was **9** yet to come in the future.

An early work of his, "Madonna and Child Enthroned," is displayed side by side with a painting of the same name by Cimabue in the Uffizi Gallery in Florence. While the composition of both is similar and they both use the gold background so typical of Byzantine art, Giotto's version takes a giant leap towards the Renaissance. The human figures have solidity and movement, unlike the stiff and flat figures in the Cimabue version. The baby Jesus looks like a real infant, not like the miniature adults so **10** commonly and frequently seen in Medieval art. There is tenderness and emotion in the faces and gestures. Even the throne itself is more convincingly three-dimensional. He makes an attempt at using linear perspective, though this concept will not be perfected for another century.

Artists, inspired by Giotto, began looking at the natural world **11** differently in new ways, closely observing and analyzing what they saw. They used statues from the ancients to perfect their depictions of the human body. Over the next centuries, an increasingly large number of artists followed his example. Masters such as Fra Angelico and Botticelli in the 15th century and Michelangelo, Leonardo, and Raphael in the 16th, owe a great debt to the innovations and accomplishments of Giotto, the first genius.

9
A) NO CHANGE
B) coming yet in the future
C) yet to come
D) yet

10
A) NO CHANGE
B) frequently common
C) frequently
D) common

11
A) NO CHANGE
B) in newly different ways
C) differently
D) DELETE the underlined portion.

Notes and Reflections

Expression of Ideas – Style 1

Modern businesses have learned the [1] unforgettable effect of data. The more a company knows about its customers, the more it can effectively advertise to them. Recent research into consumer activity revealed that more than three-quarters of online shoppers refer to reviews before making a purchase and more than half of reviews are made before customers have even used the product. Therefore, making a strong initial impression is the best way to promote good reviews, which is the best way to encourage even more purchases. Such insights into purchasing habits can lead to [2] significant gains in sales. Recognizing the power of such data, businesses are then faced with the tasks of finding sources of information, making sure the data are accurate and organized, and acting while the data are still relevant.

Data gathering takes several forms. The traditional methods are explicit; a business may ask people to fill out surveys or questionnaires in order to learn certain things about its existing customer base. Many people are [3] apprehensive to partake in this process, even if it's [4] a snap, so some incentives may be offered. Some grocery stores offer special sales for those shoppers who sign up for membership

---

1

The author wants to express a sense of importance and to avoid seeming sarcastic or overdramatic. Which of the following choices best accomplishes the author's goal?

A) NO CHANGE
B) sufficient
C) life-changing
D) impactful

2

Which of the following choices best maintains the tone of the passage?

A) NO CHANGE
B) hefty
C) whopping
D) ginormous

3

A) NO CHANGE
B) reluctant
C) spooked
D) chicken

4

A) NO CHANGE
B) a piece of cake
C) a breeze
D) simple

programs, and the shoppers allow the store to monitor their purchasing history in exchange for their discounts. More recently, businesses have used sneakier methods of gathering data. Social media sites track personal information about users and **5** hawk this data to a wide array of companies. Websites and mobile phone apps constantly gather details about our lives, useful material for businesses that can profit from knowing our routines, interests, and life events. Much of this monitoring occurs **6** behind our backs, because many people wouldn't be willing to provide the information otherwise.

For many businesses, the problem is not how to **7** score consumer data but how to sort through the incredible availability of it. There's too much to manage! With access to people's shopping habits, live status updates, social connections, hobbies, and more, businesses must invest in tools to organize and visualize all of this information. Furthermore, some of this information is more **8** accurate or useful than others, and some is particularly time-sensitive. If you are a company that sells maternity clothing for pregnant women, you might purchase client information from a

5

A) NO CHANGE
B) vend
C) sell
D) dish

6

Which of the following choices best maintains the tone of the passage?

A) NO CHANGE
B) without our awareness
C) on the downlow
D) on the sly

7

A) NO CHANGE
B) scoop up
C) acquire
D) grip

8

A) NO CHANGE
B) on the nose
C) on the money
D) on the up and up

company that sells prenatal vitamins. In this situation, you

need to advertise to your customers 9 <u>in a flash</u>; if there is a

long delay in your data gathering, processing, and reacting,

you will miss your window of opportunity. Also, some people

purchase prenatal vitamins because they need large amounts

of calcium and iron, not because they are pregnant. Data must

be used quickly and accurately to ensure that advertisements

are not 10 <u>dumped</u> by customers. Such are the complexities

of utilizing data.

As more and more businesses realize the powerful

benefits of consumer data, corporate competition is driving

advancements in how quickly data is put into action. Rather

than having employees sift through databases to find and

discuss trends, the process is being automated. Marketing is

becoming more immediately responsive. As soon as a

consumer makes a purchase, posts information online, or even

researches a product, custom marketing is instantly delivered

to them. This responsiveness effectively convinces people to

spend their money because it allows advertisements to

influence them when they are most interested and 11 <u>pumped</u>

<u>up</u>, leading to impulse-buying. In the most extreme cases,

businesses monitor consumer habits so they can sell things to

customers before the customer even knows they need the

product. The upside of this marketing is that we can be

reminded before we run out of crucial items like batteries or

toilet paper.

9
A) NO CHANGE
B) in no time flat
C) quickly
D) pronto

10
A) NO CHANGE
B) marginalized
C) disregarded
D) scrapped

11
A) NO CHANGE
B) psyched
C) excited
D) stoked

Expression of Ideas – Style 2

People tend to avoid discomfort. We seek what is soft, warm, cozy, and pleasant. This behavior extends beyond the physical to the psychological, as we tend to close ourselves off from information we find unfavorable. The phenomenon of disregarding facts is not a recent **1** look. Since the 1950s, psychologists have studied cognitive dissonance—a feeling of discomfort produced by a situation involving conflicting attitudes, beliefs, or behaviors. In many cases, cognitive dissonance leads to self-deception; people find it easier to convince themselves they believe in a lie than to confront an inconvenient truth. For example, smokers who are **2** woke that smoking is correlated with cancer may tell themselves the risks are exaggerated, their health is unimportant, or their valuing of the social or emotional aspect of the habit is a larger concern. Leon Festinger, who first investigated cognitive dissonance, theorizes that people are more likely to continue their **3** evil habits since that's the path of least resistance.

When Leon Festinger first encountered cognitive dissonance, he was conducting an observational study on a cult that believed the Earth was going to be **4** decimated by a catastrophic flood. There was no scientific basis for the belief;

1

Which of the following choices best maintains the tone of the passage?
A) NO CHANGE
B) trend
C) style
D) hit

2

A) NO CHANGE
B) sentient
C) aware
D) privy

3

A) NO CHANGE
B) unsuccessful
C) negative
D) shady

4

A) NO CHANGE
B) destroyed
C) smashed
D) beat

rather, they took it on faith. When the world-ending flood did not occur, Festinger noted the [5] emotes of the cult members, paying special attention to the ones who had already given up their homes and jobs so as to fully commit to the cult. Less [6] loving members were likely to recognize they were mistaken, whereas the devout ones attempted to reframe the evidence to show they were right all along. These stubbornly dedicated members decided the continued existence of the world was due to their great faith, rather than the [7] botched beliefs of the cult. Festinger proposed that all humans have an innate compulsion to align their beliefs and behaviors and eliminate any disharmony between them. Any inconsistency is then eliminated by a change in one or the other.

Collaborating with Carlsmith, a fellow researcher, Festinger tested his theory through a controlled experiment. The researchers [8] chopped seventy-one male students into three groups after all of them partook in a boring task. One group was given one dollar if they convinced a girl, who

5

A) NO CHANGE
B) comebacks
C) reflexes
D) reactions

6

A) NO CHANGE
B) passionate
C) rabid
D) wild

7

Which of the following choices best maintains the tone of the passage?

A) NO CHANGE
B) incorrect
C) slipshod
D) janky

8

A) NO CHANGE
B) divided
C) sliced
D) cut

who was actually an actor informed about the experiment, that

the task was fun. Another group was [9] recompensed twenty

dollars to complete the same assignment. The third group,

serving as the control, did not have to convince the actor of

anything and did not receive any type of reward.

Afterwards, the male participants completed an evaluation

of the experiment as a whole. Festinger and Carlsmith found

that participants who were paid one dollar to convince the

hired actor the [10] mind-numbing task was enjoyable were

also the same ones who claimed the task was fun. The group

who received twenty dollars to convince the girl, on the other

hand, did not assess the task as enjoyable. As expected, the

control group also admitted the task was boring. To convince

another person the boring task is actually enjoyable, the

participant will have to persuade himself. When the

participants were given more money, the reward became the

reason for persuading the hired actor, so the person did not

have to convince himself to the same degree as he would have

if the monetary amount were smaller.

As Festinger's observational study and his experiment

with Carlsmith clearly demonstrated, when people are given

evidence contradictory to what they believe, they are more

likely to ignore the evidence or reinterpret it in a favorable

manner. Self-deception becomes a defense mechanism aimed

at preserving inner [11] laxity. For many of us, we maintain

our comfort and happiness by living a lie.

9
A) NO CHANGE
B) remunerated
C) tossed
D) paid

10
A) NO CHANGE
B) snoozing
C) blunt
D) dull

11
A) NO CHANGE
B) peace
C) cool
D) chill

Notes and Reflections

Data Graphics – Passage 1

There are many ways to prevent the scourge of termites, which can quickly destroy buildings by eating channels in wood. A simple and humane solution is to choose the right type of wood, because **1** termites show preference for certain tree types.

A study of three hundred termites measured which woods termites were most likely to consume. These termites, *reticulitermes virginicus*, were placed in several types of containers where they were given access to one, two, or four types of wood. The types of wood used were pine, red oak, redwood, and poplar. All wood blocks were the same size and shape, and the termites were given the same amount of time to consume each type. Consumption was measured by wood weight loss, in grams, as well as several visual cues.

Using data like this, builders can utilize particular types of wood to deter termites. Based on the study's findings, **2** red oak lumber would be the optimal choice.

Wood Types	Weight Loss (g)	% Weight Loss
Pine	0.299	17.15
Red Oak	0.123	3.400
Pine	0.401	25.24
Redwood	0.071	1.988
Pine	0.387	22.33
Poplar	0.010	0.660
Red Oak	0.265	8.946
Redwood	0.056	3.180
Red Oak	0.304	11.42
Poplar	0.003	0.208
Redwood	0.202	13.99
Poplar	0.004	0.180

1

Which of the following choices offers an accurate interpretation of the data in the figure?

(A) NO CHANGE

(B) some wood types can cause starvation for termites.

(C) wood is the cheapest material for home construction.

(D) certain species of termites are more destructive than others.

2

The author wants to include accurate and relevant information from the table to demonstrate the point made in the previous sentence. Which of the following choices best accomplishes the author's goal?

(A) NO CHANGE

(B) pine

(C) redwood

(D) poplar

Data Graphics – Passage 2

A major part of the recycling industry, and a source of much frustration, is processing trash into pure, recyclable material. Many cities have facilities dedicated to sorting and preparation of recyclable materials to ship to China and other nations. There are standards for purity in order to reuse certain materials. For example, it may be impossible to reuse a cardboard pizza box if it has been soaked in grease. The wrong materials can contaminate large batches, rendering it all worthless. To address these problems, the industry has pushed for new standards in recyclability of paper and plastics, **1** which could raise profits as much as 31%.

The inherent imperfectness in recyclable material processing became a major problem when China upped its standards: the country will not accept waste papers, plastics, or metals unless they are 99.5% pure. This near-perfect requirement is beyond the capability of most processing plants. **2** Food residue is the most common contaminant in most processing plants. Much of the recycling in the United States is "single stream," meaning all sorts of waste products can be thrown together in the same bins. This increases the work processors must do to sort the materials and increases the risk of contamination. Also, few recycling programs require people to wash their bottles and cans, sort plastics and papers

according to types, and place different materials into different bins. These low requirements make the process very simple for people, which has aided contributions, but they also prevent processing plants from reaching high enough levels of material purity.

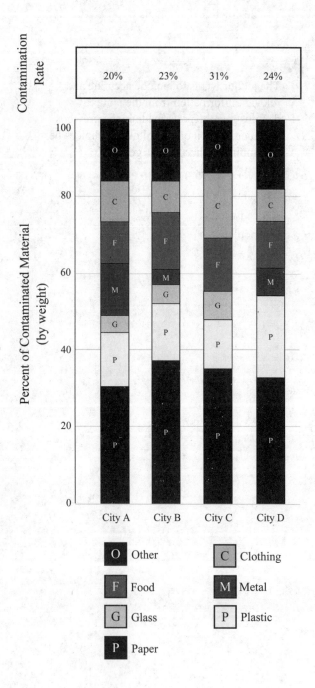

1

The writer wants to include information from the graph that is consistent with the description of recycling in the passage. Which choice most effectively accomplishes this goal?

(A) NO CHANGE

(B) which is the only way processing plants will be able to increase profits.

(C) which could eliminate the majority of contaminants in some processing plants.

(D) which would increase people's willingness to contribute recyclable materials.

2

The writer wants to support the paragraph's main idea with relevant, accurate information from the graph. Which choice most effectively accomplishes this goal?

(A) NO CHANGE

(B) Limiting options, such as restricting the recycling of metals or glass, can help reduce the rate of all contaminants.

(C) Processing plants receive batches with about 25% contaminant materials, a staggering amount to remove with such little room for error.

(D) The value of processed materials must be 20-31% higher than the cost of the processing, a level of profit that is difficult to maintain.

Data Graphics – Passage 3

When raising fish, protein management is key. Increase in dietary protein leads to increased production, particularly for carnivorous species of fish. However, providing too much protein can limit growth of some fish. This decreased growth is explained by two differing theories: the competition hypothesis and the ammonia hypothesis. The competition hypothesis suggests that carnivorous fish are limited in growth by combating over resources, which are consumed primarily by a small population of especially aggressive fish. Increasing protein availability will increase the advantages of these few fish and always decrease average weight gain in a fish population. The ammonia hypothesis attributes limited growth to changes in water conditions. The hypothesis contends that excess levels of protein will lead to increased ammonia excretion, which will deteriorate the condition of the fish culture water. The elevated levels of ammonia may harm fish growth at high levels of protein.

A group of university students conducted a study to determine the optimum protein level in fishmeal to produce maximum weight gain amongst populations of *Oplegnathus fasciatus*. *O. fasciatus*, or barred knifejaw, is a species of carnivorous fish native to the Pacific Ocean. The students created 5 different mixtures of fishmeal, each containing a different percentage of crude protein (CP) by dry weight. Protein in the meal is derived from both a commercially sourced white fishmeal and pure casein (a protein found in milk and dairy products).

Prior to beginning the experiment, the students reared a number of juvenile *O. fasciatus* in their lab, and acclimated them to a circular concrete tank containing 5000 L of water at a constant temperature of 19° C. For the two weeks leading up to the experiment, all the fish were fed the same diet of a commercially available fishmeal.

For the experiment, the concrete tank was divided into 15 sections using hanging net cages. Twenty fish, each weighing 7.1 g, were placed in each cage. The experimental feed mixtures were assigned randomly to the 15 cages, with each mixture being assigned to three of the 15 cages. The fish in each cage were fed their experimental fishmeal mixture twice a day. The students recorded the fish's percent weight gain (WG) after eight weeks and determined the optimal diet for the growth of barred knifejaw is **1** 15.8% casein. **2** **3**

Mixture	% crude protein by dry weight	% white fishmeal	% casein	% WG
1	35	25.0	15.8	163
2	40	20.0	24.5	171
3	45	15.0	33.3	181
4	50	10.0	42.0	182
5	60	5.0	55.8	162

1

Which choice provides the most accurate information from the table?

(A) NO CHANGE
(B) 10% casein
(C) 50% crude protein by weight
(D) 60% crude protein by weight

2

Based on the information in the passage, which hypothesis is better supported by the data in the table?

(A) The competition hypothesis because increase in protein availability led to decreased weight gain at lower levels and increased weight gain at higher levels.
(B) The competition hypothesis because decrease in protein availability led to increased weight gain at lower levels and decreased weight gain at higher levels.
(C) The ammonia hypothesis because increase in protein availability led to decreased weight gain at lower levels and increased weight gain at higher levels.
(D) The ammonia hypothesis because increase in protein availability led to increased weight gain at lower levels and decreased weight gain at higher levels.

3

Which choice offers an accurate interpretation of the data in the graphs?

(A) The mixture with the lowest crude protein had the highest ratio of casein to fishmeal.
(B) The mixture with the highest crude protein had the lowest ratio of casein to fishmeal.
(C) The fish with the lowest weight gain had the highest ratio of casein to fishmeal.
(D) The fish with the lowest weight gain had the lowest ratio of casein to fishmeal.

Data Graphics – Passage 4

Scientists search for ways to make fruits healthier, taking advantage of natural benefits. Strawberry plants are rich in antioxidants, substances that slow the cellular damage caused by unstable molecules known as free radicals, which accumulate over time from normal cellular processes. **1** A recent study was organized to examine the effect of adding probiotic bacteria *B. amylolequefaciens* and *P. fungorum* to strawberry plants, with the hopes of maximizing antioxidant levels. Strawberry plant growth and levels of flavonoids (a powerful class of plant antioxidant) were measured.

40-day-old strawberry plants were brought to a single plot, which contained three raised beds of equal size. Through a randomized process, 15 plants were selected and transplanted into each of the three beds, and the plants were placed in three rows of five. Rows were spaced exactly 12 inches apart. The soil used in each bed came from the same source.

There were three groups of plants, one for each bed: Group 1 was sprayed with a solution containing *B. amylolequefaciens*, Group 2 was sprayed with a solution containing *P. fungorum*, and Group 3 was sprayed with sterilized water in place of a probiotic bacteria solution. After 22 weeks of growth, effect of probiotic bacteria on the plants was studied by measuring height and root length.

Total flavonoid content was determined using established spectrophotometric methods. The measurements were reported as quercetin equivalents. Quercetin is a standard flavonoid found in plants and is used for quantifying other flavonoids.

Researchers recorded the average flavonoid levels and average plant height and root length for the three groups of strawberry plants. The results were promising, suggesting that probiotic bacteria had a positive effect on strawberry plant growth: **2** sterilized water decreased flavonoid content and brought some increase in plant height.

Plant Group	Total Flavonoid Content (μg Quercetin/g Fresh Weight)
Group 1	615.4
Group 2	774.2
Group 3	515.3

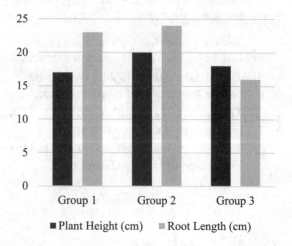

1

At this point, the writer is considering adding the following graph.

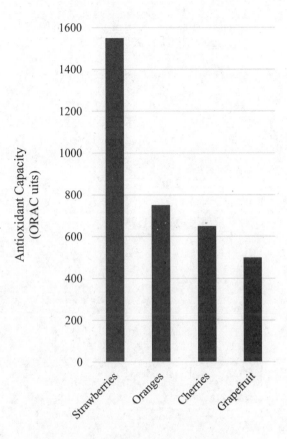

Should the writer make this addition here?

(A) Yes, because it supports the claim that strawberries contain relatively high levels of antioxidants.

(B) Yes, because it offers a relevant counterpoint to the argument that antioxidants need to be increased in fruit.

(C) No, because it presents information that is not relevant to the writer's discussion of scientific research of flavonoids.

(D) No, because it does not provide information about the impact of probiotic bacteria on fruit size.

2

Which of the following choices best demonstrates the statement made in the first part of the sentence with information from the experimental data?

(A) NO CHANGE

(B) the greatest difference was seen in the use of *B. amylolequefaciens*, which caused a 50% increase in root length.

(C) use of *P. fungorum* had the largest impact, leading to much larger plants, as well as a 50% increase in flavonoid content.

(D) while the use of *B. amylolequefaciens* brought an increase in flavonoid content, it also decreased the root length.

Notes and Reflections

Problem Solving & Data Analysis

❑ Section Quiz

❑ Percents

❑ Ratios

❑ Proportions

❑ Units & Conversion

❑ Statistics – Average

❑ Statistics – Median, Mode, & Range

❑ Probability

❑ Data Relationships

❑ Data Collection & Conclusions

Section Quiz

1

An Olympic-size pool is 50 meters in length. Approximately how long is an Olympic-sized pool in inches (1 foot ≈ 0.3048 meters)?

A) 14
B) 50
C) 164
D) 1970

2

A four-inch strand of hair grows at a rate of half an inch per month. Assuming the hair is never cut, how many inches long will the strand be in five years?

A) 20
B) 26
C) 30
D) 34

3

The total annual revenue, in millions of dollars, of Company A and Company B in 2013 through 2018 are listed in the table below. What is the absolute value of the difference between the mean revenue, in millions of dollars, of Company A and the mean revenue, in millions of dollars, of Company B during these years?

	2013	2014	2015	2016	2017	2018
Company A	14.5	15.2	17.4	13.4	10.2	11.5
Company B	10.5	11.2	13.5	15.8	17.8	18.2

A) 0.7
B) 0.8
C) 4.8
D) 10.8

4

The following table shows the approximate historical budget, in millions of dollars, for six government areas of Massachusetts over four consecutive years.

Historical Budgets ($ millions), 2015-2018

Government Area	2015	2016	2017	2018
Transportation	575	645	608	520
Public Safety	1,040	1,050	1,060	1,100
Education	6,700	6,780	6,950	7,100
Health & Human Services	18,950	20,280	21,025	21,690
Housing & Economic Development	475	480	506	524

Of the following government areas and time periods, which represents the smallest percent change from 2015 to 2017?

A) Transportation
B) Education
C) Housing & Economic Development
D) Health & Human Services

5

A movie theater sells medium and large bags of popcorn. The ratio of the number of medium bags to large bags sold on a particular day was 4:5. If the theater sold 100 medium bags of popcorn that day, how many large bags of popcorn did they sell that day?

A) 80
B) 100
C) 125
D) 225

6

A popular game store sells packs of collectible cards for two fantasy games: "Roke-Nom" and "Sorcery: The Convention". A pack of "Roke-Nom" cards contains 15 cards and sells for $3.00 per pack. A pack of "Sorcery: The Convention" cards contains 25 cards and sells for $4.50. Which game pack offers the lower price per card?

A) "Roke-Nom" packs have a lower card price.
B) "Sorcery: The Convention" packs have a lower card price.
C) The price per card is the same for both game packs.
D) There is not enough information to determine which game pack offers the lower card price.

7

City officials decide to survey 50 teachers, asking which nominated union representative they will vote for in the upcoming teachers' union election. Which of the following methods of selecting participants for the survey will result in a sample most representative of the teachers in the city district?

A) Obtain a list of all teachers in the state. Use a random number generator to select 50 teachers to participate in the survey.
B) Obtain a list of all teachers in the state. Email them the survey and record the results of the first 50 respondents.
C) Obtain a list of all teachers in the city. Use a random number generator to select 50 teachers to participate in the survey.
D) Obtain a list of all teachers in the city. Email them the survey and record the results of the first 50 respondents.

8

Below are 2 sets of numbers:

Set I {87, 87, 90, 90, 90, 94}

Set II {88, 90, 90, 90, 91, 96, 97}

Which of the following statements about the 2 sets of numbers is NOT true?

A) The mode and median of both sets is 90.
B) The range of Set II is larger than the range of Set I.
C) The mean of each set is not an integer.
D) Including 95 in each set changes their respective medians.

9

Joel is trying to determine his expenses if he purchases a new automobile. The last item on his list of expenses to figure out is the state excise tax. In Joel's state, excise tax is assessed proportionally based on the vehicle's "book value." For every $1,000 in book value of a vehicle, new or used, an excise tax of $25 is assessed. Joel's current vehicle has a book value of $3,450. The vehicle Joel wants to purchase is valued at $27,395. How much more excise tax will Joel have to pay if he goes ahead and purchases the new vehicle? Round to the nearest cent when choosing your answer.

A) $957.80
B) $684.88
C) $598.63
D) $273.95

SUMMIT
EDUCATIONAL
GROUP

10

Ava cut up pieces of red and blue construction paper and mixed them thoroughly in a bag. While her friend Carla held the bag for her, Ava drew two pieces out of the bag, one in her right hand, and one in her left hand. She recorded the color of paper in each hand and then placed the pieces back into the bag. The women repeated this process 150 times as part of an experiment. The results of the 150 trials are shown in the table below.

		Right Hand	
		Red	Blue
Left Hand	Red	37	42
	Blue	35	36

Based on the results from the experiment, what was the probability that Ava drew a red piece of paper in her left hand?

A) $\dfrac{37}{150}$

B) $\dfrac{42}{150}$

C) $\dfrac{79}{150}$

D) $\dfrac{72}{150}$

11

For the average human, the half-life of caffeine, the time it takes for the body to eliminate half of the amount of caffeine consumed, is approximately 5 hours. Alex just consumed 120 mg of caffeine in her morning coffee. Which of the following graphs best models the mass of the original 120g of caffeine still remaining in Alex's system over the 20 hours immediately following her morning coffee?

A)

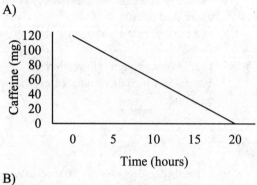

B)

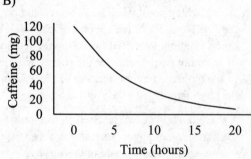

C)

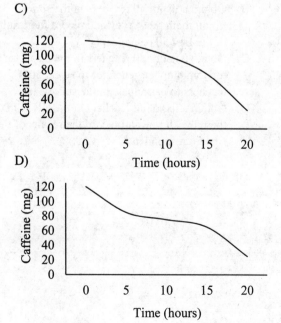

D)

12

The power needed to run a toaster is 1200 joules per second. What is the approximate power required to run the toaster in foot-pounds per minute (1 foot-pound ≈ 1.35582 joules)?

A) 885
B) 1,627
C) 53,100
D) 97,600

13

Daily rainfall in a particular city was tracked over the month of April, which has 30 days. The average rainfall for the entire month was 4.4 inches. If the average rainfall for the first ten days was 4.8 inches, which of the following must be true about the average rainfall during the last twenty days of the month?

A) It must be less than 4.4 inches.
B) It must be equal to 4.4 inches.
C) It must be between 4.4 and 5.0 inches.
D) It must be greater than 5.0 inches.

14

In a set of 15 distinct positive integers, which of the following changes can <u>not</u> affect the median of the set?

A) Increasing each of the 15 integers by 3
B) Dividing each of the 15 integers by 2
C) Increasing the largest 5 integers by 5
D) Decreasing the smallest 10 integers by 1

15

What is one possible scenario represented in the graph below?

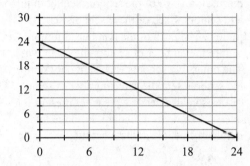

A) A food pantry is tracking their supply of food. They start with 24 storage containers, and the supply decreases by one container every two months.
B) Beth took out a loan that will require 24 annual payments. She wants to track how many payments remain after each annual payment when she makes one.
C) Jared figures it will take him two years to save up for a sailboat. He wants to track his progress as his savings grow.
D) A homeowner must put a salt product in her water softening system to maintain a potable water source. She usually puts twenty-four pounds of the salt product into the system holding tank. The holding tank empties and needs to be refilled every month and a half.

16

The price of a laptop is raised by 20% because of its popularity. This price increase causes a sharp decline in sales. Company executives decide to lower the sales price but only enough to still allow for a 15% increase over the original price. To the nearest whole number, by what percent should the price of the laptop be lowered to accomplish this?

A) 4
B) 5
C) 12
D) 15

17

Students and teachers attended a town discussion. 7 schools sent some students to the discussion. Two of the schools sent both juniors and seniors. Each of these schools sent 32 juniors. The ratio of the number of juniors they sent to the number of seniors they sent was 1:4. The other five schools each sent only seniors. All the schools sent the same number of seniors. The discussion also needed 1 teacher present for every 25 students attending. Find the total number of people at the meeting.

A) 932
B) 960
C) 998
D) 1000

18

75 people in town were surveyed about how they planned to vote on local issue questions on the upcoming ballot. The results of the survey are shown in the table.

Issue	Yes	No
Question 1: Park Land Acquisition	37	38
Question 2: School Improvement	51	24
Question 3: Lower Voting Age	29	46

Assuming that the results of the survey accurately predict the response ratios for the 2400 people who voted on these issues, how many of the voters voted Yes for School Improvement?

A) 928
B) 1184
C) 1224
D) 1632

19

The following chart shows the approximate average clock speed (in megahertz, or MHz) of the average computer processor in select years since 1975:

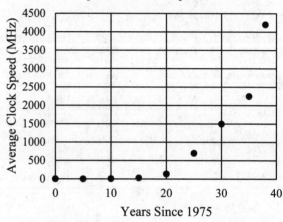

Computer Processor Speed Over Time

Which of the following best represents the average clock speed, y, after x years have passed since 1975?

A) $y = 50x + 500$
B) $y = 1.79 \times (2.72)^{0.21x}$
C) $y = 4.21x^2 - 84.05x + 214.62$
D) $y = 4.1x + 75$

20

A survey is conducted to determine whether residents of a small town want to have their high school start later. Researchers randomly selected 453 participants from a local community center, where many residents typically gather, and asked them about whether they think the start time should be earlier, later, or the same. Approximately 20 participants did not respond. Which of the following most likely explains why the data collected might not be reliable?

A) The sample size is too small.
B) There were too many people who did not respond.
C) The question that was asked guided participants toward a particular response.
D) The method of selecting participants was not random enough to ensure a reliable sample.

21

Stephen sold 11 collectible playing cards. The median selling price was $110. The mean selling price was $125. What is the lowest possible price he could have sold his most expensive card for?

A) $143
B) $152
C) $185
D) The answer cannot be determined with the information given.

22

Charisma purchases a new TV from Electronics Extravaganza. The store is having a 30% off sale. As an Extravaganza Rewards member, Charisma gets an additional 20% off the sale price. Assuming she ends up paying $450 after a 5% sales tax, which of the following is closest to the original cost of the television?

A) $250
B) $775
C) $800
D) $900

23

The following chart contains historical units of liquid measure that were used in the alcohol and spirits industry. Given the information as shown, which combination of containers, when completely emptied into 1 Tun containers with no spillage, would allow for some number of 1 Tun containers to be filled exactly to the brim with no empty space in any of the containers and no leftover liquid in the smaller containers?

Container	Equivalent
1 Tun	2 Pipes
1 Pipe	2 Hogsheads
1 Hogshead	2 Quarters
1 Quarter	2 Octaves

A) 4 Quarters, 2 Hogsheads, 2 Pipes
B) 3 Quarters, 1 Pipe, 1 Hogshead
C) 2 Quarters, 3 Hogsheads, .5 Pipes
D) 1 Quarter, 4 Pipes, 2 Octaves

24

The share price of a company's stock decreased by 50% in 2000, 35% in 2001, 25% in 2002, and then increased by 5% in 2003. Which of the following best estimates the percent increase that will restore the shares from their price in 2003 to their original price in 2000?

A) 105%
B) 115%
C) 177%
D) 291%

Notes and Reflections

Percents

Glucose is a molecule that contains only carbon, oxygen, and hydrogen atoms. The percentage composition by mass of a glucose molecule is 40% carbon, 53% oxygen, and 7% hydrogen. If you have a 250-gram sample of glucose, what is the mass in grams of the carbon atoms in the sample?

A) 40
B) 100
C) 132.5
D) 150

An integrated circuit manufacturer released data on the average gate length, in nanometers (nm), of the transistors in the microchips they produce. The data, which was collected between the years 2000 and 2010, is graphed in the scatterplot below.

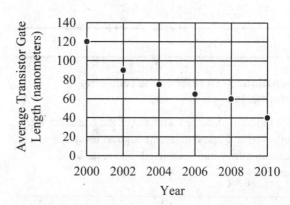

In 2012, blueberry production at a farm in Maine was affected by a fungal disease. This resulted in a 33% drop from the previous year in the amount of blueberries harvested. If the farm was able to harvest 3200 pounds of blueberries in 2011, how many pounds of blueberries did they harvest in 2012?

A) 2144
B) 3167
C) 3233
D) 4256

4

The average gate length of the transistor decreased by 20% between 2010 and 2012. What was the average length in nm of the transistor gate produced by this manufacturer in 2012?

A) 8
B) 20
C) 32
D) 48

3

A 2017 survey of local residents found that they visited a museum an average of 2.4 times in the past year. The survey was repeated in 2018 and found that the average person visited a museum 2.1 times in the past year. Based on these surveys, how did the average number of museum visits for the local residents change from 2017 to 2018? Round to the nearest tenth of a percent.

A) It decreased by 30.0%.
B) It decreased by 12.5%.
C) It decreased by 14.3%.
D) It increased by 14.3%.

5

Rounded to the closest whole number, the average transistor gate length in 2010 is what percent of the average transistor gate length produced by the manufacturer in 2000?

A) 33%
B) 40%
C) 60%
D) 69%

6

During which two-year interval did the average transistor gate length experience the greatest percentage decrease?

A) 2000 to 2002
B) 2002 to 2004
C) 2006 to 2008
D) 2008 to 2010

---▲---

---▼---

Questions 7-10 refer to the following information.

800 randomly selected adults over the age of 25 were surveyed and asked to list the highest level of education they had completed. The results are tabulated below.

Age Range	Less than High School	High School	Some College	Bachelor's Degree or Higher	Total
25-37	20	61	70	96	247
38-53	26	61	57	59	203
54-72	32	93	48	55	228
73-90	37	52	16	17	122

7

Approximately what percentage of adults aged 38-53 who participated in the survey received a Bachelor's degree or higher?

A) 7%
B) 25%
C) 26%
D) 29%

8

Of the survey participants that completed only some college, approximately what percent were between the ages of 25 and 37?

A) 9%
B) 28%
C) 37%
D) 40%

9

Which of the following is closest to the percent of all survey participants that completed at least some college?

A) 24%
B) 28%
C) 48%
D) 52%

10

Of the four age ranges studied, which has the highest percentage of adults who did not graduate high school?

A) 25-37
B) 38-53
C) 54-72
D) 73-90

---▲---

11

Cindy brings home $1800 per month after taxes. She has budgeted these funds carefully to ensure all of her expenses are fully paid. When renewing the lease for her apartment, Cindy was informed that her rent will increase in the upcoming year. Cindy calculated she would need a 5% increase in take-home pay to cover her newly anticipated living expenses. At work, she heard that this year's salary increase would raise her take take-home pay by 2.5%. Given this information, how much money, in dollars, will Cindy still need in order to cover all of her expenses once her new lease begins?

12

The amount of active ingredient in a liquid medicine is 0.12% active ingredient by volume. The medicine contains about 0.57 milliliters of that active ingredient. Which of the following is closest to the total volume, to the nearest milliliter, of the liquid medicine?

A) 5
B) 48
C) 135
D) 475

13

A company plans to buy a machine that produces plastic trays. The table below shows the average daily and 30-day outputs of three machine models along with the percentage of unusable trays that were rejected because of a production defect. The company already has one model of Machine A. If Machine A is replaced with one Machine C, what would be the approximate percent increase of <u>usable</u> trays produced in a 30-day period by Machine C?

Machine	Average Daily Output	Average 30-Day Output	Average Percent Unusable
Machine A	275 units		1%
Machine B	250 units	7500 units	.5%
Machine C	315 units		1.3%

A) .3%
B) 14%
C) 15%
D) 30%

14

Two containers contain the same amount of water. 25% of the water in container one is removed. Then, 25% of what is left in container one is added back to container one, using water from container two. Next, 50% of the water left in container one is removed. Then, 50% of what is left in container one is added back to container one using water from container two. Which of the following best approximates the amount of water in container one as a percentage of the initial amount in the container?

A) 50%
B) 67%
C) 70%
D) 100%

15

Year	Number of Customers
2017	86,540
2018	95,194

The owner of a car wash received the table above showing the amount of customers that paid for a car wash in 2017 and 2018. The owner estimates that the percent increase in customers from 2017 to 2018 is double what the percent increase in customers from 2018 to 2019 will be. How many customers did the owner expect in 2019?

A) 90,867
B) 99,954
C) 104,669
D) 114,233

16

A pair of sneakers was on sale for 15% off. After the discount and a sales tax of 8%, the final price of the sneakers was s dollars. Which of these gives the original, pre-sale price of the sneakers, in terms of s?

A) $\dfrac{s}{(0.85)(1.08)}$

B) $\dfrac{s}{(0.85)(0.92)}$

C) $s(0.85)(0.92)$

D) $s(0.85)(1.08)$

Notes and Reflections

Ratios

Questions 1-3 refer to the following information.

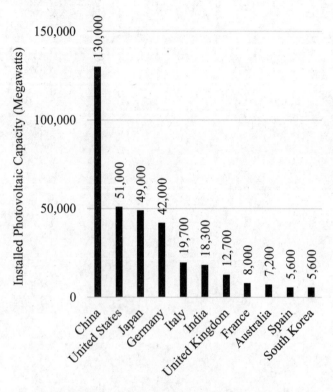

The bar graph above shows estimates from 2017 on the power output of installed photovoltaic solar cells for the top 11 solar-power-producing countries.

1

In 2017, the population of Germany was approximately 83 million people (1 million = 1,000,000). Based on this estimate, which of the following best approximates the ratio of Germany's photovoltaic capacity (in megawatts) to its population during this year?

A) 1:2000
B) 1:2
C) 2:1
D) 2000:1

2

Over the course of 2017, China added about 50,000 MW of photovoltaic capacity to its 2016 photovoltaic capacity. Which of the following best estimates the ratio of China's 2016 photovoltaic capacity to its 2017 photovoltaic capacity?

A) 5:13
B) 8:13
C) 13:8
D) 13:5

3

During 2017, the estimated total world photovoltaic capacity was 400,000 MW. Which of the following best approximates the ratio of the photovoltaic capacity of the top 11 solar energy producers to the world photovoltaic capacity during 2017?

A) 13:40
B) 7:8
C) 8:7
D) 40:13

4

It takes Jacob one hour to mow a 25,000 square-foot yard. Working together, Jacob and Sarah can mow a 200,000 square-foot yard in 3 hours. If Jacob mows at the same rate throughout, what must be the ratio of the area that Sarah will mow to the area that Jacob will mow during this task?

A) 3:8
B) 3:5
C) 5:3
D) 8:3

5

	Male	Female	Total
Brown Eyes	12	12	24
Blue Eyes	4	9	13
Green Eyes	2	1	3
Total	18	22	40

Students counted how many male and female students had each eye color in their class. What is the ratio of male students with brown eyes to female students without brown eyes?

A) 1:1
B) 5:6
C) 6:5
D) 6:11

Questions 6-8 refer to the following information.

600 randomly selected adults who regularly commute to work were surveyed and asked to list if they lived in a city, suburb, or outside of a metro area. Each was asked what method of commuting they use most often. Results are shown in the table below.

	Bike	Walk	Drive	Public Transit	Total
City	15	50	74	61	200
Suburb	19	69	148	64	300
Outside Metro Area	2	10	74	14	100
Total	36	129	296	139	600

6

Based on the data in the table, which of the following ratios is closest to the probability that a participant in the survey uses public transit to commute to work?

A) 1:10
B) 3:10
C) 7:30
D) 7:50

7

Based on the data in the table, how many times more likely is it for a city resident to regularly walk to work as it is for an outside metro resident to walk to work?

A) 1/5
B) 2/5
C) 5/2
D) 5/1

8

Based on the results of the survey, what is the ratio of the likelihood a suburb resident drives to work to the likelihood a city dweller drives to work?

A) 1:2
B) 3:4
C) 2:1
D) 4:3

9

A length of ribbon that is 8 feet long is cut into 3 pieces. The lengths of the pieces are in the ratio 2:4:6. What is the length, in inches, of the shortest piece of ribbon?

10

This season, Tree A produced 60 fruit, and Tree B produced 72 fruit. The ratio of this season's Tree A fruit yield to Tree B fruit yield is equal to the ratio of this season's Tree C fruit yield to Tree D fruit yield. If Tree D produced 120 fruit, how many individual fruits did all four trees produce in total?

11

Seth was making salad dressing in preparation for an evening get-together. His recipe was very simple: 2 parts balsamic vinegar to 5 parts extra virgin olive oil. Unfortunately, after adding 5 containers of olive oil, Seth accidentally put 3 containers of vinegar into the mix instead of 2. He does not want to throw out the dressing he has made. How many containers of olive oil must Seth add to the mix to maintain an equivalent vinegar to oil ratio, and arrive at the original flavor he wants to achieve?

A) $7\frac{1}{2}$

B) $10\frac{1}{2}$

C) $2\frac{1}{2}$

D) $\frac{1}{2}$

12

Class A has a boy to girl ratio of 3:7 and a total of 21 girls. Class B has a boy to girl ratio of 4:8 with a total of 16 boys. Both classes are moving into a new wing within the school. Classroom space is at a premium, so careful planning is required. Of the last two available classrooms, one has a capacity of 32 students and the other can hold 50. Which of the following provides accurate information that will help in classroom planning?

A) Class A will need the larger of the two available classrooms.

B) Class B will need the larger of the two available classrooms.

C) Both classes A and B will be able to function in either classroom.

D) There is not enough information to make an accurate determination.

13

Treatment	Number of patients	
	Improved	Did not Improve
Medicine	75	35
Placebo	45	55

The table above shows the results of an experiment of two treatments, either a medicine or a placebo. Based on the results what fraction of the patients who did not improve, received the medicine?

A) $\frac{7}{42}$

B) $\frac{7}{22}$

C) $\frac{7}{20}$

D) $\frac{7}{18}$

14

Kara is buying Halloween candy to give out. So far, she has bought five bags of 30 lollipops and four bags of 35 chocolate bars. If Kara wants to give out three lollipops for every two chocolate bars she gives out, how many more bags of lollipops should she buy?

A) Zero
B) One
C) Two
D) Three

15

The following table shows the approximate number of women in the United States Congress over the past decade:

Women in Congress
111th through 115th Congress

	Congress				
	111th	112th	113th	114th	115th
House of Reps	73	73	80	84	87
Senate	17	17	20	20	23
Total	90	90	100	104	110

Of the following ratios, which is closest to the ratio of the total number of women in the 111th Congress to the total number of women in the 114th Congress?

A) Women in the House of Representatives in the 111th Congress to the total number of women in the 111th Congress
B) The total number of women in the 115th Congress to women in the House of Representatives in the 115th Congress
C) Women in the House of Representatives in the 113th Congress to the total number of women in the 113th Congress
D) Women in the Senate in the 111th Congress to women in the Senate in the 112th Congress

16

Aaron is 13 years old. Baxter is 12 years old. Charlie is 10 years old. They share a sum of money in the ratio of their ages. They each give a different fraction of their shares to Damian. The fraction of the shares they give can be expressed as 1:2:3 for Aaron, Baxter, and Charlie respectively. Aaron gives 1/5 of his share. The amount of money Damian receives in total from Aaron, Baxter and Charlie is $21.44. What was the initial sum of money?

A) $8.21
B) $20.92
C) $56.00
D) $142.48

Notes and Reflections

Proportions

1

3 pounds of apples are required to produce 16 fluid ounces of apple cider. How many pounds of apples are required to produce 120 fluid ounces of apple cider?

2

A museum made a scale model of an *Escherichia coli* bacterial cell, where 1 centimeter in the model is equal to 5 nanometers in the actual bacterial cell. If the length of the actual bacterial flagellum is 24 nanometers, what is the length, to the nearest centimeter, of the flagellum in the model?

A) 5
B) 19
C) 30
D) 120

3

When at rest, Ethan's body burns 1800 calories per day to maintain basic bodily function. Assuming he rests for the first 6 hours of the day, how many calories does his body burn during this time?

A) 300
B) 450
C) 1080
D) 7200

▼

Questions 4-6 refer to the following information.

The table below shows the calorie and macromolecule content in 30g samples of a whey protein powder product and a brown rice protein powder product.

	Whey Protein	Brown Rice Protein
Calories (cal)	110	120
Total Fat (g)	1.5	0.5
Total Carbohydrate (g)	6	4
Total Protein (g)	20	25

4

How many calories are in 120g of brown rice protein powder?

A) 120
B) 144
C) 440
D) 480

5

Rounded to the nearest gram, how many more grams of protein are in 100g of the brown rice powder than there are in 100g of whey powder?

A) 5
B) 17
C) 67
D) 83

6

A 75 kg weight-lifter needs about 2 grams of protein per kg of body-weight to get the required amount of protein he needs for the day. How many grams of the whey protein powder must he consume to reach his goal protein intake for the day?

A) 150
B) 175
C) 180
D) 225

▲

SUMMIT
EDUCATIONAL
GROUP

7

The creatinine clearance rate is the rate at which kidneys filter creatinine from blood. To be considered healthy, a woman's creatinine clearance rate must fall in the range of 88-128 milliliters of blood per minute. Sandra is a woman with 5000 mL of blood. Assuming Sandra has a healthy creatinine clearance rate, which of the following could be the number of minutes it takes her kidneys to filter all of her blood of creatinine?

I.   40 min.
II. 50 min.
III. 60 min.

A) I
B) I and II
C) II and III
D) I, II, and III

8

Twice a day, Sylvia feeds her puppy 2 chewable vitamins. Sylvia is going on vacation and needs to pack enough chewables so the staff at her puppy's kennel can administer that same dose. How many chewables will Sylvia need to supply to the kennel for the two weeks she will be away?

Questions 9-10 refer to the following information.

The following table shows fuel efficiency for different types of cars in the city and on the highway. Because electric vehicles do not run on gasoline, their fuel efficiency is measured in miles per gallon equivalent, or MPGe.

Fuel Type	MPGe (City)	MPGe (Highway)
Gas only	30	40
Gas/Electric hybrid	40	50
Electric only	120	100

9

Suppose that a gas/electric hybrid vehicle is filled with 10 gallons of gas, and an electric-only vehicle is charged to the equivalent level. How much further, in highway miles, would the electric vehicle travel than the gas/electric hybrid vehicle?

A) 100 miles
B) 200 miles
C) 500 miles
D) 800 miles

10

AJ and Robbie want to take a trip to a music festival. Suppose that the cost of gas is $3.50 per gallon, and that they will need to travel 300 highway miles and 60 city miles. How much more will they save by taking AJ's gas/electric hybrid car instead of Robbie's gas only car?

A) $2.00
B) $7.00
C) $9.80
D) $28.00

11

Arnold is following a bulk recipe to make cookies.

> **Cookies**
> (Makes 180 Cookies)
>
> Sugar – 40oz
> Butter – 120oz
> Flour – 110oz
> Chocolate – 7oz

Arnold has 140oz of sugar, 500oz of butter, 420oz of flour, and 25oz of chocolate. Which one of his ingredients is limiting the amount of cookies he can make?

A) Sugar
B) Butter
C) Flour
D) Chocolate

12

Student pilot Jack was completing an assignment for his flight school where he needed to convert nautical miles to standard miles. Jack forgot his notes and could not remember the conversion factor for nautical miles to standard miles. He had, however, completed one problem in the section and could see that 110 nautical miles equals 126.5 standard miles. The next problem in the section required that Jack convert 115 nautical miles to miles. Assuming Jack answered correctly, what was his answer?

A) 133.25
B) 132.25
C) 131.5
D) 133.5

13

Runner A can run at a rate of 6.5 meters per second. Runner B can run at a rate of 7.5 meters per second. How much longer will it take runner A than runner B to run 1 mile? (1 mile = 1609 meters).

A) 0.00062 seconds
B) 30 seconds
C) 33 seconds
D) 1609 seconds

14

Rob is taking a road trip. After driving 124 miles, he has spent $48.60 on gas. If he has 208 miles left to drive, approximately how much will he spend on gas for the entire trip? (Assume that he is always able to buy gas for the same price and that he travels the same distance on a gallon of gas throughout the whole trip).

A) $81
B) $112
C) $130
D) $144

15

Olivia walks at a rate of 5 km per hour. She runs at a speed of 15 km per hour. She needs to travel to the supermarket, which is 25 km away, in 3 hours. Olivia wants to maximize the amount of time in hours that she can spend walking and still make it in time. Assuming she only walks or runs, what is the ratio of her time spent running to her time spent walking on her trip to the supermarket?

A) 2:1
B) 3:2
C) 2:3
D) 1:2

16

Mira conducted a survey asking 105 randomly chosen students from her grade whether they preferred chocolate or vanilla ice cream. 60 responded that they preferred chocolate, 32 responded that they preferred vanilla, and the rest responded that they did not like ice cream. Based on the results of Mira's survey, if there are 330 students in her grade, approximately how many students in her grade do not like ice cream?

A) 13
B) 39
C) 41
D) 51

17

A basketball team has only lost 2 games so far this year. There are only 6 more games in the regular season. If they win 15 games total, they will finish with the same winning percentage as they have now. How many games have they won so far?

(Winning percentage = $\dfrac{\text{\# of games won}}{\text{\# of games played}}$)

A) 8
B) 9
C) 10
D) 11

Notes and Reflections

Units & Conversion

1

Two units of weight used in the United Kingdom are the pound and the stone, where 14 pounds is equivalent to one stone. If a British bulldog weighs 56 pounds, what is his weight in stone?

2

The International Space Station orbits the Earth at a speed of 17,150 miles per hour. Rounded to the nearest mile, how many miles does the International Space Station travel in one minute?

A) 5
B) 172
C) 286
D) 715

3

At 25°C, the glucose solubility capacity of one liter of water is 909 grams. Assuming the temperature remains constant, what is the approximate glucose solubility capacity of one liter of water in <u>ounces</u> (1 ounce ≈ 28.3495 grams)?

A) 28
B) 32
C) 881
D) 25,770

4

Known as "the female Paul Revere," Sybil Ludington famously warned of a British attack on Danbury, Connecticut, at only sixteen years of age. Her horseback ride to deliver this news was 40 miles long. Supposing a kilometer is approximately 0.621 miles, which of the following is closest to the distance, in meters, that Sybil Ludington traveled on her ride?

A) 25,000
B) 38,500
C) 62,100
D) 64,370

5

One of the first units of measurement for medicine was the grain. You can still purchase 5-grain aspirin in most drug stores. Suppose that a grain is approximately 65 milligrams, and that a new bottle of 5-grain aspirin contains 100 5-grain aspirin pills. How many milligrams of aspirin are in the entire bottle of 5-grain aspirin pills?

A) 325 milligrams
B) 500 milligrams
C) 6,500 milligrams
D) 32,500 milligrams

6

Jill is studying for a biology final exam. She reviews 16 pages per hour and studies for 2 hours per day. If her textbook contains 8 chapters of 40 pages each, how many days will it take her to review the entire textbook?

A) 7 days
B) 10 days
C) 11 days
D) 12 days

7

A *knot* is a nautical mile per hour and is used to measure and calculate ground speed for aircraft. If 117 knots equal 134.55 standard miles per hour, by what value should one multiply to convert a measurement from knots into miles per hour?

A) 1.15
B) 11.5
C) .869
D) 17.55

8

Suppose that an airplane is flying at a constant speed of 580 miles per hour. If an airplane maintains that speed for 97 <u>minutes</u>, how many miles will it fly in that time? Round to the nearest mile.

A) 359
B) 563
C) 938
D) 1125

9

The dimensions of a rectangular desk top are 51 inches by 29 inches. What is the approximate area of the desktop in square <u>centimeters</u>? (1 in = 2.54 cm)

A) 1032
B) 1479
C) 3757
D) 9542

10

Joey is baking a cake, and the recipe calls for 3.5 tablespoons of baking soda. Joey does not have measuring spoons, but he does have a metric scale. If one teaspoon of baking soda weighs 4.8 grams, how much baking soda does Joey need for his cake (in grams)? (Note: 1 tablespoon = 3 teaspoons)

A) 5.6 g
B) 16.8 g
C) 50.4 g
D) 52.5 g

11

At room temperature, the density of liquid mercury is 13.354 g/cm^3. Rounded to the nearest cm^3, what is the volume of 2 pounds of mercury (1 pound ≈ 0.453592 kilograms) at room temperature?

A) 12
B) 27
C) 68
D) 330

12

The Earth travels approximately 584,000,000 miles to complete one revolution around the sun. Assuming Earth's orbit is circular, which of the following best approximates the distance between the Earth and the sun in kilometers (1 kilometer ≈ 0.62137 miles)?

A) 57,800,000
B) 92,900,000
C) 150,000,000
D) 859,000,000

13

The height of MIT student Oliver Smoot was used to measure the length of Harvard Bridge. Smoot measured 1.70 meters, which became known as the length of 1 Smoot. The Harvard Bridge measures 364.4 Smoots in length. If the Sydney Harbor Bridge measures 3,770ft in length and 1 meter ≈ 3.3ft, how many more Smoots, to the nearest Smoot, is the Sydney Harbor Bridge than the Harvard Bridge?

A) The bridges are the same length.
B) 20 Smoots
C) 110 Smoots
D) 308 Smoots

14

An "astronomical unit" (*au*) is a measure of distance based on the Earth's average distance from the sun. Earth is one *au* or approximately 92,955,807 miles from the sun. Jupiter is located at about 5.20 *au* from the sun, Saturn at 9.54 *au*, and Neptune at 30.06 *au*.

If a spacecraft were launched from Earth and travelled at a constant 34,600 miles per hour along a straight path into outer space (contrary to what really happens during space flight), approximately how many decades would it take for the spacecraft to reach the orbits of Jupiter, Saturn, and Neptune in that order? (One decade equals ten years)

A) 1.29, 2.62, 891.23
B) 12.9, 26.2, 8,912.34
C) .129, .262, .891
D) .129, 2.62, 8.91

15

$$1 \text{ acre} = \frac{1}{640} \text{ square miles}$$

1 hectare = 100 meters × 100 meters
1 mile = 1760 yards
1 meter ≈ 1.09 yards

Using the above unit conversions, approximately how many acres make one hectare?

A) 2.3
B) 2.5
C) 2.7
D) 2.9

16

In maritime navigation, 1 knot equals 1.85 kilometers per hour. One kilometer is 3,280.8 feet. To the nearest whole number, how fast in *statute* (land) miles per hour is a boat running at 32 knots traveling? (One statute mile = 5,280 feet)

A) 177
B) 95
C) 37
D) 12

17

	Density (grams/mL)
copper	8.96
tin	7.31

An alloy of bronze consists of a mixture with a composition of 88% copper and 12% tin by mass. Given the above data on density (density = mass/volume), what is the percent composition by volume of tin?

A) 11%
B) 12%
C) 13%
D) 14%

Notes and Reflections

Statistics – Average (Mean)

1

The following table lists the ages of the first twelve astronauts to walk on the moon. Ages shown are at the time of the astronaut's first walk on the lunar surface. According to the table, which of the answers listed below is closest to the mean age of the astronauts at the time of their first moon walk?

Astronaut	Age at First Moon Walk
Neil Armstrong	38
Buzz Aldrin	39
Pete Conrad	39
Alan Bean	37
Alan Shepherd	47
Edgar Mitchell	40
David Scott	39
James Irwin	41
John Young	41
Charles Duke	36
Eugene Cernan	38
Harrison Schmitt	37

A) 37
B) 38
C) 39
D) 40

2

2000, 6000, 9000, 12,000, x

The mean of the five numbers listed above is 9000. What must be the value of x?

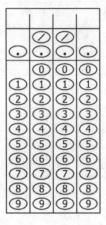

3

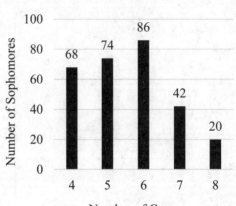

During the 2017-2018 school year, all 290 sophomores at a particular high school were asked how many courses they were taking that year. Their responses are shown in the bar graph above. Rounded to the nearest tenth, what is the average number of courses taken by a sophomore at this particular high school during this school year?

A) 5.0
B) 5.2
C) 5.6
D) 6.0

4

Wyatt and Gina went on a hike and each collected 5 wildflowers. The lengths of the flowers are recorded in the table below.

	Length (cm)				
Wyatt	12.3	15.2	5.4	x	4.4
Gina	8.7	5.6	7.4	8.3	10.5

If the mean length of the flowers Gina collected is 1 cm less than the mean length of Wyatt's flowers, what must be the value of x?

A) 4.2
B) 8.1
C) 8.2
D) 9.1

5

If a is the arithmetic mean of 11 and p, and b is the arithmetic mean of 5 and $3p$, what is the mean of a and b expressed in terms of p?

A) $4 + p$
B) $8 + p$
C) $8 + 2p$
D) $16 + 4p$

6

The average weekly temperature for a given region is normally 34°F at a certain time of year. The table below shows the daily temperature for a two-week period during that specific time of year. Assuming that the average temperature over the two weeks listed matched the average weekly temperature, what is the value of $x + y$?

Mon	Tue	Wed	Thu	Fri	Sat	Sun
34	32	33	37	28	x	30
37	y	28	34	39	37	32

A) 238
B) 33.5
C) 1364
D) 75

7

Suppose that there are five people in a social club whose mean age is 30. Suppose seven more people, whose mean age is m, join the social club. If the mean age of the social club is now 25, which of the following must be true?

A) $m = 20$
B) $10 < m < 20$
C) $20 < m < 30$
D) $m > 30$

8

Ms. O'Donnell and Mr. Larch teach chemistry. The combined average test scores for two classes is 85. Ms. O'Donnell's class of 15 students has an average of 97. Mr. Larch's class has an average of 70. How many students are in Mr. Larch's class?

A) 12
B) 13
C) 14
D) 15

SUMMIT
EDUCATIONAL
GROUP

Notes and Reflections

Statistics – Median, Mode, and Range

1

Accidents	0	1	2	3	4	5	6
Frequency	7	22	34	15	4	3	2

A car insurance company selected 87 of their customers who had at least a 10-year driving record. A data analyst tabulated the number of major traffic accidents each customer experienced in the past 10 years and recorded the data in the frequency table above. What was the median number of accidents for the 87 customers studied?

A) 1
B) 2
C) 3
D) 4

2

Country	Health Expenditure per capita (PPP international dollars)
Austria	5,227
Denmark	5,205
Germany	5,551
Ireland	5,528
Luxembourg	7,463
Netherlands	5,385
Norway	6,647
Sweden	5,488
Switzerland	7,919
United States	9,892

The table above lists the 2016 total health expenditure per capita for 10 developed countries. What is the range, in PPP international dollars, of the per capita health expenditure for the countries in the table above?

A) 2,714
B) 4,665
C) 4,687
D) 9,892

3

Three separate studies on the total number of items that grocery shoppers buy per visit were conducted at three local grocery stores: Grocery Store A, Grocery Store B, and Grocery Store C. At each grocery store, a random sample of exiting shoppers participated in a brief survey where they were asked how many items they had purchased during their visit. The distribution of total items bought for each store is shown in the table below.

Number of Items Bought	Grocery Store A	Grocery Store B	Grocery Store C
1-9	78	140	45
10-19	102	165	54
20-29	10	73	71
30-39	7	75	123
40+	3	47	107
Total Participants	200	500	400

Which of the following could be the median number of items bought at Grocery Store B?

A) 8
B) 13
C) 24
D) 31

4

Turnovers Made by Team in 37 Games								
turnovers	3	4	5	6	7	8	9	10	11
games	2	5	8	3	1	9	6	2	1

Based on the table above, in how many games did the basketball team have the median number of turnovers for the 37 games?

A) 1
B) 3
C) 8
D) 9

SUMMIT
EDUCATIONAL
GROUP

5

Age Group	Percent Voter Turnout	Percent Voting to Remain in EU
18-24	48%	73 %
25-34	52%	62 %
35-44	64%	53 %
45-54	70%	44 %
55-64	77%	43%
65+	78%	40%

The table above lists data from the 2016 United Kingdom European Union membership referendum where the United Kingdom electorate decided if the country should remain a member of the European Union (EU). The table lists percent voter turnout and the percent of voters voting to remain in the EU for various age groups that voted in the referendum.

Which of the following statements about the dataset is true?

A) The range of percent voter turnouts is lower than the range of percent voting to remain in the EU.
B) The range of percent voter turnouts is higher than the range of percent voting to remain in the EU.
C) The range of percent voter turnouts is equal to the range of the percent voting to remain in the EU.
D) There is not enough information to determine which range is lower.

6

A particular data set consists of 20 positive integers. The lowest value in the data set is 24. A new data set is constructed by taking the original data set and adding one more value to the whole set: the number 5. Which of the following measurements must be 19 more for the new data set than it was for the original data set?

A) The median
B) The mode
C) The standard deviation
D) The range

7

Set A contains elements {2, 5, 6, 7, 9, 12, 13, 15, 17, 20, 23}. A second set, B, is created by tripling the fourth element of set A and adding that number to the existing elements of set A. When comparing the new set B to set A, which of the following will result from the insertion of the additional number into set B?

A) The median will increase, but the mean will decrease.
B) The median will remain the same, but the mean will increase.
C) The median and mean will both increase.
D) The mean and median will both decrease.

8

The unified rules of mixed martial arts divide competitors into 14 different weight classes. The flyweight class is for all competitors between the weights of 116 and 125 pounds. 100 flyweight fighters were weighed on the day of a big competition, and their weights are tabulated in the frequency table below.

Weight	Frequency
116	1
117	2
118	2
119	3
120	0
121	5
122	8
123	12
124	31
125	36

Which of the answers below gives the correct order of the mode, mean, and median of the weights?

A) median < mode < mean
B) mean < mode < median
C) median < mean < mode
D) mean < median < mode

9

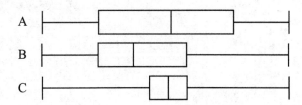

The three box-plots above represent different sets of data. Which of the following statements must be true?

I. Set B has the lowest median.
II. Set C has the lowest standard deviation.
III. Set A and Set C have the same mean.

A) I only
B) II only
C) I and II only
D) I, II and III

10

Kat is growing yams in her garden. She weighed 16 yams and recorded each of their weights (in grams):

| 131 | 133 | 140 | 140 | 141 | 148 | 149 | 150 |
| 155 | 156 | 167 | 169 | 175 | 177 | 183 | 203 |

Kat found the mean, median, mode, and range of this data set, but then discovered the yam with a weight of 203g was rotten and threw it away. Which of these values will change the most when calculated without the 203g yam?

A) Mean
B) Median
C) Mode
D) Range

11

Of 81 homeowners who live in a certain town, 20 live in a home valued between $0 and $299,999, 60 live in a home valued between $300,000 and $600,000, and the only remaining homeowner lives in a large estate that is valued at $60,000,000. Which of the following statements about the mean and median of the 80 home values is true?

A) The median is lower than the mean.
B) The mean is lower than the median.
C) The mean and the median are equal.
D) There is not enough information to determine whether the median or mean is lower.

12

Mr. Weisenfreud just finished grading his math tests and creates the following table with the scores:

40%	45%	50%	50%
60%	65%	70%	70%
75%	75%	80%	80%
80%	85%	90%	90%
95%	100%	100%	105%

As it turns out, Mr. Weisenfreud made a mistake and added an extra 75% to the table. Which of the following will change the most if one score of 75% is removed from the table?

A) Median
B) Mean
C) Mode
D) Range

Notes and Reflections

Probability

Questions 1-2 refer to the following information.

The RMS *Titanic* sank on April 15, 1912, in the Atlantic Ocean. Many passengers were put into lifeboats, and some survived after a rescue boat arrived some 9 hours after the sinking of the ship. There were three classes of passengers on the Titanic (not including the crew), and the number of passengers in each class who survived or died is listed in the table below.

	Survived	Died	Total
First Class	202	123	325
Second Class	118	167	285
Third Class	178	528	706
Total	498	818	1316

1

Based on the data, if a First Class passenger is randomly selected, which of the following is the probability that the passenger died?

A) $\dfrac{123}{202}$

B) $\dfrac{123}{325}$

C) $\dfrac{123}{1316}$

D) $\dfrac{325}{1316}$

2

Based on the data, if a random surviving passenger is selected, which of the following is the probability the survivor was in third class?

A) $\dfrac{498}{1316}$

B) $\dfrac{706}{1316}$

C) $\dfrac{498}{706}$

D) $\dfrac{178}{498}$

Questions 3-5 refer to the following information.

A spam filter is used to move unwanted email from an email inbox to a spam folder where it can be quarantined. Over a year, Anna used a particular spam filter at work and tracked all of her emails received, noting which were unwanted emails and which were legitimate work emails. She also tracked the location of where she found each message: spam folder or inbox. The data she collected is in the table below.

	Spam Folder	Inbox	Total
Unwanted Email	1100	120	1220
Work Email	25	5281	5306
Total	1125	5401	6526

3

Which of the following is the probability that an unwanted email was moved to the spam folder?

A) $\dfrac{1125}{6526}$

B) $\dfrac{1100}{1125}$

C) $\dfrac{1100}{1220}$

D) $\dfrac{1125}{1220}$

4

Which of the following is the probability that the spam filter incorrectly moved a legitimate work email to the spam folder?

A) $\dfrac{1125}{6526}$

B) $\dfrac{25}{1125}$

C) $\dfrac{1125}{5306}$

D) $\dfrac{25}{5306}$

5

For all of the emails Anna received this year, which of the following is the probability that the spam filter did not make an error and filed an email into the correct folder?

A) $\dfrac{5281}{5306}$

B) $\dfrac{1100}{1220}$

C) $\dfrac{1100}{6526}$

D) $\dfrac{6381}{6526}$

6

Maria has a rock and mineral collection that contains 14 rocks and m minerals. If she has no other items in the collection, and she picks an item at random from her collection, what is the probability that Maria will select a mineral?

A) $\dfrac{14}{14+m}$

B) $\dfrac{m}{14+m}$

C) $\dfrac{14}{m}$

D) $\dfrac{m}{14}$

Questions 7-8 refer to the following information.

Kara surveyed 250 students at random from her state university and 400 students from the neighboring community college. She asked each participant whether or not he or she was employed during the past week (employment was defined as having worked at least 10 hours in the past week). Some of her results are tabulated in the incomplete table below.

	Employed	Not Employed	Total
State University	a	b	250
Community College	320	80	400

7

Based on the data, if Kara was able to conclude that a community college student was four times as likely to be employed as a student from the state university was, how many surveyed state university students were employed?

A) 25
B) 50
C) 80
D) 200

8

If the probability that a survey participant was not employed was 26%, how many students surveyed at the state university were not employed?

A) 80
B) 89
C) 150
D) 169

Notes and Reflections

22

22

222

222

Data Relationships

Questions 1-2 refer to the following information.

The number of new patients admitted to a local emergency room (ER) each day of a week is shown in the table below.

Day	Number of New ER Patients
Monday	22
Tuesday	23
Wednesday	26
Thursday	19
Friday	44
Saturday	57
Sunday	12

1

Which of the following is true based on the data?

A) Each day from Monday through Saturday, the number of new patients admitted to the ER was greater than the previous day.
B) The hospital had the least number of newly admitted emergency room patients on Thursday.
C) The emergency room had the greatest number of new patients on Friday.
D) There were fewer newly admitted patients to the ER on Thursday than on the previous day.

2

Between which two consecutive days shown did the number of newly admitted patients increase the most?

A) Tuesday to Wednesday
B) Wednesday to Thursday
C) Thursday to Friday
D) Friday to Saturday

3

A package delivery company has 2000 packages left in its warehouse at the end of the day on Monday. On Tuesday, the company delivers 1000 packages and receives 500 new packages. On Wednesday, the company delivers 1200 packages and receives 200 packages. On Thursday, the company delivers no packages and receives no packages. On Friday, the company delivers 900 packages and receives 1400 packages. Which of the following represents the number of packages the company had in its warehouse at the end of each day?

A)
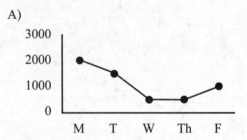

B)
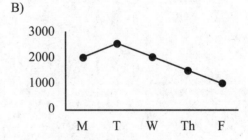

C)
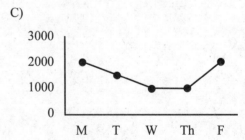

D)
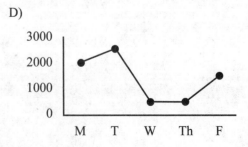

4

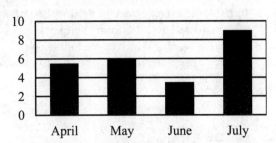

The graph above shows the monthly profits of a small business. If the business earned a total of $24,000 in profit from April to July, what would be an appropriate label for the *y*-axis of this graph?

A) Profit (in dollars)
B) Profit (in hundreds of dollars)
C) Profit (in thousands of dollars)
D) Profit (in tens of thousands of dollars)

5

Which scatter plot represents a negative strong linear correlation?

A)
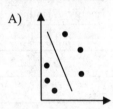

B)
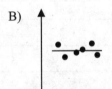

C)
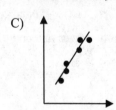

D)
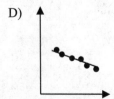

6

For thirteen different months, a homeowner tracked the number of kilowatt hours his heating system used along with the average outside temperature, in degrees Fahrenheit, for that month. The data he collected is graphed in the scatterplot below. A line of best fit is also shown.

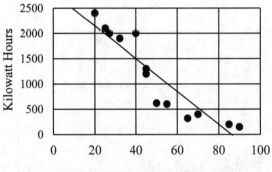

Which of the following is closest to the difference, in kilowatt hours, between the actual kilowatt hour usage and the kilowatt usage predicted by the line of best fit for the only month that recorded an average temperature of 40°F?

A) 500
B) 1000
C) 1500
D) 2000

Questions 7-9 refer to the following chart.

The line graph shows the average prices of a half-gallon of milk in a city in 2018.

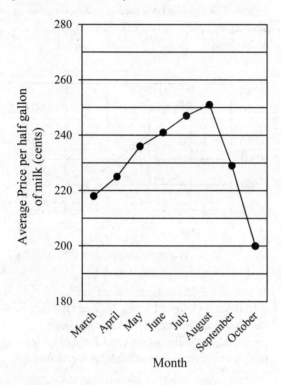

Month

7

Between which two consecutive months did the price of milk increase the most?

A) March and April
B) April and May
C) May and June
D) June and July

8

Which of the following is closest to the median price, in cents, of one half-gallon of milk between March and October of 2018?

A) 200
B) 218
C) 229
D) 233

9

In 2018, the average price of a half-gallon of milk increased by 2.9% from February (not shown) to March. Which of the following is closest to the price, in cents, of one half-gallon of milk in February 2018?

A) 194
B) 206
C) 212
D) 215

10

The elastic potential energy E, in joules, for a spring increases the greater the number of centimeters the spring is displaced from its resting position. The potential energy of a spring was measured for different displacements, d, of the spring, and the data is shown in the table below.

Spring Displacement, d (meters)	Elastic Potential Energy, E (joules)
0.00	0
0.20	2
0.40	8
0.60	18
0.80	32
1.00	50

If the relationship between E and d can be modeled by the function $E(d) = a \times d^b$, which of the following could be the values of a and b?

A) $a = 2$ and $b = 50$
B) $a = 10$ and $b = 1$
C) $a = 50$ and $b = 2$
D) $a = 250$ and $b = 3$

11

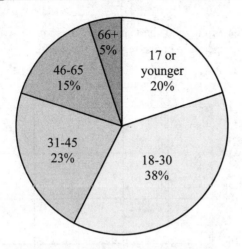

The chart above shows the approximate percentage of audience members of a certain concert that fell into each age bracket. If there were 6 audience members that were 66 or older, how many audience members were 30 or younger?

A) 48
B) 58
C) 70
D) 72

12

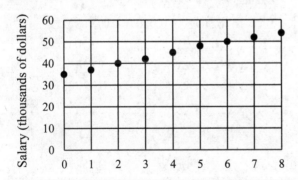

Total Years Working at Company

The above scatterplot shows Alexander's annual salary for the 9 years he worked at a particular company. What could be the slope of a line of best fit for these data points?

A) 1.25
B) 2.45
C) 4.02
D) 6.90

13

Aircraft Bank Angle	Load Factor of "Gs"	% Increase in Stall Speed
10°	<1	<1
30°	1.25	8
40°	1.5	17
60°	2	44
70°	3	72
90°	>13	>100

The chart above shows the "G-Force" or gravitational pull on a pilot as an aircraft banks at an angle to execute a turn. It also shows the percent increase in stall speed as an aircraft banks more steeply (stalling is when a plane loses its capacity for lift). Which of the following is reflected in the information provided in the chart?

A) Load factor and stall speed percents decrease in a steeper turn.
B) Load factor and stall speed percents change only slightly as turns get steeper.
C) If these data points were plotted, you would see exponential functions.
D) If these data points were plotted, you would see linear functions with negative slopes.

14

Consider the following situation:

After an initial fee, the price of a rental boat increases by a set amount each hour.

Which of the following would be true if the prices are plotted on the xy-coordinate plane, with hours along the x axis and total cost along the y axis?

I. The y-intercept would show the initial cost to rent the boat.
II. Plotting the price points for several hours' rental would yield an exponential curve.
III. A line of best fit connecting different costs would have a positive slope.

A) I, II, III
B) I, III
C) II
D) II, III

15

The following chart shows the population of Mountain View, California for the years 2005-2015.

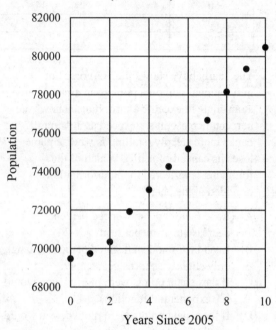

Population of Mountain View, California (2005-2015)

Which of the following best represents the population of Mountain View, California, y, after x years have passed since 2005?

A) $y = x + 68,500$

B) $y = \dfrac{1}{2}x + 68,500$

C) $y = 1200x + 68,500$

D) $y = x + 70,000$

16

The following chart shows the average temperature in one region of the world.

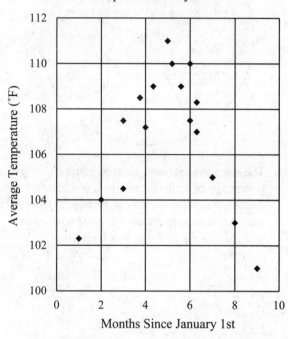

Temperature Analysis

Which of the following best represents the average temperature, y, at a point x months since January 1st?

A) $y = 0.5092x^2 + 4.9807x + 97.703$

B) $y = -0.5092x^2 + 4.9807x + 97.703$

C) $y = -0.5092x^2 - 4.9807x + 97.703$

D) $y = -0.5092x^2 + 4.9807x + 106.703$

17

A factory bought new machinery and started producing more screws. Before it bought the new machinery it could produce 10,000 screws per year. By the end of the fifth year after investing in the machinery it could produce 100,000,000 screws per year. Which of the following statements is true about the factory?

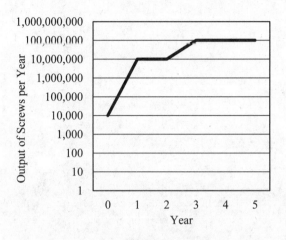

A) The greatest increase in the number of screws produced was between year 0 and year 1 and the highest percent increase in the number of screws produced was between year 2 and 3.

B) The greatest increase in the number of screws produced was between year 2 and year 3 and the highest percent increase in the number of screws produced was between year 2 and year 3.

C) No new screws were produced between year 1 and year 2 and no new screws were produced between year 4 and year 5.

D) The greatest increase in the number of screws produced was between year 2 and year 3 and the highest percent increase in the number of screws produced was between year 0 and year 1.

18

The parameters a and b of an exponential model of the form $y = a \cdot b^x$ can be altered using a computer program. At certain values of a, b, and x the model gives the horizontal straight line shown below. Which of the following values must a and b take?

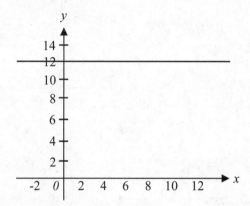

A) $a = 3, b = 4$
B) $a = 4, b = 3$
C) $a = 12, b = 1$
D) All 3 of the pairs of values of a and b work

Notes and Reflections

Data Collection & Conclusions

1

To determine if regular exercise lowers the risk of depression in women, researchers tracked a random sample of 2,600 females. Subjects wore a motion monitor, which was used to track the average level of physical activity for each participant, over the course of the study. At the conclusion of the study, the participants were identified as either regular exercisers or as occasional exercisers, based on the average motion detected by the monitors. The researchers then interviewed the participants and found that the proportion of female subjects who experienced depression was significantly higher in the "occasional exercise" group than in the "regular exercise" group. Which of the following is the most appropriate conclusion of the study?

A) Regular exercise causes a lowered risk of depression for both men and women.
B) Regular exercise causes a lowered risk of depression for women but not necessarily for men.
C) There is an association between the amount of exercise and the risk of depression for both men and women.
D) There is an association between amount of exercise and the risk of depression for women, but the association may not exist for men.

2

A wildlife group studied a random sample of 120 chimpanzees living in the wild. The group estimated that the mean lifespan of a wild chimpanzee was 42 years with a margin of error of 2.4 years. Which of the following is the most appropriate conclusion of the study?

A) Chimpanzees living in the wild have a mean lifespan of 42 years.
B) Chimpanzees living in the wild have a mean lifespan between 40.8 and 43.2 years.
C) Chimpanzees living in the wild have a mean lifespan between 39.6 and 44.4 years.
D) Chimpanzees living in the wild have a mean lifespan between 2.4 and 42 years.

3

To find if the residents of a city would approve of a proposal to spend $60,000 of local taxes to equip the high school's technology center with 10 new 3D printers, Levi surveyed 30 adults at a local PTA (Parent Teacher's Association) meeting. He found that $\frac{4}{5}$ of those surveyed approved of the proposal. Which of the following statements about the survey study must be true?

A) 80% of all city residents approve of the proposal.
B) No conclusion can be drawn from the study because the sample size is too small.
C) The sample selected is not representative of the city population, and so the result may be biased.
D) The sample selected is representative of the city population, and so the result is unbiased.

4

During May 2017, three different studies on the nightly amount of sleep that adults receive were conducted in the state of New Jersey. In each study, every participant was asked how many hours they slept the night before. Their responses are recorded in the table below.

Hours of Sleep	Study I	Study II	Study III
0-3	42	5	32
4	7	1	10
5	17	15	37
6	34	23	42
7	23	45	52
8	23	87	78
9+	4	24	49
Total Participants	150	200	300

The participants in each study were selected in the following manner:

- For Study I, 150 adult volunteers from the state of New Jersey agreed to participate.
- For Study II, 200 residents from the state of New Jersey were chosen at random to participate.
- For Study III, 300 adult residents from the state of New Jersey were chosen at random to participate.

The results of which of the studies can be generalized to all adults living in New Jersey in May 2017?

A) Study III only
B) Study I and III only
C) Study II and III only
D) Studies I, II, and III

5

A librarian tracked a random sample of library patrons' checked-out books. Based on the data, the estimated mean of books checked out per patron was found to be 3.5 books, with a margin of error of 1.5 books. Which of the statements below is the most plausible conclusion from the data?

A) All library patrons have between 2 and 5 books checked out.
B) Most library patrons have exactly 3.5 books checked out.
C) There are no library patrons with more than 6 books checked out.
D) It is likely that the mean number of books checked out per patron for all library patrons is between 2 and 5 books.

6

A sample of 25 diners was selected at random from a specific local restaurant. The 25 diners filled out a survey listing their favorite menu items. Which of the populations listed below is the largest group to which the results of the survey can be extrapolated?

A) The 25 diners who participated in the sample survey
B) All restaurant diners who go to the specific restaurant where the survey was done
C) All restaurant diners in the country
D) All citizens living in the town where the restaurant is located

7

An experimenter plans an experiment in which she will measure the volume of soft drink (in ounces) expelled from an aluminum can when the can is shaken x number of times. The experimenter considers what to use for control variables and decides the temperature of the can, the size of the can, the type of soda in the can, and the speed at which she opens the can could all be considered control variables. With repeated testing it is found that the amount of soft drink expelled from the aluminum can may be modeled by the equation $y = 0.4x + 0.3$, where y is the total volume of liquid expelled. The margin of error in the value of extra liquid per shake is 12%. Which of the following could be the true value of the volume of extra liquid expelled per shake?

A) 0.348
B) 0.048
C) 0.444
D) 0.456

8

A survey was conducted by asking 150 people at a high school baseball game if they thought local taxes should be raised in order to increase the public school sports budget. 80 people responded in favor of raising taxes, 60 said they were against raising taxes, 5 people responded that they had no strong feelings either way, and 5 people declined to answer. Which of the following factors caused the largest possible flaw in the survey results?

A) The location at which the survey was taken
B) The sample size
C) The number of people who declined to respond
D) The number of people who had no strong feelings

9

Students in a high school statistics class conducted a survey of their classmates to ask about their interest in the school's installing an indoor championship swimming pool. Over two weeks, 250 different students were polled. After the results were tabulated, the class found that 27% of students favored the addition of the pool to the school. 73% did not like the idea (the only options given were "for" or "against"). The students in the statistics class also announced that the poll had a 4% margin of error. Assuming all of this information is accurate, what would the actual poll numbers look like for initial responses of "for", initial responses of "against," lowest possible number of "against" votes, and highest possible number of "for" votes? Round to the nearest whole number for each value.

A) 68, 173, 183, 78
B) 68, 183, 173, 78
C) 183, 68, 78, 173
D) 173, 183, 68, 78

10

All visitors to a local newspaper's website on a given day are asked to answer a poll question about whether they plan to vote in the upcoming election. They reported that 90% of responses were Yes, and only 10% of responses were No. Which of the following best explains why the results are unlikely to represent all voters in a given town?

A) Those who responded are not a random sample of the population of the town.
B) The percentages do not match the percent of people who voted in the last election.
C) The percentages were not 50% Yes and 50% No.
D) The website was for a local newspaper.

Notes and Reflections

SUMMIT
EDUCATIONAL
GROUP

Heart of Algebra

- ❏ Section Quiz

- ❏ Algebraic Expressions

- ❏ Algebraic Equations & Inequalities

- ❏ Absolute Value

- ❏ Systems of Equations

- ❏ Slope

- ❏ Graphs of Linear Equations

- ❏ Systems and Graphs of Inequalities

- ❏ Creating Linear Models

- ❏ Interpreting Linear Models

Section Quiz

1

$$3x + 13 = 4$$

Which of the following equations has the same solution set as the equation above?

A) $-8 = 2x$
B) $-9 = 3x$
C) $16 = 4x$
D) $15 = 5x$

2

$$5 = 7 + |2x - 4|$$

What value of x satisfies the above equation?

A) 1
B) 2
C) 3
D) There is no such value of x

3

Line segment $\overline{AB}$ has slope 4. Line $\overline{CD}$ is the perpendicular bisector of $\overline{AB}$. What is the slope of $\overline{CD}$?

A) 4
B) $\dfrac{1}{4}$
C) -4
D) $-\dfrac{1}{4}$

4

Which of the following is the graph of the equation $y = -6 + 3x$?

A)

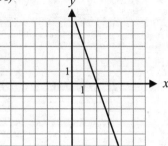

B)

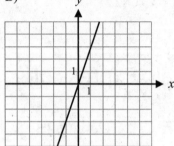

C)

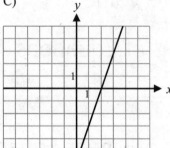

D)

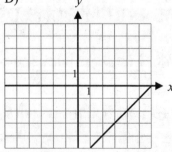

5

To get into the first floor of his office building, Jonah must climb up a set of stairs to reach the first floor, which is at a height of 7 feet above the ground. Once on the first floor, he uses the elevator to travel up to his office. Assuming the elevator ride is uninterrupted, and the elevator travels upward at a rate of 12 feet per second, which of the following equations best models Jonah's height above the ground, h, in feet, s seconds after the elevator begins moving?

A) $h = 7 + 12s$
B) $h = 7 + 84s$
C) $h = 12 + 7s$
D) $h = 12 + 84s$

6

$$x^2 + 12x + 35$$

The expression above is equivalent to which of the following expressions, for all values of x?

A) $(x + 5)(x + 7) + 23$
B) $(x - 5)(x - 7) + 12x$
C) $(x + 10)(x + 2) + 15$
D) $(x - 10)(x - 2) + 55$

7

$$x + 3y = 7$$
$$4x - y = 2$$

For the system of linear equations described above, what is the value of $x - y$?

A) -1
B) 0
C) 1
D) 2

8

$$|6 - 2x| \leq 4$$

Which of the following expresses the full solution set to the inequality shown above?

A) $x \leq -5 \text{ OR } x \geq -1$
B) $-5 \leq x \leq -1$
C) $1 \leq x \leq 5$
D) $x \leq 1 \text{ OR } x \geq 5$

 9

Below is the system of linear inequalities $y < 2x$ and $y > -\dfrac{x}{4}$. Which of the following points satisfies the system?

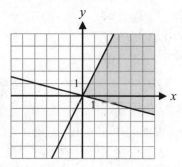

A) $(-1, -1)$
B) $(-1, 1)$
C) $(1, -1)$
D) $(1, 1)$

 10

$$h(t) = \frac{82}{625}t + 29{,}029$$

Because of the convergent movement of the Indian and Tibetan tectonic plates, Mt. Everest, the tallest mountain on Earth, is growing at a constant rate each year. A geologist uses the function above to model the height $h(t)$, in feet, of Mt. Everest t years after the present day. Assuming the model is correct, which of the following must be true?

A) Every 625 years, the height of the mountain will increase 8.2 feet.
B) Every 6250 years, the height of the mountain will increase 820 feet.
C) Every 82 years, the height of the mountain will increase 625 feet.
D) Every 820 years, the height of the mountain will increase 62.5 feet.

11

Which of the following expressions is the equivalent of
$(x^3 + x^2y^2 + xy + x) - (2x^3 - x^2y^2 - xy + x + 5)$?

A) $(x^3 - 2x^2y^2 - 2xy + 5)$

B) $(-x^3 + 2x^2y^2 - 2xy + 5)$

C) $(-x^3 + 2x^2y^2 + 2xy - 5)$

D) $(-x^3 + 2x^2y^2 + 2xy + x - 5)$

12

A widget manufacturer has a total monthly capacity of 1200 widgets with flexibility to make any mix of Advanced or Basic versions as long as the total is 1200. Last month, the company made an equal number of each type, and had sales revenue of $5400. This month, it made twice as many Advanced versions as the Basic, and had sales of $6000. What is the sum of the sales prices, in dollars, of one Advanced and one Basic widget?

13

In the xy-plane, a line k that goes through the point $(-5, -3)$ is parallel to the line with equation $y = 5x + 4$. The equation of line k can be expressed by which of the following equations?

A) $y = \dfrac{-1}{5}x - 4$

B) $y = \dfrac{1}{5}x - 2$

C) $y = 5x - 8$

D) $y = 5x + 22$

14

Donna and Barry are making energy bars to sell during the intramural volleyball tournament. They estimate it will cost them $29.78 for the materials they need, and $3.25 for the ingredients for every batch of energy bars. They make 12 energy bars from every batch and sell each bar for $0.75. Assume they have no other expenses. Which of the following represents the profit, P dollars, they will make on b batches of energy bars?

A) $P = 0.75b - 29.78$

B) $P = 3.25b - 29.78$

C) $P = 5.75b - 29.78$

D) $P = 24.03b$

15

$$x(x + 2) + 5(x + 2) = ax^2 + bx + c$$

In the equation above, a, b, and c are constants. If the equation is true for all values of x, what is the value of $a + b + c$?

A) 18

B) 19

C) 20

D) 21

16

The equation $h = 3680 - 275x$ approximates the height, h, in meters of a tram x minutes after it leaves the peak of a mountain. Which of the following is the best interpretation of 275 in this context?

A) The height of the mountain in meters
B) The time it takes the tram to descend from the mountain top in minutes
C) The number of passengers who can fit in a single tram
D) The height in meters that a tram descends in one minute

 17

-7 -6 -5 -4 -3 -2 -1 0 1 2 3 4 5 6 7

Which inequality is represented by the figure above?

A) $|x-1| - 2 < 6$

B) $|x-1| \le 7$

C) $|x-1| - 2 < 3$

D) $|x+1| < 5$

 18

In the xy-plane, a line with a positive slope goes through the points $(-2, p)$ and $(-p, 11)$. If the line also passes through $(2,6)$ what is the value of p?

A) −4
B) 8
C) −8
D) 6

19

$$4x - 3y + 4 = 17$$

$$2y + x - 16 = -10$$

In the system of equations above, what is the value of $(x + y)^2$?

A) 64
B) 25
C) 49
D) $4\sqrt{5}$

20

The air temperature in terms of "standard atmosphere" can be expressed as $t = -3.57a + 59$ where t is the air temperature and a is the altitude at which the temperature is measured in thousands of feet ("standard atmosphere" is an environment created for use in aviation and other sciences as an internationally recognized baseline). Mt. Washington is the highest mountain peak in the Northeast with an elevation of 6,288'. It is possible to drive to the top of the mountain on an auto road that begins at an elevation of 1527'. What is closest to the approximate change in temperature from the beginning of the auto road to the summit of the mountain?

A) down 16.4 degrees
B) down 46.1 degrees
C) down 4.01 degrees
D) down 17 degrees

21

Which equation is represented by the graph shown?

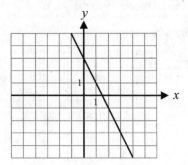

A) $2x + 4y = 6$
B) $4x + 2y = 6$
C) $\dfrac{3}{2}x + 3y = 6$
D) $3x + \dfrac{3}{2}y = 6$

22

An entrepreneur started a new company to manufacture advanced widgets. Each widget costs $2 to produce, and sells for $6. The company has $5000 in other costs each month. The entrepreneur has a monthly goal of at least $1000 profit. What is the minimum number of widgets to be produced and sold, in order to reach the profit goal?

A) 1500
B) 2500
C) 3000
D) 4000

23

Which value of x satisfies the equation
$3(2 + (-8))^2 + (5 - 3)^4 - 4x = 128$?

A) −1
B) 4
C) 12.8
D) 53

24

The slope of the line between which ordered pairs will yield the slope as shown in the equation $-x = -\dfrac{1}{2}y + \dfrac{3}{2}$?

A) $(2, 7), (11, 25)$
B) $(7, 2), (11, 25)$
C) $(13, 5), (9, 21)$
D) None of these pairs will yield the slope.

25

The graph of the following inequality has solutions in which of the 4 quadrants?

$$y < \frac{3}{4}x - 3$$

A) Quadrants I, II, and III
B) Quadrants I, II, and IV
C) Quadrants I, III, and IV
D) Quadrants I, II, III, and IV

Notes and Reflections

Algebraic Expressions

1

Which of the following expressions is equivalent to the sum of $(2x^4 + 3x^3 + 4x + 12)$ and $(2x^5 - 2x^3 - 4x - 8)$?

A) $4x^9 + x^3 + 4$
B) $2x^5 + 2x^4 + x^3 + 4$
C) $2x^5 + 2x^4 + 5x^3 + 8x + 20$
D) $2x^5 + 2x^4 + 3x^3 - 2x^2 + 4$

2

$$(4x + 5)(5x + 4)$$

The expression shown above is equivalent to which of the following expressions?

A) $4x^2 + 18x + 9$
B) $9x^2 + 18x + 9$
C) $20x^2 + 16x + 20$
D) $20x^2 + 41x + 20$

3

Which of the following expressions is equivalent to $-3(u^3 - v^2) - 2u + 2v^2 - 7u^3 + 5u^2$?

A) $-7u^3 + 5v^2$
B) $-5u^3 + 5v^2 - 2u$
C) $-10u^3 + 5u^2 - v^2 - 2u$
D) $-10u^3 + 5u^2 + 5v^2 - 2u$

4

$$(3x^2 - 6x) - 3x(x^2 - 2)$$

The expression shown above is equivalent to which of the following expressions?

A) 0
B) $-12x$
C) $-3x^3 + 3x^2$
D) $-3x^3 + 3x^2 - 12x$

5

$$-9x^2 + (-3x + 6)^2$$

Which of the following expressions is equivalent to the expression shown above?

A) $36(-x + 1)$
B) $18(-x + 2)$
C) $12(x + 3)$
D) $36(x + 1)$

6

$$x^2 - 3x - 10$$

If the expression above is equivalent to an expression of the form $(x - a)(x - b)$, what is the value of $2a - 3b$?

A) 4
B) 7
C) 12
D) 16

7

$$(a + b)(a^2 - ab + b^2)$$

Which of the following expressions is equivalent to the expression above?

A) $a^3 - b^3$
B) $a^3 - 3a^2b + 3ab^2 - b^3$
C) $a^3 + 3a^2b + 3ab^2 + b^3$
D) $a^3 + b^3$

8

$$(9x^4 + 24x^2y^2 + 16y^4)$$

Which of the following is equivalent to the expression shown above?

A) $(3x^4 + 4y^2)^2$
B) $(3x^2 + 4y^2)^4$
C) $(3x + 4y)^4$
D) $(3x^2 + 4y^2)^2$

Notes and Reflections

Algebraic Equations & Inequalities

1

$$3w + 2v = -4$$

What is the value of w in the equation above when $v = 4$?

A) -4

B) $\dfrac{-4}{3}$

C) $\dfrac{4}{3}$

D) 4

2

$$5 \times 3p = 30$$

If the equation above holds true, which of the following is equal to $5p + 4$?

A) 2
B) 6
C) 10
D) 14

3

The product of 2 and an integer p is increased by 4. The result is less than or equal to 35. What is the largest possible value for p?

A) 5
B) 6
C) 15
D) 16

4

Li has $20.00 to spend on public transportation today. A one-way bus rides costs $1.75, and a one-way subway ride costs $2.25. If he buys only three one-way bus tickets, what is the maximum number of one-way subway tickets he can purchase?

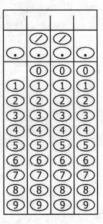

5

$$4x + 7 = 15 + 4x$$

Which of the following describes the solution set to the equation written above?

A) The equation has one solution, $x = 1$.
B) The equation has one solution, $x = 2$.
C) The equation has infinitely many solutions.
D) The equation has no solutions.

6

At the monthly swap meet, Jun sells necklaces that he makes at home. In order to make a necklace, he must purchase basic materials, which cost $0.50 for every necklace. He sells the necklaces for $5.00. In order to participate in the swap meet, he must also pay a vendor's fee of $95.00. What is the minimum number of necklaces he needs to sell in order to make more money than he will spend for the event?

A) 19
B) 20
C) 21
D) 22

7

$$3ab + 2 = 5$$

If the above equation is true, what must be the value of $9ab + 6$?

A) 4
B) 10
C) 15
D) 25

8

When you add 3 times a number x to 8, the result is 23. When you add 5 times a number y to 10, the result is 55.

What is the value of $x - y$?

A) –4
B) 4
C) 5
D) 9

9

$$(ax + 2)(7x^2 - bx + 5) = 35x^3 + 4x^2 + 21x + 10$$

The equation above is true for all x, where a and b are constants. What is the value of ab?

10

If $2r + 4s = \dfrac{t}{2}$, which of the following expressions is equivalent to $\dfrac{t^2}{4}$?

A) $r + 2s$
B) $r^2 + 4rs + 4s^2$
C) $4r^2 + 16s^2$
D) $4r^2 + 16rs + 16s^2$

 11

$$(3x + 3)(ax - 1) - x^2 + 3$$

In the expression above, a is a constant. If the expression is equivalent to bx, where b is a constant, what is the value of b?

A) –3
B) –2
C) –1
D) 1

 12

If $-3x + 14 \geq 17 - 2x$, then which of the following must be true?

A) $x \geq 3$
B) $14 \leq x \leq 17$
C) $x \neq -3$
D) $x \leq -3$

 13

Which of the following is the solution to the equation $3x - 5 = 4(x - 1) - x$?

A) The empty set (no solution)
B) {1}
C) {4}
D) The set of all real numbers

14

$$2x - 2 + c(2x + 3) = 10(x + 1)$$

c represents a constant in the equation above. If the above equation has infinitely many solutions, what must be the value of c?

A) $\dfrac{8}{3}$

B) $\dfrac{10}{3}$

C) 4

D) 5

15

$$ac + bcd = bd + bc$$

In the equation above, a, b, and d represent constants greater than 1 and $a > b$. Which of the following is equal to c?

A) $\dfrac{bd}{a - b + bd}$

B) $\dfrac{bd}{a + b + bd}$

C) $a + b$

D) $a - b + 2bd$

16

If $(ax + d)(bx + e) = 21x^2 + cx + 10$ for all values of x, and $a + b = 10$ and $d + e = 11$, what are the two possible values for c?

A) 1 and 10

B) 3 and 28

C) 15 and 105

D) 37 and 73

Notes and Reflections

Absolute Value

1

$$|4x + 2| = 6$$

The two solutions to the equation above are $x = c$ and $x = d$. Which of the following is equivalent to the value of $|c - d|$?

2

On the number line, point R has coordinate 4. Which of the below equations gives the coordinates of the two points on the number lines that are 8 units away from point R?

A) $|x - 8| = 4$
B) $|x + 8| = 4$
C) $|x - 4| = 8$
D) $|x + 4| = 8$

3

$$-5|-3x + 3| + 5 = -10$$

If $x \neq 0$, which of the following is a solution to the equation above?

A) $\dfrac{2}{3}$
B) 1
C) 2
D) There is no such value of x

4

$$|x + 2| = x + 2$$

For the equation given above, which of the following is NOT a solution for x?

A) -3
B) -2
C) 2
D) 3

5

On the real number line, which of the following inequalities describes the set of values, x, that are at most 10 units away from the point on the number line with coordinate 6?

A) $|x - 10| \leq 6$
B) $|x - 6| \leq 10$
C) $|x + 6| \leq 10$
D) $|x + 10| \leq 6$

6

If a and b are both integers and $b > a$, which of the following must be true?

A) $b - a > 0$
B) $|b| - |a| > 0$
C) $|a| - |b| > 0$
D) $|b| > |a|$

7

For which of the following equations is $y \geq -2$ for all values of x?

A) $y = -|x + 3| - 2$
B) $y = 2|x - 2| + 1$
C) $y = \dfrac{1}{2}|x - 2| - 3$
D) $y = -|x + 2| - 1$

8

Assuming $x > 0$ is an integer, which value satifies the equation $|x + 3| - 7 = -3|x - 1| + 9$?

9

For any negative real value of x, each of the following statements are true EXCEPT

A) $x^3 < 0$
B) $|x| - |2x| < 0$
C) $|x| - x = 0$
D) $\dfrac{1}{3}x < 0$

10

$$\frac{27 - 36}{|-3| - 3} = x + \left(-|36 - 27|\right)$$

Which value for x satisfies the equation above?

A) Any value of x satisfies this equation.
B) 63
C) There is no value of x that satisfies this equation.
D) .75 or −.75

11

If b is a rational number such that $-1 < b < 0$, which of the following orders the expressions $-\dfrac{1}{b}$, $-b^2$, and $|b|$ from least value to greatest value?

A) $-\dfrac{1}{b} < -b^2 < |b|$

B) $-b^2 < -\dfrac{1}{b} < |b|$

C) $-b^2 < |b| < -\dfrac{1}{b}$

D) $|b| < -b^2 < -\dfrac{1}{b}$

12

For all a, b, c, d, where $|c| \neq |d|$, which of following expressions must be equal to $\dfrac{|a - b|}{|c - d|}$?

A) $\dfrac{-a - b}{-c - d}$

B) $\dfrac{|b - a|}{|d - c|}$

C) $\dfrac{|a|}{|c - d|} - \dfrac{|b|}{|c - d|}$

D) $\dfrac{|b|}{|d - c|} - \dfrac{|a|}{|d - c|}$

13

Which inequality is NOT represented by the figure above?

A) All real numbers less than −5 or greater than −1
B) All real numbers not between −5 and −1 inclusive
C) $x < -5$ or $x \geq -1$
D) $|x + 3| > 2$

SUMMIT
EDUCATIONAL
GROUP

14

For all $x \neq 0$, compare $|x^2 + 3| - x^2$ to $|x^2 - 3| - x^2$.
Which of the following statements is true?

A) $|x^2 + 3| - x^2$ is always greater than
    $|x^2 - 3| - x^2$.

B) $|x^2 - 3| - x^2$ is always greater than
    $|x^2 + 3| - x^2$.

C) $|x^2 + 3| - x^2$ and $|x^2 - 3| - x^2$ are always
    equal.

D) Neither is always greater, and they are not
    always equal.

15

$$-|x^2 + 2| + 1 < -|x^2 - 2| + 1$$

How many solutions are there to the inequality
shown above?

A) 1
B) 2
C) There are no solutions.
D) There are infinitely many solutions.

16

What values of x will satisfy the inequality
$|-7x - 21| < 14$?

A) $-35 < x < -5$
B) $-5 < x < -1$
C) $-1 < x < 5$
D) $1 < x < 35$

17

If $a > 0$, what is the maximum value of

$$f(x) = a - \left|(x - b)^2 + c\right| ?$$

A) a
B) $a + b$
C) $a + c$
D) $a + b^2 + c$

Notes and Reflections

Systems of Equations

$$2x - \frac{2}{3}y = 5$$

$$3x + \frac{2}{3}y = 30$$

What value of x satisfies the system of equations described above?

A) 5
B) 7
C) 13.5
D) 35

2

$$x = -3y$$

$$3x + 2y = -14$$

Which of the following ordered pairs (x, y) satisfies the system of equations above?

A) $(-6, 2)$
B) $(-2, 6)$
C) $(2, -6)$
D) $(6, -2)$

3

$$3x + y = 29$$

$$2x + 2y = 26$$

The two lines described above intersect at a point (x, y). What is the value of $x - y$?

A) 2
B) 3
C) 13
D) 40

 4

$$x + y = 7$$

$$x - y = 3$$

For the system of linear equations described above, what is the value of $x^2 - y^2$?

5

$$y = 4x - 2$$

The equation above describes the line m in the xy-plane. If a line n has a slope that is one half the slope of line m and the y-coordinate of the y-intercept is triple the y-coordinate of the y-intercept of line m, at which of the following (x, y) points do the two lines intersect?

A) $(-10, -2)$
B) $(-2, -10)$
C) $(0, -2)$
D) $(0, -6)$

6

Below is a graph of a system of equations. How many solutions does the system have on the interval $-8 < x < 8$?

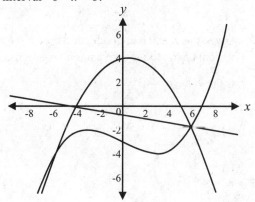

7

Consider the following three equations that form a system of equations:

I. $y = 2x + 5$
II. $y - 8 = 2x + 3$
III. $4y = 8x + 4$

How many solutions are there to this system of equations?

A) 0
B) 1
C) 2
D) Infinite

8

You are the manager of a movie theatre. You sell tickets at two prices: a regular price, r, and a matinee price, m. Last Saturday, 100 regular price tickets were sold and 150 matinee tickets were sold for a total profit of $2200. This Saturday, 150 regular price tickets were sold and 100 matinee tickets were sold for a total profit of $2300. How much less expensive is a matinee ticket than a regular price ticket?

A) $2
B) $5
C) $8
D) $10

9

$$\frac{1}{12}x + \frac{1}{6}y = \frac{3}{2}$$

$$\frac{1}{2}x + \frac{1}{6}y = -\frac{1}{6}$$

Given the system of linear equations above, what is the value of $x + y$?

A) 4
B) −11
C) 7
D) 15

10

In the xy-coordinate plane, the graph of equation $y = -8x - 15$ intersects the graph of $y = x^2$ at two points. What is the product of the x-coordinates of the two intersecting points?

11

$$y = -2x + 8$$
$$y = x^2 + 3x - 4$$

How many real solutions does the system of equations above have?

A) Zero
B) One
C) Two
D) Infinitely many

12

$$\frac{2}{3}x + \frac{1}{4}y = 12$$
$$ax - by = 8$$

Given that a and b are both constants, if the system of equations above has no solutions, what is the value of $\frac{b}{a}$?

A) $-\frac{8}{3}$

B) $-\frac{3}{8}$

C) $\frac{3}{8}$

D) $\frac{8}{3}$

13

$$ax = c - by$$
$$\frac{s}{u}x + \frac{t}{u}y = 1$$

For which set of coefficient relationships below, where b, t, and u are all non-zero, will the system of linear equations above have no solutions?

A) $at = bs$ and $bu = tc$
B) $at = bs$ and $bu \neq tc$
C) $at \neq bs$ and $bu = tc$
D) $at \neq bs$ and $bu \neq tc$

Notes and Reflections

Slope

 1

A line m in the xy-plane has an x-intercept of $(2, 0)$. If line m is perpendicular to the line with equation $y = \dfrac{1}{4}x + \dfrac{3}{4}$, what is the slope of line m?

A) -4

B) $\dfrac{-1}{4}$

C) 2

D) 4

2

$$3x - 2y + 6 = 0$$

What are the slope and y-intercept of the line with the equation that appears above?

A) The slope is $\dfrac{-3}{2}$ and the y-intercept is $(0, 3)$

B) The slope is $\dfrac{-3}{2}$ and the y-intercept is $(0, 6)$

C) The slope is $\dfrac{3}{2}$ and the y-intercept is $(0, 3)$

D) The slope is $\dfrac{3}{2}$ and the y-intercept is $(0, 6)$

 3

A line in the xy-plane passes through the origin and the point $(-3, 5)$. Which of the following is the equation of the line?

A) $y = \dfrac{-5}{3}x$

B) $y = \dfrac{-3}{5}x$

C) $y = \dfrac{3}{5}x$

D) $y = \dfrac{5}{3}x$

 4

A line in the xy-plane passes through the point $(0, -2)$ and has a slope of 2. Which of the following could represent the equation of the line?

A) $y = -2x$

B) $y = -2x + 2$

C) $y = 2x - 2$

D) $y = 2x + 4$

5

For a linear function g, $g(0) = 4$ and $g(5) = 14$. When g is plotted in the xy-plane, what is the slope of the graph?

A) -2

B) 2

C) 5

D) 10

6

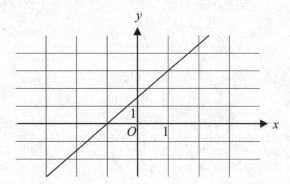

Line p, which passes through the point $(0, -4)$, is perpendicular to the line plotted in the xy-coordinate plane above. Which of the following equations describes line p?

A) $y = \dfrac{-3}{2}x - 4$

B) $y = \dfrac{-2}{3}x - 4$

C) $y = \dfrac{2}{3}x - 4$

D) $y = \dfrac{3}{2}x - 4$

7

x	$f(x)$
0	5
1	0
2	–5

Values of a function, $f(x)$, for three different values of x are listed in the table above. If $f(x)$ is a linear function that can be expressed as $f(x) = mx + n$, and m and n are constants, what must be the value of mn?

A) –25
B) –1
C) 1
D) 25

 8

Consider a square drawn in the standard (x, y) coordinate plane. One diagonal of this square lies entirely on the line with equation $y = -\frac{1}{3}x + 7$.

Which of the following could be an equation that contains the other diagonal of the square?

A) $y = -\frac{1}{3}x - 7$

B) $y = \frac{1}{3}x - 7$

C) $y = -3x - 4$

D) $y = 3x - 4$

9

In the xy-plane, the graph of line p has a slope of 0.4. Line q is perpendicular to line p and goes through the point $(5, -1)$. Which of the following is an equation of line q?

A) $y = \frac{2}{5}x - 4$

B) $y = \frac{2}{5}x - 3$

C) $5x + 2y = 23$

D) $5x - 2y = 26$

10

The graph of a linear function passes through the points $(3, p)$ and $(p, 18)$. If the slope of this line is 4, what is the value of p?

A) 3
B) 6
C) 9
D) 12

11

Suppose that f is a linear function whose graph contains the points (a, b) and (b, a), where $a + b = 0$ and $a \neq b$. Which of the following must be true about the slope of the graph of f?

A) It is positive.
B) It is negative.
C) It equals zero.
D) There is not enough information to determine the answer.

 12

A linear function f has a slope of $\frac{2}{3}$ between the points $f(-1) = -3$ and $f(a) = 1$. What is a?

13

Given the following four linear equations, which statements are true?

line r: $y = \dfrac{2}{3}x + 6$

line s: $2x - 3y - 12 = 0$

line t: $\dfrac{y-7}{x+6} = -\dfrac{3}{2}$

line u: $4x = 8 + 4y$

I. line r and line s are the same line
II. line t is perpendicular to line s
III. line t and line u have the same y-intercept

A) II only
B) I and II only
C) II and III only
D) I, II, III

14

$$5x + 7y = 35$$

In the xy-plane, the graph of which of the following equations will be perpendicular to the graph of the equation above?

A) $7x + 5y = 35$
B) $10x + 14y = 70$
C) $5x - 7y = 35$
D) $21x - 15y = 105$

15

Line l intersects the x-axis at $(p, 0)$ and intersects the y-axis at $(0, q)$. If $p = 3q$ and $p \neq q$, what is the slope of line l?

A) -3

B) $-\dfrac{1}{3}$

C) $\dfrac{1}{3}$

D) 3

16

Lines v and w are parallel. The equation of line w is $6x - 5y = 27$. Line v passes through the point $(4, -2)$. What is the value of the x-coordinate of the x-intercept of line v?

A) $-6\dfrac{4}{5}$

B) $-5\dfrac{2}{5}$

C) $4\dfrac{1}{2}$

D) $5\dfrac{2}{3}$

17

Line A has equation $4y = -\dfrac{4}{3}x + 5$. Line B is perpendicular to line A, and the y-coordinate of its y-intercept is $\dfrac{5}{4}$. Which of the following ordered pairs does *not* lie on line B?

A) $\left(0, \dfrac{5}{4}\right)$

B) $\left(3, \dfrac{41}{4}\right)$

C) $\left(-\dfrac{3}{4}, -1\right)$

D) $\left(\dfrac{5}{2}, \dfrac{1}{2}\right)$

18

$$y = 2x + 3$$

$$y - 6 = 2x$$

The system of equations above has no solutions. If the lines represented by the equations were graphed on a coordinate plane, which system of equations, when graphed with the lines represented above, would create a rectangle somewhere within the plane?

A) $y = -\dfrac{1}{2}x + 3$

    $-4y = 2x - 24$

B) $y = \dfrac{1}{2}x - 3$

    $4y = -2x + 24$

C) $2y = x + 3$

    $2y = 4x + 12$

D) $2y = -2x + 3$

    $2y = -4x + 12$

19

For any functions f and g, what is the slope of the line that is perpendicular to the line that connects the two points in the xy-coordinate plane where $f(-1) = -3$ and $g(5) = 1$?

A) $-\dfrac{3}{2}$

B) $-\dfrac{2}{3}$

C) $\dfrac{1}{3}$

D) $\dfrac{3}{2}$

Notes and Reflections

Graphs of Linear Equations

1

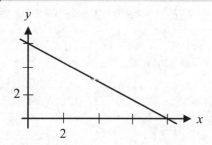

Which of the equations below best describes the graph of the linear function plotted in the above xy-plane?

A) $y = -\frac{3}{4}x + 3$

B) $y = -\frac{3}{4}x + 6$

C) $y = -\frac{4}{3}x + 3$

D) $y = -\frac{4}{3}x + 6$

2

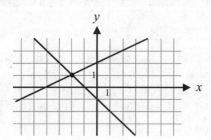

The graphs of two linear equations are plotted in the xy-plane shown above. The solution to the system formed by the linear equations is (x, y). What is the value of $x + y$?

A) −2
B) −1
C) 2
D) 3

3

In the xy-plane, which of the choices below best graphically represents the equation $y = \frac{3}{2}x + 1$?

A)

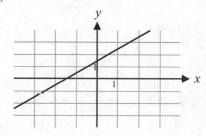

B)

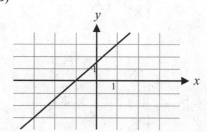

C)

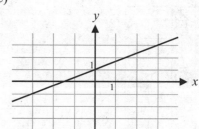

D)

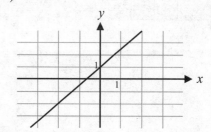

4

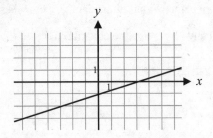

Which of the following is an equation of the line graphed in the *xy*-coordinate plane above?

A) $x - 3y = 3$

B) $x + 3y = 3$

C) $3x - y = 1$

D) $3x + y = 1$

5

In the standard coordinate plane, the line $-4x + 2y = a$ passes through the point $(1,4)$. What is the value of a?

Questions 6-7 refer to the following information.

Between the years 1995 and 2015, median monthly rent in the United Stated increased approximately $22.50 per year. The relationship between monthly rent and time in the US can be estimated using the graph below.

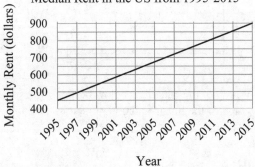

Median Rent in the US from 1995-2015

6

The relationship between monthly rent, in dollars, and time after 1995, in years, can best be modeled by which of the following equations?

A) $y = -450x + 22.5$

B) $y = -22.5x + 450$

C) $y = 22.5x + 450$

D) $y = 450x + 22.5$

7

According to the values estimated by the graph, in what year was the total rent for the year approximately $6500.00?

A) 1997

B) 1999

C) 2003

D) 2004

8

Two lines are perpendicular to one another in the *xy*-plane. One of the lines can be described by the equation $3x + 2y = 4$. If the other line passes through the point $(6, 9)$, what must be the *y*-coordinate of its *y*-intercept?

A) 2
B) 5
C) 13
D) 18

9

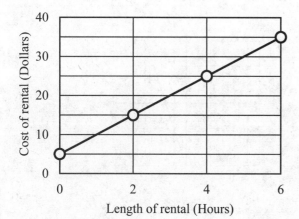

The above graph shows the cost of renting a kayak for a given number of hours. Which of the following equations gives the cost of the rental, *y*, in terms of the number of hours of the rental, *x*?

A) $y = \dfrac{2}{3}x + 5$

B) $y = \dfrac{3}{2}x + 5$

C) $y = 5x + 5$

D) $y = 10x + 5$

10

Which of the following is the graph of

$$y = -\frac{4}{3}x + 4?$$

A)

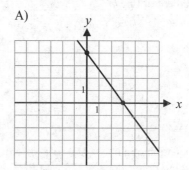

B)

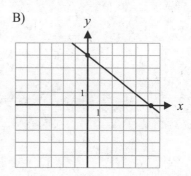

C)

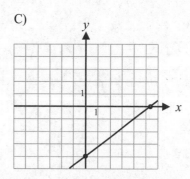

D)

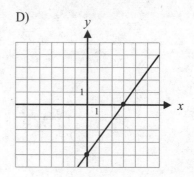

11

In the xy-plane, line m passes through the point $(-6, -2)$ and is perpendicular to line n with equation $3x - 5y = 10$. What is the y-coordinate of the y-intercept of line m?

A) −12
B) −10
C) −8
D) −6

12

Given the equation of a line, $-4x + 2y = 6$, which of the following points does NOT lie on the line?

A) $(7, 17)$
B) $(11, 13)$
C) $(\sqrt{9}, 9)$
D) $(17, 37)$

13

Which of the following graphs includes the equation $3y + x = 2y + 4x - 5$?

A)

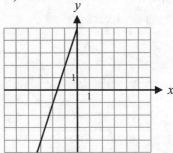

B)

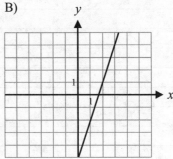

C)

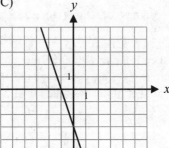

D)

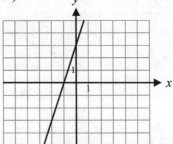

14

Y_1 and Y_2, shown below, are perpendicular straight lines. What is the product of their slopes multiplied by the product of the y–coordinates of their y-intercepts?

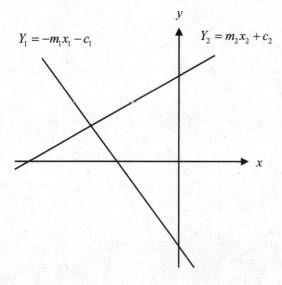

$$Y_1 = -m_1x_1 - c_1 \qquad Y_2 = m_2x_2 + c_2$$

A) c_1c_2

B) $-c_1c_2$

C) $-m_1c_1m_2c_2$

D) 1

15

In the xy-plane, the line $y = cx + d$, where both c and d are constants, is graphed. Suppose the line contains the point (a, b), where $a \neq 0$ and $b \neq 0$. What is the slope of the line in terms a, b, and d?

A) $b - d$

B) $\dfrac{d-b}{a}$

C) $\dfrac{b-d}{a}$

D) $\dfrac{d-b}{c}$

Notes and Reflections

Systems and Graphs of Inequalities

1

$$y < 2x + 3$$

$$y \geq -x - 2$$

Which of the following points is in the solution set of the system of inequalities above?

A) (1,5)
B) (2,5)
C) (3,–6)
D) (4,12)

2

An elementary school is planning a field trip to the city zoo, and children from the class as well as adult chaperones have been invited. The bus they will be traveling on can hold at most 72 individuals. In order to enter the zoo, the school must pay for everyone's ticket. The cost per child ticket is $5, and the cost per adult ticket is $13. If the school can no spend more than $500 on the zoo tickets and there are c children and a adult chaperones attending, which of the following systems of equations best reflects the constraints on the number of children and adult chaperones that can attend?

A) $\begin{aligned} c + a &\geq 72 \\ 5c + 13a &\leq 500 \end{aligned}$

B) $\begin{aligned} c + a &= 13 \\ 5c + 13a &\leq 72 \end{aligned}$

C) $\begin{aligned} c + a &\leq 72 \\ 5c + 13a &> 500 \end{aligned}$

D) $\begin{aligned} c + a &\leq 72 \\ 5c + 13a &\leq 500 \end{aligned}$

3

$$y \leq -\frac{1}{2}x + 1$$

$$2y - 3x \geq 2$$

Which of the following graphs correctly shades the region in the xy-plane that represents the solution set to the system of inequalities above?

A)
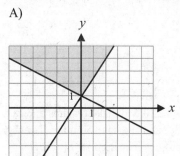

B)
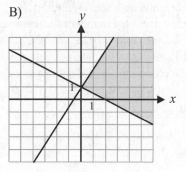

C)
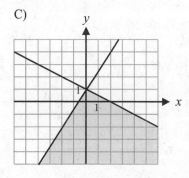

D)
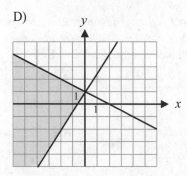

4

$$-3x < 3$$

$$y < -3x + 2$$

The above system of inequalities is graphed in the xy-plane. Which of the following defines the set of y-coordinates that satisfy the system?

A) $y < -1$
B) $y > -1$
C) $y < 5$
D) $y > 5$

5

Vivienne would like to make teacups and saucers for her family, and she has 150 ounces of clay to use for the project. The number of teacups produced should be at least equal to the number of saucers she makes. Each teacup requires 10 ounces of clay, and each saucer requires 14 ounces of clay. If t is the number of teacups she makes and s is the number of saucers she makes, which of the systems of inequalities below best describes the constraints on the number of cups and saucers that Vivienne can make?

A) $t + s \leq 150$
   $10t \geq 14s$

B) $t + s \leq 150$
   $t \geq s$

C) $10t + 14s \leq 150$
   $t \geq s$

D) $10t + 14s \leq 150$
   $t \leq s$

6

$$y \geq 3x - 4$$
$$y \geq -2x + 1$$

The system of linear inequalities shown above is graphed in the xy-plane. What is the minimum possible value of y in the set of possible solutions?

A) -2
B) -1
C) 0
D) 1

7

The point $(1, -1)$ is a solution to the system of linear inequalities shown below. Which of the following is a description of the system?

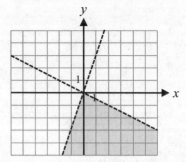

A) $y < 3x$ and $y < -\dfrac{x}{2}$

B) $y > 3x$ and $y > -\dfrac{x}{2}$

C) $y < \dfrac{1}{3}x$ and $y < -2x$

D) $y < 3x$ and $y > -\dfrac{x}{2}$

8

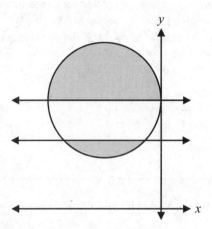

The shaded region in the graph above could represent the solution set to which of the following systems of inequalities?

A) $(x-5)^2 + (y-8)^2 \leq 25$
$|y-7| \geq 1$

B) $(x+5)^2 + (y-8)^2 \leq 25$
$|y-6| \geq 2$

C) $(x-5)^2 + (y-8)^2 \leq 25$
$y \geq 8$ or $y \leq 2$

D) $(x+5)^2 + (y-8)^2 \leq 25$
$y \leq 8$ and $y \geq 2$

9

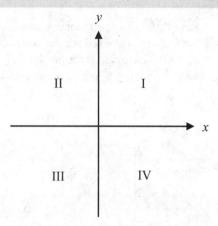

The following system of linear inequalities is graphed in the xy-plane above:

$$x + y < -2$$
$$x - 2y \geq 2$$

Which of the following is true?

I.   The solutions to the system are in Quadrants III and IV.
II. There are no solutions to the first inequality in Quadrant I.
III. There are solutions to the second inequality in all four quadrants.

A) I only
B) II only
C) I and II
D) I, II, and III

10

$$-\frac{1}{2}x - \frac{3}{4}y \geq \frac{5}{8}$$

$$\frac{2}{3}x + \frac{2}{9}y > \frac{11}{12}$$

The inequalities above are both graphed on the same xy-plane. Which of the following points will be in the region where the graphs of the inequalities overlap?

A) $(0,-1)$
B) $(2,0)$
C) $(3,-4)$
D) $(5,-6)$

11

Each of the following graphs is in the standard *xy*-coordinate plane and has the same scale on both axes. One graph is the graph of $ax + by \leq c$, where $c < b < a < 0$. Which graph could it be?

A)

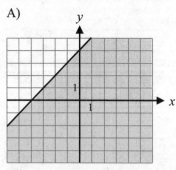

B)

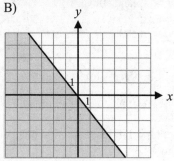

C)

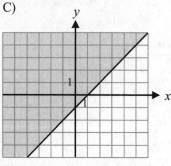

D)

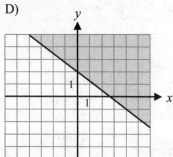

12

In the *xy* plane, point *B* is contained in the solution set of the inequality $3x - 5y < 12$. Which of the following could be the coordinates of point *B*?

A) $(-6, -8)$
B) $(-4, -4)$
C) $(-1, -3)$
D) $(2, -2)$

Questions 13-14 refer to the following graph.

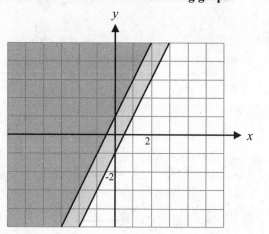

13

Which system of inequalities represents the graph pictured in the figure above?

A) $2y \geq 4x + 2$ and $3y \geq 6x - 3$
B) $y \leq 2x - 3$ and $2y \geq 2x - 3$
C) $y \leq x + 2$ and $6y \geq 3x + 3$
D) $5y \geq 5x + 3$ and $10y \leq 5x + 5$

14

Which, if any, quadrant(s) does the graph of the solution set of the system of inequalities occupy?

A) I and II
B) II and III
C) I, II, III, and IV
D) I, II, and III

15

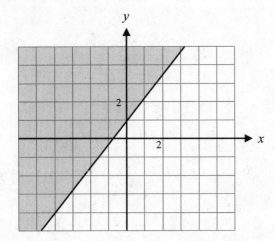

Which inequality is shown on the above graph?

A) $y \leq \dfrac{4}{5}x + 1$

B) $y \leq \dfrac{5}{4}x + 1$

C) $y \geq \dfrac{4}{5}x + 1$

D) $y \geq \dfrac{5}{4}x + 1$

Notes and Reflections

Creating Linear Models

1

While his car was in for a repair, Malik decided to rent a car for the day. The cost for the car rental included a flat fee and tax totaling $54.00. He is instructed to return the car with a full tank of gas. On his way back to return the car, he purchased gas at a nearby gas station, at a cost of $2.65 per gallon. If Malik purchased g gallons of gas, how much money, in dollars, did Malik spend on his car rental for the day?

A) $2.65g$
B) $56.65g$
C) $54.00 + 2.65g$
D) $54.00 + 51.35g$

2

Amira is an avid gardener, and she is in the midst of planting the 48 seedlings she purchased earlier that day. If it takes her 3 minutes to plant each seedling, and she has planted s seedlings already, what is an expression that represents the number of minutes she still needs to finish planting all of the seedlings she purchased that day?

A) $3s$
B) $3(48 - s)$
C) $3(s - 48)$
D) $48(s - 3)$

3

A meal delivery service charges a flat fee of $150.00 to deliver the first 20 meals in any particular month. If the price for every additional meal is $5.00, then which of the following graphs represents the cost, C, of having m meals delivered in a particular month?

A)

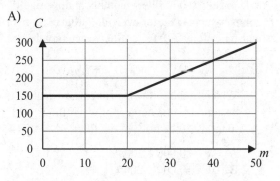

B)

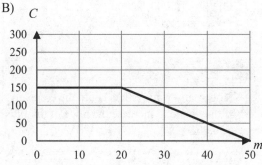

C)

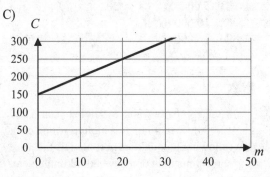

D)

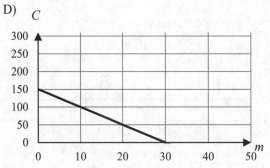

SUMMIT
EDUCATIONAL
GROUP

Questions 4-6 refer to the following information.

A company is testing consumer demand for a water filter it recently developed. The current price of the filter on the market is $25.00, and the company is able to sell 10,000 filters monthly at this price. The company notes that for every dollar increase in price, consumers buy 200 fewer filters each month.

4

Which of the following is a linear equation that best models the number of water filters sold, w, in terms of the price of the filter, p?

A) $w = 10,000 - 200p$
B) $w = 10,000 + 200p$
C) $w = 15,000 + 200p$
D) $w = 15,000 - 200p$

5

How many water filters could the company sell if they were to increase the price of the filters to $50.00?

A) 0
B) 5,000
C) 10,000
D) 15,000

6

If the company wants to sell between 7,000 and 12,000 water filters this month, which of the following inequalities best models the price constraints the company should implement?

A) $p < 15$
B) $15 \le p \le 40$
C) $35 \le p \le 60$
D) $p > 60$

7

Chelsea plans to begin baking and selling cakes. It costs her $45 for enough ingredients to make 5 cakes. She sells each cake for $15. However, she also needs to buy pans before she can get started, which will cost her $36 altogether. Which of the following equations represents the profit in dollars, P, that Chelsea would earn after selling c cakes?

A) $P = 6c - 36$
B) $P = 9c - 36$
C) $P = 15c - 36$
D) $P = 15c + 36$

8

$$h = .75(220 - n)$$

The equation above can be used to approximate the suggested heart rate, h, in beats per minute for a person n years old while exercising moderately. Which of the following is the best interpretation of the number 0.75 in this context?

A) The increase in beats per minute for each increase in a year of a person's age
B) The decrease in beats per minute for each increase in a year of a person's age
C) The suggested heart rate in beats per second for a person n years old exercising moderately
D) The suggested heart rate in beats per second for a person n years old while at rest

9

The Tokyo to Kyoto bullet train travels at 320km/h and leaves Shin-Osaka Station, which is situated in the direction of Kyoto 2 km outside of central Tokyo. Which of the following gives the distance, d, in kilometers, of the train from central Tokyo t minutes after departure from Shin-Osaka Station? (Assume the train travels in a straight line).

A) $d = 320t + 2$
B) $d = 2t + 320$
C) $d = 0.0\overline{3}t + 320$
D) $d = 5.\overline{3}t + 2$

10

Nadia must purchase new desktops and laptops for the employees of her small business. She goes to a nearby computer retailer where desktop computers are on sale for $500.00 each, and laptops are on sale for $350.00 each. If she buys d of the desktops on sale and l of the laptops on sale, and she has at most $4000.00 left on her company credit card that she can use for the purchase, which of the following inequalities must be true?

A) $350d + 500l \leq 4000$
B) $350d + 500l \geq 4000$
C) $500d + 350l \leq 4000$
D) $500d + 350l \geq 4000$

 11

Jenna runs a dog-walking business. She charges $4 per dog per hour that she walks them, plus a $2 flat fee per dog. Which of the following expressions represents the amount of money she would earn for walking d dogs for h hours?

A) $2d + 4h$
B) $4d + 2h$
C) $2dh + 4h$
D) $2d + 4dh$

12

Solubility Curve for Potassium Iodide in 100 mL of water at Standard Pressure

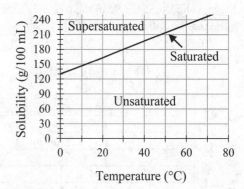

The solubility curve above describes S, how many grams of potassium iodide can be dissolved in 100 mL of liquid water at standard pressure, as the temperature, T, of the solution changes. Water is in the liquid state between 0°C and 100°C. The solution is saturated if the grams dissolved for a given temperature are on the curve. The solution is unsaturated if more potassium iodide can still be added to achieve saturation. The solution is considered supersaturated if the solution is holding more sodium iodide than the solubility curve states that it can for that temperature. Which of the systems of inequalities below best describes the region where supersaturated solutions of potassium iodide can form in 100 mL of liquid water at standard pressure?

A) $S < 1.67T + 130$
$0 \leq T \leq 100$

B) $S > 1.67T + 130$
$0 \leq T \leq 100$

C) $S < .6T + 130$
$0 \leq T \leq 70$

D) $S > .6T + 130$
$0 \leq T \leq 70$

13

A tree was purchased from a local gardening store and planted in the ground. The following graph shows the height of the tree over time after the tree was planted:

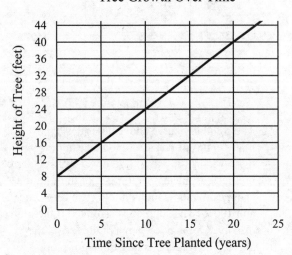

Tree Growth Over Time

Which of the following equations represents the height of the tree, y, after x years?

A) $y = 2x + 8$

B) $y = \dfrac{8}{5}x + 8$

C) $y = \dfrac{5}{8}x + 8$

D) $y = \dfrac{16}{5}x + 8$

14

In one month, a company sold 1200 bottles of hot sauce at $2.75 per bottle. With each incremental $0.15 increase in the price per bottle, the company sells 10 fewer bottles each month. Let n be the number of increases of $0.15 in the price per bottle. Which expression best represents the total monthly sales in dollars from this hot sauce?

A) $2.9(1200 + 10n)$
B) $2.9(1200 - 10n)$
C) $(2.75 + 10n)(1200 + 0.15n)$
D) $(2.75 + 0.15n)(1200 - 10n)$

 15

The number of pages of a book Tom can read per hour depends on the average number of words per page. He can read 300 words per minute and the average page of the book he is currently reading contains 500 words. He takes a 5-minute break every hour to rest his eyes. He may also take other breaks. Which of the following is a model for the number of pages Tom reads per hour for the book he is currently reading? (b = average number of minutes of breaks per hour NOT including the 5-minute break to rest his eyes; p = pages read per hour; t = average number of minutes per hour spent reading).

A) $p = \dfrac{3}{5}t$

 $t = 55 - b$

B) $p = \dfrac{5}{3}t$

 $t = 60 - b$

C) $p = \dfrac{3}{5}(t - 5 - b)$

 $t = 60 + b$

D) $p = \dfrac{5}{3}t - \dfrac{5}{60}$

 $t = \dfrac{55 - b}{60}$

16

Paul and Cyd are planning their wedding and are keeping to a strict budget. They have found a venue for their wedding reception. It will cost them a non-refundable booking fee of $250 plus a "per guest" fee of $17. The couple has decided that they will keep to their budgeted allowance of $2500 for the reception location, even if it means trimming the guest list. Which of the following most accurately represents the cost of renting the wedding venue in terms of x, the number of guests attending, while staying within the budget?

A) $2500 + 250x + 17$
B) $250 - 17x > 2500$
C) $250 + 17x \geq 2500$
D) $250 + 17x \leq 2500$

17

Nadine is organizing the volunteers at a cat shelter. The volunteers at the shelter are available for up to 40 hours each day all together. Each full-grown cat requires 1.5 hours of attention each day. Each kitten requires 3 hours of attention each day. Every day the shelter has at least 5 full-grown cats and 4 kittens. Which of the following systems of inequalities shows the number of kittens k and full-grown cats c the shelter can support?

A) $c + k \leq 40$

   $c \geq 5$

   $k \geq 4$

B) $5c + 4k \leq 40$

   $c \geq 5$

   $k \geq 4$

C) $5c + 4k \leq 40$

   $c \geq 1.5$

   $k \geq 3$

D) $1.5c + 3k \leq 40$

   $c \geq 5$

   $k \geq 4$

18

To seat a large group of guests at a restaurant, the staff take tables that normally seat 4 people and place them end to end, so that 6 people can be seated when 2 tables are together and 8 people with 3 tables together. Assuming $n \geq 1$, which expression gives the number of people who can be seated when n tables are put together?

A) $2n$
B) $2n + 2$
C) $4n$
D) $4n - 2$

▼

Questions 19-20 refer to the following information.

Nancy bought a can of sliced beets. The nutritional facts on the can state that the serving size of the beets is ½ cup and provides 40 calories, all from carbohydrates. In addition, each serving of the beets provides 250 milligrams of sodium, which is 10% of the daily allowance for adults, and 130 milligrams of potassium, which is 4% of the daily allowance for adults.

19

If s percent of an adult's daily allowance of sodium is provided by x servings of canned sliced beets per day and if p percent of an adult's daily allowance of potassium is provided by x servings of canned sliced beets per day, which of the following expresses the sum of s and p in terms of x?

A) $s + p = 0.14x$
B) $s + p = 14x$
C) $s + p = 0.14^x$
D) $s + p = (1.1)^x(1.04)^x$

20

Which of the following could be the graph of the number of calories from carbohydrates in the beets as a function of the number of 1/2 cup servings?

A)

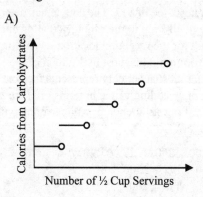

B)

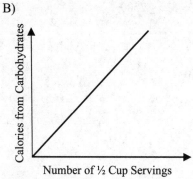

C)

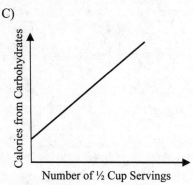

D)

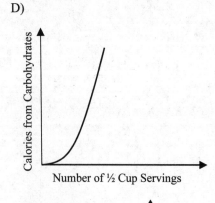

▲

21

Sydney bought a custom case for her laptop one week before an upcoming sale. One week later when the sale was officially announced, Sydney saw that the laptop case would have been a full 35% cheaper had she waited one more week to buy it. Sydney wanted to figure out how much less she would have spent if she were patient and waited for the sale. Which of the following expressions can Sydney use to discover the difference between what she paid for the laptop case and what she would have paid if she had waited for the sale? In both situations, she decided to include the 6% sales tax in her calculations and assigned s as a variable to represent her lost savings and x as the original price of the laptop case.

A) $s = 1.06x - 1.06(x - 35)$

B) $s = 0.65(1.06x) - 35$

C) $s = x - (0.65x) + 0.06(65x)$

D) $s = (1.06x) - 1.06(x - 0.35x)$

 22

Jack and Beth both obtained memberships from different health clubs. Jack paid an up-front membership fee of $34 and pays $5.50 per week to maintain his membership. Beth chose to join the club that had a less expensive membership fee but a slightly higher weekly fee. She paid an up-front cost of only $25 but pays $7.00 per week to maintain her membership. Jack and Beth were discussing their respective health clubs and found that both offer the same amenities. As they discussed the difference in pricing, they wondered how long it would take before they both had spent the same amount of money on their respective memberships. How much more than Jack will Beth have paid in <u>weekly</u> fees when they both have paid the same total amount of dollars?

A) $18.00

B) $54.00

C) $9.00

D) $12.50

23

You can determine your maximum recommended heart rate (measured in beats per minute; it is not healthy if your heart rate exceeds this number) by subtracting your age from 220. The CPAT is a multi-part examination given to those who want to become firefighters. During the fitness part of this test, firefighter candidates must perform aerobic exercises while maintaining a rate that falls between 65% and 85% of their maximum recommended heart rates. Which of the following expresses the required heart rate R for a 23-year-old firefighter candidate performing the physical part of the CPAT?

A) $65(220 + 23) \leq R \leq .85(220 - 23)$

B) $\dfrac{65}{100}(220 + 23) < R < \dfrac{85}{100}(220 + 23)$

C) $.65(197) < R < .85(243 - 46)$

D) $\dfrac{65}{100}(23) < R < \dfrac{85}{100}(23)$

Notes and Reflections

Interpreting Linear Models

$$P(t) = 22 + 12.5t$$

An algebra teacher developed the linear model shown above. The model predicts $P(t)$, a student's score on the algebra final exam, after studying t hours for the final. According to the model, which of the following is closest to the expected number of hours of studying a student must complete to achieve a final exam score of 92?

A) 3.6
B) 5.6
C) 7.4
D) 9.1

Camila orders her favorite sushi rolls for lunch at a local restaurant. The equation $m = 250 - 8.33t$ approximates the mass m, in grams, of sushi rolls remaining on her plate t minutes after they are served to Camila. Which of the following is the best interpretation of the number 250 in the context of this problem?

A) The approximate mass of the sushi rolls before Camila begins eating
B) The approximate time Camila takes to eat all of the sushi rolls
C) The approximate mass of sushi rolls Camila eats per minute
D) The approximate mass of sushi rolls Camila eats per hour

$$E = 90d - bd$$

The net earnings, E, for a person who commutes by public transit to a job working d days at the starting rate is shown, where b is a constant. If the person has net earnings of $2094 for working 24 days, what is the value of b?

$$2400 + 310t = 5500$$

In 1995, the estimated worldwide black rhino population had fallen to 2400 (down from 70,000 in 1970). Conservation efforts have helped boost the population to approximately 5500 just t years after 1995. If t satisfies the equation above, which choice below best interprets the number 310 found in the equation?

A) The number of years it took to restore the population to 5500
B) The increase in rhino population over t years
C) The average increase in black rhino population each year after 1995
D) The average decrease in black rhino population before 1995

Questions 5-6 refer to the following graph and information.

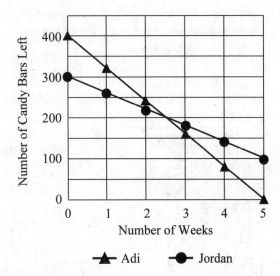

Adi and Jordan are students raising money to partially pay for a school orchestra trip. They decide to raise money in the five weeks leading up to the trip by selling candy bars. They each start with a specific supply of candy bars, and each sells his supply at a constant rate. The graphs above show the number of candy bars each student had left in his supply for the five weeks leading up to the school trip.

5

How many candy bars were in Adi's original supply at the beginning of the 5 weeks?

A) 100
B) 200
C) 300
D) 400

6

How many more candy bars did Adi sell each week than Jordan did?

A) 40
B) 80
C) 100
D) 120

7

$$P = 5000 + 200m$$

Emma recently decided to lease a car for 36 months. In the equation shown above, P represents the total amount she has paid for the lease, in dollars, m is the number of months she has been leasing her car, 200 represents her monthly lease payment, and 5000 represents her initial down payment. If Emma has paid a total of $8600, for how many months has she been leasing the car?

A) 12
B) 18
C) 24
D) 36

8

The term "standard atmosphere" is a hypothetical set of environmental conditions using air pressure, air density, and temperature. Standard atmosphere is used in aviation and in other sciences to provide a uniform baseline of atmospheric conditions recognized internationally. In the standard atmosphere environment, air temperature changes uniformly as elevation increases. In terms of standard atmosphere, the air temperature at sea level is considered to be 59° F and air pressure is 29.92 inHg (inches of mercury). The temperature at any elevation in standard atmosphere can be expressed by the equation $t + 3.57a = 59$, where t represents temperature (degrees Fahrenheit) and a represents the altitude above sea level (in thousands of units). In this equation, what does the 3.57 represent?

A) The temperature increases every 3.57 thousand feet of elevation.
B) The temperature decreases by 3.57° F for each unit of elevation.
C) The temperature decreases by 59° F for every 3.57 thousand feet of elevation.
D) The temperature increases by 3.57° F for every 3.57 feet of elevation.

9

The following graph shows the monthly bill for a customer of the N.T. Electric Company based on the number of kilowatt-hours (kWh) of electricity the customer consumed during the month:

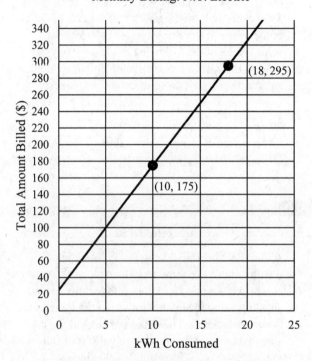

Monthly Billing: N.T. Electric

(18, 295)

(10, 175)

Total Amount Billed ($)

kWh Consumed

Janaya has a summer home and no one rents it this month. As a result, no electricity is used. If Janaya uses N.T. Electric, how much should she expect her electricity bill to be this month?

A) $20.00
B) $21.00
C) $22.50
D) $25.00

10

Jamie is a hard-working accountant that owns her own firm. The number of tax returns she has left to complete this month, r, after d days have passed in that month, can be modeled by the equation $r = 250 - \dfrac{35}{4}d$. Assume there are 30 days in a month. Which of the following must be true?

I.   Jamie completes 4 tax returns every 35 days.
II.   Jamie starts the month with 250 tax returns to complete.
III. Jamie is able to complete all of the tax returns she has to complete by the end of the month.

A) I only
B) I and II
C) II and III
D) I, II, and III

11

The volume of a carbonated soft drink that comes out of a can (in mL) when it is opened is dependent on the amount of time it is shaken (in seconds). This relationship is expressed by the equation $y = 0.8x + 10$. What is the meaning of the number 10 in this equation?

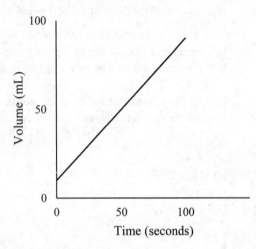

A) The volume of liquid in mL that leaves the can for every extra ten seconds the can is shaken
B) The volume of liquid leaving the can per second
C) The volume of liquid in mL that leaves the can when the can is opened without shaking
D) The volume of liquid in mL that leaves the can after 10 seconds

12

Sarah is getting her kitchen floor re-tiled. The following equation models the cost in dollars, $C(x)$, of the materials needed for tiling her floor, where x represents the area of the floor in square feet.

$$C(x) = 55 + 7.5x$$

Which of the following statements best describes the meaning of 7.5 in the equation?

A) She only has $7.50 to spend on materials.
B) Each additional square foot of tile costs $7.50.
C) The area of her floor is 7.5 square feet.
D) The area of her floor is 75 square feet.

13

Grace received a job offer from a company that sells a new health drink at local mall kiosks. The company has very good benefits, one of which is the ability for employees to choose how they are paid. One option is for employees to be paid a straight $1,040 every two weeks. The second option allows the employees to choose to be paid $500 every two weeks plus $7.50 for every bottle of the health drink (priced at $15 each) sold. Which of the following models the pay options that Grace has available? For all equations, p = pay, b = bottles, and w = weeks.

A) $p = 7.5b + 1040$ $p = 1040w$
B) $p = 7.5b + 500$ $p = 1040w$
C) $p = 7.5b + 250w$ $p = 520w$
D) $p = 250b + 7.5w$ $p = 1040w$

14

$$y = 250x + 750$$

A craft beer brewery cleans its 3,000-gallon distilling tank every month. The tank is completely emptied and then filled with a special cleaning solution suitable for use in the food and beverage industry. The tank has marks along the side that indicate the number of gallons of fluid in it at any time. Which of the following situations best represents the above linear model associated with filling the tank?

A) Because the tank has a volume of 3,000 gallons, it will take x hours before it is full if filled at 250 gallons per hour.
B) The cleaners have put 250 gallons into the tank, and it will take 750 minutes to reach the 3,000-gallon mark.
C) At 250 gallons per hour, it will take 750 minutes before the tank is full as long as the tank is filled at a uniform rate.
D) The workers stopped to estimate how much more time remained to fill the tank. When they resumed filling at 250 gallons per hour, the tank had 750 gallons of solution in it already.

15

$$F = 1.8C + 32$$

Frieda is calibrating a new temperature meter that measures in Fahrenheit (F) and Celsius (C) scales. She knows the relationship between Fahrenheit and Celsius is given by the above equation. She collects the following table of sensor temperature readings at actual temperatures of –40°C, 0°C, and 100°C.

Actual Temperature in °C	F meter reading	C meter reading
–40	–18	–40
0	32	0
100	157	100

The meter is correctly measuring temperature in Celsius scale, but the meter is incorrect for the Fahrenheit scale. Which of the following conclusions could best explain the error?

A) The °F meter reading is adding a value more than 32°F in the conversion.

B) The °F meter reading is subtracting a value more than the 32°F in the conversion.

C) The °F meter reading resulted from using a factor less than 1.8 to convert °F to °C.

D) The °F meter reading resulted from using a factor more than 1.8 to convert °F to °C.

16

The scatterplot below shows the cost C to feed a group of n people, as recorded by a family who hosted several groups of people for dinner last year. Each point represents the cost of one dinner. A line of best fit for the data is also shown. Which of the following could be an equation of the line of best fit?

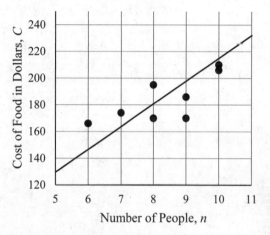

A) $C = 0.85n + 45$
B) $C = 0.85n + 130$
C) $C = 17n + 45$
D) $C = 17n + 130$

17

A researcher has been tracking the growth of an oak tree in a park by her house and has created the following equation for its growth, where $h(t)$ represents the height (in feet) of the tree t months after she began tracking it.

$$h(t) = \frac{1}{24}t + 18$$

According to the function, which of the following statements is true?

A) The tree was 24 feet tall when she began tracking it.

B) Every year, the tree will grow $\frac{1}{2}$ ft.

C) Every year, the tree will grow $\frac{1}{24}$ ft.

D) Every 18 months, the tree will grow one foot.

Notes and Reflections

Passport to Advanced Math

- Section Quiz

- Equations with Fractions

- Equations with Exponents

- Equations with Radicals

- Functions

- Graphs of Functions

- Quadratic Equations

- Graphs of Quadratics

- Polynomials

- Nonlinear Models

Section Quiz

1

If $x^6 = 9$, what must be the value of x^{-12}?

A) −81
B) −18
C) $\dfrac{1}{81}$
D) 3

2

$$\frac{1}{x+4} = -\frac{1}{x+2}$$

For the equation shown above, what must be the value of x?

A) −3
B) 1
C) 2
D) There is no value of x that satisfies the equation.

3

$$\frac{2}{5}x - 2 = \frac{1}{10}x + 1$$

In order to satisfy the equation above, what must be the value of x?

4

$$2x^2 + 3x - 2 = 0$$

Which of the choices below is a solution to the quadratic equation shown above?

A) −1
B) −0.5
C) 0.5
D) 2

5

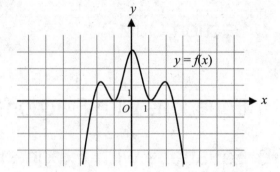

x	−2	−1	0	1	2
$g(x)$	0	−2	6	−2	−5

The graph of function f is plotted in the xy-coordinate plane above. Specific values for another function, g, are listed in the adjacent table. For which of the below values of x is $f(x) < g(x)$?

A) −2
B) −1
C) 0
D) 1

6

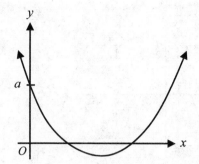

The graph of the function $f(x) = 2x^2 - 12x + 16$ is plotted in the xy-plane above. The function has a y-intercept at the point $(0, a)$. What must be the value of a?

A) 2
B) 8
C) 12
D) 16

7

$$f(x) = 3x + 2$$

$$g(x) = -2x + 1$$

The functions f and g are defined above. If $h(x) = f(x) + 2g(x)$, what is the value of $h(1)$?

8

For the equation $\dfrac{3}{25}x - 4 = \dfrac{2}{5} + 16$, what is the value of x?

A) 510
B) $20\dfrac{2}{5}$
C) $8\dfrac{2}{5}$
D) 170

9

In the xy-plane, the graph of which of the following functions is the same as the graph of $f(x) = (x - 2)^2 + 5$ shifted two units to the right?

A) $g(x) = (x - 4)^2 + 5$
B) $g(x) = x^2 + 5$
C) $g(x) = (x - 2)^2 + 3$
D) $g(x) = (x - 2)^2 + 7$

10

$$\sqrt{6x - 3} = x + 1$$

Which of the following is the solution set to the equation shown above?

A) $x = \dfrac{1}{2}$

B) $x = \dfrac{4}{5}$

C) $x = 2$

D) The equation has no real solution.

11

$$0 = x^2 - 16x + 5$$

What is the sum of all values of x that satisfy the equation above?

A) $8 + 2\sqrt{59}$
B) $16 + 4\sqrt{59}$
C) 8
D) 16

12

If $f(x) = x^2 - 3x + 4$ and d is a real number such that $f(d) < 2$, which of the following is a possible value of d?

A) 1
B) 1.5
C) 2
D) 2.5

13

Which of the following is the equation for a parabola through the points $(1, 1)$, $(0, 4)$, and $(2, 4)$?

A) $y = (x - 1)^2 + 1$
B) $y = 3(x - 1)^2 + 1$
C) $y = 4(x - 1)^2$
D) $y = 4(x - 1)^2 + 1$

14

$$f(t) = .908(1.092)^t$$

The above function can be used to estimate the total U.S. National Debt in trillions of dollars for $0 \le t \le 35$, where t is the number of years since 1980. In this context, which of the answers below gives the best interpretation of the number .908 in the function?

A) The estimated U.S. National debt, in trillions of dollars, in 1980
B) The estimated yearly increase in the U.S. National debt for each year after 1980
C) The estimated yearly percent increase in the U.S. National debt for each year after 1980
D) The estimated U.S. National debt, in trillions of dollars, t years after 1980

15

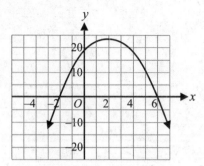

A quadratic function is graphed in the xy-plane as shown above. Which of the following could be an equation for the function?

A) $y = \dfrac{3}{2}(x - 2)(x - 6)$

B) $y = -\dfrac{3}{2}(x + 2)^2 + 24$

C) $y = \dfrac{3}{2}(x - 2)^2 + 24$

D) $y = -\dfrac{3}{2}(x + 2)(x - 6)$

16

If $x = 4$, which of the following is equivalent to the value of $9^x \cdot 9^{2x}$?

A) 3^{24}
B) 9^{24}
C) 9^{32}
D) 81^{12}

17

In the xy-plane, the horizontal line $y = k$, where k is a constant, intersects the parabola with equation $y = x^2 + 2x$ at only one point. What must be the value of k?

A) -1
B) 0
C) 1
D) 2

18

In the xy-plane, the graph of the polynomial function $y = (x - a)(x + b)(x - c)$ crosses the x-axis three times. If a, b, and c are all positive, what are the x-coordinates of the x-intercepts of the function?

A) a, b, and c
B) a, $-b$, and c
C) $-a$, b, and $-c$
D) $-a$, $-b$, and $-c$

19

If $f(x) = x^2 - 4x + 15$ and $g(x) = 3x + 14$, what is the value of $f(g(3))$?

A) 452
B) 210
C) 12
D) 512

20

The entire graph of the function $f(x)$ is shown below. What is the product of the number of x- and y-intercepts?

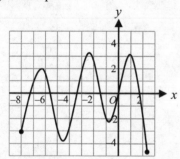

A) 7
B) 6
C) 1
D) 0

21

Kevin is deciding between two different savings accounts. The first account offers annual interest of 3.5% and the second offers annual interest of 5%. If Kevin were to deposit $400 into one of these accounts, how much more money would he have after 10 years if he chose the account with the higher annual interest rate, rounded to the nearest dollar?

A) $87
B) $164
C) $406
D) $464

22

For all $h \neq 0$ where $|h| \neq |g|$, which of the following is the equivalent of the expression $\dfrac{h - g}{h + g} + \dfrac{2g}{h}$?

A) $g^2 + 2hg + h^2$

B) $\dfrac{g^2 + 2hg + h^2}{2h + g}$

C) $\dfrac{h^2 + 2hg}{\left(h^2 - g^2\right)}$

D) $\dfrac{2g^2 + h^2 + hg}{h^2 + hg}$

23

Given the equation $x^8 + 2x^4y^3 + y^6 = 0$, where $x > 0$ and $y \neq 0$, what is the value of $\dfrac{2(x + y)}{12}$?

A) 0

B) $\dfrac{1}{2}$

C) 2

D) 1

24

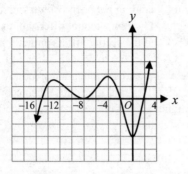

The graph of a polynomial function f was drawn in the xy-plane above. Which of the following is most likely to be the formula for f?

A) $(x - 13)(x - 8)(x - 2)(x - 1.9)$
B) $(x + 13)(x + 8)(x + 2)(x - 1.9)$
C) $(x + 13)(x + 8)^2(x + 2)(x - 1.9)$
D) $(x - 13)(x + 8)^2(x - 2)(x - 1.9)$

25

Which of the equations below defines a parabola that has no x-intercepts?

A) $y = x^2$
B) $y = x^2 - 2x$
C) $y = x^2 - 2x + 1$
D) $y = x^2 - 2x + 2$

26

Suppose that $a^{\frac{-b}{2}} = \dfrac{1}{16}$ and $4a = b$. What is the value of $a - b$?

A) -6
B) -2
C) 4
D) 6

27

If $q > 0$ and $\sqrt[3]{\dfrac{5}{2}q} = \dfrac{1}{4}q$, what is the value of q?

A) $2\sqrt{5}$
B) $4\sqrt{5}$
C) $2\sqrt{10}$
D) $4\sqrt{10}$

Notes and Reflections

Equations with Fractions

1

$$32 = \frac{16}{z}$$

What value of z satisfies the above equation?

A) 0.5
B) 2
C) 64
D) 512

2

$$\frac{x-3}{x+3} = \frac{2}{5}$$

What value of x satisfies the above equation?

A) 2
B) 3
C) 5
D) 7

3

Which of the following is equivalent to

$4 + \dfrac{1}{3x-1}$ for all $x > 1$?

A) $\dfrac{3x-4}{3x-1}$

B) $\dfrac{3x-3}{3x-1}$

C) $\dfrac{12x-4}{3x-1}$

D) $\dfrac{12x-3}{3x-1}$

4

A closed container holds 12 L of a mixture of three gases: carbon dioxide, argon, and nitrogen. The following equation can be used to calculate the partial pressure of carbon dioxide, P, in terms of the total pressure in the container, T, the volume of argon, A, and the volume of nitrogen, N.

$$P = \frac{T(12-A-N)}{12}$$

Which of the following correctly expresses T in terms of P, A, and N?

A) $T = \dfrac{P}{-A-N}$

B) $T = \dfrac{P(12-A-N)}{12}$

C) $T = \dfrac{-A-N}{P}$

D) $T = \dfrac{12P}{12-A-N}$

5

$$\frac{x^2-4}{x-2} = -1$$

Which of the following sets represents all values of x that satisfy the above equation?

A) –3
B) –2
C) –1
D) –3 and –1

6

$$\frac{4}{x+4} - \frac{2}{3(x+4)} = \frac{a}{3(x+4)}$$

If the equation above where a is a constant is true for all values of $x \neq -4$, what must be the value of a?

A) 2
B) 6
C) 10
D) 14

7

$$\frac{1}{3x} - \frac{2}{9x^2} - \frac{3}{27x^3}$$

Which of the following expressions is equivalent to the expression above for $x > 0$?

A) $\dfrac{3x^2 - x - 1}{9x^3}$

B) $\dfrac{(3x+1)(x-1)}{9x^3}$

C) $\dfrac{9x^2 - 5x - 3}{27x^3}$

D) $\dfrac{2}{9x^3}$

8

$$\frac{3}{7}x + \frac{6}{21} = x$$

For the equation above, what is the value of x?

A) $\dfrac{1}{2}$

B) 2

C) $\dfrac{1}{7}$

D) $\dfrac{6}{7}$

9

When $2 \le a \le 6$ and $8 \le b \le 12$, what is the smallest possible value of $\dfrac{4}{b-a}$?

A) $\dfrac{1}{4}$

B) $\dfrac{1}{3}$

C) $\dfrac{2}{5}$

D) $\dfrac{4}{5}$

10

If $\dfrac{x}{12} + 16 = 28 - \dfrac{x}{6}$, then what is the value of $\dfrac{x}{4}$?

11

Consider the equation $m = \dfrac{9}{4}n - 15$. For what value of n is the value of m equal to 39?

A) 11
B) 17
C) 24
D) 42

12

If $x > -3$, which of the following is equivalent to

$$\frac{x+5}{\dfrac{2}{x+3} - \dfrac{1}{x+4}}?$$

A) $x^2 + x - 12$

B) $x^2 + 7x + 12$

C) $\dfrac{x^2 + 7x + 12}{x+5}$

D) $\dfrac{x+5}{x^2 - 7x + 12}$

13

$$\frac{7}{3}y - \frac{10}{27} = y$$

What value of y satisfies the equation above?

14

$$\frac{3}{2z} + \frac{2}{z-2} = 0$$

What value of z satisfies the equation above?

15

If $\left(\dfrac{a}{c}\right)\left(\dfrac{b}{d}\right) = \dfrac{5}{18}$, what is the value of $\dfrac{3cd}{2ab}$?

A) $\dfrac{5}{27}$

B) $-\dfrac{5}{27}$

C) $\dfrac{27}{5}$

D) $-\dfrac{27}{5}$

16

For all $x \neq -3$, which of the following expressions is equal to $2x + 4 + \dfrac{x^2 - 5x - 24}{x+3}$?

A) $x - 8$
B) $3x - 4$
C) $2x^2 - 20x + 32$
D) $\dfrac{3x-4}{x+3}$

17

Which of the following is the solution to the equation $x + 2 = \dfrac{5}{x-2}$?

A) -3 only
B) -2 only
C) 3 only
D) -3 and 3 only

18

If $\dfrac{3x-4}{1-x} = 7$, what is the value of x?

A) $-\dfrac{11}{10}$

B) $-\dfrac{10}{11}$

C) $\dfrac{10}{11}$

D) $\dfrac{11}{10}$

19

If $x > -1$ and $\dfrac{x+1}{\dfrac{a}{x+3}} = \dfrac{x+5}{x+2} \div \dfrac{x+1}{x+3}$, which

expression is equal to the value of a?

A) $\dfrac{(x+2)(x+3)^2}{x+5}$

B) $\dfrac{(x+2)(x+3)}{x+5}$

C) $\dfrac{(x+1)^2(x+2)}{x+5}$

D) $\dfrac{(x+1)(x+2)}{x+5}$

20

If a quarter of a third of t is five-sixths of w and $\dfrac{3}{5}$ of t is equivalent to z, what is the ratio of w to z?

A) 1:6

B) 6:1

C) 3:5

D) 1:10

21

The expression $\dfrac{4x-3}{2x+5}$ is equivalent to which of the following?

A) $\dfrac{2-3}{5}$

B) $2 - \dfrac{3}{5}$

C) $2 - \dfrac{3}{2x+5}$

D) $2 - \dfrac{13}{2x+5}$

22

Which of the following expressions is equivalent

to $\dfrac{\left(\dfrac{x}{2}\right) + \left(\dfrac{1}{3}\right)}{\left(\dfrac{3}{4}\right) - \left(\dfrac{1}{3}\right)}$?

A) $\dfrac{12x+3}{5}$

B) $\dfrac{6x+4}{5}$

C) $6x + 4$

D) $12x + 3$

23

The following formula gives the Pressure, P, of an ideal gas when the volume, V, the number of moles of the gas, n, and the temperature, T, of the gas are known:

$$P = \frac{nRT}{V}$$

Assuming R is a constant value, which of the following expresses the temperature in terms of n, R, V, and P?

A) $T = \dfrac{P-V}{nR}$

B) $T = PV - nR$

C) $T = \dfrac{PV}{nR}$

D) $T = \dfrac{nR}{PV}$

24

For all $x \neq 7$, which of the following is equivalent to $\dfrac{2x^3 - 9x^2 - 31x - 28}{x-7}$?

A) $2x^2 + 3x - 4$

B) $2x^2 + 5x + 4$

C) $2x^2 + 7x + 4$

D) $2x^2 + 7x - 4$

25

For all $x \neq 0$, which of the following is equivalent to $\dfrac{1}{x} - \dfrac{2}{x^2} - \dfrac{4}{x^3} + \dfrac{8}{x^4}$?

A) $\dfrac{(x+2)(x-2)^2}{x^4}$

B) $\dfrac{x^3 - 2x^2 - 4x - 8}{x^4}$

C) $\dfrac{x^3 + 2x^2 - 4x + 8}{x^4}$

D) $\dfrac{(x^2+4)(x+2)}{x^4}$

26

For all $x > 7$, consider the following expression:

$$\frac{x^2 + 2x - 8}{(x-2)(x-7) - A(x-2)^2}$$

If $A = -11$, the expression can be simplified to which of the following?

A) $\dfrac{x-4}{-12x+29}$

B) 1

C) $x - 2$

D) $\dfrac{x+4}{12x-29}$

Notes and Reflections

Equations with Exponents

1

If $x > 1$ and $(x^6)^b = (x^{27})^2$, then what must be the value of b?

A) 9
B) 19
C) 23
D) 48

2

If $x > 1$, which of the following expressions is equivalent to $x^{\frac{-1}{2}}$?

A) $\dfrac{-1}{x^2}$

B) $-\sqrt{x}$

C) x^2

D) $\dfrac{1}{\sqrt{x}}$

3

For all $x > 1$, $\dfrac{x^{a^2}}{x^{6a-9}} = 1$, where a is an integer, what must be the value of a?

4

For all positive values of x and y, the rational expression $\dfrac{2^{-2}x^2 y^{\frac{3}{2}}}{3x^{-1}y^{\frac{1}{2}}}$ is equal to which of the choices below?

A) $\dfrac{-4y^3}{3x^2}$

B) $\dfrac{-4xy}{3}$

C) $\dfrac{y^3}{12x^2}$

D) $\dfrac{x^3 y}{12}$

5

If $x^{\frac{-1}{3}} = \dfrac{1}{2}$, then what must be the value of x?

A) $-\dfrac{1}{8}$

B) $\dfrac{1}{8}$

C) $\sqrt[3]{2}$

D) 8

6

If $\left(\left(y^{x-a} \right)^{x+a} \right)^{x^2 + a^2} = y^{p^{16} - a^4}$ and $y > 1$ and $x > 0$, what is the relationship between x and p?

A) $x = p^4 - 4a$
B) $x = p^4 - 4a^2$

C) $x = p^{\frac{1}{4}}$

D) $x = p^4$

7

For what real value of x is $\dfrac{64\left(4^x\right)}{256^3} = \dfrac{1}{4}$ true?

A) −3
B) 3
C) 8
D) 11

8

Which of the following is equivalent to $(3x^2yz^2)^4$?

A) $12x^6y^4z^6$
B) $12x^8y^4z^8$
C) $81x^6y^4z^6$
D) $81x^8y^4z^8$

9

For all $a > 0$ and $b \neq 0$, which of the following equations is equivalent to $\dfrac{\left(a^{\frac{1}{2}}\right)^2\left(a^2\right)^{\frac{1}{2}}}{\left(b^3\right)^{\frac{1}{3}}b^2} = 71$?

A) $\dfrac{a^2}{b^3} = 71$

B) $\dfrac{a^8}{71} = b^9$

C) $\dfrac{a^2}{2b^3} = 71$

D) $ab \cdot ab^{-2} = 71$

10

If $(x^{32})^a = (x^8)^{16}$, and $x > 1$, what is the value of a?

A) 2
B) 4
C) 6
D) 8

11

If $xyz = 12$, $x^y = 8$, $xz - y = 1$, and $y > 0$, what is the value of x^{yz}?

A) 2
B) 32
C) 64
D) Cannot be determined with the information given

12

If $x^{abcd} = y^{bcde}$ and $x = 2y$, where a, b, c, d, e, x, y are all non-zero values, which of the following is equivalent to 2^{abcd}?

A) y^{e-a}
B) y^{a-e}
C) $y^{bcd(e-a)}$
D) $y^{bcd(a-e)}$

13

Suppose that $4x - 2y = 9$. What is the value of $\left(\dfrac{625^{2x}}{25^{2y}}\right)^{-2}$?

A) 5^9
B) 5^{-9}
C) 25^{-18}
D) 25^{18}

14

For all $x > 0$ and $y > 0$, $\left(x^2y^3\right)^{\frac{3}{4}}$ is the equivalent of which of the following?

A) $\sqrt[3]{x^8y^{12}}$

B) $xy^2\left(\sqrt[4]{x^2y}\right)$

C) $6xy\left(\sqrt[4]{x^6y^9}\right)$

D) $(xy)^3$

15

If $4^{2x+3} = 8^{x+4}$ and $x - y = 4$, what is the value of $(x + y)^3$?

16

If $(3b)^{4+x} = (9b^2)^5(3b)^3$ for all values of b, what is the value of x?

A) 4
B) 6
C) 9
D) 13

17

For what real value of x is $\dfrac{2^x \cdot 2^5}{\left(4^2\right)^3} = \dfrac{1}{8}$ true?

A) 1
B) 2
C) 3
D) 4

Notes and Reflections

Equations with Radicals

1

$$\sqrt{3x} = 6$$

For the equation shown above, what must be the value of x?

A) 3
B) 6
C) 12
D) 36

2

$(36x^4y^2)^{\frac{1}{2}}$ is equal to which of the expressions listed below?

A) $6x^2 \times |y|$
B) $18x^2 \times |y|$
C) $18x^4y^2$
D) $36x^2y$

3

$$5 + \sqrt[3]{4x+2} = 7$$

What value of x satisfies the equation above?

A) $\dfrac{-5}{2}$

B) $\dfrac{3}{2}$

C) 2
D) 3

4

$$\sqrt{4x^6y^3}$$

If x and y are both integers greater than 1, which of the following expressions is equal to the expression written above?

A) $2x^{-4}y^{-1}$

B) $2x^{\frac{1}{3}}y^{\frac{2}{3}}$

C) $2x^3y^{\frac{3}{2}}$

D) $2x^4y$

5

$$\sqrt{3x+6} - 3\sqrt{x-6} = 0$$

For the equation shown above, what must be the value of x?

A) 6
B) 10
C) 14
D) There is no such value of x.

6

$$c_m = \frac{1}{\sqrt{\mu_0 \varepsilon}}$$

The equation above calculates c_m, the speed of light through a specific medium. The physical constant μ_0 represents the permeability of free space, and ε is used to represent the permittivity of the medium the light is traveling through. Which of the equations below expresses the permittivity of the medium in terms of the other variables and constants?

A) $\varepsilon = \dfrac{1}{\sqrt{\mu_0 c_m}}$

B) $\varepsilon = \dfrac{1}{c_m \sqrt{\mu_0}}$

C) $\varepsilon = \mu_0 (c_m)^2$

D) $\varepsilon = \dfrac{1}{\mu_0 (c_m)^2}$

SUMMIT
EDUCATIONAL
GROUP

7

For which value of z is the equation
$\sqrt{z-2}+3=\sqrt{25}$ true?

A) 0
B) 4
C) 6
D) 62

 8

$$\sqrt{3-x}=x+3$$

What is the solution set to the equation shown above?

A) $\{-6\}$
B) $\{-1\}$
C) $\{-6, -1\}$
D) There are no real solutions.

 9

Suppose $3r=\sqrt{5x}$ and $r=7\sqrt{5}$. What is the value of $\sqrt{x}$?

A) $21\sqrt{5}$
B) $\sqrt{5}$
C) 441
D) 21

10

What is the sum of the values of x that satisfies the equation $\left(\sqrt[3]{x-15}\right)^{2}=16$?

11

If $\sqrt[n]{y^{18}}=\left(y^{3}\right)^{2}$ for all positive values of y, what is the value of n?

A) 2
B) 3
C) 6
D) 9

12

For all non-zero a and b where $|a| \neq |b|$, which of the following is the equivalent of

$$\frac{\sqrt[3]{a^{2}-b^{2}}}{\sqrt[3]{\dfrac{ab^{2}}{ab^{2}}}} \times \frac{\sqrt[3]{\dfrac{2ab}{2ab}}}{\sqrt[3]{(a+b)(a-b)}}?$$

A) $a^{2}-b^{2}$
B) 1
C) $a^{2}+2ab+b^{2}$
D) 16

13

If $\sqrt[3]{24x^{6}y^{7}}=\sqrt[3]{py}\left(\sqrt{2}xy\right)^{2}$ for all values of x and y, what is the value of p?

A) 3
B) $8\sqrt[3]{2}$
C) 8
D) $8\sqrt{2}$

14

Any quadratic equation $y=ax^{2}+bx+c$ has no real roots if $b^{2}-4ac<0$. For the equation $y=\sqrt{2}\left(x^{2}\right)+\sqrt{2}\left(x\right)+c$, what is the range of c for which there are no real roots?

A) $c>\sqrt{2}$
B) $c<\dfrac{\sqrt{2}}{4}$
C) $c<\sqrt{2}$
D) $c>\dfrac{\sqrt{2}}{4}$

15

If $x > 0$ and $\sqrt{6x} = \sqrt[3]{x^2}$, what is the value of x?

16

Which of the following is equivalent to the inequality $-\sqrt[3]{(-t)^3} \le -\sqrt[3]{3}x < \sqrt[3]{y}$?

A) $\quad -\dfrac{t}{\sqrt[3]{3}} \ge x > -\sqrt[3]{\dfrac{y}{3}}$

B) $\quad \dfrac{t}{\sqrt[3]{3}} \ge x > -\sqrt[3]{\dfrac{y}{3}}$

C) $\quad -\dfrac{t}{\sqrt[3]{3}} \le x < -\sqrt[3]{\dfrac{y}{3}}$

D) $\quad -\dfrac{t}{\sqrt[3]{3}} \ge x > -\dfrac{\sqrt[3]{y}}{3}$

17

If $\sqrt[4]{3^2 9^3} = 3^x$, then x^3 is equivalent to what value?

A) 32
B) 8
C) 64
D) 16

Notes and Reflections

Functions

1

$$f(x) = \frac{x^2 + 2x}{2}$$

What is the value of $f(-2)$ for the function f defined above?

A) -2
B) -1
C) 0
D) 4

2

$$f(x) = 5x$$

$$g(x) = 2f(x) + 3$$

For what value of x is $g(x) = -7$?

A) -7
B) -5
C) -2
D) -1

3

$$g(x) = 3 \cdot (-2)^x$$

What is the value of $\dfrac{g(4)}{g(3)}$?

A) -6
B) -2
C) 2
D) 6

4

For functions f and g, $f(1) = 4$, $f(4) = 2$, $g(2) = -2$, and $g(4) = 1$, which of the following equals $g(f(4))$?

A) -2
B) 1
C) 2
D) 4

5

A function f is considered odd if, for all values of x, $f(-x) = -f(x)$. If f is an odd function and $f(2) = 8$, what must be the value of $f(-2)$?

A) -8
B) -2
C) 2
D) 8

6

If $f(x) = 100 - 2x + x^3$ and a is a negative integer greater than -5, what is one possible positive value of $f(a)$?

7

If $f(x) = 13 + x - 7$ and $h(x) = x^2 + 2x - 11$, what is the value of $\dfrac{2f(3)}{3h(2)}$?

A) 1
B) $-\dfrac{4}{9}$
C) -2
D) $\dfrac{9}{24}$

SUMMIT
EDUCATIONAL
GROUP

8

If $f(x) = 10 - x$ and $g(x) = (x + 2)^2$, which expression is equivalent to $g(f(x))$?

A) $-x^2 - 4x + 6$
B) $x^2 + 4x + 4$
C) $x^2 - 16x + 64$
D) $x^2 - 24x + 144$

9

Given the functions $f(x) = 2x^2$ and $g(x) = \dfrac{x}{3}$, which of the following is equal to $f(g(x))$?

A) $\dfrac{x^2}{6}$
B) $\dfrac{2x^2}{9}$
C) $\dfrac{x^2}{3}$
D) $\dfrac{2x^2}{3}$

10

If $g(x) = 3x + 5$, and $-2 = h(x)$, what is $g(g(h(x)))$?

A) $\dfrac{-7}{3}$
B) -2
C) 2
D) 38

11

Given that $f(x) = x^2 - 2x + 15$, which expression is equal to $f(x + 1)$?

A) $x^2 + 14$
B) $x^2 + 15$
C) $x^2 - 2x + 14$
D) $x^2 - 2x + 16$

12

The function g is defined by the following equation: $g(x) = x(x - 5)^2(x + 5)^3$. If $g(a - 6) = 0$, what is one possible value for a?

13

If $f(x) = 2x^2 + 7$, what is the highest exponent on the variable x for the polynomial $f(f(f(f(x))))$?

A) 2
B) 4
C) 8
D) 16

Notes and Reflections

Graphs of Functions

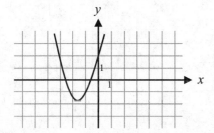

The function $y = f(x)$ is plotted in the xy-plane shown above. Based on the graph, what must be the value of $f(0)$?

2

If $g(x) = x^3 + 2x$ and $h(x) = (x + 2)^3 + 2(x + 2)$ are both graphed in the xy-plane, which of the following describes the translation of the graph of g that results in the graph of h?

A)   A shift of 2 units down in the xy-plane
B)   A shift of 2 units up in the xy-plane
C)   A shift of 2 units left in the xy-plane
D)   A shift of 2 units right in the xy-plane

Questions 3-4 refer to the following information.

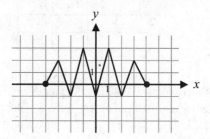

The entire graph of the function f is plotted in the xy-plane shown above.

3

For how many different values of x does $f(x) = -0.5$?

A)   1
B)   3
C)   6
D)   8

4

Function g can be defined as $g(x) = f(x) - 3$. What is the minimum value of $g(x)$?

A) -4
B) -3
C) -1
D)   0

5

x	$g(x)$
-2	v
-1	w
0	v

The above table shows some values of the function g at three different values of x. If v and w are constants and $v > w$, then which of the following could be the graph of $y = g(x)$ in the xy-plane?

A)

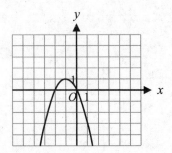

B)

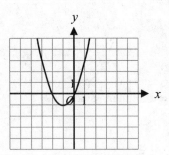

C)

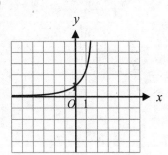

D)

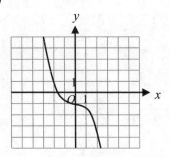

6

The graph of polynomial $y = f(x)$ is shown below for the interval $-6 \le x \le 6$.

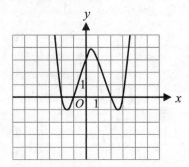

Which of the following is NOT a factor of $f(x)$?

A) $x - 2$
B) $x - 1$
C) $x + 1$
D) $x + 2$

7

A quadratic function passes through the points $(-2, 5)$ and $(-8, 5)$ and has a graph in the xy-plane that opens downward. Which of these could be the coordinates of the highest point on the graph?

A) $(5, 1)$
B) $(-5, 8)$
C) $(-5, 1)$
D) $(5, 8)$

8

In the standard xy-plane, the graph of $f(x)$ has an x-intercept at the point $(-4, 0)$. Which of the following must be the coordinates of an x-intercept of the function $g(x) = f(4 - x)$?

A) $(-8, 0)$
B) $(0, 0)$
C) $(4, 0)$
D) $(8, 0)$

9

$f(x) = ax^6 + bx^5 + cx^4 + dx^3 + ex^2 + gx + h$ is graphed below. How many double roots does $f(x)$ have?

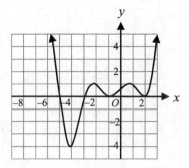

A) 0
B) 2
C) 4
D) 5

10

Pictured below are the graphs of functions $f(x)$ and $g(x)$. Which of the following expresses $g(x)$ in terms of $f(x)$?

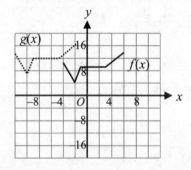

A) $g(x) = f(x + 8) + 3$
B) $g(x) = f(x) + 3$
C) $g(x) = f(x - 8) + 3$
D) $g(x) = f(x + 3) + 8$

11

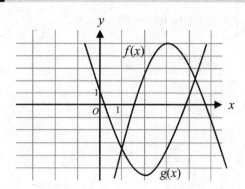

The graphs of functions f and g appear in the xy-plane above. For which of the following values of x does $f(x) - g(x) = 2$?

A) 1
B) 2
C) 3
D) 4

12

The graph of the polynomial function f is shown in the xy-plane, where $y = f(x)$. Which of the following functions could define f?

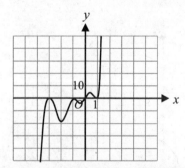

A) $f(x) = x(x - 1)^2(x + 1)(x + 3)$
B) $f(x) = x^2(x - 1)(x + 1)(x + 3)$
C) $f(x) = x(x - 1)(x + 1)^2(x + 3)^2$
D) $f(x) = x(x - 1)^2(x + 1)^2(x + 3)^2$

Consider the following function:

$$f(x) = \left(\frac{1}{2}\right)^x - 2$$

Which of the following is the graph of $-f(-x)$ in the *xy*-plane?

A)
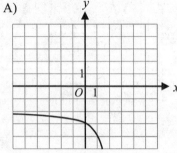

B)
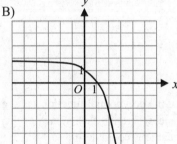

C)
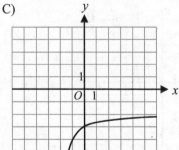

D)
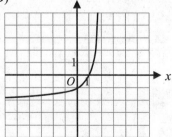

14

Based upon the graph below, which of the following is smallest?

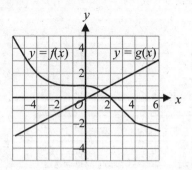

A) $f(g(4))$
B) $f(g(-4))$
C) $g(f(4))$
D) $g(f(-4))$

Notes and Reflections

Quadratic Equations

1

$$x(x + 13) = 30$$

Which of the choices below is the complete set of solutions for the quadratic equation that appears above?

A) −15 and 2
B) −2 and 15
C) −3 and −10
D) 3 and 10

2

$$(x + 3)^2 - 8(x + 3) + 16 = 0$$

For the equation shown above, what must be the value of x?

A) −3
B) −1
C) 1
D) 3

3

$$y = x^2 + x - 2$$
$$y = -3x - 6$$

What value of x satisfies both of the equations listed above?

A) −2
B) −1
C) 1
D) 4

4

$$f(x) = \frac{4x}{x^2 - x - 2}$$

For the function f defined above, what is one value of x for which the function is undefined?

A) −2
B) −1
C) 0
D) 1

5

$$-x + y = 4$$
$$x^2 - y = 2$$

Which of the following is a value of y that satisfies both of the equations listed above?

A) −7
B) −2
C) 2
D) 3

6

$$x^2 + \frac{2}{3}kx + 3 = 0$$

What are the solutions to the equation shown above?

A) $-2k \pm \dfrac{\sqrt{k^2 - 27}}{3}$

B) $-\dfrac{2}{3}k \pm \dfrac{\sqrt{k^2 - 27}}{3}$

C) $-\dfrac{1}{3}k \pm \dfrac{\sqrt{k^2 - 27}}{3}$

D) $-\dfrac{1}{6}k \pm \dfrac{\sqrt{k^2 - 27}}{3}$

7

What is the sum of all of the values of t that satisfy the equation $3t^2 - 15t + 9 = 0$?

A) 9
B) 5
C) −5
D) −9

8

$$4x^2 - y - 144p^2$$

In the equation above, p is a constant value. When graphed in the xy-plane, the graph of the function is a parabola. Which of the following is equivalent to the above equation?

A) $y = (2x - 12p)^2$
B) $y = -(2x - 12p)^2$
C) $y = (2x - 12p)(2x + 12p)$
D) $y = (4x + 16p)(x + 9p)$

9

The dimensions of a rectangular piece of card are $x - 4$ and $x + 7$. If $x > 0$ and the card has an area of 42 square inches, what is the value of x?

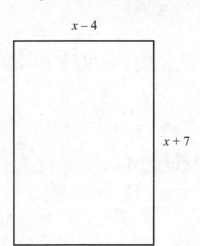

$x - 4$

$x + 7$

A) −10
B) 7
C) 10
D) 26

10

Which of the following are solutions to the equation $2x^2 - 48 = -4x$?

A) 4 and −12
B) −4 and 6
C) 2 and −8
D) 4 and −6

11

$$x^2 - 3x - 10$$

If the expression above is equivalent to an expression of the form $(x - a)(x - b)$, what is a possible value of $2a - 3b$?

A) 4
B) 7
C) 12
D) 16

12

$$\frac{(x+9)^2 - 4(x+9) - 21}{2x+3} = 0$$

What is the sum of the values of x that satisfies the equation shown above?

A) −14
B) −10
C) $-\dfrac{3}{2}$
D) 10

13

Two quadratic equations are labeled A and B. A is the equation $y = (x + p)(x - p)$ and B is the equation $y = (x + q)(x - q)$, where $p \neq q$. Which of the following statements CANNOT be true?

A) Equation A has no real roots and Equation B has no real roots.

B) Equation A has no real roots and Equation B has 1 real root.

C) Equation A has 1 real root and Equation B has no real roots.

D) Equation A has 1 real root and Equation B has 1 real root.

14

Which of the following describes the solution set for $3x^2 = -3(2x + 1)$?

A) 2 real, rational roots

B) The empty set

C) 2 real, irrational roots

D) 1 real, rational root

Notes and Reflections

Graphs of Quadratics

 1

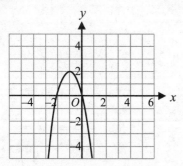

The parabola plotted in the xy-plane above is the graph of function g. Which of the following equations correctly defines the quadratic function g?

A) $g(x) = (x-1)^2 + 2$
B) $g(x) = (x+1)^2 + 2$
C) $g(x) = -2(x+1)^2 + 2$
D) $g(x) = -2(x-1)^2 + 2$

2

$$y = 2(x+1)^2 + 4$$

When the equation above is plotted in the xy-plane, the graph is a parabola. Which of the following statements is true about the graph of the parabola?

A) The minimum of the graph occurs at $(-1, 4)$.
B) The minimum of the graph occurs at $(1, 4)$.
C) The maximum of the graph occurs at $(-1, 4)$.
D) The maximum of the graph occurs at $(1, 4)$.

 3

$$f(x) = (x+a)(x-2)$$

The definition of function f is given in the above equation. Assuming a is a positive real number, which of the choices below could be the graph of $y = f(x)$ plotted in the xy-plane?

A)

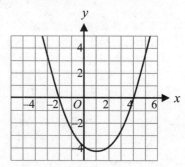

B)

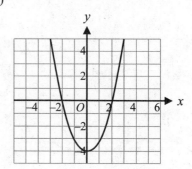

C)

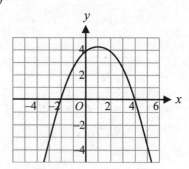

D)

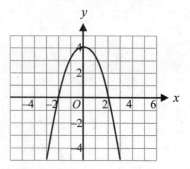

SUMMIT
EDUCATIONAL
GROUP

4

$$y = 5x^2 - 12x$$

$$y = -2x$$

The graphs of the two functions shown above are graphed in the xy-plane. The graphs intersect at two distinct points: the origin $(0,0)$ and point (a,b). Which of the following must be the value of b?

A) -4
B) -2
C) 2
D) 4

 5

$$f(x) = (x)(x + 2)$$

If the function above is plotted in the xy-plane, the graph is a parabola. Which of the intervals below contains the x-coordinate of the vertex?

A) $-4 < x < -2$
B) $-2 < x < 1$
C) $1 < x < 2$
D) $2 < x < 4$

6

When the equation $y = -4(x - 2)(x + 3)$ is graphed on an xy-plane, which of the following characteristics of the graph is displayed as a constant or coefficient in the equation?

A) x-coordinate(s) of the x-intercept(s)
B) x-value of the line of symmetry
C) y-coordinate of the vertex
D) y-coordinate of the y-intercept

7

Which of the following quadratic equations will not graph the same parabola?

A) $f(x) = 2(x - 5)(x - 3)$
B) $f(x) = 2(x - 4)^2 - 2$
C) $f(x) = 2x^2 - 16x + 30$
D) $f(x) = 2(x + 4)^2 - 14$

 8

$$f(x) = -2(x + 3)^2 + 1$$

The definition of quadratic function f is given in the above equation. Which of the graphs below could be the graph of $y = f(x)$ shifted 2 units down in the xy-plane?

A)

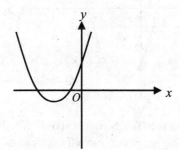

B)

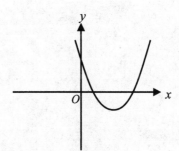

C)

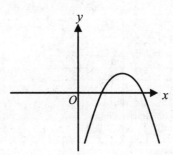

D)

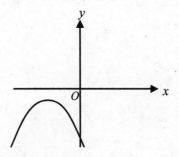

9

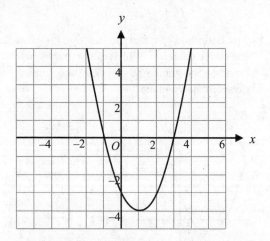

The graph of a parabola is shown above. Which of the following equations correctly represents the parabola shown, and includes the coordinates of the vertex as constants or coefficients?

A) $y = 4x^2 - 1$
B) $y = x^2 - 4$
C) $y = (x - 4)^2 - 1$
D) $y = (x - 1)^2 - 4$

10

The graph of $y = ax^2 + b$ is shown below:

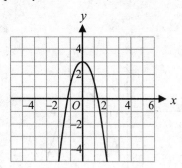

Which of the following could be the values of a and b?

A) $a = -2, b = -3$
B) $a = -2, b = 3$
C) $a = 2, b = -3$
D) $a = 2, b = 3$

11

Quadratic A has factors $(x - 2)$ and $(x + 7)$. Quadratic B has roots 2 and -3. Which of the following graphs could be a representation of both quadratic A and quadratic B?

A)

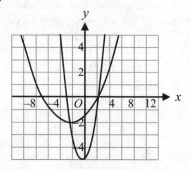

B)

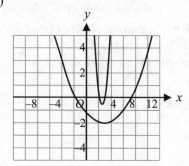

C)

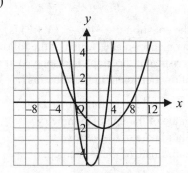

D)

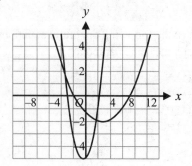

12

Below are two quadratic functions labeled M and N. Which of the following statements is true about M and N?

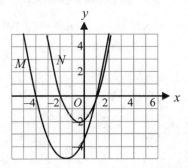

A) The roots of M are -4 and 1. The factors of N are $(x - 2)$ and $(x + 1)$.
B) The zeroes of M are -4 and 1. The factors of N are $(x + 2)$ and $(x - 1)$.
C) The zeroes of M are 4 and -1. The zeroes of N are 2 and -1.
D) The factors of M are $(x - 4)$ and $(x - 1)$. The zeroes of N are -2 and 1.

13

For function $f(x) = 3x^2 - 24x + 36$, what are the coordinates of the vertex?

A) $(4, 6)$
B) $(-4, -6)$
C) $(6, 12)$
D) $(4, -12)$

14

A parabola has a maximum value at $(3, 8)$ and crosses the x-axis at $x = 5$. What is the y-coordinate of its y-intercept?

A) 12
B) 7
C) 3
D) -10

15

$$y = \frac{3}{5}x^2 - \frac{2}{3}x + \frac{1}{15}$$

Which of the following statements is true about the graph of the above quadratic equation in the xy-plane?

I.   The y-intercept will be $\left(0, \frac{1}{15}\right)$.
II. There will be an x-intercept at $(-1, 0)$.
III. The x-value of the vertex will be a number greater than 0.

A) I only
B) I and II
C) I and III
D) I, II, and III

16

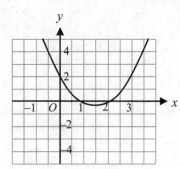

x	$f(x)$
0	0
1	4
2	6
3	6

The table gives some values of the function f, and the graph of the function g is shown in the xy-plane above. For which of the following values of x is $f(x) < g(x)$?

A) 0
B) 1
C) 2
D) 3

17

$$y = x^2 - 1$$

$$y = -\frac{1}{2}(x+3)^2 + 8$$

What is the equation of the line that connects the two points of intersection of the two quadratic equations above?

A) $y = -3x$
B) $y = -2x - 2$
C) $y = -2x + 2$
D) $y = -2x + 3$

18

Given the function $f(x) = 2x^2 + 20x + 48$, which of the following expresses the same function in vertex form?

A) $f(x) = 2(x+8)^2 - 6$
B) $f(x) = 2(x+5)^2 - 2$
C) $f(x) = 2(x-10)^2 + 48$
D) $f(x) = (x-10)^2 - 48$

19

For a quadratic function $f(x) = x^2 + bx + c$ with a y-intercept at $(0, 25)$, $b < 0$, and a discriminant of 0, what is the sum of b and c?

A) -35
B) -15
C) 15
D) 35

20

For a quadratic function $f(x) = x^2 + bx + c$, with a y-intercept at $(0, 35)$ and an x-intercept at $(-5, 0)$, what is the sum of b and c?

A) 31
B) 39
C) 47
D) 55

21

$$y = x^2$$

$$y = 6x - k$$

The above system of equations is graphed.

For what value of k will the parabola and the line be tangent to each other?

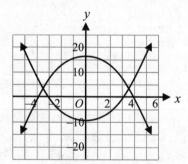

22

$y = (x-3)(x+3)$ and $y = -(x-4)(x+4)$ are both graphed in the xy-plane shown below. Over what interval is $(x-3)(x+3) < -(x-4)(x+4)$?

A) $x < -\sqrt{7}$ and $x > \sqrt{7}$

B) $x < -\dfrac{5\sqrt{2}}{2}$ and $x > \dfrac{5\sqrt{2}}{2}$

C) $-\sqrt{7} < x < \sqrt{7}$

D) $-\dfrac{5\sqrt{2}}{2} < x < \dfrac{5\sqrt{2}}{2}$

Notes and Reflections

Polynomials

$$h(x) = (3x - 4)(x + 2)^2(x - 5)$$

Which of the answers below is NOT an x-intercept of the graph of $h(x)$ plotted in the xy-plane?

A) $(-2, 0)$

B) $\left(-\dfrac{3}{4}, 0\right)$

C) $\left(\dfrac{4}{3}, 0\right)$

D) $(5, 0)$

2

$$(2x^2 - 3x + 1)(ax + 2) = 12x^3 - 14x^2 + 2$$

If the above equation holds true for all values of x, and a is a constant, what is the value of a?

3

$$\frac{x^2 + 13x + 30}{x + 10}$$

For all $x \neq -10$, the expression above is equal to which of the following expressions?

A) $x - 3$

B) $x - 2$

C) $x + 3$

D) $x + 15$

4

$$f(x) = (x - a)^3(x + b)^2(x + a)(x - b)$$

For the equation above, a and b are different positive integers. When the graph of $y = f(x)$ is plotted in the xy-plane, how many distinct x-intercepts does the graph have?

A) 2

B) 4

C) 7

D) The number of x-intercepts cannot be determined.

5

The polynomial $3w^3 + 12w^2 - 12w - 48$ can be factored and rewritten as $3(w^2 - 4)(w + 4)$. What are all of the real roots of this polynomial?

A) -4 and 4

B) $-2, 2,$ and 4

C) $-4, -2,$ and 2

D) -8 and 8

6

$$f(x) = x^3 + ax^2 + bx + c$$

For the function f shown above, a, b, c are all constants. If the x-intercepts of the graph occur at $(-1, 0)$, $(1, 0)$, and $(2, 0)$, what must be the value of $a + b + c$?

A) -5

B) -2

C) -1

D) 2

7

The polynomial function g is defined as $g(x) = 2(x - 2)^3(x + 4)^4$. If one of the x-intercepts occurs at $x = h + 2$, which of the following could be a value of h?

A) -2

B) 0

C) 2

D) 4

8

If the graph of a polynomial function $P(x)$ has x-intercepts at $x = -4$, $x = 0$, and $x = 5$, which of the following must be true of $P(x)$?

A) $(x + 5)$ is a factor of $P(x)$.
B) $(x - 4)$ is a factor of $P(x)$.
C)   The degree of $P(x)$ is 3.
D)   The degree of $P(x)$ is greater than or equal to 3.

9

Given $7x^3 - 21x = -14x^2$ and $x \neq 0$, which of the following is a solution for x in the equation?

A) -3
B) 2
C) -2
D) 7

10

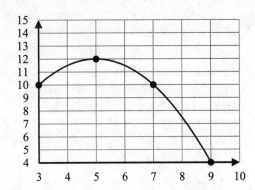

A quadratic polynomial is graphed in the xy-plane. Part of the graph is shown above. Based on the given information, which of the following must be true:

I.   The y-intercept is $(0, 10)$.
II.   For all $x < 0$, $y < 0$.
III.   For all $x > 0$, $y > 0$.

A)   I only
B)   II only
C)   II and III
D)   I, II, and III

11

Which graph shows the polynomial $f(x)$ where $f(0) < 0$ and $(x - 2)$, $(2x + 5)$, $(x - 1)$ are factors?

A)

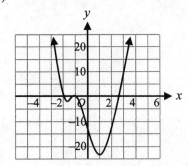

B)

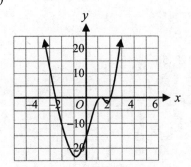

C)

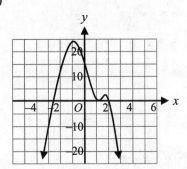

D)

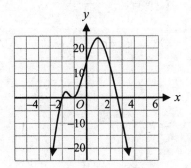

12

$f(x) = x^2 + 3x + 2$ is multiplied by the quadratic function $g(x) = x^2 + 2x + 1$. How many distinct real roots does the resulting polynomial function have?

A) 0
B) 2
C) 3
D) 4

13

For all $x > 1$, which of the following is equivalent to $\dfrac{6x^2 + 7x - 5}{3x - 1}$?

A) $4x - 5$

B) $4x - 5 + \dfrac{7}{2x - 3}$

C) $2x + 3 + \dfrac{-2}{3x - 1}$

D) $13x + \dfrac{2x - 1}{3x + 6}$

14

For all $x \neq 1$, which of the following is equivalent to $\dfrac{x^5 - 1}{x + 1}$?

A) $x^4 - x^3 + x^2 - x + 1 - \dfrac{2}{x + 1}$

B) $x^4 - x^3 - x^2 - x + 1 - \dfrac{2}{x + 1}$

C) $x^4 - x^3 + x^2 - x - 1 + \dfrac{2}{x + 1}$

D) $x^4 + x^3 + x^2 + x - 1 + \dfrac{2}{x + 1}$

15

If $Q(x) = 2x^3 + 8x^2 + 6x$ and $R(x) = x^2 + 4x + 3$, which of the following polynomials has a factor of $(2x + 3)$?

A) $Q(x) + 2R(x)$
B) $Q(x) + 3R(x)$
C) $2Q(x) + 3R(x)$
D) $3Q(x) + 2R(x)$

16

$$\frac{p(x)}{q(x)} = 3x^2 + 2x + 1 - \frac{17}{q(x)}$$

If $q(x) = x + 9$, which of the following must be true?

A) $q(x)$ is a factor of $p(x)$
B) $p(9) = -17$
C) $p(-9) = -17$
D) $p(9) = 17$

17

$$f(x) = (x - a)(x + a)^2(x - b)^3(x + b)^4$$

The equation above is graphed in the xy-plane. If a and b are positive real numbers and $a \neq b$, how many times does the graph touch the x-axis without crossing it?

Notes and Reflections

Nonlinear Models

1

Sonja started a small consulting business but could only take on 25 clients her first year. As her business grows over the next decade, she plans to increase her yearly client load by 20% over the previous year's client total. If $g(t)$ is the number of clients she takes on t years after she opens the business, which of the below statements best describes the function g?

A) g is an increasing linear function.
B) g is a decreasing linear function.
C) g is an increasing exponential function.
D) g is a decreasing exponential function.

2

$$f(x) = 0.0001202(x - 2100)^2 + 220$$

The above function f models the height, in feet, of the suspension cable that hangs above the longest span of the Golden Gate Bridge. In the function, x represents the horizontal distance, in feet, along the road after a car has entered the longest span of the bridge. The graph of the function $y = f(x)$ is plotted below.

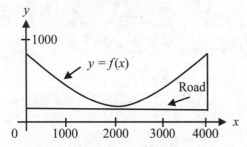

If the x-axis represents the high tide water level of the water under the bridge, what does the number 220 represent in the model?

A) The maximum height of the cable above the water level
B) The minimum height of the cable above the water level
C) The length of road along the longest span of the bridge
D) Half the length of road along the longest span of the bridge

Questions 3-4 refer to the following information.

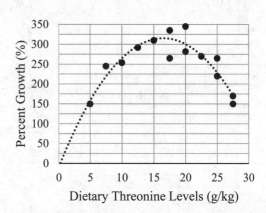

Over 90 days, experimenters fed 14 juvenile grass carp diets with specific dietary threonine levels. Their percent growth was calculated for the 90-day period. The above scatterplot shows the 14 data points collected from the experiment. The graph of the quadratic model for the data is also plotted.

3

The quadratic model underestimates the percent growth for what fraction of the 14 fish studied in the experiment?

A) $\dfrac{1}{7}$

B) $\dfrac{2}{7}$

C) $\dfrac{1}{2}$

D) $\dfrac{5}{7}$

4

Which of the following is closest to the maximum percent growth predicted by the quadratic model?

A) 17
B) 20
C) 320
D) 350

5

Jamila currently spends 2000 minutes a week on her phone. Over the next five weeks, she plans to reduce her total weekly phone usage by 5% each week. Assuming Jamila sticks to her plan, which of the following is closest to the number of minutes she will spend using her phone during the fifth week?

A) 1500
B) 1550
C) 1600
D) 1650

6

The brown tree snake was introduced to the island of Guam in 1944. With no natural predators, the Guam brown tree snake population grew to around 5,000,000 by 1980. If in 1944 the Guam brown tree snake population was 10 and the snake population grew exponentially on the island, then the average rate of population growth would correspond to approximately 33% each year. Which of the functions below best models the population $p(t)$ of brown tree snakes t years after 1944 (where $0 \le t \le 36$)?

A) $p(t) = 1.33(10)^t$
B) $p(t) = 10(.33)^t$
C) $p(t) = 10(1.33)^t$
D) $p(t) = 10(2)^{.33t}$

Questions 7-8 refer to the following information.

The force, F, in newtons (N) of a rollercoaster shooting through a circular loop can be modeled using the following equation,

$$F = m\frac{v^2}{r}$$

where m is the mass in kilograms (kg), v is the velocity in meters per second (m/s), and r is the radius of the loop in meters (m).

7

What is the force of a rollercoaster with a mass of 500,000 g, traveling at a velocity of 20 m/s, and shooting through a loop with a radius of 0.05km?

A) 4,000 N
B) 200,000 N
C) 4,000,000 N
D) 200,000,000 N

8

Engineers are designing a brand-new rollercoaster with a loop. They want it to be the fastest rollercoaster in the world. Assuming the rollercoaster will have the same mass as before, but will now travel at a velocity of 75 m/s, which of the following is closest to the maximum radius the loop can be if the maximum allowed force is 1,000,000 N?

A) 0.8 m
B) 2.8 m
C) 28,000 m
D) 280,000 m

9

$$h(t) = -5t^2 + 10t + c$$

The height of a ball shot out of a tennis ball machine can be modeled by the function h shown above, where h is the height of the ball in meters, t is the time in seconds after the ball is shot out of the machine, and c is a constant. If the function predicts the ball will have a height of 5 meters after 2 seconds, what must be the value of c?

 10

Which of the following can be modeled using an exponential function?

A) The height h of a building with n floors that are each 9 feet tall and an additional floor that is 15 feet tall
B) The amount of gasoline in a fuel tank as a vehicle drives at a constant rate
C) The speed s, of a pedestrian walking at a constant rate of 250 feet per minute after y minutes
D) The hourly pay p, after x years of a worker whose pay starts at \$9 per hour and increases by 2% each year

11

x	$f(x)$	$g(x)$	$h(x)$
0	5	12	40
1	10	18	28
2	20	27	19.6
3	40	40.5	13.72

Given the values for three functions listed in the table of data above, which of the following could be true about the functions?

I. $f(x)$, $g(x)$, and $h(x)$ are exponential functions

II. $g(x)$ has the highest growth factor

III. $h(x)$ has the highest decay factor

A) I only
B) I and II only
C) I and III only
D) I, II, and III

12

A small number of non-native fish are accidentally released into a new aquatic community. Initially its population increases at an increasing rate. Then, over time, its population grows more slowly at a gradually decreasing but positive rate. Which of the following is the best description of the model of the population of this non-native fish?

A) Linear growth followed by linear decay
B) Exponential growth followed by non-linear growth
C) Exponential growth followed by linear decay
D) Exponential growth followed by exponential decay

13

Wind Chill is a measurement of the air temperature after taking into effect a blowing wind. To find the temperature adjusted for wind chill, you can use the formula

$WC = 35.74 + 0.6215(T) - 35.75(V^{0.16}) + 0.4275(T)(V^{0.16})$

where T is the air temperature and V is the wind speed.

Given an air temperature of 27°F and a wind speed (V) of 27 mph, which of the following describes the resultant effect of the temperature adjusted for wind chill versus the ambient (without the effect of the wind) temperature?

A) The wind chill temperature will be less than one third of the ambient temperature.
B) The wind chill temperature will be 72.9 degrees less than the ambient temperature.
C) The wind chill temperature will be at 27% lower than the ambient temperature.
D) The percent decrease from ambient to wind chill temperature is about 57%

14

$$1750(1.03)^{\frac{2t}{3}}$$

The equation above can be used to model the population of a town t years after 2020. According to the model, the population is predicted to increase by 3% every n months. What is the value of n?

15

One formula for the force of gravity is $F = \dfrac{Gm_1 m_2}{r^2}$, where F is the force between two objects, G is the universal gravitational constant, m_1 is the mass of the first object, m_2 is the mass of the second object, and r^2 is the square of the distance between the two objects. If m_1 is increased by a factor of 27, by what factor would r have to change so that the overall force remains constant, and how should this be interpreted? (Assume G and m_2 remain constant throughout).

A) r would increase by a factor of $3\sqrt{3}$, and the masses are further away from one another.
B) r would increase by a factor of $3\sqrt{3}$, and the masses are closer to one another.
C) r would increase by a factor of 5, and the masses are closer to one another.
D) r^2 would increase by a factor of $9\sqrt{3}$, and the masses are closer to one another.

16

A certain species of bacteria growing in a petri dish doubles its population every 12 minutes. If 60 of the bacteria are placed in the petri dish at time $t = 0$, which of the following expressions gives the population of bacteria in the petri dish t hours later?

A) $12(2)^{\frac{t}{5}}$
B) $12(2)^{5t}$
C) $60(2)^{\frac{t}{5}}$
D) $60(2)^{5t}$

Notes and Reflections

Additional Topics in Math

- Section Quiz

- Angles

- Triangles

- Circles

- Volume & Surface Area

- Trigonometry

- Complex Numbers

Section Quiz

1

A triangle has two side lengths with lengths of 3 and 12. If the length of the third side is a, which of the following defines the set of all possible values of a?

A) $0 < a$
B) $3 < a < 12$
C) $6 < a < 15$
D) $9 < a < 15$

2

One face of a cube has a perimeter of 20. What is the surface area of the cube?

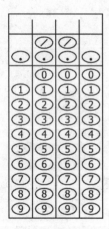

3

$$(1 + 5i) + 2(3i^2 - 2i)$$

In the expression shown above, $i = \sqrt{-1}$. Which of the complex numbers below is equal to the above expression?

A) $-5 + 9i$
B) $-5 + i$
C) $7 + 9i$
D) $7 + i$

4

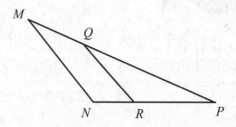

Note: Figure not drawn to scale.

In the figure shown above, line segments $\overline{MN}$ and $\overline{QR}$ are parallel. The degree measure of angle MPN is 41° and the degree measure of angle QRP is 119°. Which of the following must be the degree measure of angle NMP?

A) 20°
B) 41°
C) 60°
D) 119°

5

A circle graphed in the xy-plane has a radius of 9 and a center $(1, 2)$. Which of the following is an equation of the circle?

A) $(x - 1)^2 + (y - 2)^2 = 9$
B) $(x - 1)^2 + (y - 2)^2 = 81$
C) $(x + 1)^2 + (y + 2)^2 = 18$
D) $(x + 1)^2 + (y + 2)^2 = 81$

6

$$3i^3 + 2i^2 + 3i + 4$$

In the expression above, $i = \sqrt{-1}$. Which of the following is equal to the expression?

A) 2
B) $2 + 6i$
C) 6
D) $6 + 6i$

7

A circle with center O has a central angle POQ that measures $\dfrac{2\pi}{3}$ radians. The length of minor arc $\overset{\frown}{PQ}$ is what fraction of the total circumference of the circle?

A) $\dfrac{1}{3}$

B) $\dfrac{1}{2}$

C) $\dfrac{2}{3}$

D) $\dfrac{3}{2}$

9

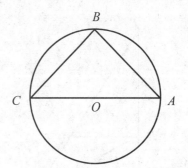

The circle above has center O and line segment $\overline{AC}$ is a diameter of the circle. If minor arcs $\overset{\frown}{AB}$ and $\overset{\frown}{BC}$ are congruent and both have length 1.5π, what is the length of line segment $\overline{AC}$?

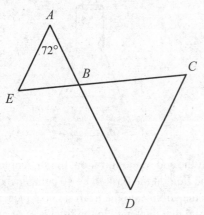

8

Note: Figure not drawn to scale.

In figure shown above, $AB = BE$ and $\overline{AE}$ is parallel to $\overline{CD}$. What is the measure of angle BCD?

A) 36°
B) 72°
C) 88°
D) 56°

10

Triangle ABC is a right triangle, and angle B measures 90°. If $\tan A = \dfrac{3}{4}$, which of the following is equal to $\cos C$?

A) $\dfrac{3}{5}$

B) $\dfrac{3}{4}$

C) $\dfrac{4}{5}$

D) $\dfrac{4}{3}$

11

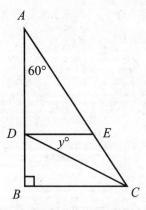

Note: The figure above is not drawn to scale.

Suppose triangles *ABC* and *ADE* are similar and that line segment $\overline{DC}$ bisects angle *ACB*. What is the value of *y*?

12

A chemistry student separates a solid out of liquid solution by using filter paper, a funnel, and a flask. She inserts a rubber stopper into the funnel and wraps filter paper into the shape of a right circular cone with a radius of 3 inches and a height of 6 inches. She then places the cone inside the funnel and pours in solution until it reaches the very top of the filter paper. She removes the stopper and waits for all of the liquid to flow through the paper and into the flask sitting below. At the end of the filtration, only the solid remains in the filter. Below is a sketch of the experimental setup once the filtration was complete:

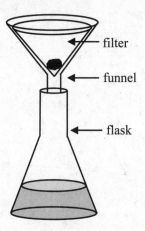

At the end of the filtration, the student measures the fluid in the flask to be 40 cubic inches. What is the volume, to the nearest cubic inch, of the solid that remained in the filter?
(volume of a cone = $(1/3)\pi r^2 h$)

A) 10
B) 17
C) 97
D) 130

13

Right triangle ABC has side lengths of 9, 12, and 15. The smallest angle in the triangle is θ, as shown in the diagram below. What is the value of the cosine of $90 - \theta$?

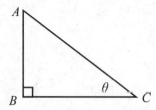

A) $\dfrac{4}{5}$

B) $\dfrac{4}{3}$

C) $\dfrac{3}{4}$

D) $\dfrac{3}{5}$

 14

The surface area of a right cylinder with radius r and height h is $2\pi rh + 2\pi r^2$, where r and h are in the same units of measure. Cylinders A and B are both right cylinders. The radius of Cylinder B is three times the radius of Cylinder A. The height of Cylinder A is one-third the height of Cylinder B. Compared to the surface area of Cylinder A, the surface area of Cylinder B is

A) the same.
B) one-ninth as great.
C) three times as great.
D) nine times as great.

15

The equation $(x - 4)^2 + (y + 3)^2 = 16$ is that of a circle that lies in the standard xy-coordinate plane. One endpoint of a diameter of the circle has y-coordinate 1. What is the y-coordinate of the other endpoint of that diameter?

A) -8
B) -7
C) 7
D) 8

16

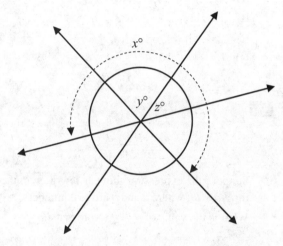

In the figure above, the three lines intersect at the center of the circle and $y = 2z$ and $6z = x$. What is the value of z?

17

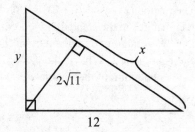

Note: The figure above is not drawn to scale.

Which of the following is the value of y in the above diagram?

A) 5

B) $1.5\sqrt{11}$

C) $2.4\sqrt{11}$

D) 13

 18

$$\frac{13-5i}{5-3i}$$

Suppose the expression above is rewritten in the form $a + bi$, where a and b are real numbers. What is the value of $a - b$? (Note that $i = \sqrt{-1}$.)

A) $\dfrac{87}{17}$

B) $\dfrac{73}{17}$

C) $\dfrac{47}{17}$

D) $\dfrac{33}{17}$

Notes and Reflections

Angles

1

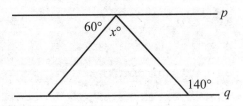

Note: Figure not drawn to scale.

Line *p* is parallel to line *q* in the figure shown above. What is the value of *x*?

A) 60°
B) 80°
C) 90°
D) 100°

2

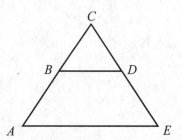

Note: Figure not drawn to scale.

In triangle *ACE*, $\overline{AC} \cong \overline{EC}$. If $\overline{BD}$ is parallel to $\overline{AE}$, and angle *ACE* measures 50 degrees, what is the measure of angle *ABD* in degrees?

A) 50
B) 65
C) 115
D) 230

3

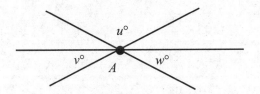

Note: Figure not drawn to scale.

Three lines intersect at point *A*. If $v = w = 40$, which of the following must be the value of *u*?

A) 40
B) 80
C) 100
D) 120

4

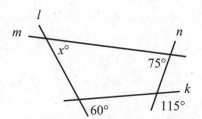

Note: Figure not drawn to scale.

The figure above shows intersecting lines *k*, *l*, *m*, and *n*. What is the value of *x*?

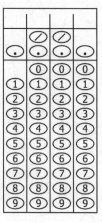

5

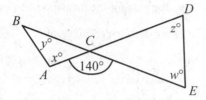

Note: Figure not drawn to scale.

In the diagram shown above, line segments $\overline{AD}$ and $\overline{BE}$ intersect at point C. Which of the following is the value of $x + y + z + w$?

A) 80
B) 140
C) 180
D) 280

6

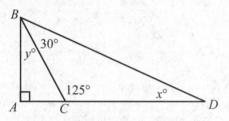

For the figure shown above, $\overline{AB}$ is perpendicular to $\overline{AD}$, and points A, C, and D are collinear. What must be the degree measure of $x + y$?

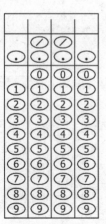

7

The intersection of lines L_1 and L_2 forms angles A, B, C, and D. If the measure of angle B is four times the measure of angle A, what is the measure of angle B?

A) 36°
B) 45°
C) 72°
D) 144°

8

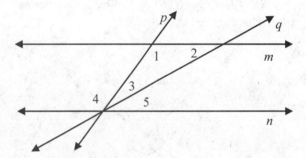

Note: Figure not drawn to scale.

Suppose that the measurement of angle 1 is 110°, the measurement of angle 5 is 45° and angles 2 and 3 are equal in measure. Which of the following must be true?

I.   Lines m and n are parallel.

II. The triangle formed by the intersection of lines p and q with line m and is isosceles.

III. The measurement of angle 4 is 100°.

A) I only
B) I and II
C) II and III
D) I, II, and III.

9

The measure of ∠C is 2.5 times the measure of ∠B in parallelogram *ABCD*. What is the measure of ∠A? Round to the nearest degree.

A) 36°
B) 51°
C) 72°
D) 129°

10

In the figure below, ∠AED is the angle labeled which includes ∠BEC. The measures of these angles are related according to the equation $m\angle AED = 3(m\angle BEC) + 44$. What is the measure of the included angle ∠BEC?

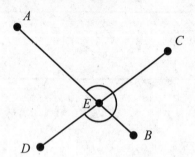

A) 29°
B) 44°
C) 79°
D) 88°

11

One formula for the measure of an exterior angle of a regular *n*-sided polygon is $\dfrac{360}{n}$. What is the sum of an exterior angle of a regular heptagon and an interior angle of a regular hexagon?

A) 51.43°
B) 11.43°
C) 171.43°
D) 188.57°

 12

One formula for the measure of an exterior angle of a regular *n*-sided polygon is $\dfrac{360}{n}$. Doubling the number of sides in a regular *n*-sided polygon has which of the following effects?

A) It doubles the sum of the interior angles.
B) It doubles the sum of the exterior angles.
C) It halves the size of each interior angle.
D) It halves the size of each exterior angle.

 13

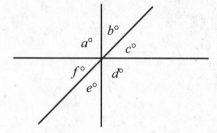

Note: Figure not drawn to scale.

Given that all three lines in the figure above intersect at the same point, and *a* = 90, which of the following statements must be true?

I. $b + c = 90$
II. $e + f = 90$
III. $b + f = d$

A) I only
B) I and II only
C) II and III only
D) I, II, and III

14

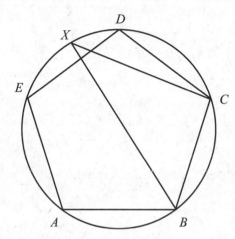

In the figure above, regular pentagon *ABCDE* is inscribed in a circle. Point *X* is on the circle between points *D* and *E*. What is the measure of ∠*BXC* in degrees?

A) 36
B) 72
C) 108
D) 144

15

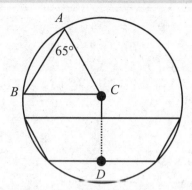

A boat is found jammed inside a bottle. The picture above is one view of what the ship looks like inside of the bottle. The flag of the boat is triangle *ABC* and it is attached to the trapezoidal body of the boat via a pole at the center of the circle, *C*, which forms a perpendicular angle where it connects to the body of the boat at *D*. The base of the flag lies parallel to the top of the body of the boat. You are able to determine that the measurement of the top angle of the flag is 65°. What is the measurement, in degrees, of angle *ACD*?

Notes and Reflections

Triangles

1

Triangles MNO and PQR are similar isosceles triangles. If $\overline{MN} \cong \overline{MO}, \overline{PQ} \cong \overline{PR}$, and the measure of angle M is 70°, what is the measure of angle R in degrees?

A) 35
B) 55
C) 70
D) 110

2

Triangles XYZ and UVW are similar. If $5XY = 2UV$ and the perimeter of triangle UVW is 50, what must be the perimeter of triangle XYZ?

A) 10
B) 20
C) 125
D) 250

3

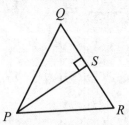

In the figure shown above, $\overline{SQ}$ and $\overline{SR}$ both have length 4. If line segment $\overline{PS}$ bisects angle QPR, which measures 60°, then what must be the perimeter of triangle PQR?

A) 8
B) 12
C) 16
D) 24

4

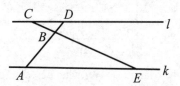

Note: Figure not drawn to scale.

In the figure shown above, points C and D lie on line l and points A and E lie on line k. If lines l and k are parallel, and line segments $\overline{AD}$ and $\overline{CE}$ intersect at point B, which of the following ratios must be equal in value to $\dfrac{DB}{DC}$?

A) $\dfrac{AE}{BE}$

B) $\dfrac{AB}{AE}$

C) $\dfrac{BE}{AE}$

D) $\dfrac{AE}{AB}$

5

Which of the following is a set of possible lengths for the three sides of a triangle in centimeters?

A) 1, 6, 7
B) 2, 9, 12
C) 3, 12, 14
D) 4, 7, 13

SUMMIT
EDUCATIONAL
GROUP

6

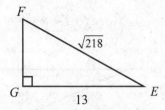

In the triangle above, what percent, rounded to the closest whole number, of the degree measure of the largest angle in the triangle is the area of the triangle?

A) 49%
B) 51%
C) 31%
D) 60%

7

Point D is the midpoint of $\overline{AC}$. $\overline{FD}$ is perpendicular to $\overline{AC}$ and $\angle F \cong \angle B$. In terms of k, what is the area of the larger triangle ABC?

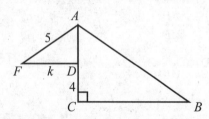

A) $\dfrac{1}{2}k^2 + 4^2$

B) $\dfrac{1}{2}k^2 + 16$

C) $8k$

D) k^2

8

A model of an iceberg consists of a cross sectional plan of the iceberg as shown below. The iceberg is modeled as a right triangle. $\dfrac{1}{9}$ of the cross-sectional area is above water, and $\dfrac{8}{9}$ of the area is below the water line. The cross-section measures 9 m by 15 m. Assume the water line is parallel to the base of the iceberg. What distance from the base of the iceberg, in meters, should the water line be drawn in the model?

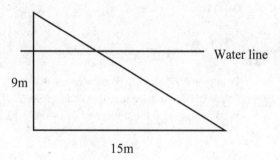

9

A kite is composed of 4 triangles, and $\overline{AC}$ is a perpendicular bisector of line segment $\overline{BD}$. The ratio of the area of triangle II to the area of triangle III is 4:7. Which of the following is equivalent to the ratio $AE:EC$?

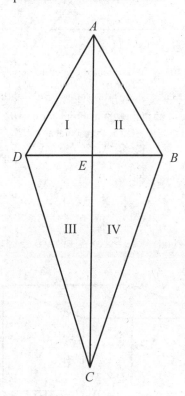

A) 1:2
B) 4:7
C) 16:49
D) 2:$\sqrt{7}$

10

The figure shows square $ABCD$, which is flanked on each side by congruent triangles.

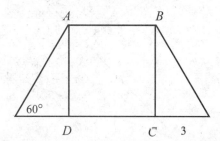

What is the value of the area of the square $ABCD$?

A) 144
B) 81
C) 27
D) $9\sqrt{3}$

11

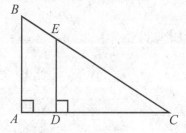

Note: Figure not drawn to scale.

In the triangle above, $AD = 3$ and $BE = 5$. If $CE = 8 + CD$, what is the length of $\overline{CD}$?

A) 12
B) 15
C) 16
D) 20

12

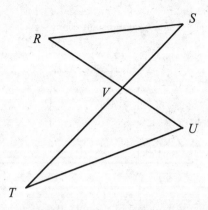

Note: The figure above is not drawn to scale.

Given that angle VUT is congruent to angle VRS, the length of $\overline{VT}$ is 12, the length of $\overline{ST}$ is 18, and the length of $\overline{RU}$ is 15, what is the length of $\overline{RV}$?

A) 5
B) 6
C) 10
D) 12

13

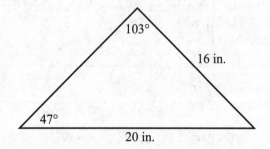

Note: The figure above is not drawn to scale.

What is the area (in square inches) of the triangle?

A) 80
B) $80\sqrt{3}$
C) 120
D) $120\sqrt{3}$

14

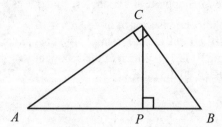

Note: The figure above is not drawn to scale.

In the figure above, a right triangle BCA with right angle C has a height at Point P on $\overline{AB}$. If AP = 720 and PB = 125, then what is CB?

A) 325
B) 360
C) 385
D) 480

15

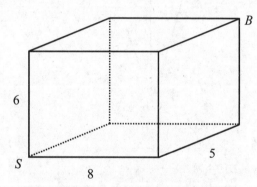

An ant is walking on the surface of a solid prism with dimensions shown above. It walks from the front left vertex S to the right back vertex B. Assuming the ant can only walk along the surface of the solid, what is the length of the shortest path it can take from S to B?

A) $8+\sqrt{41}$
B) 15
C) $6+\sqrt{89}$
D) $\sqrt{185}$

16

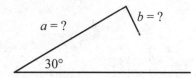

In the figure shown above with angle 30°, which lengths of *a* and *b* can form only one triangle?

A)   *a* = 11 and *b* = 5.5
B)   *a* = 14 and *b* = 6
C)   *a* = 16 and *b* = 10
D)   *a* = 19 and *b* = 18

17

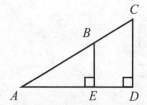

Note: Figure not drawn to scale.

In the figure above, the ratio of the length of $\overline{AE}$ to the length of $\overline{EB}$ is 12:5. If the length of $\overline{AC}$ is 39, and the length of $\overline{ED}$ is 12, what is the length of $\overline{AB}$?

Notes and Reflections

Circles

The area of a circle is 16π square units. What is the length, in units, of the diameter of the circle?

A) 2
B) 4
C) 8
D) 16

The points $(-2,0)$ and $(4,0)$ are the endpoints of a diameter of a circle in the xy-plane. Which of the following describes the equation of the circle?

A) $(x-1)^2 + y^2 = 36$
B) $(x-1)^2 + y^2 = 9$
C) $(x+1)^2 + y^2 = 36$
D) $(x+1)^2 + y^2 = 9$

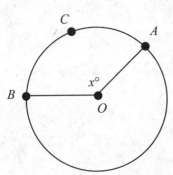

Note: Figure not drawn to scale.

The circle above has center O. If arc $\overset{\frown}{ACB}$ has length 7π and line segment $\overline{AO}$ has length 9, what is the value of x?

A) 70
B) 125
C) 140
D) 280

$$(x+2)^2 + (y-1)^2 = 9$$

When the equation above is plotted in the xy-plane, the resulting graph is a circle. Point S has coordinates $(-2, -2)$ and lies on the circle. If Point T also lies on the circle, and line segment $\overline{PT}$ passes through the center of the circle, what must be the coordinates of point T?

A) $(-5, 1)$
B) $(-2, 1)$
C) $(-2, 4)$
D) $(1, 1)$

5

In the xy-plane, the points $(2,5)$ and $(-4,-3)$ are the endpoints of a diameter of a circle. Which of the following is an equation of the circle?

A) $x^2 + y^2 = 100$
B) $x^2 + y^2 = 25$
C) $(x+1)^2 + (y-1)^2 = 25$
D) $(x-1)^2 + (y+1)^2 = 25$

6

Which of the following equations describes a circle with radius of 9 that passes through $\left(-\sqrt{7}, -\sqrt{2}\right)$ when graphed in the xy-plane?

A) $\left(x+3\sqrt{7}\right)^2 + \left(y-2\sqrt{2}\right)^2 = 9$
B) $\left(x+3\sqrt{7}\right)^2 + \left(y-2\sqrt{2}\right)^2 = 81$
C) $\left(x+4\sqrt{7}\right)^2 + \left(y-2\sqrt{2}\right)^2 = 81$
D) $\left(x+4\sqrt{7}\right)^2 + \left(y-3\sqrt{2}\right)^2 = 81$

7

The points $(2,-3)$ and $(2,11)$ are two endpoints of the same diameter of a circle that has been graphed in the xy-plane. Which of the following could be the equation of the circle?

A) $(x-2)^2 + (y-4)^2 = 3.5$
B) $(x-2)^2 + (y-4)^2 = 7$
C) $(x-2)^2 + (y-4)^2 = 10.25$
D) $(x-2)^2 + (y-4)^2 = 49$

8

A circle with radius 12 cm is divided into 6 congruent arcs. What is the length (in cm) of each of the 6 arcs?

A) 2π
B) 4π
C) 8π
D) 12π

9

The vertex v of the equilateral triangle shown in the figure below lies at the midpoint of a radius of the circle. The portion of the circle's diameter that runs along the base of the triangle is perpendicular to the radius where v lies. Which of the following is the closest approximation of the area of the triangle?

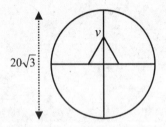

A) 43.30
B) 21.65
C) 86.60
D) 25.03

10

The circle below has an arclength $\overset{\frown}{AB}$ of 2.7π and a center angle as shown. What is the value of the radius cubed for this circle?

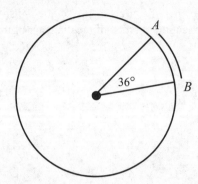

A) $27\pi^3$
B) $27^3\pi^3$
C) 5832π
D) 2460.375

11

Which equation describes a circle that when plotted in the xy-plane is tangent to the x and y axes and has a radius of 7?

A) $x^2 + y^2 = 49$
B) $x^2 + (y - 7)^2 = 49$
C) $(x + 7)^2 + y^2 = 49$
D) $(x - 7)^2 + (y + 7)^2 = 49$

12

A circle with center at Point *C* is graphed in the figure below. Points *A, B, D, E, F* all lie on the circle. If $\overline{AE}$ and $\overline{BF}$ are diameters and $\overline{AE}$ is perpendicular to $\overline{CD}$, what must be the length of arc $\overset{\frown}{BD}$?

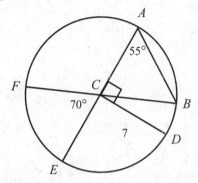

A) 18π

B) 20π

C) $\dfrac{9}{10}\pi$

D) $\dfrac{7}{9}\pi$

13

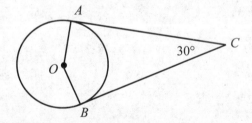

The circle above has center *O*. $\overline{BC} \cong \overline{AC}$ and the line segments are tangent to the circle at points *B* and *A* respectively. If the line segments intersect at point *C*, and the length of $\overline{OB}$ is 6, what is the area of sector *AOB*?

A) 6π
B) 9π
C) 12π
D) 15π

14

$$x^2 + 10y + y^2 - 5x - 75 = -100$$

The equation above, when graphed in the *xy*-plane, will be a circle. Which of the following will be the diameter of the circle?

A)   2.5
B)   5
C)   6.25
D)   25

15

The circle with the equation $(x + \pi)^2 + (y - 1)^2 = 1$ is graphed in the standard *xy*-coordinate plane below.

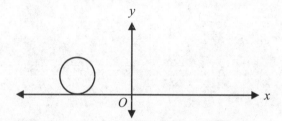

Suppose the circle rolls along the *x*-axis for 3 rotations in the positive direction and then stops. Which of the following is an equation of the circle in its new position?

A) $(x + 3)^2 + (y - 1)^2 = 1$
B) $(x + \pi)^2 + (y - 1)^2 = 1$
C) $(x - 3\pi)^2 + (y - 1)^2 = 1$
D) $(x - 5\pi)^2 + (y - 1)^2 = 1$

16

What is the shortest distance between any point on the circumference of the circle with equation $(x - 4)^2 + (y + 2)^2 = 81$ and any point on the circumference of the circle with equation $(x + 16)^2 + (y + 23)^2 = 16$?

A)   14
B)   16
C)   29
D)   65

Notes and Reflections

Volume & Surface Area

1

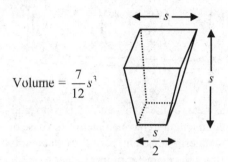

$$\text{Volume} = \frac{7}{12}s^3$$

Note: Figure not drawn to scale.

If the wastebasket above can hold a maximum of 1008 cubic inches, which of the following is closest to the length of s in inches?

A) 8
B) 10
C) 12
D) 14

2

A right circular cone has a diameter of 10 inches and a height of 10 inches. Which of the following is a correct expression for the total volume of the cone, in cubic inches?

A) $\dfrac{250\pi}{3}$

B) 250π

C) $\dfrac{1000\pi}{3}$

D) 1000π

3

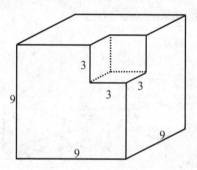

A $9 \times 9 \times 9$ cube has a cube with edge length 3 cut from one corner of the cube as shown above. This process is performed for all eight corner vertices. All cut surfaces are parallel to faces of the original cube. To the nearest 0.1%, by what percent does the surface area of the original cube change?

A) −29.6%
B) 0.0%
C) 22.2%
D) 29.6%

4

The diagram below depicts how a pyramid post cap is constructed by attaching a square right pyramid to a rectangular prism with the same base dimensions.

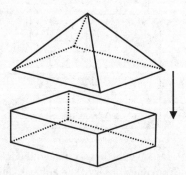

Note: Figure not drawn to scale.

The prism has a square base with an area of 9 square inches and a height of 1.5 inches. If the square pyramid's height is twice the height of the square prism, then what is the total volume, in cubic inches, of the pyramid post cap?

A) 9
B) 13.5
C) 22.5
D) 202.5

5

An oil drum is a cylindrical cargo container that can be used to transport biodiesel. A specific drum has a radius of 11.25 inches and a height of 33.5 inches. If the drum will be completely filled with biodiesel, and the density of the biodiesel is .0316 lb/in³, what will be the mass, rounded to the nearest pound (lb), of the biodiesel in the container?

A) 12
B) 134
C) 377
D) 421

6

A diagram of a cylindrical container holding three spherical tennis balls with the same diameter is shown below.

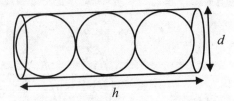

The diameter of the tennis ball, d, is 6 cm, and it is equal in length to the diameter of the base of the container. The height, h, of the container is three times the diameter of its circular base. What is the volume, in cubic centimeters, of the empty space surrounding the tennis balls in the can?

A) 54π
B) 108π
C) 126π
D) 162π

7

A company usually ships its products in crates that have a length of 24 inches, a width of 36 inches, and a depth of 18 inches. If the company switches to using crates with a 10% longer width and a 15% longer length, what would be the percent increase in volume (to the nearest 1%) of the new crates compared to the old crates?

A) 15%
B) 25%
C) 27%
D) 30%

8

A truck carries a gas canister that is in the shape of a cylinder with a hemisphere added onto either end. If the radius of the cylinder is 12 ft and the length of the entire canister is 104 ft, what is the volume of the canister in cubic feet?

A) 2,304π
B) 11,520π
C) 12,672π
D) 13,824π

9

A solid plastic box of dimensions 4 × 3 × 8 is melted down and reshaped into a sphere. What is the radius of the resulting sphere?

A) 2.84
B) 4.79
C) 2.84π
D) 4.79π

10

Zack is tasked with removing 18 inches of new snow from his family's walk and driveway. He uses a mechanical snow blower, which enables him to remove approximately 400 cubic feet of snow per hour. Zack's family has a rectangular-shaped driveway that is 70 feet long and 20 feet wide. Near the top of the driveway are parked two identical vehicles, each measuring 6 feet wide by 12 feet long. They covered part of the driveway, so no snow accumulated there. Finally, there is a walkway from the top of the driveway into the house. It measures 4 feet wide by 10 feet long. Given all of this information, approximately how many hours of Zack's snow day will be spent on removing snow? Assume that the equipment has been prepared and time starts when Zack starts the actual snow removal.

A) 4.9
B) 5.3
C) 6.2
D) 7.0

11

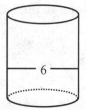

In the right cylinder shown in the figure, the length from one side to the other passing through the exact center is 6. The height of the cylinder is twice that length. The cylinder is completely filled with liquid and Jake needs to transfer the liquid into another container shaped like a cube with sides of 7.

Which of the following describes the situation resulting after Jake pours the liquid from the cylinder-shaped container into the cube?

A) The cube will be only half full once all the liquid is poured into it.
B) The cube will overflow before Jake can transfer all the liquid from the cylinder.
C) The cube will hold all of the liquid with just a small amount of room left.
D) The liquid will rise to the very top of the cube with no room to spare.

12

A handyman is hired to paint the outside surfaces of six identical storage bins. The bins are cube-shaped, each having one open surface that allows access to the interior of the cube. Each side of the cubes is 18". The color that the handyman needs is a specialty color only available in small cans. One can of this specialty color covers 40 square feet of surface. Because the handyman knows the storage cubicles will get a lot of use, he decides to put three coats of paint on all the outside surfaces. How many cans of the specialty paint will the handyman need to put three coats of paint on all the outside surfaces of all the cubes?

A) 5
B) 6
C) 7
D) 8

Questions 13-14 refer to the following figure.

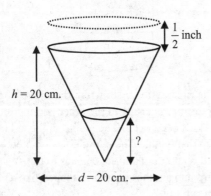

Note: Figure not drawn to scale.

13

A rain gauge to measure rainfall consists of a right circular cone with a diameter, d, of 20 cm and a height, h, of 20. As rain is collected, the level of water in the cone rises. After the first $\frac{1}{2}$ inch of rain is collected over the circular opening of the inverted cone, what will the water level be in the rain gauge, to the nearest tenth of a centimeter?

Note: 1 inch = 2.54 cm

A) 10.5
B) 11.0
C) 11.5
D) 12.0

14

The rain gauge has collected the first $\frac{1}{2}$ inch of rainfall. Another inch of rain is collected. What is the additional height of the water in the rain gauge to the nearest tenth of a centimeter?

A) 2.5
B) 3.0
C) 4.0
D) 5.1

15

The circumference of the largest cross-section of a beach ball is about 287 centimeters. What is the volume of the beach ball of the beach ball to the nearest thousand cubic <u>inches</u>?
(1 inch = 2.54 centimeters)

A) 24,000
B) 62,000
C) 158,000
D) 400,000

16

Cone Inc. makes right circular cones that are guaranteed to hold 2250π cubic centimeters of water. Each cone has a 2 centimeter diameter. Super Cone Inc., a competitor, launched a brand new right circular cone that can hold four times as much water but has the same height. What is the diameter, in centimeters, of the cone created by Super Cone Inc.?

17

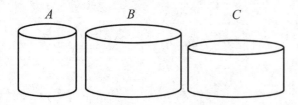

Note: Figure not drawn to scale.

You have three different cylindrical cups in your kitchen: A, B, and C. The height of A is 8 centimeters and the diameter of C is 10 centimeters. C is half the height of A but twice its diameter. B has the same radius as C and the same height as A. A recipe calls for you to use A three times, B twice, and C four times. Assuming you fill each cup to the top when you use it, which of the following is closest to the total volume of ingredients used?

A) 1000 cm^3
B) 2000 cm^3
C) 2500 cm^3
D) 3000 cm^3

18

Increasing the surface area of a solid catalyst will increase its effectiveness. A solid catalyst is in the shape of a cube with edge length s. A round hole with diameter $\dfrac{s}{4}$ is drilled completely through the cube through the center of one of the cube's faces. The lateral surface area of a cylinder is $2\pi rh$. To the nearest 0.1%, by what percent does the surface area of the catalyst increase?

A) 11.5%
B) 12.0%
C) 12.5%
D) 16.0%

19

The volume of a spherical ball A is $5\sqrt{5}$ times as large as the volume of spherical ball B. What is the ratio of the surface area of ball A to the surface area of ball B?

A) 25:1
B) $5\sqrt{5}$:1
C) $25\sqrt{5}$:1
D) 5:1

Notes and Reflections

Trigonometry

1

If an angle measure $\frac{5\pi}{4}$ radians, what is its measure in degrees?

A) 45°
B) 135°
C) 225°
D) 315°

2

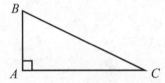

Note: Figure not drawn to scale.

In the figure depicted above, ABC is a right triangle, and the hypotenuse has a length of 5 units. If $\sin B = .85$, what must be the length of line segment $\overline{AC}$ to the nearest tenth of a unit?

A) 1.5
B) 4.3
C) 5.9
D) 8.5

3

A right triangle has two acute angles that measure $a°$ and $b°$. If $\sin a° = \frac{1}{\sqrt{5}}$, what must be the value of $\cos b°$?

A) $\frac{1}{\sqrt{5}}$

B) $\frac{2}{\sqrt{5}}$

C) $\frac{1}{2}$

D) 2

4

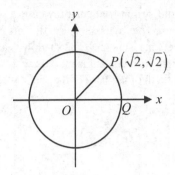

In the figure above, a circle with center O is plotted in the xy-plane. The circle contains points P and Q as shown. If Q lies on the x-axis, what is the measure of angle POQ in radians?

A) $\frac{\pi}{6}$

B) $\frac{\pi}{4}$

C) $\frac{\pi}{3}$

D) $\frac{\pi}{2}$

5

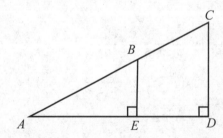

Note: Figure not drawn to scale.

In the figure, $\sin A = \frac{5}{13}$. If $CD = 25$, and $BC = 39$, what is the length of $\overline{BE}$?

A) 5
B) 10
C) 15
D) 20

6

A child's right-triangular toy casts a shadow in the sun. The toy is 3 inches tall. One of the corners measures 56. The shadow is also a right triangle with one angle measuring 21°. What is the length of the base of the shadow labeled s?

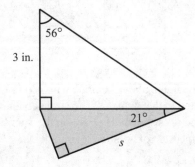

A) 1.594
B) 1.889
C) 4.152
D) 4.154

7

Suppose there is a right triangle with an angle that has a measurement of $x°$, where $0 < x < 90$, and $\tan(x°) = \frac{3}{4}$. Which of the following must be true?

A) $\sin(x°) = \frac{4}{5}$

B) $\cos(90° - x°) = \frac{3}{5}$

C) $\cos(x°) = \frac{3}{5}$

D) $\sin(90° - x°) = \frac{3}{5}$

8

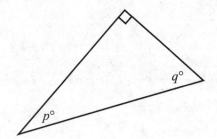

In the triangle above, $\sin q° = \frac{12}{13}$. What is the value of $\tan p°$?

A) $\frac{12}{13}$

B) $\frac{5}{13}$

C) $\frac{5}{12}$

D) $\frac{12}{5}$

9

In right triangle DEF, $m\angle F = 90°$. If $\cos E = \frac{15}{17}$, what is the value of $\cos D$?

A) $\frac{8}{17}$

B) $\frac{8}{15}$

C) $\frac{15}{17}$

D) $\frac{17}{15}$

10

When $x° = 90°$, $\dfrac{16\sin x°}{8} = \dfrac{1}{p}$, and

$p = \dfrac{0.25\sqrt{2}}{\sin y°}$. What is one possible value of y?

A) $\dfrac{\sqrt{2}}{2}$

B) $\dfrac{1}{2}$

C) 45

D) 22.5

11

Emily is standing 21 feet away from the base of a lamppost. If the angle of elevation from Emily's feet to the top of the lamppost is 48°, what is the height, in feet, of the lamppost?

A) $21\sin(48°)$

B) $21\cos(48°)$

C) $21\tan(48°)$

D) $21\cot(48°)$

12

In the right triangle shown below, the tangent of angle EFG is $\dfrac{2}{7}$. If the lengths of the legs of the right triangle must be integers, what is one possible length of the hypotenuse?

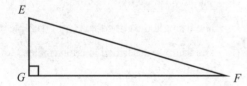

A) $3\sqrt{5}$

B) $5\sqrt{53}$

C) 14

D) $7\sqrt{2}$

13

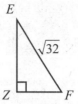

Note: Figure not drawn to scale.

In the right triangle shown above, the

$\sin F = \dfrac{5}{\sqrt{32}}$. What is the length of $\overline{ZF}$?

A) 7

B) $5\sqrt{32}$

C) $\sqrt{7}$

D) 64

14

If an angle with a measure of 1080° is expressed in radians as $x\pi$, what is the value of x?

A) 10

B) 108

C) 12

D) 6

15

For all angles $x°$, where $0 < x < 90$, which of the following is NOT equal to $\sin x°$?

A) $\tan x° \cdot \cos x°$

B) $\dfrac{1}{\csc x°}$

C) $\sqrt{1 - \cos^2 x°}$

D) $\cot x° \cdot \sin x°$

SUMMIT
EDUCATIONAL
GROUP

16

If $\cos^2 A = \dfrac{5}{12}$ and $\pi < A < \dfrac{3\pi}{2}$, what is the value of $\sin A$?

A) $-\dfrac{\sqrt{21}}{6}$

B) $-\dfrac{7}{12}$

C) $-\dfrac{\sqrt{21}}{12}$

D) $\dfrac{\sqrt{21}}{6}$

17

An ice cream cone in the shape of a right circular cone has the measurements shown in the diagram below. The height, h, shown is from the tip of the cone to the center of its opening. What is the diameter of the cone in millimeters?

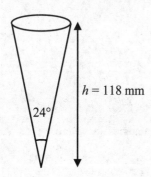

A) $\dfrac{\tan 24°}{236}$

B) $118\tan 24°$

C) $236\tan 24°$

D) $236\tan 12°$

18

In the diagram below angle $ABH = 19°$, angle $HCG = x°$, and angle $GDF = 2x°$. Side $\overline{AB}$ has length 7 cm. $ABCH$, $CDGH$, and $DEFG$ are all rectangles, and $\overline{BH}$ and $\overline{CG}$ are parallel. Rounded to the nearest hundredth of a centimeter, what is the length of side $\overline{FG}$?

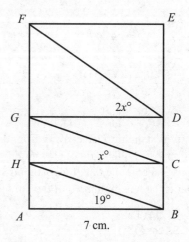

Note: Figure not drawn to scale.

A) 2.33
B) 2.41
C) 5.47
D) 10.94

19

Suppose a triangle has angles that measure $a°$, $b°$, and $(a + b)°$. Which of the following statements must be true?

I.   The triangle described is a right triangle.

II. The triangle described is an isosceles triangle.

III. $\sin(a°) = \cos(b°)$

A) I only
B) II only
C) I and III only
D) I, II, and III

Notes and Reflections

Complex Numbers

1

$$(5 + 6i) + (2 - 2i)$$

In the expression shown above, $i = \sqrt{-1}$. What is the value of the expression?

A) 11
B) 11i
C) 7 + 4i
D) 10 − 12i

2

Which complex number is equivalent to $(4 + 10i) - (4i^2 + 5i)$, where $i = \sqrt{-1}$?

A) 8 + 5i
B) 8 + 15i
C) 4 + i
D) 5i

3

$$(5 - 2i) + (3i - 6)$$

In the complex number system, which of the following is equivalent to the expression above? (Note: $i = \sqrt{-1}$)

A) 0
B) −1 + i
C) 3 − 3i
D) 8 − 8i

4

Which of the following complex numbers is equivalent to $-i(-2 + 6i)$, where $i = \sqrt{-1}$?

A) −6 + 2i
B) −2 + 6i
C) 2 − 6i
D) 6 + 2i

5

$$(2 + 3i)(1 - 2i)$$

In the expression above, $i = \sqrt{-1}$. Which of the following complex numbers is equivalent to the expression shown above?

A) −4 − i
B) 3 − i
C) 2 − 6i
D) 8 − i

6

Which complex number is equivalent to $\dfrac{2 + 4i}{i}$?

A) −4 − 2i
B) −4 + 2i
C) 4 − 2i
D) 4 + 2i

7

Which of the following is equivalent to $\sqrt{-63}$?

A) $-3\sqrt{-7}$
B) $-3i\sqrt{7}$
C) $3i\sqrt{7}$
D) $3i^2\sqrt{7}$

8

Which of the following expressions is the equivalent of $\dfrac{13}{(3+i)}$?

A) $\dfrac{13}{(3+i)^2}$

B) $\dfrac{169}{(3+i)^2}$

C) $\dfrac{(13+3i)}{(3+i)^2}$

D) $\dfrac{(39-13i)}{10}$

9

Given that $i^2 = -1$ and k is a positive integer, what is the value of $i^{(12k+3)}$?

A) 1
B) -1
C) i
D) $-i$

 10

If $i = \sqrt{-1}$, what is the value of $(3 + 2i)^2$?

A) $5 + 12i$
B) $5 - 12i$
C) $13 - 12i$
D) 5

 11

$$\frac{5+2i}{2+i}$$

Which of the following statements about the above expression is true? (Note $i = \sqrt{-1}$.)

I.   The expression is equivalent to $\dfrac{12}{5} - \dfrac{i}{5}$.

II. The expression is equilvalent to $\dfrac{8+9i}{5}$.

III. The expression is equilvalent to $2 + \dfrac{1}{2+i}$.

A) I only
B) II only
C) I and II
D) I and III

12

Given that $i^2 = -1$, which of the following is equivalent to $\dfrac{2+3i}{4-i}$?

A) $\dfrac{1}{3} + \dfrac{14}{15}i$

B) $5 + \dfrac{14}{15}i$

C) $\dfrac{5+14i}{17}$

D) $\dfrac{5+16i}{17}$

Notes and Reflections

SUMMIT
EDUCATIONAL
GROUP

Answer Explanations

Information & Ideas – Fiction – Passage 1 – Pages 2-3

1.   (A)
Category: Main Idea
Difficulty: Medium
Strategy: Map the passage by finding the main idea of each paragraph and then of the passage as a whole.
Solution: This passage describes a man who "lived entirely for his duties" and has one skill which he is dedicated to. He is given a different job and is not able to do it. He is also shown to think about his job all the time.
(B)   Incorrect. The man loves his work and thinks about it because he enjoys it.
(C)   No indication he wonders about others
(D)   Too narrow. The man likes his current job and finds the promotion too stressful.

2.   (C)
Category: Words in Context
Difficulty: Medium
Strategy: Read above and below the given lines to understand context. Think about what type of councillor this man might be.
Solution: The spelling of "councillor" refers to someone who is a member of a council. The sentence describes Akakiy's potential as a well-paid member of a state council, which would be a politician.

3.   (B)
Category: Detail
Difficulty: Easy
Solution: Process of elimination. Lines 14-15 say that "it is impossible to say that no attention was paid to him." The second paragraph showed that Akakiy's director appreciated the work that he was doing.
(A)   "If his pay was had been in proportion to his zeal…" (line 9-12)
(C)   "In his copying, he found a varied and agreeable employment." (lines 4-5)
(D)   "It would be difficult to find another man who lived so entirely for his duties." (lines 1-2)

4.   (C)
Category: Evidence
Difficulty: Medium
Solution: Answer C shows where it states that Akakiy was appreciated.
(A)   Not relevant. These lines refer to being underpaid.
(B)   Not relevant. These lines refer to being dedicated.
(D)   Not relevant. These lines refer to being content.

5.   (D)
Category: Detail
Difficulty: Easy
Strategy: Reread the given lines, try to find the answer on your own, then choose the answer choice that best answers the question.
Solution: The lines say that Akakiy's directors wanted to reward him and gave him more important work.
(A)   Not true. They promoted him because he was so good at copying.
(B)   Too negative. They wanted to give him a more difficult job, but it was a reward.
(C)   Not stated. There is no indication of their opinion.

6.   (A)
Category: Inference
Difficulty: Medium
Strategy: Use information you know about the character already. Read the lines before and after.
Solution: The paragraph where these lines appear is discussing the fact that Akakiy was oblivious to the world around him. It starts with lines 27-28 - "Outside this copying, it appeared that nothing existed for him."

(B)   Too literal. The surroundings lines are about him not paying attention.
(C)   Not true. This was never stated.
(D)   Misleading. He was anxious when his boss tried to give him different work.

7.   (C)
Category: Evidence
Difficulty: Medium
Solution: Shows where it states that Akakiy was he was constantly preoccupied with his work.
(A)   Not relevant. These lines refer to his anxiety over trying a different job.
(B)   Misleading. These lines show that he preferred copying and that "they let him copy on forever."
(D)   Misleading: Shows that he was distracted, but not by what.

8.   (A)
Category: Words in Context
Difficulty: Medium
Strategy: Read above and below the given lines to understand context.
Solution: The word inordinately, referring to his neck, means not proportional. His neck seemed oddly long. The comparison to the cats with long necks conveys this.
(B)   Not related. "Extraneous" means unrelated.
(C)   Not true. The author does explain it, so it is not inexplicable.
(D)   Not related. His neck was unusual, which has nothing to do with originality.

9.   (D)
Category: Inference
Difficulty: Medium
Solution: The author says that Akakiy's life would have continued to go on peacefully, except for the normal misfortunes that people like him experience, foreshadowing that his life would not go on in the same way.
(A)   Opposite. The narrator says that "it would have continued to flow on…were it not that there are various ills…" (lines 88-90)
(B)   Too literal/narrow. This is true, but is a stated fact, not something that is implied.
(C)   Too broad. This is only stated to imply that Akakiy will experience misfortune.

10.   (A)
Category: Main Idea
Difficulty: Medium
Strategy: Look at the beginning and end of the paragraph for clues about the main idea. Also, try to summarize the paragraph into a single sentence. This will help you narrow down the answer choices to the main idea.
Solution: The narrator compares Akakiy to his peers who go out after work. "Akakiy Akakievitch indulged in no kind of diversion…having written to his heart's content, he lay down to sleep, smiling at the thought of the coming day" (lines 80-84)
(B)   Too narrow. His peers did more fun activities, but that is not the main idea. Also, he seemed to greatly enjoy his life, even if he didn't engage in what most people would consider to be "fun" activities.
(C)   Too literal. The leisure activities are not the main idea.
(D)   Not stated. There is no opinion stated about Akakiy's lifestyle choices.

Information & Ideas – Fiction – Passage 2 – Pages 4-6

1. (D)
Category: Detail
Difficulty: Medium
Strategy: Make sure you are looking at the proper portion of the passage. Focus on the word "initial."
Solution: Her initial response is that she likes the city "very well." She supports this with several details, lending confidence to her answer.
(A) She's not neutral, but enthusiastic.
(B) She's confused by the city at first but not by her feelings for it.
(C) This is her response the second time she is asked, but not the first.

2. (C)
Category: Evidence
Difficulty: Medium
Strategy: Refer to the previous question. Evidence questions may be solved along with their paired questions, using the answer choices to search for a solution to the previous question.
Solution: Choice C is her first response to her employer.

3. (C)
Category: Generalization
Difficulty: Hard
Strategy: Deal with one part of each answer choice at a time and eliminate. Is Caline intrigued by the trains? Yes. Is she alarmed by a large event? No. Eliminate based on each portion.
Solution: The train has not stopped before as far as she knows, so the experience is "unusual"; she does travel to the city; and the ending does show her making a realization about her desires.
(A) Caline doesn't go live with a relative, even if the other parts of this answer are true/mostly true.
(B) Caline is not fulfilled by her new job, even if the other parts of this answer are somewhat true.
(D) There is no evidence of Caline being alarmed or "grappling" with her decision to move.

4. (A)
Category: Compare & Contrast
Difficulty: Medium
Strategy: Look for concrete evidence to support an answer choice. Their clothes are a good example of the contrast.
Solution: Caline has a skirt that "doesn't reach her naked ankles," while the women have "high heeled boots," and "parasols."
(B) Might be true but there isn't enough evidence.
(C) The women don't appear jaded.
(D) No evidence that Caline is fanciful or the women are practical.

5. (B)
Category: Detail – Cause & Effect
Difficulty: Medium
Strategy: Revisit paragraph four and consider their interaction.
Solution: She is interested in the passengers and answers when they "try to talk to Caline."
(A) She may be startled, but she doesn't avoid them.
(C) No evidence for concern or disruption.
(D) There is a language barrier, but Caline doesn't avoid speaking with the women from the train.

6. (C)
Category: Main Idea
Difficulty: Medium
Strategy: Look for the best fit **Solution:** A and B are too broad, while C is too narrow and incorrect.
Solution: In the last paragraph, Caline finally knows that she moved to the city in hopes of finding the boy who drew her. Since she hasn't found that boy, the move has left her feeling unhappy.

(A) Too broad. While Caline is unhappy, this is not being generalized to all women.
(B) Too extreme. While it's unlikely that she'll find this boy, there's no evidence that she won't, and that's not the main point of the paragraph.
(D) Caline's employer seems kind and genuinely interested in Caline's feelings.

7. (A)
Category: Inference
Difficulty: Medium
Strategy: There is less information about the boy, so start there and eliminate answers. There's no evidence (even if it might be true) that he sees her as "lower class," and he does pay her attention by drawing her. Then, focus on Caline. Is she "deeply effected" or "mildly concerned." Her move suggests the former.
Solution: The boy draws Caline, and Caline ends up moving based on this brief encounter.
(B) While the boy could be looking at Caline in a technical way, Caline is not alarmed.
(C) There is nothing about class in this paragraph: no evidence.
(D) The boy does pay Caline attention by drawing her, and obsession would be too extreme a word to describe Caline's feelings towards him.

8. (A)
Category: Inference
Difficulty: Easy
Strategy: Seek evidence. While these things are mentioned in the passage, which actually relates to her family's work.
Solution: There are references to the "cotton field," and "Her father had halted his mule at the end of the cotton row."
(B) While there's a mule, there's no evidence that they raise animals as a source of income.
(C) While Caline becomes interested in the trains, there's no evidence that anyone from her family works there.
(D) While Caline works as a housekeeper later on in the story, that's not her family's main mode of employment.

9. (C)
Category: Words in Context
Difficulty: Easy
Strategy: Look for other words in this area of the passage to see what Caline is feeling.
Solution: Caline is "astonished" by the stopping of the train.
(A) There's no evidence that she's in a state of disorder
(B) Alternate meaning that doesn't fit here
(D) She does not look "simple"

10. (B)
Category: Words in Context
Difficulty: Easy
Strategy: Plug in. Life plan and train car don't work, and this paragraph is focused on clothing, so bundle of cotton doesn't make sense either. Also, line 10 mentions her "cotonade skirt."
Solution: An item of clothing - use context clues to figure that clothing, most likely a dress, would be mentioned along with her "shoes" and a "shawl"
(A) She does some new plans for her life, but that's not what is being discussed here.
(C) While made of cotton, the item itself is not a bundle of cotton.
(D) She is likely getting on a train, but, again, clothing is the topic here.

Information & Ideas – Fiction – Passage 3 – Pages 7-8

1. (B)
Category: Main Idea
Difficulty: Medium
Strategy: Pay attention to word usage. Strong adjectives and verbs are good clues for identifying tone.
Solution: This passage describes a woman who cannot let go of her deceased husband and clearly loves him very much. The lines her feeling less "alive" show this and the fact that she keeps going to see the movie in which he briefly appeared.
(A) Opposite. She can barely go on living without him.
(C) Misleading. She is loving, but overly attached.
(D) Misleading. While this seems to be true, it is not the best description. She is somewhat obsessed, but not necessarily overly so.

2. (D)
Category: Detail
Difficulty: Medium
Strategy: Find the part of the passage that addresses the question, try to find the answer on your own, then choose the answer choice that best answers the question.
Solution: The narrator says that going to see the movie will "bring him back to life" and refers to a world "that had ceased to be alive."
(A) Not true. The narrator makes it clear that he has died.
(B) Not true. The woman indicates that she will never see him again.
(C) Not true. She has no hope of seeing him again.

3. (C)
Category: Evidence
Difficulty: Medium
Strategy: Evidence questions ask readers to identify a part of the text that directly supports the previous question. If you noted evidence to answer the question prior to the evidence question, check to see if those lines are given in the answer choices.
Solution: The narrator says that watching the movie will "bring him back to life", indicating that Howie is dead.
(A) Doesn't answer the question. These lines only indicate that he is gone.
(B) Doesn't answer the question. These lines only indicate that he is gone.
(D) Misleading. She is not actually meeting her husband.

4. (B)
Category: Words-in-context
Difficulty: Medium
Strategy: Read above and below the given lines to understand context. Look for other uses of the word.
Solution: Meet is used figuratively to mean that the woman would see her husband in the movie.
(A) Not logical. Her husband is dead so they could not go on a date.
(C) Not logical. She could not encounter someone who is not alive.
(D) Not logical. She is not going to join him.

5. (B)
Category: Detail
Difficulty: Medium
Strategy: Reread the given lines and the surrounding sentences, try to find the answer on your own, then choose the answer choice that best answers the question.
Solution: Howie "was one of the people passing along a street which was being taken for the picture." "Chance" indicates that this was by accident.
(A) Not true. Howie only appeared for a moment in the movie.
(C) Not true. He was not in the movie on purpose.

(D) Not true. The movie was about a robbery, there was no actual crime.

6. (A)
Category: Detail
Difficulty: Medium
Strategy: Reread the given paragraph, try to find the answer on your own, then choose the answer choice that best answers the question.
Solution: This paragraph characterizes Howie as kind and compassionate by showing his interaction with the dog.
(B) Not true. He was gentle, but not standoffish.
(C) Not true. There is no evidence that he was playful or nosy.
(D) Not true. Howie was cheerful, but there is no evidence that he was private.

7. (C)
Category: Inference
Difficulty: Medium
Strategy: Draw a conclusion from the information given. Try to find the answer on your own, then choose the answer choice that best answers the question.
Solution: "That was why she had to keep coming—constantly reaching out for something that was not hers to keep." (lines 90-92)
(A) Not true. He was not employed in the making of the movie.
(B) Not true. The narrator says that it is a "tawdry, meaningless thing"
(D) Misleading. "Meet" is used in a figurative way.

8. (D)
Category: Evidence
Difficulty: Medium
Strategy: Evidence questions ask readers to identify a part of the text that directly supports the previous question. If you noted evidence to answer the question prior to the evidence question, check to see if those lines are given in the answer choices.
Solution: "reaching out for something that was not hers to keep" implies she can't let go and can't move on after the death of her husband.
(A) Not relevant. There is no mention of her main motive for continuing to go.
(B) Not relevant. There is no mention of her main motive for continuing to go.
(C) Not relevant. There is no mention of her main motive for continuing to go.

9. (C)
Category: Words in Context
Difficulty: Medium
Strategy: Consider what the author really means in the context. What is literally stated may not be the same as what ideas the author is conveying.
Solution: "Go out" is used to refer to life and to the scene with Howie. Both are fleeting and come to an end. "Cease" matches best with this idea.

10. (A)
Category: Inference
Difficulty: Hard
Strategy: Consider the perspective of the character. How does she feel?
Solution: She asks "Why should she turn from it?" because she anticipates people would tell her to stop obsessively watching the movie.

Information & Ideas – Fiction – Passage 4 – Pages 9-11

1. (D)
Category: Detail
Difficulty: Easy
Strategy: Revisit the first paragraph. The narrator is first given to Dr. Winter for care as a small child.
Solution: This aligns with information in the first paragraph.
(A) The narrator does become a doctor, but he's not trained by Dr. Winter, nor is this period in his life when they first meet.
(B) Dr. Winter does take on this role (briefly), but the narrator has met him previously.
(C) This is also in the first paragraph, but comes after the initial meeting.

2. (B)
Category: Detail
Difficulty: Medium
Strategy: Through mapping the passage, you'll have an idea of where Dr. Winter is physically described. Go back to paragraph two and look for evidence.
Solution: From paragraph two: "His face is of a walnut brown. It looks smooth at a little distance, but as you approach him you see that it is shot with innumerable fine wrinkles like a last year's apple."
(A) This doesn't describe his physical appearance, even though it's mentioned later in the passage.
(C) Again, this is part of what describes him, but not physically. ("He would shoo Death out of the room as though he were an intrusive hen."- paragraph four)
(D) This is used as part of a synonym describing Dr. Winter in paragraph four, but it does not relate to how he looks.

3. (A)
Category: Generalization
Difficulty: Easy
Strategy: Consider how the passage describes Dr. Winter overall.
Solution: The opening paragraph describes him as harsh, but later paragraphs describe his presence as hopeful. The narrator also describes the way Dr. Winter shuns some modern advances.
(B) While his methods are somewhat outdated, the passage is characterizing him as effective, not problematic.
(C) Modern doesn't fit here, and comprehensive is ill-suited as well.
(D) Dr. Winter appears to be effective, not ineffectual, though he is described as soothing.

4. (D)
Category: Compare & Contrast
Difficulty: Medium
Solution: At the very beginning, the narrator is fearful of Dr. Winter, but he grows to appreciate Dr. Winter when he becomes a medical professional himself. Choice D is the best option available.
(A) Neither are quite true. The narrator does not show concern as an adult, and he, at least at first, does not have fond feelings for the doctor.
(B) There is no evidence that the narrator depends on the doctor, and saying he will "only seek treatment" from Dr. Winter is too extreme.
(C) At first, the narrator only expresses fear in relation to Dr. Winter, and "surly" is an inaccurate way to categorize the narrator's description of Dr. Winter.

5. (C)
Category: Detail – Cause & Effect
Difficulty: Medium
Strategy: Revisit paragraph five and find the narrator's reasoning: "It was of Patterson... something more genial."

Solution: The reasons he gives for not wanting to see Dr. Patterson all relate to Dr. Patterson being technical and cold.
(A) He does see Dr. Patterson not feeling well, but this is not his reason for requesting Dr. Winter.
(B) He does consider Dr. Patterson very capable, as is shown earlier in this paragraph.
(D) Close, but not enough evidence. He does initially consider calling for Dr. Patterson.

6. (A)
Category: Main Idea
Difficulty: Medium
Strategy: Predict your answer. What is the passage saying overall? That Dr. Winter is effective even if he isn't using every bit of current medical knowledge.
Solution: Matches the predicted answer in a more general sense.
(B) Too broad. While this may be true, it doesn't convey the overall message of the passage.
(C) Opposite. Dr. Winter does quite well without being extremely current.
(D) No evidence. Dr. Winter is older but effective.

7. (B)
Category: Inference
Difficulty: Medium
Strategy: Process of elimination. Get rid of answers that don't work.
Solution: When the narrator requests Dr. Winter, Dr. Winter is already treating another doctor, so he appears the doctors prefer Dr. Winter over each other.
(A) There is nothing to suggest that Dr. Winter is not effective.
(C) He may be in high demand, but the season is not specified.
(D) Mrs. Hudson only states that he is busy; she does make any implications about his helpfulness.

8. (D)
Category: Inference
Difficulty: Medium
Strategy: Use context clues. The next sentence, "He carries one in his hat out of deference to the expectations of his patients," implies that he has one just because his patients expect him to.
Solution: His calling it a "toy" implies that he does not find it useful.
(A) He does not seem to value it as a tool.
(B) There is no evidence that he finds it difficult to use.
(C) The word "toy" is meant to imply uselessness, not fun.

9. (D)
Category: Words in Context
Difficulty: Easy
Strategy: Predict your answer. Based on the sentence, we are looking for a word that relates to illness since it's clear that the narrator is sick and that's what he's discussing here.
Solution: Affliction aligns with illness.
(A) Related to "scour" but not "scourge"
(B) Opposite.
(C) Another definition of scourge, but not what we're looking for here.

10. (A)
Category: Words in Context
Difficulty: Medium
Solution: Periods of time. The narrator is explaining how he marked different eras in his life.
(B) This is more about time, not problems, though the things happening to the narrator are unpleasant.
(C) While the passage has much to do with illness, that is not the definition here.
(D) Similar to troubles and also not correct.

Information & Ideas – Fiction – Passage 5 – Pages 12-13

1. **(C)**
Category: Detail
Difficulty: Easy
Strategy: Consider the context in the story. Come up with your own answer and see which answer choice matches best.
Solution: Shortly before this, Martand says he wants to "speak to Naresh about us", meaning the relationship between him and the narrator, Naresh's wife.
(A) There is no deceit about this.
(B) The peaches are irrelevant to their deception.
(D) Not related. This is known, not a matter of deception.

2. **(D)**
Category: Inference
Difficulty: Medium
Strategy: Imagine being in this situation. Why would a person bring peaches to visit someone with whom she is having an affair?
Solution: At the end of her visit, she remembers why she came. She brought peaches for Martand, which was a nice gesture and a reason to visit a person she likes spending time with. It can be assumed, because of their affair, that she looks for plausible excuses to see him.
(A) She doesn't need to demonstrate this to Martand.
(B) She doesn't need to demonstrate this to Martand.
(C) Martand is not a stranger.

3. **(C)**
Category: Main Idea
Difficulty: Medium
Strategy: What's the central focus of the passage? If you told someone about this story in one sentence, what would you say it's about?
Solution: The passage mainly focuses on the struggle to maintain the narrator and Martand's affair and their hope for the future.
(A) This is the context, but not the focus.
(B) Too narrow. This is one detail of the context.
(D) Too narrow. This is one event, but not the focus.

4. **(B)**
Category: Inference
Difficulty: Easy
Strategy: Consider how the narrator feels in the moment.
Solution: After hearing that Martand is dead, she cannot be moved by anything. This suggests she is stunned and feels deadened.
(A) Incorrect. These may sound like symptoms, but they are related to an emotional reaction.
(C) Not related. This is about much more important matters than peaches.
(D) She states she still has some senses. This is also too literal. Her loss of senses reflect her emotional state.

5. **(C)**
Category: Words in Context
Difficulty: Medium
Solution: The narrator describes the refugees seeking various forms of aid. The analogy she uses is of a robot wanting resources.
(A) Too specific. Doesn't fit the robot analogy.
(B) Too specific. Doesn't fit the robot analogy.
(D) Incorrect.

6. **(B)**
Category: Inference
Difficulty: Medium
Solution: Before this line, the narrator says she will not encourage Martand to visit her because this would be part of her double life. This suggests the double life is her relationship with him, which is "double" because she is also married to Naresh.
(A) Incorrect. The double life relates to her romantic multiple relationships.
(C) Incorrect. The double life relates to her romantic multiple relationships.
(D) Incorrect. The double life relates to her romantic multiple relationships.

7. **(D)**
Category: Evidence
Difficulty: Hard
Strategy: Consider how Martand died. Were there any details earlier in the story that relate to this?
Solution: Martand is killed by an employee. Lines 77-78 show the tension that led to this event.
(A) The refugees didn't harm Martand.
(B) Her safety relates to her comforts and marriage, not her life.
(C) The danger relates to relationships and heartbreak, not their lives.

8. **(A)**
Category: Inference
Difficulty: Medium
Strategy: Consider how Naresh relates to Martand. When do we get details about both of them?
Solution: Naresh mourned Martand, so he clearly respected him.
(B) He was not apparently aware of the affair.
(C) There is no indication they were related.
(D) There is no indication they worked together.

9. **(D)**
Category: Evidence
Difficulty: Medium
Strategy: Refer to the previous question. Evidence questions may be solved along with their paired questions, using the answer choices to search for a solution to the previous question.
Solution: Choice D shows Naresh mourning Martand.

10. **(B)**
Category: Words in Context
Difficulty: Medium
Strategy: Consider what the author is talking about in this context. The literal meaning may not be the author's intended idea.
Solution: The narrator is talking about the affair she has had with Martand. The "road" is their complicated situation they are working through in their lives.
(A) Too literal
(C) Not quite. The affair isn't a lifestyle, but a path in life
(D) Too literal

Information & Ideas – Global Conversation – Passage 1 – Pages 15-16

1.   (D)
Category: Detail
Difficulty: Medium
Solution: The author states "it is the wish of most masters within my knowledge to keep their slaves thus ignorant." (lines 6-8)
(A) Too broad. While the author does state that "white children could tell their ages", this does not follow that all non-whites could not. Indeed, the author states that "the larger part of the slaves know as little of their ages as horses know of theirs", implying that most, but not all, do not know their ages.
(B) Too narrow. The author states he has not seen any "authentic record" but there is no mention of a birth certificate.
(C) Not relevant. There is no mention of a law about slaves knowing their dates of birth.

2.   (D)
Category: Detail/Evidence
Difficulty: Easy
Solution: See explanations above as to why the first 3 answer choices are incorrect, and thus the evidence lines are also incorrect.

3.   (A)
Category: Main Idea
Difficulty: Medium
Strategy: Consider the central focus of the passage.
Solution: Taken overall, the author shares his sadness at not knowing his true age in paragraph 1. Paragraphs 2-5 address the tradition of separating slave children from their mothers, and the impact this had on the author. Paragraphs 3 and 5 discuss his lack of knowledge of who his father was and the commonness of this situation among slaves.
(B) Too narrow. Cruelty is not implied. Separation of slave children from their mothers is not addressed throughout the entire passage.
(C) Too broad. The passage is more specifically about age and parentage, rather than general misery.
(D) Not true. The author states in Paragraph 5 that it was "of little consequence" to his purpose to know who his father was.

4.   (C)
Category: Detail
Difficulty: Easy
Strategy: Consider the central focus of the paragraph.
Solution: The author explains why he only saw his mother 4 or 5 times in his life.
(A) Wrong part of the passage. This is addressed in Paragraph 3.
(B) Not relevant. His mother's feelings are not discussed.
(D) Not true. Because he hardly knew her, it felt like "the death of a stranger".

5.   (B)
Category: Inference
Difficulty: Medium
Strategy: Find the relevant information. Use process of elimination to find the best answer choice.
Solution: Lines 55-56 "…a whipping is the penalty of not being in the field at sunrise"
(A) Her reasons for not visiting during the day were not just due to the amount of work she had to accomplish.
(C) Not true. Slaves could travel during the day with "special permission from his or her master…" (lines 56-57)
(D) Not relevant. His mother's feelings are not discussed.

6.   (D)
Category: Inference
Difficulty: Medium
Strategy: Find the relevant information. Use process of elimination.
Solution: Lines 43-46 suggests that the reason for the practice was "…to hinder the development of the child's affection toward its mother, and to blunt and destroy the natural affection of the mother for the child…"
(A) Not true. There is nothing in the passage that suggests that women had to return to the fields quickly after birth.
(B) Not true. There is nothing in the passage about the need for children to live without their mothers.
(C) Not true. There is nothing comparing the cost of child care between mothers and older field hands.

7.   (D)
Category: Evidence
Difficulty: Medium
Solution: See explanations above as to why lines 42-46 substantiate the answer.

8.   (A)
Category: Words in Context
Difficulty: Medium
Solution: Intimation in this instance means a "hint, or suggestion". The author receives no information about the identity of his father.
(B) No. This is closer to the meaning of intimidation, which means to frighten or compel by threat.
(C) No. This is closer to the meaning of imitation.
(D) Opposite. In context, this would imply the author was "without the slightest question" of his father's identity, when in reality, he has no idea.

9.   (B)
Category: Words in Context
Difficulty: Easy
Solution: The idea is to weaken and destroy the affection of the mother for the child.
(A) Opposite. The idea is to damage, not build up, the affection of the mother for the child.
(C) Opposite. The idea is to damage, not build up, the affection of the mother for the child.
(D) Not relevant. Decry means to speak out against, not have a negative effect upon, the affection of the mother for the child.

10.   (C)
Category: Detail – Compare & Contrast
Difficulty: Medium
Strategy: Use process of elimination.
Solution: Douglass states that most slave children were separated from their mothers and didn't know their fathers. (lines 35-38; lines 76-86)
(A) Wrong conclusion. While he didn't know his own age, this was common to most slaves.
(B) Wrong conclusion. While his mother was allowed to visit him, he only saw her 4 or 5 times, and this was common to other slave children.
(D) The discussion of his grandparents isn't connected to his treatment.

Information & Ideas – Global Conversation – Passage 2 – Pages 17-19

1.   (C)
Category: Main Idea
Difficulty: Medium
Strategy: Consider the main argument made by the passage as a whole.
Solution: Rousseau's overall premise is that "to renounce liberty is to renounce being a man, to surrender the rights of humanity and even its duties". (lines 41-43)
(A)   Too narrow. Rousseau only addresses family unit in paragraph 1.
(B)   Too narrow. Rousseau only addresses civil tranquility in response to a possible counter-argument.
(D)   Too narrow. Rousseau addresses the role of kings in part of his larger argument about liberty.

2.   (D)
Category: Inference
Difficulty: Medium
Strategy: Refer to the discussion of family in the first paragraph.
Solution: Rousseau discusses the family unit as a model for his introduction to his thoughts on liberty. (lines 11-15) He uses this as a relatable example to introduce his deeper analysis of politics.
(A)   Not true. While Rousseau sees the role of the family as a natural element of society, he notes that as soon as "need ceases", this bond is dissolved. (lines 4, 5)
(B)   Incorrect. The paragraph suggests children use family to satisfy needs.
(C)   Opposite. Rousseau notes the natural progression of children from dependence to independence.

3.   (D)
Category: Detail/Evidence
Difficulty: Medium
Solution: See explanations above as to why lines 11-15 substantiate the answer.

4.   (A)
Category: Words in Context
Difficulty: Medium
Solution: Subjects hoped to at least receive basic needs in exchange for their service.
(B)   Too abstract. Subjects were focused on receiving physical needs.
(C)   Too abstract. Subjects were not looking for privileges from kings.
(D)   Too abstract. Their focus was on basic needs for living, not honor.

5.   (B)
Category: Detail
Difficulty: Hard
Strategy: Reread the portion of the passage and consider how it relates to the author's argument.
Solution: Rousseau saw no value in civil tranquility if it resulted in misery or death. (lines 36-38)
(A)   Opposite. Rousseau saw no advantage in civil tranquility as a substitute for liberty
(C)   Irrelevant. There is no comparison between modern society and Greek civilization.
(D)   Opposite. He saw the prisoners' tranquility as absurd. (line 40)

6.   (B)
Category: Main Idea
Difficulty: Medium
Strategy: Consider the central argument made by the passage.
Solution: Wollstonecraft sees the "perfection of man" rising from the "establishment of true civilization". (lines 109-110)
(A)   Too narrow. While Wollstonecraft acknowledges her belief in the "perfection of God", she doesn't equate this belief with happiness.

(C)   Too narrow. Wollstonecraft's focus is on the benefits of civilization, not on the curse of mankind.
(D)   Too extreme. Wollstonecraft notes the presence of evil, but argues that it was "designed by God to take place" (lines 94-95)

7.   (A)
Category: Detail
Difficulty: Medium
Strategy: Use process of elimination.
Solution: Wollstonecraft states in lines 93-95, "Firmly persuaded that no evil exists in the world that God did not design to take place, I build my belief on the perfection of God."
(B)   Opposite. Wollstonecraft views Rousseau's hypothesis as false. (line 57)
(C)   Irrelevant. Wollstonecraft makes no mention of Greek philosophy.
(D)   Too broad. While Wollstonecraft addresses good and evil, they are not the basis for her argument.

8.   (D)
Category: Inference
Difficulty: Easy
Strategy: Find reference to the "natural state of mankind".
Solution: Wollstonecraft views the original state of nature as barbarism. (line 99)
Explanations:
(A)   Opposite. Wollstonecraft sees humanity as progressing towards godlike happiness, not possessing it innately.
(B)   Opposite. Wollstonecraft sees humanity as progressing towards godlike happiness, not ignorance.
(C)   Not true. This is Rousseau's argument, not Wollstonecraft's.

9.   (A)
Category: Inference
Difficulty: Easy
Strategy: Find reference to Rousseau's beliefs.
Solution: Wollstonecraft calls his arguments "plausible but unsound" and "false". (lines 57-59)
(B)   Opposite. Wollstonecraft disagrees with Rousseau throughout her argument.
(C)   Too positive. While she may see his arguments as plausible, she concludes they are both unsound and false.
(D)   Too extreme. Wollstonecraft presents a reasoned response to his claims.

10.   (B)
Category: Detail – Compare & Contrast
Difficulty: Medium
Strategy: Consider the author's central argument.
Solution: Wollstonecraft, sees "the perfection of man in the establishment of true civilization"
(A)   Not true. Wollstonecraft, sees "the perfection of man in the establishment of true civilization"
(C)   Too extreme. Wollstonecraft sees humanity as moving towards perfection (see above) not as having already achieved it.
(D)   Not stated. Wollstonecraft believes in God, but never states that only God is perfect.

11.   (B)
Category: Detail – Compare & Contrast
Difficulty: Medium
Strategy: Use process of elimination.
Solution: Both consider the role played by civilization on humanity.
(A)   Not true. Only Rousseau discusses liberty.
(C)   Not true. Rousseau makes no mention of God.
(D)   Not true. Only Rousseau addresses civil tranquility.

Information & Ideas – Global Conversation – Passage 3 – Pages 20-22

1. (D)
Category: Detail
Difficulty: Medium
Strategy: Consider the author's overall tone when discussing lives of labor. The author is critical and lamenting. He argues a farmer's life is too busy to allow the pursuit of more meaningful things.
Solution: The above quote shows that the author of passage one believes this life is empty.
(A) "Evil" is too extreme, and the author does not see it as a necessity.
(B) This passage doesn't mention government, though passage 2 does.
(C) While this may be inherited, the author doesn't view this as fortunate.

2. (B)
Category: Detail/Evidence
Difficulty: Medium
Strategy: Read each quote and select the one that best supports your answer to the previous question. If you are unsure about the previous question, look for matches between the quotes and answer selections.
Solution: See explanations above – lines 28-32 substantiate the answer. Other answer choices mention elements of this idea, but don't directly address the whole idea as well as choice B.

3. (A)
Category: Inference
Difficulty: Medium
Strategy: Reread the questions in paragraph one and consider how they contribute to the author's argument.
Solution: The author is using these sentences to question why things are done in this way.
(B) This may be true, but choice A is a more accurate fit.
(C) The author doesn't seem unsure about why people would take these jobs, just why it is done this way.
(D) The author isn't confused.

4. (B)
Category: Detail
Difficulty: Easy
Strategy: Try to locate the part of the passage where Thoreau talks about "fruit" and gentle handling and think about what that fruit would represent in this passage.
Solution: Lines 42-44
(A) Too literal
(C) Coarse labors do not need to be handled gently.
(D) This refers to the man himself; he does not have to be handled gently.

5. (A)
Category: Detail
Difficulty: Easy
Strategy: Reread the first paragraph of Passage B
Solution: In the first paragraph, Burke directly says to let government protect industry and property. Outside of his specific list of duties, he says, "the less they meddle in these affairs, the better."

6. (C)
Category: Main Idea/Generalization
Difficulty: Medium
Strategy: Reread the paragraph, think about the point Burke makes.
Solution: Burke argues that hard work is a "condition of mankind" that is "tempered with many alleviations, many comforts".
(A) Working "is the common due of man" is stated, but it is leading to the main idea.
(B) This is expressed, but it is not the main idea.
(D) This is stated, but is not the main idea.

7. (C)
Category: Evidence
Difficulty: Medium
Strategy: Read each quote and select the one that best supports your answer to the previous question. If you are unsure about the previous question, look for matches between the quotes and the answer selections.
Solution: See explanations above as to why lines 68-71 substantiate the answer.

8. (A)
Category: Detail
Difficulty: Medium
Solution: Both are addressed only in passage 2.
(B) Ignorance is mentioned in passage 1.
(C) Laziness is not mentioned in passage 2.
(D) Inheritance is discussed in passage 1.

9. (B)
Category: Detail – Compare & Contrast
Difficulty: Medium
Solution: The author of passage 1 thinks workers miss out, while the author passage 2 thinks workers are doing fine.
(A) Neither author considers the laborers themselves or the government the root of the problem.
(C) There's not enough evidence to support that the author of passage 2 finds this idea foolish.
(D) Opposite.

10. (A)
Category: Detail – Cause & Effect
Difficulty: Medium
Strategy: Reread the first paragraph of passage 1, which outlines the author's feelings on inheriting a farm.
Solution: This best matches how the author feels: "I see young men… were called to labor in."
(B) There is no mention of fortune.
(C) Too extreme.
(D) Nothing about the work being temporary, even though it is described as difficult.

11. (D)
Category: Main Idea
Difficulty: Medium
Strategy: Mapping the passage will help with this question as well as keeping in mind that you're looking for the best answer, not just a close or somewhat accurate answer.
Solution: "This affected pity only tends to dissatisfy them with their condition." (lines 83-84)
(A) While the author doesn't appear to pity the workers, the reasoning here is flawed.
(B) While this answer uses some words from the passage, it's inaccurate.
(C) This answer may seem like it could be true, there's not enough evidence to support it.

12. (C)
Category: Words in Context
Difficulty: Medium
Strategy: Predict your answer. You're looking for something that means "provoke" or "stir up."
Solution: Elicit means bring out.
(A) Galvanize is close, but c) is a better answer choice.
(B) Wrong meaning.
(D) While this word may be familiar, it is not a synonym for excite.

Information & Ideas – Global Conversation – Passage 4 – Pages 23-25

1. (C)
Category: Main Idea
Difficulty: Medium
Strategy: Reread the portion in question and summarize the main idea in your own words. Choose the answer that best answers the question.
Solution: This paragraph discusses previous instances when the US led times of innovation and uses it as encouragement and reasoning for the US to lead the age of space.
(A) Too narrow. This paragraph mentions the Industrial Revolution, but it is not the main idea.
(B) Too broad. The passage discusses the quest for knowledge and progress, but it does not discuss or focus on its timeline.
(D) Not stated. Costs were discussed previously in the passage, but are not mentioned in this paragraph.

2. (A)
Category: Detail
Difficulty: Medium
Strategy: Use the answer choices in the following Evidence question to help guide your consideration of the answer choices for this question.
Solution: In the second paragraph, the author discusses how the speed of progress must create new problems.
(B) Misleading. The author discusses desires of others to wait.
(C) Not stated. The author discusses recorded history as a metaphor, condensing the timeline to 50 years.
(D) Misleading. The author says "today" while still metaphorically talking about time in a condensed "capsule" of history.

3. (C)
Category: Evidence
Difficulty: Medium
Strategy: Use this question to help answer the previous question. Reread the given lines, and find the lines that support the answer to the previous question.
Solution: Lines 22-24 discuss the costs associated with the pace of progress.
(A) Not relevant. These lines discuss significant events of human history in the metaphorically condensed 50-year timeline.
(B) Not relevant. These lines discuss recent and possible events of human history in the metaphorically condensed 50-year timeline.
(D) Wrong part of the passage. While these lines discuss the costs, they do not discuss the incredible pace of progress.

4. (B)
Category: Inference
Difficulty: Medium
Solution: The passage states that as the US was conquered, space will also be, and he uses this as reasoning not to wait.
(A) Opposite. The author is refuting those who would wait.
(C) Wrong part of the passage. This is correct, but found in paragraph 5.
(D) Not stated. The author addresses Texas, but not necessarily because it does not support the space program.

5. (D)
Category: Words in Context.
Difficulty: Medium
Solution: In this context, "complete" most nearly means "entire" or "comprehensive."
(A) Wrong meaning. In context, "complete" is not referring to a task that can be finished. Rather, "complete" here is referring to "how much."
(B) Not a possible definition.
(C) Not a possible definition.

6. (A)
Category: Main Idea
Difficulty: Medium
Strategy: Reread the paragraph in question and summarize the main idea in one sentence. Choose the answer that best addresses the question.
Solution: The paragraph discusses many points, but the central ideas focus around the continuation of the program and the public sharing of information.
(B) Too narrow. This is only mentioned in one sentence.
(C) Wrong part of the passage. The idea of the Challenger crew leading the US is found in paragraph 4.
(D) Wrong part of the passage. This is mentioned in paragraph 4.

7. (C)
Category: Inference
Difficulty: Medium
Strategy: Use process of elimination
Solution: Lines 80-82 argues this event will pull us forward.
(A) Not stated. The statement "the future does not belong to the fainthearted" is broader than space exploration.
(B) Misleading. The paragraph addresses children, but its contents are part of the overarching argument.
(D) Wrong part of the passage. The discussion of secrets and freedom is in paragraph 5.

8. (D)
Category: Synthesis
Difficulty: Hard
Strategy: Try to answer the question on your own using the authors' arguments. Choose the option that best answers the question.
Solution: The last paragraph of Passage 1 argues that man is unstoppable in his quest for progress and knowledge. However, the author of Passage 2 does not mention anything of the sort.
(A) This is in paragraph 3 of Passage 1 and paragraph 5 of Passage 2.
(B) This is in paragraph 2 of Passage 1 and paragraph 4 of Passage 2.
(C) This idea is found in the example of William Bradford in Passage 1 and in the example of Sir Francis Drake in Passage 2.

9. (A)
Category: Synthesis
Difficulty: Medium
Strategy: Try to find your own answer using the author's arguments and descriptions. Choose the answer that best answers the question.
Solution: In paragraph 3, the author of Passage 2 describes the Challenger crew as pioneers. Later, he compares the crew to Sir Francis Drake, an explorer. This emphasizes the comparison of space exploration to exploring new lands.
(B) Misleading. The author of passage 2 refers to Sir Francis Drake as an explorer. His connection to Panama is not the focus here.
(C) Not stated.
(D) Not stated. The author mentions journeys when discussing the continuation of the space program, but he did not refer directly to space exploration in this statement.

10. (B)
Category: Words in Context
Difficulty: Medium
Strategy: Consider the context. Reread the sentence with the answer choices in the word's place and see which works best.
Solution: The narrator says great actions and difficulties must both be engaged.

Information & Ideas – Global Conversation – Passage 5 – Pages 26-28

1. **(B)**
Category: Detail
Difficulty: Medium
Solution: The author states that "In half of the world, we see rapid progress and development. However, there are many countries where millions still suffer from the very old problems of war, poverty, and injustice," (lines 33-37). This discusses the division of the world into development and war, poverty, and injustice.
(A) This text discusses the right to education, but never discusses a clear division between places with education and places where there is no education.
(C) This article discusses the transformation of Swat from a place with tourism to a place of terrorism, but the division here is between past Swat and current Swat. The author is not discussing the world at large.
(D) Not relevant. The author discusses freedom of speech when discussing her own actions.

2. **(D)**
Category: Evidence
Difficulty: Medium
Solution: Lines 33-37 discuss the world at large. The author discusses development as opposed to old problems of war, poverty, and injustice.

3. **(C)**
Category: Main Idea
Difficulty: Medium
Solution: Using rhetorical questions, the passage argues that girls should have the right to an education. This is closest to answer choice C.
(A) Opposite. The author states that education is a right.
(B) Misleading. This point is mentioned in this paragraph, but it is mentioned in order to make a point about education being a right for girls as well.
(D) Misleading. The author uses rhetorical questions to make an argument about the right to education.

4. **(B)**
Category: Main Idea
Difficulty: Medium
Strategy: Revisit each paragraph and try to summarize them into a single statement. Find the answer choice that is closest to this summary.
Solution: All of the paragraphs discuss education as a right to all students. In paragraph four, the author discusses her decision to speak up, and in the last paragraph, the author urges others to stand up as well.
(A) Too narrow. While the author discusses her experiences in Swat, she discusses education as a universal right.
(C) Too narrow. The author makes this point, but it is not the main idea of the entire passage.
(D) Not stated. The passage mentions the destruction of schools in Swat but never states that they should be rebuilt.

5. **(B)**
Category: Words in Context
Difficulty: Medium
Solution: In context, "legions" most closely means "a lot" or "many."
(A) Wrong meaning. The word cannot logically mean a group of soldiers in this context.
(C) Not logical. This does not make sense in context and is not a possible definition of the word.
(D) Opposite meaning. In context, the word must mean a large amount in order for the author to make his argument.

6. **(C)**
Category: Main Idea
Difficulty: Medium
Solution: The author includes Eugene Talmadge as an example of an intelligent man ("one of the better minds") without morals or character ("yet he contends that I am an inferior being").
(A) Opposite. The example is included to show education cannot stop at thinking critically, which was one of the capabilities of Eugene.
(B) Not stated. The author includes the rhetorical question "Are those the types of men we call educated?" anticipating negative response.
(D) Not stated. The example does not discuss how Eugene Talmadge was educated. It implies there was a lack of one aspect of his education.

7. **(D)**
Category: Inference
Difficulty: Medium
Strategy: Using the author's arguments, answer the question on your own, and then find the answer choice that best matches your answer.
Solution: Lines 102-105 support this argument.
(A) Too extreme. The author implies criticism to current education systems, but doesn't condemn all education through history.
(B) Not stated. Lines 102-105 refer to "accumulated knowledge of the race" but place it on the same level as experience of social living.
(C) Too extreme. The term "impervious" is extreme and should be a warning sign. The author argues that education should help people discern propaganda, but it does not claim that anyone could be impervious to propaganda.

8. **(B)**
Category: Detail
Difficulty: Medium
Strategy: Revisit the lines concerning the question. Try to find the answer on your own.
Solution: The author finds a "misconception" about the purpose of education in the discussions among his colleagues, which reveals choice B where he "finds faults" with their discussions as the answer.
(A) Opposite. The author does not think that the discussions concern the "proper" reasons.
(C) Opposite. The author does not agree with his colleagues.
(D) Misleading. This is the opinion of some of the author's colleagues.

9. **(A)**
Category: Synthesis
Difficulty: Medium
Strategy: Try to answer the question on your own and choose the answer choice that best answers the question.
Solution: The last paragraph argues that if we are not careful in our education, society will be full of people "consumed with immoral acts."
(B) Misleading. The author is not defending this aspect of education, but stating that it is only a part of what education needs to be.
(C) Misleading. The author is not defending this aspect of education, but stating that it is only a part of what education needs to be.
(D) Incorrect. Intelligence factors into education, but not by being measured.

10. **(D)**
Category: Synthesis
Difficulty: Easy
Solution: The thoughtful and moral components are integral to Passage 2's main point.
(A) Misleading. This is the focus of passage 1.
(B) Irrelevant. "Bull sessions" are discussed only to contrast the author's perspective with the perspectives of his peers.
(C) Irrelevant. The author occasionally mentions colleges as a place of education but does not focus on it in his argument.

Information & Ideas – Sciences – Passage 1 – Pages 30-31

1. (C)
Category: Detail
Difficulty: Easy
Strategy: Ignore "except" and scan passage for specific names. The name *not* found will be the exception.
Solution: Although, as a physician, Albert Schweitzer may have known of silver's antiseptic properties, he is not mentioned in this passage.
(A) Not true. Marion Sims pioneered suturing with silver wire (lines 57-58).
(B) Not true. Carl Nageli researched silver's oligodynamic effect (lines 50-52).
(D) Not true. Hippocrates used silver in dressing wounds (lines 54-56).

2. (B)
Category: Words in Context
Difficulty: Medium
Strategy: Replace "standard" with each answer option. Choose the best replacement given the intent of the sentence.
Solution: Since widespread, common use is implied here, norm is the best choice.
(A) Not true. Opposite of intended meaning.
(C) Wrong meaning of the word. Common usage, not quality, is the focus.
(D) Wrong meaning of the word. Tradition involves a passing on from generation to generation, while lines 66-67 speak of "new forms of antimicrobial dressings."

3. (D)
Category: Detail – Compare & Contrast
Difficulty: Easy
Strategy: Skim lines mentioned and eliminate answers that are wrong or not applicable.
Solution: Condense lines 69-73 to read: "Unlike…mercury…and lead,… silver is very low in toxicity for humans." Answer D is correct.
(A) Not true.
(B) Opposite.
(C) Not stated.

4. (B)
Category: Inference
Difficulty: Medium
Strategy: Eliminate obviously false answers.
Solution: Lines 67-68 refer to "the standard in…medicine cabinets of today," so widespread modern use is implied.
(A) Opposite.
(C) Not stated.
(D) Not stated. Usage may have improved, but silver's antiseptic properties remain unchanged.

5. (A)
Category: Main Idea
Difficulty: Medium
Strategy: Summarize the purpose of the paragraph in one sentence.
Solution: The paragraph explains theories and studies about how some materials are antibacterial.
(B) Not stated
(C) Cultural traditions are not discussed
(D) Not stated that the effects are limited to only the bacteria mentioned

6. (B)
Category: Detail
Difficulty: Easy
Strategy: Ignore "except" and scan passage beginning at line 74, where modern medicine's use of the oligodynamic effect is the focus. Narrow choices until the one remains.
Solution: Bandages lined with silver foil were phased out by the end of World War II (lines 61-63) and replaced with the "new forms of antimicrobial dressings" used today (lines 66-68).
(A) Implants and prosthetics are mentioned (lines 83-85).
(C) Infant pink eye solution is mentioned (lines 79-82).
(D) Silver sulfadiazine is mentioned (lines 75-79).

7. (D)
Category: Words in Context
Difficulty: Easy
Strategy: Replace "ubiquitous" with each answer choice. Choose the word that is closest in meaning.
Solution: Prior to the invention of digital thermometers, glass thermometers filled with mercury were the norm. Since these thermometers would be a non-functional glass tube without the enclosed mercury, the mercury was ever-present.
(A) Not true. Opposite of intended meaning.
(B) Wrong meaning. Using mercury in glass thermometers was *the* standard, it was not simply a favored choice among multiple options.
(C) Wrong meaning. While mercury-filled glass thermometers are now discouraged due to mercury's toxicity, frequency of use is the focus here.

8. (D)
Category: Main Idea
Difficulty: Easy
Strategy: Summarize the passage in one sentence.
Solution: Silver is the overwhelming passage focus, specifically its common use (paragraph 2), oligodynamic effect (paragraph 3), and function in historical and modern medicine (paragraphs 4 and 5).
(A) Partially true. Silver, however, is the overwhelming focus.
(B) False. These are only briefly mentioned
(C) False. Mentioned briefly in introduction, but not the focus.

9. (D)
Category: Detail – Cause & Effect
Difficulty: Easy
Strategy: Eliminate answers that are incorrect or not stated.
Solution: Answer D is implied in paragraph 4 and affirmed in paragraph 5.
(A) Opposite
(B) Opposite
(C) Not stated.

10. (C)
Category: Evidence
Difficulty: Medium
Strategy: Find the reference to modern medicine using silver.
Solution: Lines 74-76 state that modern medicine relies on silver.
(A) Not modern
(B) Not modern
(D) Not medical

Information & Ideas – Sciences – Passage 2 – Pages 32-33

1. (C)
Category: Detail
Difficulty: Easy
Strategy: Find references to how corn compares to teosinte.
Solution: Line 29 states corn and teosinte have identical chromosomes.
(A) Line 20 – Teosinte is green, not a common color for corn
(B) Line 21 – Teosinte seeds are triangular, unlike corn kernels, which are rounded
(D) Line 20 – Teosinte seeds are small. This isn't necessarily smaller than corn kernels, but there is no indication of similarity, and it's implied that teosinte seeds are *particularly* small. Choice C is more directly contrasted.

2. (B)
Category: Detail
Difficulty: Easy
Strategy: Find the reference to the tgal gene.
Solution: Lines 45-47 states the tgal gene is responsible for the hardness of the seed casing.
(A) Wrong part of the passage. Not related to tgal.
(C) Wrong part of the passage. Not related to tgal.
(D) Not mentioned.

3. (B)
Category: Words in Context
Difficulty: Easy
Strategy: Read the context for clues.
Solution: The sentence is about the benefit of seeds falling off. It can be inferred this would lead to more spreading of the plant.

4. (A)
Category: Main Idea
Difficulty: Medium
Strategy: Find the explanation for the evolution of teosinte.
Solution: The last paragraph describes how teosinte evolved because migratory people cultivated ideal specimens.
(B) Not performed in labs
(C) Not mentioned
(D) Climate not mentioned

5. (C)
Category: Evidence
Difficulty: Medium
Strategy: Review the answer choices to see which fits best.
Solution: Lines 56-58 directly discusses the active efforts that shaped the evolution of teosinte.

6. (D)
Category: Detail
Difficulty: Easy
Strategy: Use process of elimination.
Solution: Only D is mentioned as a trait unique to teosinte. This is described in lines 64-72.
(A) They are similar in this regard.
(B) Not mentioned.
(C) Not mentioned.

7. (D)
Category: Detail
Difficulty: Easy
Strategy: Find the reference to teosinte breeding.
Solution: The last passage begins with the origins of teosinte cultivation, stating it was 9000 years ago in Central America.
(A) Tgal was recently discovered.
(B) That was when research on teosinte began, but not its breeding.
(C) Not related.

8. (C)
Category: Words in Context
Difficulty: Medium
Strategy: Consider the context. Reread the sentence with the answer choices replacing the word.
Solution: Scientists discovered every element of the genes of the corncob. "fully documented" fits best in this context.
(A) "drawn" isn't quite right.
(B) "copied" isn't what the scientists did.
(D) The genes weren't grown but studied.

9. (C)
Category: Evidence
Difficulty: Medium
Strategy: Find a reference to an evolved trait that would not have occurred naturally.
Solution: Teosinte's seeds' tendency to fall off was valuable for the plant, but not for people, so cultivators bred the trait out of the plant.

10. (B)
Category: Main Idea
Difficulty: Medium
Strategy: Consider the central point the author is making.
Solution: Use process of elimination to find that B is the best fit.
(A) Too narrow.
(C) Not mentioned.
(D) Wrong part of the passage.

Information & Ideas – Sciences – Passage 3 – Pages 34-35

1. (B)
Category: Detail
Difficulty: Easy
Strategy: Find the reference to who brought sweet potatoes to Polynesia. Focus on the sequence of events and which came first.
Solution: Lines 61-64 state the sweet potato was first retrieved Polynesians.
(A) Lines 67-70 states this happened later (subsequently)
(C) Lines 67-70 – James Cook was a European explorer (lines 42-43) and lines 67-70 state they came later.
(D) Native Andeans grew potatoes, but the Polynesians brought them back with them.

2. (D)
Category: Evidence
Difficulty: Medium
Strategy: Review the answer choices to see which fits best.
Solution: Lines 61-64 state the sweet potato was first retrieved by Polynesians.

3. (A)
Category: Detail
Difficulty: Hard
Strategy: Find references to other experiments. Use process of elimination.
Solution: Lines 30-32 describe earlier experiments that relied on genetic profiles of modern day varieties of sweet potatoes. This fits with A.
(B) Not mentioned.
(C) Not mentioned.
(D) This is mentioned, but it's not the stated difference with the recent experiment.

4. (B)
Category: Detail
Difficulty: Hard
Strategy: Find the reference to recent evidence.
Solution: Note the question specifies *recent* evidence. Line 22-23 state archaeologists found sweet potato remnants from before 1100 C.E., which would predate Columbian contact (which the passage implies is around 1500 C.E.).
(A) The words are similar, but this doesn't indicate the time.
(C) European explorers came later that 1100 C.E.
(D) Spain and Portugal got the sweet potations after 1100 C.E.

5. (B)
Category: Inference
Difficulty: Medium
Strategy: Read the context for clues and find the most logical answer choice.
Solution: Lines 67-73 state that new varieties were created when old varieties were mixed.
(A) The sweet potato wasn't technically "reintroduced." Rather, new types were introduced to regions that already had other types.
(C) Not related.
(D) Not mentioned.

6. (D)
Category: Main Idea
Difficulty: Easy
Strategy: Consider the main focus of the passage. If you had to summarize the passage in one sentence, what would you say it is about?
Solution: The focus is on an experiment that uncovered the history of the sweet potato and how that relates to ancient people's interactions.
(A) Not about colonization directly.
(B) Not about modern routes.
(C) Not about art.

7. (A)
Category: Detail
Difficulty: Medium
Strategy: Find the reference to why the study was conducted. Use process of elimination.
Solution: Lines 12-13 state that examining agriculture, such as sweet potatoes, can reveal how people migrated.
(B) Not mentioned.
(C) Not mentioned.
(D) Not mentioned.

8. (B)
Category: Words in Context
Difficulty: Hard
Strategy: Read context for clues.
Solution: Note that lines 39-40 compare "modern" to "herbarium samples," which suggests they are not modern.

9. (A)
Category: Detail
Difficulty: Easy
Strategy: Find the reference to the introduction of sweet potatoes to Polynesia.
Solution: The earliest reference is "before 1100 C.E." so A is the best option.

10. (C)
Category: Detail
Difficulty: Easy
Strategy: Find the reference to where sweet potatoes were brought from.
Solution: Lines 61-62 state the sweet potato is native to Ecuador and Peru. Also, lines 6-7 suggest it's from South America.

Information & Ideas – Sciences – Passage 4 – Pages 36-37

1. (C)
Category: Detail
Difficulty: Medium
Strategy: Reread the description of the Burj Khalifa in paragraph 4. Find a statement about the design of spires.
Solution: Note that the uneven design is termed "unique."
(A) Many skyscrapers are built with smooth skins.
(B) The use of staggered rises makes the building resemble a lightning bolt.
(D) Burj Khalifa does not have skyscrapers around it.

2. (D)
Category: Detail
Difficulty: Medium
Strategy: Use process of elimination.
Solution: Most skyscrapers are built in cities with many other tall buildings.
(A) The article does not address the effects of skyscrapers on other buildings.
(B) Buildings are not (typically) built to lean.
(C) Only Taipei 101 is said to use a counterweight.

3. (C)
Category: Main Idea
Difficulty: Medium
Strategy: Summarize the passage as if you were telling someone what it is about.
Solution: The article focuses on different ways engineers combat the greatest danger to skyscrapers: the wind.
(A) This answer is too broad. The article does not deal with structural issues outside of wind resistance.
(B) This answer is too narrow. While the article describes the beauty and design of the Baj Khalifa, it discusses other buildings and focuses on wind.
(D) This answer is too narrow. The article mentions 3 skyscrapers and their locations in the process of making its point.

4. (D)
Category: Detail
Difficulty: Medium
Strategy: Read the answer choices carefully. Reread paragraph 3.
Solution: The wind vortices exert pressure on one side and then the other, rocking the building.
(A) The article does not discuss relative wind strengths.
(B) The article says the wind vortices pull the building in different directions.
(C) The article does not discuss wind direction.

5. (C)
Category: Words in context
Difficulty: Easy
Strategy: Read the sentence with the various word choices substituted for the word in question.
Solution: In context, "looming" refers to the great height of buildings standing above everything.
(A) Pagodas and turrets do not weave together.
(B) Sequoia trees and pagodas are not threatening.
(D) These things do not arrive while we are watching.

6. (D)
Category: Inference
Difficulty: Medium
Strategy: Find a statement that can be assumed to be true based on the article, but that is not stated within it.
Solution: The article states that there is no limit to potential future building heights.
(A) Engineers are still working on better strategies.
(B) The article states there are other effective approaches.
(C) The article states the opposite.

7. (B)
Category: Detail
Difficulty: Easy
Strategy: Find the "golden orb" and read the section around it.
Solution: Reread lines 84-87 (Termed   earthquakes)
(A) The article does not discuss decorations.
(C) The pendulum is not a timepiece
(D) The article states sideways forces (wind and shaking) are a bigger threat than downward forces (gravity).

8. (A)
Category: Main Idea
Difficulty: Medium
Strategy: Determine what the author wants you to know. What is the central focus of the passage?
Solution: The article explains the danger of wind and then how engineers have successfully dealt with it.
(B) Too narrow. This is just an introduction to the topic.
(C) Too narrow. This is used to close the article.
(D) Too broad. The focus is on one type of engineering.

9. (D)
Category: Evidence
Difficulty: Medium
Strategy: Look for lines that support your answer to #8.
Solution: The quote states that there are more than one way to combat the wind, which is the main focus of the passage.
(A) Off topic
(B) States the problem of wind pressure, but does not discuss solutions.
(C) Too narrow. Talks of one method and one building.

10. (A)
Category: Words in Context
Difficulty: Easy
Strategy: Replace the word with the answer choices and see which works best in context.
Solution: The sentence is about the force of wind impacting a building. "Assaults" isn't a perfect fit because it's a bit too extreme, but it's the best answer choice available.

Information & Ideas – Sciences – Passage 5 – Pages 38-39

1. (C)
Category: Words in Context
Difficulty: Easy
Strategy: Replace "monumental" with each answer word, looking for a synonym that retains the meaning of the sentence.
Solution: Monumental refers to the degree of difficulty of the task, which was significant.
(A) Wrong meaning.
(B) Monumental can refer to size, but not in this way.
(D) Opposite.

2. (C)
Category: Detail – Cause & Effect
Difficulty: Easy
Strategy: Skim appropriate section of passage, then eliminate wrong answers.
Solution: Lines 80-82 state that the Voyagers' nuclear batteries will fail "in only a few years, at which point we will no longer hear from them."

3. (D)
Category: Inference
Difficulty: Hard
Strategy: Consider which answer choice has the most direct support in the passage.
Solution: Specific word choice implies the author's appreciation of the Voyagers and their discs: *groundbreaking discoveries* (line 14), *precious cargo* (line 20), *serving as a legacy* (line 93).
(A) Possible, but no direct indication in the passage
(B) No indication
(C) Possible, but no direct indication in the passage

4. (A)
Category: Words in Context
Difficulty: Easy
Strategy: Consider the meaning of the word within the sentence (lines 92-96).
Solution: A legacy is something of significance (positive or negative) passed from one generation to the next.
(B) Not logical given context.
(C) Wrong meaning.
(D) Wrong connotation. A legacy implies something significant, whereas a leftover implies something insignificant.

5. (D)
Category: Detail – Compare & Contrast
Difficulty: Easy
Strategy: Eliminate obviously wrong answers. Correct answer will be mentioned in text.
Solution: Voyager 2 is described as "unlike its predecessor" (line 9) because "it still has working instruments that will be able to send back data" (lines 10-11).
(A) Not true. Both were launched in 1977 (lines 3-4, 7-8).
(B) Not stated. Both were "designed to explore the gas giants of our solar system" (lines 11-13).
(C) False. Each carries a "Golden Record" (lines 19-22).

6. (B)
Category: Evidence
Difficulty: Easy
Solution: Voyager 2 is described as "unlike its predecessor" (line 9) because "it still has working instruments that will be able to send back data" (lines 10-11).

7. (B)
Category: Detail
Difficulty: Medium
Strategy: Find the part of the passage which describes the final disc contents. Eliminate any obviously wrong elements in the four possible solutions to reveal the fully correct answer.
Solution: Lines 54-60 describe diverse music representing different genres as well as different cultures, greetings in dozens of languages, messages from "prominent" leaders, and the history of Earth.
(A) Too limited. The messages and history shared represent the world, not just America.
(C) False. Many genres of music were included, and greetings were shared in dozens of languages.
(D) False. Many genres of music were included. Messages represented "prominent" leaders, which likely included, but was not limited to, American leaders.

8. (D)
Category: Detail
Difficulty: Easy
Strategy: Find paragraph describing the creation of the "Golden Records." Look for "most challenging" or similar wording.
Solution: Lines 40-42 state that determining "what to actually put on the recording" was "most difficult of all."

9. (C)
Category: Evidence
Difficulty: Easy
Solution: Lines 40-42 state that determining "what to actually put on the recording" was "most difficult of all."

10. (C)
Category: Main Idea
Difficulty: Medium
Strategy: Rule out answers that are too extreme or don't have the right level of focus.
Solution: This paragraph paints both the intellectual curiosity in developing the Voyager program and the diverse culture documented by the discs in a positive light. The word *legacy* (line 88) affirms that something of lasting importance has been created.
(A) False. Not stated.
(B) Too extreme. The final paragraph is a positive, not negative, conclusion.
(D) Too limited. Man's intellectual curiosity is mentioned, as are man's distinctive values and culture.

Information & Ideas – Sciences – Passage 6 – Pages 40-41

1. (C)
Category: Detail
Difficulty: Easy
Solution: Lines 39-42 explain some were easy to find because of their glowing wounds.

2. (B)
Category: Detail
Difficulty: Medium
Solution: The final paragraph explains the experiment that showed the glowing was caused by the bacteria. The other answers were mentioned in the passage, but not as direct causes of the glow.

3. (A)
Category: Detail
Difficulty: Easy
Solution: The final paragraph explains how Bill and Jon, two teenagers, made the discovery.
(B) Mentioned in the passage, but this was Bill's mother, who helped them.
(C) No, because until recently the source was not understood.
(D) No, because until recently the source was not understood.

4. (D)
Category: Detail
Difficulty: Easy
Solution: Lines 81-93 explain that several conditions led to the cold environment needed for the bacteria.

5. (D)
Category: Evidence
Difficulty: Medium
Strategy: Find the best answer choice that is most relevant to the solution to the previous question.
Solution: Lines 81-93 explain the bacteria needed cold conditions, which were present on the battlefield. Lines 87-88 are the most direct reference to these conditions.
(A) Not related to the aided growth.
(B) Not related to the aided growth.
(C) This explains the bacteria needs cold temperature, but not how the bacteria's growth was aided.

6. (A)
Category: Words in Context
Difficulty: Medium
Strategy: Consider the context. Use tone to eliminate answer choices.
Solution: Based on context, the word should have a positive tone, because the "environment" was a good one for the bacteria.
(B) positive, but "courteous" is not how wounds treat bacteria
(C) not positive
(D) positive, but "congenial" is not how wounds treat bacteria

7. (B)
Category: Detail
Difficulty: Easy
Solution: Lines 30-32 explain that many soldiers died while waiting for treatments.
(A) Opposite; there weren't enough.
(C) Opposite; it was helpful.
(D) Opposite; they were untreated.

8. (C)
Category: Detail
Difficulty: Medium
Solution: The last paragraph explains how the nematodes helped by releasing the bacteria, which killed harmful bacteria.
(A) Incorrect; they don't feed on blood.
(B) Incorrect; the insect larvae weren't a threat to the soldiers.
(D) The Angel's Glow enabled them to be found by doctors, which was helpful, but the attraction of insects wasn't helpful.

9. (D)
Category: Words in Context
Difficulty: Medium
Strategy: Consider the context. Use tone to eliminate answer choices.
Solution: Based on context, the word should have a positive tone, because the bacteria is helpful to the nematode.
(A) Positive, but nematodes don't need profits.
(B) Not positive
(C) Not positive

10. (C)
Category: Words in Context
Difficulty: Medium
Solution: The sentence is discussing a general's action. "Advance" suggests something positive. A positive military action would be an army moving forward, conquering territory.
(A) Wrong meaning
(B) Wrong meaning
(D) Positive, but doesn't fit in the context

Information & Ideas – Sciences – Passage 7 – Pages 42-44

1. (A)
Category: Detail/Main Idea
Difficulty: Medium
Strategy: Be careful to keep the two scientists separate. Read carefully for their major findings.
Solution: VandenBrooks talks about the advantages of hyperoxia, while Verberk is concerned with the handling the toxicity of hyperoxia.
(B) While Verberk used stoneflies instead of VandenBrooks's dragonflies, that was a procedural question, not the heart of their disagreement.
(C) VandenBrooks did not discuss the effects of high oxygen levels on dragonfly larvae. He noted that high oxygen slowed the development of cockroach larval development.
(D) Not discussed in the article.

2. (B)
Category: Inference
Difficulty: Hard
Strategy: Reread the information on cockroaches.
Solution: High oxygen levels slows larval development and adult size. Therefore, it can be inferred that lower oxygen levels will lead to faster development and larger size.
(A) It does not say dragonflies ate cockroaches.
(C) The size of cockroach tracheal tubes is not mentioned.
(D) The size of cockroach tracheal tubes is not mentioned.

3. (C)
Category: Generalization/Main Idea
Difficulty: Medium
Strategy: Map the passage. Put the main ideas of the 4 paragraphs together and determine the main idea of the entire piece.
Solution: While the author describes the different scientific methods, the fate of the dragonfly, and the effects of hyperoxia, the passage is, in total, about the effects of oxygen levels on insect size.
(A) The methods of the two scientists are described, but the focus is on the issue they were each trying to determine: why did the dragonflies and other insects become so large during the Carboniferous Period and shrink to their current sizes.
(B) The current size of the dragonfly is known.
(D) Both scientists knew that hyperoxia made the dragonfly grow larger.

4. (B)
Category: Detail
Difficulty: Easy
Strategy: Look for discussion of insects grown in low oxygen conditions.
Solution: 10 out of 12 species of insects raised in low oxygen environments grew smaller. (Lines 35-37)
(A) Opposite.
(C) Cockroaches developed more slowly and grew smaller
(D) Used spiracles to absorb oxygen through their skin.

5. (A)
Category: Detail
Difficulty: Medium
Strategy: Read in the paragraph about VandenBrooks's studies.
Solution: In high oxygen, "[c]ockroaches... remained the same size and grew more slowly... VanderBrooks was surprised by this, as he had expected the increase in oxygen to speed up development of larvae." (Lines 39-43)
(B) Verberk did not cultivate the dragonflies, but VandenBrooks is not said to have felt that his approach was unnecessary.
(C) This is Verberk's finding.
(D) No indication in the passage.

6. (B)
Category: Words in Context
Difficulty: Medium
Strategy: Read the text surrounding the word and determine what you think would fit into the sentence properly.
Solution: The text says: "Raising dragonflies is extremely difficult." It then explains how the dragonflies had to be fed.
(A) Feeding small bugs to dragonflies is not painful.
(C) There was no mention of feeding protocols being done wrong or causing harm.
(D) If he wanted his dragonflies to live, they had to be fed in this careful manner. He was not "overly fastidious" but appropriately careful.

7. (D)
Category: Words in Context
Difficulty: Easy
Strategy: Consider alternate definitions. Reread the sentence with each answer choice.
Solution: In context, it's clear the scientists are nurturing dragonflies for their experiment. Choices A and C are too literal.

8. (D)
Category: Detail
Difficulty: Hard
Strategy: Reread to determine what VandenBrooks and Verberk disagreed about.
Solution: VanderBrooks discovered that insects raised in hyperoxic conditions had smaller tracheal tubes. "As you become a larger insect, more of your body is taken up by tracheal tubes." Verberk found that insects needed to avoid being poisoned by excessive oxygen. "If you grow larger, your surface area decreases relative to your volume."
(A) VandenBrooks believes that greater size allowed for increased tracheal tube size. Verberk does not say that larval spiracles utilize increase oxygen to promote growth.
(B) Increased food sources are not mentioned. Larval spiracles do not increase their ability to utilize increased oxygen to promote growth.
(C) VandenBrooks found that slower larval develop does not allow for greater growth and Verberk does not discuss the rate of larval development.

9. (C)
Category: Detail
Difficulty: Medium
Strategy: Reread the paragraph about Verberk's study.
Solution: Verberk found that by increasing the size of the larva, the proportion of oxygen absorbed compared to body decreases.
(A) larvae do not have spiracles.
(B) the larval stage was always in the water, and the adult stage was always on land.
(D) Verberk did not study tracheal tubes. Besides, VanderBrooks found that increased oxygen led to decreased size of tracheal tubes.

10. (D)
Category: Evidence
Difficulty: Medium
Strategy: Look for an answer that supports your answer choice to the previous question. If you do not know which to choose, look for quotes that relate to the previous question and try to find a choice that goes with an answer choice to the previous question.
Solution: Verberk: "If you grow larger, your surface area decreases relative to your volume."
(A) This just says they grew larger in an increased oxygen environment.
(B) This talks about how an adaptation affected the dragonfly.
(C) Explains why Verberk chose to work with stoneflies.

Information & Ideas – Sciences – Passage 8 – Pages 45-47

1. (B)
Category: Words in Context
Difficulty: Easy
Strategy: Find where the word appears in the passage and read lines before and after to understand its context.
Solution: The paragraph mentions "early Earth" and "the origin of life on Earth." In addition, "pre-" means "before" and "biotic" means it is pertaining to "living organisms."
(A) Incorrect. This is referring to "probiotic."
(C) Incorrect. This is referring to "robotic."
(D) Incorrect. It is before life existed, not before Earth.

2. (C)
Category: Inference
Difficulty: Medium
Strategy: Check the surrounding lines for context
Solution: According to the passage, enzymes are "molecules that speed up critical chemical reactions in biological systems," implying that they are needed to ensure that reactions are not happening too slowly.
(A) Although they are a type of molecule, there is nothing suggesting that they are needed for nutritional purposes.
(B) Although they are present in biological systems, respiration is not mentioned.
(D) Not true. There is no mention of their use in providing rigidity to cell walls.

3. (C)
Category: Detail – Compare & Contrast
Difficulty: Easy
Strategy: Search for the section of the passage that discusses RNA and DNA.
Solution: The fourth paragraph mentions the ways in which RNA is "unlike DNA." It also mentions that they carry the same type of basic information. (lines 41-43)
(A) RNA is "single-stranded." (line 44)
(B) RNA is "simpler." (line 45)
(D) RNA can "replicate on its own." (line 45)

4. (B)
Category: Detail – Compare & Contrast
Difficulty: Easy
Strategy: Find the main idea of each of the passages before determining what the difference is.
Solution: The first passage focuses on the possibility that early life originated on Earth while the second passage focuses on evidence for its origin in outer space.
(A) Both passages discuss molecules found in early life.
(C) This is not a difference between the two passages.
(D) This is not a difference between the two passages.

5. (C)
Category: Detail
Difficulty: Medium
Strategy: Read the section of the passage that mentions the potential for RNA to evolve, and anticipate an answer.
Solution: According to the end of the fourth paragraph, "sometimes different versions of the RNA enzymes would combine, forming mutant recombinant forms, demonstrating that RNA had the potential to evolve."
(A) This choice refers to DNA, not RNA.
(B) Not mentioned as evidence that RNA can evolve.
(D) Not mentioned as evidence that RNA can evolve.

6. (D)
Category: Detail – Cause & Effect
Difficulty: Medium
Strategy: Identify evidence in the second passage for the location of the origin of life; avoid attractors.
Solution: According to the fifth paragraph, "These amino acids were found in a variety of geometric configurations that do not exist on Earth, strongly suggesting the molecules originated in space and were not picked up from the Earth where the rock was found."
(A) Although the mixture of amino acids is mentioned, it is not direct evidence for an extraterrestrial origin.
(B) The ages of the amino acids are not mentioned.
(C) The sizes of the amino acids are not mentioned.

7. (A)
Category: Generalization
Difficulty: Medium
Strategy: Read the indicated statement and rephrase to ensure Information & Ideas.
Solution: According to the statement, although it seems as though nothing could survive in outer space, its large size increases the probability that life could have emerged there.
(B) The statement says it is possible that life may have emerged in space, but does not state that there are definitely different forms of life there.
(C) Although the statement says that space seems "hostile to life," it does not rule out the possibility that life could have emerged there.
(D) This is more in line with the first perspective.

8. (D)
Category: Main Idea
Difficulty: Medium
Strategy: First, try to summarize the second passage in a sentence; then, see which answer choice fits best.
Solution: This passage focuses on the possibility that early life started in outer space; in this case, the first sentence of the passage provides the most direct indication of the main idea.
(A) The passage states that the theory of an extraterrestrial origin of life is "certainly viable" but does not say that it is definitely true.
(B) This is not stated in the passage.
(C) Opposite. These are examples of evidence that life did originate in outer space.

9. (D)
Category: Evidence
Difficulty: Medium
Solution: Lines 91-95 make an argument in support of life originating in space.

10. (A)
Category: Words in Context
Difficulty: Medium
Solution: In context, it's clear the word "base" is used as "basic."

Information & Ideas – Sciences – Passage 9 – Pages 48-49

1.   (C)
Category: Detail
Difficulty: Medium
Solution: Lines 17-20 state "the simplest theory…"
(A)   Not mentioned
(B)   Microwaves are mentioned, but only as an experimental proof of the theory
(D)   Mentioned but somewhat dismissively (lines 15-17)

2.   (A)
Category: Main Idea / Detail
Difficulty: Easy
Solution: Lines 21-24 state his theory is ball lightning is caused by burning silicon.

3.   (A)
Category: Detail
Difficulty: Medium
Strategy: Find the relevant information in the correct passage.
Solution: The second paragraph (lines 63-83) explains the theory that ball lightning is initially caused by lightning striking in certain conditions.
(B)   Not mentioned
(C)   Wrong passage
(D)   Wrong passage

4.   (D)
Category: Words in Context
Difficulty: Medium
Strategy: Consider tone, based on context.
Solution: The sentence begins by mentioning how dangerous ball lightning can be, and then the conjunction "but" suggests the following detail is about a contrasting idea: how non-dangerous they can be.

5.   (C)
Category: Detail
Difficulty: Medium
Solution: The final paragraph states in lines 96-97 that "ball lightning travels parallel to the ground."
(A)   Not mentioned
(B)   Mountain tops are mentioned as an area where ball lightning does not occur
(D)   Not mentioned

6.   (C)
Category: Detail
Difficulty: Easy
Solution: Lines 55-56 state ball lightning passes through glass windows.

7.   (D)
Category: Main Idea / Detail
Difficulty: Medium
Strategy: Use process of elimination and find evidence to support the correct answer choice.
Solution: Lines 82-83 state the phenomenon has not been duplicated in a lab.
(A)   Opposite. Line 73 states it occurs in a "wide open area"
(B)   Lines 69-70 state it's a "stable mass of plasma"
(C)   Wrong passage

8.   (B)
Category: Words in Context
Difficulty: Medium
Solution: The sentence describes something the theory cannot account for. Based on this context, the "hole" is a problem with the theory.

9.   (B)
Category: Detail / Synthesis
Difficulty: Medium
Strategy: Use process of elimination.
Solution: Both passages agree ball lightning is real, though not fully understood.
(A)   Not mentioned in Passage 2
(C)   Not mentioned in Passage 2
(D)   Not mentioned in Passage 1

10.   (A)
Category: Detail / Synthesis
Difficulty: Medium
Strategy: Use process of elimination.
Solution: Both passages agree ball lightning is created by energy.
(B)   Not mentioned in Passage 2
(C)   Not mentioned in Passage 2
(D)   Neither passage states there is scientific agreement

Information & Ideas – Sciences – Passage 10 – Pages 50-52

1. **(C)**
Category: Words in Context
Difficulty: Easy
Strategy: Read the lines before and after to understand the context; try substituting the word "dramatic" with another word that could work.
Solution: In this case, the word "dramatic" is referring to how extreme the "cold snap" was.
(A) Wrong context. This meaning does not fit in with the passage.
(B) Not relevant. "Impressive" has a positive connotation that does not fit the context.
(D) Not relevant. "Vivid" does not correctly describe the temperature change.

2. **(D)**
Category: Detail
Difficulty: Easy
Strategy: Find the correct section of the passage referring to nanodiamonds.
Solution: Line 15 states the creation of nanodiamonds requires anoxic (low oxygen) conditions.

3. **(D)**
Category: Words in Context
Difficulty: Medium
Strategy: Read the lines before and after to understand the context; try substituting the word "precipitated" with another word that could work.
Solution: In this case, the sentence is discussing how the cosmic impact may have started the YD climate shift.
(A) Not relevant. There is no mention of extraction.
(B) Not relevant. "Precipitation" could refer to rain.
(C) Wrong context. This meaning refers to a chemical reaction, not a new climate shift.

4. **(A)**
Category: Main Idea
Difficulty: Medium
Strategy: Summarize the passage into a single sentence, as if you had to describe it to someone who had never read it. Pay special attention to the topic and concluding sentences.
Solution: According to the last two sentences, the evidence in the paragraph could indicate there was a cosmic impact.
(B) Not relevant. There is not a focus on the changes that were caused by the YD shift in this paragraph; there is a greater focus in the first paragraph.
(C) Too narrow. Although the sediment samples are mentioned, there is no deeper discussion of the process to obtain them.
(D) Not true. Platinum is mentioned as a form of evidence, not as a cause of climate shift.

5. **(B)**
Category: Detail – Cause & Effect
Difficulty: Medium
Strategy: Search for the section of the passage that discusses the north Atlantic. Read a few sentences before and after to understand causal relationships.
Solution: The last sentence of the fifth paragraph mentions a series of events that could potentially lead to climate shifts around the north Atlantic.
(A) Opposite. The changes mentioned in the passage occur during a deglaciation period.
(C) Opposite. The sentence mentions a high magnitude volcano.
(D) Not relevant. Electron microscopy is a tool used in research, not a cause of climate shift.

6. **(B)**
Category: Detail – Compare & Contrast
Difficulty: Hard
Strategy: Summarize the main point of each of the perspectives; next, see where platinum spikes are mentioned and what they are used as evidence for.
Solution: Platinum spikes were used as evidence for the cosmic impact hypothesis; however, the second perspective argued such indicators may be used for volcanic activity.

7. **(C)**
Category: Main Idea
Difficulty: Medium
Strategy: Summarize the passage as a whole, then see which answer is the most similar.
Solution: The focus of the passages is on potential theories for what may have caused the Younger Dryas climate shift.
(A) Although the passage mentions multiple researchers, they are not the primary focus.
(B) Too narrow. The first perspective mentions nanodiamonds, but they are just a piece of evidence for a larger theory.
(D) Only the second perspective is focused on volcanic eruptions.

8. **(B)**
Category: Evidence
Difficulty: Medium
Solution: Lines 64-68 mention pollutants (ash and smoke) causing cooling (blocking out much of the sun, triggering the cooling period).

9. **(C)**
Category: Inference
Difficulty: Medium
Strategy: Find the reference to ocean currents and use process of elimination.
Solution: Lines 72-77 explain the hypothesis linking volcanic activity to ocean currents. The passage states that this would trigger climate shifts. It can be assumed that these climate shifts are the abrupt cooling of the ice age. Also, it can be assumed that if changes in ocean currents lead to cooling, the normal path of the currents must bring warmth.

10. **(A)**
Category: Synthesis
Difficulty: Medium
Solution: Both passages explain theories. Because they are only theories, it can be inferred that they are not known to be facts.

Information & Ideas – Social Studies – Passage 1 – Pages 54-55

1. (A)
Category: Detail – Compare & Contrast
Difficulty: Medium
Strategy: Look for a section of the passage that discusses physics and math; determine what differences are given.
Solution: According to the first paragraph, math is "profitable and praiseworthy," but at the same time "stellar astronomy and atomic physics are the only sciences which stand higher in popular estimation."
(B) The first paragraph states that physics might be "higher in popular estimation."
(C) Not mentioned
(D) Not mentioned

2. (C)
Category: Detail
Difficulty: Medium
Strategy: Find specific lines about why the public does not need to be persuaded about the value of math, and anticipate the answer.
Solution: At the end of the second paragraph, the author states, "The mass of mathematical truth is obvious and imposing; its practical applications, the bridges and steam-engines and dynamos, obtrude themselves on the dullest imagination. The public does not need to be convinced that there is something in mathematics."

3. (A)
Category: Evidence
Difficulty: Medium
Solution: At the end of the second paragraph, the author states, "The mass of mathematical truth is obvious and imposing; its practical applications, the bridges and steam-engines and dynamos, obtrude themselves on the dullest imagination. The public does not need to be convinced that there is something in mathematics."

4. (D)
Category: Inference
Difficulty: Medium
Strategy: Reread the given section carefully; for possible answer choices, ensure that there is sufficient textual evidence to support it.
Solution: According to the third paragraph, mathematicians feel that "the popular reputation of mathematics is based largely on ignorance and confusion."
(A) There is no indication of this.
(B) Opposite. Hardy states that his task "should be a simpler task than Bradley's difficult apology."
(C) It is too extreme to state that it is obvious to everyone.

5. (B)
Category: Inference
Difficulty: Hard
Strategy: Reread the given line and a few sentences before and after to understand the context; anticipate the answer.
Solution: According to the sentence before, "He must shut his eyes a little and think a little more of his subject and himself than they deserve."
(A) There is no direct indication that they are trying to avoid criticism.
(C) There is no mention of others' egos.
(D) There is no indication that they are trying to be more humble.

6. (A)
Category: Main Idea
Difficulty: Medium
Strategy: Summarize the paragraph in a single statement before looking at the answer choices.
Solution: According to the sixth paragraph, "it is seldom that such differences of value will turn the scale in a man's choice of a career, which will almost always be dictated by the limitations of his natural abilities."
(B) This is not stated in the paragraph.
(C) Too general. Although he states that poetry is more valuable than cricket, this is not stated in the paragraph.
(D) Opposite. According to the paragraph, personal abilities are a greater factor in career choice than societal value.

7. (C)
Category: Generalization
Difficulty: Medium
Strategy: Find the part of the passage that best addresses reasons why a mathematician could work in a different field; anticipate the answer before looking at the answer choices.
Solution: According to the final sentence, "Such a sacrifice could be justified only by economic necessity or age."
(A) Wrong part of the passage. This is not one of the two reasons given.
(B) Wrong part of the passage. This is not one of the two reasons given.
(D) This is not one of the two reasons given.

8. (D)
Category: Words in Context
Difficulty: Medium
Strategy: Read a few lines before to understand the context. Then, try to replace the word "grossly" with another word, and see which answer choice is a potential match.
Solution: In this context, "grossly" could be replaced by "drastically."
(A) Incorrect definition.
(B) Incorrect context for the word "gross."
(C) Too extreme. Although there is a large difference, "shocking" does not properly describe the differences.

9. (A)
Category: Words in Context
Difficulty: Medium
Strategy: Carefully consider the usage of the word in the sentence. Replace the word with the answer choices and see which works best. It may help to rephrase the sentence in simpler terms.
Solution: The author is saying that if a person is a natural mathematician, they shouldn't stop "exercising" this skill. In this sense, "utilizing" works best. B and C are close, but not quite right.

10. (A)
Category: Main Idea
Difficulty: Medium
Strategy: Map the passage and find the overall point being made by the author. The main idea should have the right scope: not too broad and vague and not too narrow and specific.
Solution: A main focus of the passage is that mathematicians are people who are particularly gifted in one area and would not perform nearly as well in another profession.
(B) Mathematicians aren't the *only* people who enjoy math.
(C) The science of math isn't valueless.
(D) Mathematicians aren't more talented in general, they are just uniquely talented in one area.

Information & Ideas – Social Studies – Passage 2 – Pages 56-57

1. (C)
Category: Detail
Difficulty: Medium
Strategy: Use process of elimination and read the answer choices carefully.
Solution: Lines 26-27 state a symptom is doubting their contribution to their own successes.
(A) Not a fear of success but of fraud
(B) Not viewing failures as luck but viewing successes as luck
(D) Not improving but insufficient

2. (A)
Category: Inference
Difficulty: Easy
Strategy: Use process of elimination and read answer choices carefully.
Solution: Lines 91-94 suggest social media makes it worse.
(B) Opposite (lines 37-41)
(C) Lines 47-50 state it's about 70%.
(D) Opposite (lines 50-52)

3. (C)
Category: Evidence
Difficulty: Medium
Solution: Lines 91-94 suggest social media makes it worse.

4. (B)
Category: Words in Context
Difficulty: Medium
Solution: The sentence refers back to the previous paragraph, which discusses how common ("widespread") the issue is.

5. (D)
Category: Detail
Difficulty: Medium
Strategy: Use process of elimination and read answer choices carefully.
Solution: Lines 85-86 state it is best to be open and honest about feelings.
(A) Opposite, lines 71-73
(B) Opposite, lines 73-76
(C) Not mentioned

6. (D)
Category: Detail
Difficulty: Easy
Solution: Lines 17-19 state it's most common among high-achieving students.

7. (A)
Category: Words in Context
Difficulty: Medium
Strategy: Replace the word with the answer choices and see which works best in the context. Be mindful of tone.
Solution: The word doesn't have a positive or negative tone. Also, the "difference" isn't necessarily real, but just believed to be true.
(B) Negative tone may suit the situation, but not the word in question.
(C) Not quite right. It may not be seen, but the important part is it is believed to be there.
(D) Not related.

8. (D)
Category: Inference
Difficulty: Medium
Strategy: Use process of elimination and read answer choices carefully.
Solution: The first paragraph suggests it primarily affects top performers.
(A) Opposite, this is their fear, not the reality
(B) Opposite, they can escape
(C) Lines 47-50 state it's about 70%, not everyone

9. (A)
Category: Evidence
Difficulty: Medium
Solution: Lines 23-26 state it affects "high-achieving people", which matches with being "particularly successful and motivated."

10. (B)
Category: Main Idea
Difficulty: Medium
Strategy: Consider the central point made by the author.
Solution: The main focus of the paragraph is on how people can overcome the feelings of impostor syndrome.
(A) Too narrow. It's not just about one attribute of impostor syndrome, but how it can be overcome.
(C) Too narrow. It's not just about one attribute of impostor syndrome, but how it can be overcome.
(D) Wrong part of the passage

Information & Ideas – Social Studies – Passage 3 – Pages 58-60

1.   (C)
Category: Main Idea
Difficulty: Medium
Strategy: Use process of elimination.
Solution: Note the question asks for "a central idea", not necessarily *the* main idea. Choice C is a foundational idea behind the passage's discussion of oxytocin.
(A)   Not stated
(B)   The focus is not on disorders but behaviors in general.
(D)   Not stated

2.   (A)
Category: Evidence
Difficulty: Medium
Solution: Choice A discusses a chemical affecting the body.

3.   (A)
Category: Words in Context
Difficulty: Easy
Solution: The sentence sets up the following paragraphs, which cover different ways oxytocin may affect the mind. In this sense, "potential" means something that could be but is not certain.

4.   (D)
Category: Inference
Difficulty: Easy
Strategy: Use process of elimination. Make sure the answer is directly supported by the passage.
Solution: The last paragraph summarizes the current state of understanding, explaining that scientists still don't fully know how oxytocin works.
(A)   This may be assumed, but there is no direct suggestion of this in the passage.
(B)   Opposite. Lines 65-72
(C)   The mention of "love potions" is not a serious reference to a scientific pursuit.

5.   (D)
Category: Words in Context
Difficulty: Medium
Solution: The following information shows the study measured how oxytocin affected and changed inflammation. "Adjust" is the best answer available, though it may not be the best possible synonym.

6.   (B)
Category: Detail
Difficulty: Medium
Solution: Lines 100-103 state patients with BPD have lowered trust and cooperation. This is the opposite of the effect mentioned in lines 92-93.

7.   (A)
Category: Inference
Difficulty: Medium
Strategy: Consider the complexities of the studies and use process of elimination.
Solution: The fifth paragraph (lines 85-103) shows that oxytocin can have negative side effects for some populations, though it seems to be positive for most people. Therefore, more research is needed to be able to provide warnings for those who would use it as a drug.
(B)   Not mentioned
(C)   Opposite
(D)   If depressed people have "atypical" brains, it may have negative effects.

8.   (C)
Category: Generalization
Difficulty: Medium
Solution: Lines 41-53 explain that scientists' understanding is limited by their knowledge of how oxytocin reacts with the brain.
(A)   May be true, but not stated
(B)   Not related
(D)   Not stated

9.   (B)
Category: Evidence
Difficulty: Medium
Solution: Lines 41-53 explain that scientists' understanding is limited by their knowledge of how oxytocin reacts with the brain.

Information & Ideas – Social Studies – Passage 4 – Pages 61-62

1. (B)
Category: Detail
Difficulty: Medium
Strategy: Note *soon* in question wording.
Solution: Immediate conservation efforts were minimal and localized: "…area residents expressed their concerns in local newspapers" (lines 86-87). Lines 33-35 state roads were constructed.
(A) Line 32 refers to "a new influx of people."
(C) It would take decades for redwood conservation efforts to result in national legislation (final paragraph).
(D) Line 35 claim "Local commerce mushroomed."

2. (D)
Category: Words in Context
Difficulty: Medium
Strategy: Review the full sentence and scan the remainder of that paragraph. Look for an equivalent to the quoted phrase in the answer selections.
Solution: The massive trees were "unsuitable for construction (line 73)," much wood was wasted as the trees were harvested (lines 73-74), and the harvested wood was used for humble purposes like "shingles, fence posts, even matchsticks" (lines 78-79). Since "commercial returns" implies money made (profits), and this is "limited" (minimal), answer D is correct.
(A) Opposite. Limited commercial returns means low, not high, profits.
(B) The phrase "commercial returns" refers to financial profit, not demand.
(C) Not relevant.

3. (C)
Category: Main Idea
Difficulty: Medium
Strategy: Eliminate answers that deal with only a portion of the passage by quickly mapping the piece.
Solution: Look for an answer that corresponds to the entire passage.
(A) Only mentioned in certain paragraphs.
(B) Yosemite tribe view of redwoods only mentioned in second paragraph.
(D) Only mentioned in final two paragraphs.

4. (D)
Category: Generalization
Difficulty: Medium
Strategy: Look for a parallel, 3-part statement. Make sure points are equivalent and not opposite.
Solution: Time (years) passed, financial returns (profits) shrunk, and widespread thinking (national mindset/reigning philosophies) changed, leading to eventual conservation measures.
(A) Profits not mentioned. Politics not specifically addressed in passage.
(B) Opposite: profits decreased.
(C) National mindset not mentioned.

5. (C)
Category: Detail
Difficulty: Easy
Solution: Lines 49-51 state a passage was bored through a tree so carriages could pass through. This would be a tunnel.
(A) (line 46) – an alley, but not necessarily pins
(B) (lines 33-35) – roads were made, but not necessarily from the wood
(D) (lines 61-64) – it was a two-story home

6. (B)
Category: Inference
Difficulty: Medium
Strategy: Eliminate obviously wrong answers.
Solution: Lines 29-31 show early response to redwood commercial possibilities. Lines 65-68 state that Sierra Nevada redwoods were logged for forty years despite disappointing profits.
(A) Not stated.
(C) Both good (innovation) and bad (exploitation) aspects of the 19th-century mindset are mentioned in the passage.
(D) Not stated.

7. (B)
Category: Evidence
Difficulty: Medium
Solution: Lines 29-31 show early response to redwood commercial possibilities.

8. (B)
Category: Words in Context
Difficulty: Medium
Strategy: Substitute different answer options for "zeitgeist" while maintaining the sentence's meaning.
Solution: The word zeitgeist means mood or defining spirit. In this context it is used to describe the prevalent mindset of the 19th century.
(A) Tradition implies a continuation, not something new or unique to a time.
(C) Word does not fit since no humor or irony mentioned in passage.
(D) A consequence is a result of an action or condition. Zeitgeist is used to describe the mood current to the 19th century not something that came afterwards.

9. (B)
Category: Main Idea
Difficulty: Medium
Strategy: Map paragraphs and find commonality.
Solution: Paragraph seven begins with early conservation concerns, and paragraph eight concludes with the establishment of a state park.
(A) Too broad.
(C) Too narrow.
(D) Too narrow.

10. (C)
Category: Detail
Difficulty: Medium
Strategy: Look for comparative parallel: speculator is to Muir as ….
Solution: Speculators exploited the redwoods, while Muir fought to preserve them.
(A) Opposite.
(B) Speculators may have admired the redwoods, but Muir did not exploit them.
(D) First part incorrect: speculators did not preserve the redwoods.

Information & Ideas – Social Studies – Passage 5 – Pages 63-65

1. (A)
Category: Detail
Difficulty: Medium
Strategy: Go back to paragraph three, which discusses ways of salting a mine, and focus on the two main ways the author describes salting.
Solution: lines 49-50, "a con man might 'salt' the area by scattering bits of gold," and lines 52-53, "load a shotgun shell with gold particles and fire it against the walls of the mine."
(B) While dynamite is mentioned, there is nothing about buyers not being allowed to inspect mines.
(C) While there is some discussion of communities working together to fool others, there is nothing about false numbers.
(D) This is close, but some words make it incorrect. There's no mention of "caves," "chunks" might be too generous, and the gold isn't being shot out but shot in.

2. (D)
Category: Detail
Difficulty: Medium
Strategy: Return to the end of paragraph three and consider what a geologist might do to aid in this con:
Solution: "Even prospectors that brought… support the local communities." Choice D covers both incorrect information and the community aspect.
(A) No mention of reports.
(B) Not what the geologists did.
(C) Too extreme. While they would likely benefit, "extravagant" is too extreme.

3. (D)
Category: Detail
Difficulty: Medium
Strategy: Go back to the last paragraph to find the reason behind the inflated value
Solution: Lines 71-76 – "Michael de Guzman, a mining prospector, had promoted the portion of land as a jackpot of gold. To prove the claim's worth, he provided several core samples, which showed an abundance of gold waiting to be excavated." Later, it's noted the evidence was faked, as he used gold from his own wedding ring.
(A) No mention of fool's gold.
(B) The other company is mentioned but not as a reason to up the mine's value.
(C) Uses some words from the last paragraph, but doesn't properly answer the question.

4. (C)
Category: Evidence
Difficulty: Medium
Solution: Lines 86-89 explain how Guzman used false evidence (gold from his wedding ring, which he claimed was gold from the site).

5. (B)
Category: Generalization
Difficulty: Medium
Strategy: Reread the last paragraph and summarize it in your own words. Then, look for the answer that most closely matches your predicted answer.
Solution: Guzman did lie, estimates rose, and the truth was uncovered.
(A) There is no mention of suspicions or that the other company was brought in for this reason.
(C) Doesn't capture the main idea and is also inaccurate.
(D) There's no evidence of Guzman being encouraged or fined.

6. (D)
Category: Detail – Compare & Contrast
Difficulty: Medium
Strategy: Eliminate answers that are partially or wholly wrong.
Solution: The incidents in the 1800s are talked about as a group, while the modern scandal is a more isolated example.
(A) This sounds plausible, but there's no technological element to the modern scandal.
(B) Both are related to money, so "territorial claims" doesn't work, even though this is brought up in an earlier paragraph.
(C) Both involved spreading small amounts of gold. In the modern example, gold from a wedding ring was used.

7. (A)
Category: Detail – Cause & Effect
Difficulty: Medium
Strategy: Go to paragraph two and find evidence to answer the question. Eliminate answers that are too extreme or false.
Solution: "California was not incorporated into the United States and was under the legal control of the military. Thus, there were no mechanisms to enforce rights to land. For anyone who could find gold in those open spaces, it was free for the taking." Choice A paraphrases the evidence from paragraph two.
(B) Too extreme. While the area was under the control of the military, there's no mention of it being ineffective.
(C) Not true. California wasn't considered its own country.
(D) Inaccurate. There's no mention of conflicting governments.

8. (B)
Category: Main Idea
Difficulty: Medium
Solution: Choice B is broad enough to cover the main idea.
(A) There's no implication that miners' time should have been spent differently.
(C) Too extreme. While this is one way miners earned income, there's no evidence that it was the "primary" way.
(D) No evidence.

9. (A)
Category: Main Idea
Difficulty: Easy
Solution: The focus of the passage is on how mines were salted.
(B) Too broad. The focus is on gold mines.
(C) Incorrect. The methods are of trickery, not of actual mining.
(D) Too narrow. This is only a portion of the paragraph.

10. (C)
Category: Inference
Difficulty: Medium
Strategy: Eliminate answers that are too extreme.
Solution: Choice C is the most accurate without being too extreme.
(A) While they may tell lies, "incapable of telling the truth" is extreme.
(B) Incorrect. Given the quote, Twain doesn't appear to think that assessment is the problem.
(D) Too extreme. To say they are worth nothing isn't true.

11. (C)
Category: Words in Context
Difficulty: Medium
Strategy: Predict your answer.
Solution: A wellspring is a bounty of something, so this fits.
(A) While the trove might contain minerals, that is not the definition of trove.
(B) Chests can contain valuables, but the meaning isn't accurate.
(D) Sinkholes would be the opposite of something filled with items of value.

Rhetoric – Fiction – Passage 1 – Pages 67-68

1. **(B)**
Category: Structure
Difficulty: Medium
Strategy: Map the passage and note how the focus and tone may shift.
Solution: Lines 1-16 set the scene, and the rest of the passage describes the narrator's interaction with the old man.
(A) Not just inner thoughts
(C) It's not a lasting relationship
(D) No focus on observations of other characters

2. **(A)**
Category: Purpose
Difficulty: Medium
Strategy: Consider what the repeated line makes you feel or think as you read the story. Be careful about jumping to conclusions when considering answer choices.
Solution: By repeating the same line, the old man demonstrates his fixation. He is grappling with the horrors of war. He was taking care of animals, which are in danger now, and he's deeply troubled by his whole life seemingly reduced to one futile task.
(B) The repeated line doesn't relate to the narrator's character
(C) No strong sense of doubt
(D) No comparison is directly made

3. **(B)**
Category: Word Choice
Difficulty: Medium
Strategy: Consider the context. Be careful about jumping to conclusions when considering answer choices.
Solution: The words are used to describe the movement of the refugees.
(A) Possible, but not directly suggested
(C) Not used to describe old man
(D) Not related to politics

4. **(C)**
Category: Purpose
Difficulty: Medium
Strategy: Consider what the details suggest. Imagine the character's life and how he came to this situation.
Solution: The clothes are black but dusty, suggesting they're not usually dusty but the old man has been less careful about avoiding dust and dirt in the wartime. Also, noting he did not look like a shepherd suggests he looks like a different socioeconomic class (likely not poor, as a shepherd would be). Most likely, he has been reduced to a lower state than he is used to.
(A) Just because he's not a shepherd doesn't mean he's unemployed.
(B) Opposite.
(D) Not mentioned.

5. **(C)**
Category: Purpose
Difficulty: Medium
Strategy: Consider the impression the author is making with this sentence. Keep in mind that what seems literally stated may be different from what the author wants to convey.
Solution: By noting the old man's few bits of luck, the author is also expressing that the rest of the old man's life will be unlucky. Based on the passage, it can be inferred this is a hint the old man will die.
(A) It's directly stated cats are self-sufficient, and this isn't compared to humans.
(B) The luck concerns the old man. The reference to clouds is not related to rain.
(D) Not related

6. **(A)**
Category: Point of View
Difficulty: Medium
Solution: Lines 12-14 state the narrator's job as a scout.
(B) No mention of his attempt to help fellow citizens
(C) The old man is not related to him
(D) No sense of his contending with sympathy

7. **(D)**
Category: Purpose
Difficulty: Medium
Strategy: Summarize the paragraph and consider what effect it has on the story and on you as you read. What does it tell? How does it make you feel?
Solution: The description of the Ebro Delta and the approaching enemy create a sense of tension. The narrator seems a bit nervous and anxious to go. Meanwhile, the old man isn't moving. This contrast creates more tension.
(A) No description of native land
(B) The old man isn't attempting to resolve a problem.
(C) The war seems to be very much continuing.

Rhetoric – Fiction – Passage 2 – Pages 69-71

1. **(B)**
Category: Purpose
Difficulty: Medium
Strategy: Eliminate answers that are too extreme or too literal.
Solution: There is a contrast between the narrator's mild stress and overthinking to the barber's genial attitude towards his work.
A) Not enough evidence/too extreme. Even though the barber is jolly, there's no evidence that he takes pleasure in upsetting the narrator.
C) While this does give the reader a bit more detail about the barber's work, this is not the main purpose of including this information.
D) Too extreme. While the barber doesn't care much for what the narrator has to say, "complete" and "hostile" are too extreme given what's illustrated in the passage.

2. **(D)**
Category: Purpose
Difficulty: Medium
Strategy: Consider the wording here: "Delight of the Toilet"? Clearly, the author is bringing in some humor, so look for an answer that matches this idea.
Solution: The back and forth between the narrator and the barber, and these additional details, contribute to the humorous component.
(A) This information doesn't give specific information about time or place.
(B) It's clear that the narrator, as well as the author, does not find the barber's claims to be legitimate.
(C) There is no evidence that the writer is trying to impress the reader.

3. **(C)**
Category: Structure
Difficulty: Medium
Strategy: Through mapping the passage, you should have a solid idea of what happens in this paragraph. The narrative goes from general to specific, so you want to find an answer choice that reflects this shift.
Solution: This answer conveys the general to specific shift.
(A) The paragraph doesn't shift to a third person point of view.
(B) This paragraph doesn't focus on the interaction between the narrator and a barber; that's later in the passage.
(D Again, this is partially correct, but it misses the opening generalizations.

4. **(D)**
Category: Structure
Difficulty: Hard
Strategy: "Next!" is part of the sparse dialogue and the only repetitive part of the passage. Consider why the author may include this. What point is the author trying to drive home?
Solution: This illustrates the idea in the first paragraph that every trip to the barber is the same.
(A) While next could relate to time, this is not what it's doing here.
(B) The narrator is somewhat on edge, but the repetition is not worsening this feeling.
(C) The word doesn't appear to break the narrator's train of thought.

5. **(B)**
Category: Word Choice
Difficulty: Medium
Strategy: Consider the job these words are doing. They are making the scene at the barber shop into something of a race. But what is happening on the surface? Simply a man getting a shave.
Solution: They do add tension and drama to this ordinary situation. Even at the opening of the passage, the narrator says that things never change at the barber shop, so visiting should be an ordinary activity.
(A) There is no rivalry between the barbers as far as we know, only strong opinions presented by the narrator.
(C) This answer is too literal and inaccurate.
(D) While the narrator does have a lot going on in his mind, these words do not convey these conflicting emotions.

6. **(B)**
Category: Word Choice
Difficulty: Medium
Strategy: Consider what the words have in common; they are all related to some degree of roughness. Then, look for an answer choice that aligns with this idea.
Solution: They are all related to how the barber is jostling the narrator.
(A) While the narrator says going to the barber is always the same, he's also describing a singular experience here. He's also getting a shave here, not a haircut.
(C) "Severe pain" is too extreme. The narrator is in some discomfort but not to this degree.
(D) The narrator generally seems to understand what the barber is doing.

7. **(D)**
Category: Point of View
Difficulty: Medium
Strategy: Start with the words you know and eliminate answers. Excited and eager both don't quite fit. Complicated might be okay. If many of the other words don't look familiar, make your best guess from remaining choices.
Solution: Fraught works well since he is feeling anxious and concerned, and his feelings are complicated as he would have enjoyed seeing his favored barber.
(A) Neither work, though the words may be unfamiliar.
(B) Perturbed and excited are close but don't capture a more complex range of feelings.
(C) He is anxious, but eager doesn't fit.

8. **(A)**
Category: Argument
Difficulty: Medium
Strategy: Overall, think about how the narrator feels about visits to the barber shop. While the visit he describes isn't particularly pleasant, don't ignore the statements made in the first paragraph.
Solution: There are many factors to consider on every trip. The wait. The better or worse barber. "Multifaceted" is a good word to illustrate his feelings.
(B) Too extreme. He seems to think visits are necessary even if sometimes unpleasant.
(C) Too extreme. Even the barber he's currently visiting isn't ill tempered for the most part.
(D) Opposite. Look at the opening paragraph for evidence.

Rhetoric – Fiction – Passage 3 – Pages 72-74

1.   (C)
Category: Purpose
Difficulty: Medium
Strategy: Through mapping the passage, you should have some sense of the main idea. On the surface, the passage shows the father and daughter interacting over his visit to America. In addition to that, consider what is being illustrated about the relationship.
Solution: There is conflict between the father and daughter, but the last part of the passage also shows how they are quite similar in their tendency to be quiet.
(A) Too extreme. Also, while they may both be thinking of the divorce, they actually don't speak about it.
(B) While the father thinks the daughter is being disrespectful, the passage does not examine and analyze this.
(D) The father may think this, but this is only a small portion of the passage.

2.   (D)
Category: Purpose
Difficulty: Medium
Strategy: Eliminate answers that are too extreme. C) and B) can go, and there's no evidence for A).
Solution: Her lack of enthusiasm and departure show that she's not interested in hearing more from her father.
(A) Though she is divorced, it's unclear if she is actually lonely. We only see how her father views her.
(B) Too extreme. This sentence might show how the father's advice towards is daughter isn't welcome, but "condemn" is too strong a word to describe the purpose of this sentence.
(C) Again, too extreme. He may have damaged the relationship, but it would be hard to classify it as "ruined."

3.   (A)
Category: Structure
Difficulty: Medium
Strategy: Eliminate answers that are partially wrong. Check each statement.
Solution: It is implied that the divorce happens prior to the visit, and their relationship becomes increasingly strained as the passage progresses.
(B) The first two parts of this answer are true, but the third is incorrect.
(C) The first two parts of this answer are also correct, but not the third.
(D) This answer is mostly inaccurate. We don't really know if the daughter is isolated. Mr. Shi does try to get her to talk more, but his daughter doesn't take his advice.

4.   (A)
Category: Structure
Difficulty: Medium
Strategy: POE works well here. Eliminate all the elements that aren't present in this paragraph: sparse and simple sentences, complicated and flowery language, and incessant questions.
Solution: Many thoughts and judgements are present in this paragraph, and they do show Mr. Shi's concerns.
(B) Mr. Shi isn't disinterested in his daughter's situation.
(C) Mr. Shi's thoughts are clear, not jumbled.
(D) The questioning is in the next paragraph, not this one.

5.   (B)
Category: Word Choice
Difficulty: Medium
Strategy: Consider what it means to "run into a hidden rock." This implies that the problem was not visible from the outside, so you want an answer that matches that idea.
Solution: From the father's point of view, the marriage hadn't seemed problematic.
(A) No evidence. There is nothing to suggest that the marriage was violent.
(C) The father does not understand why they divorced, so this answer doesn't work.
(D) It is unclear what kind of damage (if any) the daughter has suffered from the divorce.

6.   (A)
Category: Word Choice
Difficulty: Medium
Strategy: Predict your answer.
Solution: First, classify each conversation. The first could be described as calm, uneventful, or civil. The second could be classified as argumentative or tense.
(B) Too extreme. "Hostile" is too strong a word to classify the second conversation.
(C) Neither word fits. There is no "force" in the first conversation or secretiveness in the second.
(D) While you may not be sure what "furtive," means, the strength of answer choice a) should help you avoid selecting this answer.

7.   (B)
Category: Point of View
Difficulty: Medium
Strategy: Figure out what the point of view is throughout the passage: 3rd person, limited. The reader hears the father's thoughts but not the daughter's.
Solution: The reader does have access to the father's thoughts, and he is concerned about and editing what he says to his daughter: "Mr. Shi knows enough not to mention the sale price."
(A) The daughter's thoughts are not given.
(C) It can't be said definitively that the father is behaving "rationally."
(D) We do hear the father's thoughts, so even though the point of view is third person, this isn't accurate.

8.   (D)
Category: Argument
Difficulty: Medium
Strategy: Consider Mr. Shi's general attitude and actions. Mr. Shi gives advice to his daughter during dinner, and when she responds directly, his reaction is, "He waits for her to apologize and change the topic, as people with good manners do when they realize they are embarrassing others with their questions."
Solution: This aligns with Mr. Shi's overall thoughts and actions.
(A) While this might be true, and illustrated here, this is not Mr. Shi's belief.
(B) Could be a possible answer, but there's not enough evidence to support it.
(C) Opposite. Mr. Shi is involved in his daughter's life.

Rhetoric – Fiction – Passage 4 – Pages 75-76

1. **(D)**
Category: Purpose
Difficulty: Hard
Strategy: Reread the paragraph, then use process of elimination.
Solution: The trees have changed over time, becoming strong where they were once small.
(A) The children are mentioned, but there's nothing about their behavior.
(B) The narrator doesn't appear to want to go back to the past, even if she wishes some things had gone differently.
(C) The narrator does seem to have changed, as shown in the last paragraph.

2. **(B)**
Category: Purpose
Difficulty: Medium
Strategy: Go back to these lines; read a little before and after these lines for context.
Solution: These lines do summarize some major events of their marriage, and they condense the timeline of their marriage into a few short phrases.
(A) There's no evidence that the narrator is seeking sympathy.
(C) While these may be viewed as excuses, their validity isn't clear.
(D) There's nothing particularly confusing about this situation.

3. **(D)**
Category: Purpose
Difficulty: Hard
Strategy: Consider what the librarian does in the passage. First, she tells the narrator what she owes, then the narrator says, "I gave the librarian a check for $32. Immediately she trusted me, put my past behind her, wiped the record clean, which is just what most other municipal and/or state bureaucracies will not do."
Solution: This answer is best because the librarian seemingly forgives the narrator while the ex-husband appears to still be upset about the past.
(A) The librarian's presence isn't really tense, and the other situation with the husband isn't comfortable.
(B) While the narrator's inability to return books on time might be considered a fault, the librarian's presence doesn't illustrate this.
(C) The ex-husband doesn't appear self-conscious or terse.

4. **(C)**
Category: Structure
Difficulty: Medium
Strategy: If there are unfamiliar words in the answer choices, deal with the words you know first and eliminate answers.
Solution: The dialogue here is direct, and the narrator does think about herself at points in the story.
(A) Description is limited, so this answer doesn't work.
(B) The story isn't muddled, and the word choice is fairly simple.
(D) The author doesn't intrude in this piece.

5. **(B)**
Category: Word Choice
Difficulty: Medium
Strategy: Reread the lines and consider the purpose of this simile. Predict an answer if you can.
Solution: These lines do show how cruel and invasive his comments felt to the narrator.
(A) It's not clear that his actions destroyed their relationship.
(C) While a plumber's snake is mentioned, the ex-husband is not being compared to an actual snake.
(D) While this could be true, there isn't enough evidence to support it.

6. **(B)**
Category: Word Choice
Difficulty: Hard
Strategy: Consider why the author may want to mention war in the passage. What context do these references add?
Solution: "War" dramatizes the nature of the relationships described. The term shows how contentious these situations were.
(A) The term doesn't relate to a broader context.
(C) They don't provide a specific time frame since a specific war isn't mentioned.
(D) They do provide some context, so they're not unnecessary.

7. **(A)**
Category: Point of View
Difficulty: Medium
Strategy: Eliminate answer that are incorrect or too extreme.
Solution: The woman is an adult, and her meeting with her ex-husband is unintentional and challenging.
(B) Too extreme. The challenges aren't crippling.
(C) Wrong time period. While there is discussion of her past, she's currently older.
(D) Not enough evidence. She is older, but not necessarily elderly.

8. **(B)**
Category: Argument
Difficulty: Medium
Strategy: Find evidence to support your answer choice.
Solution: The last paragraph shows that the narrator is optimistic about change.
(A) No evidence to support this.
(C) The narrator appears to value marriage.
(D) No evidence that children made her marriage more difficult or that she feels this way.

Rhetoric – Fiction – Passage 5 – Pages 77-78

1. (C)
Category: Purpose
Strategy: Make sure to read enough around these lines. Reading only the quoted portion may lead you to the incorrect answer.
Solution: After this quoted portion, the passage says, "This was far from the case." Showing that Bertram's conversational style doesn't mirror his actual intelligence.
(A) Opposite. The passage states that he is actually intelligent.
(B) There's no mockery here.
(D) Close, but C is a better fit, and the passage is only discussing one flaw.

2. (D)
Category: Purpose
Strategy: Look for keys words to help you eliminate answers. "Characterize" and "flood" are examples of words that don't work.
Solution: There are details here that let the reader know where the characters are and the characters names.
(A) Too literal. The author is likely doing something more complex.
(B) The characters aren't characterized here.
(C) The reader is not flooded with detail.

3. (A)
Category: Structure
Strategy: Each answer choice has a lot of information. Eliminate answers that are only partially true.
Solution: This answer accurately describes their activities.
(B) Their walk is short, and Sasha doesn't seem to care about the couple.
(C) They don't stroll through a field, and the other couple is familiar.
(D) They aren't both daydreaming at the end of the passage.

4. (D)
Category: Voice / Word Choice
Strategy: Read enough around this line to get the full context: "There they sat again, looking at the same house, the same tree, the same barrel."
Solution: Sasha is feeling that everything around her is always the same in this moment.
(A) There's not enough evidence to suggest that Bertram feels apathetic towards the couple.
(B) Too extreme and untrue.
(C) Close, but she's more noticing that things around her are the same rather than showing a lack of care.

5. (A)
Category: Voice / Word Choice
Strategy: Consider her overall mood, not just her mood at points in the passage.
Solution: She is reflective throughout the passage.
(B) Mentioned in the passage, but not her overall mood.
(C) Seems like it could be true, but she's actually quite lively at points.
(D) At points she seems joyful, but not throughout the passage.

6. (C)
Category: Point of View
Solution: The narrator is not in the passage but does have access to Sasha's thoughts.
(A) Close, but this answer is too extreme. There's no evidence that she's "severely troubled."
(B) No evidence for this answer.
(D) The narrator only appears to have access to Sasha's thoughts, not all characters.

7. (B)
Category: Argument
Strategy: Consider parts of the passage where the setting is addressed. The characters look out at London and the house they've just left.
Solution: The view of London as, "the vast inattentive impersonal world; motor omnibuses; affairs; lights before public houses; and yawning policemen." is a contrast to the small garden gathering.
(A) There's no evidence that they have limited access to other spaces.
(C) Too extreme.
(D) There's no overall mood of melancholy.

Rhetoric – Global Conversation – Passage 1 – Pages 80-81

1.   (B)
Category: Purpose
Difficulty: Medium
Strategy: Map the passage and understand the main idea. Be careful about jumping to conclusions when considering answer choices.
Solution: The narrator is describing the situation with nuclear weapons and supporting a policy of peace. Choice B is broadly stated, but it's the best fit.
(A) He considers alternate approaches to a situation, but not alternate explanations.
(C) There is no focus on particular people's actions.
(D) The focus is not on specific events but a general situation.

2.   (B)
Category: Purpose
Difficulty: Medium
Strategy: Find the main idea and consider what effect the narrator wants to make with his statements. Be careful about jumping to conclusions when considering answer choices.
Solution: The paragraph describes a current problem. Later, he proposes a stance to take.
(A) The situation is not a mistake.
(C) The narrator didn't discover a technology.
(D) The passage doesn't fully resolve a problem, but proposes a way to address one.

3.   (C)
Category: Word Choice
Difficulty: Medium
Strategy: Try to imagine the narrator speaking the paragraph with emphasis on certain words. What effect does saying "all" over and over have?
Solution: The use of "all" emphasize the incredible power of all the weapons used in WWII, which then is compared to the greater power of the nuclear arsenal.

4.   (B)
Category: Argument
Difficulty: Medium
Strategy: Consider the different answer choices.
Solution: Lines 72-77 describe why there is still a threat to the U.S., even if it has the greatest weaponry.
(A) Armed friends are not a threat.
(C) This line is about the threat to opponents of the U.S.
(D) This line is about peace, not threats.

5.   (B)
Category: Structure
Difficulty: Medium
Strategy: Map the passage and summarize the way ideas are presented.
Solution: The narrator describes a problem with many facets and proposes a stance to take.
(A) The narrator considers the future, not just the past.
(C) This is related, but it's about how to deal with the situation and not how the situation impacts daily life.
(D) The narrator's stance is not definitive and he doesn't propose questions.

6.   (D)
Category: Point of View
Difficulty: Medium
Strategy: Find words that indicate emotion and tone.
Solution: The author shows concern about the threat of nuclear war but then seems more positive in his support of peace.
(A) He doesn't show appreciation for the advancements brought by war.
(B) He expresses confidence in military strength at the beginning.
(C) Not mentioned

7.   (B)
Category: Word Choice
Difficulty: Medium
Strategy: Consider what effect these words have. How does the narrator's information make you feel?
Solution: The situation is shown to have a lot of danger.
(A) The narrator doesn't use these particular words to show a problem is impossible.
(C) The narrator is talking about a hypothetical situation, not a past event.
(D) Not mentioned

Rhetoric – Global Conversation – Passage 2 – Pages 82-83

1. (C)
Category: Purpose
Difficulty: Medium
Strategy: State the argument of the passage in one sentence. Try to answer the question on your own, and choose the choice that best answers the question.
Solution: The focus on the audience's trust for banks displays that the author is trying to persuade the audience to trust the banks once they reopen.
(A) Too narrow. While the passage does describe some of the events of the banking crisis, the passage also largely encourages readers to have trust in banks.
(B) Opposite. This passage negatively portrays this action.
(D) Incorrect. The author does not compare and contrast.

2. (B)
Category: Word choice
Difficulty: Medium
Strategy: Reread the lines surrounding the term. Understand the author's attitude toward the subject in order to evaluate the word choice.
Solution: "Hoarding" has a negative connotation, which is emphasized when the action is described as "exceedingly unpopular." The author then describes an end to fear, implying that as the reason for the hoarding. Choice B best fits this portrayal of the action.
(A) Opposite. The author is depicting a negative portrayal through the word choice of "hoarding" which is further emphasized through its description as "exceedingly unpopular."
(C) Too extreme. "Hatred" is too strong of a word to fit the tone.
(D) Irrelevant. In these lines, the author is discussing the actions of bank patrons rather that banks themselves.

3. (A)
Category: Purpose
Difficulty: Easy
Strategy: Reread the lines referenced in the question. Try to answer the question on your own.
Solution: The paragraph describes banking practices as facts without stating opinions on the practices.
(B) Wrong part of the passage. The events of the banking crisis are not described in these lines.
(C) Not relevant. The paragraph neither addresses the banks nor states that the current practices should change.
(D) Wrong part of the passage. The events of the banking crisis are not stated in these lines.

4. (D)
Category: Structure
Difficulty: Medium
Strategy: Map the passage when you are reading in order to understand how the passage develops.
Solution: The passage develops by beginning with how the events of the banking crisis developed including how the banking system works in paragraph 2 and how that impacted the events of the crisis in paragraph 3. It carries on to discuss how there must be confidence in banks to fix the financial system in paragraphs 7-12.
(A) Incorrect. Banking practices are discussed in paragraph 2 and the specific events of the banking crisis are in paragraph 3.
(B) The financial confidence is for the future, not the past.
(C) Too narrow. Currency is discussed as a component to the banking system and what happened during the crisis, but it is not the focus of the beginning of the passage.

5. (D)
Category: Point of View
Difficulty: Medium
Strategy: Pay attention to tone through the use of strong verbs and adjectives.
Solution: In the third paragraph, the author describes the role of the "undermined confidence" of the people, which created an urgent demand for banks to convert assets into currency. This implies that if the public did not have their confidence undermined, the rush and demand would not have been as extreme.
(A) Not stated. The author states that the vast majority of banks are trustworthy.
(B) Too extreme. The author describes the role of the people's undermined confidence in the events, but the author also describes the untrustworthy and incompetent actions of some bankers.
(C) Misleading. The author calls upon the audience to support the system that the government created to restore the financial system.

6. (A)
Category: Evidence
Difficulty: Medium
Strategy: This asks you to provide the section of the text that supports the previous question. Use these lines to help you answer the previous question in order to solve to questions at once.
Solution: In these lines, the author describes the role of the "undermined confidence" of the people, which created an urgent demand for banks to convert assets into currency. This implies that if the public did not have their confidence undermined, the rush and demand would not have been as extreme.
(B) Not relevant. This does not support any of the claims of the previous question.
(C) Not relevant. This does not support any of the claims of the previous question.
(D) Not relevant. This does not support any of the claims of the previous question.

7. (C)
Category: Purpose
Difficulty: Medium
Strategy: Reread the lines mentioned and try to answer the question yourself before looking at the choices. Reread the surrounding lines to better understand the context and meaning of the lines in question.
Solution: Building upon the previous paragraph, the author is urging the importance of supporting his program. He urges the audience to work by stating they share the problem.
(A) Not stated. Instead, he is urging the audience to act.
(B) Too negative. He is encouraging them to act rather than chastising them.
(D) Misleading. The claim "Together we cannot fail" is not a prediction about the future but an argument about joint actions.

Rhetoric – Global Conversation – Passage 3 – Pages 84-85

1.   (B)
Category: Purpose
Difficulty: Medium
Strategy: Find the main idea of the passage. Why is JFK making this speech? What does he hope will happen?
Solution: JFK's main point is he will not restrict the right of publishers to publish news but he hopes they will censor themselves regarding information that could jeopardize the nation.
(A)   Opposite, JFK is pointedly not imposing restrictions
(C)   Opposite
(D)   Not true

2.   (C)
Category: Structure
Difficulty: Medium
Strategy: Consider each answer choice and see which matches the structure of the passage.
Solution: The speaker mentions several things he won't do (won't censor the news or create a new Office of War Information) and instead asks the publishers to take responsibility for the effect of their work.
(A)   No anecdotes
(B)   He does not apply old solutions to modern problems, and he makes a point of that
(D)   Not mentioned

3.   (D)
Category: Argument
Difficulty: Hard
Strategy: Find the answer that best fits and use process of elimination.
Solution: Choice D notes a precedent for the need to serve the good of the nation as a whole, even if it means surrendering rights.

4.   (C)
Category: Word Choice
Difficulty: Medium
Strategy: Reread these portions and consider the effect of this word being used.
Solution: The speaker uses "we" to unite him and his audience as being a part of an open, non-secretive society and as bearing responsibilities regarding censorship. In this way, he creates a sense of being joined in a similar perspective.

5.   (A)
Category: Purpose
Difficulty: Medium
Strategy: Consider the role of the paragraph. How does it relate to the following paragraphs and the rest of the passage? How does it contribute to the main purpose of the passage?
Solution: The speaker establishes background values that serve as the basis of his arguments and states how he won't act, which is based on what he assumes his audience will worry about.
(B)   Not historical
(C)   The term "secrecy" is not defined or analyzed
(D)   The main purpose is not to just define policies but to set up the following speech by showing how conflicting policies will be applied to a situation.

6.   (A)
Category: Point of View
Difficulty: Hard
Strategy: Consider the overall message the speaker is conveying.
Solution: The speaker acknowledges the publishers' rights and will not limit them, but he hopes they will censor themselves to protect their fellow citizens. Consider tone: the speaker is not frustrated or philosophical, which rules out C and D.

7.   (A)
Category: Point of View
Difficulty: Medium
Strategy: Use process of elimination. Make sure the correct answer can be directly supported by the passage.
Solution: Lines 33-36 state that news publishers have released information to other nations that should have been kept secret.
(B)   Not stated they are unavoidable
(C)   Opposite
(D)   Not stated

8.   (C)
Category: Purpose
Difficulty: Medium
Strategy: Consider the main point the speaker is making at this point in the passage.
Solution: Lines 86-91 help clarify the speaker's main argument. He is not censoring the publishers, but hopes they will restrict the information they publish because it can compromise national security.
(A)   Opposite (lines 17-22)
(B)   Incorrect (lines 32-47)
(D)   Not quite. This refers to a different audience (lines 66-67) and is a bit too broad. It could work, but C works better.

Rhetoric – Global Conversation – Passage 4 – Pages 86-88

1. **(D)**
Category: Purpose
Difficulty: Medium
Strategy: Find the main idea of the first paragraph. Consider what the author is trying to achieve with this part of the passage.
Solution: De Tocqueville notes the negative impact of mass production on the workman's mind and body.
(A) Opposite. While De Tocqueville acknowledges some value in mass production, he sees it as detrimental to the workman (lines 11-14).
(B) Irrelevant. De Tocqueville doesn't discuss daily lives of workmen.
(C) Not true. De Tocqueville doesn't mention artisans.

2. **(B)**
Category: Argument
Difficulty: Medium
Strategy: Summarize the main point made by the author.
Solution: In lines 28-31, De Tocqueville states that "the mind of the latter (the master) is enlarged in proportion as that of the former (the workman) is narrowed.
(A) Too extreme. De Tocqueville does not compare the actual intellect of the workman or the master.
(C) Not stated. While De Tocqueville uses the word "brute" in reference to the master (line 37), he doesn't endow the workman with any specific positive qualities.
(D) Not stated. While De Tocqueville does address the workman's gain in physical strength, he doesn't mention the master's strength.

3. **(A)**
Category: Purpose
Difficulty: Hard
Strategy: Read context. Use process of elimination.
Solution: The image is used to show that "the one (the workman) is continually, closely, and necessarily dependent on the other (the master)" (lines 41, 42)
(B) Too extreme. The chains are not the chains of a slave.
(C) Opposite. The workman is dependent on the master. The master is not dependent on the workman.
(D) Too extreme. The chain is about dependence, not cruelty.

4. **(B)**
Category: Purpose
Difficulty: Medium
Solution: De Tocqueville saw the way the old aristocracy "was either bound by law, or thought itself bound by usage, to come to the relief of its serving men" (lines 47-49) while, as noted above, the new aristocracy impoverishes, debases and abandons the men who serve.
(A) Opposite. De Tocqueville believed the new aristocracy "impoverishes", "debases", and "abandons" the men who serve. (lines 50-52)
(C) Opposite. See above.
(D) Partially true. The old aristocracy may have felt "bound by law", but there is no indication the new aristocracy was shaped by ideas.

5. **(D)**
Category: Word Choice
Difficulty: Medium
Strategy: Use process of elimination.
Solution: By using the term brute, De Tocqueville is showing the unfortunate loss of intellectual challenge faced by workers who face constant repetition in their labors
(A) Too extreme. The term does not convey brutality in the sense of violence or cruelty.
(B) Too negative. De Tocqueville does not look down on the workman.
(C) Too literal. The term doesn't reduce workmen to animal status.

6. **(D)**
Category: Purpose
Difficulty: Medium
Strategy: Consider what the speaker is trying to achieve. Use process of elimination.
Solution: Roosevelt agrees with the conviction that "...combination and concentrations should be, not prohibited, but supervised and within reasonable limits controlled;" (lines 72-74)
(A) Too extreme. Roosevelt is not asking for trusts to be eliminated.
(B) Too extreme. Roosevelt is not asking for trusts to be expanded.
(C) Irrelevant. The issue is not interstate commerce.

7. **(B)**
Category: Point of View
Difficulty: Medium
Strategy: Consider the main argument. Use process of elimination.
Solution: In his judgment, their conviction "is right" (lines 74-75)
(A) Opposite. Roosevelt says their belief "springs from no spirt of envy". (line 61)
(C) Opposite. Roosevelt says their belief "does not rest upon a lack of intelligent appreciation..." (lines 64-65)
(D) Opposite. Roosevelt says their belief does not rest upon "ignorance" (line 68)

8. **(A)**
Category: Structure
Difficulty: Medium
Strategy: Summarize each paragraph. Use process of elimination.
Solution: Roosevelt begins with public opinion, shares his own beliefs that government has a right to limit public corporations, and recommends that corporations should be regulated.
(B) False. Roosevelt agrees with public opinion (lines 74-75). Denounce and demand are too extreme.
(C) False. Roosevelt neither convicts public opinion nor praises corporations
(D) False. Roosevelt does not discuss the failure of corporations.

9. **(C)**
Category: Point of View
Difficulty: Medium
Strategy: Use process of elimination.
Solution: Both authors address the social aspects of manufacturing and industry: De Tocqueville on the impact on the lives of the workmen; Roosevelt on the tendencies of corporations to hurt the general welfare.
(A) Not true. Neither addresses the economic impact of mass production of goods.
(B) Too narrow. De Tocqueville is concerned about the workman, but not a loss of individualism.
(D) Not true. Neither addresses the role of artisans.

10. **(A)**
Category: Purpose
Difficulty: Medium
Strategy: Summarize the second passage. Use process of elimination.
Solution: Roosevelt is concerned that unregulated corporations can be hurtful to the general welfare. (line 60)
(B) Irrelevant. Roosevelt does not discuss the economic principles of corporate industry.
(C) Not true. There is no indication that corporations have refused to accept limits.
(D) Not true. There is no indication that Congress has failed to take action.

Rhetoric – Global Conversation – Passage 5 – Pages 89-91

1. (D)
Category: Purpose
Difficulty: Medium
Strategy: Consider how the paragraph relates to the rest of the passage.
Solution: Wiesel uses examples of violence and cruelty in the past century to introduce an essay on the dangers of indifference to human suffering and violence.
(A) Too narrow. The passage is about the inhumanity of indifference, not just of physical violence.
(B) Not relevant. Wiesel is not writing about the new millennium.
(C) Too narrow. The passage is not merely about the two World Wars.

2. (C)
Category: Word Choice
Difficulty: Medium
Solution: Wiesel uses the term to describe a state where there is "no difference" between "light and darkness… good and evil" (lines 15-18)
(A) Not true. Wiesel doesn't say it is difficult to care about others.
(B) Too narrow. Wiesel acknowledges the etymology of the word, but only as background.
(D) Not true. While this is another common meaning of indifference, it is not the meaning used by Wiesel in the passage.

3. (A)
Category: Voice
Difficulty: Hard
Solution: Wiesel examines the moral and metaphysical implications of indifference towards suffering and violence
(B) Too narrow. Wiesel uses historical examples, but the passage is not a historical analysis.
(C) Too extreme. While Wiesel clearly sees indifference as an evil, but his tone is not one of anger.
(D) Too narrow. While Wiesel clearly sees indifference as something to be regretted, he does not express sorrow.

4. (B)
Category: Argument
Difficulty: Medium
Strategy: Use process of elimination.
Solution: Wiesel acknowledges that indifference can be "tempting" and "seductive" (lines 24-25)
(A) Too extreme. In paragraph 2, Wiesel infers that at times indifference may be "necessary at times to…keep one's sanity" (line 21)
(C) Not true. Wiesel does not state or infer that indifference is necessary for humanity
(D) Not true. Wiesel states clearly that indifference is both a "sin" and a "punishment". (lines 56 and 57)

5. (B)
Category: Purpose
Difficulty: Medium
Strategy: Summarize the passage and its main points.
Solution: Wiesel defines indifference in paragraph 2, and describes its negative impact on individual relationships and on humanity as a whole.
(A) Not true. Wiesel is clear that, despite temptations towards indifference, indifference has no redeeming value
(C) Too narrow. Wiesel mentions violence but his focus is on indifference.
(D) Too extreme. Wiesel calls indifference a "punishment" in line 57, but doesn't call for it to be punished.

6. (A)
Category: Argument
Difficulty: Medium
Strategy: Summarize the passage.
Solution: Roosevelt states (lines 72-74): "It is hard to fail but it is worse never to have tried to succeed. In this life we get nothing save by effort."
(B) Too literal. Roosevelt is not talking about physical labor.
(C) Too narrow. Roosevelt mentions toil and labor in lines 61-62, but this is not the focus of his essay
(D) Not true. While mention is made of both work and leisure, there is no discussion of balancing the two.

7. (B)
Category: Structure
Difficulty: Hard
Strategy: Summarize the passage.
Solution: Roosevelt introduces the concept of the strenuous life in paragraph 1; he then considers the argument that a life of ease might seem beneficial; he concludes with the historical example of the Civil War when the nation took action against slavery.
(A) Roosevelt does not question the ideal of the strenuous life in paragraph 1. He does not continue by contemplating its effects; neither does he conclude with a counterargument
(C) Not true. Roosevelt does not begin with a historical background of the strenuous life.
(D) Not true. While Roosevelt does compare a life of ease to the strenuous life, he does not accept there is value in a life of ease.

8. (D)
Category: Point of View
Difficulty: Hard
Strategy: Use process of elimination.
Solution: Roosevelt's focus is to proudly reflect on the time when the United States as a nation took action against slavery, despite the negative consequences of war. "…for in the end the slave was freed, the Union restored, and the mighty American republic placed once more as a helmeted queen among nations". (End of the final paragraph)
(A) There is no indication that Roosevelt wrote this while President. In addition, there is no specific call for action.
(B) Too literal. While preaching is mentioned at the beginning of the passage, there is no reference to a minister or congregation.
(C) Not relevant. There is no effort to persuade to follow a cause.

9. (C)
Category: Argument
Difficulty: Medium
Solution: Both support the ideal that we must not be indifferent toward evil (Wiesel) or choose peace over fighting for what is right (Roosevelt).
(A) Opposite. Both Wiesel and Roosevelt object to "indifference towards" (Wiesel) or "inaction against" (Roosevelt) evil.
(B) Not relevant. Neither sees war as a means towards comfort or ease.
(D) Too narrow. Wiesel doesn't address the United States specifically.

10. (A)
Category: Purpose
Difficulty: Hard
Strategy: Use process of elimination.
Solution: Wiesel looks back at the violence of the 20th century as a warning against continued indifference, while Roosevelt is focused on his pride in his country for taking action against slavery ("Thank God for the iron in the blood of our fathers…", lines 116-117)
(B) Not true. Wiesel is not writing about individual actions.
(C) Too extreme. Wiesel is not condemning worldwide suffering, merely considering humanity's response to suffering.
(D) Not true. Neither is persuading an audience to take specific action.

Rhetoric – Science – Passage 1 – Pages 93-94

1. (D)
Category: Purpose
Difficulty: Medium
Strategy: Consider the author's overall purpose in the passage, looking at the broad view, rather than at narrow details.
Solution: The passage opens with a claim that photosynthesis has "brought death and decay across the world" and that, therefore, "scientists aim to make the process more efficient." The body of the passage describes the inefficiencies of photosynthesis in more detail, and the final paragraphs describe how "molecular biologists have been searching for ways to address rubisco's problems."
(A) Not relevant. No experiment is described.
(B) Not relevant. The passage discusses how rubisco is wasteful, not people.
(C) Too narrow. The passage discusses possible future technology, but none of them are prevalent and this only makes up a small part of the passage.

2. (C)
Category: Argument
Difficulty: Hard
Strategy: Consider how the author supports her claims about the inefficiencies of photosynthesis and rubisco.
Solution: In Paragraphs 3-5 (Lines 38-86), the author provides technical -descriptions of how photosynthesis and rubisco work, and then uses numbers (Lines 60-62, 70-71, 80-81, 83-86) to drive home the point.
(A) Not true. The author makes no such comparisons.
(B) Not true. The author does not make use of analogies.
(D) Not true. The author does not challenge common beliefs.

3. (B)
Category: Point of View
Difficulty: Easy
Strategy: Consider the author's purpose in choosing to use the exclamation point. Reread several lines before the sentence in question to understand the context of the exclamation.
Solution: In this paragraph, the author is describing the annoying problem of rubisco's "lack of discernment" (line 67) and its consequences. The author lists increasingly frustrating consequences, leading up to the exasperating climax of "rendering the metabolic sequence entirely ineffectual!" Note the first line of the paragraph sets the tone of frustration.
(A) The author is not surprised, as she is an expert.
(C) "Fury" is an even more extreme form of answer choice (B).
(D) There is no evidence to support a joyful tone. If anything, the author is expressing a fascinated surprise.

4. (B)
Category: Argument
Difficulty: Medium
Strategy: Consider which of the answer choices best reflects the main idea of the passage and author's purpose in a broader context.
Solution: The author concludes with the statement, "Similarly, if scientists can improve the process's efficiency, there may be an immense impact on our society" (lines 108-109) and goes on to describe specific positive potential impacts such as "combatting hunger across the world." (lines 113-114)
(A) Opposite of what the author states. While this may be true, the author focuses on the negatives of the biology itself and the positives of tampering.
(C) Opposite of what the author states. The author expresses hope that progress can have a positive influence on the environment.
(D) Opposite of the what the author states. The main purpose of the passage is to highlight an inefficiency of evolution.

5. (C)
Category: Argument
Difficulty: Medium
Strategy: Reread the lines in the answer choices and consider which one best answers the question of how a more efficient photosynthesis could impact hunger.
Solution: Answer C refers to the negative impact that rubisco's inefficiency has on food crops.
(A) Not relevant. These lines refer to the oxygen produced by the first photosynthetic algae.
(B) Not relevant. These lines refer to the rate at which rubisco processes molecules relative to other enzymes.
(D) Not relevant. This is a general statement about the overall impact of photosynthesis.

6. (A)
Category: Word Choice
Difficulty: Easy
Strategy: Reread the lines cited in the question along with a few lines before and after them. Consider the main idea of this part of the passage and how these words contribute to that main idea. What would be lost if the author used less impactful words?
Solution: Here, the author is discussing the impact of the sudden introduction of oxygen caused by photosynthesis. One result of the increased oxygen levels was "a horrible ice age that persisted for hundreds of millions of years." (lines 25-26) The author supports her assertion that the ice age was "horrible" by describing some of the conditions as "toxic" and "frigid".
(B) Not relevant. Rubisco has not been introduced in the passage yet.
(C) Not relevant. The main idea revolves around natural processes.
(D) Not relevant. The main idea revolves around natural processes.

7. (D)
Category: Purpose
Difficulty: Medium
Strategy: Reread the third paragraph and consider its role in the context of the passage as a whole. Consider what would happen if you removed the third paragraph. What void would that leave in the passage?
Solution: The third paragraph describes the technical processes that take place in photosynthesis. Furthermore, it mentions rubisco and its role in photosynthesis for the first time in the passage, thereby laying the groundwork for subsequent paragraphs to address the impact of rubisco's inefficiencies.
(A) Not relevant. The paragraph simply describes a biological process.
(B) Not true. The paragraph describes a known process.
(C) Not true. The problem is discussed before and after, but not in this paragraph.

Rhetoric – Science – Passage 2 – Pages 95-96

1.   (D)
Category: Purpose
Difficulty: M
Strategy: Consider the author's overall purpose in the passage, looking at the broad view, rather than at narrow details.
Solution: The passage begins with the assertion that "IBM's name is historically tied to the birth of computing." (lines 1-2) The passage then describes primitive computing systems and explains how engineer Herman Hollerith was inspired by Jacquard's automated loom. (lines 78-85)
(A) Not relevant. While the reader may be surprised at the origins described in the passage, the author does not mention any kind of misunderstanding.
(B) Not relevant. No ongoing problems are discussed.
(C) Too narrow. Close, but not quite right. The passage focuses on the origins of computing. It only mentions possible future advancements in passing.

2.   (A)
Category: Point of View
Difficulty: E
Strategy: Pay attention to word usage. Strong adjectives and verbs are good clues for identifying tone.
Solution: Jacquard's invention is discussed in the final paragraph. The author makes very clear how he feels about the invention when he declares, "To say this invention revolutionized the world would be no exaggeration." (lines 80-81) The author continues by describing the impact of Jacquard's invention as "profound" (line 82) and "inspiring" (line 83).
(B) Not true. There is no smugness or ambivalence in the author's descriptions.
(C) Not true. The author is overwhelmingly positive and shows no indication of being annoyed or critical.
(D) Not true. While the author could be described as curious (though this is not well supported), he shows no indication of being puzzled.

3.   (C)
Category: Structure
Difficulty: E
Strategy: Consider the way the passage flows and identify where there is a shift in main idea.
Solution: The shift occurs sharply between paragraphs 2 and 3 (line 46). The author abruptly goes from chronicling the early days of computer technology to discussing the complexity of the weaving process.
(A) Not true. While the beginning of the answer is right, the passage never suggests that computer technology will become irrelevant.
(B) Not true. While the first half of the passage might be described as chronicling a series of accomplishments, the second half does not discuss how they can be improved upon.
(D) Not true. The first part of the passage is not an anecdote, and the latter part of the passage does not provide various ways something is remembered.

4.   (B)
Category: Word Choice
Difficulty: H
Strategy: Reread the third paragraph and consider the effect of the word "we" (along with "us"). Consider how the paragraph would be different if a different pronoun had been used. What would it lack?
Solution: The writer is describing the weaving process, something that affects all of us but with which many of us are unfamiliar. In order to invoke a sense of connection between the reader and the topic, he repeatedly includes the reader in the description by using second person pronouns.
(A) Not true. If anything, "we" creates a positive, inclusive tone.
(C) Not relevant. The "group" to which the question would be referring is unclear.
(D) Not relevant. The author does not indicate that he is a member of the profession being discussed, so the "we" is not meant to refer to his relationship to weavers.

5.   (A)
Category: Purpose
Difficulty: M
Strategy: Reread the first paragraph, paying special attention to the main idea of the paragraph and the point at which the analogy to the music box is made (lines 10-13). Consider what the description of the computing machines would be lacking if the reference to the music box was removed.
Solution: The author is describing a technical process with which most people are probably not familiar. In order to make the description more accessible to a larger audience, he includes an analogy to the workings of a music box, something with which people are more commonly familiar.
(B) Not relevant. The analogy is purely mechanical in nature and does not imply a deeper relationship between science and art. Furthermore, no hypothesis is being forwarded here.
(C) Not relevant. The passage does not address theoretical technologies.
(D) Not relevant. Similar to Answer Choice B, the analogy is purely mechanical in nature and does not imply a deeper relationship between science and art.

6.   (B)
Category: Purpose
Difficulty: H
Strategy: Consider the main idea of the passage as a whole and the role that the final paragraph plays in that main idea. How does the quotation at the end serve to summarize that connection and tie up loose ends?
Solution: The author leads into the quotation by explaining that the analytical engine modeled on Jacquard's loom "served as the inspiration for Hollerith's computational machines." (lines 83-89) The quotation at the end closes out the passage by drawing a final connection between the automated loom and computer technology.
(A) Opposite of what is true. The author actually suggests similarities.
(C) Not relevant. The passage and quotation focus on the connections between Jacquard's design and computer technology, not on any flaws in the design.
(D) Misleading. While the quotation does mention "leaves and flowers," it does so in order to draw an analogy between the intricacies of the "Analytical Engine" and its "algebraical patterns" and the "Jacquard-loom".

7.   (C)
Category: Word Choice
Difficulty: E
Strategy: Reread the paragraph where these words appear. Consider the context surrounding the words and the purpose of the paragraph of which they are a part. Remove the words from the paragraph and consider what would be lost without them.
Solution: These words appear in Paragraph 3, lines 54-63, in the context of describing the process of weaving with a loom. The topic sentence of the paragraph establishes the fact that "weaving is a tedious process" (line 46) and the remainder of the paragraph provides details to support that claim. If we remove the words in question, we lose some sense of the meticulousness that is required.
(A) Not relevant. While the passage later describes a more automated process, these words do not refer to the currency of the weaving process.
(B) Not relevant. Although the reader might consider such a complex process to be obnoxious, there is no evidence in the passage to support this.
(D) Not relevant. While the loom may weave comfortable clothes, the words are used to describe the process itself, which is tedious and difficult.

8.   (C)
Category: Argument
Difficulty: H
Strategy: Consider the author's overall purpose in the passage, looking at the broad view, rather than at narrow details. Sometimes it helps to reread the first and last sentence or two of each paragraph to crystallize the main point.
Solution: The author details the innovation of the first computing machines, then details the process of hand-weaving on a loom, and then uses the final paragraph to make the connections between these seemingly unrelated topics. Lines 74 onward really crystallize the argument.
(A) Not relevant. There is nothing in the passage about rediscovering previously forgotten advancements.
(B) Not relevant. While the passage describes how a process for creating a kind of art (weaving) inspired innovations in modern technology, it does not suggest that the machines themselves are art.
(D) Too broad. While the passage describes the chronology of a couple of particular innovations, it goes too far to say that it suggests that all ideas take generations to be realized.

Rhetoric – Science – Passage 3 – Pages 97-99

1.   (D)
Category: Purpose
Difficulty: H
Strategy: Consider the author's overall purpose in the passage, looking at the broad view, rather than at narrow details.
Solution: The passage introduces the role of energy efficiency research and goes on to delineate some of the subjects of study, their history, their possible future, and the challenges involved.
(A) Not true. The passage does not describe experiments.
(B) Too broad. The focus is not on any one profession, but instead on the evolving landscape of energy efficiency.
(C) Too extreme. While the author outlines challenges that a lack of energy efficiency will bring, his tone is neutral and informative, not critical.

2.   (C)
Category: Word Choice
Difficulty: M
Strategy: Reread the paragraph where the phrase appears. Consider the context surrounding the phrase and the purpose of the paragraph of which it is a part. Remove the phrase from the paragraph and consider what would be lost without it.
Solution: The author is being a bit tongue-in-cheek here, referring back to the previous paragraph where she described a theoretical situation where an EROEI of 1:2 would eventually result in starvation (lines 11-14). By using the phrase "you know," she is attempting to make a technical subject a little more relatable to the average reader. We can all relate to the objective of not starving!
(A) Not relevant. While the paragraph goes on to explain efficiency in terms of mathematical relationships, the phrase in question does not refer to these.
(B) Not true. The author is not casting doubt on anything here.
(D) Not true. The author is clearly invested in this research, and there is no evidence that he finds it to be dull.

3.   (D)
Category: Purpose
Difficulty: H
Strategy: Reread the sentences around "*somehow*", paying special attention to the context surrounding the word. Consider the words used around "*somehow*" and the tone that they express.
Solution: In this paragraph, the author is describing a theoretical ideal EROEI. The words "fantasies"/"fantasize" (lines 25 & 29), "impossible" (line 29), and "magical imp" (line 31) convey the fanciful nature of the ideal. Furthermore, the subsequent sentence draws a contrast between the "somehow" scenario and what is likely when using "more practical sources" "in the real world" (lines 31-33).
(A) While we learn about cold fusion and its near zero-point energy later in the passage, it is not analogous to the fantastical scenario described here.
(B) Not true. The author states that "our experience and understanding of physics rule[s] out such notions as impossible" (lines 27-29).
(C) Not true. Scientists have "fantasized" about the ways to create infinite energy, not kept them secret.

4. (C)
Category: Purpose
Difficulty: M
Strategy: Reread the sentences around "*less*", paying special attention to the context surrounding the word. Think about why the author is emphasizing the word.
Solution: The author is explaining a surprising fact – that the total mass of an atom is less than the sum of its parts. Common sense would typically tell us that the atom's mass should equal the sum of its parts exactly, so the author uses italics to emphasize the word "less" and draw the reader's attention to the seeming contradiction.
(A) Opposite of true. It would seem obvious that the mass of the atom should equal the sum of its parts, not be less than it.
(B) Not relevant. The author is not discussing disappointment or a failed technology.
(D) Not relevant. The author's tone is informative, not frustrated.

5. (C)
Category: Structure
Difficulty: M
Strategy: Use process of elimination to consider the presence of each strategy throughout the passage.
Solution: The author regularly uses math to show the practicality of ideas and simplify ideas.
(A) Not true. The author does not use personification.
(B) The author does not counter assumptions.
(D) Not true. While the author generally mentions "anecdotes of scientists claiming they have achieved cold fusion" (lines 97-98), she does not actually share these anecdotes, nor does she refer to them "throughout the passage."

6. (A)
Category: Argument
Difficulty: M
Strategy: Consider the main idea of the statement and choose the lines that best support that idea.
Solution: The quotation in answer choice A directly relates our knowledge of physics to the impossibility of producing "endless energy without additional fuel spent."
(B) This serves to conclude the description of what EROEI is.
(C) This serves to provide an example of how energy efficient cold fusion could be.
(D) This serves to compare the energy efficiency of cold fusion to non-renewable resources.

7. (B)
Category: Point of View
Difficulty: M
Strategy: Consider the way the passage is written and who might be the intended audience.
Solution: The high level of detail presented in the passage indicates that the author is an expert in her field, while phrases like "you know" (line 19) and "you see" (line 61), definitions (lines 26-27), explanations (lines 39-43), and the questions the author anticipates in lines 45-46 and 94-95 indicate that the author is trying to simplify the passage for a less scientific audience.
(A) Not mentioned. There is not a focus on human culture throughout history.
(C) Not true. The level of detail belies the author's expertise, and the main idea of the passage revolves around surveying topics of energy efficiency, not persuading the reader to find it interesting.
(D) Not true. While the author does mention how EROEI is related to goods that can be sold for profit, the focus is not on the profitability of the industry, but on its sustainability. Furthermore, there is no evidence to indicate that the author is an investor.

8. (A)
Category: Purpose
Difficulty: H
Strategy: Reread the lines before and after the question appears. Consider the context surrounding the question and the purpose of the paragraph of which it is a part. Remove the question from the paragraph and consider what would be lost without it.
Solution: As discussed in Question 5, the author poses questions that she anticipates a reader might ask. She is acknowledging that the facts she just presented (the continuous fall of domestic oil's EROEI) may seem contradictory and may not make sense to someone who is not an expert in the field.
(B) Not true. The question is not referring to a problem posed earlier in the passage.
(C) Not relevant. There is no evidence to suggest that these facts cause difficulties in others accepting new ideas.
(D) Not relevant. There is no experiment discussed.

9. (B)
Category: Argument
Difficulty: M
Strategy: Consider the main idea of the statement and choose the evidence that best supports that idea.
Solution: The author concludes the 5th paragraph by saying, "…while cold fusion is not an endless source of energy, its remarkably high EROEI makes it an attractive candidate to tackle not-too-distant energy problems."
(A) While Einstein's equation is mentioned (lines 59-61), it is in the context of explaining why cold fusion has such a high EROEI, not why it is a superior alternative to fossil fuels.
(C) While this analogy is used throughout the passage, it is done so in the context of explaining what a favorable EROEI means. It should not be taken literally.
(D) While this is true, it is only an example of "one potential form of cold fusion" (lines 71-72) used to illustrate just how much energy it can produce.

10. (A)
Category: Purpose
Difficulty: H
Strategy: Reread the lines around the section where "nuclear fission" appears. Consider the main idea and the purpose of the paragraph of which it is a part. Remove the reference from the paragraph and consider what would be lost without it.
Solution: The author is comparing and contrasting cold fusion to nuclear fission, introducing the comparison with "in spite of" the similarities before drawing a sharp contrast between the two – that "meltdowns and radiation…do not apply to cold fusion" (lines 87-88).
(B) Not relevant. Wheat production is not discussed here.
(C) Not true. The author mentions nuclear power plants in order to orient the reader to nuclear fission, but she does not advocate for building more of them.
(D) Not true. The author mentions nuclear power plants in order to orient the reader to nuclear fission, but she does not discuss their EROEI.

Rhetoric – Sciences – Passage 4 – Pages 100-102

1. (B)
Category: Purpose
Difficulty: Medium
Strategy: Consider how the paragraph relates to the development of the passage as a whole. Use process of elimination.
Solution: The first paragraph addresses the mystery of the high temperatures of the sun's corona
(A) Wrong part of passage. Evidence comes in paragraph 3.
(C) Not relevant. Other theories are not mentioned.
(D) Wrong part of passage. A new theory is suggested in paragraph 2.

2. (C)
Category: Structure
Difficulty: Medium
Strategy: Summarize each paragraph.
Solution: The author begins by introducing the mystery of the heat of the sun's corona, proposes the wave heating theory in paragraph two, and provides evidence for the theory in paragraph three.
(A) Not true. No evidence for a theory is given in paragraph one.
(B) Not true. No new theory is proposed in paragraph one.
(D) Not true. No past theory is questioned in the passage.

3. (D)
Category: Point of View
Difficulty: Hard
Strategy: Use process of elimination.
Solution: The piece is written to explain, in language accessible to non-scientists, a theory about the heat of the sun's corona.
(A) False. There is no critique in passage one.
(B) False. There is no indication that this is the author's personal theory.
(C) False. A scientist would not need to explain the mystery of the sun's corona to peers

4. (A)
Category: Argument
Difficulty: Medium
Strategy: Use process of elimination.
Solution: The author of passage 2 suggests that nanoflares may "account for the heat discrepancy" in the mystery of the heat of the sun's corona.
(B) False. While the author mentions the principles of thermodynamics in lines 1 and 2, they are not noted as an explanation for the heretofore unexplained heat of the sun's corona
(C) Opposite. Nanoflares may be an explanation for the heretofore unexplained heat of the sun's corona, not the sun's core.
(D) Irrelevant. Heat discrepancy is the mystery being explored, not a possible solution.

5. (B)
Category: Purpose
Difficulty: Medium
Strategy: Summarize the paragraph. Use process of elimination.
Solution: The paragraph addresses the link between solar flares and magnetic reconnection. (lines 68-71)
(A) Wrong part of the passage. The argument for nanoflares is in paragraph four.
(C) Not true. The author does not mention the wave heating theory.
(D) Wrong part of the passage. The argument and evidence for nanoflares is in paragraph four.

6. (C)
Category: Word Choice
Difficulty: Medium
Solution: Corroborate implies support for the nanoflare theory, based on evidence.
(A) Too strong. Corroborate means "to make more certain", not to prove.
(B) Too negative. Corroboration implies support for a theory, not argument against a theory.
(D) Irrelevant. The author does not express a personal opinion.

7. (B)
Category: Argument
Difficulty: Medium
Strategy: Use process of elimination.
Solution: Both state that the heat of the sun's corona has been a mystery to scientists.
(A) Opposite. Both state that the heat of the sun's corona is hotter than that of its surface.
(C) False. While both make a note of magnetism, the focus is on the mystery of the heat of the sun's corona.
(D) Not true. Only the author of passage two mentions nanoflares as a possible solution.

8. (B)
Category: Argument
Difficulty: Medium
Strategy: Summarize the second passage. Use process of elimination.
Solution: The author argues that nanoflares may explain the corona's high temperatures (lines 26-28)
(A) Not true. The IRIS is used to observe the sun's pattern of ultraviolet emissions. It does not contribute to the corona's high temperature
(C) Not true. While the author describes Hard-X-rays as " a type of emission unique to solar flares" (lines 24-25) there is no mention of the location of hard X-rays within the sun's core
(D) Not stated. While the author mentions magnetic reconnection in line 20, it is connection with models from the University of Oslo. The main argument is that nanoflares may explain the corona's high temperatures.

Rhetoric – Science – Passage 5 – Pages 103-104

1. (A)
Category: Purpose
Difficulty: E
Strategy: Consider the author's overall purpose in the passage, looking at the broad view, rather than at narrow details. It may help to review the first and last sentence from each paragraph.
Solution: The passage begins by asserting, "Here on Earth, we have certain ideas about what constitutes life…" (lines 1-2) before introducing several examples of life that don't fit our common definition. It goes on to discuss the conditions we consider when looking for life on other planets.
(B) Not relevant. The passage does not discuss the development of a technology.
(C) Opposite of what is true. The author acknowledges that there are many life forms that fall outside of the common definition and that there is much we do not yet know.
(D) Not true. While some of the facts in the passage may be surprising to the reader, the passage does not focus on any particular recent or surprising discovery.

2. (D)
Category: Structure
Difficulty: M
Strategy: Consider how the passage flows between main ideas.
Solution: The passages surveys our conceptions about life on Earth in order to extend them to and consider them in the context of our search for extraterrestrial life.
(A) While the passage provides a somewhat detailed description of the forms of life on Earth, it does not do so "across the universe" and does not consider how forms of life across the universe impact biological research.
(B) While there are some overviews of familiar knowledge, the passage does not apply it to everyday situations (unless searching for life on Mars is an everyday situation!)
(C) While the passage discusses the possibility of life on Mars, it uses Mars as an example to illustrate a larger point.

3. (C)
Category: Argument
Difficulty: M
Strategy: Identify Cox's theory and crystallize its main idea in your mind. Then, consider which answer choice would contradict it.
Solution: Cox's theory can be found in lines 78-89. In sum, Cox argues that the evolutionary accident that resulted in eukaryotes was a singular event in the history of the universe, so any extraterrestrial life we might find would likely be primitive and unicellular. If, as in answer choice C, complex, multicellular life was found to be able to evolve a variety of different ways, then his theory would no longer be supported.
(A) Not relevant. Cox's theory revolves around a chance event in the universe and is not predicated on a large number of planets hospitable to life.
(B) Not relevant. That life can now be found in a wide variety of environments does not disprove the idea that the evolution of the first eukaryote was a highly unlikely chance occurrence.
(D) Opposite. Cox's theory predicts that extraterrestrial life will be basic, so this would support his theory.

4. (A)
Category: Argument
Difficulty: H
Strategy: Consider the main idea of the passage and the sections of the passage that directly discuss the search for life on other planets. Select the answer choice that best reflects the ideas expressed in the passage.
Solution: The passage describes the current search for life on other planets, explaining in Paragraph 2 that it is "still based on substances

that are crucial to life on Earth: liquid water and carbon" (lines 25-27). Later, in Paragraph 3, the author describes scientists who postulate that "a focus on liquid water or carbon will blind us to the other possibilities of life" (lines 55-56) and suggest that other solvents or elements be considered instead. Thus, there are many things to consider in the search for extraterrestrial life.
(B) No evidence that the author thinks the search is impractical.
(C) Too narrow. The author says "it may be shortsighted to only look for life as it exists on Earth" (lines 68-69), but does not believe the search itself is shortsighted.
(D) No evidence that the author thinks the search is inevitable. Rather, physicist Brian Cox simply believes that there is a "chemical inevitability for life on other planets" (line 79).

5. (D)
Category: Argument
Difficulty: H
Strategy: Use process of elimination to consider the presence of each strategy throughout the passage.
Solution: This happens in several places: first, when the author presumes the reader's definition of life in Paragraph 1 (lines 1-7) and again when the author cautions that "before we imagine a *Star Trek*-ian future…temper our expectations" (lines 76-77).
(A) Too extreme. The definitions of life are not "entirely" incorrect, and while various perspectives are introduced, none is directly proposed by the author.
(B) Misleading. The author does not propose any ways to view the situation, but instead considers a variety of different views espoused by others.
(C) The author provides only a few snippets of quotes from one scientist, and they are not in response to commonly held opinions.

6. (A)
Category: Purpose
Difficulty: H
Strategy: Reread the lines around the section where "wires" and "splinter" appear. Consider how you may read or understand the sentences differently if the words were not in quotation marks.
Solution: The author is describing the actions of some forms of life that she expects will be unfamiliar to the reader. In order to do so in a way that most readers can understand, she uses common terms instead of scientific jargon.
(B) Not mentioned. There no reference to an established scientist.
(C) Not true. These words are describing "organisms discovered on Earth in recent decades" (line 13)
(D) Not true. These are not common slang terms.

7. (C)
Category: Purpose
Difficulty: M
Strategy: Reread the third paragraph and consider its role in the context of the passage as a whole. Consider what would happen if you removed the third paragraph.
Solution: The author begins the paragraph with the phrase "To further complicate matters…" (line 54). After detailing the complications, she summarizes the paragraph by stating, "For these reasons, life could take on many forms and make use of a variety of elements, so it may be shortsighted to only look for life as it exists on Earth."
(A) Too extreme. The paragraph does not suggest that the endeavor is impossible, just that it is complicated.
(B) Not true. No calculations are described.
(D) Not true. There is no evidence that the author is questioning the field of study.

Rhetoric – Science – Passage 6 – Pages 105-106

1. **(D)**
Category: Purpose
Difficulty: E
Strategy: Consider the author's overall purpose in the passage, looking at the broad view, rather than at narrow details. It may help to review the first and last sentence from each paragraph.
Solution: The author concludes the first paragraph with a fairly concise summary of his purpose: "…let's attempt to understand what quantum entanglement is so we can speculate on how it may be utilized and whether it is worth investment" (lines 20-22)
(A) Too narrow. While the passage mentions early 20th Century scientists, it does so only to provide historical context. In addition, nothing is mentioned about those scientists' "creativity".
(B) Not true. The passage's explanation of entanglement builds off of Heisenberg's principle (lines 23-48).
(C) Not true. Einstein's theories are mentioned in order to provide historical context, but the author is not out to prove them.

2. **(D)**
Category: Purpose
Difficulty: M
Strategy: Reread the first paragraph and consider its role in the context of the passage as a whole. Consider what would happen if you removed the first paragraph. What void would that leave in the passage?
Solution: The author concludes the first paragraph with a fairly concise summary of her purpose: "…let's attempt to understand what quantum entanglement is so we can speculate on how it may be utilized and whether it is worth investment" (lines 20-22)
(A) Not relevant. The author makes clear he is interested in scientific investment and is simply looking to gain a basic understanding of a potentially profitable phenomenon.
(B) Not mentioned. The author does not mention any controversy in the first paragraph.
(C) Not mentioned. The author does not identify any difficulties that are due to the nascent state of the science; he simply admits that the field of study itself is confusing (11).

3. **(D)**
Category: Point of View
Difficulty: E
Strategy: Consider the way the passage is written and who might be the intended audience.
Solution: The author identifies his perspective in the first paragraph – "speculators should consider investing" (line 6), "there is vast potential for new commercial opportunities to arise" (lines 15-16), and "…whether it is worth investment" (line 22) – and last paragraph – "Such technologies could be incredibly valuable…there is money to be made" (lines 118-122).
(A) Not mentioned. There is no indication that the author is a journalist. Instead, he is an investor himself.
(B) Not true. The author admits that the field is "confusing" (line 11) and uses an entire paragraph (lines 73-101) to explain the phenomenon with a simple analogy.
(C) Not mentioned. There is no indication that the author is a historian. Though the author uses history for context, he does not "explore different theories for the origins of particle physics discoveries".

4. **(B)**
Category: Structure
Difficulty: E
Strategy: Consider the way the passage flows and identify where there is a shift in main idea.
Solution: The first paragraph outlines the author's purpose in writing the piece. The passage then shifts for several paragraphs into a discussion of the background of quantum physics and a description of what is meant by "entanglement" (lines 22-101). Another shift occurs in the final paragraph, where the author places the focus on how the described phenomenon might be used in practical technologies.
(A) Too narrow. While various scientists and their discoveries are mentioned, the focus is not on describing the life or accomplishments of any one scientist.
(C) Not mentioned. While various scientists and their discoveries are mentioned, the focus is not on describing the accomplishments or goals of any one person.
(D) Not true. The passage mentions past innovations and anticipates future innovations, but the focus is not on an innovation itself, but on understanding the scientific principles behind innovations that have not yet occurred.

5. **(B)**
Category: Word Choice
Difficulty: Easy
Strategy: Reread the lines around "well". Consider the context surrounding the word and the purpose of the paragraph of which it is a part. Remove "well" from the paragraph and consider what would be lost without it.
Solution: The sentence using "well" is followed by the question, "Not too spooky yet, right?" (line 78) The "yet" implies that something is about to change. Indeed, it does, when the author declares that "things get odder" (line 79) and introduces a situation where the outcome is not predictable. Thus, the predictable "well" scenario is in contrast to one for which the outcome is not obvious.
(A) Not relevant. While "entanglement" is being explained via analogy here, it is not being directly discussed.
(C) Not relevant. There is no element of "unfairness" here.
(D) Not mentioned. There is no evidence that the narrator is annoyed.

6. **(D)**
Category: Argument
Difficulty: M
Strategy: Use process of elimination to consider the presence of each strategy throughout the passage.
Solution: The author uses analogies throughout the passage. In Paragraph 1, "As you surely know…just as the creation of the steam engine…brought sudden wealth…" (lines 15-19); in Paragraph 2, "The physical state…can be likened to something like a coin toss…all the different potential states of the particle, just as the flipped coin's ultimate fate…"(lines 35-41); and most notably in Paragraph 5, "To demonstrate this phenomenon, imagine we have two friends…" (lines 73-95).
(A) Not true. The author does not introduce conflicting ideas or express an opinion about the superiority of one idea or another.
(B) Too narrow. While the author adds some narration to the scientific history, this does not play a significant role in "dramatizing" the piece.
(C) Too narrow. While the author poses some questions that researchers hope to answer (lines 105-110), he does not answer them.

Rhetoric – Sciences – Passage 7 – Pages 107-108

1.   (B)
Category: Purpose
Difficulty: E
Strategy: Consider the author's overall purpose in the passage, looking at the broad view, rather than at narrow details.
Solution: The author uses the 2nd paragraph to discuss the discovery that living organisms generate electricity, the 3rd paragraph to introduce the first time that "scientists began using organisms as generators of electricity" (lines 29-30), the 4th – 6th paragraphs to discuss "renewed interest in revisiting…generation of electricity through biological processes" (lines 38-39), and the final paragraph to explain that "this technology is still developing" (lines 98-99).
(A)   Opposite. The author suggests ways microbial fuel cells may be used in the future and views these possibilities as "revolution[ary]" (line 102) and potentially able to "reshape our lives" (line 105).
(C)   Too narrow/not relevant. While experiments are described, the passage does not focus on one experiment, and there are no experiments that "contradict a widely held belief".
(D)   Not relevant. While a history of the science is provided, various explanations for it are not.

2.   (C)
Category: Word Choice
Difficulty: M
Strategy: Consider the context surrounding the word and the purpose of the paragraph of which it is a part. Remove "visionaries" from the paragraph and consider what would be lost without it.
Solution: In the topic sentence of the paragraph, the author claims that "some great ideas take a long time to gain support" (lines 1-2). In the several sentences that follow, the author offers examples of ideas that did not catch on immediately, including that of the "visionaries who first used umbrellas" (lines 5-6).
(A)   Not relevant. The word "visionaries" refers to insightful people who recognize the utility of new ideas before others. It does not have to do with physically seeing people.
(B)   Not true. If anything, the passage discusses the foresight of successful scientists, not the lack thereof of unsuccessful ones.
(D)   Not mentioned. While there is a discussion of new technologies, there is no discussion of profits.

3.   (C)
Category: Purpose
Difficulty: M
Strategy: Reread the lines around "macabre" and "eerily". Consider the context surrounding the words and the purpose of the paragraph of which they are a part. Remove "macabre" and "eerily" from the paragraph and consider what would be lost without them.
Solution: Galvani uses electrical stimulation to make frog corpses twitch. The author describes the "experimental setup" as "disturbingly morbid" (lines 14-15) before describing the "odd, macabre material: frog skin" (line 17). Thus, the author is clearly disgusted.
(A)   Wrong part of the passage. Rittman is not introduced until Paragraph 6 (line 86).
(B)   Too extreme. While the author finds the experimental materials to be gross, she does not have a sinister attitude toward it.
(D)   Not relevant. While the author invokes Frankenstein in an analogy, she is not actually talking about the book.

4.   (D)
Category: Argument
Difficulty: M
Strategy: Identify the author's argument and crystallize its main idea in your mind. Then, consider which answer choice would weaken it.
Solution: The author asserts that there are extensive possibilities to use bacteria in microbial fuel cells that would convert waste into energy. If it's true that bacteria are fragile, these possibilities would be limited.
(A)   Not relevant. Just because there are other systems does not mean that a new system cannot also be put into place.
(B)   Not relevant. The author specifically refers to the "enormous variety of bacterial species" and their ability to specialize. His argument does not depend on one species doing all the work.
(C)   Opposite. That the need for energy sources will only increase supports the author's argument of finding new ways to release energy.

5.   (A)
Category: Argument
Difficulty: E
Strategy: Use process of elimination to consider the presence of each strategy throughout the first paragraph.
Solution: The author lists several scenarios involving well-known objects – the telephone, umbrellas, and the electric car – that were mocked or ignored when first introduced. This provides a familiar framework for her to connect with the delayed popularity of a lesser known entity – biological fuel cells.
(B)   Not true. The author is not proposing any ideas on her own and she does not directly criticize anyone.
(C)   Not true. While the author describes a common behavior (the extended time it takes for "some great ideas…to gain support" (lines 1-2), it would be a stretch to categorize this as "well-known".
(D)   Not true. While the author lists a few different examples, they are not sequential (the electric car was first invented before the telephone). They do not cause each other.

6.   (B)
Category: Structure
Difficulty: H
Strategy: Consider the way the passage flows and identify where it transitions between main ideas.
Solution: Paragraphs 2 and 3 explain the phenomenon of bioelectricity and its discovery. In the fourth paragraph (lines 37-60), the author describes renewed interest in the topic. For the remainder of the passage, the author connects bacteria to the previous ideas of electrical generation and describes possibilities for harnessing energy using bacteria.
(A)   Not relevant. Even though the discoveries the author discusses could certainly be profitable, the author does not mention this.
(C)   The first half is not an overview of modern research, but a historical background.
(D)   Not true. The author does not provide a description of personal experiences.

7.   (A)
Category: Purpose
Difficulty: E
Strategy: Reread the last paragraph and consider its role in the context of the passage as a whole. Consider what would happen if you removed the last paragraph. What void would that leave in the passage?
Solution: The paragraph begins with "This technology is still developing" (line 98) and goes on to describe several possibilities, using the phrases "in the future", "would be revolutionized", "would be formed", "could reshape", and "until then".
(B)   Not true. This paragraph supports the argument biological fuel cells could play an important role in energy generation in the future.
(C)   Not true. There is no controversy introduced in this paragraph.
(D)   Opposite. The paragraph lists potential future events.

Rhetoric – Sciences – Passage 8 – Pages 109-110

1.   (C)
Category: Purpose
Difficulty: H
Strategy: Consider the author's overall purpose in the passage, looking at the broad view, rather than at narrow details. It may help to review the first and last sentence from each paragraph.
Solution: The author provides an overview of nanorobots – how they have developed, the similarities they have to familiar "macro" robots, some recent research into them, and possible applications for the future.
(A) Too narrow. While the author discusses the use of enzymes as nanobots in Paragraph 4 (lines 72-102), this is only a part of the larger discussion about nanorobotics in general.
(B) Too broad. While the passage highlights some recent discoveries, they are specific to nanorobotics and do not span the field of biology in general.
(D) Too narrow AND too broad. While the passage addresses future applications of nanorobotic technology, it focuses on other aspects as well. Considered another way, the passage only focuses on nanorobotic technology, not on future applications of technology in general.

2.   (A)
Category: Structure
Difficulty: H
Strategy: Consider the way the passage flows and identify where it transitions between main ideas.
Solution: The passage opens with a description of the structure and function of ATP synthase (lines 1-11), then describes the benefits of robots (lines 18-26), and then introduces the idea of nanorobots and how they blend aspects of biological mechanisms and robotic engineering (lines 26 onward).
(B) There is no indication that scientists have failed to replicate it. The author only says, "By *observing* the mechanisms of molecular wonders such as ATP synthase, chemists can devise new machines" (lines 13-16).
(C) Not true. The passage does not present a problem that needs to be solved.
(D) Not true. While the passage mentions several technologies, there is no discussion of any being superior to any others.

3.   (D)
Category: Argument
Difficulty: H
Strategy: Use process of elimination to consider the presence of each strategy throughout the passage.
Solution: On several occasions, the author references common things to which the reader can relate: "ten thousand times smaller…sheet of paper" (lines 8-9), "a billion machines…a grain of rice" (lines 36-37), multiple analogies in the quotation by David Leigh (lines 45-62) and "Similar to…large robots…nanomachines need such standardized components" (lines 105-108).
(A) Too narrow. While the author does highlight features of nanobots, he does not do this throughout the passage. In addition, he does not explain historical influences behind their developments.
(B) Not true. While the author tries to predict some problems that nanobots might help solve, he does not develop the passage through a series of problems and resolutions.
(C) Not true. The author does not describe personal experiences.

4.   (D)
Category: Word Choice
Difficulty: M
Strategy: Reread the third paragraph with special focus on the lines around the words indicated. Consider the context surrounding the words and the purpose of the paragraph of which they are a part. Remove "individual," "specific," and "exact" from the paragraph and consider what would be lost without them.
Solution: The purpose of the 3rd paragraph is to introduce the concept of nanorobots and the unique tasks they are able to perform. It follows a paragraph that provides an introduction to robots "on a macro scale" and differentiates nanobots' ability to "perform chemical operations that are entirely beyond the scope of human labor" (lines 28-29). The highlighted words appear in lines 37-43 and emphasize the precision employed by nanobots on that small scale.
(A) Misleading. In context, these words are highlighting strengths of nanobots, not challenges.
(B) Not relevant. The words are being applied to the work nanobots perform, not to the research required to create them.
(C) Not relevant. The words are being applied to the work nanobots perform, not to the challenges of an experiment.

5.   (C)
Category: Argument
Difficulty: E
Strategy: Consider which answer choice best reflects Leigh's quotation and work.
Solution: The author quotes Leigh at length, describing his work around nanomachines. Towards the end of the quotation, Leigh expresses his belief in the potential for the advancement of robotics: "Our aim is to design and make the smallest machines possible. This is just the start, but we anticipate that within 10 to 20 years molecular robots will begin to be used to build molecules and materials on assembly lines in molecular factories" (lines 57-63).
(A) No evidence that Leigh believes that enzymes cannot be used.
(B) No evidence that Leigh prioritizes "the artistry of human labor".
(D) While this may be true, again there is no evidence to support this.

6.   (C)
Category: Argument
Difficulty: E
Strategy: Consider the main idea of the statement and choose the lines that best support that idea.
Solution: The quotation in Answer Choice C directly addresses a task that nanobots can perform that "[would] allow for treatment of illnesses before our senses could even detect them," thereby drawing a contrast between the capabilities of nanobots and those of the humans.
(A) This is describing how robots play a role in assembly lines.
(B) This explains how scientists are able to control nanobots.
(D) This is describing a new discovery about the behavior of enzymes.

7.   (A)
Category: Purpose
Difficulty: M
Strategy: Reread the analogy and consider its role in the context of the paragraph. Consider what would happen if you removed the analogy. What void would that leave in the paragraph?
Solution: This analogy appears in lines 50-57, where David Leigh is describing how nanorobots are controlled and what they are able to do. He draws a comparison with the operation of a car assembly line – a machine that readers can relate to and understand.
(B) Not true. The analogy is only a comparison to improve understanding. There is no evidence – and it is unreasonable – that nanobots would replace automobile assembly lines.
(C) Not mentioned. There is no discussion of robots replacing human jobs.
(D) Not true. Like in B, the analogy is only a comparison to improve understanding. There is no discussion of nanobots being involved in actual industrial assembly lines.

Rhetoric – Sciences – Passage 9 – Pages 111-113

1. (C)
Category: Word Choice
Difficulty: Medium
Strategy: Use context to consider the intended meaning.
Solution: The idea is that concepts at the subatomic are not "intuitive", or "easily perceived."
(A) Too broad. The term is not being applied to all of scientific research.
(B) Too broad. The term is not being applied to all of scientific research.
(D) Opposite. The idea is that concepts at the subatomic level are not "intuitive", or "easily perceived".

2. (A)
Category: Purpose
Difficulty: Medium
Strategy: Summarize the paragraph. Use process of elimination.
Solution: In paragraph 2, the author compares the way both electrons and olfactory receptors travel through barriers.
(B) Opposite. The author is focused on the similarities, not the differences, between the two.
(C) Wrong part of the passage. The shape theory is not discussed in paragraph two.
(D) Wrong part of the passage. The shape theory is not discussed in paragraph two.

3. (B)
Category: Argument
Difficulty: Medium
Strategy: Summarize the passage. What is the key point the author is making?
Solution: The author addresses flaws in the shape theory, then explains how vibrational theory can solve those flaws.
(A) Too narrow. While the author addresses flaws in the shape theory of olfaction, the focus of the argument is on the way vibrational theory solves those flaws.
(C) Too broad. While the author addresses both theories, the focus of the argument is on the way vibrational theory solves problems found in shape theory.
(D) Too extreme. While neither theory has been "proven", the author's focus is not on lack of sufficient evidence for either.

4. (A)
Category: Structure
Difficulty: Hard
Strategy: Summarize each paragraph. Use process of elimination.
Solution: Paragraph 1 provides information on electrons and quantum tunneling. Paragraph 2 introduces the vibration theory. Paragraph 3 provides evidence for the vibration theory. Paragraph 4 concludes that the vibration theory "must be" (last sentence) the explanation for odor discernment.
(B) False. No theory is introduced in Paragraph 1.
(C) False. There is no critique of any theory in Paragraph 1.
(D) False. While the author provides background on a concept and develops a theory based on that concept, there is no acknowledgment of a counter argument, and the author does not conclude that more evidence is needed. Rather, the author concludes with a positive assessment of the theory.

5. (D)
Category: Point of View
Difficulty: Hard
Strategy: Consider the tone of the passage. Use process of elimination.
Solution: The author briefly explains vibrational and shape theory, comparing them to each other.
(A) Too narrow. There is no indication the writer has pursued his/her own research.
(B) Too narrow. The writer notes flaws with vibrational theory, but also defends shape theory.
(C) The terminology and explanations are in line with explaining a concept to those unfamiliar with the topic, but the tone is not as casual as what would be expected in a popular magazine.

6. (A)
Category: Word Choice
Difficulty: Hard
Strategy: Consider tone. Use process of elimination.
Solution: The use of the term infers that the theory is outside the range of probability, with an ironic, negative connotation.
(B) Too literal. The theory is not foreign, as in "from another place"
(C) Opposite. The author does not use the term in a positive way and disproves its legitimacy.
(D) Too extreme. While the author infers the theory is outside the range of probability, he/she doesn't discount the theory altogether as ridiculous.

7. (C)
Category: Argument
Difficulty: Medium
Strategy: Use process of elimination.
Solution: Both authors acknowledge research into both theories.
(A) Not true. The author of passage 2 defends shape theory.
(B) Not true. The author of passage 1 concludes that "the different vibrations in the bonds must be triggering odor discernment in animals". (last sentence)
(D) Too extreme. There is no indication that either has been discredited by the scientific community.

8. (B)
Category: Argument
Difficulty: Medium
Strategy: Use process of elimination.
Solution: Both authors cite specific examples of flaws in the opposing theory and offer examples of solutions to these flaws in his/her preferred theory
(A) Not stated. Neither recommends further research.
(C) Not stated. Neither suggests that a new theory is needed.
(D) Opposite. Each notes flaws in the other's theory, not his/her preferred theory.

Rhetoric – Sciences – Passage 10 – Pages 114-115

1.   (D)
Category: Purpose
Difficulty: Medium
Strategy: Consider how the paragraph relates to the rest of the passage. What does it achieve?
Solution: The author mentions transit photometry, RV surveys, astrometry, and the microlensing technique.
(A) Not true. The author is merely introducing the transit photometry method
(B) Too narrow. The author mentions a number of methods used in the search for exoplanets.
(C) Irrelevant. There is no definition of exoplanets in the paragraph.

2.   (A)
Category: Word Choice
Difficulty: Medium
Strategy: Consider the way the word is used in relation to information around it. Use process of elimination.
Solution: All current techniques employ indirect methods. (lines 4-11)
(B) Not true. While none of the listed techniques are perfect, each contributes to the search for exoplanets.
(C) Too extreme. Each of the techniques has advantages, as well as disadvantages.
(D) Too negative. There is no criticism here, but rather an acknowledgment that direct detection is "exceedingly difficult to perform". (lines 12-13)

3.   (B)
Category: Structure
Difficulty: Medium
Strategy: Summarize each paragraph.
Solution: The first paragraph provides an overview. Paragraphs 2 and 3 consider the pros and cons of the RV method and the transit photometry method
(A) Not true. The author does not introduce the concept of the search for exoplanets, but rather begins with explanations of various techniques currently used in the search. He also provides both advantages and disadvantages for each.
(C) Not true. The author does not define a dilemma in the first paragraph. In addition, he considers the potential of two possible solutions in the final paragraph.
(D) Not true. There is no historical overview of the search for exoplanets.

4.   (D)
Category: Argument
Difficulty: Medium
Strategy: Summarize the paragraph. What is the main point the author is making?
Solution: The author indicates that both methods have strong potential in the search for exoplanets. (lines 53-54; 62-68)

5.   (C)
Category: Purpose
Difficulty: Medium
Strategy: Summarize the passage. What is the author achieving?
Solution: Both pros and cons are given for the various methods described
(A) Too negative. The author is examining the pros and cons, not just the cons.
(B) Not relevant. There is no effort to persuade scientists to choose a specific method
(D) Not relevant. There is no mention of why we must search for exoplanets.

6.   (C)
Category: Word Choice
Difficulty: Hard
Strategy: Be careful of other meanings of "obscure." Use process of elimination.
Solution: Exoplanets are hidden "in the stellar light of their own stars".
(A) Wrong meaning of obscure. The focus is on the fact that exoplanets are hidden, not that results are vague.
(B) Opposite. Exoplanets are hidden due to the brightness of light around them
(D) Not relevant. The term is not used to describe the properties of exoplanets.

7.   (A)
Category: Point of View
Difficulty: Hard
Strategy: Consider the author's tone. How does he feel about the topic as a whole? Use process of elimination.
Solution: The author concludes in paragraph 4 with the strong potential for two specific methods in the search for exoplanets
(B) Too negative. While the author does include some problems with current methods, he is generally positive about the future of the search.
(C) Too negative. See above.
(D) Too extreme. The author uses positive words -"potential", "powerful" "advantageous" – but does not share a personal fascination with the methods described.

8.   (B)
Category: Voice
Difficulty: Hard
Strategy: Consider the author's tone. How does he feel about the topic as a whole? Be careful of answer choices that are too extreme.
Solution: The author offers a scientific analysis of the pros and cons of the various methods.
(A) Too extreme. The author does not convey personal excitement.
(C) Too negative. The author ends with optimism, not pessimism.
(D) Too extreme. The author does not convey a sense of curiosity.

Rhetoric – Social Studies – Passage 1 – Pages 117-118

1. (D)
Category: Argument/Point of View
Difficulty: M
Strategy: Consider the entire passage. The author never treats it as unimportant and writes about its modern application. Look out for overly stated responses and only partially correct answers.
Solution: The first two paragraphs talk about this problem as an intellectual puzzle, and the last two paragraphs talk about modern solutions and applications.
(A) The author never suggests the question is silly.
(B) Overstated. The author does not suggest it is extremely important
(C) The author neither suggests it was superficial., nor that it was before its time.

2. (B)
Category: Words in Context
Difficulty: M
Strategy: A conundrum is a complex puzzle
Solution: Reread the sentence as a fill-in-the-blank and decide what you think belongs in the blank. Then consider the option choices.
(A) It is a question - not an argument.
(C) It is an intellectual question - not a wrestling match.
(D) Overstated. It is an intriguing question, but it is not of extreme importance.

3. (C)
Category: Purpose/Point of View
Difficulty: M
Strategy: Reread the last paragraph.
Solution: The text states that Molyneux's problem contributed to expanding new treatments to older patients.
(A) It does not restate the first paragraph
(B) It does not talk about that.
(D) It shows that abstract questions can have a practical benefit.

4. (C)
Category: Words in context
Difficulty: M/H
Strategy: Read the sentence with each of the answer choices in the place of the word "viable". Consider the main idea of the rest of the paragraph.
Solution: It is a practical solution.
(A) A solution to a problem cannot be lively.
(B) The study does not grow
(D) It does not offer a contrast, and there was no assertion the debate couldn't be resolved.

5. (A)
Category: Structure
Difficulty: H
Strategy: Reread the third paragraph and determine the main idea.
Solution: The first two paragraphs talk about philosophical debate in the past. This paragraph shifts to a modern, practical application of the problem.
(B) John Locke is not attacked in the article.
(C) That information is in paragraph four.
(D) It does not talk about that.

6. (C)
Category: Point of View
Difficulty: E
Strategy: Think about how each of these literary styles would read.
Solution: The article offers information in a straightforward manner.
(A) There is nothing personal about this.
(B) Legal briefs are very technical and formal.
(D) The author is not trying to persuade his readers, just inform them.

7. (C)
Category: Point of View
Difficulty: M
Strategy: Consider the main idea and the tone of the article.
Solution: The article reports that philosophers considered this an important question for centuries and then shows that it has a practical application in modern life.
(A) The author considered this a worthwhile problem.
(B) The opposite.
(D) Blind people can distinguish object shapes by touch.

8. (D)
Category: Evidence
Difficulty: M
Strategy: Read each quote and relate it to the answer to the previous question.
Solution: Molyneux's problem suggested the experiment which led to better treatments.
(A) Locke was not thinking about this problem at that point.
(B) The philosophers were unable to solve the problem, but it does not say it was a waste of time.
(C) It explains the experiment but not the author's opinion.

Rhetoric – Social Studies – Passage 2 – Pages 119-120

1. (C)
Category: Purpose
Difficulty: E
Strategy: Consider the author's overall purpose in the passage, looking at the broad view, rather than at narrow details. It may help to review the first and last sentence from each paragraph.
Solution: The author introduces ambergris and describes in detail the way that it is thought to be created.
(A) Not true. The author only presents one theory and does not compare the accuracy of multiple theories.
(B) Not true. While the author explores the origin of the phenomenon itself, he does not explore the history of research into it.
(D) Not true. The author's tone is informative, not persuasive.

2. (B)
Category: Word Choice
Difficulty: E
Strategy: Reread the third paragraph, with particular focus on the second half, where the author repeats the word "seems". Consider what the author says before he uses the word. Consider what this part of the paragraph would lose if you removed each instance of the word.
Solution: The author leads into the first "seems" with the following sentence: "Here is where our knowledge of the development of ambergris is limited to speculation" (lines 50-52). The repetition of "seems" drives home this point about speculation – that we are making our best guess but aren't entirely sure of the origins of ambergris.
(A) Too extreme. The author is not suggesting the information is incorrect, just that we are not entirely sure that the details are correct.
(C) Not true. The author does not include analogies here.
(D) Not true. The author is describing a process, not comparing multiple theories.

3. (A)
Category: Structure
Difficulty: M
Strategy: Consider the way the passage flows and identify where there is a shift in main idea.
Solution: After a very brief introduction to the mysterious ambergris, the 2nd and 3rd paragraphs (lines 7-61) are devoted to describing the best theory as to how ambergris is produced. The 4th paragraph (lines 62-74) represents a shift to a discussion about the physical characteristics of ambergris, the 5th (lines 75-92) a discussion about the unique smell, and the 6th (lines 93 onward) a summary of how it is used.
(B) Partially correct. While the passage does describe a mystery, it does not address how its solution would affect various professions.
(C) Not true. The author does not provide a personal account.
(D) Not true. The author does not summarize historical research or modern discoveries.

4. (B)
Category: Purpose
Difficulty: M
Strategy: Consider the main idea of the paragraph that contains the quotations. Why are the quotations important? If you removed them, what void would that leave in the paragraph?
Solution: The 4th paragraph leads into the 5th paragraph when it asserts, "...one trait distinguishes ambergris as extraordinary: the smell" (lines 73-74). The 5th paragraph continues to drive home the point, claiming, "'Unique' is the most common description..." (line 75). The author supports these claims about the smell by then providing a litany of quotations from a wide variety of sources.
(A) Partially correct, but the author is not supporting his own experiences.

(C) Not true. The explanations are similar and do not address a problem.
(D) Wrong part of the passage. The description of how ambergris is created occurs in Paragraphs 2 and 3.

5. (D)
Category: Point of View
Difficulty: H
Strategy: Consider which answer choice is best supported by statements made by the author. Use process of elimination.
Solution: The author repeatedly refers to the mysteriousness of ambergris and its popularity. It can be inferred there is a connection between the two. Also, all other answer choices can be solidly eliminated.
(A) Too extreme. While the author muses at the end of the passage that, as with other rare substances, people prefer natural to synthetic ambergris, he does not go so far as to say that synthetic products are inferior.
(B) Too extreme. There is no indication it will "always" remain a mystery.
(C) No evidence. While the author mentions that ambergris is "incredibly expensive" (line 6), he never expresses the opinion that it is too expensive.

6. (B)
Category: Argument
Difficulty: M
Strategy: Identify the theory described in the 3rd paragraph, and crystallize its main idea in your mind. Then, consider which answer choice would weaken it.
Solution: The heart of the theory is that ambergris results from a lubricant that whale digestive systems secrete in order to facilitate the passing of squid beaks. If it were a fact that whale digestive systems do not produce a lubricant, the theory would lose its footing.
(A) Opposite. The fact that something else may be hard to digest might support the theory as more digestive lubricant may need to be secreted.
(C) Not relevant. The fact that a different rare item can be manmade does not impact the plausibility of the whale digestive lubricant – ambergris theory.
(D) Not relevant. The theory is not predicated on the number of stomachs.

7. (B)
Category: Purpose
Difficulty: E
Strategy: Reread the first paragraph and consider its role in the context of the passage as a whole. Consider what would happen if you removed the first paragraph. What void would that leave in the passage?
Solution: The first paragraph introduces ambergris as an intriguing substance and hints at the bizarre way that it is produced. This paragraph serves as a "hook" to lure the reader in to reading the rest of the passage.
(A) Not relevant. The passage does not have a controversy.
(C) Too broad. While the first paragraph mentions sperm whales as part of a mysterious process, the focus is strictly on ambergris, not on studying ocean life in general.
(D) No evidence to support the idea of "an ongoing debate" even though the origins of ambergris are mysterious.

Rhetoric – Social Studies – Passage 3 – Pages 121-122

1.   (D)
Category: Purpose
Difficulty: E
Strategy: Consider the author's overall purpose in the passage, looking at the broad view, rather than at narrow details. It may help to review the first and last sentence from each paragraph.
Solution: The author shares several anecdotes about Lustig and his exploits through most of the passage (lines 1-89) before ending with a fable-like moral (lines 90-102).
(A)   Not relevant. There is no discussion of charity in the passage.
(B)   Not supported. While the passage describes confidence as a way to convince people of lies (lines 98-102), it does not examine *why* people believe those lies.
(C)   Too narrow. While the passage discusses the Eiffel Tower, it does so only in the context of describing Lustig's exploits (lines 45-89).

2.   (D)
Category: Point of View
Difficulty: M
Strategy: Consider the way the passage is written and who might be the intended audience.
Solution: The background for the passage describes it as being "adapted from an article about the history of the Eiffel Tower". Throughout the passage, the author chronicles the acts of a famous con man and playfully interacts with readers via rhetorical questions.
(A)   Not supported. While the author describes mechanisms involved in the Rumanian money box, this is the only such instance of this.
(B)   Not supported. The crimes discussed are in the 1920s and 1930s, so they are not current.
(C)   Not supported. While some social phenomena is discussed, the tone is playful and does not match the formal tone of a researcher.

3.   (C)
Category: Word Choice
Difficulty: M
Strategy: Reread the lines that include "surely" as well as a few lines before and after each instance. Consider the context surrounding the words and the purpose of the paragraph of which they are a part.
Solution: In both instances, the author is channeling the probable thought process of the people who were conned by Lustig. The inclusion of "surely" adds to the sense that we can all relate to Lustig's victims and would all likely think the same way if in their shoes.
(A)   Wrong part of the passage. While the author does voice his criticism of Lustig's behavior toward the end of the passage, this part of the passage focuses on telling the stories of his exploits.
(B)   No evidence for this. The author does not promote any theories about Lustig's life.
(D)   Misleading. While these lines emphasize the certainty with which people were tricked into believing things, the perceived facts turned out to be falsehoods.

4.   (D)
Category: Argument
Difficulty: H
Strategy: Use process of elimination to consider the presence of each strategy throughout the passage.
Solution: The author directly addresses the reader on several occasions, asking him/her to consider situations and how s/he would respond: "Imagine a small…" (lines 1-3), "How much would you pay for the device?" (lines 12-13), "Would you have suspected…casually wiping the windows?" (lines 88-89), and the entire final paragraph (lines 90-101), where the author refers to "we" and "you" several times.
(A)   Misleading. While the author uses numbers on several occasions (and especially when describing the Rumanian music box), he does

not perform any math and only uses the numbers descriptively, not in service to an argument.
(B)   Partially correct. While the author asks rhetorical questions, he does not answer them but leaves the reader to consider them.
(C)   Misleading. While the author describes situations one might consider challenging, he does not consider how he would react.

5.   (A)
Category: Point of View
Difficulty: M
Strategy: Pay attention to word usage. Strong adjectives and verbs are good clues for identifying tone.
Solution: While the author expresses distaste for Lustig's lies at the end of the passage, his tone throughout the passage clearly indicates that he is impressed with the lengths Lustig went to and the success that he had. The author describes Lustig's "criminal profession" as "impressive" in lines 90-91 and our reaction to it as "amazed" in line 94 and declares Lustig to possibly "be the greatest scam artist to have ever lived"
(B)   Wrong part of the passage. While the author does warn that Lustig "is hardly a role model" (line 91), this only occurs at the end of the passage. His descriptions of Lustig's exploits are full of words that indicate he was amazed by the acts themselves.
(C)   No evidence. The author does not employ any words that indicate he is ashamed of Lustig's exploits.
(D)   Misleading. While the author's tone when describing Lustig's exploits is one of awe, he never goes so far as to indicate he is jealous or envious. In fact, he includes a warning at the end of the passage that "we must also resist the temptation of similarly robbing gullible strangers (lines 94-95).

6.   (C)
Category: Purpose
Difficulty: H
Strategy: Reread the second paragraph and consider its role in the context of the passage as a whole. Consider what would happen if you removed the second paragraph.
Solution: The main idea of the passage as a whole is that Victor Lustig successfully orchestrated a series of elaborate hoaxes. The second paragraph contributes to this main idea by showing us that that is all Lustig did. It lays Lustig bare for who he is and removes any doubts the reader might have had about Lustig's intentions or motivations (he wasn't selling the Rumanian money boxes for charity, for example!)
(A)   Misleading. The descriptions of Lustig's exploits serve to provide breadth and depth far better than the list of disguises and fake identities in Paragraph 2.
(B)   Too narrow. This answer may reflect the main idea of the paragraph, but it does not explain the role the paragraph plays in service to the passage as a whole.
(D)   Too narrow. While the author lists a few of Lustig's victims (lines 45-47) he does so in order to support the idea that Lustig "may have been the greatest scam artist to have ever lived," (lines 42-44) which is the larger point (and purpose) of the paragraph.

7.   (A)
Category: Purpose
Difficulty: M
Strategy: Reread the sentence with the exclamation point and consider its role in the context of the paragraph. Consider what would happen if the author had just ended the sentence with a period.
Solution: The author has just used 2 paragraphs (lines 45-76) to describe the complexity of the Eiffel Tower scam and the enormous losses incurred by its first victim, Andre Poisson. The reader (and author) expect that Poisson will report the crime and Lustig will be caught. Unexpectedly, Poisson flees the country. The reader (and author) then expect Lustig to count his blessings, but both are surprised when he boldly commits the complex scam for a second time (!)

Rhetoric – Social Studies – Passage 4 – Pages 123-124

1. (A)
Category: Word Choice
Difficulty: E
Strategy: Consider the context surrounding the words and the purpose of the passage. Replace "birthed" and "born" with less descriptive verbs and consider what would be lost without them.
Solution: The passage describes a seminal event in the history of American football that created "the first professional American football player" (lines 96-97). Along with phrases like "new era" (lines 4-5) and "pivotal in sports history" (line 8), "birthed" and "born" alert the reader to the passage's focus on the start of something new.
(B) Not relevant.
(C) Not relevant. While the words may loosely be associated with an exciting event, they do not invoke excitement themselves.
(D) Opposite.

2. (C)
Category: Purpose
Difficulty: M
Strategy: Reread the third paragraph and consider its role in the context of the passage as a whole. Consider what would happen if you removed the third paragraph. What void would that leave in the passage?
Solution: The paragraph lists some of the ways that players were "awarded" or compensated – with "jobs," trophies, watches, and "double expenses". It is important to note that the paragraph emphasizes that the AAA "challenged these practices" (line 27) because the "athletes…were supposed to be amateurs" (line 29).
(A) Partially correct. The paragraph describes amateur compensation.
(B) Not mentioned. While the paragraph mentions several forms of compensation, it never mentions cash or salaries.
(D) Not true. The paragraph informs but does not try to persuade.

3. (B)
Category: Structure
Difficulty: H
Strategy: Consider the way the paragraph flows and identify where there is a shift in main idea. Take a broad view of the themes of the paragraph rather than obsessing over small details.
Solution: The paragraph begins by discussing the rivalry between the AAA and PAC and the controversy stemming from the AAA's arguing that the PAC's top player was a professional (lines 35-39). Though the teams are at odds, they then both employ the same strategy of "scouting" the Chicago Athletic Association team for new players (lines 37-42). Thus, the paragraph shifts from a controversy between the teams to an identical action taken by both.
(A) Opposite.
(C) Misleading. While the AAA accuses the PAC of having a professional player, there are no professional players or teams.
(D) Misleading. Though there is controversy between a Pittsburgh-based team and the AAA, the passage does not detail where the controversy takes place.

4. (B)
Category: Argument
Difficulty: H
Strategy: Consider which answer choice is best supported by statements made by the author.
Solution: The text best supports the assertion that the Nov. 12, 1892 game was a significant for professional sports. The author directly describes the game as "significant" in line 32. He further asserts the game's importance at the close of the passage, saying, "The November 12, 1892, AAA-PAC game opened the door to the professional sport. And football as we know it today was born" (lines 98-100).

(A) Too extreme. While it's true that the evolution wasn't planned, the author chronicles how it took place over the 1880s (Paragraph 3, lines 20-30), so it's not accurate to characterize it as a mistake.
(C) Not mentioned. While the author discusses the controversy over betting, he does not assert judgment about betting.
(D) Not supported. Though the reader may have never heard of the Nov 12 game, the author provides no evidence he believes it is "obscure". He only says it was "no ordinary day" (line 1) in the context that it was a special day in the history of football.

5. (C)
Category: Word Choice
Difficulty: M
Strategy: Reread the first paragraph with particular focus on the line that includes "pivotal". Consider the context surrounding the word and the purpose of the passage. Replace "pivotal" with a less descriptive adjective and consider what would be lost without it.
Solution: As described in Paragrah 1, the word "pivotal" is used with a couple of other strong words in the introductory paragraph – "birthed," "born," and "new era" – to indicate the passage's purpose of describing the start of something.

6. (D)
Category: Purpose
Difficulty: E
Strategy: Reread the final paragraph and consider its role in the context of the passage as a whole. Consider what would happen if you removed the final paragraph. What void would that leave in the passage?
Solution: In the final paragraph, the author details a piece of evidence from the National Football Hall of Fame that confirms that Heffelfinger was paid $500 for the Nov 12th game. The author summarizes the impact of this evidence: "The truth was finally clear. William "Pudge" Heffelfinger was the first professional American football player".
(A) Opposite. The purpose is to confirm.
(B) Opposite. The purpose is to confirm.
(C) Not true. He was the first *professional* American football player.

7. (B)
Category: Structure
Difficulty: H
Strategy: Consider how the author progresses from one main idea to the next as the passage unfolds.
Solution: The early days are described in Paragraph 2, compensation and clubs are described in Paragraphs 3-5, the game is described in Paragraph 6, and the new precedent is described in Paragraph 7.

8. (B)
Category: Argument
Difficulty: M
Strategy: Consider the context around the claim "a new precedent was set." Which answer choice provides the most accurate support for this?
Solution: The paragraph containing the phrase details the controversy immediately following the Nov 12th game over the AAA offering payment to Heffelfinger. Though proof of that transaction would not appear until decades later, the author supports his claim of a new precedent by explaining, "…within four years every AAA player would be paid" (line 87).
(A) Not true. The passage states that "Heffelfinger kept mum on the subject" (line 79).
(C) Too extreme. Though this event spurred the development of the first professional teams, the passage does not state that amateur football clubs disappeared.
(D) Misleading. While the cash payment was not proven definitively until 68 years later (lines 90-100), it was ultimately proven. Furthermore, inability to prove a payment is not the precedent to which the author is referring.

Rhetoric – Social Studies – Passage 5 – Pages 125-127

1. (D)
Category: Purpose
Difficulty: E
Strategy: Consider the author's overall purpose in the passage, looking at the broad view, rather than at narrow details.
Solution: The author describes a common human experience in the first paragraph, chronicles a bit of its history in the second paragraph, and then describes current research on the reasons behind the phenomenon.
(A) Not mentioned. Memories and their development are not described.
(B) Not relevant. Though the author mentions Edgar Allen Poe's use of the phenomenon, he does so in order to establish the commonality of the phenomenon, not for connecting psychology and art.
(C) Not mentioned. Though the author introduces researchers who study the phenomenon, no experiments are described.

2. (B)
Category: Structure
Difficulty: M
Strategy: Consider the way the passage flows and identify where there is a shift in main idea.
Solution: The first paragraph recounts the experience of having an intrusive thought. The second paragraph establishes the fact that the experience is normal. The remainder of the passage invokes researchers who provide various possible explanations for the phenomenon.
(A) Not true. The passage states intrusive thoughts "are nothing to worry about" (lines 96-97)
(C) Not mentioned. The events that are described are general experiences, not historical events.
(D) Misleading. The author mentions Edgar Allen Poe's story (lines 19-26) to explain how common the phenomenon is. The story is not addressed any further.

3. (C)
Category: Argument
Difficulty: M
Strategy: Reread the lines in the answer choices and consider which one best supports the idea that intrusive thoughts are not dangerous.
Solution: The quotation in C explains that though intrusive thoughts make us uncomfortable, they are not usually something to worry about.

4. (B)
Category: Point of View
Difficulty: M
Strategy: Pay attention to word usage. Strong adjectives and verbs are good clues for identifying tone.
Solution: The author dispels fears she predicts the reader may have on several occasions: "If you've ever felt… you're not alone" (lines 16-17), "Scary though it may seem…neither uncommon nor dangerous" (lines 31-33), "This sense of uncertainty… occur only occasionally" (lines 56-58), and "But… they are nothing to worry about" (lines 94-99).
(A) No evidence of appreciation toward the reader.
(C) Opposite.
(D) Opposite.

5. (A)
Category: Purpose
Difficulty: E
Strategy: Reread the first paragraph and consider its role. Consider what would happen if you removed the first paragraph.
Solution: The first paragraph of the passage recounts the experience of an intrusive thought to establish the topic to which most can relate.
(B) Not mentioned. No experimental results are described.
(C) Misleading. While the author includes the pronoun "we" (line 1), she is not sharing a personal experience, but instead including herself in the common experience being described.

(D) Wrong part of the passage. The author attempts to do this in Paragraphs 3-5.

6. (C)
Category: Purpose
Difficulty: M
Strategy: Reread the second paragraph and consider its role in the context of the passage as a whole. Consider what would happen if you removed the second paragraph.
Solution: In the second paragraph, the author surveys a number of different names that have been given to the experience: "The Imp of the Perverse" (line 20), "l'appel du vide" (line 27), "high place phenomenon" (line 30), and "intrusive thought" (line 31).
(A) Not relevant. There is no description of mechanics of a problem.
(B) Misleading. While the paragraph details names that others have called the phenomenon, it does not describe experiences of others.
(D) Not relevant. No explanations are provided here – only names.

7. (C)
Category: Word Choice
Difficulty: M
Strategy: Consider the main idea of what is being described and how "in fact" is used to transition in this instance.
Solution: The "in fact" is part of Professor Smith's theory about what occurs in the brain during an intrusive thought. Smith describes a situation where "we may be misinterpreting" (line 38) and further explains that "the rational mind… begins to overanalyze them" (lines 46-47). Thus, the "in fact" in context is the brain drawing an inappropriate conclusion as the result of misinterpretation.
(A) Not relevant. The phrase is part of a theory about the brain, nothing to do with the artists or scientists.
(B) Not relevant. The phrase is part of a theory about how the brain produces the phenomenon, but there is no experiment described.
(D) Misleading. While the brain believes the following statement is accurate, it is a misinterpretation by the brain.

8. (C)
Category: Purpose
Difficulty: M
Strategy: Consider the information in parentheses in the context of the lines surrounding it. Remove the information in the parentheses from the passage and consider what would be lost without it.
Solution: The information defines the previous term – "clinically normal". This term could be unknown by a nonmedical audience.
(A) Misleading. While the information helps define a prior term, it does not provide an analogy.
(B) Not mentioned. While the information helps define a prior term, it does not tell us where the term comes from.
(D) Not true. The information supports the prior term by defining it, not offering an alternative.

9. (A)
Category: Argument
Difficulty: E
Strategy: Consider the way the author constructs her argument and the progression of ideas throughout the passage.
Solution: Similar to paragraph 2, the first paragraph of the passage recounts the experience of having an intrusive thought. The second paragraph establishes the fact that the experience is normal. The remainder of the passage invokes researchers who provide various possible explanations for the phenomenon.
(B) Not true. The author does not describe one person's experiences, but instead the common experiences of many people.
(C) Partially true. The author does assume the reader has had similar experiences, but does not invoke or criticize any counterarguments.
(D) Partially true. The author presents a puzzling phenomenon and describes theories, but no experiments are described.

Reading – Data Graphics – Passage 1 – Pages 129-130

1. (A)
Category: Data Graphics
Difficulty: Easy
Strategy: Find the relevant data in the figure.
Solution: Use figure 1, which indicates BAI. 2001-2002 shows all plots decreasing. Note that if you incorrectly use figure 2, choice B is an attractor answer.

2. (C)
Category: Data Graphics
Difficulty: Medium
Strategy: Use process of elimination. Check trends in Figure 1, which measures growth.
Solution: Plot 1 shows the most growth, overall, in Figure 1. Since Figure 1 was not shoveled, it had the most snow cover.

3. (B)
Category: Data Graphics
Difficulty: Medium
Strategy: Find the relevant data in the figures.
Solution: Plot 1 had its greatest freeze depth in 2007. Figure 1 shows its BAI in this year had a -20% increase.

Reading – Data Graphics – Passage 2 – Pages 131-132

1. (B)
Category: Data Graphics
Difficulty: Medium
Strategy: Use process of elimination.
Solution: The figure shows Spanish traveling from North America to east Asia, with "secondary spreading" to Japan. It can be assumed that the spread of words for sweet potatoes also occurred with the spread of actual sweet potatoes.

2. (B)
Category: Data Graphics
Difficulty: Medium
Solution: Spanish brought sweet potatoes to east Asia and Hawaii. However, South Americans had already brought sweet potatoes to Hawaii.

3. (A)
Category: Data Graphics
Difficulty: Medium
Solution: Rouiller states that linguistic evidence and the sweet potato show the connection between Polynesians and South Americans. The figure shows how terms for sweet potatoes were spread among nations.

Reading – Data Graphics – Passage 3 – Pages 133-134

1. (A)
Category: Data Graphics
Difficulty: Medium
Solution: The quoted lines refer to the number of people employed in factories. This data is not shown in the figure.

2. (D)
Category: Data Graphics
Difficulty: Medium
Strategy: Use process of elimination.
Solution: The highest increase has been in productivity. Different calculations of compensation show different levels of increase, but none come close to matching the increase in productivity.
(A) No indication of causation. Also, wages decreased.
(B) Total compensation increased.
(C) No indication of employment rates in the figure

3. (C)
Category: Data Graphics
Difficulty: Easy
Solution: 2000-2005 had an approximately 25% increase in the difference between wages and productivity.

Reading – Data Graphics – Passage 4 – Pages 135-136

1. (A)
Category: Data Graphics
Difficulty: Medium
Strategy: Use process of elimination.
Solution: The figure shows 2016 having an extremely high number of discoveries. The passage states this is the year Kepler was revived to search for more exoplanets.
(B) Kepler uses transit photometry, which isn't new.
(C) No indication it didn't find any exoplanets.
(D) Kepler uses transit photometry.

2. (A)
Category: Data Graphics
Difficulty: Medium
Solution: Lines 10-13 express the difficulty of direct detection and imaging. The figure shows very low numbers of exoplanets discovered through this technique.
The rest of the answer choices describe characteristics of detection methods, but these descriptions don't relate to the data in the figure.

3. (C)
Category: Data Graphics
Difficulty: Medium
Strategy: Use process of elimination.
Solution: The relative numbers of detections by each method shows their effectiveness.

Standard English Conventions 1 – Pages 140-142

1. (C)
Category: Diction, Pronouns, Verb Tense
Difficulty: Medium
Strategy: "Loose" is not tight. "Lose" is to not win or to not possess. "Their" is a possessive pronoun. "There" refers to a place.
Solution: Based on context, it is clear the sentence refers to the humors' loss of standing. The pronoun should be possessive. Also, the verb should be in past tense, because it's in the eighteenth century.

2. (C)
Category: Modifiers
Difficulty: Medium
Strategy: Descriptions must be placed next to the things they describe. When a sentence begins with a descriptive phrase, ask who or what is being described.
Solution: The "student of medicine" is Galen, so he should come after the comma.

3. (C)
Category: Pronouns
Difficulty: Medium
Strategy: The pronoun "who" refers to the subject. The pronoun "whom" refers to an object. To determine whether a pronoun is a subject or object, plug in an easier pronoun and see which works better. "Whose" is possessive.
Solution: Rewrite as "he is credited" to see the pronoun is a subject, so "who" should be used.

4. (D)
Category: Semicolons & Colons
Difficulty: Hard
Strategy: Semicolons, like periods, are used between independent clauses.
Solution: A semicolon is needed to separate the independent clauses. Consider where "however" is needed; if part of the first clause, it suggests a contrast between Galan promoting humors and being interested in anatomy, which doesn't make sense. There is, however, a contrast between his interest in anatomy and inability to dissect.

5. (A)
Category: Subject-Verb Agreement, Commas
Difficulty: Medium
Strategy: Singular subjects require singular verbs, and plural subjects require plural verbs. Extra information set off by commas is not a part of the independent clause.
Solution: The "theory" is the subject singular. No comma is needed because it would separate the subject from the verb.

6. (D)
Category: Commas
Difficulty: Medium
Strategy: Commas set of extra information.
Solution: "As well" can be set off with commas, but this would create a run-on.

7. (C)
Category: Apostrophes
Difficulty: Easy
Strategy: When the possessor is a plural noun ending in *s*, possession can be shown by adding an apostrophe after the *s*.
Solution: The treatments are the possession of the patients, which is a plural noun.

8. (C)
Category: Comparisons, Diction
Difficulty: Hard
Strategy: Make sure that comparisons are logical and parallel. The same types of ideas should be compared to each other. "Than" is for comparisons. "Then" is for time.
Solution: Without "to", the comparison states bathing is more harmful to men than women are harmful to men. Use "to" to make it logical. Use "than" for a comparison.

9. (B)
Category: Subject-Verb Agreement, Commas
Difficulty: Hard
Strategy: Singular subjects require singular verbs, and plural subjects require plural verbs. Extra information set off by commas is often not a part of the independent clause, which has the subject and verb.
Solution: The comma after "Shakespeare" begins a parenthetical phrase with extra information. Add another comma to completely set off the phrase. "Chaucer and other famous writers" are not included in the subject because they are a part of this extra information, which can be eliminated from the sentence. Therefore, the subject is "Shakespeare", which is singular.

10. (D)
Category: Comparisons
Difficulty: Hard
Strategy: Make sure that comparisons are logical and parallel. The same types of ideas should be compared to each other.
Solution: "Medicine in the United States used" is compared to what the Royal College of Physicians used. A noun and verb should be parallel with another noun and verb. Choice D uses "did" in place of "used".

11. (C)
Category: Run-ons
Difficulty: Medium
Strategy: When two independent clauses are joined with a comma but without a conjunction, the mistake is called a comma splice.
Solution: A period is needed to separate the independent clauses. Choice D creates a fragment.

Standard English Conventions 2 – Pages 143-145

1. (C)
Category: Subject-Verb Agreement, Comparisons
Difficulty: Medium
Strategy: Singular subjects require singular verbs.
Use the comparative form when comparing two things. Use the superlative form when comparing more than two things.
Solution: Ignore the information set off by commas, so "Amsterdam" is the singular subject. There are more than two cities in Europe, so use the superlative form: "most".

2. (D)
Category: Verb Tense, Fragments, Subject-Verb Agreement
Difficulty: Hard
Strategy: A verb ending in *ing* is not complete.
Solution: Use a past tense verb. The subject is "one", which is singular.

3. (B)
Category: Comparisons
Difficulty: Hard
Strategy: When comparing something to a group that it is part of, you can't just compare it to the whole group.

Solution: The word "other" is needed to separate multicolored varieties from the rest of them. Otherwise, multicolored varieties are compared to all varieties, including themselves. This is a tricky logical rule.
A verb is needed to keep the comparison parallel. C and D compare the action of trading, but the comparison should be between varieties.

4. (C)
Category: Parallelism
Difficulty: Medium
Strategy: Use parallel structure with elements in a list or series.
Solution: The structure of the previous sentence was to name a variety of tulip, have a verb, then mention features of the variety.

5. (C)
Category: Commas
Difficulty: Hard
Strategy: Use commas between coordinate adjectives, but not between cumulative adjectives.
Solution: These are coordinate adjectives, so a comma is needed. A good test for coordinate adjectives is you can use "and" between them: "the rare and treasured bulbs" works.

6. (C)
Category: Diction
Difficulty: Medium
Strategy: Consider context and the definitions of each word. Be wary of words that sound similar.
Solution: "Might" can be used for something possible. "Have" is an auxiliary verb. "Of" is a preposition.

7. (D)
Category: Pronouns
Difficulty: Hard
Strategy: Use a form of "who" when referring to people. "That" is a relative pronoun connecting a noun to essential information. "Which" is a relative pronoun connecting a noun to nonessential information and is usually preceded by a comma.
Solution: The traders are the subject referred to. Since these are people, use "who" or "whom". Replace with a simpler verb to test subject/object: "he could make the equivalent" works better than "him could make the equivalent", so use "who", which is a subject pronoun.

8. (C)
Category: Fragments, Semicolons
Difficulty: Medium
Strategy: Semicolons separate independent clauses. A verb ending in *ing* is not a complete verb.
Solution: "fearing they were likely to die" is not an independent clause. Use a comma to connect it to an independent clause.

9. (A)
Category: Verb Tense
Difficulty: Medium
Strategy: The past perfect tense is used for actions that were ongoing in the past and are now completed.
Solution: In the past, there was a time when the tulip market had an effect on economies. This is in the past and is completed now. Choice C would mean the tulip market still has this effect, which is not true because, as the passage states, the market collapsed.

10. (C)
Category: Apostrophes
Difficulty: Medium
Strategy: Apostrophes are used for abbreviations and possession.
Solution: "'20s" is an abbreviation of "1920s." There is no apostrophe before the *s* because it is not possessive.

11. (D)
Category: Idioms
Difficulty: Medium
Strategy: Idioms must be both proper and logical. Try to hear which idiom sounds correct. If you see an underlined verb and preposition, or just an underlined preposition, look for an idiom error.
Solution: "Compared to" is a proper idiom.

Standard English Conventions 3 – Pages 146-148

1. (A)
Category: Commas
Difficulty: Medium
Strategy: Use commas between coordinate adjectives, which each modify the noun. Do not use commas between cumulative adjectives.
Solution: "Old" and "unused" are coordinate adjectives, so a comma is needed. A good test for coordinate adjectives is you can use "and" between them: "old and unused buildings" works. Note that "many and old and unused buildings" does not work.

2. (B)
Category: Semicolons & Colons, Run-ons
Difficulty: Medium
Strategy: Semicolons, like periods, are used between independent clauses.
Solution: The first sentence is not a question. A semicolon is needed to separate the independent clauses.

3. (A)
Category: Pronouns
Difficulty: Easy
Strategy: "Its" is the possessive form of "it." "It's" is short for "it is." "There" refers to a place. "Their" is a possessive pronouns.
Solution: The pronoun refers back to the jungle, which is singular.

4. (C)
Category: Subject-Verb Agreement, Verb Tense
Difficulty: Hard
Strategy: Singular subjects require singular verbs, and plural subjects require plural verbs. To simplify sentences, remove all extra information between the subject and the verb, and then make sure they agree.
Solution: Simplify and rewrite as "Knowledge was nearly lost." Prepositional phrases (such as "of the achievements of the Mayan people", which begins with the preposition "of") are not a part of the subject. Use context to determine the verb should be past tense.

5. (D)
Category: Diction
Difficulty: Medium
Strategy: Consider context and the definitions of each word. Be wary of words that sound similar.
Solution: "Altogether" means "completely".

6. (A)
Category: Commas
Difficulty: Hard
Strategy: When a description or title is combined with a name, use commas to set off the name only when the name is not necessary to specify exactly who is being mentioned. If the name is necessary, do not use commas.
Solution: With the use of "a", the description is limited to one person, so the name isn't necessary to further limit it.

7. (D)
Category: Modifiers
Difficulty: Medium
Strategy: Descriptions must be placed next to the things they describe. When a sentence begins with a descriptive phrase, ask who or what is being described.
Solution: Stephens was who was "guided only by the vague accounts", so he should come immediately after the comma.

8. (D)
Category: Idioms
Difficulty: Easy
Strategy: Idioms must be both proper and logical. Try to hear which idiom sounds correct. If you see an underlined verb and preposition, or just an underlined preposition, look for an idiom error.
Solution: "Capable of" is a proper idiom.

9. (A)
Category: Fragments, Run-ons
Difficulty: Medium
Strategy: A verb ending in *ing* is not a complete verb.
Solution: The previous comma in the sentence is used to set off a parenthetical phrase with nonessential information. Use another comma to set it off. Choices B and C create fragments after the punctuation.

10. (D)
Category: Run-ons
Difficulty: Medium
Strategy: When two independent clauses are joined with a comma but without a conjunction, the mistake is called a comma splice. Fix a comma splice by replacing the comma with a semicolon, a period, or a comma and a conjunction.
Solution: Choice D correctly uses a comma and conjunction to fix the comma splice. Choice B uses a semicolon, but there needs to be a reference back to the Mayan population to make the following independent clause logical.

11. (B)
Category: Semicolons & Colons
Difficulty: Hard
Strategy: A colon should only be used at the end of a complete sentence. Colons may be used present information that elaborates on the independent clause.
Solution: The clause after the punctuation expands on the previous information and is not independent.

Standard English Conventions 4 – Pages149-151

1. (A)
Category: Subject-Verb Agreement
Difficulty: Medium
Strategy: Subjects grouped by "and" are plural, even if the "and" joins two singular words.
Solution: "Individualism and autonomy" works as a plural subject. Ignore the extra information set off by commas. To simplify, you can replace the grouped nouns with "they" and rewrite as "They are at the center of modern life."

2. (D)
Category: Diction, Pronouns
Difficulty: Medium
Strategy: Consider context and the definitions of each word. Be wary of words that sound similar.
Be consistent with use of "one" or "you".

Solution: "Loose" is not tight. "Lose" is to not possess. The sentence uses "one's" later, so use "oneself" for consistency.

3. (C)
Category: Fragments
Difficulty: Medium
Strategy: A complete sentence needs a main subject and verb. A verb ending in *ing* is not a complete verb.
Solution: Simplify and rewrite as "The classic story of the Manchurian Candidate just one of the many books or films" to see a verb needs to be added.

4. (C)
Category: Modifiers, Run-ons, Fragments
Difficulty: Hard
Strategy: Descriptions must be placed next to the things they describe.
Solution: The fungus is "perfectly adapted", so it should appear next to that description. Choice B creates a fragment. Choice D creates a run-on.

5. (D)
Category: Pronouns
Difficulty: Hard
Strategy: A pronoun must have a clear antecedent.
Solution: There are several singular nouns that "it" could refer to: the fungus, process, spore, plant growth, and exoskeleton. Directly name the spore for the sake of clarity.

6. (A)
Category: Apostrophes
Difficulty: Medium
Strategy: When the possessor is a singular noun, possession can be indicated by adding 's.
Solution: Based on context, it's clear the sentence is describing a single insect, which possesses behaviors.

7. (D)
Category: Commas
Difficulty: Medium
Strategy: Use commas to set off nonessential information. Use commas between independent and dependent clauses.
Solution: Use a comma after "University" to set off a phrase of unnecessary information. Use a comma after "agrees" to separate the preceding independent clause from the following dependent clause.

8. (C)
Category: Commas, Apostrophes
Difficulty: Medium
Strategy: Use commas or dashes to set off nonessential information. "Its" is a possessive pronoun. "It's" is a contraction of "it is".
Solution: Dashes can be used like commas to set off nonessential information. Do not mix commas and dashes; be consistent. "its" should be used because "it is muscles" doesn't make sense.

9. (D)
Category: Diction
Difficulty: Medium
Strategy: Consider context and the definitions of each word. Be wary of words that sound similar. Some distinctions between words are based on logic and literal definitions.
Solution: Use "between" for something in the midst of two things. Use "among" for something in the midst of more than two things.

10. (D)
Category: Run-ons
Difficulty: Medium
Strategy: When two independent clauses are joined with a comma but without a conjunction, the mistake is called a comma splice.
Solution: The following information about the ant climbing a leaf is followed with a comma, suggesting this is extra information that should be set off by commas. Use "since", which is a conjunction, to make the following clause dependent to avoid a run-on.

11. (D)
Category: Parallelism
Difficulty: Medium
Strategy: Use parallel structure with elements in a list or series.
Solution: The previous two examples in the list have *ing* verbs.

Expression of Ideas 1 – Pages 153-157

1. (C)
Category: Addition & Deletion
Difficulty: Medium
Strategy: Sentences should be deleted if they're not relevant to the focus or do not support and strengthen the passage's ideas.
Solution: The fact that "Dark Ages" has a negative-sounding name isn't relevant to the paragraph, which in the first half is describing the age.

2. (D)
Category: Transitions
Difficulty: Medium
Strategy: Transitions show contrast, support, or cause. Choose the most appropriate and logical way to shift from one idea to another.
Solution: Both this sentence and the previous one are positive in their description of the time. The ideas build on each other, rather than being just similar ideas, so choice D works better than choice C.

3. (D)
Category: Organization
Difficulty: Hard
Strategy: Combined sentences should have proper modifiers, complete ideas, and logical structure.
Solution: Choice A is a fragment. Choice B has an illogical order of information, with Islam conquering empires and then emerging. Choice C has a modifier error with the first description relating to other empires rather than to Islam.

4. (C)
Category: Main Idea
Difficulty: Medium
Strategy: Questions may provide key information about what a portion should achieve. To determine the main idea, consider the central claim, issue, argument, or message that the author wants to communicate.
Solution: The focus of the rest of passage is about the importance of Islamic scholars who recorded and expanded upon Greek and Roman knowledge and thereby contributed to an era of progress for Islamic nations.

5. (D)
Category: Style
Difficulty: Easy
Strategy: Make sure the language of passages is consistent in tone. Avoid language that is too complex or too informal.
Solution: Choices A and B are too informal. Choice C doesn't work in context.

6. (B)
Category: Addition & Deletion
Difficulty: Medium
Strategy: Consider how the sentence relates to the sentences around them and the paragraph's main idea.
Solution: The first sentence of the paragraph states Arabs preserved ancient texts. The added sentence builds on this and leads to the next sentence, which summarizes the idea.

7. (D)
Category: Main Idea
Difficulty: Medium
Strategy: Questions may provide key information about what a portion should achieve in the passage.
Solution: The preceding sentence is about the connection between religion and science. Choice D demonstrates this idea through the design of cities, with the buildings that house these studies being close.

8. (B)
Category: Transitions
Difficulty: Hard
Strategy: Combined sentences should have proper transitions, as well as no run-on or fragment errors.
Solution: Choices A, C, and D have run-on errors.

9. (A)
Category: Main Idea
Difficulty: Medium
Strategy: Questions may provide key information about what a portion should achieve in the passage.
Solution: The previous sentence states Al-Razi made significant discoveries", so the following example should detail one of these discoveries. Choices B and C are too broad. Choice D isn't a discovery.

10. (D)
Category: Main Idea
Difficulty: Medium
Strategy: Questions may provide key information about what a portion should achieve in the passage.
Solution: There should be a contrast described. Choices A and B only show one side. Choice C shows no contrast.

11. (B)
Category: Organization
Difficulty: Hard
Strategy: Combined sentences should have proper modifiers, complete ideas, and logical structure.
Solution: Choice A suggests sciences are never supported. Choice C has a modifier error. Choice D is a fragment.

Expression of Ideas 2 – Pages 158-162

1. (C)
Category: Main Idea, Transitions
Difficulty: Medium
Strategy: Questions may provide key information about what a portion should achieve. To determine main idea, consider the central claim, argument, or message that the author wants to communicate.
Solution: The main idea is *Howl* had a big impact on society. The other options may be true but are minor ideas in the passage.

2. (C)
Category: Transitions
Difficulty: Medium
Strategy: Transitions show contrast, support, or cause. Choose the most appropriate and logical way to shift from one idea to another.
Solution: The first half of the sentence is positive, but the second half is negative. Use a contrasting transition.

3. (D)
Category: Wordiness
Difficulty: Easy
Strategy: Eliminate details that are unnecessarily repeated. Look out for synonyms that do not add new information.
Solution: "Recognize" and "acknowledge" are synonyms, so there's no need to use both.

4. (D)
Category: Organization, Main Idea
Difficulty: Medium
Strategy: Every portion of the passage should contribute to the main idea.

Solution: The information in sentence 3 is not relevant to the paragraph's focus on the societal and personal inspiration behind Ginsberg's poem.

5. (A)
Category: Main Idea
Difficulty: Medium
Strategy: The main idea is the central claim, issue, argument, or thought. It is the overall message that the author wants to communicate. The main idea tells what the passage or paragraph is essentially about.
Solution: The main idea of the paragraph is that multiple things contributed to the success of Ginsberg's poem.

6. (C)
Category: Transitions
Difficulty: Medium
Strategy: Transitions show contrast, support, or cause. Choose the most appropriate and logical way to shift from one idea to another.
Solution: There is a list of things that made the poem successful. Use a transition that connects items in a list.

7. (D)
Category: Addition & Deletion
Difficulty: Easy
Strategy: Sentences should be deleted if they are not relevant to the focus of the passage or do not support and strengthen the passage's ideas.
Solution: The paragraph begins by defining a generation, but it doesn't discuss the process of defining a generation. The main idea of the paragraph is that *Howl* helped shape this generation. Choice C is not quite correct because the added sentence may discredit the author's legitimacy, but it does not directly contradict this paragraph's main idea.

8. (A)
Category: Addition & Deletion
Difficulty: Easy
Strategy: Sentences should be deleted if they are not relevant to the focus of the passage or do not support and strengthen the passage's ideas.
Solution: The paragraph is not about *Howl*'s style but its cultural impact.

9. (D)
Category: Wordiness
Difficulty: Medium
Strategy: Eliminate details that are unnecessarily repeated. Look out for synonyms that do not add new information.
Solution: "Real" and "truthful" are synonyms. Based on the context, it is clear that the "account" is not a fantasy, so neither word is needed.

10. (D)
Category: Organization
Difficulty: Medium
Strategy: When organized properly, an essay's ideas should build upon each other and transition naturally.
Solution: Sentence 4 notes "court" and sentence 5 mentions "this celebrity" (in this usage, "celebrity" is a synonym for "fame"), so the sentence fits logically between these.

11. (B)
Category: Style
Difficulty: Medium
Strategy: Make sure the language of passages is consistent in tone. Avoid language that is too complex or too informal.
Solution: Choice A is too informal. Choices C and D don't work in this context.

ANSWER EXPLANATIONS **571**

Expression of Ideas 3 – Pages 163-167

1. (A)
Category: Main Idea
Difficulty: Medium
Strategy: Every portion of the passage should contribute to the main idea. To determine the main idea, consider the central claim, issue, argument, or message that the author wants to communicate.
Solution: The focus of this part of the paragraph is on the problem of malnutrition. Note the following sentence mentions "this problem", which suggests this sentence further explains the problem.

2. (A)
Category: Style
Difficulty: Easy
Strategy: Consider context for words that have similar meanings.
Solution: Choices B, C, and D have similar meanings, but do not work in the context.

3. (C)
Category: Main Idea
Difficulty: Hard
Strategy: The main idea is the central claim, issue, argument, or thought. It is the overall message that the author wants to communicate. The main idea tells what the passage or paragraph is essentially about.
Solution: The main idea of the paragraph is that malnutrition is a serious, widespread problem. Choice C states this and substantiates it with a relevant fact.

4. (D)
Category: Addition & Deletion
Difficulty: Medium
Strategy: Consider how the sentence relates to the sentences around it and the paragraph's main idea.
Solution: The sentence provides a fact supporting the idea that malnutrition is a serious issues.

5. (D)
Category: Addition & Deletion
Difficulty: Medium
Strategy: Sentences should be deleted if they are not relevant to the focus of the passage or do not support and strengthen the passage's ideas.
Solution: The previous sentence already states vitamin A is stored or converted, and there's no need for more information about that.

6. (D)
Category: Addition & Deletion
Difficulty: Medium
Strategy: Consider how the portion relates to the information around it and the paragraph's main idea.
Solution: The first half of the sentence brings up an outside detail, and this portion ties it back to the central topic.

7. (C)
Category: Transitions
Difficulty: Hard
Strategy: Transitions show contrast, support, or cause. Choose the most appropriate and logical way to shift from one idea to another.
Solution: The previous sentence states there is need for several nutrients. This next sentence notes the problem that golden rice only provides one nutrient. Use a contrasting transition to show the disconnect between these statements.

8. (B)
Category: Organization
Difficulty: Hard

Strategy: When organized properly, an essay's ideas should build upon each other and transition naturally.
Solution: The reference to "other modifications" suggests the previous sentence discusses modifications to rice.

9. (D)
Category: Wordiness
Difficulty: Easy
Strategy: Eliminate details that are unnecessarily repeated. Look out for synonyms that do not add new information.
Solution: "Limit" and "obstruction" are synonyms. There is no need to use both.

10. (B)
Category: Main Idea
Difficulty: Medium
Strategy: Questions may provide key information about what a portion should achieve in the passage.
Solution: The preceding portion of the paragraph mentions different issues with golden rice, including increasing poverty and negatively impacting our health or environment. Choice B best summarizes this by noting the "risk of creating other problems".

11. (A)
Category: Main Idea
Difficulty: Medium
Strategy: The main idea is the central claim, issue, argument, or thought. It is the overall message that the author wants to communicate. The main idea tells what the passage or paragraph is essentially about.
Solution: The main idea of the passage is that golden rice may help with malnutrition but there are currently some issues.

Expression of Ideas 4 – Pages 168-171

1. (A)
Category: Main Idea
Difficulty: Medium
Strategy: Every portion of the passage should contribute to the main idea.
Solution: The paragraph notes primitive air conditioning systems were used exclusively by wealthy people.

2. (D)
Category: Wordiness
Difficulty: Easy
Strategy: Eliminate details that are unnecessarily repeated. Look out for synonyms that do not add new information.
Solution: "Remarkable" and "impressive" are synonyms. There is no need to use both.

3. (D)
Category: Style
Difficulty: Medium
Strategy: Consider context for words that have similar meanings.
Solution: All of the choices have similar meanings, but only choice D works in the context. Choice A is for flashy things, choice B is for things that actively show something, choice C is for people using weapons or tools.

4. (B)
Category: Main Idea, Transitions
Difficulty: Medium
Strategy: Questions may provide key information about what a portion should achieve in the passage.

To determine the main idea, consider the central claim, issue, argument, or message that the author wants to communicate.
Solution: The previous paragraph was about ways wealthy people used air conditioning. This paragraph is about how common people used other methods.

5. (C)
Category: Style
Difficulty: Easy
Strategy: Consider context for words that have similar meanings.
Solution: Temperatures can be reduced, but they can't be shrunk (made smaller), curtailed (made shorter), or dipped (made lower in height).

6. (A)
Category: Transitions
Difficulty: Easy
Strategy: Transitions show contrast, support, or cause. Choose the most appropriate and logical way to shift from one idea to another.
Solution: The paragraph lists several features of homes. Use a transition that links items in a list.

7. (B)
Category: Addition & Deletion
Difficulty: Medium
Strategy: Consider how the sentence relates to the sentences around them and the paragraph's main idea.
Solution: The information isn't as detailed or in-depth as choice A would suggest. The rest of the passage focuses primarily on the impact of air conditioning, so choice C does not work. Choice D doesn't match.

8. (A)
Category: Addition & Deletion
Difficulty: Medium
Strategy: Consider how information relates to the information around it.
Solution: The previous paragraph was about cooling methods in the South. This added sentence would transition between paragraphs.

9. (A)
Category: Transitions
Difficulty: Easy
Strategy: Transitions show contrast, support, or cause. Choose the most appropriate and logical way to shift from one idea to another.
Solution: The preceding sentence has a broad statement that is supported by this sentence.

10. (C)
Category: Transitions
Difficulty: Medium
Strategy: Transitions show contrast, support, or cause. Choose the most appropriate and logical way to shift from one idea to another.
Solution: Consider how the two parts of the sentence relate. The first half is positive, but the second half is negative. This sentence links the positive tone of the previous paragraph to the negative tone of this one. Use a contrasting transition. Choice D doesn't work because it would suggest there are no positive consequences of air conditioning.

11. (A)
Category: Organization
Difficulty: Medium
Strategy: When organized properly, an essay's ideas should build upon each other and transition naturally.
Solution: The use of "thus" suggests the previous sentence explains why air conditioning caused a "vicious cycle." This cycle is the fact that CFCs used in air conditioning can cause higher environmental temperatures, which leads to even more use of air conditioning.

Pronouns 1 – Pages 173-175

1. (B)
Category: Pronouns
Difficulty: Medium
Strategy: In "whomever" and "whoever," the pronoun follows the same rules as "whom" and "who." The pronoun "who" always refers to the subject. The pronoun "whom" always refers to an object. In order to determine whether a pronoun is a subject or object, try plugging in an easier pronoun (such as "he/him" or "they/them") and see which works better. Just as people are not referred to as "that," they are not referred to as "whatever."
Solution: Test whether "he" or "him" would work best. "He lost the race…" makes more sense, so the pronoun would be "who" or "whoever."

2. (A)
Category: Pronouns
Difficulty: Easy
Strategy: The pronoun "who" always refers to the subject. The pronoun "whom" always refers to an object. In order to determine whether a pronoun is a subject or object, try plugging in an easier pronoun and see which works better.
Solution: "He marched from Austin" works better than "Him marched from Austin." Also, "he followed" is better than "him followed," so "who" works better.

3. (C)
Category: Pronouns
Difficulty: Medium
Strategy: A pronoun must have a clear antecedent.
Solution: It's not clear what "they" refers to, because the only nouns referred to previously were Gridley, the saloon, and the parade, which are all singular. "He" clearly refers to Gridley.

4. (D)
Category: Pronouns
Difficulty: Medium
Strategy: A pronoun must have a clear antecedent. It must match the antecedent in being singular or plural.
Solution: The pronoun should refer to the bag of flour.

5. (D)
Difficulty: Hard
Category: Pronouns
Strategy: A pronoun must have a clear antecedent. It must match the antecedent in being singular or plural.
Solution: "They" may refer to the mines, the residents, or their pockets. A specific noun works better because it's clear.

6. (C)
Category: Pronouns
Difficulty: Medium
Strategy: A pronoun must have a clear antecedent. It must match the antecedent in being singular or plural.
Solution: A specific pronoun works best. Omitting the underlined portion results in a fragment.

7. (A)
Category: Pronouns
Difficulty: Medium
Strategy: A pronoun must have a clear antecedent. It must match the antecedent in being singular or plural.
Solution: "it was" is sometimes used as an idiom. In this case, the pronoun "it" refers to a noun that appears later within the same sentence: the millman. Omitting will result in a fragment.

8. (B)
Category: Pronouns
Difficulty: Medium
Strategy: "Its" is the possessive form of "it." "It's" is short for "it is."
Solution: The phrase would be "it is rumored," so "it's" works best.

9. (D)
Category: Pronouns
Difficulty: Medium
Strategy: A pronoun must have a clear antecedent.
Solution: Using "him" may refer to Clemens or Gridley, so using the name is clearer. A comma is needed to create a parenthetical phrase.

10. (C)
Category: Pronouns
Difficulty: Medium
Strategy: Use a form of "who" when referring to people.
Solution: "Who" works because we're referring to a person and it's not possessive.

11. (D)
Category: Pronouns
Difficulty: Medium
Strategy: A pronoun must match the antecedent in being singular or plural.
Solution: The pronoun refers back to the cakes, which are plural.

Pronouns 2 – Pages 176-178

1. (D)
Category: Pronouns
Difficulty: Easy
Strategy: A pronoun must match the antecedent in being singular or plural.
Solution: The pronoun refers to Petra, which is singular.

2. (C)
Category: Pronouns
Difficulty: Hard
Strategy: A pronoun must have a clear antecedent.
Solution: Petra was "long hidden," but the pronoun may also refer to Jordan, so a clear noun is better.

3. (D)
Category: Pronouns
Difficulty: Hard
Strategy: A pronoun must have a clear antecedent.
Solution: They protected the city from looting. A singular pronoun may refer to other nouns, such as the path.

4. (C)
Category: Pronouns
Difficulty: Easy
Strategy: A pronoun must match the antecedent in being singular or plural.
Solution: The pronoun refers to Petra, which is singular.

5. (B)
Category: Pronouns
Difficulty: Medium
Strategy: "Its" is the possessive form of "it." "It's" is short for "it is."
Solution: The pronoun is possessive, so it should be "its".

6. (D)
Category: Pronouns
Difficulty: Hard
Strategy: A pronoun must have a clear antecedent.
Solution: The first phrase in the sentence modifies the next subject. A pronoun would have no clear antecedent.

7. (D)
Category: Pronouns
Difficulty: Medium
Strategy: A pronoun must have a clear antecedent.
Solution: He was obsessed with finding the city, and there is no pronoun to clearly refer to that.

8. (A)
Category: Pronouns
Difficulty: Medium
Strategy: A pronoun must have a clear antecedent.
Solution: None of the pronouns clearly refer to the false identity.

9. (D)
Category: Pronouns
Difficulty: Easy
Strategy: When a pronoun is paired with another noun, ignore the other noun to see which pronoun works best.
Solution: "He went straight through the ruins" works best.

10. (A)
Category: Pronouns
Difficulty: Medium
Strategy: A pronoun must match the antecedent in being singular or plural.
Solution: The pronoun refers to Al-Khazneh, which is singular.

11. (B)
Category: Pronouns
Difficulty: Hard
Strategy: A pronoun must match the antecedent in being singular or plural.
Solution: The pronoun refers to Al-Khazneh, which is singular.

Pronouns 3 – Pages 179-181

1. (D)
Category: Pronouns
Difficulty: Hard
Strategy: A pronoun must have a clear antecedent.
Solution: The pronoun "them" may refer to the farmers, relatives, or graves. A clear noun is better.

2. (A)
Category: Pronouns
Difficulty: Hard
Strategy: A pronoun must have a clear antecedent.
Solution: None of the pronouns would clearly refer to the investigations.

3. (C)
Category: Pronouns
Difficulty: Medium
Strategy: "There" refers to a place. "Their" is a possessive pronouns. "They're" is short for "they are."
Solution: The pronoun should be possessive.

4. (D)
Category: Pronouns
Difficulty: Medium
Strategy: "There" refers to a place. "Their" is a possessive pronouns. "They're" is short for "they are."
Solution: The sentence should say "they are feeding".

5. (C)
Category: Pronouns
Difficulty: Medium
Strategy: A pronoun must match the antecedent in being singular or plural.
Solution: "Community" is singular, so a singular pronoun is needed.

6. (D)
Category: Pronouns
Difficulty: Medium
Strategy: A pronoun must match its antecedent in being singular or plural.
Solution: The "infected person" is singular, so a singular pronoun is needed. C doesn't work when referring to a person.

7. (C)
Category: Pronouns
Difficulty: Hard
Strategy: "Them" is an object pronoun. "Themselves" is an object when the same thing is the subject.
Solution: To keep the sentence parallel, it should say that the locals have addled minds. In this case, "the locals" can be replaced with "them."

8. (C)
Category: Pronouns
Difficulty: Medium
Strategy: Use of "one" should be consistent.
Solution: Because the sentence refers to "one" at the beginning, continue this by using "oneself."

9. (A)
Category: Pronouns
Difficulty: Medium
Strategy: Use of "one" should be consistent.
Solution: Because the sentence refers to "one" at the beginning, continue this by using "one." "One" is singular, which works with "resorts."

10. (D)
Category: Pronouns
Difficulty: Hard
Strategy: A pronoun must have a clear antecedent.
Solution: What is being combated? They are battling the situation of having a dwindling population.

11. (D)
Category: Pronouns
Difficulty: Hard
Strategy: A pronoun must have a clear antecedent.
Solution: What were they trying to save? There is no pronoun that clearly refers to their peers, so use a clear noun.

Subject-Verb Agreement 1 – Pages 183-185

1. (C)
Category: Subject-Verb Agreement
Difficulty: Medium
Strategy: When the subject follows the verb, flip the sentence to put the subject first.
Solution: Rewrite as "The Cuban Revolution was just four years prior."

2. (C)
Category: Subject-Verb Agreement
Difficulty: Hard
Strategy: Singular subjects require singular verbs, and plural subjects require plural verbs. To simplify sentences, remove all extra information between the subject and the verb, and then make sure they agree. Extra information set off by commas is often not a part of the subject.
Solution: Rewrite as "Her faith was deeply reflective," because her art is extraneous information in the sentence.

3. (C)
Category: Subject-Verb Agreement
Difficulty: Medium
Strategy: Subjects grouped by "and" are plural, even if the "and" joins two singular words.
Solution: "Homeland" and "faith" are grouped to form a plural subject.

4. (B)
Category: Subject-Verb Agreement
Difficulty: Medium
Strategy: When the subject follows the verb, flip the sentence to put the subject first.
Solution: Rewrite as "A cloudy reflection was on one of the panels".

5. (B)
Category: Subject-Verb Agreement
Difficulty: Medium
Strategy: Extra information set off by commas is often not a part of the subject.
Solution: The Rome Prize is the singular subject, because "numerous grants" is set off by commas.

6. (D)
Category: Subject-Verb Agreement
Difficulty: Medium
Strategy: When the subject follows the verb, flip the sentence to put the subject first.
Solution: Rewrite as "The Sistine Chapel, St. Peter's Basilica, and Vatican Museums are in this site."

7. (C)
Category: Subject-Verb Agreement
Difficulty: Hard
Strategy: To simplify sentences, remove all extra information between the subject and the verb, and then make sure they agree.
Solution: Rewrite as "The sight of relics was an inspiring confluence of religion and design." The pronoun should be plural because the containers held multiple things.

8. (A)
Category: Subject-Verb Agreement
Difficulty: Easy
Strategy: Singular subjects require singular verbs, and plural subjects require plural verbs.
Solution: The subject, Renaissance paintings, is plural. Also, use the correct phrase of "certainly influential."

9. (B)
Category: Subject-Verb Agreement
Difficulty: Medium
Strategy: Subjects grouped by "and" are plural, even if the "and" joins two singular words.
Solution: "Spiked wheel" and "gridiron" are grouped to form a plural subject. Also, the two objects of the sentence, St. Catherine and St. Lawrence, need a plural pronoun.

10. (B)
Category: Subject-Verb Agreement
Difficulty: Hard
Strategy: To simplify sentences, remove all extra information between the subject and the verb, and then make sure they agree.
Solution: Rewrite as "A set appears on white pedestals."

11. (C)
Category: Subject-Verb Agreement
Difficulty: Medium
Strategy: Singular subjects require singular verbs, and plural subjects require plural verbs.
Solution: The different professions are not multiple people. There is only one subject: Maria. Also, remove the comma to create a single modifying phrase.

Subject-Verb Agreement 2 – Pages 186-188

1. (D)
Category: Subject-Verb Agreement
Difficulty: Easy
Strategy: Singular subjects require singular verbs, and plural subjects require plural verbs. To simplify sentences, remove all extra information between the subject and the verb, and then make sure they agree. Extra information set off by commas is often not a part of the subject.
Solution: "One" is a singular pronoun and is the subject. The phrase "of his pieces" and everything else before "being" is extra information that can be removed to simplify the sentence. Rewrite as "One is a modified water tower."

2. (B)
Category: Subject-Verb Agreement
Difficulty: Medium
Strategy: Singular subjects require singular verbs, and plural subjects require plural verbs.
Solution: The subject is Finkel, which is singular. Choices A, C, and D are all plural.

3. (D)
Category: Subject-Verb Agreement
Difficulty: Hard
Strategy: To simplify sentences, remove all extra information between the subject and the verb, and then make sure they agree. Collective nouns are singular (technically, collective nouns can be considered plural in some situations, but not on this test).
Solution: Rewrite as "A group assembled." Choice A results in a fragment, as –ing verbs often do. Choices B and C are plural. Rather than use a singular verb, choice D eliminated the "to be" verb, which works in this case.

4. (A)
Category: Subject-Verb Agreement
Difficulty: Easy
Strategy: Subjects grouped by "and" are plural, even if the "and" joins two singular words.

Solution: "The construction" and "the effect" are joined to create a plural subject. Choice D is also a plural verb, but it doesn't work with "certain" following.

5. (B)
Category: Subject-Verb Agreement
Difficulty: Medium
Strategy: When the subject follows the verb, flip the sentence to put the subject first.
Solution: Rewrite as "Many people have been there." A plural verb is needed. "Were" is plural, but it doesn't work with "been" following.

6. (D)
Category: Subject-Verb Agreement, Fragments
Difficulty: Medium
Strategy: To simplify sentences, remove all extra information between the subject and the verb, and then make sure they agree. Relative pronouns may create fragments.
Solution: Rewrite as "The goals sound lofty."

7. (B)
Category: Subject-Verb Agreement
Difficulty: Easy
Strategy: To simplify sentences, remove all extra information between the subject and the verb, and then make sure they agree.
Solution: Rewrite as "Completed projects include some spaces."

8. (A)
Category: Subject-Verb Agreement
Difficulty: Medium
Strategy: To simplify sentences, remove all extra information between the subject and the verb, and then make sure they agree.
Solution: "One" is a singular pronoun and is the subject. Rewrite as "One has an open air stage."

9. (A)
Category: Subject-Verb Agreement
Difficulty: Hard
Strategy: To simplify sentences, remove all extra information between the subject and the verb, and then make sure they agree.
Solution: Prepositional phrases are extra information and can be ignored when identifying the subject. "of local plants, stories, buildings, and traditions" is a prepositional phrase. Rewrite as "the legacy has been preserved." It doesn't matter if "tradition" or "traditions" is used.

10. (B)
Category: Subject-Verb Agreement
Difficulty: Hard
Strategy: To simplify sentences, remove all extra information between the subject and the verb, and then make sure they agree.
Solution: Though it appears there are two subjects ("the dam" and "parks and art installations"), there is only one: "the building." This is a gerund, an –ing verb used as a noun. Rewrite as "the building has had lasting impact."

11. (D)
Category: Subject-Verb Agreement, Verb Tense
Difficulty: Medium
Strategy: To simplify sentences, remove all extra information between the subject and the verb, and then make sure they agree.
Solution: Rewrite as "Finkel is still working." In context, it is clear this verb should be present tense.

Comparisons 1 – Pages 190-192

1. (A)
Category: Comparisons
Difficulty: Medium
Strategy: Make sure that comparisons are logical and parallel. The same types of ideas should be compared to each other.
Solution: The sentence compares "the noble character of George Washington" to the character of Cincinnatus.

2. (C)
Category: Comparisons
Difficulty: Medium
Strategy: Use the comparative form of an adjective to compare two things. Comparative forms add either "-er" or are preceded by "more." Use the superlative form of an adjective to compare three or more things. Superlative forms add "-est" or are preceded by "most."
Solution: The comparison is between two choices, so the comparative form is used.

3. (B)
Category: Comparisons
Difficulty: Medium
Strategy: When comparing something to a group that it is part of, you can't just compare it to the whole group. Remember to use "other," comparing it to the rest of the group, not to itself.
Solution: Compare integrity to other characteristics.

4. (C)
Category: Comparisons
Difficulty: Hard
Strategy: When comparing something to a group that it is part of, you can't just compare it to the whole group.
Solution: Cincinnatus cannot be compared to anyone, because he is included in that group. "Anyone else" works better.

5. (B)
Category: Comparisons
Difficulty: Hard
Strategy: Make sure that comparisons are logical and parallel. The same types of ideas should be compared to each other.
Solution: Compare our law to Rome's law.

6. (B)
Category: Comparisons
Difficulty: Hard
Strategy: Make sure that comparisons are logical and parallel. The same types of ideas should be compared to each other.
Solution: Compare the dictators' corruptible characters to Cincinnatus' character.

7. (C)
Category: Comparisons
Difficulty: Hard
Strategy: Make sure that comparisons are logical and parallel. The same types of ideas should be compared to each other.
Solution: Compare Cincinnatus' reputation to the reputations of saviors or masters.

8. (D)
Category: Comparisons
Difficulty: Medium
Strategy: Make sure that comparisons are logical and parallel. The same types of ideas should be compared to each other.
Solution: When the sentence is properly parallel, it compares the importance of two things: preserving laws and preserving his power.

9. (C)
Category: Comparisons
Difficulty: Medium
Strategy: Make sure that comparisons are logical and parallel. The same types of ideas should be compared to each other.
Solution: The story of Washington is said to resemble the story of Cincinnatus.

10. (A)
Category: Comparisons
Difficulty: Medium
Strategy: Make sure that comparisons are logical and parallel. The same types of ideas should be compared to each other.
Solution: When the sentence is properly parallel, it states two ways Washington was remembered: as a defender and as a commander.

11. (C)
Category: Comparisons
Difficulty: Hard
Strategy: Use the comparative form of an adjective to compare two things. Comparative forms add either "-er" or are preceded by "more." Use the superlative form of an adjective to compare three or more things. Superlative forms add "-est" or are preceded by "most."
Solution: There are two paths given, so the comparative form is used.

Comparisons 2 – Pages 193-195

1. (C)
Category: Comparisons
Difficulty: Hard
Strategy: Make sure that comparisons are logical and parallel. The same types of ideas should be compared to each other.
Solution: The comparison is how commonly the opinion is held by different groups.

2. (A)
Category: Comparisons
Difficulty: Medium
Strategy: Make sure that comparisons are logical and parallel. The same types of ideas should be compared to each other.
Solution: Compare Cezanne's reputation to other artists' reputations.

3. (B)
Category: Comparisons
Difficulty: Medium
Strategy: Use the comparative form of an adjective to compare two things. Comparative forms add either "-er" or are preceded by "more." Use the superlative form of an adjective to compare three or more things. Superlative forms add "-est" or are preceded by "most."
Solution: His paintings are compared to others, establishing two subjects to compare.

4. (A)
Category: Comparisons
Difficulty: Medium
Strategy: Use the comparative form of an adjective to compare two things. Use the superlative form of an adjective to compare three or more things.
Solution: Two things are compared: subject matter and the act of painting.

5. (C)
Category: Comparisons
Difficulty: Hard
Strategy: Make sure that comparisons are logical and parallel. The same types of ideas should be compared to each other.
Solution: Cezanne was more concerned than other artists were concerned.

6. (A)
Category: Comparisons
Difficulty: Medium
Strategy: Use the comparative form of an adjective to compare two things. Use the superlative form of an adjective to compare three or more things.
Solution: There are three traits compared, so use the superlative.

7. (C)
Category: Comparisons
Difficulty: Medium
Strategy: Make sure that comparisons are logical and parallel. The same types of ideas should be compared to each other.
Solution: The sentence compares the two ways he approached her.

8. (A)
Category: Comparisons
Difficulty: Hard
Strategy: Make sure that comparisons are logical and parallel. The same types of ideas should be compared to each other.
Solution: The sentence compares the length of time Hortense could pose to the length of time most people could pose.

9. (D)
Category: Comparisons
Difficulty: Easy
Strategy: Use the comparative form of an adjective to compare two things. Use the superlative form of an adjective to compare three or more things.
Solution: The sentence compares two things: their relationship and most relationships.

10. (C)
Category: Comparisons
Difficulty: Medium
Strategy: Make sure that comparisons are logical and parallel. The same types of ideas should be compared to each other.
Solution: The sentence compares "to ensure" to "to show".

11. (B)
Category: Comparisons
Difficulty: Medium
Strategy: Make sure that comparisons are logical and parallel. The same types of ideas should be compared to each other.
Solution: The sentence compares when success came to Cezanne to when it comes to most artists.

Idioms 1 – Pages 197-199

1. (B)
Category: Idioms
Difficulty: Easy
Strategy: Idioms must be both proper and logical. Try to hear which idiom sounds correct. If you see an underlined verb and preposition, or just an underlined preposition, look for an idiom error.
Solution: "Discovery of" is the only proper idiom.

2. (C)
Category: Idioms
Difficulty: Medium
Strategy: Idioms must be both proper and logical.
Solution: "Curiosity about" is a proper idiom, but doesn't fit in the context. "Curious about" works better.

3. (C)
Category: Idioms
Difficulty: Easy
Strategy: Idioms must be both proper and logical.
Solution: "Spread on" is a proper idiom, but doesn't fit in the context. "Spread to" works better.

4. (D)
Category: Idioms
Difficulty: Medium
Strategy: Idioms must be both proper and logical.
Solution: "On the grounds" is the proper idiom. "For the grounds" isn't right in this context, but it's a good attractor, considering the women for divorce their husbands for the coffee "grounds."

5. (C)
Category: Idioms
Difficulty: Medium
Strategy: Idioms must be both proper and logical.
Solution: "Methods of preparing" is the proper idiom.

6. (B)
Category: Idioms
Difficulty: Medium
Strategy: Idioms must be both proper and logical.
Solution: In the context, "known as" works best because a name follows.

7. (D)
Category: Idioms
Difficulty: Hard
Strategy: Idioms must be both proper and logical.
Solution: Consider the whole sentence. None of the idioms work with "would spread" at the end, so the prepositions should be omitted.

8. (C)
Category: Idioms
Difficulty: Medium
Strategy: Idioms must be both proper and logical.
Solution: "Subject of controversy" is the proper idiom.

9. (A)
Category: Idioms
Difficulty: Easy
Strategy: Idioms must be both proper and logical.
Solution: "Put an end to" is the proper idiom.

10. (C)
Category: Idioms
Difficulty: Easy
Strategy: Idioms must be both proper and logical.
Solution: In the context, "give up" is the proper idiom.

11. (D)
Category: Idioms
Difficulty: Medium
Strategy: Idioms must be both proper and logical.
Solution: In the context, "in defense of" is the proper idiom.

Idioms 2 – Pages 200-202

1. (C)
Category: Idioms
Difficulty: Easy
Strategy: Idioms must be both proper and logical. Try to hear which idiom sounds correct. If you see an underlined verb and preposition, or just an underlined preposition, look for an idiom error.
Solution: The idiom, broken up in the sentence, is "so accredited that…"

2. (C)
Category: Idioms
Difficulty: Easy
Strategy: Idioms must be both proper and logical.
Solution: In the context, "working on" is the proper idiom.

3. (A)
Category: Idioms
Difficulty: Easy
Strategy: Idioms must be both proper and logical.
Solution: "Interested in" is the proper idiom.

4. (C)
Category: Idioms
Difficulty: Easy
Strategy: Idioms must be both proper and logical.
Solution: In the context, "position as" is the proper idiom.

5. (B)
Category: Idioms
Difficulty: Medium
Strategy: Idioms must be both proper and logical.
Solution: "Set up", "left out", and "left over" are proper idioms, but in the context "set out" works best.

6. (D)
Category: Idioms
Difficulty: Easy
Strategy: Idioms must be both proper and logical.
Solution: In the context, "gave to" works best.

7. (C)
Category: Idioms
Difficulty: Medium
Strategy: Idioms must be both proper and logical.
Solution: In the context, "due to" works best.

8. (D)
Category: Idioms
Difficulty: Medium
Strategy: Idioms must be both proper and logical.
Solution: "Ability to adapt to" is the proper idiom.

9. (B)
Category: Idioms
Difficulty: Easy
Strategy: Idioms must be both proper and logical.
Solution: In the context, "pass on" works best.

10. (B)
Category: Idioms
Difficulty: Easy
Strategy: Idioms must be both proper and logical.
Solution: In the context, "sought advice from" works best.

11. (C)
Category: Idioms
Difficulty: Easy
Strategy: Idioms must be both proper and logical.
Solution: "As a result of" is the proper idiom.

Diction 1 – Pages 204-206

1. (A)
Category: Diction
Difficulty: Easy
Strategy: Consider context and the definitions of each word. Be wary of words that sound similar.
Solution: "Rights" are entitlements. "Rites" are a custom or religious act. "Writes" is a verb for writing. "Wrights" are builders.

2. (B)
Category: Diction
Difficulty: Hard
Strategy: Consider context and the definitions of each word. Be wary of words that sound similar.
Solution: "Ensure" is to guarantee. "Fair" is in accordance with rules. "Insure" is to arrange compensation for a loss. "Fare" is an expense.

3. (C)
Category: Diction
Difficulty: Medium
Strategy: Consider context and the definitions of each word. Be wary of words that sound similar.
Solution: "Break" is to bring an end to, in this context. "Brake" is to slow down.

4. (C)
Category: Diction
Difficulty: Medium
Strategy: Consider context and the definitions of each word. Be wary of words that sound similar.
Solution: "Descent" is lineage. "Decent" is of permissible quality. "Dissent" is to disagree. "Docent" is a guide or teacher.

5. (A)
Category: Diction
Difficulty: Medium
Strategy: Consider context and the definitions of each word. Be wary of words that sound similar.
Solution: "Losing" is to have less. "Loosing" is to set loose. "Patience" is ability to wait. "Patients" visit doctors.

6. (D)
Category: Diction
Difficulty: Medium
Strategy: Consider context and the definitions of each word. Be wary of words that sound similar.
Solution: "Peace" is without conflict. "Piece" is a portion. "Lead" is present tense, "led" is past tense.

7. (B)
Category: Diction
Difficulty: Medium
Strategy: Consider context and the definitions of each word. Be wary of words that sound similar.
Solution: "A lot" is a large amount. "Allot" is to give a task. "Alot" is not a word.

8. (C)
Category: Diction
Difficulty: Medium
Strategy: Consider context and the definitions of each word. Be wary of words that sound similar.
Solution: "Some" is an amount. "Sum" is the result of an addition. "Felled" is past tense of "fell," as in cutting down trees. "Felt" is past tense of "feel."

9. (B)
Category: Diction
Difficulty: Medium
Strategy: Consider context and the definitions of each word. Be wary of words that sound similar.
Solution: "Mind" is a person's thoughts. "Mined" is past tense of "mine." "Soul" is an intangible part of a person. "Sole" is the bottom of a foot.

10. (A)
Category: Diction
Difficulty: Hard
Strategy: Consider context and the definitions of each word. Be wary of words that sound similar.
Solution: "Number" is used for a countable quantity. "Amount" is used for something that can only be measured, not counted. For people, use "number." "Effect" is a noun and "affect" is a verb.

11. (C)
Category: Diction
Difficulty: Medium
Strategy: Consider context and the definitions of each word. Be wary of words that sound similar.
Solution: "Especially" means "particularly." "Specially" is an adverb for something done uniquely. "Specific" things are particular and clearly defined. "Special" is an adjective for unique things.

Diction 2 – Pages 207-209

1. (B)
Category: Diction
Difficulty: Hard
Strategy: Consider context and the definitions of each word. Be wary of words that sound similar.
Solution: "Between" is used with two items. "Among" is used for more than two. "Principles" are truths or concepts. "Principals" run schools.

2. (C)
Category: Diction
Difficulty: Medium
Strategy: Consider context and the definitions of each word. Be wary of words that sound similar.
Solution: "Fewer" is used when a thing can be counted. "Less" is used when a thing cannot be counted. "There" is used for places. "Their" is a possessive pronoun.

3. (A)
Category: Diction
Difficulty: Hard
Strategy: Consider context and the definitions of each word. Be wary of words that sound similar.
Solution: "Where" is used for places. "Were" is a past-tense verb. "Too" means "in addition" or "extremely".

4. (C)
Category: Diction
Difficulty: Medium
Strategy: Consider context and the definitions of each word. Be wary of words that sound similar.
Solution: "Would have" is the proper idiom. "Scene" is a place. "Seen" is the past participle of "see."

5. (D)
Category: Diction
Difficulty: Medium
Strategy: Consider context and the definitions of each word. Be wary of words that sound similar.
Solution: "Spored" is not a word. "Spared" is left aside. "Sparred" is battled. "Spurred" is urged.

6. (A)
Category: Diction
Difficulty: Medium
Strategy: Consider context and the definitions of each word. Be wary of words that sound similar.
Solution: "Fewer" is used when a thing can be counted. "Less" is used when a thing cannot be counted. "Accept" is to approve. "Except" is to exclude.

7. (D)
Category: Diction
Difficulty: Hard
Strategy: Consider context and the definitions of each word. Be wary of words that sound similar.
Solution: "Maybe" means "possibly." "May be" means it might be. "Based" is having a foundation on something. "Baste" is to pour juices over something.

8. (C)
Category: Diction
Difficulty: Medium
Strategy: Consider context and the definitions of each word. Be wary of words that sound similar.
Solution: "Threw" is the past tense of "throw." "Through" is moving past. "There" is for places. "Their" is a possessive pronoun.

9. (B)
Category: Diction
Difficulty: Medium
Strategy: Consider context and the definitions of each word. Be wary of words that sound similar.
Solution: "Device" is a tool. "Devise" is to invent. "New" means "original." "Knew" is the past tense of "know."

10. (C)
Category: Pronouns
Difficulty: Hard
Strategy: Consider context and the definitions of each word. Be wary of words that sound similar.
Solution: "Between" is used with two items. "Among" is used for more than two. "Number" is used for a countable quantity. "Amount" is used for something that can only be measured, not counted.

11. (C)
Category: Diction
Difficulty: Hard
Strategy: Consider context and the definitions of each word. Be wary of words that sound similar.
Solution: "Ensuring" is to make sure. "Insuring" is to invest money in preparation for a loss. "Compliment" is a nice thing to say. "Complement" is to work well with something else.

Fragments 1 – Pages 211-213

1. (D)
Category: Fragments
Difficulty: Medium
Strategy: Be careful with relative pronouns, such as *who, which,* and *that.* They may create incomplete ideas by changing how the action of the sentence relates to the subject.
Solution: "Where" is used as a relative pronoun and creates a fragment. "If" creates a conditional phrase rather than an independent clause.

2. (D)
Category: Fragments
Difficulty: Medium
Strategy: Be careful with relative pronouns, such as *who, which,* and *that.* They may create incomplete ideas.
Solution: "Which" creates a fragment.

3. (D)
Category: Fragments
Difficulty: Easy
Strategy: Commas may create parentheticals that do not form independent clauses.
Solution: The sentence needs a main verb. Get rid of the comma.

4. (A)
Category: Fragments
Difficulty: Medium
Strategy: Commas may create parentheticals that do not form independent clauses.
Solution: The sentence needs a main verb and no excessive commas.

5. (C)
Category: Fragments
Difficulty: Medium
Strategy: Verbs can be part of a descriptive phrase rather than part of an independent clause.
Solution: Choices A and B use "placed" to describe the shades. Choice C is passive but a complete idea.

6. (D)
Category: Fragments
Difficulty: Medium
Strategy: Be careful with relative pronouns, such as *who, which,* and *that.* They may create incomplete ideas. A verb ending in *ing* is not a complete verb. An *ing* verb creates a fragment if the sentence does not include another, complete verb.
Solution: Don't use "that" or *ing* verbs.

7. (A)
Category: Fragments
Difficulty: Medium
Strategy: Complete sentences need a main verb.
Solution: The "of" following the underlined portion requires a proper idiom. Choice B does not have a main verb.

8. (D)
Category: Fragments
Difficulty: Medium
Strategy: Prepositional phrases do not create independent clauses.
Solution: The sentence begins with "in," creating a prepositional phrase, so it needs to be joined to an independent clause with a comma.

9. (D)
Category: Fragments
Difficulty: Medium
Strategy: "When" is a relative pronoun. "Since" and "so" are conjunctions. These do not begin independent clauses.
Solution: Delete the words that create fragments.

10. (A)
Category: Fragments
Difficulty: Easy
Strategy: Prepositional phrases do not create independent clauses.
Solution: The phrase "near the baoli" is a prepositional phrase, which doesn't create a complete sentence, so the following part needs to be an independent clause.

11. (C)
Category: Fragments
Difficulty: Medium
Strategy: Be careful with relative pronouns, such as *who, which,* and *that.* They may create incomplete ideas.
Solution: Choices A and D use "who" to create fragments. Choice C uses "who" but also has an independent clause with "It was architect Manit Rastogi".

Fragments 2 – Pages 214-216

1. (D)
Category: Fragments
Difficulty: Medium
Strategy: Be careful with relative pronouns, such as *who, which,* and *that.* They may create incomplete ideas.
Solution: This is a complicated sentence, so try simplifying it. Rewrite as "The flowers close and then reopen." "That" and "which" create a fragment.

2. (D)
Category: Fragments
Difficulty: Medium
Strategy: Past tense verbs may be used as descriptions rather than main verbs.
Solution: The sentence needs a main verb, such as "is."

3. (D)
Category: Fragments, Subject-Verb Agreement
Difficulty: Medium
Strategy: A verb ending in *ing* is not a complete verb. An *ing* verb creates a fragment if the sentence does not include another, complete verb.
Solution: Don't use "that," which is a relative pronoun, or an *ing* verb. The subject is plural, so "follow" works best.

4. (D)
Category: Fragments
Difficulty: Hard
Strategy: Be careful with relative pronouns, such as *who, which,* and *that.* They may create incomplete ideas. A verb ending in *ing* is not a complete verb.
Solution: This is a tricky sentence. Choices A, B, and C use "fruit" as a noun, but Choice D would use it as a verb. In this context, the verb works and creates a complete sentence.
Don't use "that," which is a relative pronoun, or an *ing* verb.

5. (C)
Category: Fragments
Difficulty: Medium
Strategy: Complete sentences need a main verb.
Solution: Use "have" as the main verb. The "have" that is part of "they've" is an auxiliary verb to be used with another verb, so it doesn't work.

6. (B)
Category: Fragments
Difficulty: Medium
Strategy: A verb ending in *ing* is not a complete verb.
Solution: The initial clause needs a subject and verb.

7. (A)
Category: Fragments
Difficulty: Medium
Strategy: The initial clause needs a subject and verb.
Solution: "It is" can serve as the subject and verb.

8. (D)
Category: Fragments
Difficulty: Medium
Strategy: Be careful with relative pronouns, such as *who, which,* and *that.* They may create incomplete ideas.
Solution: Don't use "that."

9. (A)
Category: Fragments
Difficulty: Medium
Strategy: Be careful with relative pronouns, such as *who, which,* and *that.* They may create incomplete ideas. A verb ending in *ing* is not a complete verb.
Solution: Choice B uses a relative pronoun. Choice C uses an *ing* verb. Choice D has a modifier error.

10. (D)
Category: Fragments
Difficulty: Medium
Strategy: Parentheticals do not create independent clauses.
Solution: Add a comma to separate the parenthetical from the independent clause. Choice C is an *ing* verb.

11. (C)
Category: Fragments
Difficulty: Medium
Strategy: Past tense verbs may be used as descriptions rather than main verbs. A verb ending in *ing* is not a complete verb.
Solution: Choice C has both a subject and verb to create an independent clause.

Run-Ons 1 – Pages 218-220

1. (D)
Category: Run-Ons
Difficulty: Medium
Strategy: When two independent clauses are joined with a comma but without a conjunction, the mistake is called a comma splice. Fix a comma splice by replacing the comma with a semicolon, a period, or a comma and a conjunction.
Solution: This sentence contains two independent clauses, so split with a period, semicolon, or colon.

2. (C)
Category: Run-Ons
Difficulty: Medium
Strategy: When two independent clauses are joined with a comma but without a conjunction, the mistake is called a comma splice.
Solution: This sentence contains two independent clauses. Choice D creates a fragment.

3. (A)
Category: Run-Ons
Difficulty: Hard
Strategy: When two independent clauses are joined with a comma but without a conjunction, the mistake is called a comma splice.
Solution: The question is long and complex, but the comma is not a comma splice but a parenthetical.

4. (B)
Category: Run-Ons
Difficulty: Medium
Strategy: When two independent clauses are joined with a comma but without a conjunction, the mistake is called a comma splice.
Solution: Add a conjunction.

5. (B)
Category: Run-Ons
Difficulty: Hard
Strategy: When two independent clauses are joined with a comma but without a conjunction, the mistake is called a comma splice.
Solution: "Because" is not a regular conjunction but a subordinating conjunction. It connects an independent clause to a subordinating clause, which doesn't necessitate a comma. "Too," however, does need commas in this case.

6. (B)
Category: Run-Ons
Difficulty: Medium
Strategy: When two independent clauses are joined with a comma but without a conjunction, the mistake is called a comma splice.
Solution: This sentence contains two independent clauses, so split with a period, semicolon, or colon.

7. (B)
Category: Run-Ons
Difficulty: Medium
Strategy: When two independent clauses are joined with a comma but without a conjunction, the mistake is called a comma splice.
Solution: This is a complex sentence. The comma is not a comma split but part of a parenthetical.

8. (A)
Category: Run-Ons
Difficulty: Hard
Strategy: When two independent clauses are joined with a comma but without a conjunction, the mistake is called a comma splice.
Solution: Note that the second clause is a dependent clause before an independent. Choice B has no conjunction. Choice C merges the clauses, but then creates a comma splice later in the sentence. Choice D creates a comma splice after the semicolon, too.

9. (D)
Category: Run-Ons
Difficulty: Medium
Strategy: When two independent clauses are joined with a comma but without a conjunction, the mistake is called a comma splice.
Solution: The first clause must be a dependent clause because an independent clause follows.

10. (A)
Category: Run-Ons
Difficulty: Medium
Strategy: "Which" is used to link to nonrestrictive clauses, which are nonessential dependent clauses.
Solution: A comma comes before the clause, so it needs to be an independent clause or a dependent clause beginning with a conjunction.

11. (D)
Category: Run-Ons
Difficulty: Medium
Strategy: "Which" is used to link to nonrestrictive clauses, which are nonessential dependent clauses.
Solution: Before a clause with "which," use a comma.

Run-Ons 2 – Pages 221-223

1. (D)
Category: Run-Ons
Difficulty: Medium
Strategy: If a sentence contains two independent clauses, split with a period, semicolon, or colon.
Solution: Choices B and C don't have an independent clause before the semicolon or colon. Choice A has a main verb, but there's another main verb later in the sentence.

2. (D)
Category: Run-Ons
Difficulty: Medium
Strategy: When two independent clauses are joined with a comma but without a conjunction, the mistake is called a comma splice.
Solution: Choice D gets rid of the second verb to create a dependent clause.

3. (D)
Category: Run-Ons
Difficulty: Medium
Strategy: Independent clauses have one main verb.
Solution: Choice D turns the following information into a parenthetical.

4. (B)
Category: Run-Ons
Difficulty: Medium
Strategy: If a sentence contains two independent clauses, split with a period, semicolon, or colon.
Solution: There are two independent clauses, so a semicolon works to split them.

5. (C)
Category: Run-Ons
Difficulty: Medium
Strategy: Subordinating conjunctions lead to dependent clauses.
Solution: "If" creates a conditional clause, which is dependent. "While" and "since" are subordinating conjunctions.

6. (D)
Category: Run-Ons
Difficulty: Medium
Strategy: When two independent clauses are joined with a comma but without a conjunction, the mistake is called a comma splice.
Solution: "In addition" is not a conjunction that can join two sentences. When starting a sentence, it can be set off by a comma and serve as its own introductory phrase, but in this case, it is part of a larger phrase.

7. (C)
Category: Run-Ons
Difficulty: Medium
Strategy: An independent clause has a main subject and verb.
Solution: "It" is unnecessary because the subject is already stated: "the area containing the facility." A verb is necessary.

8. (C)
Category: Run-Ons
Difficulty: Medium
Strategy: When two independent clauses are joined with a comma but without a conjunction, the mistake is called a comma splice.
Solution: A semicolon is needed to separate the two sentences. The tricky part of this question is determining whether "in fact" fits better with the first or second sentence. The phrase implies a fact is interesting, and the second sentence is most appropriate.

9. (A)
Category: Run-Ons
Difficulty: Easy
Strategy: When two independent clauses are joined with a comma but without a conjunction, the mistake is called a comma splice.
Solution: A period is needed to split two sentences.

10. (D)
Category: Run-Ons
Difficulty: Medium
Strategy: When two independent clauses are joined with a comma but without a conjunction, the mistake is called a comma splice.
Solution: A period is needed to split the sentences. Choice C creates a parenthetical and gets rid of the main verb.

11. (C)
Category: Run-Ons
Difficulty: Hard
Strategy: Split sentences with periods, semicolons, or colons.
Solution: There are two independent clauses: "Helium is still being discovered" and "Researchers found a helium gas field." Split these.

Parallelism 1 – Pages 225-227

1. (D)
Category: Parallelism
Difficulty: Medium
Strategy: Conjunctions used in pairs (e.g., not only...but also, both...and) require that the words following each conjunction be parallel.
Solution: "encountering" should be parallel with "overcoming"

2. (C)
Category: Parallelism
Difficulty: Hard
Strategy: Comparisons should be logical and parallel.
Solution: O'Connor's action (having insecurity) should be compared to student's actions (do). Choice C uses the proper idiom of "as much as."

3. (C)
Category: Parallelism
Difficulty: Medium
Strategy: Use parallel structure with elements in a list or series.
Solution: The list is of items he is known for. Choice B and D are actions. Choice A uses "as well as," which should not be used to finish a list; "and" should be used instead.

4. (B)
Category: Parallelism
Difficulty: Medium
Strategy: Use parallel structure with elements in a list or series.
Solution: The list is of nouns. Choice D doesn't fit the structure.

5. (D)
Category: Parallelism
Difficulty: Medium
Strategy: Conjunctions used in pairs (e.g., not only...but also, both...and) require that the words following each conjunction be parallel.
Solution: "A seminal artist" would be parallel with "a defining voice."

6. (C)
Category: Parallelism
Difficulty: Hard
Strategy: Use parallel structure with elements in a list or series.
Solution: Note the previous two sentences: "Fans have wished" and "Writers have wanted." "Publishers have desired" fits these best.

7. (C)
Category: Parallelism
Difficulty: Hard
Strategy: Use parallel structure with elements in a list or series.
Solution: "Her desire" should be parallel with "her anxiety."

8. (D)
Category: Parallelism
Difficulty: Medium
Strategy: Conjunctions used in pairs (e.g., not only...but also, both...and) require that the words following each conjunction be parallel.
Solution: "Worries about acceptance" should be parallel with "doubts her abilities."

9. (C)
Category: Parallelism
Difficulty: Medium
Strategy: Use parallel structure with elements in a list or series.
Solution: The list is of nouns. Choice C best matches the structure.

10. (A)
Category: Parallelism
Difficulty: Medium
Strategy: Match the structure, according to the question.
Solution: "Adult accomplishments" should be parallel with "eighteen-year-old musings" because they both fit the adjective-noun structure.

11. (B)
Category: Parallelism
Difficulty: Hard
Strategy: Comparisons should be logical and parallel.
Solution: The comparison is between the older O'Connor's action (she entertained) and her college-age self's action (she did). Choice B is clunky, but it's the only option with an action.

Parallelism 2 – Pages 228-230

1. (B)
Category: Parallelism
Difficulty: Medium
Strategy: Use parallel structure with elements in a list or series.
Solution: The list is of actions: "made," "filled," and "painted."

2. (C)
Category: Parallelism
Difficulty: Medium
Strategy: Use parallel structure with elements in a list or series.
Solution: Note the previous sentences, which begin with "There are some who believe" and "There are others who believe". Choice C matches this form best.

3. (B)
Category: Parallelism
Difficulty: Hard
Strategy: Comparisons should be logical and parallel.
Solution: The expense of leaving wood unprotected should be compared to the expense of protective paint. "That" refers to this expense.

4. (D)
Category: Parallelism
Difficulty: Medium
Strategy: Use parallel structure with elements in a list or series.
Solution: The list is of verbs. Choice D fits the structure best.

5. (D)
Category: Parallelism
Difficulty: Medium
Strategy: Use parallel structure with elements in a list or series.
Solution: The list is of nouns. Seasonal is an adjective, so it should be grouped with a noun.

6. (C)
Category: Parallelism
Difficulty: Medium
Strategy: Use parallel structure with elements in a list or series.
Solution: The list has a form: an item produced from a source. Don't use "as well as" to complete a list; use "and."

7. (B)
Category: Parallelism
Difficulty: Medium
Strategy: Use parallel structure with elements in a list or series.
Solution: Note the beginnings of each paragraph. Each one begins with a question.

8. (D)
Category: Parallelism
Difficulty: Medium
Strategy: Use parallel structure with elements in a list or series.
Solution: The sentences before and after have similar structures: one type of atom is used to make another. Choice D best follows this structure.

9. (B)
Category: Parallelism
Difficulty: Hard
Strategy: Comparisons should be logical and parallel.
Solution: The amount of energy for iron fusion is compared to the amount of energy from iron fusion. "That" represents the amount.

10. (C)
Category: Parallelism
Difficulty: Medium
Strategy: Conjunctions used in pairs (e.g., not only...but also, both...and) require that the words following each conjunction be parallel.
Solution: "simple to procure" would be parallel with "easy to grind and mix".

11. (A)
Category: Parallelism
Difficulty: Medium
Strategy: Use parallel structure with elements in a list or series.
Solution: The list is of adjectives: "simple", "affordable", and "protected".

Modifiers 1 – Pages 232-234

1. (B)
Category: Modifiers
Difficulty: Medium
Strategy: Descriptions must be placed next to the things they describe. When a sentence begins with a descriptive phrase, ask who or what is being described.
Solution: "As a child" sets the time for the details of the sentence, and it matches with the following subject.

2. (D)
Category: Modifiers
Difficulty: Hard
Strategy: Descriptions must be placed next to the things they describe.
Solution: The action "before pursuing this art" should be attributed to Kandinsky.

3. (D)
Category: Modifiers
Difficulty: Hard
Strategy: Descriptions must be placed next to the things they describe.
Solution: The underlined portion should end in Monet to fit the following description. Choice A is not a complete sentence.

4. (C)
Category: Modifiers
Difficulty: Hard
Strategy: Descriptions must be placed next to the things they describe.
Solution: The underlined portion should relate to his work or should establish a context for the following information.

5. (B)
Category: Modifiers
Difficulty: Easy
Strategy: Descriptions must be placed next to the things they describe.
Solution: The underlined portion should describe Kandinsky and set a context for the following information.

6. (D)
Category: Modifiers
Difficulty: Medium
Strategy: Descriptions must be placed next to the things they describe.
Solution: The action of "while watching a performance" should be followed by Kandinsky, who performed this action.

7. (A)
Category: Modifiers
Difficulty: Easy
Strategy: Descriptions must be placed next to the things they describe.
Solution: The underlined portion should begin by relating back to Schoenberg.

8. (D)
Category: Modifiers
Difficulty: Medium
Strategy: Descriptions must be placed next to the things they describe.
Solution: The underlined portion should begin by relating back to Beethoven.

9. (C)
Category: Modifiers
Difficulty: Medium
Strategy: Descriptions must be placed next to the things they describe.
Solution: The description of "an influential artist" should be followed by the artist himself.

10. (C)
Category: Modifiers
Difficulty: Medium
Strategy: Descriptions must be placed next to the things they describe.
Solution: The underlined portion is followed by "Kandinsky", so it should describe him.

11. (A)
Category: Modifiers
Difficulty: Medium
Strategy: Descriptions must be placed next to the things they describe.
Solution: The underlined portion is followed by "Kandinsky", so it should describe him.

Modifiers 2 – Pages 235-237

1. (C)
Category: Modifiers
Difficulty: Hard
Strategy: Descriptions must be placed next to the things they describe.
Solution: The preceding description of popularity should be describing the porch.

2. (A)
Category: Modifiers
Difficulty: Medium
Strategy: Descriptions must be placed next to the things they describe.
Solution: The underlined portion should describe vestibules.

3. (D)
Category: Modifiers
Difficulty: Medium
Strategy: Descriptions must be placed next to the things they describe.
Solution: The underlined portion should begin by relating back to Italy.

4. (C)
Category: Modifiers
Difficulty: Medium
Strategy: Descriptions must be placed next to the things they describe.
Solution: The underlined portion should begin with who was "motivated".

5. (D)
Category: Modifiers
Difficulty: Medium
Strategy: Descriptions must be placed next to the things they describe.
Solution: The underlined portion should begin with who was "familiar with wide porches".

6. (C)
Category: Modifiers
Difficulty: Medium
Strategy: Descriptions must be placed next to the things they describe.
Solution: The description before the underlined portion is about the buildings, which should begin the underlined portion.

7. (A)
Category: Modifiers
Difficulty: Medium
Strategy: Descriptions must be placed next to the things they describe.
Solution: The underlined portion should begin with the front porch, which is described by the preceding portion of the sentence.

8. (D)
Category: Modifiers
Difficulty: Medium
Strategy: Descriptions must be placed next to the things they describe.
Solution: Reorder the information. Note "they" comes next and must relate clearly to the families.

9. (C)
Category: Modifiers
Difficulty: Medium
Strategy: Descriptions must be placed next to the things they describe.
Solution: The underlined portion should lead to the following information about traffic noise and exhaust fumes. Pay attention to causality and logic.

10. (D)
Category: Modifiers
Difficulty: Hard
Strategy: Descriptions must be placed next to the things they describe.
Solution: The underlined portion should begin with what "started in 2007".

11. (A)
Category: Modifiers
Difficulty: Medium
Strategy: Descriptions must be placed next to the things they describe.
Solution: Based on the context of the passage, determine that "adaptability" is attributed to the front porch.

Verb Tense 1 – Pages 239-241

1. (B)
Category: Verb Tense
Difficulty: Medium
Strategy: Present tense is used for actions occurring now.
Solution: The growing season isn't in the past; the cycle of these seasons continues.

2. (C)
Category: Verb Tense
Difficulty: Easy
Strategy: Present tense is used for actions occurring now.
Solution: Stating "currently" means the action is in the present.

3. (D)
Category: Verb Tense
Difficulty: Medium
Strategy: Present tense is used for actions occurring now.
Solution: The growing season isn't in the past; the cycle of these seasons continues.

4. (C)
Category: Verb Tense, Subject-Verb Agreement
Difficulty: Hard
Strategy: The growing season isn't in the past; the cycle of these seasons continues.
Solution: The first half of the sentence makes it clear the action is in the present. There are two subjects, frost and snow, making it plural, so "are" works best.

5. (C)
Category: Verb Tense
Difficulty: Medium
Strategy: Past tense is used for actions completed in the past.
Solution: The earlier part of the sentence makes it clear the action is in the past. Choice B would mean they had already brought their love of avocados at the time they migrated.

6. (B)
Category: Verb Tense
Difficulty: Medium
Strategy: The present perfect continuous tense is used for actions that occurred in the past and continue to occur.
Solution: The use of "now" means the action continues into the present.

7. (C)
Category: Verb Tense
Difficulty: Hard
Strategy: Present tense is used for actions occurring now.
Solution: Using "would not have been" suggests this fact is no longer valid because it is in the past; it suggests that now, without modern technologies, it is possible to keep produce fresh.

8. (A)
Category: Verb Tense
Difficulty: Medium
Strategy: Present tense is used for actions occurring now.
Solution: The following verb is in present tense, which also places the underlined verb in the present.

9. (D)
Category: Verb Tense
Difficulty: Medium
Strategy: Present tense is used for actions occurring now.
Solution: The following sentence is in present tense, which also places the underlined verb in the present. Also, the information in the sentence did not cease to be true.

10. (A)
Category: Verb Tense
Difficulty: Medium
Strategy: The future tense is used for actions that will occur.
Solution: The sentence states a truth about fruits. The future tense works because it establishes an outcome that can always be anticipated.

11. (D)
Category: Verb Tense
Difficulty: Medium
Strategy: Present tense is used for actions occurring now.
Solution: The rest of the sentence is in present tense, which places the underlined verb in the present.

Verb Tense 2 – Pages 242-244

1. (D)
Category: Verb Tense
Difficulty: Hard
Strategy: The past perfect tense is used for actions that were ongoing in the past.
Solution: The sentence describes a time in the past when scientists had been dreaming of harvesting resources for a while already.

2. (D)
Category: Verb Tense
Difficulty: Medium
Strategy: The future tense is used for actions that will occur.
Solution: The sentence mentions "the future," which clearly indicates the action should be in the future tense.

3. (A)
Category: Verb Tense, Subject-Verb Agreement
Difficulty: Medium
Strategy: Actions in the present or future tense lead to actions in the future tense.
Solution: The first part of the sentence notes an action in the future: humans colonizing space. The second part notes an action, new industries becoming available, that will lead to this future. These new industries can be becoming available now or in the future. Also, the subject that matches with the verb is "industries," which is plural, so "become" works better than "becomes."

4. (C)
Category: Verb Tense
Difficulty: Medium
Strategy: The present tense is used for actions occurring now.
Solution: The resources, or "harvests", in space are available now. Note, "lay" is to place and "lie" is to exist.

5. (A)
Category: Verb Tense
Difficulty: Easy
Strategy: Maintain verb tense based on context clues in the passage.
Solution: The passage mentions the speech occurring in 2010, in the past.

6. (D)
Category: Verb Tense
Difficulty: Medium
Strategy: The future tense is used for actions that will occur.
Solution: Based on context, it is clear that companies believe humans will colonize space in the future. This is a prediction, as it is not happening yet.

7. (B)
Category: Verb Tense
Difficulty: Easy
Strategy: The future tense is used for actions that will occur.
Solution: Based on context, it is clear that this is an idea about the future. The previous sentence notes "DSI envisions", which indicates this is something they believe will happen. Also, the verb must work with the following verb, "aggregate".

8. (D)
Category: Verb Tense
Difficulty: Medium
Strategy: The words "when" and "while" sometimes create reduced adverbial clauses, in which the subject and "be" verb are eliminated, and the clause describes an action that is in addition to another verb in the sentence. In these reduced adverbial clauses, -ing verbs are used.
Solution: The sentence's phrase "while also delivering valuable materials to Earth" is a reduced form of "while they are also delivering…", an action that is occurring in addition to "these depots can supply resources".

9. (C)
Category: Verb Tense
Difficulty: Easy
Strategy: The future tense is used for actions that will occur.
Solution: Based on context, it is clear that this is an idea about the future. The sentence notes "Planetary Resources is betting", which indicates this is something they believe will happen.

10. (A)
Category: Verb Tense, Subject-Verb Agreement
Difficulty: Medium
Strategy: The present tense is used for actions occurring now.
Solution: The "customers" are in space now. Note the subject is "customers," which is plural.

11. (D)
Category: Verb Tense
Difficulty: Medium
Strategy: The present tense is used for actions occurring now.
Solution: The sentence has another verb in the present tense, which makes it clear this action also occurs in the present.

Commas 1 – Pages 246-248

1. (C)
Category: Commas
Difficulty: Medium
Strategy: When naming a city and its state, place commas around the state name.
Solution: Place commas around "Virginia".

2. (A)
Category: Commas
Difficulty: Easy
Strategy: Reduced adverbial clauses are set off by commas.
Solution: The phrase "her dream of becoming an entertainer seemingly unrealizable" is an adverbial clause that describes the action of "living on the streets."

3. (C)
Category: Commas
Difficulty: Medium
Strategy: Unessential words and clauses may be set off with commas.
Solution: "however" is an unnecessary word and should be set off with commas.

4. (A)
Category: Commas
Difficulty: Medium
Strategy: Unessential words and clauses may be set off with commas.
Solution: "at the last minute" is an unnecessary phrase and should be set off with commas.

5. (D)
Category: Commas
Difficulty: Hard
Strategy: When a description or title is combined with a name, use commas to set off the name only when the name is not necessary to specify exactly who is being mentioned. If the name is necessary, do not use commas.
Solution: Mentioning a "drummer" is not enough to know exactly who is being mentioned, so the name is necessary and should not be set off with commas. The phrase "as a singer" is a part of the verb phrase with "joined" and should not be set off with commas.

6. (B)
Category: Commas
Difficulty: Hard
Strategy: Use a comma before "which" if the word introduces a nonessential phrase.
Solution: The information following "which" is not essential to the sentence, so use a comma before "which".

7. (A)
Category: Commas
Difficulty: Medium
Strategy: Use commas between coordinate adjectives, which each modify the noun. Do not use commas between cumulative adjectives, which may modify a series of modified nouns.
Solution: The adjectives are cumulative. "Jazz music" describes the "scene." "American" describes the "Jazz music scene." "Evolving" describes the "American Jazz music scene." A good test for cumulative adjectives is that you cannot use "and" between them: "the evolving and American and Jazz and music scene" doesn't make sense.

8. (C)
Category: Commas
Difficulty: Hard
Strategy: Use commas between coordinate adjectives, which each modify the noun. Do not use commas between cumulative adjectives, which may modify a series of modified nouns.
Solution: Some of the adjectives are coordinate. "Boisterous" and "playful" are coordinate adjectives describing the "big-band piece." A good test is to see where you could use the word "and" and place a comma there: "a boisterous and playful big-band piece" would work.

9. (B)
Category: Commas
Difficulty: Medium
Strategy: Use commas to set off nonessential phrases.
Solution: "And sense of rhythm" is a nonessential phrase.

10. (D)
Category: Commas
Difficulty: Medium
Strategy: Use commas between coordinate adjectives, which each modify the noun. Do not use commas between cumulative adjectives, which may modify a series of modified nouns.
Solution: The adjectives are cumulative. The phrase beginning with "while" should be set off with a comma.

11. (D)
Category: Commas
Difficulty: Medium
Strategy: Use commas to set off nonessential phrases.
Solution: None of the phrases are nonessential, so no commas are needed. Choice C is not correct because "and" isn't connecting two independent clauses.

Commas 2 – Pages 249-251

1. (D)
Category: Commas
Difficulty: Medium
Strategy: Use commas between coordinate adjectives, which each modify the noun. Do not use commas between cumulative adjectives.
Solution: These are cumulative adjectives, so no commas are needed. A good test for cumulative adjectives is that you cannot use "and" between them: "the ancient and world's and great wonders" doesn't make sense.

2. (D)
Category: Commas
Difficulty: Medium
Strategy: Do not use a comma to separate independent clauses without conjunctions. Dashes can be used to separate nonessential clauses and as semicolons separating independent clauses.
Solution: There are two independent clauses without a conjunction, so separate with a dash.

3. (C)
Category: Commas
Difficulty: Easy
Strategy: Commas separate items in a list.
Solution: Don't separate nouns from adjectives, unless there are coordinate adjectives. Note the sentence indicates there are three categories, which is a clue about the following list.

4. (C)
Category: Commas
Difficulty: Medium
Strategy: Commas separate items in a list.
Solution: The first list ends with "trapezoids." You can continue with additional items after "as well as," which needs a comma before it, because it is a nonessential phrase.

5. (D)
Category: Commas
Difficulty: Easy
Strategy: Use "which" to introduce a nonessential clause after a comma.
Solution: Using a comma and "which" is the only option that doesn't cause a run-on.

6. (D)
Category: Commas
Difficulty: Hard
Strategy: Use commas to set off nonessential information.
Solution: The phrase "as with most other wonders of the ancient world" is nonessential. Nonessential phrases can be set off with either commas or dashes, but not a mix of both.

7. (A)
Category: Commas
Difficulty: Hard
Strategy: When a description or title is combined with a name, use commas to set off the name when the name isn't necessary to specify who is mentioned. If the name is necessary, don't use commas.
Solution: "Peruvian archaeologist" is not enough to determine exactly who is mentioned, so the name is necessary.

8. (B)
Category: Commas
Difficulty: Medium
Strategy: Commas separate items in a list. Use commas after introductory phrases that set time of place.
Solution: A comma is needed after 1930s, because this is the end of an introductory phrase. Commas are needed after "explorers" and "researchers" because they are part of a list.

9. (C)
Category: Commas
Difficulty: Hard
Strategy: When a description or title is combined with a name, use commas to set off the name when the name isn't necessary to specify who is mentioned. If the name is necessary, don't use commas.
Solution: A comma is needed after "Stonehenge" to set off a nonessential phrase. Commas are needed around "Maria Reiche" because the sentence mentions a specific archaeologist; the use of "a" already makes it a specific person, so the name doesn't further increase its specificity and is unnecessary information.

10. (D)
Category: Commas
Difficulty: Medium
Strategy: Use commas or dashes to set off nonessential information.
Solution: Nonessential phrases can be set off with commas or dashes, but not a mix of both.

11. (B)
Category: Commas
Difficulty: Hard
Strategy: Use commas to set off nonessential information.

Solution: If there were an option with commas on either side of "like aqueducts did," it would be a valid choice. Without such option, no punctuation is needed.

Commas 3 – Pages 252-254

1. (B)
Category: Commas
Difficulty: Medium
Strategy: Use commas or dashes to set off nonessential information.
Solution: "In her time" is a nonessential phrase and should be set off with commas.

2. (D)
Category: Commas
Difficulty: Hard
Strategy: Use commas to separate items in a list of more than two items.
Solution: Look carefully at the sentence to determine what parts are in a list. Note that items in a list should be parallel. The final item, "they entered a covenant" is not a part of the list of what women became. If the sentence ended in "nun" instead, choice A would work (wives, mothers, or nuns). As it is, the sentence lists two items and then adds another independent clause.

3. (B)
Category: Commas
Difficulty: Hard
Strategy: When a description or title is combined with a name, use commas to set off the name only when the name is not necessary to specify exactly who is being mentioned. If the name is necessary, do not use commas. Use commas between coordinate adjectives, which each modify the noun. Do not use commas between cumulative adjectives.
Solution: There's no need for commas with "famed older painter", as you would not say "famed and older painter." No comma is needed after painter, because the name is essential for specifying who is mentioned.

4. (C)
Category: Commas
Difficulty: Hard
Strategy: Do not use a comma to separate independent clauses without conjunctions. Dashes can be used to separate nonessential clauses and as semicolons separating independent clauses.
Solution: In this case, "however" comes between two independent clauses, so a period, semicolon, colon, or dash is needed. Choice D doesn't work because two dashes are only used for nonessential phrases, not to separate independent clauses. Choice A needs a comma after "However"; without it, the following clause is not a complete sentence.

5. (C)
Category: Commas
Difficulty: Medium
Strategy: Commas set off items in a list.
Solution: Keep nouns and their adjectives grouped, unless there are coordinate adjectives.

6. (A)
Category: Commas
Difficulty: Medium
Strategy: Use commas before conjunctions joining independent clauses.
Solution: The clause following "and" is not an independent clause, so no comma is necessary.

7. (A)
Category: Commas
Difficulty: Easy
Strategy: Use commas after introductory phrases that establish time or place.
Solution: "Upon receiving this honor" establishes the time, so a comma is needed after it.

8. (A)
Category: Commas
Difficulty: Medium
Strategy: Use a comma to set off unnecessary information.
Solution: "the great scientist" is extra information and is not needed to clarify who is being mentioned.

9. (D)
Category: Commas
Difficulty: Medium
Strategy: Use a comma to set off unnecessary information.
Solution: "rather than her talent" is extra information.

10. (B)
Category: Commas
Difficulty: Medium
Strategy: Use a comma to set off unnecessary information. Use commas before conjunctions joining independent clauses.
Solution: "by Agnes Merlet" is extra information. "and" combines two independent clauses and should be preceded by a comma.

11. (C)
Category: Commas
Difficulty: Hard
Strategy: When a description or title is combined with a name, use commas to set off the name only when the name is not necessary to specify exactly who is being mentioned. If the name is necessary, do not use commas.
Solution: By specifying "her muse," the sentence doesn't need to name the person, so "Caravaggio" is extra information. Rather than "as well," the sentence uses the phrase "as well as", so it doesn't need to be set off with commas.

Semicolons & Colons 1 – Pages 256-258

1. (D)
Category: Semicolons & Colons
Difficulty: Medium
Strategy: Semicolons, like periods, are used between independent clauses.
Solution: The following clause, beginning with "coffee", is an independent clause.

2. (C)
Category: Semicolons & Colons
Difficulty: Medium
Strategy: Semicolons, like periods, are used between independent clauses.
Solution: The following clause is dependent, so a comma should be used instead of a semicolon.

3. (C)
Category: Semicolons & Colons
Difficulty: Medium
Strategy: Semicolons, like periods, are used between independent clauses.
Solution: Use context clues to determine "however" should be a part of the following independent clause.

4. (C)
Category: Semicolons & Colons
Difficulty: Hard
Strategy: A colon should only be used at the end of a complete sentence. Colons may be used to introduce lists or present information that clarifies or elaborates on the independent clause.
Solution: Choices C and D begin with an independent clause, but choice D is not valid because an independent clause must follow a semicolon.

5. (B)
Category: Semicolons & Colons
Difficulty: Hard
Strategy: Semicolons, like periods, are used between independent clauses.
Solution: "yet" is used as a conjunction, so it should be preceded by a comma when joining two independent clauses.

6. (D)
Category: Semicolons & Colons
Difficulty: Medium
Strategy: Dashes can be used to separate nonessential clauses or as semicolons separating independent clauses.
Solution: The preceding dash in the sentence is used to set off a phrase with unnecessary information, so there must be another dash to follow that phrase.

7. (A)
Category: Semicolons & Colons
Difficulty: Medium
Strategy: A colon should only be used at the end of a complete sentence. Colons may be used to introduce lists or present information that clarifies or elaborates on the independent clause.
Solution: Following the punctuation, there is no independent clause, so a colon works best.

8. (D)
Category: Semicolons & Colons
Difficulty: Hard
Strategy: Semicolons, like periods, are used between independent clauses.
Solution: Without a conjunction to join the independent clauses, a semicolon works. Choice A would work if there were a comma after "published."

9. (B)
Category: Semicolons & Colons
Difficulty: Hard
Strategy: Semicolons, like periods, are used between independent clauses.
Solution: Use a semicolon to split the independent clauses. The phrases "aside from serving the greater good of the scientific process" is unessential and should be set off with commas.

10. (A)
Category: Semicolons & Colons
Difficulty: Medium
Strategy: Semicolons, like periods, are used between independent clauses.
Solution: There are two independent clauses, so use a semicolon.

11. (D)
Category: Semicolons & Colons, Commas
Difficulty: Hard
Strategy: Colons can be used to introduce quotes.
Solution: Commas are needed to set of "Brian Nosek" because the name is unnecessary. The quote could be introduced with "argues that" or "argues," or "argues:".

Semicolons & Colons 2 – Pages 259-261

1. (D)
Category: Semicolons & Colons
Difficulty: Easy
Strategy: A colon should only be used at the end of a complete sentence. Colons may be used to introduce lists or present information that clarifies or elaborates on the independent clause.
Solution: The clause preceding the colon doesn't work well as an independent clause, so no punctuation works best.

2. (A)
Category: Semicolons & Colons
Difficulty: Medium
Strategy: A colon should only be used at the end of a complete sentence. Colons may be used to introduce lists or present information that clarifies or elaborates on the independent clause.
Solution: Choice A works best because the others have semicolons or colons following clauses that are not independent clauses.

3. (A)
Category: Semicolons & Colons
Difficulty: Medium
Strategy: A colon should only be used at the end of a complete sentence. Colons may be used to introduce lists or present information that clarifies or elaborates on the independent clause.
Solution: An independent clause precedes a list, so a colon works best.

4. (C)
Category: Semicolons & Colons
Difficulty: Medium

Strategy: Semicolons, like periods, are used between independent clauses.
Solution: There are two independent clauses, so they should be separated with a colon. Use context clues to determine that "however" is connected to the second independent clause.

5. (D)
Category: Semicolons & Colons
Difficulty: Hard
Strategy: Semicolons, like periods, are used between independent clauses. A dash can be used as a semicolon.
Solution: What follows the underlined portion is a dependent clause connected to an independent clause, which work together as a sentence. Set off with a semicolon or dash.
This question can be tricky because "for" can be used like "because" to link to an explanation. In this case, that use of "for" would result in a run-on, which is why A is not a valid answer choice.

6. (C)
Category: Semicolons & Colons, Commas
Difficulty: Medium
Strategy: Semicolons, like periods, are used between independent clauses.
Solution: "Though" can be used to start a dependent clause, but here it is a nonessential phrase in the sentence, so it should be set off with commas.

7. (C)
Category: Semicolons & Colons, Commas
Difficulty: Medium
Strategy: Nonessential phrases should be set off by commas.
Solution: "unlike areas meant purely for diversion" is extra information that should be set off with commas.

8. (A)
Category: Semicolons & Colons
Difficulty: Medium
Strategy: Semicolons, like periods, are used between independent clauses.
Solution: Following the underlined portion is an independent clause, so a semicolon works.

9. (D)
Category: Semicolons & Colons
Difficulty: Medium
Strategy: Semicolons and colons must be preceded by independent clauses.
Solution: The preceding clause is not independent, so no punctuation is needed.

10. (C)
Category: Semicolons & Colons
Difficulty: Hard
Strategy: Semicolons, like periods, are used between independent clauses.
Solution: The clause up to "decisions" is independent, so a period or semicolon would work. "For example" should be set off with a comma, because it is an introductory phrase.

11. (A)
Category: Semicolons & Colons
Difficulty: Medium
Strategy: Colons, like semicolons, can split independent clauses.
Solution: A period or semicolon should come after "employees" to split the independent clauses, and a colon would also work. There is no need for a comma after "in order" because it is part of a larger phrase.

Apostrophes 1 – Pages 263-265

1. (B)
Category: Apostrophes
Difficulty: Medium
Strategy: When the possessor is a plural noun ending in *s*, possession can be shown by adding an apostrophe after the *s*.
Solution: The model is owned by the two scientists, so use a plural possessive.

2. (D)
Category: Apostrophes
Difficulty: Medium
Strategy: When the possessor is a singular noun, possession can be indicated by adding *'s*.
Solution: "historic discoveries" is owned by "mankind".

3. (C)
Category: Apostrophes
Difficulty: Easy
Strategy: When the possessor is a singular noun, possession can be indicated by adding *'s*.
Solution: The "inventions" are owned by "Edison".

4. (C)
Category: Apostrophes, Pronouns
Difficulty: Medium
Strategy: "Who's" is a contraction for "who is". "Whose" is the possessive of "who".
Solution: The contributions are owned by the scientists, so use a possessive pronoun.

5. (B)
Category: Apostrophes
Difficulty: Medium
Strategy: When nouns are grouped as both being possessive of something, there are two options: Make both possessive or make the last noun possessive.
Solution: Choice B is the only one that correctly makes either both or the last possessive noun possessive.

6. (D)
Category: Apostrophes
Difficulty: Easy
Strategy: Pronouns can be possessive without needing apostrophes.
Solution: "His" is the only possessive, and it doesn't need an apostrophe.

7. (A)
Category: Apostrophes
Difficulty: Easy
Strategy: When the possessor is a singular noun, possession can be indicated by adding *'s*.
Solution: The "components" are owned by "DNA".

8. (D)
Category: Apostrophes
Difficulty: Medium
Strategy: Pronouns can be possessive without needing apostrophes.
Solution: The "structure" is owned by "it", which doesn't need an apostrophe to be possessive.

9. (D)
Category: Apostrophes
Difficulty: Medium
Strategy: When the possessor is a plural noun ending in *s*, possession can be shown by adding an apostrophe after the *s*.

Solution: The only possessive is the molecules, which own the bonds.

10. (D)
Category: Apostrophes, Pronouns
Difficulty: Easy
Strategy: Pronouns can be possessive without needing apostrophes.
Solution: "Their" is possessive.

11. (D)
Category: Apostrophes
Difficulty: Medium
Strategy: Apostrophes can be used for contractions.
Solution: The sentence could read "who is most deserving", so what's needed is "who's", a contraction of "who is".

Apostrophes 2 – Pages 266-268

1. (B)
Category: Apostrophes
Difficulty: Easy
Strategy: Pronouns can be possessive without needing apostrophes.
Solution: The only possessive is "your", which doesn't need an apostrophe.

2. (A)
Category: Apostrophes
Difficulty: Medium
Strategy: When the possessor is a plural noun ending in *s*, possession can be shown by adding an apostrophe after the *s*.
Solution: Because there is no "a" before "customers", it must be plural, so the apostrophe goes after the *s*.

3. (D)
Category: Apostrophes
Difficulty: Medium
Strategy: Apostrophes can be used for contractions.
Solution: The sentence could be written as "from your home, it is close to rush hour". Use a contraction for "it is".

4. (A)
Category: Apostrophes
Difficulty: Easy
Strategy: Apostrophes can be used for contractions.
Solution: "Workers" is not possessive. Use a contraction for "who have".

5. (D)
Category: Apostrophes
Difficulty: Medium
Strategy: Pronouns can be possessive without needing apostrophes.
Solution: The "name" is owned by "it", but an apostrophe is not needed.

6. (D)
Category: Apostrophes
Difficulty: Hard
Strategy: Apostrophes can be used for contractions.
Solution: Apostrophes can be used for contraction with years (such as '90s). In this case, it is not a contraction.

7. (B)
Category: Apostrophes
Difficulty: Easy
Strategy: Apostrophes can be used for contractions.
Solution: The sentence could be written as "it is sometimes described".

8. (D)
Category: Apostrophes
Difficulty: Easy
Strategy: Apostrophes can be used for contractions.
Solution: The sentence could be written as "it remains unclear", which could have no contractions.

9. (B)
Category: Apostrophes
Difficulty: Easy
Strategy: When the possessor is a singular noun, possession can be indicated by adding 's. Apostrophes can be used for contractions.
Solution: The "workers" are owned by the "gig economy". "Don't" is a contraction for "do not".

10. (C)
Category: Apostrophes
Difficulty: Hard
Strategy: When the possessor is a plural noun ending in *s*, possession can be indicated by adding an apostrophe after the *s*..
Solution: The "rights" are owned by the "workers".

11. (D)
Category: Apostrophes
Difficulty: Medium
Strategy: When the possessor is a plural noun ending in *s*, possession can be shown by adding an apostrophe after the *s*.
Solution: The "options" are owned by "Americans".

Main Idea 1 – Pages 270-272

1. (C)
Category: Main Idea
Difficulty: Easy
Strategy: Questions may provide key information about what an underlined portion should achieve in the passage.
Solution: The preceding idea is about sharks being menacing, which is reinforced by their jagged teeth.

2. (B)
Category: Main Idea
Difficulty: Hard
Strategy: Every portion of the passage should contribute to the main idea.
Solution: The main idea is that mantis shrimp are fierce predators.

3. (A)
Category: Main Idea
Difficulty: Medium
Strategy: Every portion of the passage should contribute to the main idea. To determine the main idea, consider the central claim, issue, argument, or message that the author wants to communicate.
Solution: The main idea is that mantis shrimp are fierce predators.

4. (D)
Category: Main Idea
Difficulty: Medium
Strategy: Every portion of the passage should contribute to the main idea.
Solution: This portion of the paragraph is describing the two types of appendages. Choice A repeats earlier information. Choice D maintains the focus on the function of the appendage.

5. (A)
Category: Main Idea
Difficulty: Hard
Strategy: Each paragraph should develop a distinct main idea.
Solution: The main idea is that the mantis shrimp's appendages make it very dangerous.

6. (B)
Category: Main Idea
Difficulty: Hard
Strategy: Questions may provide key information about what an underlined portion should achieve in the passage.
Solution: The preceding paragraph was about appendages. The following is about eyes. Both paragraphs describe features of mantis shrimps that make them good hunters. Choice B makes this connection; the phrase "beyond even their appendages" suggests there are other features which will be covered in the next paragraph.

7. (C)
Category: Main Idea
Difficulty: Medium
Strategy: Questions may provide key information about what an underlined portion should achieve in the passage.
Solution: The preceding paragraph is about the mantis shrimp's dangerous appendages, and the following paragraph is about another trait that makes them good hunters: their unique eyes.

8. (D)
Category: Main Idea
Difficulty: Medium
Strategy: Questions may provide key information about what an underlined portion should achieve in the passage.
Solution: The point of the description of mantis shrimps' eyes is they are useful for hunting prey.

9. (B)
Category: Main Idea
Difficulty: Medium
Strategy: Questions may provide key information about what an underlined portion should achieve in the passage.
Solution: The previous information was about how mantis shrimp interact, which requires adaptations because they are so dangerous.

10. (A)
Category: Main Idea
Difficulty: Medium
Strategy: Questions may provide key information about what an underlined portion should achieve in the passage.
Solution: The main idea of the passage is that studying mantis shrimps is valuable but tricky.

11. (A)
Category: Main Idea
Difficulty: Medium
Strategy: Questions may provide key information about what an underlined portion should achieve in the passage. To determine the main idea, consider the central claim, issue, argument, or message that the author wants to communicate.
Solution: The main idea of the passage is that mantis shrimp is the top predator, in addition to the stated idea that it has a lot to teach us.

Main Idea 2 – Pages 273-275

1. (B)
Category: Main Idea
Difficulty: Easy
Strategy: Questions may provide key information about what an underlined portion should achieve in the passage. To determine the main idea, consider the central claim, issue, argument, or message that the author wants to communicate.
Solution: The paragraph, as well as the following sentence, is about prices rising (whereas Coke stayed the same). The question asks for a "specific example."

2. (C)
Category: Main Idea
Difficulty: Hard
Strategy: Questions may provide key information about what an underlined portion should achieve in the passage.
Solution: Coke prices remained the same, but the world around them changed. Choice C emphasizes change.

3. (D)
Category: Main Idea
Difficulty: Hard
Strategy: Questions may provide key information about what an underlined portion should achieve in the passage.
Solution: The passage is about why the Coke price remained the same, which is all tied to the business deal that Candler made.

4. (A)
Category: Main Idea
Difficulty: Medium
Strategy: Questions may provide key information about what an underlined portion should achieve in the passage.
Solution: The paragraph is about the deal that Candler made, and the following paragraph is about dealing with that.

5. (A)
Category: Main Idea
Difficulty: Medium
Strategy: Each paragraph should develop a distinct main idea.
Solution: The paragraph is about how Coke dealt with their business arrangement and the economy.

6. (C)
Category: Main Idea
Difficulty: Hard
Strategy: Each paragraph should develop a distinct main idea.
Solution: The paragraph is about how Coke managed to make profits, in spite of their bad deal. It's not about "varying effectiveness".

7. (C)
Category: Main Idea
Difficulty: Medium
Strategy: Every portion of the passage should contribute to the main idea.
Solution: The paragraph is about how vending machines made it difficult to raise prices.

8. (C)
Category: Main Idea
Difficulty: Medium
Strategy: Questions may provide key information about what an underlined portion should achieve in the passage.
Solution: The previous sentence states that vending machines could only process single coins. Choice C supports this with a specific detail, noting the machines could only accept nickels.

9. (C)
Category: Main Idea
Difficulty: Medium
Strategy: Questions may provide key information about what an underlined portion should achieve in the passage.
Solution: The "complication" the author wants to emphasize is how it would negatively affect business.

10. (C)
Category: Main Idea
Difficulty: Medium
Strategy: Every portion of the passage should contribute to the main idea.
Solution: The main idea of the paragraph is about the complications Coca-Cola faced with raising prices. Eisenhower contributed to these complications by not helping.

11. (D)
Category: Main Idea
Difficulty: Medium
Strategy: Every portion of the passage should contribute to the main idea. To determine the main idea, consider the central claim, issue, argument, or message that the author wants to communicate.
Solution: The focus of the passage was on Coca-Cola making the best of a bad situation. In the end, these efforts led to their incredible success.

Organization 1 – Pages 277-281

1. (C)
Category: Organization
Difficulty: Medium
Strategy: Combined sentences have proper modifiers, complete ideas, and logical structure.
Solution: Make sure pronouns, such as "they", clearly refer to nouns.

2. (B)
Category: Organization
Difficulty: Medium
Strategy: When organized properly, an essay's ideas should build upon each other and transition naturally.
Solution: The reference to "means of survival" relates directly to the slaves dancing to stay healthy, so the sentence should appear after sentence 4, where this is mentioned.

3. (A)
Category: Organization
Difficulty: Medium
Strategy: Combined sentences have proper modifiers, complete ideas, and logical structure.
Solution: Pay attention to how the order of information suggests causality. For example, choice B suggests the Irish became women and children after some went to Spain.

4. (D)
Category: Organization
Difficulty: Medium
Strategy: When organized properly, an essay's ideas should build upon each other and transition naturally.
Solution: "For example" should relate back to a mention of Irish and African music. This is mentioned in sentence 5.

5. (C)
Category: Organization
Difficulty: Medium
Strategy: Combined sentences have proper modifiers, complete ideas, and logical structure.
Solution: Choice A is an incomplete sentence. Choice B has a modifier error. Choice D has the wrong sequence of events.

6. (C)
Category: Organization
Difficulty: Medium
Strategy: When organized properly, an essay's ideas should build upon each other and transition naturally.
Solution: "One such place" should relate back to a mention of a location where Irish and African music blended. This is referenced in sentence 2, and it works with the reference to "here" in sentence 3.

7. (A)
Category: Organization
Difficulty: Hard
Strategy: When organized properly, an essay's ideas should build upon each other and transition naturally.
Solution: This is a tricky question. "As such" should relate back to a reason why performers mimicked others. Note sentence 3 refers to "this organic transferal of the form, with dancers continually copying and trying to improve on each other's performances", and the use of "this" suggests the situation was mentioned earlier. For these two reasons, sentence 2 fits very well where it already is.

8. (C)
Category: Organization
Difficulty: Hard

Strategy: When organized properly, an essay's ideas should build upon each other and transition naturally.
Solution: "These performers" should relate back to a reference to dancers. Sentence 3 mentions performers.

9. (D)
Category: Organization
Difficulty: Medium
Strategy: Combined sentences have proper modifiers, complete ideas, and logical structure.
Solution: Avoid cumbersome and wordy sentences. Choice D uses phrases set off with commas to organize and separate information, making the sentence easy to follow.

10. (D)
Category: Organization
Difficulty: Medium
Strategy: Combined sentences have proper modifiers, complete ideas, and logical structure.
Solution: Choice A is repetitive and the use of "it" is somewhat unclear. Choice B has a modifier issue. Choice C's has an illogical contradiction.

11. (C)
Category: Organization
Difficulty: Medium
Strategy: When organized properly, an essay's ideas should build upon each other and transition naturally.
Solution: "This attention" should relate back to tap dancing's rise. This is mentioned in sentences 2, 3, and 4.

Organization 2 – Pages 282-286

1. (A)
Category: Organization
Difficulty: Medium
Strategy: Combined sentences have proper modifiers, complete ideas, and logical structure.
Solution: Choice B needs a verb in the first phrase of the sentence. Choice C says the apprentices were distributed, not the patterns. Choice D is too complicated.

2. (A)
Category: Organization
Difficulty: Medium
Strategy: When organized properly, an essay's ideas should build upon each other and transition naturally.
Solution: "And yet" should refer back to information that seemingly contradicts the information in Sentence 2. It works best where it is now.

3. (C)
Category: Organization
Difficulty: Medium
Strategy: Combined sentences have proper modifiers, complete ideas, and logical structure.
Solution: Choice A has two uses of "if," which makes the sentence confusing. Choice B is too complicated. Choice D is not a complete sentence. Choice C has a simple "if this, then this" structure.

4. (C)
Category: Organization
Difficulty: Medium
Strategy: When organized properly, an essay's ideas should build upon each other and transition naturally.
Solution: "More importantly" should relate back to another profitable benefit. Sentence 1 mentions "making artists of amateurs".

5. (B)
Category: Organization
Difficulty: Medium
Strategy: Combined sentences have proper modifiers, complete ideas, and logical structure.
Solution: Choice A is too clunky and would be improved with phrases set off with commas. Choice C is awkwardly constructed. Choice D has two descriptive phrases between the verb and object, which is confusing.

6. (C)
Category: Organization
Difficulty: Medium
Strategy: When organized properly, an essay's ideas should build upon each other and transition naturally.
Solution: "Subsequently" suggests this sentence comes after the description of another event in which "all the right boxes" were not checked. This would be after sentence 5.

7. (B)
Category: Organization
Difficulty: Hard
Strategy: Combined sentences have proper modifiers, complete ideas, and logical structure.
Solution: Choice A has a cumbersome noun phrase: "Customers who had painted the bulls green and asked for refunds from Kresge". Choices C and D become complicated and confusing because they initially focus on the bulls when the sentence is mainly about customers and Kresge.

8. (C)
Category: Organization
Difficulty: Hard
Strategy: When organized properly, an essay's ideas should build upon each other and transition naturally.
Solution: "To make matters worse" should relate back to another bad situation. It may be inferred that "promptly blew it" will be directly followed by a description of how Craft Master made further mistakes. It works best after sentence 3, which finishes up the description of one issue before going into another.

9. (B)
Category: Organization
Difficulty: Medium
Strategy: Combined sentences have proper modifiers, complete ideas, and logical structure.
Solution: Choice A is too wordy and complicated. Choice C isn't logically constructed. Choice D is complicated and awkward. The use of a colon keeps choice B simple and easy to understand.

10. (C)
Category: Organization
Difficulty: Hard
Strategy: When organized properly, an essay's ideas should build upon each other and transition naturally.
Solution: Sentence 7 describes a later step in Klein's plan. Also, the reference to 200 kits is mentioned in sentence 5 ("those 200 sales"), which suggests it should come earlier.

11. (A)
Category: Organization
Difficulty: Medium
Strategy: Combined sentences have proper modifiers, complete ideas, and logical structure.
Solution: Choice B's use of "being" is awkward. Choices C and D are clunky.

Addition & Deletion 1 – Pages 288-292

1. (B)
Category: Addition & Deletion
Difficulty: Medium
Strategy: Consider how the sentence relates to the sentences around them and the paragraph's main idea.
Solution: The "symbolism" of the dodo is "awkwardness and stupidity", as mentioned in the next sentence. Noting the dodo was called a "fool" contributes to this idea.

2. (D)
Category: Addition & Deletion
Difficulty: Hard
Strategy: Sentences should be deleted if they are not relevant to the focus of the passage or do not support and strengthen the passage's ideas.
Solution: The previous sentence already mentions there are skeleton remains, so the information about subfossils is unnecessary, as is the species and genus.

3. (D)
Category: Addition & Deletion
Difficulty: Medium
Strategy: Consider how the sentence relates to the sentences around them and the paragraph's main idea.
Solution: The next two paragraphs expand on the idea that dodos has ample nourishment and no dangers.

4. (A)
Category: Addition & Deletion
Difficulty: Medium
Strategy: Sentences should be deleted if they are not relevant to the focus of the passage or do not support and strengthen the passage's ideas.
Solution: The fact that the dodo is related to pigeons is not important to any other information in the passage. Do not leap to the conclusion that being related to pigeons explains how the dodo evaded predators; there is no logical connection to these.

5. (B)
Category: Addition & Deletion
Difficulty: Hard
Strategy: Added sentences must logically connect to the sentences around them.
Solution: "Accordingly" suggests the preceding sentence mentions a reason dodos were defenseless.

6. (D)
Category: Addition & Deletion
Difficulty: Easy
Strategy: Added sentences must logically connect to the sentences around them.
Solution: The added sentence summarizes several points about dodo vulnerability, so it should come after these points.

7. (D)
Category: Addition & Deletion
Difficulty: Easy
Strategy: Added sentences must be relevant to the focus of the passage and should support and strengthen the passage's ideas. It does not matter if the addition is interesting or well-stated; it must makes sense where it would be added in the passage.
Solution: The paragraph is about the dodo's falling prey to new threats. The popular image of the dodo is irrelevant.

8. (B)
Category: Addition & Deletion
Difficulty: Easy
Strategy: Consider how information relates to the information around it.
Solution: Choice A is wrong because the behavior isn't "natural," as the dodo's typical life is being disrupted. Choice C is the opposite, as the information is about humans hunting dodos. Choice D is irrelevant. Choice B works because the information further explains the dodo's "lack of self-protection".

9. (D)
Category: Addition & Deletion
Difficulty: Easy
Strategy: Consider how the sentence relates to the sentences around them and the paragraph's main idea.
Solution: The sentence should appear after a reference to "these animals" that preyed on dodos.

10. (B)
Category: Addition & Deletion
Difficulty: Easy
Strategy: Consider how the sentence relates to the sentences around them and the paragraph's main idea.
Solution: The introduction to the paragraph establishes the main idea about how the dodo's extinction caused other changes. The added information clarifies a specific example of this.

11. (D)
Category: Addition & Deletion
Difficulty: Medium
Strategy: Sentences should be deleted if they are not relevant to the focus of the passage or do not support and strengthen the passage's ideas.
Solution: The paragraph's main idea is about how the dodo's extinction caused other changes. The information about gizzard stones is irrelevant.

Addition & Deletion 2 – Pages 293-297

1. (A)
Category: Addition & Deletion
Difficulty: Medium
Strategy: Consider how the sentence relates to the sentences around them and the paragraph's main idea.
Solution: The paragraph's focus transitions from school learning to ancient learning, and this added sentences makes that transition more smooth. Choice B is incorrect because there is no "specific example."

2. (B)
Category: Addition & Deletion
Difficulty: Medium
Strategy: Added sentences must be relevant to the focus of the passage and should support and strengthen the passage's ideas.
Solution: The rest of the passage is about Eratosthenes, so a reference to him in the introduction is a good idea.

3. (C)
Category: Addition & Deletion
Difficulty: Easy
Strategy: Sentences should be deleted if they are not relevant to the focus of the passage or do not support and strengthen the passage's ideas.
Solution: The paragraph sets up Eratosthenes' mission to map the Earth. His other interests and library position aren't relevant to this focus.

4. (C)
Category: Addition & Deletion
Difficulty: Medium
Strategy: Sentences should be deleted if they are not relevant to the focus of the passage or do not support and strengthen the passage's ideas.
Solution: Syene is not referred to as Aswan anywhere in the passage, so this is unnecessary information.

5. (B)
Category: Addition & Deletion
Difficulty: Hard
Strategy: Consider how information relates to the information around it.
Solution: The previous sentence mentions "one fiftieth of a circle", which suggests this is how Eratosthenes had to make his calculation. Be careful with the answer choices, which involve making assumptions. You may be able to find some justification for choices A, C, or D, but they are not necessarily suggested by the underlined information.

6. (B)
Category: Addition & Deletion
Difficulty: Medium
Strategy: Sentences should be deleted if they are not relevant to the focus of the passage or do not support and strengthen the passage's ideas.
Solution: This information has importance because it substantiates the earlier claim that "measuring distance at that time was not easy."

7. (D)
Category: Addition & Deletion
Difficulty: Medium
Strategy: Consider how information relates to the information around it.
Solution: The reference to stadia is important because the end of the paragraph mentions it. Without an earlier reference, readers may be confused. Choices A and C are clearly not correct. Choice B is nearly correct, because the reference to Greek footraces is unnecessary, but the other information in the sentence is useful.

8. (B)
Category: Addition & Deletion
Difficulty: Medium
Strategy: Consider how information relates to the information around it.
Solution: The sentence explains Eratosthenes' calculation. Be careful about making assumptions, such as with choices A and D.

9. (B)
Category: Addition & Deletion
Difficulty: Medium
Strategy: Consider how information relates to the information around it.
Solution: The reference to "this measurement" should relate back to this information in the underlined sentence. Be careful about making assumptions, such as with choices A and C.

10. (B)
Category: Addition & Deletion
Difficulty: Hard
Strategy: Consider how information relates to the information around it.
Solution: The precision of Eratosthenes calculation is most relevant to sentences 2 and 3.

11. (D)
Category: Addition & Deletion
Difficulty: Medium
Strategy: Consider how information relates to the information around it.
Solution: Choice C is partially correct, but the sentence doesn't have "a description of an event". Choice A is incorrect and choice B is not directly stated.

Transitions 1 – Pages 299-301

1. (C)
Category: Transitions
Difficulty: Medium
Strategy: Transitions show contrast, support, or cause. Choose the most appropriate and logical way to shift from one idea to another.
Solution: The preceding sentence focuses on negative portrayals of AI in film, and the following contrasts with more positive uses of AI in other settings.

2. (A)
Category: Transitions
Difficulty: Medium
Strategy: Transitions show contrast, support, or cause. Choose the most appropriate and logical way to shift from one idea to another.
Solution: The following information builds on the preceding but isn't "particular" or "similar".

3. (C)
Category: Transitions
Difficulty: Medium
Strategy: Consider main ideas when creating transitions between paragraphs.
Solution: The previous paragraph concludes with a consideration of AI as good or bad. The next paragraph mentions "both of these perspectives". Choice C is the best fit because it maintains this focus.

4. (D)
Category: Transitions
Difficulty: Medium
Strategy: Transitions show contrast, support, or cause. Choose the most appropriate and logical way to shift from one idea to another.
Solution: There is a contrast between GPUs having benefits and them not leading to General AI. "On the contrary" doesn't quite work because the link is causal.

5. (C)
Category: Transitions
Difficulty: Medium
Strategy: Combined sentences should have proper transitions, as well as no run-on or fragment errors.
Solution: Choice A is a run-on. The phrase "and it is most important" in choice B is awkward and wordy. In choice D, "despite this" sets up a contrast, which isn't right.

6. (D)
Category: Transitions
Difficulty: Medium
Strategy: Combined sentences should have proper transitions, as well as no run-on or fragment errors.
Solution: Choice A is repetitive. Choices B and C don't introduce the proper subject: machine learning.

7. (B)
Category: Transitions
Difficulty: Hard
Strategy: Transitions show contrast, support, or cause. Choose the most appropriate and logical way to shift from one idea to another.
Solution: The following sentence provides an example that is an exception to the previous idea. This is a tricky question that may be clearer with simplified sentences: "Computers need traditional coding to see things, but this coding doesn't work sometimes." This should help illustrate the contrast.

8. (A)
Category: Transitions
Difficulty: Medium
Strategy: Transitions show contrast, support, or cause. Choose the most appropriate and logical way to shift from one idea to another.
Solution: In context, it's clear this example is supposed to be different from the earlier one about computer vision. Choices B, C, and D would suggest Artificial Neural Networks work similarly to traditional coding, which isn't true.

9. (B)
Category: Transitions
Difficulty: Easy
Strategy: Transitions show contrast, support, or cause. Choose the most appropriate and logical way to shift from one idea to another.
Solution: The transition should set up a contrast between a "yes or no" answer and a probability. In context, "instead" is best because it sets up a comparison.

10. (D)
Category: Transitions
Difficulty: Medium
Strategy: Transitions show contrast, support, or cause. Choose the most appropriate and logical way to shift from one idea to another.
Solution: The sentence already has a contrast transition, "but," so another isn't necessary.

11. (D)
Category: Transitions
Difficulty: Easy
Strategy: Transitions show contrast, support, or cause. Choose the most appropriate and logical way to shift from one idea to another.
Solution: Choice D is the only option that doesn't set up a contrast. The information before and after all supports the idea that AI will have positive effects, so there should not be a contrast.

Transitions 2 – Pages 302-304

1. (C)
Category: Transitions
Difficulty: Medium
Strategy: Transitions show contrast, support, or cause. Choose the most appropriate and logical way to shift from one idea to another.
Solution: The previous sentence mentions cold, whereas the following sentence discusses heat. "Granted" can be used to establish contrasts.

2. (B)
Category: Transitions
Difficulty: Medium
Strategy: Transitions show contrast, support, or cause. Choose the most appropriate and logical way to shift from one idea to another.
Solution: The previous sentence discusses heat, whereas the following sentence restates that most space is cold, so a contrasting transition is needed.

3. (C)
Category: Transitions
Difficulty: Medium
Strategy: Transitions show contrast, support, or cause. Choose the most appropriate and logical way to shift from one idea to another.
Solution: This sentence builds on the ideas of the previous sentence. There are ideas that seem to contrast, but the focus is on building a sequence of ideas.

4. (A)
Category: Transitions
Difficulty: Hard
Strategy: Transitions show contrast, support, or cause. Choose the most appropriate and logical way to shift from one idea to another.
Solution: The previous sentence discusses typical lakes, whereas the following states Lake Mercer is not typical. A contrasting transition is needed.

5. (A)
Category: Transitions
Difficulty: Medium
Strategy: Combined sentences should have proper transitions, as well as no run-on or fragment errors.
Solution: Choice B is a run-on. Choice C needs a verb. Choice D has a pronoun referring back to the salt rather than the lake.

6. (D)
Category: Transitions
Difficulty: Easy
Strategy: Transitions show contrast, support, or cause. Choose the most appropriate and logical way to shift from one idea to another.
Solution: The following information is a specific example to support the previous statement.

7. (C)
Category: Transitions
Difficulty: Medium
Strategy: Consider main ideas when creating transitions between paragraphs.
Solution: Consider the focus of the paragraphs and the logical link between the introductory phrase and the rest of the sentence.

8. (D)
Category: Transitions
Difficulty: Medium
Strategy: Transitions show contrast, support, or cause. Choose the most appropriate and logical way to shift from one idea to another.
Solution: The use of a comma can set off a phrase as unnecessary information. Without a comma, "because" or "that" would work.

9. (A)
Category: Transitions
Difficulty: Medium
Strategy: Transitions show contrast, support, or cause. Choose the most appropriate and logical way to shift from one idea to another.
Solution: The following description is an example to show the previous idea. "Just imagine" is repetitive because the sentence also states "consider".

10. (B)
Category: Transitions
Difficulty: Medium
Strategy: Transitions show contrast, support, or cause. Choose the most appropriate and logical way to shift from one idea to another.
Solution: The second clause of the sentence begins with "others," which suggests there is a contrast between two groups. "On one hand" would need to be paired with another contrasting phrase, such as "while on the other hand."

11. (A)
Category: Transitions
Difficulty: Medium
Strategy: Combined sentences should have proper transitions, as well as no run-on or fragment errors.
Solution: Avoid wordiness and unnecessary repetition.

Wordiness 1 – Pages 306-308

1. (D)
Category: Wordiness
Difficulty: Easy
Strategy: Eliminate details that are unnecessarily repeated. Look out for synonyms that do not add new information.
Solution: "Benefits" and "advantages" are synonyms, so there's no reason to have both.

2. (D)
Category: Wordiness
Difficulty: Medium
Strategy: Eliminate details that are unnecessarily repeated. Look out for synonyms that do not add new information.
Solution: "Fully" and "entirely" are synonyms, so there's no reason to have both.

3. (D)
Category: Wordiness
Difficulty: Easy
Strategy: Eliminate details that are unnecessarily repeated. Look out for synonyms that do not add new information.
Solution: "true" and "factual" are synonyms, so there's no reason to have both.

4. (C)
Category: Wordiness
Difficulty: Medium
Strategy: Eliminate details that are unnecessarily repeated. Look out for synonyms that do not add new information.
Solution: "that existed" is not necessary. Choice D eliminates necessary information.

5. (C)
Category: Wordiness
Difficulty: Medium
Strategy: Eliminate details that are unnecessarily repeated. Look out for synonyms that do not add new information.
Solution: "it eventually occurred" is not necessary because it's implied. Choice D eliminates necessary words.

6. (B)
Category: Wordiness
Difficulty: Hard
Strategy: Eliminate details that are unnecessarily repeated. Look out for synonyms that do not add new information.
Solution: The sentence states "annually," so it's not necessary to say it occurs each year again.

7. (D)
Category: Wordiness
Difficulty: Easy
Strategy: Eliminate details that are unnecessarily repeated. Look out for synonyms that do not add new information.
Solution: The sentence already states that recycled products are cheaper, so it's not necessary to restate that others sources are more expensive.

8. (C)
Category: Wordiness
Difficulty: Medium
Strategy: Eliminate details that are unnecessarily repeated. Look out for synonyms that do not add new information.
Solution: "likely" and "probably" are synonyms, so there's no reason to have both.

9. (D)
Category: Wordiness
Difficulty: Medium
Strategy: Eliminate details that are unnecessarily repeated. Look out for synonyms that do not add new information.
Solution: "imperfect" and "flawed" are synonyms, so there's no reason to have both.

10. (B)
Category: Wordiness
Difficulty: Easy
Strategy: Eliminate details that are unnecessarily repeated. Look out for synonyms that do not add new information.
Solution: "a small number" and "few" are synonyms, so there's no reason to have both.

11. (C)
Category: Wordiness
Difficulty: Medium
Strategy: Eliminate details that are unnecessarily repeated. Look out for synonyms that do not add new information.
Solution: "leads to" and "brings about" are synonyms, so there's no reason to have both. Choice D does not work because the proper verb would be "leads to"; "leads" has a different meaning without the preposition.

Wordiness 2 – Pages 309-311

1. (D)
Category: Wordiness
Difficulty: Easy
Strategy: Eliminate details that are unnecessarily repeated. Look out for synonyms that do not add new information.
Solution: "watch" and "observe" are synonyms, so there's no reason to have both.

2. (C)
Category: Wordiness
Difficulty: Medium
Strategy: Eliminate details that are unnecessarily repeated. Look out for synonyms that do not add new information.
Solution: Both "during the time" and "when" establish a time. There's no reason to have both.

3. (D)
Category: Wordiness
Difficulty: Medium
Strategy: Eliminate details that are unnecessarily repeated. Look out for synonyms that do not add new information.
Solution: Based on context, it's clear where Cimabue returned to without restating "the place of his workshop".

4. (C)
Category: Wordiness
Difficulty: Medium
Strategy: Eliminate details that are unnecessarily repeated. Look out for synonyms that do not add new information.
Solution: "try" and "attempt" are synonyms, so there's no reason to have both. "several times" and "repeatedly" are synonyms, so there's no reason to have both.

5. (D)
Category: Wordiness
Difficulty: Easy
Strategy: Eliminate details that are unnecessarily repeated. Look out for synonyms that do not add new information.
Solution: "perfect" and "flawless" are synonyms, so there's no reason to have both.

6. (D)
Category: Wordiness
Difficulty: Medium
Strategy: Eliminate details that are unnecessarily repeated. Look out for synonyms that do not add new information.
Solution: "of all time" and "ever" are synonyms, so there's no reason to have both.

7. (D)
Category: Wordiness
Difficulty: Medium
Strategy: Eliminate details that are unnecessarily repeated. Look out for synonyms that do not add new information.
Solution: The sentence states interest "increased", so restating it "rose" is unnecessary. Choices B and C incorrectly use words from the underlined portion.

8. (C)
Category: Wordiness
Difficulty: Medium
Strategy: Eliminate details that are unnecessarily repeated. Look out for synonyms that do not add new information. Do not get rid of necessary information.
Solution: The sentence states the change in outlook "eventually" led to the Protestant Reformation, so restating it occurred "after some time" is unnecessary. It is necessary to mention the Protestant Reformation to finish the sentence.

9. (C)
Category: Wordiness
Difficulty: Easy
Strategy: Eliminate details that are unnecessarily repeated. Look out for synonyms that do not add new information.
Solution: "Yet to come" and "in the future" are synonyms, so there's no reason to have both.

10. (C)
Category: Wordiness
Difficulty: Medium
Strategy: Eliminate details that are unnecessarily repeated. Look out for synonyms that do not add new information.
Solution: "Commonly" and "frequently" are synonyms, so there's no reason to have both. "Frequently" works better than "common" because an adverb is needed to pair with "seen."

11. (C)
Category: Wordiness
Difficulty: Medium
Strategy: Eliminate details that are unnecessarily repeated. Look out for synonyms that do not add new information. Do not get rid of necessary information.
Solution: "Differently" and "in new ways" are synonyms, so there's no reason to have both.

Style 1 – Pages 313-315

1. (D)
Category: Style
Difficulty: Medium
Strategy: Questions may provide key information about what an underlined portion should achieve in the passage.
Solution: Choice A doesn't fit the context and seems a bit overstated. Choice B understates the "sense of importance." Choice C is far too dramatic and feels sarcastic. Choice D fits well.

2. (A)
Category: Style
Difficulty: Easy
Strategy: Make sure the language of passages is consistent in tone. Avoid language that is too complex or too informal.
Solution: Choices B, C, and D are too informal.

3. (B)
Category: Style
Difficulty: Medium
Strategy: Make sure the language of passages is consistent in tone. Avoid language that is too complex or too informal. Consider context for words that have similar meanings.
Solution: "Apprehensive" isn't quite the right word, and it should be paired with "about" rather than "to". Choices C and D are too informal.

4. (D)
Category: Style
Difficulty: Easy
Strategy: Make sure the language of passages is consistent in tone. Avoid language that is too complex or too informal.
Solution: Choices A, B, and C are too informal.

5. (C)
Category: Style
Difficulty: Medium
Strategy: Make sure the language of passages is consistent in tone. Avoid language that is too complex or too informal.
Solution: Choices A and D are too informal. "Vend" isn't quite the right word in this context. Consider context for words that have similar meanings.

6. (B)
Category: Style
Difficulty: Easy
Strategy: Make sure the language of passages is consistent in tone. Avoid language that is too complex or too informal.
Solution: Choices A, C, and D are too informal.

7. (C)
Category: Style
Difficulty: Easy
Strategy: Make sure the language of passages is consistent in tone. Avoid language that is too complex or too informal.
Solution: Choices A, B, and D are too informal.

8. (A)
Category: Style
Difficulty: Easy
Strategy: Make sure the language of passages is consistent in tone. Avoid language that is too complex or too informal.
Solution: Choices B, C, and D are too informal.

9. (C)
Category: Style
Difficulty: Easy
Strategy: Make sure the language of passages is consistent in tone. Avoid language that is too complex or too informal.
Solution: Choices A, B, and D are too informal.

10. (C)
Category: Style
Difficulty: Medium
Strategy: Make sure the language of passages is consistent in tone. Avoid language that is too complex or too informal. Consider context for words that have similar meanings.
Solution: Choices A and D are too informal. "Marginalized" doesn't work in this context.

11. (C)
Category: Style
Difficulty: Easy
Strategy: Make sure the language of passages is consistent in tone. Avoid language that is too complex or too informal.
Solution: Choices A, B, and D are too informal.

Style 2 – Pages 316-318

1. (B)
Category: Style
Difficulty: Medium
Strategy: Consider context for words that have similar meanings.
Solution: In context, "trend" works best.

2. (C)
Category: Style
Difficulty: Medium
Strategy: Consider context for words that have similar meanings.
Solution: In context, "aware" works best.

3. (C)
Category: Style
Difficulty: Medium
Strategy: Consider context for words that have similar meanings.
Solution: "Evil" is too negative. "Shady" and "unsuccessful" don't work in this context.

4. (B)
Category: Style
Difficulty: Hard
Strategy: Consider context for words that have similar meanings.
Solution: "Decimated" means reduced to one tenth. "Smashed" and "beat" don't work in this context.

5. (D)
Category: Style
Difficulty: Medium
Strategy: Consider context for words that have similar meanings.
Solution: In context, "reactions" works best.

6. (B)
Category: Style
Difficulty: Medium
Strategy: Make sure the language of passages is consistent in tone. Avoid language that is too complex or too informal. Consider context for words that have similar meanings.
Solution: In context, "passionate" works best. "Rabid" is too extreme.

7. (B)
Category: Style
Difficulty: Medium
Strategy: Make sure the language of passages is consistent in tone. Avoid language that is too complex or too informal. Consider context for words that have similar meanings.
Solution: Choices C and D are too informal. In context, "botched" doesn't work as well as "incorrect".

8. (B)
Category: Style
Difficulty: Medium
Strategy: Consider context for words that have similar meanings.
Solution: Choice D is too informal. In context, "divided" works best (we should assume, for the sake of the participants, that choices A and C aren't appropriate descriptions of what the researchers did to them!)

9. (D)
Category: Style
Difficulty: Medium
Strategy: Make sure the language of passages is consistent in tone. Avoid language that is too complex or too informal.
Solution: Choices A and B are too formal. Choice C is too informal.

10. (D)
Category: Style
Difficulty: Medium
Strategy: Make sure the language of passages is consistent in tone. Avoid language that is too complex or too informal. Consider context for words that have similar meanings.
Solution: Choices A and B are too informal. "Blunt" doesn't work in this context.

11. (B)
Category: Style
Difficulty: Medium
Strategy: Make sure the language of passages is consistent in tone. Avoid language that is too complex or too informal.
Solution: Choice A is too formal. Choices C and D are too informal.

Data Graphics – Passage 1 – Pages 320-321

1. (A)
Category: Data Graphics
Difficulty: Medium
Strategy: Consider the trends shown in the data and determine which answer choice best matches.
Solution: The data shows termites have a strong preference for some woods over others (pine is preferred, whereas poplar is not). Choice B may be true, but is a bit of a leap (it's also an attractor based on the weight loss label).

2. (D)
Category: Data Graphics
Difficulty: Hard
Strategy: Read the previous sentence and find the data that best matches.
Solution: To "deter" termites, builders should use wood that termites do not prefer. Note the weight loss in the table is not loss for termites but loss of wood due to consumption by termites; therefore, the lower weight loss, the less the termites ate, showing they didn't like it as much. Based on this, poplar is the best wood to deter termites.

Data Graphics – Passage 2 – Pages 322-323

1. (C)
Category: Data Graphics
Difficulty: Medium
Strategy: Use process of elimination, and do not jump to conclusions to justify answers.
Solution: In cities B and D, plastic and paper make up more than 50% of contaminants.
(A) There is a 31% contamination rate at one city, but this doesn't necessarily mean it would raise profits that much.
(B) There may be other ways to raise profits.
(D) No connection between these standards and willingness to contribute.

2. (C)
Category: Data Graphics
Difficulty: Medium
Solution: The contamination rates at the top of the figure range from 20-31%, which is about 25% on average.
(A) Food residue makes up only 10-15% of contaminants.
(B) It may be assumed that cities C and D restricted metal and glass, respectively. If so, it didn't seem to lower contaminants much, because city C has the highest contamination rate.
(D) The contamination rate is not the same as the necessary increase in value of materials. These aren't necessarily connected.

Data Graphics – Passage 3 – Pages 324-325

1. (C)
Category: Data Graphics
Difficulty: Easy
Strategy: Find the relevant data in the table.
Solution: The highest weight gain was for mixture 3 and 4.

2. (D)
Category: Data Graphics
Difficulty: Hard
Strategy: Identify the premise of each hypothesis and test which matches the data trends.
Solution: The competition hypothesis states that increasing protein decreases overall weight. The ammonia hypothesis states that only "excess" protein will decrease weight. The data shows weight increase until it reaches a point where it begins decreasing, which matches the ammonia hypothesis.

3. (C)
Category: Data Graphics
Difficulty: Medium
Strategy: Use process of elimination.
Solution: The lowest weight gain was with mixture 5, which had the highest ratio of casein to fishmeal.

Data Graphics – Passage 4 – Pages 326-327

1. (A)
Category: Data Graphics
Difficulty: Easy
Strategy: Use process of elimination.
Solution: The chart shows strawberries having the highest antioxidant levels of the fruits shown, which strengthens choice A.

2. (C)
Category: Data Graphics
Difficulty: Hard
Strategy: Read the previous part of the sentence and find the relevant data in the figures.
Solution: The sentence states probiotic bacteria benefited plant growth. The bar graph on the bottom shows plant growth, with Group 2 having the most growth. Group 2 was sprayed with a solution containing *P. fungorum*.

Problem Solving & Data Analysis – Section Quiz – Pages 330-335

1. (D)

Difficulty: E

Category: Units and Conversion

Strategy: Multiply by the correct conversion factor to convert meters into feet. Then, multiply by the correct conversion factor to convert feet into inches.

Solution: There are 0.3048 meters in one foot, so use this proportion to convert 50 meters to feet. To do so, multiply by the conversion proportion so that meters cancel in the units:

$$50\ meters \cdot \frac{1\ foot}{0.3048\ meters} \approx 164.04\ \text{feet}.$$

To convert this value into inches, use the fact that one foot is equivalent to 12 inches. Convert to inches by multiplying by the conversion factor so that feet cancel in the units:

$$164.04\ feet \cdot \frac{12\ inches}{1\ foot} \approx 1970\ \text{inches}.$$

2. (D)

Difficulty: E

Category: Proportions

Strategy: Set up a proportion to solve for how much the hair grows. Add this value to the original length of the hair.

Solution: To find how many inches the hair will grow over the next five years, first find how many months are in 5 years. 5 years = 5 years · 12 months/1year = 60 months. Set up the following proportion:

$$\frac{.5\ inches}{1\ month} = \frac{x\ inches}{60\ months}$$. Cross multiply to get $x = 30$ inches. The

hair started at 4 inches, so with 30 inches of growth, it should be 4 + 30 = 34 inches long after 5 years.

3. (B)

Difficulty: E

Category: Statistics-Averages (Mean)

Strategy: Use the average formula to find the average revenue for each company, and then take the absolute value of the difference.

Solution: Average Revenue for Company A:

$$\frac{14.5 + 15.2 + 17.4 + 13.4 + 10.2 + 11.5}{6} = \$13.7\ \text{million}$$

Average Revenue for Company B:

$$\frac{10.5 + 11.2 + 13.5 + 15.8 + 17.8 + 18.2}{6} = \$14.5\ \text{million}$$

The absolute value of the difference is |13.7 – 14.5| = $0.8 million.

4. (B)

Difficulty: E/M

Category: Percents

Strategy: Use the percent change formula and apply it to each of the four government areas in the answer choices. Then, compare values to pick the smallest percent change.

Solution: Calculate the percent change in 2015 budgets to 2017 budgets for each government area indicated.

In general, percent change in budget = (Change in Budget/Original Budget) × 100%. Use this formula to calculate the percent change in the transportation budget from 2015 to 2017, which is

$\frac{608 - 575}{575} \cdot 100\% \approx 5.7\%$. The percent change in the education

budget from 2015 to 2017 is $\frac{6950 - 6700}{6700} \cdot 100\% \approx 3.7\%$. The

percent change in the Housing and Economic Development budget

from 2015 to 2017 is $\frac{506 - 475}{475} \approx 6.5\%$. The percent change in the

Health and Human Services budget from 2015 to 2017 is

$\frac{21025 - 18950}{18950} \approx 10.9\%$. Of these percentages, the percent change in

the Education budget is the smallest.

5. (C)

Difficulty: E

Category: Ratios

Strategy: Set up a proportion to solve for the unknown.

Solution: The ratio of medium to large cups is 4:5. If 100 medium cups were sold that day, set up a proportion to solve for how many

large cups were sold: $\frac{4}{5} = \frac{100}{x}$. Cross multiply to get $4x = 500$. Solve

for x to get x, the number of large cups sold, is 125.

6. (B)

Difficulty: E

Category: Ratios

Strategy: Find the cost of a card from each pack and compare.

Solution: The price per card for the Roke-Nom packs is $3.00/(15 cards) = $0.20/card. The price per card for the Sorcery: the Convention game packs is $4.50/(25 cards) = $0.18/card. Overall, the card price for the Sorcery: the Convention packs is lower.

7. (C)

Difficulty: E

Category: Data Collection and Conclusions

Strategy: Know that a good sample (one that can be generalized for a population) is a random sample that is selected from only members of the population the sample is meant to represent.

Solution: Answer choices A and B select from lists of all teachers in the state, not from the city district, which is the population of interest in this study. A sample taken from a list of all state teachers will not necessarily represent the opinions of teachers from the specific city district of interest. Answer choices C and D choose from the correct population of interest, city district school teachers, but only answer choice C randomizes the selection process. By only recording the first 50 email responses in answer choice D, bias may be introduced into the sample.

8. (D)

Difficulty: E/M

Category: Statistics – Median, Mode, and Range

Strategy: Know the definition of mean, mode, median, and range. Use process of elimination by trying each choice to find the one that is false.

Solution: The mode is the most common occurring number; it is 90 in both cases. The median is the middle number when the items in the lists are ordered by ascending value. In both sets, the median is 90. Thus, A is true. The range, or difference between highest and lowest values, of Set II is $97 - 88 = 9$, and the range of Set I is $94 - 87 = 7$. B is true. The mean of Set I is the average of the set, which is $\frac{87 + 87 + 90 + 90 + 90 + 94}{6} \approx 89.7$ and the mean of Set II is $\frac{88 + 90 + 90 + 90 + 91 + 96 + 97}{7} \approx 91.7$, so C is true. Including 95 in Set I does not change the median, but adding it to Set II raises the median to 90.5. D is not true.

9. (C)

Difficulty: M

Category: Proportions

Strategy: Find the difference in book value between the new and current vehicle. Set up a proportion to find the excise tax needed to pay for the difference in book value.

Solution: First, find the difference in book value between the new and current vehicle = $27395 - $3450 = $23945. Next, set up a proportion to determine how much excise tax, x, should be paid for the difference in book value:

$\frac{\$25 \; tax}{\$1000} = \frac{x}{23945}$. Cross-multiply to find $1000x = 598625$. Solve for x to find $x = \$598.625$.

10. (C)

Difficulty: E/M

Category: Probability

Strategy: Find the size of the sample space, the group that you are selecting from. Find the number of ways a certain event occurs within that sample space. Divide the numbers to determine the probability of the event.

Solution: The probability will be equal to the number of times Ava drew a red piece of paper using her left hand divided by the total number of trials (the sample space). There were 150 total trials. Of those trials, she drew a red piece of paper with her left hand $37 + 42 = 79$ times. Therefore, the probability that she drew a red piece of paper in her left hand was $\frac{79}{150}$.

11. (B)

Difficulty: E/M

Category: Data Relationships

Strategy: Determine the relationship between the amount of caffeine left in Alex's system and the time after her coffee. Choose the graph with the correct shape that matches the model. Alternatively, use process of elimination by finding how much caffeine she will have in her body after 5 hours.

Solution: The problem is describing an exponential rate, where every five hours, the amount of caffeine is halved (rate is a 50% decrease every 5 hours). Only graph B shows the shape of an exponential graph, specifically the function

$C = 120\left(\frac{1}{2}\right)^{\frac{t}{5}}$ where C represents the amount of caffeine left in Alex's body and t is time in hours since drinking the coffee. Alternatively, reason that after 5 hours, Alex only has 60 mg of the original caffeine in her body. Only graph B goes through this point.

12. (C)

Difficulty: M

Category: Units and Conversion

Strategy: Convert units one at a time by multiplying by the correct conversion factors. Convert from Joules per second into foot-pounds per second. Then convert seconds into minutes to convert into foot-pounds per minute. Set up the conversion factors so that the relevant units cancel.

Solution: First, convert from Joules per second into foot-pounds per second:

$\frac{1200J}{s} \cdot \frac{1ft - lb}{1.35582J} \approx 885$ ft-lb/s.

Next, convert ft-lb/s to ft-lb/min:

$\frac{885ft - lb}{s} \cdot \frac{60s}{1min} = 53100$ ft-lb/min.

13. (A)

Difficulty: M

Category: Statistics-Averages (Mean)

Strategy: Reasoning and process of elimination are effective here as only one of the choices can be correct, given that the average for the entire month is lower than the average for the first ten days. Alternatively, use the average formula to calculate the total rainfall for the first ten days and for the month. Use these numbers to find the average rainfall for the last 20 days of the month.

Solution: If the month average is 4.4 inches of rain, and the average rainfall for the first ten days was higher than 4.4 inches (at 4.8 inches), then deduce that the remainder of the days must have an average rainfall lower than the monthly average, to overall get an average of 4.4. Thus, A must be correct.

Alternatively, calculate the total rainfall for the first ten days and for the month by applying the average formula:

First 10-day rainfall = x. Then, $\frac{x}{10} = 4.8 \rightarrow x = 48$ inches.

Month Rainfall = y. Then, $\frac{y}{30} = 4.4 \rightarrow y = 132$ inches.

The rainfall for the last 20 days must be the difference:

Total Rainfall for last 20 days = 132 in – 48 in = 84 inches.

Average rainfall for last 20 days = $\frac{84}{20} = 4.2$ inches.

14. (C)

Difficulty: M

Category: Statistics – Median, Mode, and Range

Strategy: Know the definition of a median. Either use reasoning and process of elimination or create a data set with 15 positive integers and test each answer choice to see which will not change the median.

Solution: The median of a set of 15 integers will be the 8th integer when the integers are listed from smallest to largest. If each integer is increased by 3, the median (or 8th value) will also increase by 3. Similarly, dividing each of the integers by 2 will result in the median being halved. If the largest 5 integers are increased by 5 however, the 8th largest integer will be unchanged. Decreasing the smallest 10 integers by 1 will drop the median by 1, since the 8th largest integer is in the set of the smallest 10 integers of the set. If needed, create a set of numbers to test these scenarios, for example, the natural numbers 1 through 15. Test each answer choice to find choice C will not affect the median.

15. (B)

Difficulty: M

Category: Graphs of Linear Equations

Strategy: Determine the slope and y-intercept of the graph. Review each choice to determine the function which could model each situation described. Use process of elimination.

Solution: The graph has a y-intercept, or starting point, of (0, 24) and a slope of -1, which means one variable, y, will decrease by 1 as the other variable, x, increases by 1. Eliminate answer choice A, since it has a slope of $-1/2$ (down one container for every two months). Choice B works, since the starting number of annual payments is 24, and each year, the number of payments left will decrease by 1. Choice C can be eliminated because Jared's savings are increasing, not decreasing. Choice D describes a situation where the weight of the salt product will fluctuate between decreases (as the salt is used over the month and a half) and sudden increases when the salt is replenished.

16. (A)

Difficulty: M

Category: Percents

Strategy: When no prices (starting, ending, or intermediate) are given in a percent problem, choosing your own number for the starting price is often an effective strategy. Know how to find what percent one number is of another and how to use the percent change formula.

Solution: Let l = the original price of the laptop. The increased price will be $l + 0.2l = 1.2l$. After decreasing the price, the final price must be $l + 0.15l = 1.15l$. Percent change = (difference in price/original price) $\cdot 100\%$. In this case, the percent decrease in price from the increased to the final price should be

$$\frac{1.2l - 1.15l}{1.2l} \cdot 100\% = \frac{0.05l}{1.2l} \cdot 100\% \approx 4\% .$$

If choosing numbers, choose 100 for the original price of the laptop and follow the same procedure.

17. (C)

Difficulty: H

Category: Ratios

Strategy: Using the ratio, set up a proportion to find the number of seniors that attended from each school. Find the total number of students, and then calculate the number of teachers needed to find the total.

Solution: For the two schools that sent both juniors and seniors the ratio was 1:4. Since each school sent 32 juniors, set up a proportion to find the number of seniors sent from each school: $\frac{1}{4} = \frac{32}{s}$. Solve to find the number of seniors, $s = 128$. Therefore, the number of students sent from the two schools is $32 \cdot 2 + 128 \cdot 2 = 320$ students. Each of the five other schools also sent 128 seniors, yielding an additional $128 \cdot 5 = 640$ students. The total number of students was $320 + 640 = 960$. The number of teachers needed is 960 students $\cdot$ 1 teacher/25 students = 38.4 teachers. Thus, 38 teachers are needed (since there are only 38 groups of 25 in 960), and the total number of people attending is $960 + 38 = 998$ people.

18. (D)

Difficulty: M/H

Category: Proportions

Strategy: Use the relevant data from the data to set up a proportion and solve.

Solution: In the survey, 51 of 75 people said they would support Question 2 for School Improvement. Set up a proportion to find the number of voters, x, who voted yes on this question:

$$\frac{51}{75} = \frac{x}{2400} \rightarrow 75x = 51(2400) \rightarrow x = 1632.$$

19. (B)

Difficulty: H

Category: Data Relationships

Strategy: Draw a sketch of a curve that best fits the points. Identify the best type of model that matches the shape of the sketch, and then determine the appropriate equation.

Solution: Answer choices A and D are examples of linear models. Answer choice B shows an exponential model, and answer choice C is a quadratic model. A linear model is not best for this graph given the other options, as the points appear to follow a curve rather than a line. To determine whether the quadratic or exponential model is better suited, plug in some values of x into the model, and see if they closely match the graph. An easier value to test is $x = 0$ (the y-intercept). The exponential model has a y-intercept of (0, 1.790), which matches the data more accurately than the quadratic model's y-intercept of (0, 214.62).

20. (D)

Difficulty: M/H

Category: Data Collection and Conclusions

Strategy: Read the question carefully and determine all aspects of how the survey data was collected. Then identify one clear source of bias.

Solution: The researchers wanted to survey the attitudes of an entire town, yet they surveyed people at one location. This method of sampling makes the conclusion less reliable because the sample is less likely to be representative of the population. There is not enough information about the population to determine whether the sample size is too small. Less than 5% of people not responding isn't significant enough to make a difference. Finally, there is not enough information about the question to determine whether it was asked in a biased way.

21. (A)

Difficulty: H

Category: Statistics – Median, Mode, and Range

Strategy: Assume all of the first 6 cards were sold for the maximum price and that the last 5 cards were sold for the same lowest possible price. Know the definition of median and mode.

Solution: In order to calculate the minimum possible maximum price, assume the first 6 cards (all the cards up to and including the median) were sold for the maximum price possible, i.e. the median price of $110. In this case, Stephen made 6 · $110 = $660 from the 6 lowest-priced playing cards. Since the mean selling price was $125 in total, Stephen made 11·$125 = $1375 selling all 11 cards. He made $1375 − $660 = $715 selling the remaining 5 cards. To get the minimum possible maximum price, assume all of 5 cards were sold for the same price. Thus, the lowest price of the most expensive card would be $715 / 5 = $143.

22. (B)

Difficulty: H

Category: Percents

Strategy: Create an equation relating the original price to the final price that Charisma ends up paying, or carefully work backwards, one step at a time, from the final payment to the original price.

Solution: The original 30% decrease is the same as finding 70% of the original price (100% − 30% = 70%). The rewards membership gives her another 20% discount, which is the same as finding 80% of her new price. Finally, adding a 5% tax is equivalent to finding 105% of the price before tax. Multiplying these percentages by the original price should give the final price, $450, which can be expressed using the following equation:

Original Price·(.7)(.8)(1.05) = $450. Solve for the original price:

Original Price = $\dfrac{\$450}{(.7)(.8)(1.05)} \approx$ $765.00. Of all the answer choices listed, (B) is the closest.

23. (A)

Difficulty: M

Category: Units and Conversion

Strategy: Go through each answer choice and convert all measurements into Tun by multiplying by the correct conversion factors. Sum up the totals to see if they yield a whole number of Tuns.

Solution: Begin with answer choice A, and convert each measurement into Tuns:

$$4 \; quarters \cdot \frac{1 \; hogshead}{2 \; quarters} \cdot \frac{1 \; pipe}{2 \; hogshead} \cdot \frac{1 \; tun}{2 \; pipe} = 0.5 \; tun.$$

$$2 \; hogshead \cdot \frac{1 \; pipe}{2 \; hogshead} \cdot \frac{1 \; tun}{2 \; pipe} = 0.5 \; tun$$

$2 \; pipe \cdot \dfrac{1 \; tun}{2 \; pipe} = 1 \; tun$. Add the three values to get 2.0 tun, which will fill 2 1.0-Tun containers to the top. All other answers will yield total volumes measuring non-integer Tun values.

24. (D)

Difficulty: H

Category: Percents

Strategy: If choosing numbers, use 100 units as the initial share price and carry out each percentage increase or decrease sequentially. Use the percent change formula.

Solution: Let s = original share price. The 50% drop in share price leaves 50% of the original price. The 35% drop in share price the following year is the same as 65% of the new price (100% − 35% = 65%). The following 25% drop in share price is the same as 75% of the year prior. Finally, the increase by 5% the final year is the same as finding 105% of the last year's price. Therefore, the price of the shares by the end of 2003 will be $s(0.5)(0.65)(0.75)(1.05) \approx .256s$. Percent change = (change in price)/initial price x 100%. To restore the price back to s, apply the percent change formula (the initial price will be the 2003 price): $\dfrac{s - .256s}{.256s} \cdot 100\% = \dfrac{.744s}{.256s} \cdot 100\% \approx 291\%$.

Problem Solving & Data Analysis – Percents – Pages 337-340

1. (B)
Difficulty: E
Category: Percents
Strategy: Either set up a proportion for this problem or convert 40% into a decimal and multiple by the total mass.
Solution: The glucose sample has a mass of 250g, and 40% of that mass comes from the Carbon atoms. Therefore, the mass of the Carbon atoms in the sample (in grams) is 40% of 250, which is

$$\frac{40}{100} \cdot 250 = 100 \, .$$

2. (A)
Difficulty: E
Category: Percents
Strategy: Use the percent change formula. Eliminate choices C and D since they represent an increase in the number of blueberries.
Solution: The number of blueberries harvested in 2011 was 3200 pounds. If there was a 33% decrease in the blueberry harvest in 2012, then first calculate 33% of 3200 = $.33 \cdot 3200 = 1056$. Subtract this from 3200 to get the answer, which is 2144. Alternatively, reason that a 33% decrease is equivalent to finding $(100 - 33)\% = 67\%$ of the 3200 pounds = 2144 pounds.

3. (B)
Difficulty: E
Category: Percents
Strategy: Use the percent change formula. Eliminate answer choice D, since it represents an increase.
Solution: Apply the percent change formula here:

$$\frac{\text{new - original}}{\text{original}} \cdot 100\% = \frac{2.1 - 2.4}{2.4} \cdot 100\% = -12.5\% \, .$$

Since the percent change is negative, it represents a decrease. This means that the average visits to the museum per resident decreased by 12.5%.

4. (C)
Difficulty: E
Category: Percents
Strategy: Use the percent change formula. Eliminate choice D, since it is higher than the length in 2010. A and B can both be eliminated by inspection since they represent a percent decrease greater than 50%.
Solution: The average length of a transistor gate produced by this manufacturer in 2010 was 40 nm. The length was decreased by 20% between 2010 and 2012, so to calculate the new average length, find 20% of 40, which is $.2 \cdot 40 = 8$. Subtract this value from 40 to get 32 nm. Alternatively, a 20% decrease is the same as finding of 80% of the original length in 2010. 80% of 40 is $.8 \cdot 40 = 32$.

5. (A)
Difficulty: E
Category: Percents
Strategy: Divide the average transistor length in 2010 by the average transistor gate length in 2000. Then multiply by 100 to convert to a percent.
Solution: According to the graph, in 2010, the average transistor gate length was 40 nm. In 2000, the length was 120 nm. Calculate what percent 40 is of 120, which is $\frac{40}{120} \cdot 100\% \approx 33\%$.

6. (D)
Difficulty: M
Category: Percents
Strategy: Use the percent change formula for each of the four two-year intervals mentioned in the answer choices. Then, compare values to pick the largest percent decrease.
Solution: In general, percent decrease = Change in Length/Original Length. Use this equation to calculate the percent decrease between 2000 and 2002, which is $\frac{120 - 90}{120} = 25\%$. The percent decrease in length between 2002 and 2004 is $\frac{90 - 75}{90} \approx 17\%$ The percent decrease in length between 2006 and 2008 is $\frac{65 - 60}{65} \approx 8\%$. The percent decrease in length between 2008 and 2010 is $\frac{60 - 40}{60} \approx 33\%$. Of these percentages, the percent decrease between 2008 and 2010 is the greatest.

7. (D)
Difficulty: E
Category: Percents
Strategy: Divide the number of 38-53-year-olds that completed a Bachelor's Degree by the number of 38-53-year-olds (the sample space). Multiply this decimal by 100 to convert to a percent.
Solution: Of the 203 adults aged 38-53 that participated in the survey, 59 completed at least their Bachelor's degree. Therefore, the percentage of adults aged 38-53 that completed college is $\frac{59}{203} \approx 29\%$.

8. (C)
Difficulty: M
Category: Percents
Strategy: Divide the number of 25-37-year-olds that completed some college by the number of people who completed some college (the sample space). Multiply this decimal by 100 to convert to a percent.
Solution: Of the $70 + 57 + 48 + 16 = 191$ adults that only completed some college, 70 were between the ages of 25 and 37. Therefore, the percentage of adults that completed only some college that are between the ages of 25 and 37 is $\frac{70}{191} \approx 37\%$.

9. (D)
Difficulty: M
Category: Percents
Strategy: Find the number of people in the survey who completed *at least* some college and divide by 800, the total number of participants (the sample space). Multiply this decimal by 100 to convert to a percent.
Solution: Interpret that adults who completed at least some college must be those that were in the "Some College" or "Bachelor's Degree or Higher" categories. Next, calculate the percentage of the 800 adults surveyed who completed some college or a bachelor's degree or higher, which is

$$\frac{70+57+48+16+96+59+55+17}{800} = \frac{418}{800} \approx 52\%.$$

10. (D)
Difficulty: M
Category: Percents
Strategy: Find the percent of adults who did not graduate high school for all four age groups. Compare these percentages, and find the highest among them.
Solution: Interpret that adults who did not graduate high school must be those that were marked in the "Less than High School" category of the survey. Next, calculate the percentage of adults that completed less than high school for each age group. For the 25-37 age range,

$\frac{20}{247} \cdot 100\% \approx 8.1\%$ did not finish high school.

$\frac{26}{203} \cdot 100\% \approx 12.8\%$ of people in the 38-53 group did not finish

high school. For the 54-72 age group, $\frac{32}{228} \cdot 100\% \approx 14.0\%$ did not

finish high school. For the 73-90 age group, $\frac{37}{122} \cdot 100\% \approx 30.3\%$ did

not finish high school. Of the four percentages calculated, the 73-90 age cohort has the largest percentage of adults surveyed that did not graduate high school.

11. (45)
Difficulty: M
Category: Percents
Strategy: Know how to express percents as decimals and how to take the percent of a number.
Solution: Cindy finds that she will need $1800 plus 5% of $1800 to meet her anticipated expenses. To find the percent of a number, multiply that number by the percent expressed as a decimal: $1800 × .05 = $90. $90 represents the *additional* money Cindy will need. Thus, her new monthly required funds must be $1890. Because she will get a salary increase that gives her a 2.5% increase in take home pay, she will get 2.5% of 1800 = (.025) · $1800 = $45 additional monthly pay. Cindy can anticipate having an additional $45 per month in take home pay but needs $90 to meet all of her future expenses. The difference of these two numbers, $90 – $45 = $45, represents how much money she will still need to raise in order to cover all of her expenses once the new lease begins.

12. (D)
Difficulty: M
Category: Percents
Strategy: Write a percent equation relating the volume of the liquid medicine to the volume of the active ingredient. Alternatively, plug in the answer choices, finding 0.12% of each answer to see which choice results in 0.57.
Solution: The 0.57 milliliters of active ingredient is 0.12% of V, the volume of the liquid medicine. Translate this statement into an equation (using the decimal version of the percent) and solve for the total volume:

$0.57 = 0.0012 \cdot V$. Solve to get $V = \frac{0.57}{0.0012} = 475$ mL.

13. (B)
Difficulty: M
Category: Percents
Strategy: Know how to fill in data using other data provided in a graphic. Ignore irrelevant information. Know how to take the percent of a number. Use the percent change formula.
Solution: Find the number of useable plastic trays produced in a thirty-day month by both Machines A and C. In this problem, information related to Machine B is irrelevant – although you can see that the daily output was multiplied by 30 to get the monthly output. Machine A will have an average 30-day output of 275 · 30 = 8250 trays. Machine C will have an average 30-day output of 315 · 30 = 9450 trays. Now, calculate the number of unusable trays. Multiply each total by the respective rejection percentage and subtract that value to find the actual number of useable trays produced by each machine. Alternatively, you could save a step by realizing that 99% (100% – 1%) of Machine A trays will be useable and 98.7% (100% – 1.3%) of Machine C trays will be useable. Use this method to find that there will be .987 · 9450 ≈ 9327 useable trays that Machine C will produce and .99 · 8250 ≈ 8168 useable trays that Machine A will produce. Take the difference between the usable output numbers of Machines A and C to get 1159. Put that difference over the original number – the Machine A monthly usable output – and convert to a

percent: $\frac{1159}{8168} \cdot 100\% \approx 14\%$.

14. (C)
Difficulty: H
Category: Percents
Strategy: If choosing numbers, choose 100 units as the initial amount in each container and carry out each step sequentially.
Solution: Let w = initial amount of water in both containers. When 25% of the water is removed there is $w - .25w = .75w$ left in container one. 25% of what is left in container one (.75w) is added back in, now leaving $.75w + .25(.75w) = .9375w$ in container 1. Next, 50% of what is left is removed leaving $.9375w - .5(.9375w) = .46875w$ in container 1. Next, 50% of what is left is added back in leaving $.46875 + 0.5(.46875) = .703125w$ in container 1. $0.703125w$ is what percent of w? Divide the expressions by each other and

multiply by 100% to find out: $\frac{.703125w}{w} \cdot 100\% \approx 70\%$.

If choosing numbers, choose 100 units as the initial amounts in each container and carry out each step sequentially to arrive at the same answer.

15. (B)

Difficulty: H

Category: Percents

Strategy: Use the percent change formula. You can also plug in answer choices and apply the percent change formula.

Solution: First, calculate the percentage increase in customers from 2017 to 2018: $\frac{95194-86540}{86540}\cdot 100\% = 10\%$. Therefore, there was a 10% increase in customers from 2017 to 2018. The owner estimated that this would be double the percent increase from 2018 to 2019, which means there is expected to be a 5% increase from 2018 to 2019. Therefore, the expected number of customers in 2019 should be $95194 + 95194(0.05) \approx 99954$ customers.

16. (A)

Difficulty: H

Category: Percents

Strategy: Choose numbers using 100 as your initial price, and solve for s, going through each percentage change sequentially. Then, plug in your value for s into the answer choices and test to see which answer gets you back your original price of 100 dollars.

Otherwise, write an algebraic equation relating the original price, p, with the final price, s, and solve for p.

Solution: Call the original price of the sneakers p and create an equation that shows the relationship between p and s. The 15% discount leaves 85% of the original price. Then, an additional 8% tax must be applied, which is equivalent to finding 108% of the discounted price. Therefore, $p(.85)(1.08) = s$. Then, rearrange this equation to isolate the original price, p, in terms of s:

$$p = \frac{s}{(0.85)(1.08)}.$$

Problem Solving & Data Analysis – Ratios – Pages 342-345

1. (A)

Difficulty: E

Category: Ratios

Strategy: Find the photovoltaic capacity from the graph and divide by the population.

Solution: The ratio of Germany's photovoltaic capacity to its population is 42,000 MW:83,000,000 people. Dividing these two numbers on the calculator gives approximately the decimal 0.000506. Of all the ratios listed, this value is closest to 1:2000, or 0.0005:1.

2. (B)

Difficulty: E

Category: Ratios

Strategy: Find the photovoltaic capacity from the previous year (2016) and divide by the capacity from 2017. Reduce the fraction.

Solution: In 2017, the photovoltaic capacity of China was 130,000 MW. If in 2017, China added 50,000 MW to its 2016 capacity, then China's 2016 solar output was 130,000 – 50,000 = 80,000 MW. The ratio of 2016 to 2017 photovoltaic capacity is 80,000:130,000 = 8:13.

3. (B)

Difficulty: M

Category: Ratios

Strategy: Find the total photovoltaic capacity of the top 11 producers from the figure. Divide by the world capacity.

Solution: The 2017 total photovoltaic capacity of the top 11 solar energy producers is the sum of their individual capacities, which is 349,100 or approximately 350,000. Thus, the ratio of this total to the world estimate given is about 350,000:400,000, which reduces to 7:8.

4. (C)

Difficulty: M

Category: Ratios

Strategy: Find the area that Jacob will mow in three hours, and then find the area that Sarah will complete. Divide the numbers and reduce the fraction.

Solution: Jacob's rate of work is 25,000 ft²/hr. In 3 hours, he will mow a total of 25,000 ft²/hr × 3hr = 75,000 ft². This leaves 200,000 – 75,000 = 125,000 ft² for Sarah to mow. The ratio of Sarah's area to Jacob's area is then 125,000:75,000, which reduces to 5:3.

5. (C)

Difficulty: E

Category: Ratios

Solution: There are 12 male students with brown eyes, and 22 – 12 = 10 female students without brown eyes. This gives a ratio of 12:10, which reduces to 6:5.

6. (C)
Difficulty: E
Category: Ratios
Strategy: Find the probability that a participant in the survey uses public transit to commute to work. Then, compare this value to the ratios in the answer choices.
Solution: The probability that a survey participant uses public transit = (number of survey participants who use public transit)/(number of survey participants). Based on the data, this probability is 139/600 ≈ .232:1. Of all the ratios, this value is closest to 7:30 ≈ .233:1.

7. (C)
Difficulty: M
Category: Ratios
Strategy: Find the probability that a city resident walks to work and the probability that an outside metro resident walks to work. Divide the values.
Solution: Based on the data, the probability that a city resident walks to work is 50/200 = .25. The probability that a resident from outside of a metro area walks to work is 10/100 = 0.1. To find how many times more likely it is for a city resident to walk than for the other group, divide the probabilities: .25/.1 = 2.5 = 5/2.

8. (D)
Difficulty: M
Category: Ratios
Strategy: Find the probability that a suburb resident drives to work and a city dweller drives to work. Divide the values.
Solution: The probability that a suburb resident drives to work is 148/300 ≈ .493. The probability that a city resident drives to work is 74/200 = 0.37. To find how many times more likely it is for a suburban resident to drive than a city dweller, divide the probabilities: .493/.37 = 4/3.

9. (16)
Difficulty: M
Category: Ratios
Strategy: Write an equation relating the lengths of the cuts to the full ribbon. Convert from feet into inches.
Solution: The length of ribbon is 8 feet or 8 ft · 12 in/1 ft = 96 inches. To find the length of the shortest piece, write an equation that relates the size of each piece to the whole. Since the ratio between the parts is 2:4:6, the cuts have lengths $2x$, $4x$, and $6x$. Therefore, $2x + 4x + 6x = 96$. Solve for $2x$ to find the length of the shortest piece: $12x = 96$. Divide by 6 on both sides to find $2x = 16$ inches.

10. (352)
Difficulty: M
Category: Ratios
Strategy: Find the ratio of Tree A to Tree B fruit and reduce. Set up a proportion to solve for the fruit yield of Tree C.
Solution: The ratio of Tree A fruit yield to Tree B fruit yield is 60:72 = 5:6. This is the same as the ratio of fruit yields for Tree C to Tree D. Set up a proportion to solve for x, number of fruit Tree C produced this season: $\frac{5}{6} = \frac{x}{120}$. Cross multiply to get $6x = 600$. Solve for x to get $x = 100$. Add up the number of fruit produced by each tree to get $60 + 72 + 100 + 120 = 352$ total fruit.

11. (C)
Difficulty: M
Category: Ratios
Strategy: Set up a proportion.
Solution: Use a proportion to determine the number of containers of extra olive oil needed, x, to be added to the mix: $\frac{2}{5} = \frac{3}{5+x}$. Cross multiplying yields the equation $2(5+x) = 15$. Distribute to get $10 + 2x = 15$. Solve for x to get $x = 2.5$.

12. (B)
Difficulty: M
Category: Ratios
Strategy: Set up proportions to solve for unknown values.
Solution: For class A, the number of boys is unknown. Set up a proportion to solve for it:
$\frac{3}{7} = \frac{b}{21}$. Cross multiply to find $7b = 63$. Divide by 7 to find the number of boys in class A = 9. The number of students in class A is 9 + 21 = 30.
For class B, the number of girls is unknown. Set up a proportion to solve for it:
$\frac{4}{8} = \frac{16}{g}$. Cross multiply to find $4g = 128$. Divide by 4 to find the number of girls in class B is 32. The number of students in class B is 16 + 32 = 48, which is larger than class A.

13. (D)
Difficulty: M
Category: Ratios
Strategy: Find the number of patients who did not improve. Of those, find the number who received medicine. Divide the numbers and reduce the fraction.
Solution: The number of patients who received the medication and did not improve was 35. The number of patients who did not improve is 35 + 55 = 90. Therefore, the fraction of patients who did not improve and received the medication is $\frac{35}{90} = \frac{7}{18}$.

14. (C)
Difficulty: M
Category: Ratios
Strategy: Find the total number of lollipops and chocolate bars Kara has already bought. Set up a proportion to solve for how many remaining lollipops she needs to purchase.
Solution: So far, Kara has 5·30 = 150 lollipops and 4·35 = 140 chocolate bars. Let x = the number of additional lollipops she needs to purchase. Set up a proportion relating the number of lollipops to chocolate bars using the ratio given in the problem: $\frac{150+x}{140} = \frac{3}{2}$.
Cross multiply to get the equation $300 + 2x = 420$. Solve for x to get $x = 60$. Since each bag of lollipops holds 30 lollipops, she needs 60/30 = 2 more bags.

15. (A)

Difficulty: M

Category: Ratios

Strategy: Either calculate the ratios in the answer choices or use a combination of estimation and process of elimination.

Solution: The number of women in the House of Representatives in the 111th congress = 73. The number of women in the 111th congress = 90. The ratio of these two values is 73:90 ≈ 0.865:1.

Eliminate D since the two quantities in question are the same, yielding a ratio of 1:1.

Eliminate B because the ratio is greater than 1.

A and C are very close with the ratio in A = 73:90 ≈ 0.81:1. The ratio in C is 80:100 = 0.8:1. The closest to 0.865 is answer choice A.

16. (C)

Difficulty: H

Category: Ratios

Strategy: Set up an equation relating how much money each child receives. Set up an additional equation with the amounts each child gives Damian. Alternatively, plug in the answer choices and work backwards.

Solution: Let the initial sum of money = x. If the ratio of the shares is 13:12:10, then the total amounts of each share can be expressed as $13s$, $12s$, and $10s$, where $x = 13s + 12s + 10s = 35s$. If Aaron gives 1/5 of his share, then Baxter must give twice the fraction or 2/5 of his share, and Charlie gives 3/5 of his share. So, the amount Damian receives can be expressed as $\frac{1}{5} \cdot 13s + \frac{2}{5} \cdot 12s + \frac{3}{5} \cdot 10s = 21.44$.

Multiply through by 5 to get $13s + 24s + 30s = 107.2$. Group like terms to get $67s = 107.2$. Solve to get $s = 1.6$. Recall that the initial sum of money = $x = 35s = 35(1.6) = \$56.00$.

Problem Solving & Data Analysis – Proportions – Pages 347-350

1. (22.5 or 45/2)

Difficulty: E

Category: Proportions

Strategy: Set up a proportion and solve for the missing value or use estimation.

Solution: Set up a proportion to find how many pounds of apples are needed to make 120 fluid ounces of apple cider:

$\frac{3\ lb}{16\ oz} = \frac{x}{120\ oz}$. Cross multiple to get the equation $16x = 360$.

Divide by 16 on both sides to get the pounds of apples needed, x, is equal to 22.5.

2. (A)

Difficulty: E

Category: Proportions

Strategy: Set up a proportion and solve for the missing value or use estimation.

Solution: Set up a proportion to find how large the flagellum will be in the model:

$\frac{1\ cm}{5\ nm} = \frac{x}{24\ nm}$. Cross multiply to find $5x = 24$. Divide by 5 on both

sides to find the flagellum will have a length of 4.8 cm, or approximately 5 cm.

3. (B)

Difficulty: E

Category: Proportions

Strategy: Set up a proportion and solve for the missing value or use estimation.

Solution: Set up a proportion to find how many calories Ethan burns through for the first 6 hours of the day:

$\frac{1800\ cal}{24\ hr} = \frac{x}{6hr}$. Cross multiply to find $24x = 10800$. Divide by 24

on both sides to get the calories burned for the first 6 hours, x, is 450 calories.

4. (D)

Difficulty: E

Category: Proportions

Strategy: Set up a proportion to solve.

Solution: According to the table, there are 120 calories in 30g of brown rice protein powder. Set up a proportion to find how many calories are in 120g of brown rice protein powder:

$\frac{120\ cal}{30\ g} = \frac{x\ calories}{120\ g}$. Cross multiply to get $14400 = 30x$. Divide by

30 on both sides, and you will find there are 480 calories in 120g of brown rice protein powder.

5. (B)
Difficulty: M
Category: Proportions
Strategy: Set up a proportion to solve for how much protein would be in each sample. Subtract the two values.
Solution: Set up a proportion to find how many grams of protein are in a 100g sample of brown rice protein powder: $\frac{25}{30} = \frac{b}{100}$. Cross multiply and solve to find $b \approx 83.3$ g of protein. Set up a similar proportion to find how many grams of protein are in a 100g sample of whey protein powder: $\frac{20}{30} = \frac{w}{100}$. Cross multiply and solve to find $w \approx 66.7$g of protein. To find how much more protein is in 100g of brown rice powder than 100g of whey powder, subtract w from b, which will yield approximately 16.7g, which rounds to 17g. Alternatively, you can notice that for 30g of powder, brown rice powder has 5 more grams than whey protein powder ($25 - 20 = 5$). So, you could set up one proportion to solve for the difference in 100g of each sample: $\frac{5}{30} = \frac{x}{100}$. Cross multiply and solve for x to get approximately 17g.

6. (D)
Difficulty: M
Category: Proportions
Strategy: Set up a proportion to solve for how much protein the weight-lifter needs. Then, using this value, set up another proportion to determine how much whey protein powder he would need to consume.
Solution: Set up a proportion to find how many grams of protein the weight-lifter needs: $\frac{2g}{1\ kg} = \frac{x}{75\ kg}$. Cross multiplying yields $x = 150$g of protein. To find how much whey protein he needs to consume 150g of protein, set up the following proportion: $\frac{20g}{30g} = \frac{150g}{x}$. Cross multiply and solve to get $x = 225$g.

7. (B)
Difficulty: M
Category: Proportions
Strategy: Set up two proportions to solve for the lowest and largest amount of time it would take a healthy woman to filter her blood. Check which answers fall into the range.
Solution: The lowest creatinine clearance rate that would still be considered healthy is 88 mL/min. Calculate the time it would take to filter 5000 ml of blood using a proportion:
$\frac{88\ ml}{1\ min} = \frac{5000\ ml}{x\ min}$. Cross multiply to get $88x = 5000$. Solve to get $x \approx 56.82$ min., the maximum time it takes a healthy woman to filter 5000 mL. The highest creatinine clearance rate for a healthy woman is 128 ml/min. Calculate the time it would take to filter 5000 mL of blood at this rate:
$\frac{128\ ml}{1\ min} = \frac{5000\ ml}{x\ min}$. Cross multiply to get $128x = 5000$. Solve to get $x \approx 39.06$ min, the minimum time it takes a healthy woman to filter 5000 milliliters of blood. To have a healthy creatinine clearance rate, Sandra can take 39.06 min-56.82 min to filter 5000 mL of blood. Only answers I and II fall within that range.

Alternatively, test each Roman Numeral. For each option, set up a proportion to solve for Sandra's creatinine filtration rate, and check if it falls in the healthy range.

8. (56)
Difficulty: E
Category: Proportions
Strategy: Find how many chewables the puppy eats in one day. Find how many days Sylvia will be away. Set up a proportion and solve.
Solution: In one day, the puppy consumes $2 \cdot 2 = 4$ chewables. Because she will be away for two weeks, Sylvia needs to provide a fourteen-day supply. Set up a proportion to solve for the number of chewables she needs to supply: $\frac{4\ chewables}{1\ day} = \frac{x}{14\ days}$. Cross multiply to find $x = 56$ chewables.

9. (C)
Difficulty: M
Category: Proportions
Strategy: Set up proportions to calculate the total highway miles traveled for each vehicle. Find the difference.
Solution: Set up proportions to find how many highway miles the two vehicles will travel with 10 gallons of gas:
Electric: 100 mi/gallon × 10 gallons = 1000 miles
Gas/Electric: 50 miles/gallon × 10 gallons = 500 miles
Difference: 1000 miles – 500 miles = 500 miles.

10. (B)
Difficulty: M
Category: Proportions
Strategy: Calculate the amount of fuel used for each type of car based on the number of highway/city miles. Take the difference to find the gallons saved. Then, set up a proportion to convert to money saved.
Solution: Calculate the total gas used by each car.
Gas Car: 300 highway miles · 1 gallon/40 highway miles = 7.5 gallons, 60 city miles · 1 gallon/30 city miles = 2 gallons. Total gallons = 7.5 + 2 = 9.5 gallons.
Hybrid: 300 highway miles · 1 gallon/50 highway miles = 6.0 gallons, 60 city miles · 1 gallon/40 city miles = 1.5 gallons. Total gallons = 6.0 + 1.5 = 7.5 gallons.
Gas Saved: 9.5 gallons – 7.5 gallons = 2.0 gallons
Money saved: $3.50/gallon · 2.0 gallons = $7.00.

11. (A)

Difficulty: M

Category: Proportions

Strategy: For each ingredient, set up a proportion to determine how many cookies the given amount could make. Determine which sample makes the least number of cookies. This ingredient will determine the largest number of cookies that can be made from the available ingredients.

Solution: The limiting factor is the one that will make the fewest cookies. Set up a proportion to determine how many cookies can be made from each of the ingredients:

140oz sugar · 180 cookies/40oz sugar = 630 cookies

500oz butter · 180 cookies/120oz butter = 750 cookies

420oz flour · 180 cookies/110oz flour ≈ 687 cookies

25oz chocolate · 180 cookies/7oz chocolate ≈ 643 cookies

The 140oz of sugar makes the least amount of cookies, so it must be the ingredient limiting the maximum number of cookies that can be made.

12. (B)

Difficulty: (M)

Category: Proportions

Strategy: Set up a proportion.

Solution: Set up a proportion to find how many standard miles are in 115 nautical miles. Be sure that both ratios are set up the same.

$\frac{110}{126.5} = \frac{115}{x}$. Cross-multiply to get $110x = 115(126.5)$. Divide by 110 to find $x = 132.25$ standard miles.

13. (C)

Difficulty: M

Category: Proportions

Strategy: Set up proportions to find the time each runner took to complete a mile. Find the difference.

Solution: To complete one mile, the runners must run 1609 meters.

Mile Time for Runner A: 1609m · 1s/6.5m ≈ 247.5 seconds

Mile Time for Runner B: 1609m · 1s/7.5m ≈ 214.5 seconds

Runner A will take an additional 247.5 – 214.5 = 33 seconds to run the mile.

14. (C)

Difficulty: M

Category: Proportions

Strategy: Find the total distance traveled. Set up a proportion to find the total cost of gas for the trip.

Solution: First, add together the two parts of the trip to find the total distance of the road trip is 124 + 208 = 332 miles. Then, set up a proportion to solve for x, the total amount paid for gas:

$\frac{\$48.60}{124\ miles} = \frac{x}{332\ miles}$. Cross-multiply and solve to find $x = \$130.12$.

15. (D)

Difficulty: M

Category: Proportions

Strategy: To maximize the amount of time spent walking, reason that she should take the full 3 hours to walk 25 miles. Use the distance = rate · time formula to write expression for the distances traveled walking and running. Then, set up an equation and solve for the time spent running or walking.

Solution: Let t = the time in hours spent walking. To maximize this time, she should spend the full 3 hours traveling. So, the time spent running should be $(3 - t)$ hours. The total distance traveled, 25 km, should be equal to her distance walking plus her distance running:

$5t + 15(3 - t) = 25$

Solve for t to find $t = 2$ hours.

If she spends 2 hours walking and 1 hour running, the ratio of time spent running to walking is 1:2.

16. (C)

Difficulty: M

Category: Proportions

Strategy: Find the number of survey participants that responded they did not like ice cream. Set up a proportion to solve for the value asked for and solve.

Solution: First, determine how many students from the original survey did not like ice cream: 105 – 60 – 32 = 13 students. Next, set up a proportion relating the sample of students surveyed to the entire grade: $\frac{13}{105} = \frac{x}{330}$. Cross-multiply and solve to find $x \approx 41$. About 41 students in the whole grade could be expected to dislike ice cream.

17. (C)

Difficulty: H

Category: Proportions

Strategy: Set up a proportion and solve or plug in the answer choices.

Solution: Let x be the number of games the team has won, so they have played $x + 2$ games, and at the end of the season will have played $(x + 2) + 6 = x + 8$ games. Write a proportion equating the winning percentage now and at the end of the season and solve for x:

$$\frac{x}{x+2} = \frac{15}{x+8} \rightarrow 15(x+2) = x(x+8) \rightarrow 15x + 30 = x^2 + 8x \rightarrow$$
$$0 = x^2 - 7x - 30 = (x-10)(x+3) \rightarrow x = 10, x = -3.$$

Since x must be positive, the answer is 10. Alternatively, try plugging in answers and work backwards.

Problem Solving & Data Analysis – Units & Conversion – Pages 352-354

1. (4)
Difficulty: E
Category: Units and Conversion
Strategy: Either set up a proportion or multiply by the correct conversion factor.
Solution: To find the dog's weight in stone, multiply by the conversion proportion so that pounds cancel in the units:

$$56 \text{ lb} \cdot \frac{1 \text{ stone}}{14 \text{ lb}} = 4 \text{ stone}.$$

2. (C)
Difficulty: E
Category: Units and Conversion
Strategy: Multiply by the correct conversion factor to convert miles per hour into miles per minute.
Solution: There are 60 minutes in 1 hour, so use this proportion to convert the ISS's speed from miles per hour to miles per minute. To find the how fast the ISS travels in one minute set up the initial rate and multiply by the conversion proportion so that hours cancel in the units:

$$\frac{17150 \text{ mi}}{1 \text{ hour}} \cdot \frac{1 \text{ hour}}{60 \text{ min}} \approx 286 \text{ mi/min}.$$ Therefore, the ISS travels approximately 286 miles in one minute.

3. (B)
Difficulty: E
Category: Units and Conversion
Strategy: Multiply by the correct conversion factor to convert grams into ounces.
Solution: There are 28.3496 grams in one ounce. Use this proportion to convert 909 grams to ounces. To do so, multiply by the conversion proportion so that grams cancel in the units:

$$909 \text{ grams} \cdot \frac{1 \text{ ounce}}{28.3496 \text{ grams}} \approx 32 \text{ ounces}.$$

4. (D)
Difficulty: M
Category: Units and Conversion
Strategy: Multiply by the correct conversion factor to convert miles into kilometers. Then, use the kilo/unit conversion rate to convert from kilometers to meters.

Solution: $40 \text{ miles} \times \frac{1 \text{ km}}{0.621 \text{ mile}} \times \frac{1000 \text{ m}}{1 \text{ km}} = 64,412 \text{ m}.$

5. (D)
Difficulty: M
Category: Units and Conversion
Strategy: Use the given conversion rate to convert from grains to milligrams. Then, use the information about the pills in a bottle to calculate the milligrams of aspirin in the entire bottle.
Solution: First, find how many milligrams are in one pill:

$$\frac{5 \text{ grain}}{1 \text{ pill}} \cdot \frac{65 \text{ mg}}{1 \text{ grain}} = 325 \text{ mg/pill}.$$ Next, find how many milligrams are in the whole bottle of 100 pills:

$$1 \text{ bottle} \cdot \frac{100 \text{ pills}}{\text{bottle}} \cdot \frac{325 \text{ mg}}{1 \text{ pill}} = 32,500 \text{ mg of aspirin}.$$

6. (B)
Difficulty: M
Category: Units and Conversion
Strategy: Multiply by the correct series of conversion factors to convert from book chapters into days.
Solution: 8 chapters · (40 pages / 1 chapter) · (1 hour / 16 pages) • (1 day / 2 hours) = 10 days.

7. (A)
Difficulty: M
Category: Units and Conversion
Strategy: Use the information provided to evaluate the conversion factor from knots into miles per hour.
Solution: To convert a measurement from knots into miles per hour, one must multiply by $\frac{134.55 \text{ mph}}{117 \text{ knots}} \approx 1.15$ mph/knots. Thus, multiplying by this factor will cancel knot units and convert to mph.

8. (C)
Difficulty: M
Category: Units and Conversion
Strategy: Multiply by the correct conversion factors to convert 97 minutes into miles the plane will travel.
Solution: Remember that there are 60 minutes in one hour.

$$97 \text{ min} \cdot \frac{1 \text{ hr}}{60 \text{ min}} \cdot \frac{580 \text{ mi}}{1 \text{ hr}} \approx 938 \text{ miles}.$$

9. (D)
Difficulty: M
Category: Units and Conversion
Strategy: Convert each of the dimensions into centimeters. Them, multiply the two values to find the area.
Solution: Multiply by the correct conversion factors to convert each of the measurements into centimeters:

$$51 \text{ in.} \cdot \frac{2.54 \text{ cm}}{\text{in.}} = 129.54 \text{ cm} \quad \text{and} \quad 29 \text{ in.} \cdot \frac{2.54 \text{ cm}}{\text{in.}} = 73.66 \text{ cm}$$

Next, multiply the two values to find the area in square cm:
73.66 cm · 129.54 cm $\approx$ 9542 cm^2.

10. (C)
Difficulty: M
Category: Units and Conversion
Strategy: Multiply by the correct conversion factor to convert tablespoons into teaspoons. Then, multiply by the correct conversion factor to convert teaspoons into grams.
Solution: 3.5 tablespoons · (3 teaspoons / 1 tablespoon) · (4.8 g / 1 teaspoon) = 50.4 g.

11. (C)
Difficulty: M
Category: Units and Conversion
Strategy: Convert units one at a time by multiplying by the correct conversion factors. Convert pounds of mercury to kilograms of mercury. Next, convert kilograms into grams. Use the density to convert the measurement into cm³.

Solution: Convert from 2 pounds of mercury into kilograms of mercury. To do so, multiply by the conversion factor so that pounds cancel in the units:

$$2 \text{ lb} \cdot \frac{0.453592 \text{ kg}}{1 \text{ lb}} = .907184 \text{ kg}.$$

Next, convert kilograms to grams; you will need to use the fact that 1000 grams = 1 kg:

$$.907184 \text{ kg} \cdot \frac{1000 \text{ g}}{1 \text{ kg}} = 907.184 \text{ g}.$$

Use the density to convert this mass of mercury into its volume in cubic centimeters:

$$907.184 \text{g} \cdot \frac{1 \text{cm}^3}{13.354 \text{g}} \approx 68 \text{ cm}^3.$$

12. C
Difficulty: M
Category: Units and Conversion
Strategy: The length of Earth's path around the sun is a circumference measurement, and the distance from the Earth to the Sun is the radius of that orbit. Use the formula for circumference to calculate the radius, and then convert the measurement to kilometers.

Solution: 584,000,000 miles is the circumference of the Earth's orbit, and circumference = $2\pi r$. Set up an equation to solve for the radius of the Earth's orbit (the distance between the sun and the Earth): 584,000,000 = $2\pi r$. Divide by 2π on both sides to solve for the radius: $r \approx 92,946,487$ miles. Use the conversion factor to convert this measurement into kilometers.

$$92,946,487 \text{ miles} \cdot \frac{1 \text{km}}{0.62137 \text{ miles}} \approx 150,000,000 \text{ km}.$$

13. (D)
Difficulty: M
Category: Units and Conversion
Strategy: Convert the length of the Sydney Harbor Bridge into meters. Then, convert this measurement to Smoots. Find the difference in length between the two bridges.

Solution: The length of the Sydney Harbor Bridge =

$$3770 \text{ feet} \cdot \frac{1 \text{ m}}{3.3 \text{ feet}} \cdot \frac{1 \text{ Smoot}}{1.7 \text{ m}} \approx 672.0 \text{ Smoots}.$$ The length of the Harvard Bridge is 364.4 Smoots. Find the difference to see how much longer the Sydney Harbor Bridge is: 672 Smoots – 364.4 Smoots ≈ 308 Smoots.

14. (C)
Difficulty: H
Category: Units and Conversion
Strategy: Find the distances the spacecraft must travel to each planet in *au*. Multiply by the correct conversion factors and rates to convert from *au* into decades of space travel.

Solution: Start with Jupiter first. The distance from Earth to the orbit of Jupiter would be 5.2 au – 1 au = 4.2 au. Next, convert this measurement into miles:

$$4.2 \text{ au} \cdot \frac{92955807 \text{ miles}}{1 \text{ au}} = 390414389.4 \text{ miles}$$

Use the rate of the spacecraft to determine how many hours it would take to travel this distance:

$$390414389.4 \text{ miles} \cdot \frac{1 \text{ hour}}{34600 \text{ miles}} \approx 11284 \text{ hours}.$$ Next, convert this measurement into decades:

$$11284 \text{ hours} \cdot \frac{1 \text{ day}}{24 \text{ hours}} \cdot \frac{1 \text{ year}}{365 \text{ days}} \cdot \frac{1 \text{ decade}}{10 \text{ years}}$$

≈ .129 decades. This eliminates answers A and B. Since Saturn is close to twice the distance away from Earth as Jupiter is, then the time the spacecraft would take to reach Saturn must be about twice the time to reach Jupiter. Only answer choice C has a value about twice Jupiter's value. Answer choice D can be eliminated because the measurement for Saturn is more than 10 times the measurement for Jupiter.

15. (B)
Difficulty: H
Category: Units and Conversion
Strategy: Convert units one at a time by multiplying by the correct conversion factors. Convert from square meters into square yards. Then convert square yards into square miles, and convert square miles into acres. Set up the conversion factors so that the relevant units cancel.

Solution: First, convert from hectares (100m x 100m) into square yards (you will need to convert *both* 100 m measurements into yards):

$$100\text{m} \cdot 100\text{m} \cdot \frac{1.09 \text{ yards}}{1\text{m}} \cdot \frac{1.09 \text{ yards}}{1\text{m}} = 11881 \text{ yd}^2$$

Convert from square yards into square miles next:

$$11881 \text{ yard}^2 \cdot \frac{1 \text{ mile}}{1760 \text{ yards}} \cdot \frac{1 \text{ mile}}{1760 \text{ yards}} \approx 0.0038555 \text{ mi}^2$$

Finally, convert this measurement into acres:

$$0.0038555 \text{ miles}^2 \cdot \frac{1 \text{ acre}}{\frac{1}{640} \text{ miles}^2} \approx 2.5 \text{ acres}$$

16. (C)

Difficulty: H

Category: Units and Conversion

Strategy: Convert units one at a time by multiplying by the correct conversion factors. Convert from knots into kilometers per hour. Then convert from kilometers per hour into feet per hour. Finally, convert feet per hour into statutes per hour. Set up the conversion factors so that the relevant units cancel.

Solution: Convert 32 knots into kilometers per hour:

$$32 \text{ knots} \cdot \frac{1.85 \text{ km/h}}{1 \text{ knot}} = 59.2 \text{ kilometers per hour}$$

Use the kilometer to feet conversion factor to convert this rate into feet per hour:

$$\frac{59.2 \text{ km}}{1 \text{ hr}} \cdot \frac{3280.8 \text{ feet}}{1 \text{ km}} = 194,223.36 \text{ feet per hour}$$

Finally, convert to statute miles per hour:

$$\frac{194223.36 \text{ feet}}{1 \text{ hour}} \cdot \frac{1 \text{ statute mile}}{5280 \text{ feet}} \approx 37 \text{ statute mi per hour.}$$

17. (D)

Difficulty: H

Category: Units and Conversion

Strategy: Assume the problem involves 100 g of bronze. Find the mass of copper and tin in the alloy first. Then, use the densities to convert the masses into volumes. Find the percent composition by volume of tin.

Solution: Assume a 100 g sample of bronze. There are $.88 \cdot 100 = 88$g of copper and $.12 \cdot 100 = 12$g of tin in the sample. Convert these measurements into volume by using the density of the material:

Volume of copper = $88\text{g} \cdot \dfrac{1\text{mL}}{8.96\text{g}} \approx 9.82$ mL of copper

Volume of tin = $12\text{g} \cdot \dfrac{1\text{mL}}{7.31\text{g}} \approx 1.64$ mL of copper

Total Volume ≈ 9.82 mL $+ 1.64$ mL $= 11.46$ mL

% Tin by Volume = $\dfrac{1.64\text{mL}}{11.46\text{mL}} \cdot 100\% \approx 14\%$

Problem Solving & Data Analysis – Average (Mean) – Pages 356-357

1. (C)

Difficulty: E

Category: Statistics-Averages (Mean)

Strategy: Use the average formula.

Solution: The mean, or average, of a set of numbers is their sum divided by how many numbers there are. The average of the ages listed in the table is

$(38 + 39 + 39 + 37 + 47 + 40 + 39 + 41 + 41 + 36 + 38 + 37)/12 \approx 39.$

2. (16,000)

Difficulty: E

Category: Statistics-Averages (Mean)

Strategy: Use the average formula.

Solution: Set up an equation for the mean of the data set:

$$\frac{2000 + 6000 + 9000 + 12000 + x}{5} = 9000 \rightarrow \frac{29000 + x}{5} = 9000$$

Multiply both sides by 5 to get $29000 + x = 45,000$. Solve for x to find $x = 16,000$.

3. (C)

Difficulty: E

Category: Statistics-Averages (Mean)

Strategy: Understand how to read a bar graph. Find the total number of courses taken by all 290 sophomores. Then, use the average formula to find the average.

Solution: Use the bar graph to calculate the total number of courses taken by all 290 students, which is $68(4) + 74(5) + 86(6) + 42(7) + 20(8) = 1612$ courses.

Use the average formula to find the average number of courses taken per sophomore:

(1612 courses)/(290 sophomores) ≈ 5.6 courses/sophomore.

4. (C)

Difficulty: M

Category: Statistics-Averages (Mean)

Strategy: Calculate Gina's average using the average formula. Then, either plug in answers or use the average formula to find the sum of wildflower lengths that Wyatt would need. Use this information to calculate the value asked for in the problem.

Solution: Gina's average flower length = $\dfrac{8.7 + 5.6 + 7.4 + 8.3 + 10.5}{5} = 8.1$ cm. Thus, Wyatt's average flower length should be 9.1 cm. Try plugging in the answer choices for x or use the average formula to find x:

$$\frac{12.3 + 15.2 + 5.4 + x + 4.4}{5} = 9.1 \rightarrow \frac{37.3 + x}{5} = 9.1$$

Multiply by 5 on both sides to get $37.3 + x = 45.5$. Solve for x to find $x = 8.2$ cm.

5. (A)

Difficulty: M

Category: Statistics-Averages (Mean)

Strategy: Use the average formula to write expressions for a and b in terms of p. Then, use the average formula to express the average of a and b in terms of p. Choose a number for p if needed.

Solution: Use the average formula to write expressions for a and b in terms of p:

$$a = \frac{11+p}{2} \text{ and } b = \frac{5+3p}{2}$$

The average of a and b must be their sum divided by two:

$$\frac{a+b}{2} = \frac{\frac{11+p}{2} + \frac{5+3p}{2}}{2} = \frac{\frac{16+4p}{2}}{2} = \frac{8+2p}{2} = 4+p$$

If needed, choose a number for p, such as $p = 5$, and solve the problems step by step. Your final answer should be 9. Plug in 5 into the answer choices, and you will find only choice A yields the correct solution.

6. (D)

Difficulty: M

Category: Statistics-Averages (Mean)

Strategy: Use the average formula to express the average temperature over the two weeks in terms of the sum of x and y. Rearrange the equation to find the sum.

Solution: Use the average formula to set up an equation for the average temperature for the two weeks:

$(34 + 32 + 33 + 37 + 28 + x + 30 + 37 + y + 28 + 34 + 39 + 37 + 32)/14 = 34$. Simplify this equation to $\frac{401+x+y}{14} = 34$. Multiply both sides by 14 to get $401 + x + y = 476$, which yields $x + y = 75$.

7. (C)

Difficulty: M

Category: Statistics-Averages (Mean)

Strategy: Use reasoning and process of elimination. Alternatively, use the average formula to express the mean age of the 12 people in terms of m and solve for m.

Solution: Use reasoning to deduce the correct answer:

It's not A since there are more people in the group joining than the club currently, so the new mean couldn't be exactly in the middle of 20 and 30.

It's not B since if m was less than 20, because the joining group has more people than the club currently, the new mean would be less than 25, the midway point of 20 and 30.

It's not D because then their new members brought down the total age. Their average age could not be higher than the original average.

Alternatively, use the average formula to express the average age of the new joggers:

t = total age of 7 new joggers. Thus, $\frac{t}{7} = m \rightarrow t = 7m$.

Total age of first 5 joggers = $30 \cdot 5 = 150$.

Thus, the average age of the 12 joggers is $\frac{150+7m}{12} = 25$. Multiply by 12 on both sides to find $150 + 7m = 300$. Solve for m to find $m \approx 21.4$ years.

8. (A)

Category: Statistics-Averages (Mean)

Difficulty: H

Strategy: Find the sum of all test scores in Ms. O'Donnell's class. Find an expression for the sum of all test scores in Mr. Larch's class in terms of s, the number of students in his class. Then, use the average formula to write an equation for the average of students in both classes in terms of s. Solve for s. Alternatively, work backwards by plugging in the answer choices into the problem.

Solution: First, solve for o, the sum of test scores in Ms. O'Donnell's class:

$$\frac{o}{15} = 97 \rightarrow o = 1455$$

Next, find an expression for l, the sum of test scores in Mr. Larch's class, in terms of s, the number of students in his class:

$$\frac{l}{s} = 70 \rightarrow l = 70s$$

Write an equation for the average of both classes in terms of s (note that the total number of students = $15 + s$ and the total sum of test scores = $1455 + 70s$):

$\frac{1455+70s}{15+s} = 85$. Multiply both sides by $15 + s$ to get the equation

$1455 + 70s = 1275 + 85s$. Combine like terms to get $180 = 15s$. Solve for s to find $s = 12$.

Problem Solving & Data Analysis – Mean, Mode, and Range – Pages 359-361

1. (B)
Difficulty: E
Category: Statistics – Median, Mode, and Range
Strategy: Know the definition of a median. Know how to interpret a frequency table.
Solution: There were 87 customers studied. If all 87 drivers are organized in terms of their number of accidents by ascending value, the median will be the 44th number. The table tells us that there are 7 drivers with 0 accidents, and there are another 22 with 1 accident, which means the 29 drivers with the least amount of accidents had one accident or less. There are 34 drivers who had two accidents, which means that the median value must fall in this range, since the 30th-63rd driver when arranged by ascending number of accidents will all have 2 accidents in their 10-year record. Therefore, the median of the data set must be 2.

2. (C)
Difficulty: E
Category: Statistics – Median, Mode, and Range
Strategy: Know the definition of range. Sort the health expenditures from smallest to largest.
Solution: The range of a data set is the difference between the largest and smallest values in the data set. According to the table, the largest health expenditure per capita is for the United States, which is $9,892. The smallest health expenditure per capita is for Denmark, at $5,205. The range is the difference in these values = $9892 – $5205 = $4687.

3. (B)
Difficulty: E
Category: Statistics – Median, Mode, and Range
Strategy: Know the definition of a median. Use the data in the table to find the range of possible values for the median.
Solution: There were 500 exiting shoppers surveyed at Grocery Store B. If all 500 item totals are listed by ascending value, the median will be the average of the 250th and 251st totals. The table lists 140 numbers in the smallest range of values (1-9). There are 165 items in the second range of values (10-19). Since 140+165 > 251 and 250, then the 250th and 251st terms must both be in the 10-19 range. Therefore, their average, the median of this dataset, must be between 10 and 19 as well. The only answer choice in the range of 10-19 is 13.

4. (A)
Difficulty: E
Category: Statistics – Median, Mode, and Range
Strategy: Know the definition of a median. Know how to interpret a frequency table.
Solution: To find the median, find the middle data value when all data values are in ascending order. Since there are 37 data values, the median must be the 19th data value.
2 + 5 + 8 + 3 + 1 = 19, so the 19th data value is 7 turnovers. There is only one game that had 7 turnovers.

5. (A)
Difficulty: E
Category: Statistics – Median, Mode, and Range
Strategy: Know the definition of range. Find the range for percent voter turnout and the range for percent voting to remain in UK. Compare these ranges.
Solution: The range of a data set is the difference between the largest and smallest values in the data set. The highest voter turnout was for the oldest age group, at 78%. The lowest voter turnout was for the youngest age group, 48%. The range for voter turnout was 78% – 48% = 30%. Next, calculate the range of percent voting to remain in the EU for the age groups listed. The highest percent voting to remain in the EU was for the 18-24-year-olds, where 73% voted to remain. The lowest percent voting to remain in the EU was for the oldest age group, where 40% voted to remain. The range is the difference = 73% - 40% = 33%. This range is slightly larger than the range of voter turnouts.

6. (D)
Difficulty: M
Category: Statistics – Median, Mode, and Range
Strategy: Know the definition of median, mode, standard deviation, and range.
Solution: If the number 5 is added to the original data set, the minimum value will decrease from 24 to 5, which drops the minimum value by 19. Since the maximum value is unchanged, the range, which is the difference in maximum and median values, must widen by 19.

7. (C)
Difficulty: M
Category: Statistics – Median, Mode, and Range
Strategy: Know the definition of mean and median. Find the mean and median for set A. Next, construct set B and find its mean and median.
Solution: To find the median of set A, find the middle value of the set, which is already listed by ascending value. The median of set A should be its 6th element, which is 12. The mean, or average of set A = (2 + 5 + 6 + 7 + 9 + 12 + 13 + 15 + 17 + 20 + 23) / 11 ≈ 11.7.

Next, construct set B by taking the fourth element of set A, 7, and multiply it by 3. The resulting 21 is placed in its appropriate spot among the ordered numbers in new set B: {2, 5, 6, 7, 9, 12, 13, 15, 17, 20, 21, 23}.

The two middle values are 12 and 13, so the median is found by taking their average: (12 + 13) / 2 = 12.5. The median increased from set A to set B.

Now, find the mean, or average of set B, which is (2 + 5 + 6 + 7 + 9 + 12 + 13 + 15 + 17 + 20 + 21+ 23) / 12 = 12.5. The mean has also increased. Note that any number added to the sum will cause the mean to increase if the number is greater than the mean for the set. In this question, you just need to know if the mean goes up, down, or stays the same, so the exact calculation of mean for Set B is not necessary.

8. (D)

Difficulty: M

Category: Statistics – Median, Mode, and Range

Strategy: Know how to interpret a frequency table. Know the definition of mode, mean, and median. Find each for the dataset.

Solution: The mode is the most common weight among the competitors. The weight with the highest frequency count was 125 pounds (36 competitors had this weight, more than for any other weight in the table), so it is the mode. There were 100 competitors weighed. Therefore, if all competitors are organized by ascending weight, the median will be the average of the 50th and 51st weights. The table shows there is one person who weighs 116, two who weigh 117, two who weigh 118, three who weigh 119, none who weigh 120, 5 who weigh 121, 8 who weigh 122, and 12 who weight 123. A total of 33 competitors weigh 123 or less. The median must still be higher. There are 31 competitors who weigh 124. This means that the 34th - 64th competitor when arranged by ascending weight weigh 124 pounds. The 50th and 51st competitor both fall in this range, so the median must be 124. Thus, the median is less than the mode. To calculate the mean (average), first find the total weight of all the competitors =

$116 \cdot 1 + 117 \cdot 2 + 118 \cdot 2 + 119 \cdot 3 + 120 \cdot 0 + 121 \cdot 5 + 122 \cdot 8 +$

$123 \cdot 12 + 124 \cdot 31 + 125 \cdot 36 = 12344$. There were 100 competitors, so divide this number by 100 to get the average weight = 123.44. This number is less than the median, which is less than the mode.

9. (A)

Category: Statistics – Median, Mode, and Range

Difficulty: H

Strategy: Know how to interpret a box plot and what data it gives. Know the definition of a median, mean, and standard deviation. Work through each choice one by one.

Solution: The middle line in the box of a box and whisker plot represents the median value. The ends of the box represent the 25th and 75th quartiles. The ends of the plot represent the lowest and highest points in the dataset. While a box and whisker plot is useful for calculating range and median, it gives no definitive data about the mean.

I is true because Set B has the midline furthest to the left indicating the lowest median.

II is tempting but is not necessarily true. Remember, a box and whisker plot gives no information about the mean, and standard deviation measures deviation from the mean, not deviation from the median. Here is a counter-example that shows B can potentially have a lower standard deviation. Let Set B = {0, 6, 7, 7, 8, 8, 15, 15, 15, 24}. Let Set A = {0, 9, 12, 15, 24}. Both sets have the same range, 75th percentile, and their box and whisker plots roughly match the images when placed side by side (namely set B has a much larger and lower interquartile range). The mean of set B = 10.5. Its standard deviation is approximately 6.7. Meanwhile, the mean of set A = 12, and its standard deviation is 8.8.

III is not necessarily true as box and whisker plots give no definitive information about the mean. Here is a counterexample which shows they do not necessarily have the same mean: Let Set A = {0, 2, 4, 6, 8}, which has a mean of 4. Let Set C = {0, 3, 3.5, 3.5, 4, 4.5, 4.5, 8, 8}, which has a mean of about 4.3.

10. (D)

Difficulty: H

Category: Statistics – Median, Mode, and Range

Strategy: Know the definition of mean, median, mode, and range. Find each value before and after the 203g weight is thrown away. Determine which value changes the most.

Solution: Find the mean mass of the original data set: (131 + 133 + 140 + 140 + 141 + 148 + 149 + 150 + 155 + 156 + 167 + 169 + 175 + 177 + 183 + 203) / 16 = 157.3125g

The mean mass after the 203g yam is thrown out is (131 + 133 + 140 + 140 + 141 + 148 + 149 + 150 + 155 + 156 + 167 + 169 + 175 + 177 + 183) / 15 ≈ 154.27g. The difference in the mean after the yam is thrown out is about

3.045g. The median of the original data set is (150 + 155)/2 = 152.5g. The median after the 203g yam is thrown out is 150g. The difference in medians is 2.5g. The mode in both cases will remain unchanged (140g). The difference in modes is 0g. The range in the original data set is 203 – 131 = 72g. After the 203g yam is thrown out, the range becomes 183 – 131 = 52g. The change in range is 72 – 52 = 20g. The range changed the most overall.

11. (A)

Difficulty: H

Category: Statistics – Median, Mode, and Range

Strategy: Know the definition of mean and median. Know that a single outlier has a larger impact on a mean than it does on a median. Alternatively, find a range of possible values for the median. Then, find a range of possible mean values and compare.

Solution: The median value must be somewhere between $300,000 and $600,000, since the middle home value would end up falling in that range if home values were arranged from lowest to highest.

The minimum mean home value for the 81 people can be determined by assuming the 20 people with home values in the $0-$299,999 range all have a home value of $0 and by assuming the 60 people with home values in the $300,000-$600,000 range all have a home value at the low end of the range, $300,000. The minimum home value of all 81 homes would be $\frac{0 \cdot 20 + 300000 \cdot 60 + 60000000}{81} \approx$ $962,963. Since the minimum home value is already larger than the maximum median home value (i.e. 962,963 > 600,000), then the median home value must be lower than the mean home value for the 80 homeowners.

12. (A)

Difficulty: H

Category: Statistics – Median, Mode, and Range

Strategy: Know the definition of mean, median, mode, and range. Use reasoning to determine which answer will change most. Alternatively, calculate mean, median, mode, and range for the original data set and the new one, and find which value changes the most.

Solution: The original mean is (40 + 45 + 50 + 50 + 60 + 65 + 70 + 70 + 75 + 75 + 80 + 80 + 80 + 85 + 90 + 90 + 95 + 100 + 100 + 105) / 20 = 75.25%. The original median is (75 + 80) / 2 = 77.5%. The original mode is 80%, and the range is 105% – 40% = 65%. Removing one score of 75%

- will have no impact on the range, since the largest and smallest values will be unchanged.

- will have no impact on the mode, since the mode was 80% and no score of 80% was removed.

- will change the median from 77.5% to 80%, a change of 2.5%.

- will change the mean less than the median, since the mean is already 2.5% away from 75% and a score of 75% is removed.

Problem Solving & Data Analysis – Probability – Pages 363-364

1. (B)
Difficulty: E
Category: Probability
Strategy: Find the size of the sample space, the group that you are selecting from. Find the number of ways a certain event occurs within that sample space. Divide the numbers to determine the probability of the event.
Solution: The probability will be equal to the number of First Class passengers that died divided by the number of First Class passengers (the sample space). There were 325 first class passengers on the Titanic. Of those, 123 died. Therefore, the probability that a randomly selected first class passenger died is $\frac{123}{325} \approx .38$.

2. (D)
Difficulty: E
Category: Probability
Strategy: Find the size of the sample space, the group that you are selecting from. Find the number of ways a certain event occurs within that sample space. Divide the numbers to determine the probability of the event.
Solution: The probability will be equal to the number of third-class passenger survivors divided by the number of survivors (the sample space). There were 498 surviving passengers on the Titanic. Of those, only 178 were third class passengers. Therefore, the probability that a surviving passenger was in third class is $\frac{178}{498}$.

3. (C)
Difficulty: E
Category: Probability
Strategy: Find the size of the sample space, the group that you are selecting from. Find the number of ways a certain event occurs within that sample space. Divide the numbers to determine the probability of the event.
Solution: The probability will be equal to the number of unwanted emails that were found in the spam folder divided by the number of unwanted emails (the sample space). There are 1220 unwanted emails that Anna received this year. Of those, 1100 were moved to the spam folder. Therefore, the probability that an unwanted email was moved to the spam folder is $\frac{1100}{1220}$.

4. (D)
Difficulty: E
Category: Probability
Strategy: Find the size of the sample space, the group that you are selecting from. Find the number of ways a certain event occurs within that sample space. Divide the numbers to determine the probability of the event.
Solution: The probability will be equal to the number of work emails that were found in the spam folder divided by the number of work emails (the sample space). There are 5306 total work emails that Anna received this year. Of those, only 25 were moved to the spam folder. Therefore, the probability that an unwanted email was moved to the spam folder is $\frac{25}{5306}$.

5. (D)
Difficulty: M
Category: Probability
Strategy: Find the size of the sample space, the group that you are selecting from. Find the number of ways a certain event occurs within that sample space. Divide the numbers to determine the probability of the event.
Solution: If the spam filter acted correctly, then it either filed work email into the inbox OR it filed unwanted email into the spam folder. There are 5281 work emails that were kept in the inbox and 1100 unwanted emails that were moved to the spam folder. Therefore, the spam filter acted correctly a total of 5281 + 1100 = 6381 times. There were 6526 total emails that Anna received this year, so the probability that the spam filter acted correctly is $\frac{6381}{6526}$.

6. (B)
Difficulty: M
Category: Probability
Strategy: Find the size of the sample space, the group that you are selecting from. Find the number of ways a certain event occurs within that sample space. Divide the numbers to determine the probability of the event. If needed, the problem can be numerically evaluated by choosing a number for m.
Solution: The probability will be equal to the number of minerals divided by the total number of items in the collection (the sum of her rocks and minerals). There are m minerals and $14 + m$ items in her collection. Therefore, the probability that she will pick a mineral from the collection is $\frac{m}{14 + m}$.

7. (B)
Difficulty: M
Category: Probability
Strategy: Use the table to find the probability that a surveyed community college student was employed. Divide this value by 4. Write an expression for the probability that a state university student surveyed was employed in terms of the variable a. Set the expression equal to the numerical probability that he/she is employed. Solve for a. Alternatively, plug in the answer choices for a and use process of elimination.
Solution: The probability that a surveyed community college student was employed is equal to the number of community college students that were employed over the number of community college students surveyed = 320/400 = 0.8. If this value is four times the probability that a surveyed state university student was employed, then the probability that a surveyed state university student was employed is 0.8/4 = 0.2. If a state university student that were surveyed were employed, then the probability that state university student was employed was $a/250$. Thus, $a/250 = 0.2$. Multiply both sides by 250 to find $a = 50$.

8. (B)

Difficulty: M

Category: Probability

Strategy: Find 26% of the total number of survey participants. Subtract the number of them that were community college students to find the number that were state university students. Alternatively, plug in the answer choices for *b* and use process of elimination.

Solution: There were a total of 650 students surveyed. If 26% of them reported being not employed, then $.26 \cdot 650 = 169$ students surveyed reported not being employed. According to the table, 80 of those students were from the community college. Therefore $169 - 80 = 89$ of the non-employed students must have come from Kara's state university.

Problem Solving & Data Analysis – Data Relationships – Pages 366-371

1. (D)

Difficulty: E

Category: Data Relationships

Strategy: Use process of elimination as you review each answer choice. If any part of the answer is incorrect, it can be eliminated.

Solution: Answer choice A is incorrect because the number of new ER patients drops between Wednesday and Thursday. Answer choice B is incorrect because the lowest number of admitted patients was on Sunday, not Thursday. Answer choice C is incorrect because the greatest number of patients were admitted on Saturday, not Friday. Only answer choice D is correct according to the table.

2. (C)

Difficulty: E

Category: Data Relationships

Strategy: Use process of elimination as you review each answer choice. Calculate the increase in patients admitted for the pairs of days listed and then compare to select the largest increase.

Solution: By inspection, one will probably notice that the increase between Thursday and Friday is the greatest, but each increase can also be calculated. The increase in admitted patients between Tuesday and Wednesday is $26 - 23 = 3$ patients. There is a decrease in patients between Wednesday and Thursday, so B can be eliminated. Between Thursday and Friday, the increase is $44 - 19 = 25$ patients. Between Friday and Saturday, the increase in admitted patients is $57 - 44 = 13$ patients. The largest increase was between Thursday and Friday.

3. (A)

Difficulty: E

Category: Data Relationships

Strategy: Use process of elimination. Find the number of packages that will remain in the warehouse by Tuesday to eliminate two of the answers. To do this, you will need to subtract the number of deliveries and add the number of packages received Do this one more time for Wednesday, and eliminate one more answer choice to find the answer.

Solution: The company starts with 2000 packages at the beginning of the day on Tuesday. After delivering 1000 packages, it is down to 1000, but the company receives 500, so the total number of packages in the warehouse by the end of Tuesday should be 1500. Eliminate graphs B and D, since they show 2500 as the total on Tuesday. On Wednesday, the company delivers 1200 packages, which brings the total packages down from 1500 to 300, but 200 packages are added, leaving the total in the warehouse at 500 for the end of the day on Wednesday. Of the remaining options, only graph A shows this total for Wednesday

4. (C)

Difficulty: E

Category: Data Relationships

Strategy: Find the total profit based on the units used in the unlabeled graph. Then, divide the actual profit by this number to determine the units used for the *y*-axis.

Solution: Total profit from unlabeled graph $= 6.5 + 6 + 3.5 + 9 = 24$. The actual profit is \$24,000. \$24,000/24 = \$1000. Thus, the units on the *y*-axis should indicate profit in thousands of dollars.

5. (D)
Difficulty: E
Category: Data Relationships
Strategy: Know the definition of a negative correlation. Know the definition of a strong correlation. Use process of elimination.
Solution: Negative correlation means the best fit line has a negative slope. Eliminate answers B and C, which have best fit lines with slopes that are either zero or positive. A strong correlation occurs when data points are scattered close to the best fit regression line. Of the remaining options, graph D shows the strongest correlation.

6. (A)
Difficulty: E
Category: Data Relationships
Strategy: Use the graph to find the month that had an average temperature of 40°F and determine the actual kilowatt hour usage. Find the point on the line of best fit where average temperature is 40°F and note the predicted kilowatt hour usage. Find the difference.
Solution: The actual kilowatt hours used for the month that has an average temperature of 40°F is 2000. The line of best fit predicts approximately 1500 kilowatt hours for this average monthly temperature. The difference between these two values, the residual, is $2000 - 1500 = 500$.

7. (B)
Difficulty: E
Category: Data Relationships
Strategy: Since the slope of the graph is positive for all of the intervals, find the part with the steepest slope to find where the price increased the most. Alternatively, estimate the increases in milk price for each pair of months listed.
Solution: The steepest part of the graph is between April and May, where the price increases by just over 10 cents in one month. All other increases are below 10 cents.

8. (D)
Difficulty: M
Category: Data Relationships
Strategy: Know the definition of a median. Arrange the prices from smallest to largest to determine the median.
Solution: Make a list of the prices in ascending order and find the average of the middle two prices, since there are 8 months of prices shown:
200, 218, 225, **229, 236,** 241, 247, 251
The average of the two middle prices is 232.5. The median can also be determined directly from the graph by crossing out the lowest and highest values and working inward.

9. (C)
Difficulty: M
Category: Data Relationships
Strategy: Use the graph to find the price of milk in March. Write a percent equation to determine the February price or plug in answers and work backward through the problem.
Solution: The price in March is about 218 cents. If x = price of the milk in February, then $218 = x + 0.029x$. Combine like terms to find $218 = 1.029x$. Solve for x to find $x \approx 212$ cents.

10. (C)
Difficulty: M
Category: Data Relationships
Strategy: Use process of elimination and plug in the values from the answer choices into the equation. Use the last data point with the displacement of 1 meter and plug in the respective values of E and d into the function to find only one of the possible answer choices could work.
Solution: Plug in some of the data points into the equation to determine which combination of constants is correct. Plug in the last data point (where $d = 1.00$ and $E = 50J$), to get the equation $50 = a(1.00)^b$. Simplify to find $50 = a$. Only answer choice C lists 50 as a value for a.

11. (C)
Difficulty: M
Category: Data Relationships
Strategy: Set up a percent equation to find the total number of audience members. Calculate the percent of audience members that are 30 or younger. Then, calculate this percentage of the total audience members.
Solution: Let x = total number of audience members. The graph shows 5% of the total are 66 or older, so $.05x = 6$. Solve to find $x = 120$ audience members.

Add together the 0-17 and 18-30 brackets to find that 58% of the total audience was 30 or younger. Find 58% of the total audience members to find the number that were 30 or younger: $.58 \cdot 120 = 69.6$, which is closest to 70.

12. (B)
Difficulty: M
Category: Data Relationships
Strategy: Sketch an approximate line of best fit through the points and calculate the slope. Know how to calculate a slope between two points.
Solution: The points have a very strong linear relationship, but it still may be worthwhile to sketch a line of best fit between the points of the scatterplot.

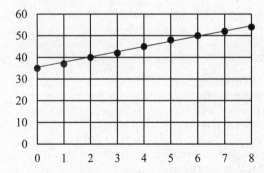

The line sketched above approximately connects the points (0, 35) and (8, 54). The slope of the line between any two points is $\frac{y_2 - y_1}{x_2 - x_1}$.

This means that the slope of the estimated line of best fit $\approx \frac{54-35}{8-0} = \frac{19}{8} = 2.375$. This value is closest to answer choice B.

13. (C)

Difficulty: M

Category: Data Relationships

Strategy: Use process of elimination. Plot out points from the data table to see how a graph will look.

Solution: By examining the table, A can be eliminated since load factor and stall speeds both increase with steeper angles. Choice B is not true since the increases get larger and larger as angles get steeper. Examine the table to see that most of the data points are close in value, but not all of them are. Roughly sketch out a coordinate plane and plot points and notice the shape resembles an exponential function. Alternatively, when values go from small and close together and then make a sudden large increase, the graph will resemble an exponential function.

14. (B)

Difficulty: M

Category: Data Relationships

Strategy: Recognize key words that reveal the type of function being described. Relate how different aspects of the situation pertain to the graph. Use process of elimination.

Solution: Look carefully to see "*increase by a set amount,*" which indicates a linear function. Note that to rent the boat, there is an initial fee that is charged before any time has elapsed for the rental. This describes the starting cost, or the y-intercept. The longer the boat is rented, the higher the price. Consequently, a line connecting hourly costs would go up and to the right: a positive slope. Because the rental price increases uniformly (by a set amount), eliminate II, which eliminates choices A, C, and D.

15. (C)

Difficulty: M

Category: Data Relationships

Strategy: Draw an approximate line of best fit through the data points. Find the slope and y-intercept. Then, find the equation that contains these approximate values.

Solution: By inspection, it appears that the y-intercept is around 68,500, so D cannot be the correct answer because it does not have the correct y-intercept. Using any two points on the approximate line, for example (8, 78000) and (2, 70000), calculate the slope to be approximately $8000/6 \approx 1300$, which is closest to the slope in C.

16. (B)

Difficulty: H

Category: Data Relationships

Strategy: Identify the model as quadratic (either by inspection or drawing on the paper), then determine which equation is best based on the coefficients. Use process of elimination.

Solution: By inspection, it appears that the best type of curve to model this data is a parabola that opens downward and has a y-intercept somewhere below 102.

- Eliminate A because the leading coefficient is positive, which would indicate an upward opening parabola.

- Eliminate C because the x-coordinate of the vertex, which can be found using $x = \dfrac{-b}{2a}$ where $b = -4.9807$ and $a = -0.5092$, must be negative. Clearly, the x coordinate of the vertex is positive.

- Eliminate D because the y-intercept of that equation's curve would be (0, 106.703), which is higher than the upper bound on the y-intercept.

17. D

Difficulty: H

Category: Data relationships

Strategy: Use process of elimination. Pay attention to the scale on the y-axis. Determine the increase in screws produced for the years listed. Determine the percent increase in screw output for each year by using the percent change formula.

Solution: According to the graph, there are only two years when screw output increased: the years between year 0-1 and year 2-3. The greatest absolute increase in the number of screws produced per year was $100,000,000 - 10,000,000 = 90,000,000$ between years 2 and 3 (The absolute increase in output of screws between years 0 and 1 was 9,990,000). The greatest percent increase was between years 0 and 1, from 10,000 to 10,000,000. The percent increase in output was $\dfrac{10,000,000 - 10,000}{10,000} \cdot 100\% = 99,900\%$. For the year between 2 and 3 the percent increase was lower at $\dfrac{100,000,000 - 10,000,000}{10,000,000} \cdot 100\% = 900\%$.

18. C

Difficulty: H

Category: Data relationships

Strategy: Find the equation of the horizontal line on the graph. Test the answers and use process of elimination. Plug in the values for a and b into the exponential equation to see which combination results in the equation of the line.

Solution: The equation of the line shown in the graph is $y = 12$. Answer choice A results in the exponential model $y = 3 \cdot 4^x$, which is not the equation of the line. Answer choice B results in the model $y = 4 \cdot 3^x$, which is not the equation of a line. Answer choice C results in $y = 12 \cdot 1^x$. Since 1^x is always equal to 1, then the equation can be simplified to just $y = 12$, the equation of the line in the graph.

Problem Solving & Data Analysis – Data Collection and Conclusions – Pages 373-375

1. (D)
Difficulty: E
Category: Data Collection and Conclusions
Strategy: Know that correlation does not imply causation. Understand that a random sample is only representative of the population from which the sample is drawn.
Solution: A sample is meant to be representative of a larger population. Because only a random sample of women participated in this study, any conclusion drawn can only apply to the population of women from which the sample was drawn. Since no men were sampled, any conclusion drawn in this experiment cannot apply necessarily to men. Also, any experiment can only show a possible relationship, correlation, or association between variables, but causation can never be inferred from a study. Therefore, we can say there is a correlation between amount of exercise and depression in women, but we cannot say that one causes the other. D draws the only valid conclusion that can be supported from the data.

2. (C)
Difficulty: E
Category: Data Collection and Conclusions
Strategy: Know the definition of margin of error.
Solution: The mean lifespan for the wild chimpanzees in the study was 42 years. Since the margin of error was 2.4 years, the true average lifespan for the population of chimpanzees in the wild can be anywhere between 42 ± 2.4 years. Hence, the true average lifespan of a chimpanzee in the wild is anywhere between $42 - 2.4 = 39.6$ years and $42 + 2.4 = 44.4$ years.

3. (C)
Difficulty: E
Category: Data Collection and Conclusions
Strategy: Know that a good sample (one that can be generalized for a population) is a random sample that is selected from all members of the population the sample is meant to represent.
Solution: Survey participants were selected from adults attending a PTA meeting. Since the people attending the meeting are teachers and parents of students, they are not a representative sample of the entire city. If the purpose of the study is to find if all residents approve of the proposal, it would be more appropriate to survey a random sample of all city residents, not those in a particular interest group. By only surveying the PTA, the results are likely biased.

4. (A)
Difficulty: E
Category: Data Collection and Conclusions
Strategy: Know that a good sample (one that can be generalized for a population) is a random sample that is selected from only members of the population the sample is meant to represent.
Solution: Study I selected participants who volunteered to participate. Volunteering introduces bias into any sample, since the true distribution of amounts of sleep in adults is not necessarily the same as that for those who would volunteer for a study on sleep (for example, a person may be more likely to volunteer if he has problems sleeping and thus has lower levels of sleep). Thus, Study I cannot be generalized to all adults living in NJ that month. Study II selected random residents from the state of New Jersey, but no age limit is specified; thus, children may have been interviewed as well. A sample that may include children will not be representative of the population of New Jersey adults. Only Study III chose random adult participants living in New Jersey, so only Study III could be a representative sample that may be generalized to all adults living in New Jersey in May 2017.

5. (D)
Difficulty: E
Category: Data collection and Conclusions
Strategy: Know the definition of margin of error.
Solution: The mean number of books checked out per patron is 3.5 books. Since the margin of error was 1.5 books, the actual average number of books checked out per patron is likely to be between 3.5 ± 1.5 books, which is between 2 and 5 books. This is an estimate for the average of all patrons, but it does not mean that every patron has this many book checked out from the library.

6. (B)
Difficulty: E
Category: Data collection and Conclusions
Strategy: Know that a good sample (one that can be generalized for a population) is a random sample that is selected from all members of the population the sample is meant to represent.
Solution: The random sample was a random sample of diners at a specific restaurant. Therefore, the results of the survey can be applied to the population of diners who attend the specific restaurant, but cannot be applied to any larger group.

7. (C)
Difficulty: M
Category: Data Collection and Conclusions
Strategy: Know the definition of margin of error. Use the linear model to find the predicted value of the extra liquid expelled per shake. Find 12% of this value. Determine the range of possible values for the extra liquid expelled per shake.
Solution: The slope of the linear equation lists how much y, the total volume of liquid expelled, increases as x, the number of shakes, increases by one. Thus, the model predicts that the extra liquid expelled per shake is 0.4. The margin of error is 12%, and 12% of 0.4 is $.12 \cdot (0.4) = 0.048$. Thus, the true value of the volume of extra liquid expelled per shake is anywhere between $0.4 - 0.048 = 0.352$ and $0.4 + 0.048 = 0.448$. The only value within this range is 0.444.

8. (A)

Difficulty: M

Category: Data Collection and Conclusions

Strategy: Know that a good sample (one that can be generalized for a population) is a random sample that is selected from only members of the population the sample is meant to represent.

Solution: A sample is meant to be representative of a larger population. The survey was taken at a high school baseball game, which is not truly representative of the population of interest in the study, residents of the local area. Since people attending a baseball game are more likely to support the measure, some bias may have been introduced into the sample by surveying at this location.

9. (B)

Difficulty: H

Category: Data Collection and Conclusions

Strategy: Know the definition of margin of error. Understand how to find the percent of a number.

Solution: If 250 students were polled and 27% voted "for" then $.27 \cdot 250 \approx 68$ students voted for the installation. The 73% that voted "against" results in $.73 \cdot 250 \approx 183$ student who voted against the pool. The margin of error was 4%, thus the true percentage of students that would vote "against" could be anywhere between 73% - 4% = 69% and 73% + 4% = 77%. The lowest possible number of "against" votes is then $.69 \cdot 250 \approx 173$. Similarly, the true percentage of students that would vote "for" could be anywhere between 27% - 4% = 23% and 27% + 4% = 31%. The highest possible number of "for" votes is thus $.31 \cdot 250 \approx 78$.

10. (A)

Difficulty: M

Category: Data Collection and Conclusions

Strategy: Know that a good sample (one that can be generalized for a population) is a random sample that is selected from only members of the population the sample is meant to represent.

Solution: Selecting poll participants from those who visit a local website is not a true random sampling of the town, the population of interest.

Heart of Algebra – Section Quiz – Pages 378-382

1. (B)
Difficulty: E
Category: Algebraic Equations & Inequalities
Strategy: Solve the equation for x. Then, plug in the solution to the answer choices. Use process of elimination.
Solution: Subtract 13 from both sides to get $3x = -9$. Divide by 3 on both sides to find $x = -3$. This is the same solution to the equation in answer choice B: $-9 = 3(-3)$.

2. (D)
Difficulty: E
Category: Absolute Value
Strategy: Isolate the absolute value on one side and solve, or plug in the answers and use process of elimination.
Solution: Subtract 7 from both sides to get the following equation: $-2 = |2x - 4|$. An absolute value can never be negative, so there is no solution to this equation.

3. (D)
Difficulty: E
Category: Slope
Strategy: Perpendicular lines have slopes that are negative reciprocals of one another.
Solution: Since the slope of $\overline{AB}$ is 4 and line $\overline{CD}$ is perpendicular to $\overline{AB}$, the slope of $\overline{AB}$ must be $-1/4$.

4. (C)
Difficulty: E
Category: Graphs of Linear Equations
Strategy: Find the slope and y-intercept of the equation. Review each answer choice to see if it has the correct slope and y-intercept. Use process of elimination.
Solution: The line $y = 3x - 6$ has a slope of 3 and a y-intercept of (0, -6). A and B show the wrong y-intercept, so eliminate them. Choice D has a slope of 1 (up one, over one); only the line in C has the right slope and y-intercept.

5. (A)
Difficulty: E
Category: Creating Linear Models
Strategy: Determine the slope (rate of change) and h-intercept (starting value of h) of the linear model. Alternatively, choose a number for s and evaluate h.
Solution: The h-intercept of the linear model should be the height of the elevator at 0 seconds, which is 7 feet. Answers C and D can immediately be eliminated. The elevator goes up 12 feet in height for every 1 second, so the slope must be 12. Thus, A is correct.

6. (C)
Difficulty: E
Category: Algebraic Expressions
Strategy: Check each answer choice and use process of elimination. Expand each expression using the distributive property. Combine like terms to find the equivalent expression. Alternatively, choose a number for x and evaluate the expression for this value.
Solution: Go through the answers, distribute and simplify each answer choice. You will find only answer choice C yields the equivalent expression:
$(x+10)(x+2)+15 = x^2 + 2x + 10x + 20 + 15 = x^2 + 12x + 35$.

7. (A)
Difficulty: E
Category: Systems of Linear Equations
Strategy: Use elimination or substitution to solve the system. Then, subtract the variables.
Solution: Multiply the bottom equation by three, and add the two equations to each other to eliminate y:
$$\begin{aligned} x + 3y &= 7 \\ +12x - 3y &= 6 \\ \hline 13x &= 13 \end{aligned}$$
Solve for x to get $x = 1$. Plug this value into either of the original equations to solve for y: $1 + 3y = 7$. Solve for y to get $y = 2$. Thus, $x - y = 1 - 2 = -1$.

8. (C)
Difficulty: E/M
Category: Absolute Value
Strategy: Plug in numbers from different ranges in the answers and use process of elimination or solve the inequality using algebra.
Solution: Through plugging in values from each solution set in the answers, you should find that C is the solution. Try $x = 4$, which is only in the interval described in this answer choice, and plug it into the original inequality: $|6 - 2(4)| = 2 \le 8$. Any numbers unique to the other intervals listed will not work in the original inequality. Alternatively, solve using algebra: $-4 \le 6 - 2x \le 4$. Subtract 6 from all three sides to get $-10 \le -2x \le -2$. Divide by -2, remembering to flip the direction of the inequality signs to find $5 \ge x \ge 1$.

9. (D)
Difficulty: M
Category: Graphs of Linear Inequalities
Strategy: Check each answer to determine if it lies in the shaded region of the graph. Use process of elimination.
Solution: Only the point (1, 1) lies in the shaded region.

10. (B)
Difficulty: M
Category: Interpreting Linear Models
Strategy: Understand the meaning of slope and y-intercept in a linear model. Plug in the years given in the answer choices to see how much growth will occur in each case. Use process of elimination.
Solution: Check each answer choice one at a time:
The slope of the graph is 82/625. This means that for every 625 years, the height should increase 82 feet. Choice A is wrong since it underestimates the growth by a factor of 10. Answer choice B works, since $\dfrac{82ft}{625years} = \dfrac{820ft}{6250years}$.

11. (C)
Difficulty: M
Category: Algebraic Expressions
Strategy: Distribute the minus sign at the end of the expression. Combine like terms.
Solution: Distribute the minus sign to eliminate the parentheses:
$(x^3 + x^2y^2 + xy + x) - (2x^3 - x^2y^2 - xy + x + 5) = x^3 + x^2y^2 + xy + x - 2x^3 + x^2y^2 + xy - x - 5$. Next, carefully combine like terms to get $-x^3 + 2x^2y^2 + 2xy - 5$.

12. (9)
Difficulty: M
Category: Systems of Linear Equations
Strategy: Determine how many of each type of widget were made last month and this month. Then, set up equations for the total sales revenue for each month. Solve for the expression asked for in the problem directly.
Solution: Capacity can be expressed as $x + y = 1200$ where $x =$ number of advanced versions and $y =$ number of basic versions. Revenue can be expressed as $ax + by = R$ where $a =$ price of advanced versions and $b =$ price of basic version.
Last Month: $x = y = 600$
Last Month Revenue: $a600 + b600 = 5400$
This Month: $x = 2y$, so $2y + y = 1200$, and $y = 400$ and $x = 800$. This Month's Revenue is $a800 + b400 = 6000$.
All that is left is to solve the following system of equations: $600a + 600b = 5400$ and $800a + 400b = 6000$.
Divide the top equation by 600 to get $a + b = 9$. The problem asks for the value of this expression, so there is no need to solve for the individual variables further.

13. (D)
Difficulty: M
Category: Slope
Strategy: Find the slope of the parallel line. Know the relationships between the slopes of parallel lines. Plug in the point into the answers choices and use process of elimination.
Solution: The line described by the equation $y = 5x + 4$ has slope 5. Since parallel lines have equal slopes, the slope of line k must also be 5. Only answers C and D have equations with slope 5. Plug in the point into the two remaining equations to determine which lines contains the point $(-5, -3)$. The point is on the line in choice D: $-3 = 5(-5) + 22$.

14. (C)
Difficulty: M
Category: Creating Linear Models
Strategy: Find how much each batch of 12 bars is sold for, and then write an expression for the revenue made from selling b batches. Write an expression for the total cost to make b batches. Subtract the expressions to find an expression for profit (Profit = Revenue – Cost). Alternatively, choose a number for b and solve.
Solution: There are 12 bars in each batch, so a single batch of bars is sold for $(\$0.75)/(1 \text{ bar}) \cdot 12 \text{ bars/batch} = \$9/\text{batch}$. Thus, the total revenue made from selling b batches is $9b$. The total cost to make b batches is $29.78 + 3.25b$.
Thus, $P = 9b - (29.78 + 3.25b) = 5.75\ b - 29.78$.

15. (A)
Difficulty: M
Category: Algebraic Equations & Inequalities
Strategy: Use the distributive property to expand the left side of the equation and combine like terms. Set corresponding coefficients on either side of the equation equal to one another to solve for the variables.
Solution: Expand the left-hand side to get
$x^2 + 2x + 5x + 10 = x^2 + 7x + 10$. Since $x^2 + 7x + 10 = ax^2 + bx + c$, then $a = 1$, $b = 7$, and $c = 10$. Thus, $a + b + c = 1 + 7 + 10 = 18$.

16. (D)
Difficulty: M
Category: Interpreting Linear Models
Strategy: Understand what slope and y-intercept represent in the linear model.
Solution: The slope of the linear model is -275, which indicates that the height of the tram decreases by 275 meters as x (time in minutes) increases by 1.

17. (C)
Difficulty: M
Category: Absolute Value
Strategy: Know how to interpret a number line. Understand the relationship between absolute value and distance to find the inequality directly. Alternatively, plug in values from the solution set into the answer choices and use process of elimination.
Solution: The range between circles is 10 with midpoint at $x = 1$. Thus, all point in the solution are a distance less than 5 away from 1. The distance between x and 1 can be expressed as the absolute value of their difference, so $|x - 1| < 5$. Subtract 2 from both sides to get answer choice C.

18. (A)
Difficulty: M
Category: Graphs of Linear Equations
Strategy: Know that slope between any two points on a line remains constant. Use the formula for the slope between two points to find two different expressions for the slope in terms of p. Set them equal to each other and solve for p. For each solution, check that the slope is positive.
Solution: The slope of the line $m = \dfrac{p-6}{-2-2} = \dfrac{p-6}{-4}$ and
$m = \dfrac{6-11}{2+p} = \dfrac{-5}{2+p}$. Thus, $\dfrac{p-6}{-4} = \dfrac{-5}{2+p}$. Cross-multiply to get $20 = p^2 - 4p - 12$. Set the equation equal to zero to get $p^2 - 4p - 12 = 0$. Factor to find $(p - 8)(p + 4) = 0$, which has solutions $p = -4$ and $p = 8$. Find the slope in each case. If $p = 8$, then the slope is $(8 - 6)/-4 = -1/2 < 0$, so eliminate this option. If $p = -4$, then the slope is $(-4 - 6)/-4 = 10/4 = 5/2 > 0$. Thus, $p = -4$.

19. (B)
Difficulty: M
Category: Systems of Linear Equations
Strategy: Combine any like terms in both equations first. Then, solve the system using either the elimination or substitution method. Plug in the solutions for each variable into the final expression.
Solution: The equations can be simplified into $4x - 3y = 13$ and $x + 2y = 6$. Solve for x in terms of y in the second equation to find $x = 6 - 2y$. Substitute this expression in for x into the top equation: $4(6 - 2y) - 3y = 13$. Expand to get $24 - 8y - 3y = 13$. Combine like terms to get $-11y = -11$. Solve to find $y = 1$. Plug this value back into the earlier expression to solve for x directly: $x = 6 - 2(1) = 4$. Thus, $(x + y)^2 = (4 + 1)^2 = 25$.

20. (A)
Difficulty: M/H
Category: Interpreting Linear Models
Strategy: Convert the elevations to thousands of feet and find their difference. Multiply by the slope to find the difference in temperature between these elevations. Alternatively, find the temperature at each elevation and subtract the resulting values.
Solution: The elevation of Mt. Washington is 6.288 thousand feet, and the elevation of the beginning of the auto road is 1.527 thousand feet. The difference is 6.288 – 1.527 = 4.761 thousand feet. The change in temperature should be this value times the slope, –3.57, which is 4.761(–3.57) ≈ –17°F. Therefore, the temperature should drop about 17°F.

21. (B)
Difficulty: M
Category: Graphs of Linear Equations
Strategy: Find the slope and y-intercept of the line in the graph. Determine its equation in slope-intercept form. Rearrange the equation to match one of the answers. Alternatively, plug in points from the graph into the answer choices and use process of elimination.
Solution: The slope of the graph is –2 (down 2, right 1), and its y-intercept is (0, 3). Thus, the equation of the line $y = -2x + 3$. Rearrange this equation to get $y + 2x = 3$. Multiply by 2 on both sides to get $2y + 4x = 6$.

22. (A)
Difficulty: M
Category: Creating Linear Models
Strategy: Find expressions for the total revenue and cost in terms of w, number of widgets sold. Subtract the expressions to find an expression for profit (profit = revenue – cost), and write an inequality for total profit. Solve to find the range of possible values for w.
Solution: revenue = $6w$ and cost = $2w + 5000$
Thus profit = $6w – (2w + 5000) \geq 1000$. Rearrange to get $4w \geq 6000$. Divide by 4 to find $w \geq 1500$.

23. (A)
Difficulty: M/H
Category: Algebraic Equations & Inequalities
Strategy: Understand Order of Operations (PEMDAS). Simplify and solve for x. Alternatively, plug in the answer choices and use process of elimination.
Solution: Using PEMDAS, the left side of the equation can be simplified by evaluating what is in the parentheses first:
$3(2 + (-8))^2 + (5 - 3)^4 - 4x = 3(-6)^2 + (2)^4 - 4x$.
Evaluate any exponents next to get $3(36) + 16 - 4x = 128$. Evaluate any multiplication next to get $108 + 16 - 4x = 128$. Combine terms to get $124 - 4x = 128$. Solve for x to find $x = -1$.

24. (A)
Difficulty: M/H
Category: Slope
Strategy: Rearrange the equation given into slope-intercept form by solving for y. Determine the slope of the line. Use the formula to evaluate the slope between two points to find the slope for each pair of points.
Solution: To rearrange the linear equation given into slope-intercept form, multiply by –2 on both sides to eliminate any fractions: $2x = y - 3$, or $y = 2x + 3$. The slope of this line is 2. Apply the slope formula $m = \dfrac{y_2 - y_1}{x_2 - x_1}$ to each pair of points in the answers to see which has an equivalent slope. Answer choice A gives the correct slope since $(25 - 7)/(11 - 2) = 18/9 = 2$.

25. (C)
Difficulty: H
Category: Graphs of Linear Inequalities
Strategy: Sketch the graph of the inequality. Draw the boundary line first and shade below the line.
Solution: To sketch the inequality, draw the boundary line first. Since the inequality is for all y values below the line, shade the area below (or use a test point like (0,0) to determine which side to shade).

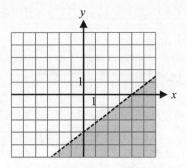

The shaded region goes through quadrants I, III, and IV.

Heart of Algebra – Algebraic Expressions – Page 384

1. (B)
Difficulty: E
Category: Algebraic Expressions
Strategy: Know the definition of a sum. Combine like terms together.
Solution: Add the expressions to find their sum:
$(2x^4 + 3x^3 + 4x + 12) + (2x^5 - 2x^3 - 4x - 8)$. Remove the parentheses since neither expression is being multiplied by anything other than 1. Combine like terms to get the solution:
$2x^5 + 2x^4 + 3x^3 - 2x^3 + 4x - 4x + 12 - 8 = 2x^5 + 2x^4 + x^3 + 4$.

2. (D)
Difficulty: E
Category: Algebraic Expressions
Strategy: Use the distributive property to expand the product. Combine all like terms. Alternatively, choose a number for x and evaluate the expression for this value.
Solution: Use the distributive property or FOIL to expand the product: $(4x + 5)(5x + 4) = 20x^2 + 16x + 25x + 20$. Combine like to terms to get $20x^2 + 41x + 20$. The problem can be solved by choosing a number for x as well.

3. (D)
Difficulty: E
Category: Algebraic Expressions
Strategy: Use the distributive property to expand the product at the beginning of the expression. Then, combine all like terms. Alternatively, choose a number for x and evaluate the expression for this value.
Solution: Use the distributive property to expand the product at the beginning of the expression:
$-3(u^3 - v^2) - 2u + 2v^2 - 7u^3 + 5u^2 = -3u^3 + 3v^2 - 2u + 2v^2 - 7u^3 + 5u^2$. There are four different types of terms. Combine any like terms to get the answer, which is $-10u^3 + 5u^2 + 5v^2 - 2u$.

4. (C)
Difficulty: E
Category: Algebraic Expressions
Strategy: Use the distributive property to expand the product at the end of the expression. Combine like terms. Alternatively, choose a number for x and evaluate the expression for this value.
Solution: Use the distributive property to expand the product at the end of the expression:
$(3x^2 - 6x) - 3x(x^2 - 2) = 3x^2 - 6x - 3x^3 + 6x$. Combine like to terms to get $-3x^3 + 3x^2$.

5. (A)
Difficulty: M
Category: Algebraic Expressions
Strategy: Use the distributive property to expand the product at the end of the expression. Combine like terms. Factor the expression or expand the answer choices. Alternatively, choose a number for x and evaluate the expression for this value.
Solution: Use the distributive property to expand the product at the end of the expression:
$-9x^2 + (-3x + 6)(-3x + 6) = -9x^2 + 9x^2 - 18x - 18x + 36$.
Combine like to terms to get $-36x + 36$.
The greatest common factor of this expression is 36. Factor it out to get the result $36(-x + 1)$.

6. (D)
Difficulty: M
Category: Algebraic Expressions
Strategy: Factor the expression to find the values of a and b. Substitute these values into the expression asked for.
Solution: Factor the quadratic first to find the values of a and b:
$x^2 - 3x - 10 = (x - 5)(x + 2) = (x - 5)(x - (-2))$.
Thus, $a = 5$ and $b = -2$. Substitute these values into the expression asked for: $2a - 3b = 2(5) - 3(-2) = 16$.

7. (D)
Difficulty: M
Category: Algebraic expressions
Strategy: Use the distributive property to expand the product. Combine all like terms. Alternatively, choose numbers for a and b and evaluate the expression.
Solution: Use the distributive property to expand the expression:
$(a + b)(a^2 - ab + b^2) = a^3 - a^2b + ab^2 + a^2b - ab^2 + b^3$. Combine like terms to simplify: $a^3 - a^2b + ab^2 + a^2b - ab^2 + b^3 = a^3 + b^3$.

8. (D)
Difficulty: M
Category: Algebraic Expressions
Strategy: Factor the top expression or use the distributive property to expand each answer choice and use process of elimination.
Solution: Use the distributive property for each answer chance. Eliminate A and B as these answers will raise x and y to the incorrect powers. Eliminate choice C since it will result in a leading term of $81x^4$. Answer choice D expands to a yield an equivalent expression: $(3x^2 + 4y^2)(3x^2 + 4y^2) = 9x^4 + 12x^2y^2 + 12x^2y^2 + 16y^4 = 9x^4 + 24x^2y^2 + 16y^4$.

Heart of Algebra – Algebraic Equations & Inequalities – Pages 386-388

1. (A)
Difficulty: E
Category: Algebraic Equations & Inequalities
Strategy: Plug in the value given and solve for w.
Solution: Plug in $v = 4$ into the equation to get
$3w + 2(4) = -4$ or $3w + 8 = -4$. Subtract 8 from both sides and solve for w to get $w = -4$.

2. (D)
Difficulty: E
Category: Algebraic Equations & Inequalities
Strategy: Solve the equation for p and plug in the value into the expression asked for in the problem. You can skip one step in this process by solving for $5p$ directly.
Solution: Divide the equation by 3 to solve for $5p$: $5p = 10$. Add 4 to get the value of $5p + 4 = 10 + 4 = 14$.

3. (C)
Difficulty: E
Category: Algebraic Equations & Inequalities
Strategy: Translate the word problem and set up an inequality. Solve for the set of solutions for p. Find the largest integer that is in the set.
Solution: The product of 2 and an integer p is $2p$. Increasing the product by 4 results in the expression $2p + 4$. The expression is less than or equal to 35. Rewrite as an inequality: $2p + 4 \leq 35$. Subtract four from both sides:
$2p \leq 31$. Divide by two on both sides: $p \leq 15.5$. Since p must be an integer, the greatest value it can be is 15.

4. (6)
Difficulty: E
Category: Algebraic Equations & Inequalities
Strategy: Plug in answer choices or set up an inequality for his total fare, and find the solution set for x = number of subway tickets. Find the largest integer in the set.
Solution: Li has at most $20 he can spend. Set up an inequality for the amount of money he can spend and let b = the number of bus tickets and s = the number of subway tickets: $1.75b + 2.25s \leq 20$. The problem states that $b = 3$. Plug in for b: $1.75(3) + 2.25s \leq 20$. Simplify to get $5.25 + 2.25s \leq 20$. Subtract 5.25 from both sides to isolate s: $2.25s \leq 14.75$. Divide by 2.25 to find $s \leq 6.556$. Since s must be an integer, the maximum value it can be is 6.

5. (D)
Difficulty: E
Category: Algebraic Equations & Inequalities
Strategy: Group like terms together and solve or plug in the answers and use process of elimination.
Solution: Subtract $4x$ from both sides to get $7 = 15$. This statement is false and never true, so there must be no solution to the equation. This makes sense because the two expressions on either side represent equations of parallel lines, which never intersect to yield a solution.

6. (D)
Difficulty: E
Category: Algebraic Equations & Inequalities
Strategy: Set up an inequality and solve. Alternatively, plug in answer choices and work backwards.
Solution: If Jun sells n necklaces, he will make a total of $5n$. His total cost will be $0.50 per necklace plus the flat $95.00 vendor fee, or $95 + 0.50n$. To make a profit, his revenue (how much he makes) minus his cost (how much he must spend) must be larger than 0. Set up the inequality $5n - (95 + 0.50n) > 0$. Distribute and simplify to get $4.5n - 95 > 0$. Add 95 to get $4.5n > 95$. Divide by 4.5 on both sides to find $n > 21.1$. Since Jun must sell an integer quantity of necklaces, then he must sell at least 22 necklaces to make a profit.

7. (C)
Difficulty: E
Category: Algebraic Equations & Inequalities
Strategy: While solving for ab and plugging back into the expression will work, the expression the problem asks for is a multiple of the expression on the left side of the equation. For this reason, the problem can be solved in one step.
Solution: $9ab + 6$ is three times the expression on the left side of the equation, $3ab + 2$.
Since $3ab + 2 = 5$, then $9ab + 6 = 3(3ab + 2) = 3(5) = 15$.

8. (A)
Difficulty: M
Category: Algebraic Equations & Inequalities
Strategy: Translate the word problem into two equations. Solve for x and y. Find the difference.
Solution: The first sentence can be translated into the equation $3x + 8 = 23$. Subtract 8 from both sides to get $3x = 15$. Solve to find $x = 5$. The other equation is $5y + 10 = 55$. Subtract 10 from both sides to get $5y = 45$, or $y = 9$.
$x - y = 5 - 9 = -4$.

9. (10)
Difficulty: M
Category: Algebraic Equations & Inequalities
Strategy: Use the distributive property to expand the expression on the left side of the equation. Combine like terms on the left side. Then set corresponding coefficients on either side of the equation equal to one another.
Solution: Use the distributive property to expand the left-hand side and combine any like terms:
$(ax + 2)(7x^2 - bx + 5) = 7ax^3 - abx^2 + 5ax + 14x^2 - 2bx + 10$
$= 7ax^3 + (14 - ab)x^2 + (5a - 2b)x + 10$. Then, compare the resulting expression to the right-hand side:
$7ax^3 + (14 - ab)x^2 + (5a - 2b)x + 10 = 35x^3 + 4x^2 + 21x + 10$
Thus, $7a = 35 \rightarrow a = 5$. Also, $14 - ab = 4$. Plug in the value found for a to get $14 - 5b = 4$. Solve to find $b = 2$. Thus, $ab = 5(2) = 10$.

10. (D)
Difficulty: M
Category: Algebraic Equations & Inequalities

Strategy: Find the relationship between $\frac{t}{2}$ and $\frac{t^2}{4}$. Express the latter in terms of r and s. Alternatively, choose numbers for r and s, and solve for t. Plug the value into the final expression.

Solution: Note that $\frac{t^2}{4} = \left(\frac{t}{2}\right)^2$. Thus, $\frac{t^2}{4} = (2r + 4s)^2$. Write out this product and use FOIL to distribute:
$(2r + 4s)(2r + 4s) = 4r^2 + 16rs + 16s^2$.

11. (B)
Difficulty: M
Category: Algebraic Equations & Inequalities
Strategy: Use the distributive property to expand the expression and then combine like terms. Set the resulting expression equal to bx. Set corresponding coefficients equal to each other to solve for b.
Solution: $(3x + 3)(ax - 1) - x^2 + 3 = 3ax^2 - 3x + 3ax - 3 - x^2 + 3 = (3a - 1)x^2 + (3a - 3)x$.
Set this equal to bx: $(3a - 1)x^2 + (3a - 3)x = bx$. Corresponding coefficients must be equivalent. Thus, $3a - 1 = 0$. Solve for a to find $a = 1/3$. Also, $3a - 3 = b$.
Plug in the value for a to find $b = 3(1/3) - 3 = 1 - 3 = -2$.

12. (D)
Difficulty: M
Category: Algebraic Equations & Inequalities
Strategy: Combine like terms and solve for the solution set to the inequality. Alternatively, plug in some values from the answer choices and use process of elimination.
Solution #1: Solve the inequality for x: $-3x + 14 \geq 17 - 2x$. Add $2x$ to both sides to get $-x + 14 \geq 17$. Subtract 14 from both sides to get $-x \geq 3$. Multiply by -1 on both sides (remember to flip the inequality sign when multiplying or dividing by a negative) to get $x \leq -3$.

13. (A)
Difficulty: M
Category: Algebraic Equations & Inequalities
Strategy: Use the distributive property to expand the right side. Combine like terms and solve. Alternatively, plug in the answer choices and use process of elimination.
Solution: Use the Distributive Property to rewrite the right side: $4(x - 1) - x = 4x - 4 - x = 3x - 4$. Thus, $3x - 5 = 3x - 4$. Subtract $3x$ from both sides to get the result $-5 = -4$. This statement is never true, so there is no solution.

14. (C)
Difficulty: M
Category: Algebraic Equations & Inequalities
Strategy: Use the distributive property to expand each side of the equation and combine like terms. To obtain infinite solutions, the two sides must be equal for all values of x. Set corresponding coefficients equal to one another.
Solution: Expand both the left and right sides of the equation to get $2x - 2 + 2cx + 3c = 10x + 10$.
Next, combine like terms: $x(2 + 2c) + (3c - 2) = 10x + 10$. To have infinite solutions, the right and left sides of the equation must be exactly equal. Therefore, $2 + 2c = 10$ and $-2 + 3c = 10$. Solve either equation to find $c = 4$.

15. (A)
Difficulty: H
Category: Algebraic Equations & Inequalities
Strategy: Rearrange the equation so all terms containing c appear on one side. Factor out c. Solve for c.
Solution: Begin by moving all terms containing c to one side: $ac + bcd - bc = bd$. Factor out c from each term to get $c(a + bd - b) = bd$.

Solve for c to get $c = \dfrac{bd}{a - b + bd}$.

16. (D)
Difficulty: H
Category: Algebraic Equations & Inequalities
Strategy: Use the distributive property to expand the left side of the equation and combine like terms. Set corresponding coefficients equal to one another. Solve for all solutions for a, b, d, and e first. Use these values to solve for all possible values of c.
Solution: Expand the left side of the equation and combine like terms: $(ax + d)(bx + e) = abx^2 + (ae + bd)x + de = 21x^2 + cx + 10$.
Thus, $ab = 10$, $ae + bd = 21$, and $de = 10$. Solve for a and b first using the following system of equations: $a + b = 10$ and $ab = 21$. Solve for a in the first equation and substitute the resulting expression in to the second equation: $a = 10 - b$.
Thus, $b(10 - b) = 21$. Expand and set the resulting quadratic equation equal to zero: $b^2 - 10b + 21 = 0$. Factor to get $(b - 3)(b - 7) = 0$, which yields the solutions $b = 3$ (and $a = 7$) or $b = 7$ (and $a = 3$).
Next, solve for d and e by solving the following system of equations: $d + e = 11$ and $de = 10$. Using the same approach as with the last system, we find $(11 - e)e = 10$. Set this quadratic equal to zero to find $e^2 - 11e + 10 = 0$. Factor to get $(e - 1)(e - 10) = 0$, which results in solutions $e = 1$ (and $d = 10$) or $e = 10$ (and $d = 1$).
Recall that $c = ae + bd$.
Thus, $c = 3(10) + 7(1) = 37$, $c = 7(10) + 3(1) = 73$, $c = 3(1) + 7(10) = 73$, or $c = 7(1) + 3(10) = 37$.
Therefore, c can equal 37 or 73.

Heart of Algebra – Absolute Value – Pages 390-392

1. (3)
Difficulty: E
Category: Absolute Value
Strategy: Set up two equations to solve for the solutions. Then, evaluate the expression asked for in the problem.
Solution: Note that you can eliminate answer choice A right away, since the problem asks for an absolute value, which cannot be negative. Set up two equations to solve for the solutions to the absolute value equation: $4x + 2 = 6$ and $4x + 2 = -6$. Solve each equation for x to find $x = 1$ and $x = -2$. Plug in these values into the expression asked for in the problem: $|1 - (-2)| = 3$.

2. (C)
Difficulty: E
Category: Absolute Value
Strategy: Find the two points that are 8 units away from 4 and plug them into the answers. Alternatively, use your knowledge of distance to set up the correct absolute value equation.
Solution: The two points on the number line that are exactly 8 units away from 4 are $4 + 8 = 12$ and $4 - 8 = -4$.
These solutions only work in answer choice C.
The distance away from a value x and the point 4 on the number line is the absolute value of their difference: $|x - 4|$. The problem states the distance must be 8, so $|x - 4| = 8$.

3. (C)
Difficulty: E
Category: Absolute Value
Strategy: Isolate the absolute value on one side and solve. Alternatively, plug in the answer choices into the equation and use process of elimination.
Solution: Subtract 5 from both sides to get the equation $-5|-3x + 3| = -15$. Divide by -5 to get $|-3x + 3| = 3$. Set up two separate equations: $-3x + 3 = 3$ and $-3x + 3 = -3$.
Solve to find $x = 0$ and $x = 2$. Since $x \neq 0$, then x must be 2.

4. (A)
Difficulty: E/M
Category: Absolute Value
Strategy: Plug in the answers.
Solution: If you plug in answers, you can quickly get to the solution. Plugging in -3 gets you the solution right away:
$|-3 + 2| = |-1| = 1 \neq -3 + 2 = -1$.
Alternatively, recognize that an absolute value can only result in a non-negative number (a number greater than or equal to zero). Therefore, this equation should have no solutions when $x + 2 < 0$, or when $x < -2$. The only answer choice that satisfies the solution set is choice A.

5. (B)
Difficulty: E/M
Category: Absolute Value
Strategy: Plug in values that you know are within 10 units of 6 on the number line and use process of elimination. Alternatively, use your knowledge of distance to set up the correct absolute value inequality.
Solution: 16 is exactly 10 units away from 6, so it must be part of the solution set. Plugging in 16 eliminates answer choices C and D. -2 is 8 units away from 6, so it must also be part of the solution set. Answer choice A can be eliminated, so B must be correct.
The distance between a point x on the number line and 6 is the absolute value of their difference: $|x - 6|$. The distance must be at

most 10 units away, so the distance must be less than or equal to 10. Thus, $|x - 6| \leq 10$.

6. (A)
Difficulty: E/M
Category: Absolute Value
Strategy: Test each statement with a variety of integers to see if it must be true. Use process of elimination.
Solution: Choice A, $b - a > 0$, will always be true with any pair of integers such that $b > a$. Answer choice B, $|b| - |a| > 0$, is not true if you choose two negative integers such as $|-3| - |-4| = -1$. Answer choice C, $|a| - |b| > 0$, is not true if you choose two positive integers such as $|3| - |4| = -1$. Answer choice D, $|b| > |a|$, is not necessarily true if you choose a negative integer for a with a larger absolute value than that of a positive b: $|5| > |-10|$, for example, is not true.

7. (B)
Difficulty: M
Category: Absolute Value
Strategy: Choose numbers for x to test the answer choices and use process of elimination, or use your knowledge of absolute value functions to determine the minimum or maximum value for each function.
Solution: Each absolute value function will have a minimum or maximum value at its vertex. Answer choice A has a vertex at $(-3, -2)$, and it will open downward, so $y \leq -2$ for all values of x. Answer choice B has a vertex at $(2, 1)$ and opens upward. Thus, $y \geq 1$ for all values of x, and so B is correct.
If choosing numbers, choose $x = 2$. Answer choice A will yield $y = -|2+3| - 2 = -7 < -2$, so A can be eliminated. Answer B will yield $y = 2|2 - 2| + 1 = 1 \geq -2$, so keep this choice. Answer choice C will result in $y = (1/2)|2 - 2| - 3 = -3 < -2$, so eliminate C. Answer choice D will yield $y = -|2 - 2| + 1 = -3 < -2$, so eliminate D. Infer that B must be the answer since all other choices have been eliminated.

8. (4)
Difficulty: M
Category: Absolute Value
Strategy: Consider the restrictions on x. Rewrite the absolute value equation and then solve. Alternatively, plug in the choices and use process of elimination.
Solution: If $x > 0$ and is an integer (meaning it has a minimum value of 1), then $|x + 3| = x + 3$ and $|x - 1| = x - 1$, so
$|x + 3| - 7 = -3|x - 1| + 9 \rightarrow x + 3 - 7 = -3(x - 1) + 9$
$\rightarrow x - 4 = -3x + 12 \rightarrow 4x = 16 \rightarrow x = 4.$

9. (C)
Difficulty: M
Category: Absolute Value
Strategy: Choose a number for x and plug into the answer choices. Use process of elimination.
Solution: Choose a negative real value for x, like $x = -2$, and plug it into each answer choice: $(-2)^3 = -8 < 0$, so choice A is true. $|-2| - |2(-2)| = -2 < 0$, so choice B is true. $|-2| - -2 = 4 \neq 0$, so choice C is NOT true. Thus, C must be the answer.

10. (C)
Difficulty: M
Category: Absolute Value
Strategy: Understand the concept of absolute value and order of operations. Know when a fraction is undefined.

Solution: Simplify the left side of the equation to get $\frac{27-36}{|-3|-3} = \frac{-9}{0}$.

A fraction is undefined if the denominator is zero. Thus, there is no value of x that satisfies the equation.

11. (C)
Difficulty: M
Category: Absolute value
Strategy: Choose a number for b and evaluate each expression. Order from smallest to largest.

Solution: Choose $b = -1/2$. Then, $\frac{-1}{b} = \frac{-1}{-\frac{1}{2}} = 2$.

$-b^2 = -\left(-\frac{1}{2}\right)^2 = -\frac{1}{4}$. Finally, $|b| = \left|-\frac{1}{2}\right| = \frac{1}{2}$.
In this case, $-b^2 < |b| < -1/b$. Thus, C must be correct.

12. (B)
Difficulty: M
Category: Absolute value
Strategy: Know the definition of an absolute value. Plugging in numbers for the variables and using process of elimination will work here too.
Solution: $|x - y|$ is the positive difference between x and y. So, $|x - y| = |y - x|$. Because of this fact, then $|b - a| = |a - b|$ and $|c - d| = |d - c|$, so answer B must always be correct for the values defined. All other choices are not true for all possible values of a, b, c, and d. Answer choice A is not correct in the case where $a > b$ and $c < d$ (or vice versa). Answer choice C is not correct when $a > 0$ and $b < 0$ or in any case where $b > a$. Answer choice D is not correct when $b > 0$ and $a < 0$ or in any case where $a > b$.

13. (C)
Difficulty: M
Category: Absolute Value
Strategy: Consider each answer choice and use process of elimination. Know how to interpret a number line.
Solution: The range between circles is 4 with midpoint at $x = -3$. All points are at distance greater then 2 away from -3. The distance between x and -3 is the absolute value of their difference. Thus, $|x + 3| > 2$, which is answer D.

Answers A and B correctly describe the set of numbers in the solution. Answer C is almost correct, but it contains the solution $x = -1$, which is not a solution on the number line.

14. (A)
Difficulty: H
Category: Absolute value
Strategy: Consider what expressions have in common and how they differ. Cancel the $-x^2$ outside the absolute value signs before comparing. Alternatively, plug in some non-zero value for x and use process of elimination.
Solution: $|x^2 + 3| - x^2$ and $|x^2 - 3| - x^2$ have the $-x^2$ in common (outside the absolute value signs), so this can be discounted to make the problem easier. Now compare $|x^2 + 3|$ and $|x^2 - 3|$. Since x^2 is always positive for all non-zero x, the absolute value of $x^2 + 3$ is always greater than the absolute value of $x^2 - 3$ when $x \neq 0$.

15. (D)
Difficulty: H
Category: Absolute value
Strategy: Consider what the two expressions have in common and what is different. Don't forget the negative sign at the front of both expressions.
Solution: Subtract one from both sides of the inequality to get $-|x^2 + 2| < -|x^2 - 2|$. Multiply by -1 on both sides (remember to flip the inequality sign) to get $|x^2 + 2| > |x^2 - 2|$. Since x^2 is positive for all $x \neq 0$, then for all non-zero x, the distance from x^2 to $-2 = |x^2 + 2|$ will always be grater than the distance from x^2 to $2 = |x^2 - 2|$. They are only equal when $x = 0$. Thus, D is correct.

16. (B)
Difficulty: H
Category: Absolute Value
Strategy: Solve for the solution set of the inequality. Find which answer choice is contained in the set of solutions. Alternatively, pick a value for x in each range given and test to see if it works in the original inequality.
Solution: Set up two inequalities to solve for the solution set: $-7x - 21 < 14$, $-7x - 21 > -14$. Solve each inequality separately (begin by adding 21 to each side): $-7x > 35$, $-7x < 7$. Divide by -7 on both sides (remember to flip the inequality sign) to get $x < -5$ or $x > -1$. Only answer choice B contains values of x in the solution set.

17. (A)
Difficulty: H
Category: Absolute value
Strategy: Consider the range of possible values of the absolute value expression. From here, determine the maximum value of the function.
Solution: The absolute value changes any value inside the absolute value to a non-negative number. Subtracting any positive number from a positive a would result in a value less than a, but when the absolute value is equal to zero, then the function will reach its maximum value, $a - 0 = a$.

So, the maximum value of $f(x)$ occurs when $\left|(x - b)^2 + c\right| = 0$, which can occur when $c = -(x - b)^2$.

Heart of Algebra – Systems of Equations – Pages 394-396

1. (B)
Difficulty: E
Category: Systems of Equations
Strategy: Add the equations to solve directly for x. Plug in the answer choices and use process of elimination.
Solution: Add the two equations to eliminate y: $5x = 35$. Divide both sides by 5 to get $x = 7$.

2. (A)
Difficulty: E
Category: Systems of Equations
Strategy: Use substitution to solve the system of equations or plug in the points in the answer choices into the system.
Solution: The top equation expresses x in terms of y, so plug in $-3y$ for x into the lower equation: $3(-3y) + 2y = -14$. Solving this equation gives $y = 2$. Plug this value back into the top equation to get $x = (-3)(2) = -6$. Therefore, the point of intersection for the two lines is $(-6, 2)$.

3. (B)
Difficulty: E
Category: Systems of Equations
Strategy: Subtract the equations to solve directly for the expression.
Solution: If you subtract the bottom equation from the top one, you will solve for the expression directly:

$$\begin{aligned} 3x + y &= 29 \\ -(2x + 2y) &= -26 \\ \hline x - y &= 3 \end{aligned}$$

Therefore, $x - y = 3$. Note that while substitution or graphing can be used to solve this problem, both methods take much longer.

4. (21)
Difficulty: E
Category: Systems of Equations
Strategy: Know how to factor a difference of squares. The expression asked for in the problem can be factored into the expressions in the system of equations. Alternatively, use elimination to solve for x and y and plug into the expression to solve.
Solution: $x^2 - y^2 = (x + y)(x - y)$. We know from the system that $x + y = 7$ and $x - y = 3$. Thus, $x^2 - y^2 = 7 \cdot 3 = 21$.
This is the easiest way to solve the problem, but the problem can also be solved quickly through using elimination to solve for each of the variables.

5. (B)
Difficulty: M
Category: Systems of Equations
Strategy: Know the slope-intercept form of the line. Find the equation of the other line. Solve the system of equations to find their intersection.
Solution: The slope of line m is 4 and the y-intercept is $(0, -2)$. Thus, the slope of line n is 2 and the y-intercept is $(0, -6)$. The slope-intercept forms of the two lines are $y = 4x - 2$ and $y = 2x - 6$. Since both equations are set equal to y, set the two expressions equal to each other: $4x - 2 = 2x - 6$. Solve this equation to get $x = -2$. Only answer choice B has that x-value, so it must be correct.

6. (1)
Difficulty: M
Category: Systems of Equations
Strategy: Know that a solution for a system is the same as a point on intersection. Count how many times *all* of the lines intersect at the same point.
Solution: The solution to a system of equations is a point where all graphs intersect. In this question, all of the graphs only intersect once (at an x-value of around 6).

7. (A)
Difficulty: M
Category: Systems of Equations
Strategy: Rearrange each equation into slope-intercept form. Check their slopes to see if they intersect.
Solution: In slope-intercept form, equation I remains $y = 2x + 5$; equation II becomes $y = 2x + 11$; and equation III becomes $y = 2x + 1$. All three lines have the same slope of 2. Therefore, they are all parallel, and since none of them are the same line, there are no solutions to this system (no points of intersection).

8. (A)
Difficulty: M
Category: Systems of Equations
Strategy: Write equations for the total profits for last Saturday and this Saturday in terms of r and m. Solve the system to find the difference in price.
Solution:

$$\begin{aligned} 100r + 150m &= 2200 \\ -(150r + 100m) &= -2300 \\ \hline -50r + 50m &= -100 \end{aligned}$$

Divide by -50 on both sides to get the answer directly: $r - m = 2$. Alternatively, solve the system by elimination or substitution to find the values of r and m and find the difference.

9. (C)
Difficulty: M
Category: Systems of Equations
Strategy: Multiply the equations by the common denominators of the fractions to clear the fractions. Then, solve using the elimination or substitution methods.
Solution: Multiply the top by 12 and the bottom by 6 on both sides. Solve for y in the second equation:

$$\frac{1}{12}x + \frac{1}{6}y = \frac{3}{2} \rightarrow x + 2y = 18$$

$$\frac{1}{2}x + \frac{1}{6}y = -\frac{1}{6} \rightarrow 3x + y = -1 \rightarrow y = -3x - 1$$

Substitute into the first equation to get $x + 2(-3x - 1) = 18$. Expand to get $x - 6x - 2 = 18$. Combine like terms to get $-5x = 20$ or $x = -4$. Now, plug back in to solve for y: $y = -3(-4) - 1 = 11$. Thus, $x + y = -4 + 11 = 7$.

10. (15)
Difficulty: M
Category: Systems of Equations, Quadratic Equations
Strategy: Since both equations are set equal to y, set the expressions equal to each other to find their intersection. Set the resulting equation equal to zero and factor to solve for the x-coordinates of the points of intersection.
Solution: Set the expressions equal to each other to find points of intersection: $x^2 = -8x - 15$. Set the quadratic equation equal to zero to get $x^2 + 8x + 15 = 0$. Factor to find $(x + 3)(x + 5) = 0$. Set each factor equal to zero to find the two solutions $x = -3$, $x = -5$. Their product is 15.

11. (C)
Difficulty: H
Category: Systems of Equations, Quadratic Equations
Strategy: Since both equations are set equal to y, set the expressions equal to each other to find their intersection. Set the resulting equation equal to zero and use the quadratic formula to solve for the x-coordinates of the points of intersection.
Solution: Set the two expressions for y equal to each other: $x^2 + 3x - 4 = -2x + 8$. Set the equation equal to zero to get $x^2 + 5x - 12 = 0$. Find the discriminant to find how many solutions exist: $b^2 - 4ac = 25 + 48 = 73 > 0$, so there must be two solutions.

12. (B)
Difficulty: H
Category: Systems of Equations
Strategy: If a system of linear equations has no solutions, the system must represent two parallel lines. Rearrange each equation into slope-intercept form and set the slopes equal to each other. Solve for the expression.
Solution: If two lines have no solution (are parallel), the two lines have the same slope. Rearrange each equation into slope-intercept form. To do so, multiply the top equation by 12 to eliminate all fractions: $8x + 3y = 144$. Solve for y to put into slope-intercept form. $y = -(8/3)x + 48$. Now, solve the bottom equation for y: $y = (a/b)x - 8/b$.

Set the slopes of the two lines equal to one another: $-\dfrac{8}{3} = \dfrac{a}{b}$. The problem asks for b/a, the reciprocal of the a/b, so $b/a = -3/8$.

13. (B)
Difficulty: H
Category: System of Equations
Strategy: Convert the linear equations into slope-intercept form. If there is no solution, the lines must be parallel. Set the slopes equal to each other. Make sure the y-intercepts are NOT equal. Rearrange to arrive at the answer choice. Alternatively, choose numbers for a, b, c, s, t, and u that fit each answer choice and work backwards.
Solution: Solve for y in both equations to convert into slope-intercept form. $ax - c = -by$ becomes $y = (-a/b)x + (c/b)$. For the second equation, multiply through by u to eliminate all fractions: $sx + ty = u$. Solve for y to find $y = (-s/t)x + u/t$. Parallel lines have equal slopes, so set the slopes equal to each other: $-\dfrac{a}{b} = -\dfrac{s}{t} \rightarrow at = bs$

Parallel lines must have different y-intercepts, which means $\dfrac{c}{b} \neq \dfrac{u}{t} \rightarrow bu \neq ct$. Thus, B is correct.

Heart of Algebra – Slope – Pages 398-401

1. (A)
Difficulty: E
Category: Slope
Strategy: Find the slope of the line given. Know how the slopes of perpendicular lines are related.
Solution: The slopes of perpendicular lines are negative reciprocals of each other. The slope of the line perpendicular to line m is 1/4. Thus, the slope of line m must be –4.

2. (C)
Difficulty: E
Category: Slope
Strategy: Rearrange the equation into slope-intercept form.
Solution: Solve the equation for y in terms of x: $-2y = -3x - 6$. Divide by –2 on both sides to get $y = (3/2)x + 3$. The slope of this equation is 3/2 and the y-intercept is (0, 3).

3. (A)
Difficulty: E
Category: Slope
Strategy: Use the formula for evaluating a slope between two points to calculate the slope. Alternatively, plug in the known points into the answer choices and use process of elimination.
Solution: Calculate the slope point two points by using the slope = $\dfrac{y_1 - y_2}{x_1 - x_2}$ formula. The slope is $\dfrac{5 - 0}{-3 - 0} = -\dfrac{5}{3}$. Only answer choice A has this slope.

4. (C)
Difficulty: E
Category: Slope
Strategy: Know the slope-intercept form of the equation of a line. Recognize that you are given both the slope and the y-intercept in the problem. Alternatively, plug in the point into the answer choices and use process of elimination.
Solution: The problem gives you both the y-intercept, (0, –2), and the slope, $m = 2$. Plug these in to get the slope-intercept form of the equation of the line: $y = 2x - 2$.

5. (B)
Difficulty: E
Category: Slope
Strategy: Recognize that you are given two points in the problem. Know how to evaluate a slope from two points.
Solution: If $g(0) = 4$ and $g(5) = 14$, then the points (0, 4) and (5, 14) must both be on the graph of the function. The function is linear, so its slope can be calculated using the $m = \dfrac{y_2 - y_1}{x_2 - x_1}$ formula. Using the two points known, the slope must be $\dfrac{14 - 4}{5 - 0} = \dfrac{10}{5} = 2$.

6. (B)
Difficulty: E
Category: Slope
Strategy: Find the slope of the line in the graph. Know the relationship between the slopes of perpendicular lines. Identify the choice with the correct slope.
Solution: Slope is rise over run. Use this fact to determine the slope of the line in the graph is 3/2 (up three, over two). The slope can also be calculated by picking two points on the graph, such as (-1, 0) and (1, 3). Perpendicular lines have slopes that are negative reciprocals of each other. Hence, the slope of line p should be –2/3. The only answer choice with this slope is choice B.

7. (A)
Difficulty: M
Category: Slope
Strategy: The table lists three points of the function. Use the formula for evaluating a slope between two points to calculate the slope. Find the y-intercept from the points given. Find the expression asked for in the problem.
Solution: The table gives us the y-intercept of the line, which is the value of y when $x = 0$. The y-coordinate of the y-intercept is 5. The slope can be calculated using any of the two points. Slope $= \dfrac{y_2 - y_1}{x_2 - x_1}$
$= \dfrac{f(x_2) - f(x_1)}{x_2 - x_1}$. Plug in any two of the points to find the slope: $(0 - 5)/(1 - 0)$. Therefore, $m = -5$ and $n = 5$. Thus, mn must be –25.

8. (D)
Difficulty: M
Category: Slope
Strategy: The diagonals of a square are always perpendicular. Know the relationship between the slopes of perpendicular lines. Find the choice with the correct slope.
Solution: The two diagonals of a square must be perpendicular, and lines that are perpendicular have slopes that are negative reciprocals of each other. Since the first diagonal lies on a line with slope –1/3, the other diagonal must lie on a line with slope 3. Choice D is the only option with this slope.

9. (C)
Difficulty: M
Category: Slope
Strategy: Know the relationship between the slopes of perpendicular lines. Find the slope of line q. Rearrange the answers into slope-intercept form to find the equation with the correct slope.
Solution: The slopes of perpendicular lines are negative reciprocals of each other. The slope of line p is 0.4 = 2/5. Thus, the slope of line q must be –5/2. Answers A and B have different slopes, so eliminate both. Answers C and D are in standard form and should be rearranged into slope-intercept form: Answer choice C can be rearranged into $y = (-5/2)x + 23/2$, which has the correct slope. Answer choice D in slope-intercept form is $y = (5/2)x - 13$, which has a different slope. Only answer choice C has a slope that is perpendicular to the slope of line p.

10. (B)
Difficulty: M
Category: Slope
Strategy: Use the formula for evaluating the slope of a line between two points to find an expression for the slope in terms of p. Set the expression equal to 4 and solve for p. Alternatively, plug in the values in the answer choices for p and work through the problem backwards.

Solution: Set up an equation for the slope: $\dfrac{18 - p}{p - 3} = 4$. Multiply both sides by $(p - 3)$ to get $18 - p = 4(p - 3)$. Expand the right side to get $18 - p = 4p - 12$. Rearrange to get $30 = 5p$. Solve for p to find $p = 6$.

11. (B)
Difficulty: M
Category: Slope
Strategy: Solve for a in terms of b, and find an expression for the slope all in terms of one variable. Alternatively, plug in some values for a and b that meet the restrictions and determine the sign of the slope.
Solution: If $a + b = 0$, then $a = -b$. Thus, the line contains points $(-b, b)$ and $(b, -b)$. The slope of the line must be $\dfrac{-b - b}{b - -b} = \dfrac{-2b}{2b} = -1$ for all $b \neq 0$.

12. (5)
Difficulty: M
Category: Slope
Strategy: Find the two points given. Write an expression for slope in terms of a. Set it equal to 2/3 and solve for a.
Solution: The points given in the problem are $(-1, -3)$ and $(a, 1)$. Slope $m = \dfrac{y_2 - y_1}{x_2 - x_1} = \dfrac{1 - -3}{a - -1} = \dfrac{4}{a + 1} = \dfrac{2}{3}$. Cross-multiply to get $12 = 2a + 2$. Solve for a to find $a = 5$.

13. (C)
Difficulty: M
Category: Slope
Strategy: Rewrite each linear equation into slope-intercept form. Know the relationship between slopes of perpendicular lines.
Solution: Rewrite each linear equation into slope-intercept form:
line r: $y = (2/3)x + 6$
line s: $2x - 3y - 12 = 0$ can be rewritten as $-3y = -2x + 12$. Divide by –3 to get $y = (2/3)x - 4$
line t: Cross-multiply to get $2y - 14 = -3x - 18$. Solve for y to find $y = (-3/2)x - 2$
line u: $y = x - 2$
lines r and s are parallel (same slope) but different (different y-intercepts), so I is false.
line s and line t are perpendicular, since their slopes are negative reciprocals of each other, so II is true.
line t and line u have same y-intercept, so III is true.

14. (D)
Difficulty: M
Category: Slope
Strategy: Rearrange the top equation into slope-intercept form to determine the slope of the line. Use the relationship between the slopes of perpendicular lines to determine the slope of a perpendicular line. Rearrange the equations in the solutions into slope-intercept form to find the choice with the correct slope.
Solution: Rearrange the top equation into slope-intercept form by solving for y: $7y = -5x + 35$. Divide by 7 to get $y = (-5/7)x + 5$. The line has a slope of –5/7. Perpendicular lines have slopes that are negative reciprocals to one another, so the slope of the correct answer should be 7/5. Rearrange the equations in the answer choices into slope-intercept form to find the linear equation with slope 7/5:
A: $5y = -7x + 35$, or $y = (-7/5)x + 7$, which has slope –7/5.
B: $14y = -5x + 70$, or $y = (-5/7)x + 5$, which has slope –5/7.
C: $-7y = -5x + 35$, or $y = (5/7)x - 5$, which has slope 5/7.
D: $-15y = -21x + 105$, or $y = (7/5)x + 7$, which has slope 7/5, the correct slope.

15. (B)
Difficulty: H
Category: Slope
Strategy: Substitute the expression for p in terms of q into the x-intercept to express both points in terms of q. Use the formula to evaluate the slope between two points to express the slope in terms of q. Reduce the fraction. Alternatively, choose numbers for p and q that fit the restrictions and solve for the slope with your numbers.
Solution: Since $p = 3q$, then line l must go through points $(3q, 0)$ and $(0, q)$. The slope between these two points is $\dfrac{q-0}{0-3q} = \dfrac{q}{-3q} = -\dfrac{1}{3}$.

16. (D)
Difficulty: H
Category: Slope
Strategy: Rewrite the equation of line w in slope-intercept form to find its slope. Use the relationship between the slopes of parallel lines to determine the slope of line v. Use the point given to find the equation of line v. Plug in $y = 0$ to determine the x-coordinate of the x-intercept of line v.
Solution: Rearrange the equation of line w into slope-intercept form: $-5y = -6x + 27$, or $y = (6/5)x - (27/5)$, which has slope $6/5$. Lines that are parallel have equal slopes, so line v must have slope $6/5$ also. In slope-intercept form, the equation of line v must be $y = (6/5)x + b$. Plug in the point $(4, -2)$ to determine, b, the y-coordinate of the y-intercept: $-2 = (6/5)(4) + b$. Solve for b to get $b = -34/5$. Thus, the equation of line v is $y = (6/5)x - 34/5$. The x-intercept occurs when $y = 0$, so plug in 0 for y to find the answer: $0 = (6/5)x - 34/5$. Multiply by 5 on both sides to get $0 = 6x - 34$.

Solve for x to find $x = 34/6 = 17/3 = 5\dfrac{2}{3}$.

17. (D)
Difficulty: H
Category: Slope
Strategy: Rewrite the equation for line A in slope-intercept form and determine its slope. Use the relationship of slopes of perpendicular lines to determine the slope of line B. Write the equation of line B in slope-intercept form. Plug in the points from the answer choices into the equation to find the point that does not lie on the line.
Solution: Rewrite the equation for line A in slope-intercept form by dividing by 4 to get $y = (-1/3)x + (5/4)$. Perpendicular lines have slopes that are negative reciprocals of each other, so the slope of line B should be 3. The y-coordinate of the y-intercept is $5/4$, so the slope-intercept form of the equation for line B is $y = 3x + (5/4)$. From here, simply plug in the coordinate pairs to find which does not lie on the line. Eliminate choice A, which is the y-intercept. Check choice B by plugging in the point into the equation: $41/4 = 3(3) = 5/4$, so eliminate answer B. Check choice C next: $-1 = 3(-3/4) + 5/4$m so eliminate this choice. Check choice D to make sure it does not lie on the line. $1/2 \neq 3(5/2) + 5/4$, so the point does not lie on the line.

18. (A)
Difficulty: H
Category: Slope
Strategy: Rewrite the equations in the system into slope-intercept form. Know that the adjacent sides of a rectangle are perpendicular. Use the relationship between slopes of perpendicular lines to determine the slope of the lines in the solution. Rewrite the equations in the solutions into slope-intercept form to find which contain the correct slopes. Use process of elimination.
Solution: The original system of equations can be rewritten entirely in slope intercept form as $y = 2x + 3$ and $y = 2x + 6$, which are parallel lines with slope 2. The other two sides of the rectangle must lie on perpendicular lines to these ones. Since perpendicular lines have slopes that are negative reciprocals of one another, then the slope of the other pair of lines must be $-(1/2)$. Only choice A has two lines with this slope. The top equation in the system is already in slope-intercept form, so its slope is clearly $-(1/2)$. The second equation can be rewritten as $y = -(1/2)x + 6$, which has the correct slope. All other answer choices contain at least one incorrect slope.

19. (A)
Difficulty: H
Category: Slope
Strategy: Use the values of the functions to determine the two points that are connected by the line. Use the formula to evaluate the slope between two points to find the slope of the line that connects the points. Use the relationship between slopes of perpendicular lines to determine the slope of the perpendicular line.
Solution: $f(-1) = -3$ occurs at point $(-1, -3)$ and $g(5) = 1$ occurs at point $(5, 1)$. Slope $m = \dfrac{y_2 - y_1}{x_2 - x_1} = \dfrac{-3-1}{-1-5} = \dfrac{-4}{-6} = \dfrac{2}{3}$.

A line that is perpendicular will have a slope equal to the negative reciprocal of $2/3$. Thus, the slope of the line must be $-3/2$.

Heart of Algebra – Graphs of Linear Equations – Pages 403-407

1. (B)
Difficulty: E
Category: Graphs of Linear Equations
Strategy: Note the scale on the axes of the graph. Use the graph to find the slope and y-intercept of the line. Identify the correct slope-intercept equation of the line.
Solution: Two points easily identified on the graph are the x and y-intercepts, which are $(8, 0)$ and $(0, 6)$ respectively. The slope can be found using the formula slope $= \dfrac{y_2 - y_1}{x_2 - x_1} = (6 - 0)/(0 - 8) = -6/8 =$
$-3/4$. The y-intercept is $(0, 6)$, so the solution is B.

2. (B)
Difficulty: E
Category: Graphs of Linear Equations
Strategy: Find the point of intersection on the graph. Add the two coordinates.
Solution: Based on the graph, the solution to the system is $(-2, 1)$. Therefore, $x + y = -2 + 1 = -1$.

3. (D)
Difficulty: E
Category: Graphs of Linear Equations
Strategy: Know the slope-intercept form of the equation of the line. Find which graphs contain the correct y-intercept. From there, use rise over run to see which graph has the correct slope. Use process of elimination.
Solution: The line has a y-intercept of $(0, 1)$, so A and B can be eliminated. Choice C has a slope of 2/3 (up two, right three), while choice D has the correct slope of 3/2.

4. (A)
Difficulty: E
Category: Algebraic Expressions
Strategy: Determine the equation of the graphed line in slope-intercept form. Then, rearrange into the standard form of the line. Alternatively, plug in a point or two on the line into the answer choices and use process of elimination.
Solution: Note that the slope of the line is 1/3 (up one, right three), and that the y-intercept is $(0, -1)$. Thus, the slope-intercept form of the equation of this line is $y = (1/3)x - 1$. Multiply by 3 on both sides to find $3y = x - 1$. Rearrange to get $3y - x = -1$. Multiply through by -1 to get answer choice A.

5. (4)
Difficulty: E
Category: Graphs of Linear Equations
Strategy: Plug the x and y-coordinates of the point into the equation and solve for a.
Solution: $-4(1) + 2(4) = a$. Thus, $a = 4$.

6. (C)
Difficulty: E
Category: Graphs of Linear Equations
Strategy: Find the y-intercept on the graph and find the slope from the information in the problem. Know the slope-intercept form of the equation of the line.
Solution: The graph shows you the y-coordinate of the y-intercept (median rent in 1995) is approximately 450. Eliminate choices A and D. The slope represents the increase in the y-coordinate as x increases by 1. The information at the beginning gives this value: the slope must be 22.5 (it is positive since median rent is increasing). Of the remaining choices, only C is possible.

7. (B)
Difficulty: M
Category: Graphs of Linear Equations
Strategy: Convert yearly rent to monthly rent. Find the point on the graph with this monthly rent value to determine the year in which it occurred.
Solution: If the total rent for the year is \$6500.00, then monthly rent should be $\dfrac{\$6500}{year} \cdot \dfrac{1 year}{12 months} \approx 542.00$ per month. Based on the graph, the year with the closest median monthly rent was in 1999.

8. (B)
Difficulty: M
Category: Graphs of Linear Equations
Strategy: Rearrange the equation given into slope-intercept form. Use the relationship between slopes of perpendicular lines to determine the slope of the perpendicular line. Plug in the point to find the y-intercept of the line.
Solution: Rearrange the equation of the first line given, putting it into slope-intercept form: $y = (-3/2)x + 2$. The slope of this line is $-3/2$. Since the other line is perpendicular to this one, its slope is the negative reciprocal of $-3/2$. Thus, the slope of the perpendicular line is 2/3. In slope-intercept form, its equation must be $y = (2/3)x + b$. Plug in the point $(6, 9)$ into the equation and solve for b, the y-coordinate of the y-intercept: $9 = (2/3) \cdot 6 + b$. Thus, $b = 5$.

9. (C)
Difficulty: M
Category: Graphs of Linear Equations
Strategy: Note the scale on the axes of the graph. Find the slope and y-intercept of the line. Choose the equation with the correct slope and y-intercept.
Solution: The y-intercept of the line is $(0, 5)$. Note that the cost increases by \$10 over each 2-hour interval, giving a slope of $10/2 = 5$. The equation for this line is: $y = 5x + 5$.

10. (A)
Difficulty: M
Category: Graphs of Linear Equations
Strategy: Know the slope-intercept form of the equation of the line to determine the y-intercept and slope. Identify the graph with the correct y-intercept and slope.
Solution: The linear equation given has a slope of $-4/3$ and a y-intercept at $(0, 4)$. Only graphs A and B have the correct y-intercept. Choice A has the correct slope (down 4, right 3). Choice B has a slope of $-4/5$ instead.

11. (A)
Difficulty: M
Category: Graphs of Linear Equations
Strategy: Rearrange the equation of line n into slope-intercept form. Determine the slope of line n. Use the relationship between slopes of perpendicular lines to determine the slope of line m. Plug in the point to determine the y-intercept of line m.
Solution: The slope-intercept form of line n is $y = (3/5)x - 2$, which has a slope of 3/5. Since line m is perpendicular, its slope is the negative reciprocal, which is $-5/3$. Thus, the equation of line m is $y = (-5/3)x + b$, where b is the y-coordinate of the y-intercept. Plug in the point $(-6, -2)$ into the equation: $-2 = (-5/3) \cdot (-6) + b$. Solve to find $b = -12$.

12. (B)
Difficulty: M
Category: Graphs of Linear Equations
Strategy: Plug in the x and y-coordinates of the points into the equation and use process of elimination.
Solution: Plug in $(7, 17)$ first to get $-4(7) + 2(17) = -28 + 36 = 6$. Since the statement is true, the point must lie on the line, and so choice A can be eliminated. Plug in $(11, 13)$ next to get $-4(11) + 2(13) = -44 + 26 = 18 \neq 6$. Since the statement is not true, then $(11, 13)$ must not lie on the line.

13. (B)
Difficulty: E
Category: Graphs of Linear Equations
Strategy: Rearrange the equation into slope-intercept form. Find the slope and y-intercept of the linear equation. Find the graph with the correct y-intercept.
Solution: Subtract $2y$ and x from both sides to get $y = 3x - 5$. The slope of this line is 3 and the y-intercept is $(0, -5)$. Only graph B has the correct y-intercept (and slope).

14. (A)
Difficulty: H
Category: Graphs of Linear Equations
Strategy: Use the relationship between the slopes of perpendicular lines to determine the product of the slopes. Find the y-intercepts to find the product asked for.
Solution: Perpendicular lines have slopes that are negative reciprocals of each other. Therefore, the product of their slopes, $-m_1 m_2 = -1$. The y-coordinate of the y-intercept of line Y_1 is $-c_1$ and is c_2 for line Y_2. The product of the slopes and y-intercepts is $-1(-c_1)(c_2) = c_1 c_2$.

15. (C)
Difficulty: H
Category: Graphs of Linear Equations
Strategy: Plug in the point into the equation, and solve for c, the slope of the line, in terms of the other variables. Alternatively, choose numbers for a, b, and d, and solve for the slope.
Solution: The slope of the line is c. Plug in the point given to get $b = ca + d$. Solve for c: $b - d = ca$, or $c = (b - d)/a$.

Heart of Algebra – Systems and Graphs of Inequalities – Pages 409-413

1. (B)
Difficulty: E
Category: Systems of Linear Inequalities
Strategy: Plug in the x and y coordinates of the points in the answer choices into the system of inequalities. Use process of elimination.
Solution: Plug in the point $(1, 5)$ into the system first: $5 = 2(1) + 3$, which violates the first inequality. Eliminate choice A. The point $(2,5)$ works in both inequalities: $5 < 2(2) + 3$ and $5 \geq -2 - 2$. Therefore, choice B is correct.

2. (D)
Difficulty: E
Category: Systems of Linear Inequalities
Strategy: Translate the word problem into a system of inequalities. One inequality should account for the number of people attending the field trip, and one inequality should account for the cost constraints.
Solution: The max number of people the bus can hold is 72, so the number of people attending, $c + a$, must be at most 72, or $c + a \leq 72$. Eliminate A and B. The total cost of the tickets will be $5c + 13a$. This value can be at most 500, so $5c + 13a \leq 500$.

3. (D)
Difficulty: E
Category: Graphs of Linear Inequalities
Strategy: Choose points in each region shaded in the answers and plug them into the system to see which one satisfies the set of inequalities. Use process or elimination.
Solution: A point that satisfies the system of inequalities is $(-1,0)$ since $0 \leq -(1/2) \cdot (-1) + 1 = 3/2$ and $2(0) - 3(-1) = 3 \geq 2$. The only graph that shades the region containing the point $(-1,0)$ is answer choice D, so it must be correct.

4. (C)
Difficulty: E
Category: Graphs of Linear Inequalities
Strategy: Solve the system of inequalities to find the range of possible y values (can be done via graphing or substituting the first inequality directly into the second).
Solution: The system of inequalities states $-3x < 3$. Notice the term $-3x$ occurs in the second inequality, $y < -3x + 2$. If $-3x$ is at most 3, then y must be less than $3 + 2 = 5$. Therefore, answer choice C is correct. The system can also be solved by graphing the solution set and finding the maximum possible value of y.

5. (C)
Difficulty: E
Category: Systems of Linear Inequalities
Strategy: Translate the word problem into a system of inequalities. One inequality should account for the amount of clay she can use, and the other should account for the relationship between the number of teacups and saucers.
Solution: The number of teacups must be at least the number of saucers, thus $t \geq s$. Eliminate A and D. The ounces of clay that Vivienne will use for the project will be $10t + 14s$. She has at most 150 ounces of clay to use. Thus, $10t + 14s \leq 150$.

6. (B)
Difficulty: M
Category: Graphs of Linear Inequalities
Strategy: Graph the system of inequalities and determine the lowest value of y that is in the solution set.
Solution: Graph the solution set to the system of equations:

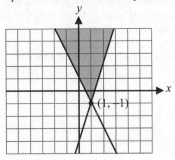

The lowest value of y that is part of the solution occurs at the intersections of the lines, where $y = -1$.

7. (A)
Difficulty: M
Category: Graphs of Linear Inequalities
Strategy: Find the equations of the lines and then consider where y is shaded relative to the lines (above or below). Alternatively, plug in the point into the answer choices and use process of elimination.
Solution: The y-intercept of both lines is $(0,0)$. The slope of the line going from the bottom left to top right is 3 and the slope of the line going from top left to bottom right is $-1/2$. $(1, -1)$ is *below* the corresponding y-coordinates of each of the lines at $x = -1$, so in both cases y is less than the equation of each line, or $y < 3x$ and $y < (-1/2)x$.

8. (B)
Difficulty: H
Category: Graphs of Linear Inequalities
Strategy: Determine the signs of the x and y coordinates of the center of the circle. Choose the correct equation of a circle with a center in the second quadrant. Of the choices remaining, determine which splits up the circle into two different ranges of y-value, instead of only one range.
Solution: The figure shows no scale on the axes, but the center (h, k) is clearly in quadrant II, where $h < 0$ and $k > 0$. The shaded region inside the circle represents all the points less than or equal to a distance r away from the center.
The best choice of a set of points inside a circle in the second quadrant would be $(x + 5)^2 + (y - 8)^2 \leq 25$, which represents the set of points inside a circle centered at $(-5, 8)$ with radius = 5. Eliminate A and C. The top line is $y = k = 8$ crossing through center of circle. The bottom line could be $y = 4$, less than 5 units below diameter at $y = 8$. Thus, the best choice for solution set of lines is absolute value inequality: $|y - 6| \geq 2$. Choice D contains a set of points between the lines instead.

9. (C)
Difficulty: H
Category: Graphs of Linear Inequalities
Strategy: Sketch the graph of the system and use process of elimination.
Solution: To sketch the system of inequalities, draw the boundary lines first (the graph that would result if the inequality were replaced with an equal sign) and use $(0, 0)$ as a test point to determine which side to shade:

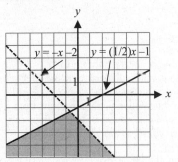

From the sketch, note that all solutions to the system of inequalities will be in Quadrants III and IV. I is true. II is also true, since all the points below $y = -x -2$ are in quadrants II, III, and IV. None are in quadrant I. III is not true because the set of points below $y = (1/2)x -1$ are only in quadrants I, III, and IV. None are in quadrant II. Thus, only statements I and II are true, so C is the answer.

10. (C)
Difficulty: M
Category: Graphs of Linear Inequalities
Strategy: Multiply the inequalities by the lowest common denominator to eliminate the fractions. Then, plug in the points and use process of elimination.
Solution: Multiply both sides of the first inequality by 8 and both sides of the second inequality by 36 to get $-4x - 6y \geq 5$ and $24x + 8y > 33$. The point $(0, -1)$ violates the second inequality since $24(0) + 8(-1) = -8 < 33$. The point $(2, 0)$ violates the first inequality since $-4(2) - 6(0) = -8 < 5$. The point $(3, -4)$ violates neither inequality since $-4(3) -6(-4) = 12 \geq 5$ and $24(3) + 8(-4) = 72 - 32 = 50 > 33$, so $(3, -4)$ will be in the solution set of the system.

11. (D)
Difficulty: H
Category: Graphs of Linear Inequalities
Strategy: Solve the inequality for y (remember to flip the sign when dividing by b, which is negative). Consider the signs of the y-intercept and the slope of the boundary line. Only one graph will show a boundary line with the correct sign of both slope and y-intercept. Alternatively, choose values for a, b, and c that fit the constraints and find the graph most similar to it.
Solution: $by \leq -ax + c$. Divide by b on both sides. Remember, b is negative, so the inequality sign should be flipped: $y \geq (-a/b)x + (c/b)$. a, b, and c are all negative, so the boundary line's slope = $-a/b$ should also be negative (positive/negative is negative). The boundary line's y-intercept = c/b should be positive (negative/negative is positive). The only graph that shows a boundary line with a negative slope and a positive y-intercept is choice D.

12. (B)
Difficulty: M
Category: Graphs of Linear Inequalities
Strategy: Plug the points into the inequality and use process of elimination.
Solution: Plug (–6, –8) into the inequality first to get $3(-6) - 5(-8) = -18 + 40 = 22 > 12$, which violates the inequality. Eliminate choice A. Next, test the point (–4, –4): $3(-4) - 5(-4) = -12 + 20 = 8 < 12$. Thus, (–4, –4) could be point B.

13. (A)
Difficulty: M
Category: Graphs of Linear Inequalities
Strategy: Find the equations of the boundary lines for each inequality. Determine which side is shaded to determine the direction of the inequality sign. Solve the inequalities in the answer choices for y and use process of elimination. Alternatively, plug in points from the solution set into the answers and use process of elimination.
Solution: The top line has y-intercept (0, 1) and slope 2. Since only the area above it is graphed, then $y \geq 2x + 1$. The bottom line has y-intercept (0, –1) and slope 2. Only the area above it is shaded, so $y \geq 2x - 1$. Check the answers to see which one matches this set of inequalities. For answer choice A, divide both sides of the first inequality by 2 to get $y \geq 2x + 1$. Divide both sides of the second inequality by 3 to get $y \geq 2x - 1$. These inequalities match the solution set, so A is correct.

14. (D)
Difficulty: M
Category: Graphs of Linear Inequalities
Strategy: Determine the area the overlap of the solution set for each inequality, or check the graph to see which quadrants the darker region (the overlap of the two inequalities) goes through.
Solution: The overlap of the two inequalities is the darker region above the top graph. Thus, the entire solution set is contained in quadrants I, II, and III.

15. (D)
Difficulty: M
Category: Graphs of Linear Inequalities
Strategy: Find the equation of the boundary line by determining its slope and y-intercept. Identify which side is shaded to determine the direction of the inequality sign.
Solution: Find the slope of the line, which is 5/4 (up 5, over 4), and the y-intercept is (0, 1). Thus, the boundary line has equation $y = (5/4)x + 1$. Note that the shaded region is *above* the line, so it represents all y-values greater than or equal to the line. Thus, the inequality represented is $y \geq (5/4)x + 1$.

Heart of Algebra – Creating Linear Models – Pages 415-421

1. (C)
Difficulty: E
Category: Creating Linear Models
Strategy: Malik's total cost included the flat fee and gas purchase. Express his gas purchase in terms of g. Then express his total cost in terms of g. Alternatively, choose a number for g and determine his total cost as a number.
Solution: The fixed, non-variable cost is $54.00 and the amount spent on gas is $g \cdot \$2.65$. Therefore, the total spent on the car rental is $54.00 + 2.65g$.

2. (B)
Difficulty: E
Category: Creating Linear Models
Strategy: Express how many seedlings she still has left to plant in terms of s. Use this to write an expression for the time she will need to plant this quantity of seedlings. Alternatively, choose a number for s and solve for the time she will need to plant the rest of the seedlings.
Solution: If Amira has planted s seedlings already, then she has $48 - s$ seedlings left to plant. Each takes three minutes to plant, so the total time she needs to finish planting her seedlings is $3(48 - s)$.

3. (A)
Difficulty: E
Category: Creating Linear Models
Strategy: Find the value of the total monthly cost for different values of m and use process of elimination.
Solution: For all values of m from 0 to 20, the monthly cost stays flat at $150.00. Choices C and D can be eliminated right away. When $m > 20$, the total monthly cost should begin to rise (since the cost of each additional meal will add to the flat fee). Eliminate B, since its graph decreases after 20.

4. (D)
Difficulty: M
Category: Creating Linear Models
Strategy: Plug in the stated price and units sold into the answers. Use process of elimination.
Solution: When $p = 25.00$, $w = 10,000$. Plugging in this ordered pair into the four equations eliminates all choices except for D, which will yield a true statement: $10,000 = 15,000 - 200(25) = 10,000$.

5. (B)
Difficulty: E
Category: Creating Linear Models
Strategy: If you chose the correct answer in the last problem, plug in 50 into the correct variable and solve. Alternatively, determine the price increase from $25.00 and calculate the decrease in the number of water filters sold. Use the value to find the total units sold.
Solution: If you picked the correct answer in the previous question, which was answer choice D, then plug in $50.00 for p and solve for w to get $w = 15,000 - 200(50) = 5,000$. Alternatively, reason that $50.00 is $25.00 more than $25.00. Therefore, the number of units sold at a $50.00 price should be $25 \cdot 200 = 5,000$ units less than the amount sold at the $25.00 price. This gives $10,000 - 5,000 = 5,000$ water filters sold.

6. (B)
Difficulty: M
Category: Creating Linear Models
Strategy: Find the two prices of water filters that would result in 7,000 and 12,000 water filters sold by using the correct linear model from question 5. Any price in between should result in filters sold within the desired range. Alternatively, plug in values unique to each inequality into the linear model to determine if the units sold falls within the correct range. Use process of elimination.
Solution: The correct linear model for predicting number of water filters sold is $w = 15,000 - 200p$. When $w = 7000$, then $7,000 = 15,000 - 200p$. Solve for p to find $p = \$40$. When $w = 12,000$, then $12,000 = 15,000 - 200p$. Solve for p to find $p = \$15$. Therefore, any price between \$15 and \$40 should result in the desired range of units sold.

7. (A)
Difficulty: M
Category: Creating Linear Models
Strategy: Find the cost to make one cake. Write an expression for her revenue, the amount she makes, in terms of c. Write an expression for her total cost in terms of c. Subtract the two to find an expression for her profit. Alternatively, choose a number for c and find her profit.
Solution: The cost of ingredients per cake is $\$45/5 = \$9.00$. Her total cost is the cost of ingredients to make c cakes plus the cost of the pans, or $9c + 36$. Her revenue, the amount she makes from selling c cakes, is $15c$. Thus, her net profit $P = 15c - (9c + 36) = 6c - 36$.

8. (B)
Difficulty: M
Category: Creating Linear Models
Strategy: Expand the expression in the model. Find the slope and y-intercept and interpret .75 in this context.
Solution: Use the distributive property to find $h = -.75n + 150$. The slope of the line is $-.75$, which means that suggested heart rate decreases by 0.75 beats per minute for each year a person gets older (h decreases by .75 as n increases by one.).

9. (D)
Difficulty: M
Category: Creating Linear Models
Strategy: Convert the train's rate from km per hour to km per minute. Find an expression for the distance traveled from Shin-Osaka Station, in terms of t. Consider the distance between the station and central Tokyo to find an expression for the distance from central Tokyo.
Solution: $(320 \text{ km})/(1 \text{ hr}) \cdot (1\text{hr})/(60 \text{ min}) \approx 5.3 \text{ km/min}$. The total distance the train will travel t minutes after departure will be $d = r \cdot t \approx 5.3t$. The station is 2 km from central Tokyo, so the distance from central Tokyo is $d = 5.3t + 2$.

10. (C)
Difficulty: M
Category: Creating Linear Models
Strategy: Write an expression for how much Nadia spends in terms of d and l. Use her card limit to write an inequality for how much she can spend.
Solution: If Nadia buys d desktops that cost \$500.00 each, then she will spend $500d$ dollars on her desktop purchase. Similarly, if she buys l laptops at \$350.00 each, then she will spend $350l$ dollars on all of the laptops she purchases. In total, she will spend $500d + 350l$. She can use at most \$4000.00 for the purchase, so $500d + 350l \leq 4000$.

11. (D)
Difficulty: M
Category: Creating Linear Models
Strategy: Write an expression for the amount she earns for walking one dog for h hours. Then, write an expression for the amount she earns from walking d dogs for h hours. Alternatively, choose numbers for d and h to solve.
Solution: To walk one dog, she will charge a \$2 fee plus \$4 per hour. Thus, she will charge $2 + 4h$ to walk one dog for h hours. Therefore, she will charge $(2 + 4h)d = 2d + 4hd$ to walk d dogs for h hours.

12. (B)
Difficulty: M
Category: Creating Linear Models
Strategy: Find the equation of the solubility curve. Reason that y-values above the curve lie in the supersaturated region. Choose the answer choice that reflects this inequality. Alternatively, plug in points that are clearly in the supersaturated region of the graph into the system of inequalities and use process of elimination.
Solution: The slope of the solubility curve is approximately 5/3 (up 50, right 30), and the y-intercept is (0, 130). The equation of the solubility curve is $S = 1.67T + 130$. The supersaturated region is the region above the line, or where $S > 1.67T + 130$. The solution is liquid between 0°C and 100°C, so the other restriction on T is $0 \leq T \leq 100$.

13. (B)
Difficulty: M
Category: Creating Linear Models
Strategy: Determine the slope (rate of tree growth) and y-intercept (height of the tree once planted) of the graph. Note the scale on the axes. Alternatively, plug in points on the graph into the equations and use process of elimination.
Solution: The y-intercept of the graph is (0, 8), but all of the linear model equations have the same y-intercept. The slope is 8/5 (up 8, right 5), so the correct answer is B.

14. (D)
Difficulty: M
Category: Creating Linear Models
Strategy: Find an expression for the price per bottle in terms of n. Find an expression for the number of bottles sold per month in terms of n. Use these expressions to find an expression for the total monthly sales. Alternatively, choose a number for n to solve.
Solution: The price per bottle is $2.75 + .15n$. The total bottles sold per month is $1200 - 10n$. Therefore, total monthly sales = $(2.75 + 0.15n)(1200 - 10n)$.

15. (A)
Difficulty: H
Category: Creating linear models
Strategy: Each answer has an expression for p and an expression for t. Convert Tom's words per minute rate into pages per minute. Then, express the number of pages he reads in t minutes. Finally, express t in terms of b, using the information given in the problem. Alternatively, choose numbers for b and t. Solve and use process of elimination.
Solution: Tom reads 300 words per minute, and the book has an average of 500 words per page. Therefore, Tom reads (300 words)/(1 min) · (1 page)/(500 words) = (3/5 page)/minute = 0.6 pages/minute. Thus, the total pages Tom will read in t minutes of reading is $p = 0.6t$. Every hour (60 min), Tom spends 5 minutes resting his eyes and b minutes for other rests. Therefore, the average time spent reading per hour, $t = 60 - 5 - b = 55 - b$.

16. (D)
Difficulty: M
Category: Creating Linear Models
Strategy: Write an expression for the total cost of the weeding reception. Use the restriction on the budget given to write an inequality for the cost.
Solution: The total cost of the wedding reception will be the booking fee plus the guest fee times the number of guests attending, $250 + 17x$. Paul and Cyd's budget allows for up to $2500. Therefore, $250 + 17x \le 2500$.

17. (D)
Difficulty: M
Category: Creating Linear Models
Strategy: Write an expression for the total hours of attention spent on the cats and kittens. Then, use the information in the problem to write inequalities for the numbers of hours spent giving attention to the cats, the number of full-grown cats, and the number of kittens.
Solution: The time spend giving attention to the cats can be expressed as $1.5c + 3k$. There is a maximum of 200 hours that the volunteers can devote to this, so $1.5c + 3k \le 200$. There are at least 5 full-grown cats, so $c \ge 5$, and there are at least 4 kittens, so $k \ge 4$.

18. (B)
Difficulty: M
Category: Creating Linear Models
Strategy: Write the number of tables and guests as ordered pairs (number of tables, number of people). Find the slope and y-intercept of the line between these points. Note the y-intercept is no included in the solution set (since $n \ge 1$).
Solution: As ordered pairs of the form (tables, people), the relation must go through (1, 4), (2, 6), and (3, 8). The slope is 2, so number of people $= 2n + b$. Plug in any of the points to find $b = 2$.

19. (B)
Difficulty: M
Category: Creating Linear Models
Strategy: Determine the daily serving size of sodium and potassium for an adult. Write an expression relating s to x. Solve for s in terms of x. Write an expression relating p to x. Solve for p in terms of x. Add the two expressions.
Solution: If 250 mg of sodium is 10% of the daily allowance, m, for adults, then $250 = .10 \cdot m$, and $m = 2500$ mg. Similarly, if 130 mg of potassium is 4% of the daily allowance, n, for adults, then $130 = .04 \cdot n$ and $n = 3250$ mg. If s % of m is provided by x servings of beets, then $(s/100) \cdot 2500 = 250 \cdot x$, which means $25s = 250x$. Solve for s to get $s = 10x$. If p % of n is provided by x servings of beets, then $(p/100) \cdot 3250 = 130x$, or $32.5p = 130x$. Solve for p to get $p = 4x$. Thus, $s + p = 10x + 4x = 14x$.

20. (B)
Difficulty: M
Category: Creating Linear Models
Strategy: Write an expression for the number of calories, C, in terms of number of servings, x. Choose the graph that has the correct shape and y-intercept.
Solution: The equation for calories as a function of 1/2 cup servings of beets is $C = 40x$. The graph starts at (0,0) and is a line that slopes upward. Note that n need not be an integer, so the graph should be continuous.

21. (D)
Difficulty: M
Category: Creating Linear Models
Strategy: Write an expression for the amount Sidney paid in terms of x. Write an expression for what she would have paid had she waited for the sale. Find the difference. Alternatively, choose a value for x, like $x = 100$ and solve.
Solution: Sidney paid the price of the laptop, x, plus a 6% tax, which is $x + 06x = 1.06x$. The 35% off sale price of the case was $(x - .35x)$. She would have paid a 6% tax on this, bringing the amount paid to $1.06(x - .35x)$. Thus, her lost savings $= 1.06x - 1.06(x - 0.35x)$.

22. (C)
Difficulty: H
Category: Creating Linear Models
Strategy: Write an expression for Jack's gym costs in terms of x, and one for Beth's cost. Set the expressions equal to each other and solve for x. Determine how much more Beth pays in weekly fees than Jack does. Multiply this number by your solution for x.
Solution: Jeff's membership cost is $34 + 5.5x$, and Beth's cost is $25 + 7x$. If their total costs are the same, then $34 + 5.5x = 25 + 7x$. Rearrange the equation to get $9 = 1.5x$. Divide both sides by 1.5 to find $x = 6$. Thus, the two will have paid the same amount toward their gym memberships after 6 weeks. For each week, Beth pays $7.00 - $5.50 = $1.50 more in weekly fees than Jack does. So, after 6 weeks, she will have paid $6 \cdot $1.50 = $9.00 more in weekly fees than Jack has. Alternatively, reason that the amount Beth pays more in weekly fees (at the time when memberships costs are equal) is equal to the difference in their fixed costs ($34.00 - $25.00 = $9.00).

23. (C)
Difficulty: M
Category: Creating Linear Models
Strategy: Find the maximum recommended heart rate for a 23-year-old. Determine 65% and 85% of this value to find the range of heart rates required of a 23-year-old firefighter candidate. Use process of elimination on the answer choices.
Solution: The maximum recommended heart rate for a 23-year-old is $220 - 23 = 197$ beat/minute. 65% of 197 $= .65 \cdot 197 = 128.05$, which is the lowest acceptable heart rate. Eliminate choice A (100 times the lower limit), B (too high a lower limit), and choice D (too low a lower limit), to find C must be correct. The upper limit is correct also since $.85(197) = .85(243 - 46)$.

Heart of Algebra – Interpreting Linear Models – Pages 423-427

1. (B)
Difficulty: E
Category: Interpreting Linear Models
Strategy: Understand what the variables represent in the model. Plug in the value given for the appropriate variable and solve for the quantity asked for in the problem. Alternatively, plug in the answers and work backward.
Solution: To achieve an exam score of 92, $P(t) = 92$. Therefore, $22 + 12.5t = 92$, or $12.5t = 70$. Solve to get $t = 5.6$ hours.

2. (A)
Difficulty: E
Category: Interpreting Linear Models
Strategy: Identify the slope and the m-intercept in the linear model. Understand what slope and m-intercept represent in a linear model.
Solution: The m-intercept of the equation is 250. The m-intercept indicates the value of m when $t = 0$. When $t = 0$, the plate is first served to Camila (before she begins eating), and the mass of the sushi rolls is 250g.

3. (2.75 or 11/4)
Difficulty: M
Category: Interpreting Linear Models
Strategy: Understand what the variables represent in the model. Plug in the values given for the appropriate variables and solve for the relevant quantity.
Solution: The problem gives $E = 2094$ and $d = 24$. Thus, $2094 = 90(24) - b(24)$. Rearrange to get $-66 = -24b$. Solve for b to find $b = 2.75$.

4. (C)
Difficulty: E
Category: Interpreting Linear Models
Strategy: Understand what slope and y-intercept represent in a linear model.
Solution: The equation listed in the problem describes a linear model for a specific value of $y = 5500$. The starting population, 2400, is the y-intercept in the equation, and 310 represents the slope. The slope indicates how much y, the population, will increase every year.

5. (D)
Difficulty: E
Category: Interpreting Linear Models
Strategy: Find which points on the graph correspond to the starting supply for Adi.
Solution: Adi's starting supply is the y-intercept of his graph, which is 400 candy bars.

6. (A)
Difficulty: E
Category: Interpreting Linear Models
Strategy: Understand the meaning of slope and y-intercept in a linear model. Use the graphs to find how many candy bars each student sold per week. Find the difference.
Solution: The change in the number of candy bars per week is the slope of each graph.
The slope of Adi's graph is $(0 - 400)/(5 - 0) = -80$ candy bars per week, which means he sells 80 candy bars per week.
The slope of Jordan's graph is $(100 - 300)/(5 - 0) = -40$ candy bars per week, which means he sells 40 candy bars per week.
The difference is $80 - 40 = 40$ candy bars per week.

7. (B)
Difficulty: E
Category: Interpreting Linear Models
Strategy: Plug in the value given in the problem into the equation. Solve for m. Alternatively, plug in the answer choices and work backwards.
Solution: The total paid toward the lease is $8600.00. Plug this value in for P into the equation to get $8600 = 5000 + 200m$. Subtract 5000 from both sides to get $3600 = 200m$. Divide by 200 on both sides to find $m = 18$ months.

8. (B)
Difficulty: M
Category: Interpreting Linear Models
Strategy: Solve the temperature-altitude equation for t. Interpret slope and y-intercept in this linear model.
Solution: Solving the temperature-altitude equation for t yields the equation $t = -3.57a + 59$. Thus, the 3.57 in the equation is representative of the slope of this line. Since the slope is negative, then t, temperature, must decrease by 3.57 degrees Fahrenheit for every unit increase in altitude.

9. (D)
Difficulty: M
Category: Interpreting Linear Models
Strategy: Determine the slope of the line given the two points. Plug in one of the points to determine the equation of the line and its y-intercept.
Solution: slope $= \dfrac{295 - 175}{18 - 10} = \dfrac{120}{8} = 15$. The equation of the line must be $y = 15x + b$. Plug in one of the points to solve for b, the value of y when x (kWh usage) is 0: $175 = 15(10) + b$. Solve for b to find $b = 25$. The problem asks for the value of y when $x = 0$, which is $25.00.

10. (C)
Difficulty: M
Category: Interpreting Linear Models
Strategy: Understand what slope and r-intercept represent in the linear model. Determine whether or not each statement is true using this information.
Solution: The slope of the linear model is $-35/4$, which means that Jamie completes 35 tax returns every 4 days. Statement I is false. The r-intercept of $(0, 250)$ means that Jamie starts each month with 250 tax returns to complete. Statement II is true. To check if statement III is true, solve for how many days it would take her to have 0 left to complete: $0 = 250 - (35/4)(d)$. Solve for d to find $d \approx 29 < 30$, so she has enough time to complete the 250 she begins with in the month. Statement III is true.

11. (C)
Difficulty: M
Category: Interpreting Linear Models
Strategy: Understand what slope and y-intercept represent in the linear model.
Solution: In the equation, 10 is the y-coordinate of the y-intercept. The y-intercept occurs when $x = 0$, or when the can is shaken for 0 seconds. Thus, 10 mL represents the volume of liquid that comes out when the can is not shaken.

12. (B)
Difficulty: M
Category: Interpreting Linear Models
Strategy: Understand what slope and C-intercept represent in the linear model.
Solution: 7.5, the slope of the linear model, indicates that the cost of the kitchen re-tiling increases by $7.50 for every additional square foot of area.

13. (C)
Difficulty: M
Category: Interpreting Linear Models
Strategy: Write an expression for the amount Grace would be paid in terms of w, the number of weeks she works. Be mindful of units.
Solution: If Grace chooses the option where she is paid $1040 every two weeks, then she is paid half of that in one week, or $520.00 weekly. With this option, $p = 520w$. If she picks the other option, she will be paid $7.5b$ for the bottles she sells, plus $250 per week ($500 for two weeks), or $p = 7.5b + 250w$.

14. (D)
Difficulty: M
Category: Interpreting Linear Models
Strategy: Understand what slope and y-intercept represent in the linear model. Use process of elimination.
Solution: The slope, 250, represents the rate at which y increases as x increases incrementally. Thus, there is an activity taking place at a rate of 250 units per some unit (in this case, hours). The y-intercept indicates that when $x = 0$, $y = 750$. Only answer choice D lists 250 as a volumetric rate and 750 as a starting volume.

15. (C)
Difficulty: M/H
Category: Interpreting Linear Models
Strategy: Write the Celsius and Fahrenheit temperatures measured by the meter as a set of ordered pairs (temp in °C, temp. in °F). Find the slope and y-intercept of the meter readings, and compare this to the conversion equation given at the top.
Solution: The ordered pairs of readings are $(-40, -18)$, $(0, 32)$, and $(100, 157)$. The y-coordinate of the y-intercept is 32. The slope, or change in Fahrenheit readings per unit increase in Celsius is $(32 - 18)/(0 - 40) = 50/40 = 1.2$.
Therefore, the meter readings can be found using the incorrect equation $F = 1.2C + 32$. Thus, the meter is incorrect because it is using a factor less than 1.8 to convert from Celsius to Fahrenheit.

16. (C)
Difficulty: H
Category: Interpreting Linear Models
Strategy: Find the slope of the line. Plug in a point on the line to determine the line's y-intercept (note that the y-intercept does not appear on the graph, since n does not begin at 0) or use process of elimination.
Solution: Use points that appear to be on the line at about $(5, 130)$ and $(8, 180)$ to estimate the slope:
slope $\approx (180 - 130)/(8 - 5) = 50/3 \approx 17$. Only choices C and D have the correct slope. The line of best fit goes through about the point $(5, 130)$, which is not the y-intercept. So, the y-coordinate of the y-intercept must be less than 130. The only possible answer choice is C.

17. (B)
Difficulty: H
Category: Interpreting Linear Models
Strategy: Understand what slope and h-intercept represent in the linear model. Since t is measured in months, plug in $t = 12$ to find yearly growth. Use process of elimination.
Solution: The y-intercept indicates that the tree was 18 ft tall when the researcher began tracking it ($t = 0$). Eliminate choice A. The slope of 1/24 indicates that the tree grows 1 ft every 24 *months*. Thus, every year (12 months), the tree will grow 1/2 foot.

Passport to Advanced Math – Section Quiz – Pages 430-434

1. (C)
Difficulty: E
Category: Equations with Exponents
Strategy: Raise each side of the equation to the appropriate exponent to get the value of the desired result. Use exponent rules to evaluate.
Solution: To convert x^6 to x^{-12}, the exponent must be multiplied by –2. This is equivalent to raising x^6 to the power of –2. $\left(x^6\right)^{-2} = 9^{-2}$.

Thus, $x^{-12} = \dfrac{1}{9^2} = \dfrac{1}{81}$.

2. (A)
Difficulty: E
Category: Equations with Fractions
Strategy: Find the domain of any rational expressions. Multiply both sides by a common denominator and solve. Check the solution is in the domain. Alternatively, plug in the answer choices.
Solution: The rational expressions exist for all values of $x \neq -4, -2$. Cross multiply to get $x + 2 = -(x + 4)$. Distribute the minus sign and combine like terms to get $2x = -6$. Divide by 2 to find $x = -3$. This solution is in the domain.

3. (10)
Difficulty: E
Category: Equations with Fractions
Strategy: Multiply both sides by a common denominator and solve. Alternatively, plug in the answer choices.
Solution: Multiply both sides of the equation by 10 to eliminate all the fractions: $\dfrac{10}{1} \cdot \dfrac{2}{5} x - 20 = \dfrac{10}{1} \cdot \dfrac{1}{10} x + 10$. Cancel any common factors and simplify to get $4x - 20 = x + 10$. Collect like terms and solve for x to find $x = 10$.

4. (C)
Difficulty: E
Category: Quadratic Equations
Strategy: Factor the quadratic equation first. Then, set each factor equal to zero to solve for all solutions for x. Alternatively, use the quadratic formula, or simply plug in the answer choices.
Solution: $2x^2 + 3x - 2 = (2x - 1)(x + 2)$. Set each factor equal to zero and solve to get the solutions to the equation: $2x - 1 = 0$ results in the solution $x = 1/2$. If $x + 2 = 0$, then $x = -2$. Only one of these solutions shows up in the answer choices, so C must be correct.

5. (C)
Difficulty: E
Category: Graphs of Functions
Strategy: Know how to interpret the values of a function from both its graph and a table of values. Evaluate both functions for each answer choice, and check which pair of resulting values satisfies the inequality condition. Use process of elimination.
Solution: To find the value of a function at a specific x-value, find the ordered pair on the graph with the same x-value. The value of f at this number is the y-coordinate of the point. Find $f(x)$ for each of the values listed in the answers and compare them to the corresponding value of $g(x)$ found in the table.

$f(-2) = 1 > g(-2) = 0$
$f(-1) = 0 > g(-1) = -2$
$f(0) = 3 < g(0) = 6$
$f(1) = 0 > g(1) = -2$
Only answer choice C satisfies the inequality.

6. (D)
Difficulty: E/M
Category: Graphs of Quadratics
Strategy: Plug in the appropriate value of x into the function to find the y-intercept.
Solution: The y-intercept is the point where the graph intersects the y-axis, i.e. the point on the graph where $x = 0$. Plug in $x = 0$ into the equation of the function to find the y-coordinate of the y-intercept: $a = f(0) = 2(0)^2 - 12(0) + 16 = 16$. Alternatively, reason that the function is expressed in the standard form of a quadratic function. Thus, the constant term should be the y-coordinate of the y-intercept.

7. (3)
Difficulty: E/M
Category: Functions
Strategy: Write an expression for $h(x)$ in terms of x. Plug in $x = 1$ into the resulting expression to find the solution.
Solution: $h(x) = f(x) + 2\,g(x) = 3x + 2 + 2(-2x + 1) = -x + 4$. Thus, $h(1) = -(1) + 4 = 3$. The problem can also be solved by evaluating $f(1) + 2g(1)$ directly.

8. (D)
Difficulty: M
Category: Equations with Fractions
Strategy: Multiply both sides by a common denominator and solve for x. Alternatively, plug in the values in the answers and use process of elimination.
Solution: Multiply by 25 to get $3x - 100 = 10 + 400$. Combine like terms to get $3x = 510$. Solve to find $x = 170$.

9. (A)
Difficulty: E/M
Category: Graphs of Functions
Strategy: Determine the algebraic expression for the function that would result in the graph of f shifted 2 units to the right. Alternatively, graph the functions in the answer choices on a graphing calculator. Compare them to the graph of $f(x)$. Use process of elimination.
Solution: The graph of $f(x - 2)$ is the graph of $f(x)$ shifted two units to the right. To find an expression for $f(x - 2)$, plug in $(x - 2)$ wherever x appears in the original function:
$f(x - 2) = ((x - 2) - 2)^2 + 5 = (x - 4)^2 + 5$.

10. (C)
Difficulty: M
Category: Equations with Radicals
Strategy: Square both sides. Set the equation equal to zero and factor to find solutions for x. Check for extraneous solutions. Alternatively, plug in answers to solve.
Solution: Squaring both sides to find $6x - 3 = (x + 1)^2$. Expand the right side to get $6x - 3 = x^2 + 2x + 1$. Set the quadratic equation equal to zero next: $x^2 - 4x + 4 = 0$. Factor to find $(x - 2)(x - 2) = 0$, which gives the solution $x = 2$. The solution works in the original equation.

11. (D)

Difficulty: M

Category: Quadratic Equations

Strategy: Use the quadratic formula to find the solutions for x. Add the solutions.

Solution: To solve, apply the quadratic formula

$\left(x = \dfrac{-b \pm \sqrt{b^2 - 4ac}}{2a} \right)$, where $a = 1$, $b = -16$, and $c = 5$.

$x = \dfrac{16 \pm \sqrt{(-16)^2 - 4(5)}}{2}$. Note that there is no need to solve for the two individual solutions since the problem asks for the SUM of the possible solutions. Add the two solutions, which will result in canceling the radical expression:

$\dfrac{16 + \sqrt{(-16)^2 - 4(5)}}{2} + \dfrac{16 - \sqrt{(-16)^2 - 4(5)}}{2} = \dfrac{32}{2} = 16.$

12. (B)

Difficulty: M

Category: Functions

Strategy: Evaluate the function for each value of x in the answer choices. Alternatively, graph the function on a graphing calculator. Find which value of d makes $f(d) < 2$.

Solution: Evaluate the function for each answer choice.

$f(1) = (1)^2 - 3(1) + 4 = 2$, which is not less than 2.

$f(1.5) = (1.5)^2 - 3(1.5) + 4 = 1.75 < 2$. B is correct.

$f(2) = (2)^2 - 3(2) + 4 = 2$, which is not less than 2.

$f(2.5) = (2.5)^2 - 3(2.5) + 4 = 2.75$, which is not less than 2.

13. (B)

Difficulty: M

Category: Graphs of Quadratics

Strategy: Note that the answer choices are in vertex form. Use the symmetry of a parabola and the set of points to determine that one of the three points must be the vertex. Write the vertex form of the quadratic function. Plug in either of the non-vertex points to solve for a, the leading coefficient. Alternatively, plug the points on the parabola into the answer choices and use process of elimination.

Solution: Since the points $(0, 4)$ and $(2, 4)$ have the same y-value, the axis of symmetry and the vertex must be at the x-value halfway between them, or $x = 1$. Therefore, the point $(1, 1)$ must be the vertex of the parabola. The vertex form of the quadratic function for a parabola with vertex at (h, k) is $y = a(x - h)^2 + k$. Thus, the parabola must have a quadratic function of $y = a(x - 1)^2 + 1$. Plug in the y-intercept $(0, 4)$ to solve for a: $4 = a(0 - 1)^2 + 1 = a + 1$. Solve to find $a = 3$. Hence, the equation for this parabola is $y = 3(x - 1)^2 + 1$.

14. (A)

Difficulty: M

Category: Nonlinear Models

Strategy: Understand the components of an exponential function.

Solution: For an exponential function $f(t) = a\left(1 + \dfrac{b}{100}\right)^t$, a represents the y-intercept of the function, or the value of y when $t = 0$. The value of b represents the percent yearly growth (if positive) or percent yearly decay (if b is negative) for the function. The value of a in the function given in the problem is .908, which is a number given

in units of trillions of dollars. Therefore, .908 must be the value of the US National debt when $t = 0$. The variable t represents the number of years after 1980. Thus, the value of the U.S. National Debt in 1980 must have been approximately .908 trillion dollars, or $908,000,000,000.

15. (D)

Difficulty: M

Category: Graphs of Quadratics

Strategy: Identify the x-intercepts of the graph, the vertex, and the sign of the leading coefficient. Use process of elimination based on this information.

Solution: The x-intercepts are $(-2, 0)$ and $(6, 0)$. The vertex is approximately $(2, 24)$. The graph opens downward, which means the quadratic function must have a negative leading coefficient. Eliminate A and C, since they have positive leading coefficients. Eliminate B because the vertex of the quadratic function is $(-2, 24)$, which does not match the graph. Answer choice D shows factors which reflect the correct x-intercepts, so it must be the correct answer.

16. (A)

Difficulty: M

Category: Equations with Exponents

Strategy: Plug in the value of x into the expression. Rewrite the expression as a power of 9 using relevant exponent rules. If needed, rewrite the expression as a power of 3 or 81 using relevant exponent rules. Use process of elimination.

Solution: Plug in $x = 4$ into the expression to get $9^4 \cdot 9^8$. When multiplying two powers of the same base, the exponents can be added: $9^4 \cdot 9^8 = 9^{12}$. This value is clearly less than the values in answer choices B, C, and D, so A must be correct. To prove that A is correct, rewrite 9^{12} as a power of 3:

Since $9 = 3^2$, then $9^{12} = (3^2)^{12} = 3^{24}$.

17. (A)

Difficulty: M

Category: Quadratic Equations / Graphs of Quadratics

Strategy: Since both equations are set equal to y, set the two expressions for y equal to each other. Set the resulting quadratic equation equal to zero and express the discriminant in terms of k. Set the discriminant equal to zero and solve for k.

Solution: Set the expressions for y equal to each other to get $x^2 + 2x = k$. Subtract k from both sides to get $x^2 + 2x - k = 0$. For the equation to have only one real solution (a double root), the discriminant, $b^2 - 4ac$ where $a = 1$, $b = 2$, and $c = -k$, must be equal to zero.

Thus, $4 + 4k = 0$. Solve to find $k = -1$.

18. (B)

Difficulty: M

Category: Polynomials

Strategy: Set each factor equal to zero to find the x-coordinates of the x-intercepts.

Solution: The polynomial function has x-intercepts when $x - a = 0$ (or when $x = a$), $x + b = 0$ (or when $x = -b$), and when $x - c = 0$ (or when $x = c$).

19. (A)
Difficulty: M
Category: Functions
Strategy: Start on the inside of the compound function and work your way outward. Begin by evaluating $g(3)$. Plug in the resulting value into the expression for f. Use PEMDAS to evaluate numerically.
Solution: $g(3) = 3 \cdot 3 + 14 = 9 + 14 = 23$.
Thus, $f(g(3)) = f(23) = 23^2 - 4 \cdot 23 + 14 = 529 - 92 + 14 = 452$.

20. (B)
Difficulty: M
Category: Graphs of Functions
Strategy: Locate the x-intercept(s) and count them. Locate the y-intercept(s) and count them. Find the product of these numbers.
Solution: The y-intercepts are the points where the graph crosses the y-axis ($x = 0$). This occurs at one point, the point $(0, 0)$. The x-intercepts are the points where the graph crosses the x-axis ($y = 0$). The graph crosses the x-axis 6 times, so there are 6 x-intercepts. The product is $6 \cdot 1 = 6$.

21. (A)
Difficulty: M/H
Category: Nonlinear Models
Strategy: Determine the correct exponential model that describes the amount of money in both savings accounts, using the original deposit and percent rate of growth. Evaluate each model to determine the amount in each account after 10 years. Subtract the values.
Solution: The general formula for an exponential model is $p(t) = ab^t$, where a represents the original deposit, b represents the percent rate of growth, and t represents time. The function $p(t)$ represents the amount in the account after t years. For the account with 3.5% interest, $p_1(t) = 400(1.035)^t$. For the account with 5% interest, $p_2(t) = 400(1.05)^t$. Plug in $t = 10$ for x into each of the models and find the difference:
$400(1.05)^{10} - 400(1.035)^{10} \approx 651.56 - 564.24 = \$87.32$. Rounded to the nearest dollar, the answer is $87.00.

22. (D)
Difficulty: M
Category: Equations with Fractions
Strategy: Convert all fractions into fractions with a common denominator and simplify. Alternatively, choose numbers for h and g and solve.
Solution: Rewrite both fractions as fractions over the common denominator $h(h + g)$:

$$\frac{h}{h} \cdot \frac{h - g}{h + g} + \frac{2g}{h} \cdot \frac{h + g}{h + g} = \frac{h(h - g) + 2g(h + g)}{h(h + g)}$$

$$= \frac{h^2 + gh + 2g^2}{h^2 + hg}.$$

23. (A)
Difficulty: M/H
Category: Polynomials
Strategy: Factor the expression on the left (it is a perfect square). Set the factor equal to zero. Find all values for x and y that satisfy the equation. Plug in these vales for x and y into the rational expression asked for in the problem.
Solution: The left-hand side of the equation can be re-written as $(x^4)^2 + 2x^4y^3 + (y^3)^2 = (x^4 + y^3)^2 = 0$. Set the factor equal to zero to get $x^4 + y^3 = 0$ or $x^4 = -y^3$. The only values for which this function is true is if $x = 0$, $y = 0$ (which violates the restrictions in the problem), if $x = -1$, $y = -1$ (which violates the restriction on x), or if $x = 1$, and $y = -1$. This is the only case that meets all the requirements in the problem, so $x + y = 0$. Therefore, $(1/6)(x + y) = 0$.

24. (C)
Difficulty: M/H
Category: Graphs of Functions
Strategy: Identify all x-intercepts. Rewrite the x-intercepts as factors of the polynomial. Know how to recognize the difference between a root of even vs. odd multiplicity. Identify each root from the graph as having odd or even multiplicity, and then determine the nature of the powers of the corresponding factors. Use process of elimination.
Solution: The graph has x-intercepts at $(-13, 0)$, $(-8, 0)$, $(-2, 0)$, and $(1.9, 0)$. Thus, the polynomial function must have factors of $(x + 13)$, $(x + 8)$, $(x + 2)$, and $(x - 1.9)$. Choices A and D can be eliminated, since they show incorrect factors. Roots where the graph is tangent to the x-axis must have even multiplicity (i.e. corresponding polynomial factors must be raised to an even power), whereas zeros where the graph crosses through the x-axis must have odd multiplicity (i.e. corresponding polynomial factors must be raised to an odd power). The graph is tangent to the x-axis at $x = 8$ only, and crosses through the x-axis at all other zeros. Hence, the $(x - 8)$ factor must be raised to an even power, while all others should be raised to an odd power. Only answer choice C has this particular set of characteristics.

25. (D)
Difficulty: M/H
Category: Quadratic Equations
Strategy: Determine the discriminant of each answer choice. The sign of the discriminant should determine how many x-intercepts exist in the xy-coordinate plane.
Solution: For a parabola to have no x-intercepts, then there are no real solutions when the function is set equal to zero. Instead of solving each answer choice separately for solutions, it is faster to determine the discriminant for each quadratic function, which tells the nature of the solution set. When the discriminant, $b^2 - 4ac$, is negative, then there are no real solutions. The discriminant in answer choice A is $0 - 4(1)(0) = 0$. This graph must have one x-intercept (a double root). It can be eliminated. Answer choice B has a discriminant of $(-2)^2 - 4(1)(0) = 4$, which is positive, so it must have 2 real solutions, and thus two x-intercepts. Only answer choice D results in a negative discriminant: $(-2)^2 - 4(1)(2) = -4$. Thus, it has no x-intercepts when graphed in the xy-plane.

26. (A)

Difficulty: H

Category: Equations with Exponents

Strategy: Use a substitution to rewrite the left-hand side all in terms of a. Raise each side to the -1 power. Find the value of a for which the resulting equation is true. Determine the value of b, and the find the difference.

Solution: $a^{-\frac{b}{2}} = a^{-\frac{4a}{2}} = \frac{1}{16} \rightarrow a^{-2a} = \frac{1}{16} \rightarrow a^{2a} = 16$

For this equation to be true, a must be 2 ($2^4 = 16$). Thus, $b = 4(2) = 8$, and $a - b = 2 - 8 = -6$.

27. (D)

Difficulty: H

Category: Equations with Radicals

Strategy: Cube both sides and solve for q.

Solution: Cube both sides to get $\frac{5}{2}q = \frac{1}{64}q^3$.

Then, divide both sides by q (this is possible since $q \neq 0$): $\frac{5}{2} = \frac{1}{64}q^2$.

Multiply both sides by 64 to get $160 = q^2$. Find the square root to find $q = \sqrt{160} = \sqrt{16}\sqrt{10} = 4\sqrt{10}$.

Passport to Advanced Math – Equations with Fractions – Pages 436-440

1. (A)

Difficulty: E

Category: Equations with Fractions

Strategy: Find the domain of any rational expressions. Multiply both sides by a common denominator and solve. Check the solution is in the domain. Alternatively, plug in the answer choices.

Solution: The rational expression on the right exists for all values of $z \neq 0$. Multiply both sides of the equation by z to eliminate any fractions: $32z = 16$. Divide both sides by 32 to find $z = 0.5$. This number is in the domain.

2. (D)

Difficulty: E

Category: Equations with Fractions

Strategy: Find the domain of any rational expressions. Multiply both sides by a common denominator and solve. Check the solution is in the domain. Alternatively, plug in the answer choices.

Solution: The rational expression on the left exists for all values of $x \neq -3$. Cross-multiply to get $5(x - 3) = 2(x + 3)$. Distribute to get $5x - 15 = 2x + 6$. Rearrange and solve to find $x = 7$. This number is in the domain.

3. (D)

Difficulty: E

Category: Equations with Fractions

Strategy: Convert all terms into fractions with a common denominator and simplify. Alternatively, choose a number for x and solve.

Solution: Convert all terms into fractions over $3x - 1$:

$\frac{4(3x-1)}{3x-1} + \frac{1}{3x-1}$. Combine the fractions by adding the numerators:

$\frac{12x-4+1}{3x-1} = \frac{12x-3}{3x-1}$.

4. (D)

Difficulty: E

Category: Equations with Fractions

Strategy: Multiply both sides by the denominator. Divide by the appropriate expressions to solve for T. Alternatively, plug in numbers for P, A, and N, and solve for T. Use process of elimination.

Solution: Multiply both sides by 12 to eliminate all fractions: $12P = T(12 - A - N)$. Divide by $12 - A - N$ on both sides to get

$T = \frac{12P}{12 - A - N}$.

5. (A)

Difficulty: M

Category: Equations with Fractions

Strategy: Find the domain of the rational expression. Factor the numerator and cancel any common factors in the denominator. Solve and check that the solution is in the domain. It is also possible to solve by multiplying by the denominator and solving the final quadratic equation. However, this method will result in an extraneous solution.

Solution: The rational expression on the left exists for all values of $x \neq 2$. Factor the numerator and cancel any factors to find $\dfrac{x^2-4}{x-2} = \dfrac{(x+2)(x-2)}{x-2} = x+2 = -1$. Solve to find $x = -3$, which is in the domain of all the original expressions.

6. (C)

Difficulty: M

Category: Equations with Fractions

Strategy: Multiply both sides by a common denominator and solve for a. Alternatively, choose a number for x and solve for a.

Solution: Multiply both sides by $3(x+4)$ to get $\dfrac{3(x+4)\cdot 4}{(x+4)} - \dfrac{3(x+4)\cdot 2}{3(x+4)} = \dfrac{3(x+4)\cdot a}{3(x+4)}$. Cancel to get $12 - 2 = a$. Therefore, $a = 10$.

7. (B)

Difficulty: M

Category: Equations with Fractions

Strategy: Convert all terms into fractions with a common denominator and simplify. Alternatively, choose a number for x and solve.

Solution: Rewrite fractions with a common denominator of $27x^3$, then simplify:

$$\frac{1}{3x} - \frac{2}{9x^2} - \frac{3}{27x^3} = \left(\frac{9x^2}{9x^2}\right)\left(\frac{1}{3x}\right) - \left(\frac{3x}{3x}\right)\left(\frac{2}{9x^2}\right) - \frac{3}{27x^3}$$

$$= \frac{9x^2}{27x^3} - \frac{6x}{27x^3} - \frac{3}{27x^3} = \frac{9x^2 - 6x - 3}{27x^3} = \frac{3(3x^2 - 2x - 1)}{27x^3}$$

$$= \frac{3(3x+1)(x-1)}{27x^3} = \frac{(3x+1)(x-1)}{9x^3}.$$

8. (A)

Difficulty: M

Category: Equations with Fractions

Strategy: Multiply both sides by a common denominator and solve for x. Alternatively, plug in the answer choices.

Solution: Multiply both sides by 21 to get the equation $9x + 6 = 21x$. Rearrange to get $12x = 6$. Solve to find $x = 1/2$.

9. (C)

Difficulty: M

Category: Equations with Fractions

Strategy: To obtain the smallest possible value of the fraction, the denominator must be as large as possible (in this case, the denominator can never be negative, so we need not consider this possibility). Consider which values of a and b will result in a difference with the largest value.

Solution: To achieve the largest possible positive denominator, choose the largest possible value for b and the smallest possible value for a. Plug in 12 for b and 2 for a to get $4/(12 - 2) = 4/10 = 2/5$.

10. (12)

Difficulty: (M)

Category: Equations with Fractions

Strategy: Combine any constant terms. Multiply both sides by a common denominator and solve for x.

Solution: Subtract 16 from both sides to get the equation $\dfrac{x}{12} = 12 - \dfrac{x}{6}$. Multiply both sides by 12 to find $x = 144 - 2x$. Add $2x$ to both sides to get $3x = 144$. Solve for x to find $x = 48$. Thus, $x/4 = 48/4 = 12$.

11. (C)

Difficulty: E/M

Category: Equations with Fractions

Strategy: Plug in the value given for m into the equation and solve for n.

Solution: $m = \dfrac{9}{4}n - 15 \rightarrow 39 = \dfrac{9}{4}n - 15 \rightarrow 54 = \dfrac{9}{4}n$. Divide both sides by 9/4 (the same as multiplying both sides by 4/9) to find $n = 24$.

12. (B)

Difficulty: M

Category: Equations with Fractions

Strategy: Convert all fractions in the denominator into fractions with a common denominator and simplify. Cancel any common factors along the way. Alternatively, choose a number for x and solve.

Solution: Rewrite the denominator as a single fraction over a common denominator and simplify:

$$\frac{x+5}{\dfrac{2}{x+3} - \dfrac{1}{x+4}} = \frac{x+5}{\dfrac{2(x+4) - 1(x+3)}{(x+3)(x+4)}} = \frac{x+5}{\dfrac{2x+8-x-3}{x^2+7x+12}} =$$

$$\frac{x+5}{\dfrac{x+5}{x^2+7x+12}} = \frac{x+5}{1}\cdot\frac{x^2+7x+12}{x+5} = x^2+7x+12.$$

13. $\dfrac{5}{18}$ or .277 or .278

Difficulty: M

Category: Equations with Fractions

Strategy: Multiply both sides by a common denominator and solve for y.

Solution: Multiply both sides by 27 to get $63y - 10 = 27y$.

Combining like terms to find $36y = 10$. Solve to find $y = 10/36 = 5/18$ or .277 or .278.

14. $\dfrac{6}{7}$ or .857

Difficulty: M

Category: Equations with Fractions

Strategy: Find the domain of any rational expressions. Multiply both sides by a common denominator and solve. Check the solution is in the domain.

Solution: The rational expressions in the equation for all values of z $\neq 0$ or -2. Multiply both sides by the common denominator $2z(z-2)$ to get $3(z-2) + 2 \cdot 2z = 0$. Distribute the products to get $3z - 6 + 4z = 0$. Combine like terms to get $7z = 6$. Solve to get $z = 6/7$ or $.857$. This solution is in the set of values of z for which the equation is defined.

15. (C)

Difficulty: M

Category: Equations with Fractions

Strategy: Find the value of the reciprocal of the expression on the left side of the equation. Then, multiply and divide by the relevant quantities. Alternatively, find values of a, b, c, and d, for which the original equation is true. Then, evaluate the expression asked for in the problem.

Solution: $\left(\dfrac{a}{c}\right)\left(\dfrac{b}{d}\right) = \dfrac{ab}{cd} = \dfrac{5}{18}$. Thus, the reciprocal, $\dfrac{cd}{ab} = \dfrac{18}{5}$.

Finally, $\dfrac{3cd}{2ab} = \dfrac{3}{2} \cdot \dfrac{cd}{ab} = \dfrac{3}{2} \cdot \dfrac{18}{5} = \dfrac{27}{5}$.

16. (B)

Difficulty: M

Category: Equations with Fractions

Strategy: Factor the numerator of the fraction and cancel any common factors in the denominator. Combine like terms. Alternatively, choose a number for x and solve.

Solution: $2x + 4 + \dfrac{x^2 - 5x - 24}{x+3} = 2x + 4 + \dfrac{(x-8)(x+3)}{x+3}$

$= 2x + 4 + x - 8 = 3x - 4$.

17. (D)

Difficulty: M

Category: Equations with Fractions

Strategy: Find the domain of any rational expressions. Multiply both sides by a common denominator and solve. Check the solution is in the domain. Alternatively, plug in the answer choices and work backward.

Solution: The equation is defined for all values of $x \neq 2$. Multiply both sides by $(x-2)$ to get $(x+2)(x-2) = 5$. Distribute the expression on the left to get $x^2 - 4 = 5$, or $x^2 = 9$. This is true when $x = 3$ or -3. Both solutions are in the set of values of x for which the original equation is defined.

18. (D)

Difficulty: M

Category: Equations with Fractions

Strategy: Find the domain of any rational expressions. Multiply both sides by a common denominator and solve. Check the solution is in the domain. Alternatively, plug in the answer choices and work backward.

Solution: The equation is defined for all values of $x \neq 1$. Multiply both sides of the equation by $(1 - x)$ to get $3x - 4 = 7(1 - x)$.

Distribute the expression on the right side to get $3x - 4 = 7 - 7x$. Combine like terms to get $10x = 11$. Solve to find $x = 11/10$.

19. (C)

Difficulty: M

Category: Equations with Fractions

Strategy: Rearrange all quotients of fractions into products of fractions. Cancel any common terms in the denominators and numerators. Rearrange and solve for a. Alternatively, choose a number for x and solve for a.

Solution: Rewrite the left-hand side first as a product of fractions, and express as a single fraction: $\dfrac{\dfrac{x+1}{a}}{\dfrac{x+3}{}} = \dfrac{x+1}{1} \cdot \dfrac{x+3}{a} = \dfrac{(x+1)(x+3)}{a}$.

Do the same for the right side:

$\dfrac{x+5}{x+2} \div \dfrac{x+1}{x+3} = \dfrac{x+5}{x+2} \cdot \dfrac{x+3}{x+1} = \dfrac{(x+5)(x+3)}{(x+2)(x+1)}$. Set the two sides equal

to each other to get $\dfrac{(x+1)(x+3)}{a} = \dfrac{(x+5)(x+3)}{(x+2)(x+1)}$. Divide both sides

by their common factor of $(x + 3)$ to find $\dfrac{(x+1)}{a} = \dfrac{(x+5)}{(x+2)(x+1)}$.

Cross multiply to get $a(x+5) = (x+1)^2(x+2)$. Divide both sides by

$(x + 5)$ to find $a = \dfrac{(x+1)^2(x+2)}{x+5}$.

20. (A)

Difficulty: M

Category: Equations with Fractions

Strategy: Write an equation that relate the variables t and w. Write another that relates the variables t and z. Solve for w and z in terms of t. Find the ratio. Alternatively, choose a number for t and find the ratio for that specific value of t.

Solution: The first sentence states $\dfrac{1}{4} \cdot \dfrac{1}{3} t = \dfrac{5}{6} w$ and that $\dfrac{3}{5} t = z$. Solve

for w in terms of z by multiplying both sides by 6/5: $\dfrac{t}{10} = w$. z is

already in term of t. Thus, w: $z = \dfrac{\dfrac{t}{10}}{\dfrac{3t}{5}} = \dfrac{t}{10} \cdot \dfrac{5}{3t} = \dfrac{5}{30} = \dfrac{1}{6} = 1:6$.

21. (D)

Difficulty: M/H

Category: Algebraic Expressions

Strategy: Perform polynomial long division or synthetic division. Alternatively, choose a number for x and solve.

Solution:

$$
\begin{array}{r}
2 r = -13 \\
2x+5 \overline{)\ 4x - 3} \\
\underline{-4x - 10} \\
-13
\end{array}
$$

Thus, $\dfrac{4x-3}{2x+5} = 2 - \dfrac{13}{2x+5}$.

22. (B)

Difficulty: M/H

Category: Equations with Fractions

Strategy: Convert all fractions in the numerator into fractions with a common denominator and simplify. Do the same for the denominator. As a last step, take the numerator and multiply by the reciprocal of the denominator, cancelling any common factors as they occur. Alternatively, choose a number for x and solve.

Solution: Rewrite both fractions in the numerator as fractions over 6:

$\frac{3}{3} \cdot \frac{x}{2} + \frac{2}{2} \cdot \frac{1}{3} = \frac{3x+2}{6}$. Rewrite the fractions in the denominator as fractions over 12:

$\frac{3}{4} - \frac{1}{3} = \frac{9}{12} - \frac{4}{12} = \frac{5}{12}$.

Finally, $\dfrac{\dfrac{3x+2}{6}}{\dfrac{5}{12}} = \dfrac{3x+2}{6} \cdot \dfrac{12}{5} = \dfrac{6x+4}{5}$.

23. (C)

Difficulty: M/H

Category: Equations with Fractions

Strategy: Multiply both sides by the denominator. Then, divide by the relevant variables to solve for T.

Solution: Multiply both sides by V to get $PV = nRT$. Divide both sides by nR to solve for $T = (PV)/(nR)$.

24. (B)

Difficulty: M/H

Category: Equations with Fractions

Strategy: Use polynomial long division or synthetic division. Alternatively, choose a number for x and solve.

Solution:

$$
\begin{array}{r}
2x^2 + 5x + 4 \\
x-7 \overline{\smash{\big)}\, 2x^3 - 9x^2 - 31x - 28} \\
\underline{-\left(2x^3 - 14x^2\right)} \\
5x^2 - 31x - 28 \\
\underline{-\left(5x^2 - 35x\right)} \\
4x - 28 \\
\underline{-\left(4x - 28\right)} \\
0
\end{array}
$$

Or use synthetic division:

$$
\begin{array}{r|rrrr}
7 & 2 & -9 & -31 & -28 \\
  &   & 14 & 35 & 28 \\
\hline
  & 2 & 5 & 4 & 0
\end{array}
$$

To get the solution $2x^2 + 5x + 4$.

25. (A)

Difficulty: H

Category: Equations with Fractions

Strategy: Convert all terms into fractions with a common denominator and combine into one fraction. Factor the numerator by grouping. Alternatively, choose a number for x and solve.

Solution: Rewrite each fraction as a fraction over x^4:

$\dfrac{x^3}{x^3} \cdot \dfrac{1}{x} - \dfrac{x^2}{x^2} \cdot \dfrac{2}{x^2} - \dfrac{x}{x} \cdot \dfrac{4}{x^3} + \dfrac{8}{x^4} = \dfrac{x^3 - 2x^2 - 4x + 8}{x^4}$

$= \dfrac{(x^3 - 2x^2) + (-4x + 8)}{x^4} = \dfrac{x^2(x-2) - 4(x-2)}{x^4} =$

$\dfrac{(x^2 - 4)(x - 2)}{x^4} = \dfrac{(x-2)^2(x+2)}{x^4}$.

26. (D)

Difficulty: H

Category: Equations with Fractions

Strategy: Plug in the value of A into the expression. Factor the numerator and denominator. Cancel any common factors and simplify. Alternatively, choose a number for x and solve.

Solution: $\dfrac{x^2 + 2x - 8}{(x-2)(x-7) + 11(x-2)^2} = \dfrac{(x+4)(x-2)}{(x-2)(x-7+11(x-2))}$

$= \dfrac{x+4}{x-7+11x-22} = \dfrac{x+4}{12x-29}$.

Passport to Advanced Math – Equations with Exponents – Pages 442-444

1. (A)
Difficulty: E
Category: Equations with Exponents
Strategy: Apply the appropriate exponent rule to simplify. Since the bases are equal, set exponents equal to each other and solve for b.
Solution: When raising a power of a base to another power, the exponents can be multiplied:
$(x^6)^b = x^{6b}$ and $(x^{27})^2 = x^{54}$. Thus, $x^{6b} = x^{54}$. Set the exponents equal to each other: $6b = 54$. Divide by 6 on both sides to find $b = 9$.

2. (D)
Difficulty: E
Category: Equations with Exponents
Strategy: Apply the appropriate exponent rules to rewrite the expression.
Solution: $x^{-a} = \dfrac{1}{x^a}$. Therefore, $x^{-\frac{1}{2}} = \dfrac{1}{x^{\frac{1}{2}}}$.

In general, $x^{\frac{a}{b}} = \sqrt[b]{x^a}$, so $x^{-\frac{1}{2}} = \dfrac{1}{x^{\frac{1}{2}}} = \dfrac{1}{\sqrt{x}}$.

3. (3)
Difficulty: E/M
Category: Equations with Exponents
Strategy: Rewrite both sides of the equation as powers of x using relevant exponent rules. Set the exponents equal to each other and solve for a.
Solution: The quotient of two powers of the same base is equal to the base raised to the difference of its powers. The number one is equal to any base raised to the zero power. Thus, the equation can be rewritten as $x^{a^2-6a+9} = x^0$. Since both bases are the same, the exponents must be equal: $a^2 - 6a + 9 = 0$. Factor the quadratic equation to get $(a-3)(a-3) = 0$. Set factors equal to 0 and solve to find $a = 3$.

4. (D)
Difficulty: M
Category: Equations with Exponents
Strategy: Use exponent rules to simplify the rational expression.
Solution: The quotient of two powers of a base is equal to the base raised to the difference of the powers. Apply this rule to simplify the rational expression first:
$$\frac{2^{-2}x^2 y^{\frac{3}{2}}}{3x^{-1}y^{\frac{1}{2}}} = \frac{2^{-2}x^{2-(-1)}y^{\frac{3}{2}-\frac{1}{2}}}{3} = \frac{2^{-2}x^3 y}{3}.$$

Anything raised to a negative exponent can be moved to the opposite side of the fraction with a positive exponent since
$x^{-n} = \dfrac{1}{x^n}$. Therefore, $\dfrac{2^{-2}x^3 y}{3} = \dfrac{x^3 y}{2^2 \cdot 3} = \dfrac{x^3 y}{12}$.

5. (D)
Difficulty: M
Category: Equations with Exponents
Strategy: Raise both sides to the appropriate exponent to solve for the variable x directly. Apply relevant exponent rules to simplify the expression on the right-hand side.
Solution: To convert $x^{-1/3}$ to x^1, the exponent must be multiplied by -3. Raise both sides of the equation to the -3 power to achieve this result:
$$\left(x^{-\frac{1}{3}}\right)^{-3} = x^{\frac{-1}{3}\cdot\frac{-3}{1}} = x = \left(\frac{1}{2}\right)^{-3} = (2)^3 = 8.$$ Thus, $x = 8$.

6. (D)
Difficulty: M
Category: Equations with Exponents
Strategy: Rewrite the left-hand side of the equation as a single power of y using relevant exponent rules. Set the exponents equal to each other. Simplify and solve for x in terms of p. Alternatively, choose a number for p and solve for x. Use process of elimination.
Solution: Simplify the left-hand side to get
$$\left(\left(y^{x-a}\right)^{x+a}\right)^{x^2+a^2} = \left(y^{x^2-a^2}\right)^{x^2+a^2} = y^{x^4-a^4}.$$ Set the expression equal to the right-hand side: $y^{x^4-a^4} = y^{p^{16}-a^4}$, so $x^4 - a^4 = p^{16} - a^4$. Add a^4 to both sides to get $x^4 = p^{16}$. Take the fourth root of both sides, and consider only positive real solutions to find $x = (p^{16})^{1/4} = p^4$.

7. (C)
Difficulty: M/H
Category: Equations with Exponents
Strategy: Rewrite each constant in the left-hand side as a power of 4. Use exponent rules to simplify and rewrite as a single power of 4. Rewrite the right side as a power of 4. Set the exponents equal to each other and solve for x. Alternatively, plug in answer choices.
Solution: Rewrite the left-hand side as a power of 4:
$$\frac{64\left(4^x\right)}{256^3} = \frac{4^3 \cdot 4^x}{\left(4^4\right)^3} = \frac{4^{3+x}}{4^{12}} = 4^{3+x-12} = 4^{x-9}$$

Rewrite the right-hand side as a power of 4: $1/4 = 4^{-1}$.
Set them equal to each other to get $4^{x-9} = 4^{-1}$. Thus, $x - 9 = -1$. Solve to find $x = 8$.

8. (D)
Difficulty: M
Category: Equations with Exponents
Strategy: Apply the relevant exponent rule to raise the expression to the 4th power. Alternatively, choose numbers for x, y, and z, and solve for the value of the expression.
Solution: When raising a product to a power, each factor in the product must be raised to the power.
Thus, $(3x^2 yz^2)^4 = 3^4 x^8 y^4 z^8 = 81x^8 y^4 z^8$.

9. (A)

Difficulty: (M)
Category: Equations with Exponents
Strategy: Use exponent rules to express the numerator as a power of a. Use the same rules to express the denominator as a power of b. Rewrite the left-hand side of the equation.
Solution: The numerator is $(a^{1/2})^2 \cdot (a^2)^{1/2} = a \cdot a = a^2$. The denominator is $(b^3)^{1/3} \cdot b^2 = b^1 \cdot b^2 = b^3$. Thus, the equation can be rewritten as $\dfrac{a^2}{b^3} = 71$.

10. (B)

Difficulty: M
Category: Equations with Exponents
Strategy: Use the relevant exponent rule to rewrite both sides of the equation as a single power of x. Set the exponents equal to each other and solve for a.
Solution: Raising a power to another power is the same as raising the base to the product of the powers. Therefore, $(x^{32})^a = x^{32a}$, and $(x^8)^{16} = x^{128}$. Since $x^{32a} = x^{128}$, then $32a = 128$. Divide by 32 to find $a = 4$.

11. (C)

Difficulty: M/H
Category: Equations with Exponents
Strategy: Use the first and third equation to find y. Then, plug in the value of y to solve for the other variables. Plug in each value into the final expression.
Solution:

Rearrange $xyz = 12$ to $xz = 12/y$. Substituting this into $xz - y = 1$ gives $\dfrac{12}{y} - y = 1$. Multiplying through by y yields the equation $12 - y^2 = y$.

Set the quadratic equal to zero by moving all terms to the right: $y^2 + y - 12 = 0$. Factor to find $(y + 4)(y - 3) = 0$, which has solutions $y = -4$ and 3. Since $y > 0$, then $y = 3$. Plug this value in for y into the second equation to find $x^3 = 8$. Take the third root of both sides to find $x = 2$. Finally, $xyz = 12$, so $(2)(3)z = 12$. Solve for z to find $z = 2$. Plug in to find $x^{yz} = 2^{2\cdot3} = 64$.

12. (C)

Difficulty: H
Category: Equations with Exponents
Strategy: Replace x with $2y$ on the left-hand side of the expression. Rewrite as a product of a power of 2 and a product of y. Bring the power of y to the other side of the equation and rewrite the right side as a single power of y. Factor the power.
Solution: Plug in $x = 2y$ to rewrite the equation as $(2y)^{abcd} = y^{bcde}$. A product raised to an exponent is the product of each factors raised to the exponent. Therefore, $(2y)^{abcd} = 2^{abcd}y^{abcd} = y^{bcde}$. Divide both sides by y^{abcd} to get the equation $2^{abcd} = y^{bcde}/y^{abcd} = y^{bcde - abcd}$. Factor the power on the right side to find $2^{abcd} = y^{bcde - abcd} = y^{bcd(e - a)}$.

13. (C)

Difficulty: H
Category: Equations with Exponents
Strategy: Rewrite the numerator and denominator as powers of 5 or 25. Apply exponent rules to rewrite as a single power of 5 or 25.

Solution: $\left(\dfrac{625^{2x}}{25^{2y}}\right)^{-2} = \left(\dfrac{\left(5^4\right)^{2x}}{\left(5^2\right)^{2y}}\right)^{-2} = \left(\dfrac{5^{8x}}{5^{4y}}\right)^{-2}$

$= \left(\dfrac{5^{4y}}{5^{8x}}\right)^2 = \left(\dfrac{5^{8y}}{5^{16x}}\right) = 5^{8y - 16x} = 5^{-4(4x - 2y)} = 5^{-4\cdot9} = 5^{-36}$. This is not a solution, so express as a power of 25 instead: $5^{-36} = (5^2)^{-18} = 25^{-18}$.

14. (B)

Difficulty: H
Category: Equations with Exponents
Strategy: Rewrite as a radical. Move any fourth power factors outside of the radical.
Solution: With fractional exponents, the denominator indicates which root is expressed, and the numerator indicates the power to which everything under the radical is raised. Thus, $(x^2y^3)^{3/4}$ can be written as $\sqrt[4]{\left(x^2y^3\right)^3}$. Raising a product to an exponent is equal to raising each factor of the product to the exponent. Hence, $\sqrt[4]{\left(x^2y^3\right)^3} = \sqrt[4]{x^6y^9}$. Any fourth power factor in the fourth root can be moved outside the radical, so the expression can be re-written further as $\sqrt[4]{x^4x^2y^8y} = \sqrt[4]{x^4} \cdot \sqrt[4]{y^8} \cdot \sqrt[4]{x^2y} = xy^2\sqrt[4]{x^2y}$.

15. (512)

Difficulty: H
Category: Equations with Exponents
Strategy: Rewrite both sides of the exponent equation as powers of the same base. Set the exponents equal to each other to solve for x. Use the other equation to solve for y. Plug in the values of x and y into the expression.
Solution: Both 4 and 8 are powers of 2, so both sides of the equation can be expressed powers of 2: $4^{2x+3} = (2^2)^{2x+3} = 2^{4x+6}$, and $8^{x+4} = (2^3)^{(x+4)} = 2^{3x+12}$. Since $2^{4x+6} = 2^{3x+12}$, the exponents must be equal. Thus, $4x + 6 = 3x + 12$. Rearrange to find $x = 6$. The other equation states $x - y = 4$. Therefore, $6 - y = 4$. Solve to find $y = 2$. Finally, $(x + y)^3 = (6 + 2)^3 = 8^3 = 512$.

16. (C)

Difficulty: H
Category: Equations with Exponents
Strategy: Rewrite each side as a power of 3b. Then, set the exponents equal to each other and solve for x. Alternatively, plug in a value for b and solve for x.
Solution: Note that $9b^2 = (3b)^2$. The right side of the equation can be rewritten as $(9b^2)^5(3b)^3 = ((3b)^2)^5(3b)^3 = (3b)^{10}(3b)^3 = (3b)^{13}$. Set this equal to the left-hand side to get $(3b)^{4+x} = (3b)^{13}$. Set the exponents equal to each other to get $4 + x = 13$. Solve to find $x = 9$.

17. (D)

Difficulty: H
Category: Equations with Exponents
Strategy: Using relevant exponent rules, rewrite the left and right sides as powers of 2. Set the exponents equal to each other and solve for x. Alternatively, plug in the answer choices and work backward.
Solution: $4 = 2^2$ and $8 = 2^3$: Therefore, the left-hand side of the equation $\dfrac{2^x \cdot 2^5}{\left(4^2\right)^3} = \dfrac{2^{x+5}}{\left(\left(2^2\right)^2\right)^3} = \dfrac{2^{x+5}}{2^{12}} = 2^{x-7}$. The right-hand side of the equation $1/8 = 2^{-3}$. Since $2^{x-7} = 2^{-3}$, then $x - 7 = -3$. Solve to find $x = 4$.

**Passport to Advanced Math – Equations with Radicals –
Pages 446-448**

1. (C)
Difficulty: E
Category: Equations with Radicals
Strategy: Square both sides and solve for x. Alternatively, plug in the answer choices and use process of elimination.
Solution: Square both sides to find $3x = 36$. Divide by 3 on both sides to find $x = 12$.

2. (A)
Difficulty: E
Category: Equations with Radicals
Strategy: Understand how to interpret a fractional exponent. Apply any relevant exponent rules. The problem can also be done with choosing numbers for x and y.
Solution: Raising an expression to the 1/2 power is equivalent to taking the square root. Apply exponent rules first to simplify the expression:
$(36x^4y^2)^{1/2} = 36^{1/2}(x^4)^{1/2}(y^2)^{1/2} = 6x^2|y|$. Note the absolute value notation for y is necessary since $\sqrt{y^2} \geq 0$, and y is not necessarily a positive number.

3. (B)
Difficulty: E
Category: Equations with Radicals
Strategy: Isolate the radical and raise both sides to the power that eliminated any roots in the equation. Solve for x. Alternatively, plug in the answers to solve.
Solution: Subtracting 5 from both sides to get $\sqrt[3]{4x+2} = 2$. To eliminate the cube root, raise each side to the third power:
$\left(\sqrt[3]{4x+2}\right)^3 = 2^3$, or $4x + 2 = 8$. Solve to find $x = 6/4 = 3/2$.

4. (C)
Difficulty: E
Category: Equations with Radicals
Strategy: Rewrite the root as a fractional exponent and apply relevant exponent rules to simplify the expression.
Solution: A square root of an expression is equivalent to raising the expression to the 1/2 power. Therefore, the expression can be rewritten as $(4x^6y^3)^{1/2}$. A product raised to an exponent is the same as the product of each factor raised to the exponent: $(4x^6y^3)^{1/2} = 2x^3y^{3/2}$.

5. (B)
Difficulty: M
Category: Equations with Radicals
Strategy: Isolate each radical on opposite sides and raise both sides to the power that will eliminate all roots. Alternatively, plug in the answers to solve.
Solution: Move each radical to its own side of the equation. This way, each radical is isolated:
$\sqrt{3x+6} = 3\sqrt{x-6}$. Square both sides to get $3x + 6 = 9(x - 6)$. Distribute the right side to get $3x + 6 = 9x - 54$. Combine like terms to get $6x = 60$, or $x = 10$.

6. (D)
Difficulty: M
Category: Equations with Radicals
Strategy: Square both sides. Then, carefully solve for ε, the permittivity of the medium.
Solution: Square both sides of the equation first to find
$(c_m)^2 = \dfrac{1}{\mu_0 \varepsilon}$. Next, multiply by the denominator on both sides to get rid of the fraction: $(c_m)^2 \mu_0 \varepsilon = 1$. Solve for epsilon to find
$\varepsilon = \dfrac{1}{\mu_0 (c_m)^2}$.

7. (C)
Difficulty: M
Category: Equations with Radicals
Strategy: Simplify the right side and isolate the root. Square both sides and solve for z. Alternatively, plug in the answers to solve.
Solution: $\sqrt{z-2} + 3 = 5 \to \sqrt{z-2} = 2$. Square both sides to get $z - 2 = 4$. Solve to find $z = 6$.

8. (B)
Difficulty: M
Category: Equations with Radicals
Strategy: Square both sides. Set the equation equal to zero and factor to find solutions for x. Check for extraneous solutions. Alternatively, plug in answers to solve.
Solution: First, square both sides of the equation: $3 - x = x^2 + 6x + 9$.
Move all terms to one side: $0 = x^2 + 7x + 6$.
Factor to find $(x + 6)(x + 1) = 0$, to find $x = -6$, or -1. Check if the solutions are extraneous by plugging them back into the original equation. Plugging in -6 gives $\sqrt{3-(-6)} = -6 + 3 \to 3 = -3$, which is not true. Thus, -6 is an extraneous solution. Plugging in -1 gives $\sqrt{3-(-1)} = -1 + 3 \to 2 = 2$, so -1 is a real solution.

9. (D)
Difficulty: M
Category: Equations with Radicals
Strategy: Substitute the value of r in for r. Rewrite the right side as a product of two square roots. Solve for square root of x.
Solution: $r = 7\sqrt{5} \to 3r = 21\sqrt{5} = \sqrt{5x}$. Rewrite the right side as a product of two roots to get $21\sqrt{5} = \sqrt{5}\sqrt{x}$. Divide by the square root of 5 on both sides to find $\sqrt{x} = 21$.

10. (30)
Difficulty: M/H
Category: Equations with Radicals
Strategy: Take the square root of both sides, to find the two solutions for the cube root. Then, for each solution, cube both sides and solve for the two solutions for x. Find their sum.
Solution: $\sqrt{\left(\sqrt[3]{x-15}\right)^2} = \pm\sqrt{16} \to \sqrt[3]{x-15} = \pm 4$. Cube both sides to find $x - 15 = \pm 64$. Add 15 to both sides to find $x = -49$ or 79. $-49 + 79 = 30$.

11. (B)

Difficulty: M

Category: Equations with Radicals

Strategy: Rewrite the left side as a fractional power of y. Use exponent rules to express the right side as a power of y. Set exponents equal to each other and solve for n.

Solution: $\sqrt[n]{y^{18}} = y^{\frac{18}{n}} = (y^3)^2 = y^6$. Thus, $y^{18/n} = y^6$. Set the exponents equal to each other to get $18/n = 6$. Solve to find $n = 3$.

12. (B)

Difficulty: M

Category: Equations with Radicals

Strategy: Simplify all fractions in the roots by canceling any common factors between numerators and denominators. Factor the difference of squares under one of the roots. Cancel any common factors between the numerator and denominator.

Solution: The fractions under cube roots can both be simplified to just 1, since the numerator and denominator of both fractions is the same. Therefore,

$$\frac{\sqrt[3]{a^2 - b^2}}{\sqrt[3]{\frac{ab^2}{ab^2}}} \times \frac{\sqrt[3]{\frac{ab^2}{ab^2}}}{\sqrt[3]{(a+b)(a-b)}} = \frac{\sqrt[3]{a^2 - b^2}}{\sqrt[3]{1}} \times \frac{\sqrt[3]{1}}{\sqrt[3]{(a+b)(a-b)}}$$

Since $a^2 - b^2 = (a + b)(a - b)$, substitute this expression into the root on the top left to get

$$\frac{\sqrt[3]{(a+b)(a-b)}}{1} \times \frac{1}{\sqrt[3]{(a+b)(a-b)}} = \frac{\sqrt[3]{(a+b)(a-b)}}{\sqrt[3]{(a+b)(a-b)}} = 1$$

13. (A)

Difficulty: H

Category: Equations with Radicals

Strategy: Remove all perfect cube factors from the root on the left-hand side. Simplify the right-hand side and compare the two simplified sides to solve for p.

Solution: Rewrite the left side as the root of a product of perfect cube factors and any remaining factors:

$$\sqrt[3]{24x^6 y^7} = \sqrt[3]{8x^6 y^6 \cdot 3y} = \sqrt[3]{8x^6 y^6} \cdot \sqrt[3]{3y} = 2x^2 y^2 \sqrt[3]{3y}.$$

Now, simplify the right-hand side of the equation:

$$\sqrt[3]{py}\left(\sqrt{2xy}\right)^2 = \sqrt[3]{py} \cdot 2x^2 y^2.$$ Set the two sides equal to each other and cancel any common factors:

$$2x^2 y^2 \sqrt[3]{3y} = \sqrt[3]{py} \cdot 2x^2 y^2 \rightarrow \sqrt[3]{3y} = \sqrt[3]{py}.$$ Cube both sides to get $3y = py$. Divide by y on both sides to find $p = 3$.

14. (D)

Difficulty: H

Category: Equations with Radicals

Strategy: Substitute the values for a, b, and c form the equation into the inequality. Solve for c.

Solution: $b^2 - 4ac < 0$ becomes $(\sqrt{2})^2 - 4 \cdot \sqrt{2} \cdot c < 0$.

Simplify to get $2 - 4c\sqrt{2} < 0$. Subtract 2 from both sides to get $-4c\sqrt{2} < -2$. Divide both sides by -4 (remember to flip the inequality sign) to get $c\sqrt{2} > \frac{1}{2}$. Divide by root 2 to get $c > \frac{1}{2\sqrt{2}}$. Rationalize the denominator by multiplying the numerator and denominator both by square root of two to find $c > \frac{1}{2\sqrt{2}} \cdot \frac{\sqrt{2}}{\sqrt{2}} = \frac{\sqrt{2}}{4}$.

15. (216)

Difficulty: H

Category: Equations with Radicals

Strategy: Raise both sides to the sixth power to eliminate all roots. Solve for x.

Solution: Raise both sides to the 6th power to get

$$\left((6x)^{\frac{1}{2}}\right)^6 = \left((x)^{\frac{2}{3}}\right)^6,$$ or $6^3 x^3 = x^4$. Divide both sides by x^3 to find $x = 6^3 = 216$.

16. (A)

Difficulty: H

Category: Equations with Radicals

Strategy: Simplify the left side of the inequality. Then, rearrange the inequality to solve for the possible range of x values.

Solution: First simplify the left side: $-\sqrt[3]{(-t)^3} = --t = t$. The inequality is now $t \leq -\sqrt[3]{3}x < \sqrt[3]{y}$. Now divide through by -1 and remember to flip the signs: $-t \geq \sqrt[3]{3}x > -\sqrt[3]{y}$. Finally, divide by $\sqrt[3]{3}$ to get the inequality found in A.

17. (B)

Difficulty: H

Category: Equations with Radicals

Strategy: Raise both sides to the 4th power to eliminate all radicals. Rewrite the left side as a power of 3. Set the exponents equal to each other and solve for x.

Solution: Raise both sides to the fourth power to get $3^2 9^3 = 3^{4x}$. Since $9 = 3^2$, the equation can be rewritten as $3^2(3^2)^3 = 3^{4x}$. Simplify the left side to find $3^2 \cdot 3^6 = 3^8 = 3^{4x}$. Set the exponents equal to each other to get $8 = 4x$. Solve to find $x = 2$. Thus, $x^3 = 2^3 = 8$.

Passport to Advanced Math – Functions – Pages 450-451

1. (C)
Difficulty: E
Category: Functions
Strategy: Plug in –2 in for x into the expression for f and evaluate.

Solution: $f(-2) = \dfrac{(-2)^2 + 2(-2)}{2} = \dfrac{4-4}{2} = 0$.

2. (D)
Difficulty: E/M
Category: Functions
Strategy: Write an expression for $g(x)$ in terms of x. Set the expression equal to –7 and solve for x. Alternatively, plug in the answer choices into the expression to see which value of x yields a result of –7.
Solution: $g(x) = 2f(x) + 3 = 2(5x) + 3 = 10x + 3$. Since $g(x) = -7$, then $10x + 3 = -7$. Solve to find $x = -1$.

3. (B)
Difficulty: E
Category: Functions
Strategy: Plug in the x-values 3 and 4 into the function. Then, divide the results, canceling all common factors that occur in both the numerator and denominator.
Solution: $g(4) = 3 \cdot (-2)^4$. Similarly, $g(3) = 3 \cdot (-2)^3$.

Divide the results: $\dfrac{g(4)}{g(3)} = \dfrac{3 \cdot (-2)^4}{3 \cdot (-2)^3} = -2^{4-3} = -2$.

4. (A)
Difficulty: E
Category: Functions
Strategy: Start on the inside of the compound function, substituting the value of the inner function at the specific x-value given. Then, work your way outward.
Solution: To evaluate $g(f(4))$, start on the inside and evaluate $f(4)$ first. Since $f(4) = 2$, then $g(f(4)) = g(2) = -2$.

5. (A)
Difficulty: M
Category: Functions
Strategy: Use the rule given for odd functions and plug in $x = 2$ to solve.
Solution: The function is odd, so $f(-x) = -f(x)$. Plug in $x = 2$ to find $f(-2) = -f(2)$. Since $f(2) = 8$, then $f(-2) = -8$.

6. (44,79,96,101)
Difficulty: E
Category: Functions
Strategy: Choose any negative integer greater than –5, and plug in the value for x into the expression for the function. Evaluate numerically.
Solution: There are 4 negative integers greater than –5, which are –4, –3, –2, and –1. The four possible solutions arise from each possible value for x (any one of these solutions would be considered correct):
$f(-4) = 100 - 2(-4) + (-4)^3 = 100 + 8 - 64 = 44$
$f(-3) = 100 - 2(-3) + (-3)^3 = 100 + 6 - 27 = 79$

$f(-2) = 100 - 2(-2) + (-2)^3 = 100 + 4 - 8 = 96$
$f(-1) = 100 - 2(-1) + (-1)^3 = 100 + 2 - 1 = 101$

7. (C)
Difficulty: M
Category: Functions
Strategy: Plug in 3 into the expression for f to evaluate $f(3)$. Plug in 2 into the expression for h to find $h(2)$. Plug in the results into the final expression and evaluate.
Solution: $f(3) = 13 + 3 - 7 = 9$ and $h(2) = 2^2 + 2 \cdot 2 - 11 = -3$. Plug these values into the final expression to find $\dfrac{2f(3)}{3h(2)} = \dfrac{2 \cdot 9}{3 \cdot -3} = -2$.

8. (D)
Difficulty: M
Category: Functions
Strategy: To find an expression for the compound function in terms of x, plug in the inner function as the input (x-value) for the outer function. Alternatively, choose a number for x and evaluate the compound function for this x-value. See which answer choice gives the same result.
Solution: Substitute the function for f into the function for g, then rewrite the function in standard form to match the answers.
$g(f(x)) = g(10 - x) = ((10 - x) + 2)^2 = (12 - x)^2 = (12 - x)(12 - x) = 144 - 24x + x^2$.

9. (B)
Difficulty: M/H
Category: Functions
Strategy: To find an expression for the compound function in terms of x, plug in the inner function as the input (x-value) for the outer function. Alternatively, choose a number for x and evaluate the compound function for this x-value. See which answer choice gives the same result.
Solution: To find the composite function, substitute in the entire function of $g(x)$ wherever an x appears in $f(x)$:

$$f\big(g(x)\big) = f\left(\frac{x}{3}\right) = 2\left(\frac{x}{3}\right)^2 = \frac{2x^2}{9}.$$

10. (C)
Difficulty: M/H
Category: Functions
Strategy: To find an expression for the compound function in terms of x, plug in the inner function as the input (x-value) for the next innermost function. Work this way outwards. Alternatively, choose a number for x and evaluate the compound function for this x-value. See which answer choice yields the same result.
Solution: $(g(g(h(x)))) = (g(g(-2))) = g(3 \cdot -2 + 5) = g(-1) = 3 \cdot -1 + 5 = 2$.

11. (A)
Difficulty: M/H
Category: Functions
Strategy: Substitute $(x + 1)$ wherever x appears in the expression for f and simplify. Alternatively, choose a number for x and evaluate the function for the value of $x + 1$. Check which answer choice yields the same result.
Solution: $f(x + 1) = (x + 1)^2 - 2(x + 1) + 15 = x^2 + 2x + 1 - 2x - 2 + 15 = x^2 + 14$.

12. (1, 6 ,11)

Difficulty: H

Category: Functions

Strategy: Plug in $(a - 6)$ into the expression for g and simplify each factor. Set the resulting expression equal to zero. Set each factor equal to zero and solve for a.

Solution: $g(a - 6) = (a - 6)((a - 6) - 5)^2((a - 6) + 5)^3 = (a - 6)(a - 11)^2(a - 1)^3$. Since $g(a - 6) = 0$, then $(a - 6)(a - 11)^2(a - 1)^3 = 0$, which means $a = 6, 11,$ or 1.

Alternatively, the problem can be approached the following way: Set each factor of the function g equal to zero to find the zeros of g, which are 5, 0, or –5. Thus, when $(a - 6)$ equals 5, 0, or –5, $g(a - 5) = 0$. Set $a - 6$ equal to 5, 0, –5, to find $a = 11, 6,$ or 1.

13. (D)

Difficulty: H

Category: Functions

Strategy: Do not evaluate the compound function exactly; this approach is too time consuming. Instead, note that the highest power term in the expression for f is $2x^2$. Consider the function $g(x) = x^2$, and find the power of $g(g(g(g(x))))$. Since all other terms in f are a lower power of x, then conclude the highest power of $g(g(g(g(x)))) =$ the highest power of $f(f(f(f(x))))$.

Solution: If $g(x) = x^2$, then $g(g(g(g(x)))) = g(g(g(x^2))) = g(g(x^4)) = g(x^8) = x^{16}$. The polynomial expression has a highest power of 16. Since the highest power term in f is an x^2 term, then $f(f(f(f(x))))$ must have the same highest power term, an x^{16} term. All other terms in the polynomial expression for $f(f(f(f(x))))$ have a lower power for x.

Passport to Advanced Math – Graphs of Functions – Pages 453-456

1. (2)

Difficulty: E

Category: Graphs of Functions

Strategy: Find the point on the graph where $x = 0$. The y-value of this point is equivalent to the function evaluated for this x-coordinate.

Solution: When $x = 0$ on this graph of the function, the y-coordinate is 2. Therefore, $f(0) = 2$.

2. (C)

Difficulty: E/M

Category: Graphs of Functions

Strategy: Rewrite the function h in terms of the function g. The graph of the resulting expression for h should yield a simple translation of the original graph of g. Determine which translation would result.

Solution: $h(x) = g(x + 2)$. In general, $g(x + n)$ shifts the graph of g to the left by n. Hence, $h(x)$ should shift the graph of g two units to the left.

3. (C)

Difficulty: E

Category: Graphs of Functions

Strategy: Know how to interpret the value of a function from its graph. Find the point(s) on the graph where $y = -0.5$. Count how many such points exist.

Solution: Since $f(x) = y$, the question is asking how many different values of x on the graph have a y-value equal to –0.5. There are 6 different points with this y-value, so there must be 6 different values of x for which $f(x) = -0.5$.

4. (A)

Difficulty: E/M

Category: Graphs of Functions

Strategy: Determine which translation of the graph of $f(x)$ would result in the graph of $g(x)$. If helpful, sketch the graph of g. The minimum value of $g(x)$ should be equivalent to the lowest value of y on the graph.

Solution: The minimum value of the function f is the lowest value of y on the graph, which is –1. Since $g(x) = f(x) - 3$, the graph of $g(x)$ is the graph of $f(x)$ shifted three units downward. If the minimum value of f was –1, then the minimum value of g must be –4.

5. (B)

Difficulty: M

Category: Graphs of Functions

Strategy: Use the relationship between the constants to help guide your understanding of where the y-values should fall relative to each other for each value of x listed.

Solution: The chart shows that $f(-2) = f(0)$, since they are both equal to the constant v. Therefore, the y-coordinates for these two points should be the same. This only occurs in answer choices A and B, and so C and D can be eliminated right away. The problem also states that $v > w$, which means that $f(-1) < f(0)$. Thus, the y-coordinate of the point on the graph where $x = -1$ should be less than the y-coordinate of the point on the graph where x is –2 or 0. This only occurs in answer choice B.

6. (B)
Difficulty: M
Category: Graphs of Functions
Strategy: Each factor of a function can be used to find a zero, or an x-intercept of the graph of the function. Find the x-intercepts of the graph of f to determine which factors the polynomial function must have. Use process of elimination.
Solution: The x-intercepts of the graph of $f(x)$ occur when $x = -2$, -1, or 2. These are the solutions for x when any factor of the polynomial function is set equal to zero (resulting in zero as the value of the function). Thus, $x + 2$ (which is equal to zero for $x = -2$), $x + 1$, and $x - 2$ are all factors of the function. Since the function has no x-intercept at $x = 1$, then $x - 1$ cannot be a factor.

7. (B)
Difficulty: M
Category: Graphs of Functions
Strategy: Note that both points given have the same y-coordinate. Use the vertical axis symmetry of a downward facing vertical parabola to determine the x-coordinate of the parabola's vertex. Determine if the y-coordinate of the vertex should be higher or lower than the y-coordinates of the points given in the problem. Use process of elimination.
Solution: Parabolas that open downward or upward have a vertical axis of symmetry. Since both points given have the same y-coordinate, the vertical axis of symmetry must lie halfway between $x = -2$ and $x = -8$, which is $x = -5$. The vertex must lie on the vertical axis of symmetry, so the x-coordinate must be -5. Eliminate choices A and D. The problem states that the parabola is downward facing, so the vertex must have the highest y-coordinate out of all points on the graph. Of the points remaining, only choice B has a y-coordinate > 5 (the y-coordinate of the two points given), so it is the only possible vertex.

8. (D)
Difficulty: M
Category: Graphs of Functions
Strategy: Use the x-intercept given to determine which value of x will make $g(x) = f(4 - x) = 0$.
Solution: Since $(-4, 0)$ is on the graph of $f(x)$, then $f(-4) = 0$. Thus, $g(x) = f(x - 4) = 0$ when $x - 4 = -4$. Solve for x to find $x = 8$. Hence, $g(8) = f(8 - 4) = f(4) = 0$. Therefore, the point $(8, 0)$ must be an x-intercept of $g(x)$.

9. (B)
Difficulty: M/H
Category: Graphs of Functions
Strategy: Know the definition of a double root and how to recognize it on the graph of a polynomial.
Solution: An even powered root (double roots are an example) is a zero of the function where the graph does not cross the x-axis, but is tangent to the axis. Double roots are any solutions that arise from perfect square factors of the polynomial. The graph is tangent to the x-axis at zeros $(-1, 0)$ and $(2, 0)$. All other roots cross the x-axis and cannot be considered double or roots of even multiplicity. Since there are 2 linear roots and at most 6 real roots (because the function is a 6th degree polynomial), then the two roots of even multiplicity must be double roots. If the roots were quartic roots for example (multiplicity 4 instead of 2), then the possible number of total roots would exceed 6, which is not possible for a 6th degree polynomial.

10. (A)
Difficulty: M/H
Category: Graphs of Functions
Strategy: Find how many units $f(x)$ must be shifted vertically and horizontally to match the graph of $g(x)$. If useful, track a "corner" point on the graph to see how many units it moves in each direction. Determine which translation(s) of the graph of $f(x)$ would result in the graph of $g(x)$.
Solution: Note that both graphs have the same shape and size, but only differ in their position. Choose an easily identifiable point on the graph of $f(x)$, like the minimum point at $(-2, 4)$. The minimum on the graph of $g(x)$ is $(-10, 7)$. This point is the original point on $f(x)$ shifted 8 units to the left and three units up. The function $f(x) + 3$ represents a vertical shift of the graph of $f(x)$ three units upward, and $f(x + 8)$ represents a horizontal shift 8 units to the left. Thus, $g(x) = f(x + 8) + 3$.

11. (D)
Difficulty: M/H
Category: Graphs of Functions
Strategy: Know how to interpret the value of a function from its graph. Interpret the difference in the values of the function as the difference in y-coordinates between corresponding points on each graph. Alternatively, go through the answer choices and find the values of f and g for each x-value. Subtract the values and use process of elimination.
Solution: To find the value of a function at a specific x-value, find the ordered pair on the graph with the same x-value. The value of a function at this number is the y-coordinate of the point.
Thus $f(x) - g(x) = 2$ for values of x where $f(x)$ is higher than $g(x)$ by two units. At $x = 1$, $f(x) - g(x) = 0$, since the graphs intersect here. Answer choice A can be eliminated.
$f(2) - g(2) \approx 3 - -5.5 = 8.5 > 2$. Eliminate choice B.
$f(3) - g(3) = 5 - -3.5 = 8.5 > 2$, so eliminate choice C.
$f(4) - g(3) = 3 - 1 = 2$, so D is correct.

12. (D)
Difficulty: M/H
Category: Graphs of Functions
Strategy: Identify all x-intercepts. Rewrite the x-intercepts as factors of the polynomial. Know how to recognize the difference between a root of even vs. odd multiplicity. Identify each root from the graph as having odd or even multiplicity, and then determine the nature of the powers of the corresponding factors. Use process of elimination.
Solution: Since the graph of the function has x-intercepts at $x = -3$, -1, 0, and 1, the function must have factors of $x + 3$, $x + 1$, x, and $x - 1$. Roots where the graph is tangent to the x-axis must have even multiplicity (i.e. corresponding polynomial factors must be raised to an even power), whereas zeros where the graph crosses through the x-axis must have odd multiplicity (i.e. corresponding polynomial factors must be raised to an odd power). The graph is tangent to the x-axis at $x = -3$, -1 and 1, and crosses through the x-axis at $x = 0$. Hence, the $x + 3$, $x + 1$, and $x - 1$ factors must be raised to an even power, while the x factor must be raised to an odd power. Only answer choice D has this set of characteristics.

13. (B)

Difficulty: M/H

Category: Graphs of Functions

Strategy: Find an expression for $-f(-x)$. Then, plug in some values of x to find some points on its graph. Use process of elimination.

Solution: $f(x) = \left(\frac{1}{2}\right)^x - 2 \rightarrow f(-x) = \left(\frac{1}{2}\right)^{-x} - 2 \rightarrow$

$-f(-x) = -\left(\frac{1}{2}\right)^{-x} + 2$. Test some values for x and evaluate the function at these values. If $x = 0$, then $-f(0) = -(1/2)^0 + 2 = 1$. Thus, $(0, 1)$ must be the y-intercept of the graph. Only choice B has a graph that does through this point.

14. (C)

Difficulty: H

Category: Graphs of Functions

Strategy: Evaluate each answer choice. Start on the inside of the compound function, substituting the value of the inner function at the specific x-value given. Then, work your way outward. Know how to interpret the value of a function from its graph. Compare the values.

Solution: Each answer choice must be evaluated and compared. To evaluate a value of a compound function, find the value of the inside function and work your way outward. To find the value of a function at a specific x-value from a graph, find the ordered pair on the graph with the same x-value. The value of a function at this number is the y-coordinate of the point.

Answer choice A: $f(g(4)) = f(2) = 0$

Answer choice B: $f(g(-4)) = f(-2) = 1$

Answer choice C: $g(f(4)) = g(-2) = -1$

Answer choice D: $g(f(-4)) = g(2) = 1$

Of all these answers, answer choice C is the smallest.

Passport to Advanced Math – Quadratic Equations – Pages 458-460

1. (A)

Difficulty: E

Category: Quadratic Equations

Strategy: Distribute the product and set the equation equal to zero. Factor and solve for all solutions for x. Alternatively, plug in the answer choices.

Solution: Distribute the product on the left side of the equation first to get $x^2 + 13x = 30$. Set the expression equal to zero to get $x^2 + 13x - 30 = 0$. Factor to find $(x + 15)(x - 2) = 0$. Set each factor equal to zero and solve to find $x = -15$ or $x = 2$.

2. (C)

Difficulty: E

Category: Quadratic Equations

Strategy: Note that the expression on the left side of the equation is a perfect square. Factor it appropriately to determine the solution. Alternatively, graph the parabola that would result from graphing $y =$ the expression on the left and determine where any zeros occur. It is also possible to plug in the answer choices into the equation.

Solution: In general, $(a + b)^2 = a^2 + 2ab + b^2$. Notice that the expression on the left side of the equation stated in the problem is the perfect square of the binomial $(a + b)$ where $a = x + 3$ and $b = -4$. Therefore, the equation in the problem can be rewritten as $((x + 3) - 4)^2 = 0$. Simplifying yields the equation $(x - 1)^2 = 0$. Set the factor equal to zero to find $x = 1$. Alternatively, one can distribute out all products in the equation and solve for x by factoring, but this approach is more time consuming.

3. (A)

Difficulty: E

Category: Quadratic Equations

Strategy: Set the expressions for y equal to each other and solve the resulting quadratic equation. Alternatively, plug the answer choices in for x to see which value yields the same result for both expressions of y.

Solution: For x to satisfy both equations, it must be an x-coordinate of the point of intersection, where the corresponding values of y should be equal on both graphs. Since both equations are set equal to y, the point of intersection can be found by setting the expressions for y equal to each other: $x^2 + x - 2 = -3x - 6$. Set the equation equal to zero to get $x^2 + 4x + 4 = 0$. Factor the expression on the left to get $(x + 2)(x + 2) = 0$. Set each factor to zero to find $x = -2$.

4. (B)

Difficulty: E/M

Category: Quadratic Equations

Strategy: Know in which cases a rational function is undefined (i.e. when the denominator = 0). Set the denominator equal to zero and solve the resulting quadratic equation. Alternatively, plug in the answer choices to find at which value the function is undefined.

Solution: The function is undefined when $x^2 - x - 2 = 0$. Factor the quadratic equation to find $(x - 2)(x + 1) = 0$. Set each factor equal to zero and solve to find $x = 2$ and $x = -1$. Since only -1 appears in the answer choices, B is correct.

5. (C)

Difficulty: M

Category: Quadratic Equations

Strategy: Solve the top equation for y in terms of x and substitute the expression for y into the second equation (alternatively, add the equations to eliminate the variable y). Solve the resulting quadratic equation. Alternatively, graph both equations on a graphing calculator and find any points of intersections between the two graphs.

Solution: While substitution is a valid technique, a faster approach to solving the system is through the elimination method. Add the two equations together to eliminate the variable y: $x^2 - x = 6$. Set the equation equal to zero to get $x^2 - x - 6 = 0$. Factor to get $(x - 3)(x + 2) = 0$. There are two solutions for x: 3 and -2. Next, plug each of these answers back into any of the original equations to solve for y. If $x = 3$, then $-3 + y = 4$. Solving this yields the solution $y = 7$, which is not an answer choice. Plug in the other solution for x into either equation to solve for the other point of intersection: $-(-2) + y = 4$ yields the solution $y = 2$. This is an answer, so it must be the correct choice.

6. (C)

Difficulty: M

Category: Quadratic Equations

Strategy: Use the quadratic formula to write an expression for the solutions. Simplify the expression.

Solution: First, multiply both sides of the original equation by 3 to eliminate any fractions: $3x^2 + 2kx + 9 = 0$. Then, apply the quadratic formula $\left(x = \dfrac{-b \pm \sqrt{b^2 - 4ac}}{2a} \right)$, where $a = 3$, $b = 2k$, and $c = 9$.

$x = \dfrac{-2k \pm \sqrt{4k^2 - 4(27)}}{6} = -\dfrac{1}{3}k \pm \dfrac{\sqrt{4(k^2 - 27)}}{6}$

$= -\dfrac{1}{3}k \pm \dfrac{2\sqrt{(k^2 - 27)}}{6} = -\dfrac{1}{3}k \pm \dfrac{\sqrt{k^2 - 27}}{3}$. Note that in order to solve the problem efficiently, the radical does not need to be simplified, since the same radical expression appears in all answer choices.

7. (B)

Difficulty: M

Category: Quadratic Equations

Strategy: Use completing the square or the Quadratic Formula to find the solutions for t. Add the solutions.

Solution: Completing the square: $3t^2 - 15t + 9 = 0$. Divide by three to get $t^2 - 5t + 3 = 0$. Move 3 to the other side to get $t^2 - 5t = -3$. $t^2 - 5t + 6.25 = -3 + 6.25 = 3.25$. $(t - 2.5)^2 = 3.25$. Take the square root of both sides to get $t - 2.5 = \pm\sqrt{3.25}$. Thus, $t = 2.5 \pm \sqrt{3.25}$. Add the two solutions to get $2.5 + \sqrt{3.25} + 2.5 - \sqrt{3.25} = 5$.

8. (C)

Difficulty: M

Category: Quadratic Equations

Strategy: Solve the equation for y in terms of x and p. The expression for y should be a difference of squares. Factor the difference of squares. Alternatively, choose a number for p and solve the problem for this value.

Solution: $4x^2 - y = 144 p^2$ can be rewritten as $y = 4x^2 - 144p^2$. Since $a^2 - b^2 = (a - b)(a + b)$, then y can be expressed as $(2x - 12p)(2x + 12p)$.

9. (B)

Difficulty: M

Category: Quadratic Equations

Strategy: Find an expression for the area of the rectangle in terms of x. Set the expression equal to 42 and solve the resulting quadratic equation. Alternatively, plug in the answer choices and see which value of x will result in a rectangle area of 42.

Solution: Area of a rectangle is (length)·(height). Thus, the area of the rectangle can be expressed as $(x - 4)(x + 7) = 42$. Distribute the product to get $x^2 + 3x - 28 = 42$. Set the equation equal to zero: $x^2 + 3x - 70 = 0$. Factor to find $(x + 10)(x - 7) = 0$. Thus, $x = -10$ or $x = 7$. However, $x > 0$, so x must be equal to 7.

10. (D)

Difficulty: M

Category: Quadratic Equations

Strategy: Set the equation equal to zero and factor out any common factors. Factor the resulting quadratic equation and solve.

Solution: Set the equation equal to zero to get $2x^2 + 4x - 48 = 0$. Factor out 2 to get $2(x^2 + 2x - 24) = 0$. Factor the inner quadratic expression to get $2(x + 6)(x - 4) = 0$. Set each factor equal to zero to find the solutions are $x = -6$ and $x = 4$.

11. (D)

Difficulty: M

Category: Quadratic Equations

Strategy: Factor the quadratic expression to find values of a and b. Then, plug the values into $2a - 3b$.

Solution: Factor the quadratic to get $(x - 5)(x + 2)$. Given the expression must equal $(x - a)(x - b)$, a and b can equal 5 or -2. Plugging these values into $2a - 3b$ can give either $2(5) - 3(-2) = 16$ or $2(-2) - 3(5) = -19$. 16 is the only option available.

12. (A)

Difficulty: H

Category: Quadratic Equations

Strategy: Note for which values of x the left-side of the equation is undefined. Set the numerator equal to 0. Factor and solve for x. Check that the solutions are values of x for which the rational expression is defined. Sum the solutions.

Solution: The rational expression on the left is undefined when the denominator $2x + 3 = 0$, or when $x = -3/2$. If the value of a fraction is 0, then the value of its numerator must be 0. Thus, $(x + 9)^2 - 4(x + 9) - 21 = 0$. Factor this quadratic to get $((x + 9) - 7)((x + 9) + 3) = 0$. Simplify to get $(x + 2)(x + 12) = 0$, which yields solutions $x = -2$ and $x = -12$. Both solutions are in the set of x-values for which the original fraction is defined, so they are both solutions. $-2 + -12 = -14$.

13. (D)

Difficulty: H

Category: Quadratic Equations

Strategy: Consider the possible values of p and q. Consider what happens when either value is equal to zero, or is not real. Use process of elimination.

Solution: Answer choice A is possible if both p and q are not real numbers. Answer choice B is possible if p is not a real number and $q = 0$. Answer choice C is possible if $p = 0$ and q is not a real number. Answer choice D is only possible if both p and q equal zero, but since $p \neq q$, then the statement cannot be true.

14. (D)

Difficulty: H

Category: Quadratic Equations

Strategy: Distribute the expression on the right and set the equation equal to zero. Divide out any common factors and factor the resulting expression, or use the quadratic formula to find the roots. Determine the nature of the roots.

Solution: Use the distributive property to expand the expression on the right side to get $3x^2 = -6x - 3$. Set the equation equal to zero to get $3x^2 + 6x + 3 = 0$. Divide by 3 on both sides to get $x^2 + 2x + 1 = 0$. Factor to find $(x + 1)(x + 1) = 0$, which gives one real, rational root: $x = -1$.

Passport to Advanced Math – Graphs of Quadratics – Pages 462-466

1. (C)

Difficulty: E

Category: Graphs of Quadratics

Strategy: Look at the answer choices and note that they all express the vertex form of the quadratic function. Find the vertex from the graph and eliminate all choices with the incorrect vertex. Determine the sign of the outside coefficient based on the direction the parabola opens. Alternatively, plug points on the parabola into answer choices.

Solution: The parabola is pointing downward. Hence, the outside coefficient must be negative, and answers A and B can be eliminated. The vertex of the parabola is $(-1, 2)$. Only answer B and C show the correct vertex, but B has been eliminated, so answer choice C must be correct.

2. (A)

Difficulty: E

Category: Graphs of Quadratics

Strategy: Determine the vertex of the graph. Find which direction the parabola opens to determine whether the vertex is considered a maximum or a minimum. Alternatively, graph the equation on a graphing calculator and find the maximum or minimum point.

Solution: The equation of the parabola is given in vertex form. From the equation, determine that the vertex occurs at $(-1, 4)$. The vertex is always the maximum or the minimum point, depending on how the parabola is oriented. The coefficient in front of the x^2 term is 2, which is positive, so the parabola opens upward. Thus, the vertex is the minimum point of the parabola.

3. (B)

Difficulty: E

Category: Graphs of Quadratics

Strategy: Note that the quadratic function is given in intercept form. Consider the signs of the x-coordinates of the two x-intercepts. Then, determine in which direction the parabola should open. Use process of elimination.

Solution: The quadratic function has a leading coefficient (coefficient on the square term) that is positive, and so the parabola must open upward. Choices C and D can be eliminated. The x-intercepts should be $(2, 0)$ and $(-a, 0)$. Since $a > 0$, then $-a$ must be negative. Only answer choice B contains the x-intercept $(2,0)$. Furthermore, the other x-intercept occurs at a negative value of x.

4. (A)

Difficulty: E

Category: Graphs of Quadratics

Strategy: Set the expressions for y equal to each other and solve for x. Determine the value of a. Plug in this value for x into either equation to determine the value of b. Alternatively, plug the answer choices in for y and solve.

Solution: Solve the system of equations to find any points of intersection. Since both equations are equal to y, set the expressions for y equal to each other and solve for x first: $5x^2 - 12x = -2x$. Set the equation equal to zero to get $5x^2 - 10x = 0$. Factor to get $5x(x - 2) = 0$. Set each factor equal to zero to get $x = 0$ or $x = 2$. Ignore the $x = 0$ solution, since that one is tied to the origin intersection point, which is not asked for in the problem. Thus, a must equal 2. Plug in $x = 2$ into either equation and solve for b, the y-coordinate of the other intersection point: $y = -2(2) = -4$.

5. (B)

Difficulty: E

Category: Graphs of Quadratics

Strategy: Determine the x-intercepts of the quadratic function. Use this information to find the axis of symmetry for the parabola, which must intersect with the vertex. Find the x-coordinate of the vertex.

Solution: The quadratic function is given in intercept form. Set each factor equal to zero to determine that the x-intercepts are $(0, 0)$ and $(-2, 0)$. Parabolas are symmetrical with respect to their axis of symmetry, which intersects the vertex. Therefore, the x-coordinate of the vertex should lie half way between the x-coordinates of the x-intercepts, so it should be half-way between $x = -2$ and $x = 0$. Thus, the x-coordinate of the vertex must be $x = (-2 + 0)/2 = -1$. Of all the intervals listed, only choice B contains the solution.

6. (A)

Difficulty: M

Category: Graphs of Quadratics

Strategy: Determine which form of the quadratic function is shown in the equation.

Solution: Compare the form of the equation to known forms of quadratic equations. The factored form of a quadratic equation provides the x-coordinates of the x-intercepts of the function. This is because for an expression written as $y = a(x - p)(x - q)$, the x-coordinates of the $x$intercepts are p and q. Thus, the function $y = -4(x - 2)(x + 3)$ has x-intercepts $(2, 0)$ and $(-3, 0)$, so the function displays the x-coordinates of the x-intercepts as constants.

7. (D)

Difficulty: M

Category: Graphs of Quadratics

Strategy: Note that two of the answer choices are in vertex form and show different vertices. Thus, they cannot both be correct. Use either of the other answer choices to determine the x-coordinate of the vertex, and use process of elimination. Another approach would be to use the distributive property to express all of the answer choices in standard form. Compare to find the one choice that shows a different expression for the quadratic function.

Solution: The answer must be either B, which has a vertex of $(4, -2)$ or D, which has a vertex of $(-4, -14)$. Answer choice A shows a parabola with x-intercepts at $(3, 0)$ and $(5, 0)$. Due to the symmetry of a parabola, the vertex must have an x-coordinate of $x = 4$. Therefore, D must display a quadratic equation that does NOT graph the same parabola.

8. (D)

Difficulty: E

Category: Graphs of Quadratics

Strategy: Find the vertex of the quadratic function (note the function is given in vertex form). Shift the point 2 units down and determine in which quadrant the vertex must lie. Then, look at the sign of the leading coefficient to determine in which direction the parabola should open. Use process of elimination.

Solution: The leading coefficient on the quadratic is a negative number, so the parabola must open downward. Eliminate choices A and B. For a quadratic function with vertex (h, k), the vertex form of the equation is $f(x) = a(x - h)^2 + k$. Thus, the vertex of $f(x)$ is $(-3, 1)$. If the graph is shifted two units down, the new vertex must also be shifted the same amount, and would move to the point $(-3, -1)$. Thus, the vertex must be in the third quadrant. Of the remaining choices, D must be correct.

9. (D)

Difficulty: M

Category: Graphs of Quadratics

Strategy: Determine the vertex of the parabola. Express the vertex form of the quadratic function. Use process of elimination.

Solution: In order to write the equation that includes the coordinates of the vertex, the equation must be expressed in vertex form, which is $y = a(x - h)^2 + k$, where the vertex is (h, k). Since the vertex of this parabola is $(1, -4)$, the equation in vertex form is $y = a (x - 1)^2 - 4$. Only answer choice D gives a version of this equation.

10. (B)

Difficulty: M

Category: Graphs of Quadratics

Strategy: Identify the y-intercept to determine the value of b. Determine the sign of a based on the direction the parabola opens. Use process of elimination.

Solution: The parabola opens downward, so the value of the leading coefficient a must be negative. The y-intercept is $(0, 3)$, so $b = 3$. Choice B is the only combination of values that meet these criteria.

11. (A)

Difficulty: M

Category: Graphs of Quadratics

Strategy: Use the fact that if $(x - a)$ is a factor of the quadratic, then $x = a$ is a root, zero, or x-intercept.

Solution: If $(x - a)$ is a factor, then $x = a$ is a zero. So, we are looking for a graph with x-intercepts for quadratic A at $(2, 0)$ and $(-7, 0)$ and x-intercepts for quadratic B at $(2, 0)$ and $(-3, 0)$. Only answer choice A shows parabolas with these features.

12. (B)

Difficulty: M

Category: Graphs of Quadratics

Strategy: Use the fact that if $(x - a)$ is a factor of the quadratic, then $x = a$ is a root, zero, or x-intercept. The converse is also always true. Use process of elimination.

Solution: M has roots at $x = -4$ and $x = 1$ (the x-coordinates of the x-intercepts), so it has factors $(x + 4)$ and $(x - 1)$. N has roots at $x = -2$ and $x = 1$, so it has factors $(x + 2)$ and $(x - 1)$. Since zeros are the same as roots, the answer is B.

13. (D)

Difficulty: M

Category: Graphs of Quadratics

Strategy: Factor the quadratic function. Note the x-intercepts. Use the symmetry of the parabola to find the x-intercept of the vertex. Plug the x-value into the function to determine the y-coordinate of the vertex.

Solution: The quadratic function is given in standard form. While it is possible to find the x-coordinate of the vertex by using $x = -b/2a$ (where a is the leading coefficient of the function and b is the coefficient on the x term), it can also be evaluated quickly by factoring the function.

$3x^2 - 24x + 36 = 3(x^2 - 8x + 12) = 3(x - 6)(x - 2)$.

The function has x-intercepts at $(2, 0)$ and $(6, 0)$. Due to the symmetry of the parabola, the x-coordinate of the vertex must lie halfway between, at $x = 4$. Since $f(4) = 3(4 - 6)(4 - 2) = -12$, the coordinates of the vertex are $(4, -12)$.

14. (D)
Difficulty: M/H
Category: Graphs of Quadratics
Strategy: Since the vertex is known, write an expression for the quadratic function in terms of a, the leading coefficient. Plug the coordinates of the x-intercept given into the function to solve for a. Then, let $x = 0$ and solve to find the y-coordinate of the y-intercept.
Solution: The vertex form of the quadratic function is $y = a(x - 3)^2 + 8$. Plug in the point $(5, 0)$, the x-intercept listed in the problem, to solve for a: $0 = a(5 - 3)^2 + 8$, or $0 = 4a + 8$. Solve to find $a = -2$. Thus, the quadratic function is $y = -2(x - 3)^2 + 8$. To find the y-coordinate of the y-intercept, plug in $x = 0$ to find $y = -2(0 - 3)^2 + 8 = -18 + 8 = -10$.

15. (C)
Difficulty: M/H
Category: Graphs of Quadratics
Strategy: Use process of elimination to see whether each statement is true.
Solution: The quadratic function is given in standard form. To find the y-intercept, plug in $x = 0$ to find $y = 1/15$. Statement I is true. To test if statement II is true, plug in $x = -1$:
$$y = \frac{3}{5}(-1)^2 - \frac{2}{3}(-1) + \frac{1}{15} = \frac{3}{5} + \frac{2}{3} + \frac{1}{15} > 0,$$ and thus $(-1, 0)$ cannot be the x-intercept. Statement II is false. For a quadratic written as $y = ax^2 + bx + c$ (standard form), the x-coordinate of the vertex can be found using the formula $x = -b/2a$. Thus, $x = \dfrac{\frac{2}{3}}{2 \cdot \frac{3}{5}} > 0$, so statement III is true.

16. (A)
Difficulty: M/H
Category: Graphs of Quadratics
Strategy: Know how to interpret the values of a function from both its graph and a table of values. Evaluate both functions for each answer choice, and check which pair of resulting values satisfies the inequality condition. Use process of elimination.
Solution: To find the value of a function at a specific x-value, find the ordered pair on the graph with the same x-value. The value of g at this number is the y-coordinate of the point. Find $g(x)$ for each of the values listed in the answers and compare them to the corresponding value of $f(x)$ found in the table.
$g(0) = 2 > f(0) = 0$
$g(1) = 0 < f(1) = 4$
$g(2) = 0 < f(2) = 6$
$g(3) = 2 < f(3) = 6$
Only answer choice A satisfies the inequality.

17. (C)
Difficulty: H
Category: Graphs of Quadratics
Strategy: To find the points of intersection, set the two quadratic functions equal to each other. Solve for the two values of x and their corresponding y-values. Then, find the slope between the points and write the equation for the line between the points in slope-intercept form.
Solution: Set the two expressions for y equal to each other to solve for the x-coordinates of their intersections: $x^2 - 1 = -(1/2)(x + 3)^2 + 8$. To eliminate all fractions, multiply both sides by -2:
$-2x^2 + 2 = x^2 + 6x + 9 - 16$.
Set the equation equal to zero to get $3x^2 + 6x - 9 = 0$.
Factor to find $3(x^2 + 2x - 3) = 0$ or $3(x + 3)(x - 1) = 0$.
Set each factor equal to zero to find $x = -3$ or $x = 1$.
If $x = -3$, then $y = (-3)^2 - 1 = 8$. Therefore, $(-3, 8)$ is one point of intersection. If $x = 1$, then $y = (1)^2 - 1 = 0$, and $(1, 0)$ must be a point of intersection. To find the equation of the line that connects $(-3, 8)$ and $(1, 0)$, find the slope first. Slope $= (8 - 0)/(-3 - 1) = -2$. Therefore, the slope-intercept form of the line is $y = -2x + b$. Plug in one of the points to determine the value of b: $0 = -2(1) + b$. Solve to get $b = 2$. Thus, the equation of the line is $y = -2x + 2$.

18. (B)
Difficulty: H
Category: Graphs of Quadratics
Strategy: Either complete the square to rewrite in vertex form or use the formula to find the x-coordinate of the vertex from the standard form of the quadratic function. If using the latter method, remember to plug the x-coordinate of the vertex back into the function to find the y-coordinate as well. Then, rewrite in vertex form.
Solution: The vertex form of a quadratic function is $y = a(x - h)^2 + k$, where a is the leading coefficient of the function and (h, k) is the vertex. To put the standard form of the equation $f(x) = 2x^2 + 20x + 48$ into vertex form, complete the square. As a first step, move the 48 to the other side and factor out 2 on the right side of the equation:
$f(x) - 48 = 2(x^2 + 10x)$. Rewrite the expression on the right side as a perfect square by adding the square of half of 10 into the parentheses. Remember to add this term to the other side to keep the equation balanced: $f(x) - 48 + 2 \cdot 25 = 2(x^2 + 10x + 25)$, which can be re-written as $f(x) + 2 = 2(x + 5)^2$.
Solve for $f(x)$ to get $f(x) = 2(x + 5)^2 - 2$.

19. (C)
Difficulty: H
Category: Graphs of Quadratics
Strategy: Plug the y-intercept into the quadratic function to solve for c. Write an expression for the discriminant and set it equal to zero. Solve for b. Find the sum of b and c.
Solution: Plug in the y-intercept to find $25 = (0)^2 + b(0) + c$. Therefore, $c = 25$. For the quadratic $ax^2 + bx + c$, the discriminant is the expression $b^2 - 4ac$. Therefore, the discriminant for the quadratic function in the problem must be $b^2 - 4(1)(25) = b^2 - 100$. Set this expression equal to zero to get $b^2 - 100 = 0$. Solve to find $b = \pm 10$. Since $b < 0$, then $b = -10$. Therefore, $b + c = -10 + 25 = 15$.

20. (C)

Difficulty: H

Category: Graphs of Quadratics

Strategy: Plug the y-intercept into the quadratic function to solve for c. Then, plug the x-intercept into the quadratic function to solve for b. Find the sum of b and c.

Solution: Plug in the y-intercept to find $35 = (0)^2 + b(0) + c$. Therefore, $c = 35$. Plug in the x-intercept next to find $0 = (-5)^2 + b(-5) + 35$. Therefore, $0 = 25 - 5b + 35$. Solve to find $b = 12$. Therefore, $b + c = 12 + 35 = 47$.

21. (9)

Difficulty: H

Category: Graphs of Quadratics

Strategy: If the parabola and the line are tangent, their graphs will have one intersection point. Set the expressions for y equal to each other and set the resulting quadratic equal to zero. To have one solution, the quadratic must be a perfect square (i.e. the discriminant must be equal to zero). Set the discriminant equal to zero and solve for k.

Solution: To solve the system of equations, set the equations to each other: $x^2 = 6x - k$. Set the equation equal to zero to get $x^2 - 6x + k = 0$. For this to quadratic to have one solution, the discriminant = 0. Thus, discriminant = $b^2 - 4ac = (-6)^2 - 4k = 0$. Solve to find $k = 9$.

22. (D)

Difficulty: H

Category: Graphs of Quadratics

Strategy: Use the distributive property to rewrite the products on either side of the inequality and solve for x. Use the graph to check or determine in which interval the solutions lie. Use process of elimination.

Solution: Expand both sides of the inequality to get $x^2 - 9 < -x^2 + 16$. Combine like terms to get $2x^2 < 25$. Divide by 2 to find $x^2 < 25/2$. Find where $x^2 = 25/2$ first, and then go back to the inequality.

If $x^2 = 25/2$, then $x = \pm\sqrt{\dfrac{25}{2}} = \pm\dfrac{5}{\sqrt{2}} = \pm\dfrac{5\sqrt{2}}{2}$.

These are the x-coordinates of the points of intersection of the two curves. Eliminate choices A and C, since they contain the incorrect points of intersection. Note that $y = (x - 3)(x + 3)$ is the upward opening curve and $y = -(x - 4)(x + 4)$ is the downward opening graph. The upward opening parabola is below the downward facing parabola (i.e. $(x - 3)(x + 3) < -(x - 4)(x + 4)$) between the points of intersection. Thus, D is correct.

Passport to Advanced Math – Polynomials – Pages 468-470

1. (B)

Difficulty: E

Category: Polynomials

Strategy: Set each factor equal to zero to find the x-intercepts. Alternatively, plug in answer choices and use process of elimination.

Solution: To find the x-intercepts of the polynomial, set each factor equal to zero: $3x - 4 = 0$ gives $x = 4/3$. Therefore, $(4/3, 0)$ is an x-intercept. If $(x + 2)^2 = 0$, then $x = -2$, and $(-2, 0)$ must be an x-intercept. If $x - 5 = 0$, then $x = 5$, and $(5, 0)$ is an x-intercept. The only point not listed is answer choice B.

2. (6)

Difficulty: E

Category: Polynomials

Strategy: Distribute the product on the left side of the equation and collect like terms. Set the coefficients of corresponding terms on each side of the equation equal to each other. Alternatively, plug in the answer choices and use process of elimination.

Solution: Distribute the left side of the equation to get $2ax^3 + 4x^2 - 3ax^2 - 6x + ax + 2 = 2ax^3 + x^2(4 - 3a) + x(a - 6) + 2 = 12x^2 - 14x^2 + 2$. In order for this equation to be true for all values of x, each coefficient on each term on the left must be equal to each coefficient of each respective term on the right.

Thus, $2a = 12$, $4 - 3a = -14$, $a - 6 = 0$, and $2 = 2$. Each of the first three equations gives $a = 6$. To complete the problem faster, observe the x^3 term on both sides to find $2a = 12$ or $a = 6$.

3. (C)

Difficulty: E

Category: Polynomials

Strategy: Factor the numerator and cancel any common factors. Alternatively, plug in a number for x and evaluate numerically.

Solution: Factor the numerator to get $\dfrac{x^2 + 13x + 30}{x + 10} = \dfrac{(x + 3)(x + 10)}{x + 10}$.

Cancel the $x + 10$ factor to get the expression $x + 3$.

4. (B)

Difficulty: E

Category: Polynomials

Strategy: Set each factor of the polynomial equal to zero to determine the x-intercepts. Count how many there are.

Solution: Note that the equation of the function is factored. To find the x-intercepts, set each factor equal to zero and solve for x: If $(x - a)^3 = 0$, then $x = a$. If $(x + b)^2 = 0$, then $x = -b$. $(x + a) = 0$, then $x = -a$. If $(x - b) = 0$, then $x = b$. Since a and b are not equal and are positive, all four zeros listed above are distinct. The graph will have four x-intercepts at the points $(a, 0)$, $(-b, 0)$, $(-a, 0)$, and $(b, 0)$.

5. (C)

Difficulty: M

Category: Polynomials

Strategy: Continue to factor the rewritten expression. Set each factor equal to zero. Alternatively, plug in answer choices.

Solution: One of the factors in the rewritten expression is a difference of squares and can be factored further: $2(w^2 - 4)(w + 4) = 2(w - 2)(w + 2)(w + 4)$. Set each factor equal to zero to determine the real roots, which are $w = 2$, $w = -2$, and $w = -4$.

6. (C)

Difficulty: M

Category: Polynomials

Strategy: Use the x-intercepts to find three linear factors of $f(x)$. Write an expression for $f(x)$ as a product of these factors. Distribute the product to rewrite the polynomial in standard form and solve for a, b, and c. Find the sum. Alternatively, plug in the three x-intercepts and solve the resulting system of equations.

Solution: If $(n, 0)$ is an x-intercept of a polynomial, then $(x - n)$ is a factor of the polynomial. Therefore, three factors of the cubic polynomial must be $(x + 1)$, $(x - 1)$, and $(x - 2)$.
Since the leading coefficient of the polynomial is 1, then
$f(x) = 1(x + 1)(x - 1)(x - 2) = (x^2 - 1)(x - 2) = x^3 - 2x^2 - x + 2$.
Therefore, $a = -2$, $b = -1$, and $c = 2$. So, $a + b + c = -2 + -1 + 2 = -1$.

7. (B)

Difficulty: M

Category: Polynomials

Strategy: Find the zeros of the polynomial and set them equal to the expression $h + 2$. Solve for h. Alternatively, plug the answer choices in for h to solve.

Solution: The real zeros of the function are the same as the x-intercepts, and they occur when the factors are equal to zero. This happens at $x = 2$ and at $x = -4$. Set $h + 2$ equal to these values and solve for h: $2 = h + 2$ and $-4 = h = 2$ yield the solutions $h = 0$ or -6. Only 0 appears in the answer choices, so it must be correct.

8. (D)

Difficulty: M/H

Category: Polynomials

Strategy: Use the x-intercepts given to determine what factors $P(x)$ must have. Determine the minimum number of factors the polynomial has to determine the minimum degree of the function. Based on this information, consider each choice and use process of elimination.

Solution: The x-intercepts occur at $x = -4$, $x = 0$, and $x = 5$. Thus, the polynomial function must have factors $(x + 4)$, x, and $(x - 5)$. Answers A and B can be eliminated, since they do not need to be true. Since $P(x)$ has at least three factors, then it must have a degree (the degree is the value of the highest power in the polynomial) of at least three. It does not need to be exactly three however, since one of the roots may be a double or higher order root, which would yield a higher degree polynomial. Thus, only D must be true.

9. (A)

Difficulty: M

Category: Polynomials

Strategy: Set the equation equal to zero. Factor out any common divisors of all terms. Then, factor the resulting quadratic factor. Set each factor equal to zero and solve for x. Alternatively, plug in the answer choices to solve.

Solution: Set the equation equal to zero to get $7x^3 + 14x^2 - 21x = 0$. Factor out $7x$ to get $7x(x^2 + 2x - 3) = 0$. Factor the quadratic expression to get $7x(x + 3)(x - 1) = 0$. Set each factor equal to zero to find $x = 0$, $x = -3$, and $x = 1$. Only answer choice A lists one of the solutions for x.

10. (B)

Difficulty: M/H

Category: Polynomials

Strategy: Note that the x-axis does not begin at the origin. Consider the symmetry of the parabola to determine if statements I, II or III are true. Use process of elimination.

Solution: Statement I is false. The graph goes through the point $(3, 10)$, not $(0, 10)$. Therefore, the y-intercept occurs below the point $(0, 10)$. Based on the symmetry of the parabola, which has a vertex at $(5, 12)$ and an x-intercept at $(9, 0)$, the other x-intercept must occur at $(1, 0)$. Since the parabola opens downward, then $y > 0$ only when $1 < x < 9$, between the x-intercepts. Thus, statement II MUST be true because the parabola should be negative for all $x < 1$, which means for all $x < 0$, then $y < 0$ as well. Statement III is not true. y is positive only when $1 < x < 9$. Only II is true.

11. (B)

Difficulty: M

Category: Polynomials

Strategy: Use the factors to determine what the x-intercepts of the polynomial must be. Eliminate any choices without these intercepts. Between the remaining options, select the answer which has a negative value for $f(0)$.

Solution: Set each factor equal to zero to determine the x-coordinates of the x-intercepts: If $x - 2 = 0$, then $(2, 0)$ must be an x-intercept. If $2x + 5 = 0$, then $(-2.5, 0)$ must be an x-intercept. If $x - 1 = 0$, then $(1, 0)$ must be an x-intercept. Eliminate choices A and D, which show the incorrect intercepts. The problem also states that $f(0) < 0$. Thus, the y-coordinate of the y-intercept must be negative. Of the remaining choices, the statement is only true for answer B.

12. (B)

Difficulty: M

Category: Polynomials

Strategy: Factor each quadratic function first. Determine how many distinct roots there must be for the product.

Solution: $f(x) = x^2 + 3x + 2 = (x + 1)(x + 2)$ and $g(x) = x^2 + 2x + 1 = (x + 1)^2$. Therefore, $f(x) \cdot g(x) = (x + 1)^3(x + 2)$. This polynomial function has roots at $x = -1$ (a triple root) and at $x = -2$. Thus, there are two distinct roots.

13. (C)

Difficulty: M/H

Category: Polynomials

Strategy: Use polynomial long division. Alternatively, choose a number for x and solve.

Solution:

$$\begin{array}{r} 2x + 3 \\ 3x - 1 \overline{) 6x^2 + 7x - 5} \\ -\left(6x^2 - 2x\right) \\ \hline 9x - 5 \\ -(9x - 3) \\ \hline -2 \end{array}$$

The quotient yields $2x + 3$ with remainder -2, which can be rewritten as $\dfrac{6x^2 + 7x - 5}{3x - 1} = 2x + 3 + \dfrac{-2}{3x - 1}$.

14. (A)

Difficulty: H

Category: Polynomials

Strategy: Use polynomial long division or synthetic division. Alternatively, choose a number for x and solve.

Solution:

$$
\begin{array}{r}
x^4 - x^3 + x^2 - x + 1 \\
x+1{\overline{\smash{\big)}\,x^5 + 0x^4 + 0x^3 + 0x^2 + 0x - 1}} \\
\underline{-(x^5 + x^4)} \\
x^4 + 0x^3 + 0x^2 + 0x - 1 \\
\underline{-(x^4 - x^3)} \\
x^3 + 0x^2 + 0x - 1 \\
\underline{-(x^3 + x^2)} \\
-x^2 + 0x - 1 \\
\underline{-(-x^2 - x)} \\
x - 1 \\
\underline{-(x+1)} \\
-2
\end{array}
$$

Or use synthetic division:

$$
\begin{array}{r|rrrrr}
-1 & 1 & 0 & 0 & 0 & -1 \\
   &   & -1 & 1 & -1 & 1 & -1 \\
\hline
   & 1 & -1 & 1 & -1 & 1 & -2
\end{array}
$$

The quotient yields $x^4 - x^3 + x^2 - x + 1$ with remainder -2, which can be rewritten as $\dfrac{x^5 - 1}{x+1} = x^4 - x^3 + x^2 - x + 1 + \dfrac{-2}{x+1}$.

15. (B)

Difficulty: H

Category: Polynomials

Strategy: Rewrite $Q(x)$ in terms of $R(x)$. Substitute this expression into the answer choices and factor out $R(x)$. Determine which answer choice has a factor of $(2x + 3)$.

Solution: Note that $Q(x) = 2x(x^2 + 4x + 3) = 2x \cdot R(x)$. Also, note that $R(x)$ has factors $(x + 1)$ and $(x + 3)$, but is not divisible by $(2x + 3)$. Substitute $Q(x) = 2x \cdot R(x)$ into each of the answer choices and factor out $R(x)$ in each choice:

A: $Q(x) + 2R(x) = 2x \cdot R(x) + 2R(x) = R(x)(2x + 2)$, which has factors $(x + 1)$ and $(x + 3)$

B: $Q(x) + 3R(x) = 2x \cdot R(x) + 3R(x) = R(x)(2x + 3)$

Answer choice B has a factor of $2x + 3$, so it must be correct.

C: $2Q(x) + 3R(x) = 4x \cdot R(x) + 3R(x) = R(x)(4x + 3)$, which has factors $(x + 1)$, $(x + 3)$, and $(4x + 3)$.

D: $3Q(x) + 2R(x) = 6x \cdot R(x) + 2R(x) = R(x)(6x + 2)$, which has factors $(x + 1)$, $(x + 3)$, and $(3x + 1)$.

16. (C)

Difficulty: H

Category: Polynomials

Strategy: Use the polynomial remainder theorem.

Solution: The equation states that the remainder when $p(x)$ is divided by $q(x)$ is -17. The remainder theorem states that the remainder of the division of a polynomial $f(x)$ by a linear factor $x - n$ is equal to $f(n)$. Since the remainder of $p(x)$ when divided by linear factor $x + 9$ is -17, then $p(-9) = -17$. All other statements are false or not necessarily true.

17. (2)

Difficulty: H

Category: Polynomials

Strategy: Note that the polynomial function is in factored form. Know how to recognize the difference between a root of even vs. odd multiplicity. Identify each root from the function as having odd or even multiplicity, and then determine which of the roots will result in an x-intercept that is tangent to the axis (i.e. will not cross the x-axis).

Solution: All x-intercepts that occur where the graph is tangent to the x-axis must arise from roots with even multiplicity (i.e. corresponding polynomial factors must be raised to an even power). The only roots with even multiplicity come from the factors $(x + a)^2$ and $(x + b)^4$. Thus, there are two times when the graph touches the x-axis without crossing it, when $x = -a$ and when $x = -b$.

Passport to Advanced Math – Nonlinear Models – Pages 472-475

1. (C)
Difficulty: E
Category: Nonlinear Models
Strategy: Since the number of Sonja's clients will grow, two of the choices can be eliminated right away. A linear function has a constant rate of change, while an exponential function has a rate of change that is proportional to the value of the function.
Solution: The number of Sonja's clients is increasing, so choices B and D can be eliminated right away. Furthermore, she is increasing her client load by 20% yearly, which represents an exponential growth rate of 1.2, and so answer choice C is correct.

2. (B)
Difficulty: E/M
Category: Nonlinear Models
Strategy: Recognize that the function is a quadratic function, and it is given in vertex form. Use the fact that the vertex is either the lowest or highest point on a parabola to determine which answer choice is correct.
Solution: The quadratic model is written in vertex form, which means that 220 represents the y-coordinate of the vertex of the parabola. Because the parabola opens upward, the value of the function at the vertex must be a minimum value. Therefore, 220 represents the height above the water level of the lowest point on the suspension cable.

3. (B)
Difficulty: E
Category: Nonlinear Models
Strategy: Compare the data points in the scatterplot to the smooth curve quadratic model. Identify how many points are underestimated by the graph.
Solution: If a data point is underestimated, then the data point should lie above the graph of the quadratic model. This occurs at four points: (7.5, 245), (17.5, 335), (20, 345), and (25, 270). Since there are 14 data points in total, the fraction of the points that are underestimated is 4/17 = 2/7.

4. (C)
Difficulty: E
Category: Nonlinear Models
Strategy: Find the largest percent growth found on the smooth curve quadratic model.
Solution: The quadratic model has a maximum at the vertex of the parabola. This occurs very close to the point (17.5, 320). The problem asks for the maximum percent change predicted by the graph, so the y-coordinate is needed, and thus 320 must be the best estimate. Note that 350% is close to the maximum percent growth on the scatterplot, but it is not predicted by the model.

5. (B)
Difficulty: M
Category: Nonlinear Models
Strategy: Write an expression for the appropriate function to model Jamila's minutes of phone usage in terms of time in weeks. Evaluate the function for week 5.
Solution: The problem describes an exponential function (since the rate of change is proportional to the value of the function). The original starting value is Jamila's current weekly phone usage, which is 2000 minutes. The weekly rate of decay is 95% = 1 − 0.05 = .95. Time can be expressed in weeks by the variable t. Thus, the exponential model for the number of minutes, M, Jamila uses each week is $M = 2000 \cdot (.95)^t$. The problem asks how many minutes will Jamila spend on her phone by the 5th week, so plug in $t = 5$ into the model to solve for her weekly minutes: $M = 2000 \cdot (.95)^5 \approx 1550$ minutes.

6. (C)
Difficulty: M
Category: Nonlinear Models
Strategy: Determine the correct exponential model, using the original population and the rate of growth. Alternatively, choose a number for t to solve.
Solution: The general formula for an exponential model is $p(t) = ab^t$, where a represents the original population, b represents the rate of growth, and t represents time. The original population in 1944 is 10, and since there is 33% growth, this means the rate of growth is 1.33 (133%). Therefore, the correct population model should be $p(t) = 10(1.33)^t$.

7. (A)
Difficulty: M
Category: Nonlinear Models
Strategy: Convert the measurements given to the correct units needed in the equation. Plug in the values to evaluate the force in Newtons.
Solution: The mass given in grams must be converted to kilograms first. There are 1000 grams in 1 kg:
500,000 g · (1 kg/1000 g) = 500 kg. The radius of the loop must be converted from kilometers to meters:
0.05 km · (1000 m)/(1 km) = 50 m. Velocity is in the correct set of units, so plug in to the equation to evaluate:
$$F = m\frac{v^2}{r} = 500 \cdot \frac{20^2}{50} = 500 \cdot \frac{400}{50} = 10 \cdot 400 = 4000N.$$

8. (B)
Difficulty: M
Category: Nonlinear Models
Strategy: Plug in the values given for mass, velocity, and force into the equation. Solve for r.
Solution: $F = m\frac{v^2}{r} \rightarrow 1,000,000 = 500\frac{(75)^2}{r} = \frac{2,812,500}{r}$
Multiply by r to get $1,000,000r = 2,812,500$, or $r \approx 2.8$ m.

9. (5)
Difficulty: M
Category: Nonlinear Models
Strategy: Plug in the values given for h and t in the problem and solve for c.
Solution: The problem states that when $t = 2$, h is equal to 5. Plug these values into the quadratic model given to get $5 = -5(2)^2 + 10(2) + c$. Simplify to find $5 = c$. Therefore, $c = 5$ meters (incidentally, this value must be the height of the tennis ball machine from which the balls are shot).

10. (D)

Difficulty: M

Category: Nonlinear Models

Strategy: A linear function has a constant rate of change, while an exponential function has a rate of change that is proportional to the value of the function.

Solution: The situation in A is a linear model that can be written as an equation $h(n) = 15 + 9n$. For each incremental increase in n, the height increases by a constant amount (9). The situation in B also describes a linear model, with a constant rate of change. The situation in C is a linear model that can be written as an equation $s = 250y$. The situation in D is an exponential model that can be written as an equation $p = 9(1.02)^x$.

11. (C)

Difficulty: M/H

Category: Nonlinear Models

Strategy: To determine if the functions could be exponential, divide the value of the function for $x = n$ by the value of the function for $x = n-1$, and check to see that the percent growth/decay remains constant (if so, the value of the quotient is the percent rate of growth or decay). Find the rate of growth/decay for all of the functions that could be exponential and use process of elimination.

Solution: Exponential functions have the general form

$y = a \cdot b^x$, where a is the value of y when $x = 0$, and b represents the percent rate of growth/decay (i.e. growth/decay factor). To find the value of b, take the value of the function for $x = n$ and divide by the value of the function for $x = n-1$. To make sure the function is exponential, the value of b should remain constant.

Note that $f(1)/f(0) = f(2)/f(1) = f(3)/f(2) = 2$. Therefore, $f(x)$ could be the function $f(x) = 5 \cdot 2^x$. It could represent an exponential function with growth factor $b = 2$.

Also, $g(1)/g(0) = g(2)/g(1) = g(3)/g(2) = 1.5$. Therefore, $g(x)$ could be the function $g(x) = 12 \cdot 1.5^x$. It could represent an exponential function with growth factor $b = 1.5$.

Finally, $h(1)/h(0) = h(2)/h(1) = h(3)/h(2) = 0.7$. Therefore, $h(x)$ could be the function $h(x) = 40 \cdot 0.7^x$. It could represent an exponential function with decay factor $b = 0.7$.

Therefore, statement I is true. Statement II is not true because $f(x)$ has a higher growth factor ($2 > 1.5$). Statement III is true because $h(x)$ is the only one of the functions with a decay factor.

Alternative reasoning: For each function, to determine the growth/decay factor, calculate the percent change with each increment of x. Each exponential function will have the same percent change for each increment of x.

$f(x)$ doubles for each increment of x, so $b = 2$.

$g(x)$ increases by a factor of $b = 1.5$.

$h(x)$ decreases by a factor of $b = 0.7$.

12. (B)

Difficulty: M

Category: Nonlinear Models

Strategy: A linear function has a constant rate of change, while an exponential function has a rate of change that is proportional to the value of the function. Exponential growth is always increasing, while exponential decay is always decreasing. Use process of elimination.

Solution: The rate of growth is either increasing or decreasing, but never constant. Therefore, the best model should not include linear growth or decay. Eliminate choices A and C. The population is always increasing, so exponential decay cannot describe any part of the model. Eliminate choice D. The only option left is B.

13. (D)

Difficulty: M/H

Category: Nonlinear Models

Strategy: Plug in the air temperature into the formula to evaluate the wind chill temperature. Find the percent decrease from ambient to wind chill temperature.

Solution: Plug $V = 27$ and $T = 27$ into the formula for wind chill to find the wind chill temperature:

$WC = 35.74 + 0.6215(27) - 35.75(27^{0.16}) + 0.4275(27)(27^{0.16}) \approx 35.74 + 16.7805 - 60.5751 + 19.5577 = 11.5031°F$. 11.5031 is not less than $1/3$ of $27 = 9$, so choice A can be eliminated. Choice B is also incorrect. The wind chill temperature is $27 - 11.5 \approx 15.5$ degrees less than the ambient temperature. The percent decrease in temperature is the change over the air temperature times $100\% \approx ((27 - 11.5)/27) \cdot 100\% \approx 57\%$ decrease.

14. (18)

Difficulty: M/H

Category: Nonlinear Models

Strategy: Compare the given equation to the standard form of an exponential model. Find what t must equal for the population to increase by 3%. Then, convert this value into months to find the value of n.

Solution: The equation given models 3% growth for every increase of 1 in the expression $2t/3$. Let $(2t)/3 = 1$ to find $t = 3/2$. Therefore, for every $3/2$ years, there is a 3% increase. Convert to months to find $3/2$ years $= 18$ months for each 3% increase.

15. (A)

Difficulty: H

Category: Nonlinear Models

Strategy: Rewrite the expression for gravitational force in the second scenario, using r_2 to denote the new distance between the objects. Set the expression equal to the original gravitational force. Cancel any common factors on both sides and solve for r_2 in terms of the original distance, r_1. Alternatively, choose numbers for the original masses and radius, and calculate the gravitational force. Do the same for the second scenario, and set the forces equal to each other. Solve for the new distance and compare to what it was originally in the problem.

Solution: The original gravitational force can be expressed as

$\frac{Gm_1m_2}{(r_1)^2}$. The gravitational force in the second scenario is $\frac{27Gm_1m_2}{(r_2)^2}$.

Set the forces equal to each other to get $\frac{Gm_1m_2}{(r_1)^2} = \frac{27Gm_1m_2}{(r_2)^2}$. Divide

both sides by the common factor Gm_1m_2 to get $\frac{1}{(r_1)^2} = \frac{27}{(r_2)^2}$. Cross-

multiply to get $r_2^2 = 27 r_1^2$. Take the square root of both sides (ignoring the negative solution, since physical distance must be positive) to find $r_2 = \sqrt{27}r_1 = 3\sqrt{3}r_1$. Since $3\sqrt{3} > 1$, this represents an elongation in distance between the objects, so the masses are further away from one another.

Alternatively, reason that if the numerator increases by a factor of 27, then the denominator must also increase by a factor of 27. This means r^2 must increase by a factor of 27, or r must increase by a factor of $3\sqrt{3}$.

16. (D)

Difficulty: H

Category: Nonlinear Models

Strategy: Compare the equations in the answer choices to the standard form of an exponential model. Find what t must equal for the population to double once. Use process of elimination. Alternatively, choose a number for t to solve numerically.

Solution: For an exponential function $f(x) = a\left(1 + \dfrac{b}{100}\right)^x$, a represents the y-intercept of the function, or the value of y when $t = 0$. The value of b represents the percent yearly growth (if positive) or percent yearly decay (if b is negative) for the function, and when the exponent $t = 1$, the function should increase by b%. Since the bacterial population starts at 60, then $a = 60$. Eliminate choices A and B. To double, the percent rate of growth must be 100%, so the value inside the parentheses is 2. Finally, the population should double when the exponent equals 1. In answer choice C, if $t/5 = 1$, then $t = 5$, which means the population doubles every 5 hours, which is not true. In answer choice D, if $5t = 1$, then $t = 1/5$ hour = 12 minutes. This means the population doubles every 12 minutes, so choice D must be correct. Alternatively, choose numbers. After $t = 1$ hour, the population would have doubled 5 times, resulting in 1920 bacteria, so plug in 1 for t to each expression and see which gives a result of 1920.

Additional Topics in Math – Section Quiz – Pages 478-482

1. (D)
Difficulty: E
Category: Triangles
Strategy: Use the triangle inequality law to set up three inequalities relating the sides of the triangle. Solve each inequality for a to determine the range of possible values for a.
Solution: The triangle inequality law states that the sum of any two sides of a triangle must be greater than the length of the third side. Thus, one can set up three inequalities for the triangle defined in the problem: $a < 3 + 12$, $3 < a + 12$, and $12 < 3 + a$. Solve each of these inequalities for a to find $a < 15$, $-9 < a$, and $9 < a$. Therefore, $9 < a < 15$.

2. (150)
Difficulty: E/M
Category: Volume & Surface Area
Strategy: Use the formula for the perimeter of a square to solve for the length of a side of one face. Calculate the area of one face. Then, multiply by 6 to find the total surface area of the cube.
Solution: The face of a cube is a square. The perimeter of a square is $4s$, where s is the length of one side. Thus, $4s = 20$, or $s = 5$, so each side length of the cube has length 5. The area of one square face is $s^2 = 25$. There are 6 faces on a cube, so the total surface area is $25 \cdot 6 = 150$.

3. (B)
Difficulty: E
Category: Complex Numbers
Strategy: Expand the product using the distributive property and group together like terms. Convert i^2 to its equivalent real number value.
Solution: Use the distributive property to expand the expression: $(1 + 5i) + 2(3i^2 - 2i) = 1 + 5i + 6i^2 - 4i$. Since $i = \sqrt{-1}$, $i^2 = -1$. Substitute this value into the expression: $1 + 5i + 6i^2 - 4i = 1 + i - 6 = -5 + i$.

4. (A)
Difficulty: E
Category: Angles
Strategy: Mark the figure with all known angles and parallel sides. Use the fact that the three angles of a triangle must sum to 180° to find the measure of angle RQP. There are two transversal lines intersecting the parallel lines. Find the relationship between angles RQP and NMP to solve for the measure of angle NMP.
Solution: Two of the angles in triangle RQP are known. Therefore, the third angle in the triangle (angle RQP) can be determined by solving the equation $x + 41 + 119 = 180$. Solve to find the measure of angle RQP is 20°. Line segments QR and MN are parallel and are intersected by the transversal line MP. Because corresponding angles of parallel lines intersected by a transversal must be congruent, then conclude that angle NMP is congruent to angle RQP, and so its measure must also be 20°.

5. (B)
Difficulty: E
Category: Circles
Strategy: Use the center-radius form of the equation of a circle. Plug in the coordinates of the center and the radius given into the equation.
Solution: The center-radius equation for a circle is $(x - h)^2 + (y - k)^2 = r^2$, where the center is at (h, k) and r = radius. Therefore, the correct equation of the circle should be $(x - 1)^2 + (y - 2)^2 = 81$.

6. (A)
Difficulty: E
Category: Complex Numbers
Strategy: Rewrite each term as a real number or as a multiple of i. Combine like terms.
Solution: Since $i = \sqrt{-1}$, squaring both sides yields the equation $i^2 = -1$. Therefore, $i^3 = i \cdot i^2 = i \cdot (-1) = -i$.
Hence, $3i^3 + 2i^2 + 3i + 4 = -3i - 2 + 3i + 4$. Combine like terms to get the solutions $-3i - 2 + 3i + 4 = 2$.

7. (A)
Difficulty: E
Category: Trigonometry
Strategy: Convert the angle into degrees. Determine what fraction of the whole circumference the length of the arc occupies.
Solution: To convert from radians into degrees, multiply by $(180/\pi)$. $(2\pi/3) \cdot (180/\pi) = 120°$. The full circle is 360° around, so the arc only sweeps through $120/360 = 1/3$ of the full circumference.

8. (B)
Difficulty: M
Category: Angles
Strategy: Use the relationship between angles of an isosceles triangle to find the measures of each angle in triangle BAE. Determine the measure of angle BCD by noting its relationship to angle AEB as angles formed by a transversal intersecting parallel lines.
Solution: The problem states that $AB = BE$. Therefore, triangle ABE is isosceles, and angle E must have measure 72°, since it is congruent to angle A. Angles BEA and BCD are alternating interior angles along transversal line segment EC, which intersects parallel lines. Therefore, the two angles must be congruent, and so angle BCD must measure 72°.

9. (6)
Difficulty: M
Category: Circles
Strategy: Note that the sum of the lengths of the minor arcs should equal half the circumference of the circle. Write an equation setting their sum equal to half the formula for circumference and solve for the length of the radius. Multiply by 2 to find the length of the diameter.
Solution: Line segment AC is a diameter, and therefore must go through the center. This means that arc ABC must represent half of the circumference of the circle, since the central angle associated with it is 180 degrees. Minor arcs AB and BC both have length 1.5π and together add up to arc ABC, which is half the circumference of the circle. Thus, $1.5\pi + 1.5\pi = 3\pi = (1/2)2\pi r = \pi r$. Therefore, $r = 3$. The diameter AC must be twice this and has length 6.

10. (A)

Difficulty: E/M

Category: Trigonometry

Strategy: Draw the triangle and use SOH CAH TOA to write out possible lengths for the sides based on the values given in the problem. Use these lengths to determine the trigonometric function asked for in the problem.

Solution: Draw a sketch of the triangle, labeling all of the vertices. Since tan A = 3/4, assume that two of the sides of the triangle are 3 and 4 (although they can be any multiple of these two values). SOH CAH TOA states that tan A = opposite/adjacent (TOA). Therefore, the side opposite to angle A can be labeled 3, and the side adjacent to angle A can be labeled 4.

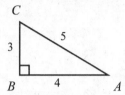

Use the Pythagorean Theorem (or your knowledge of the 3-4-5 Pythagorean triple) to find that the hypotenuse is 5. The problem asks for cos C = (adjacent/hypotenuse) = 3/5.

11. (15)

Difficulty: M

Category: Triangles

Strategy: Find the measure of angle ACB using the fact that the sum of the interior angles in triangle ACB is 180°. Find the measure of angle BCD using the information given in the problem. Find the measure of angle BDC using the other two known angles in triangle BDC. Determine the measure of angle BDE and subtract the measure of angle BDC from it to solve for y.

Solution: If $m(\angle BAC)$ = 60° and $m(\angle ABC)$ = 90°, then $m(\angle ACB)$ = 180 − 60 − 90 = 30° (the sum of the measures of the interior angles of a triangle must be 180). Since line segment DC bisects angle ACB, then $m(\angle BCD)$ = 30/2 = 15°. Thus, $m(\angle BDC)$ = 180 − 90 − 15 = 75°. Triangles ABC and ADE are similar, so angle ADE must measure 90°. Thus, angle BDE must measure 180 − 90 = 90°, and y = 90 − 75 = 15.

12. (B)

Difficulty: M

Category: Volume & Surface Area

Strategy: Find the volume of the cone filter using the formula for the volume of a cone given on the test form. Subtract the volume of the liquid captured in the flask to find the volume of the solid remaining in the filter.

Solution: The volume of a cone is $(1/3)\pi r^2 h$, where r is the radius, and h is the height. Note that this formula is listed at the beginning of every math section on the test. Since the cone filter will be completely filled, the volume of the solid plus the liquid (i.e. the mixture poured into the filter) should equal the volume of the filter. Therefore, the volume of the mixture = $(1/3)\pi(3)^2(6) \approx 56.5$ in^3. The volume of the liquid that was in the mixture is 40 in^3. The volume of the solid must be the volume of the mixture minus the volume of the liquid filtrate ≈ 56.5 − 40 = 17 cubic inches.

13. (D)

Difficulty: (M)

Category: Trigonometry

Strategy: The smallest angle is opposite the smallest side, and the hypotenuse must be the longest side. Use these facts to label the lengths of the right triangle. Use the sinΘ = cos(90 − Θ) identity and SOH CAH TOA to evaluate the solution.

Solution: The smallest angle in a triangle is always opposite the smallest side, so angle theta must be opposite the side with length 9. Since sinΘ = cos(90 − Θ), then only sinΘ needs to be computed. Use SOHCAHTOA to find that $\sin\theta = \dfrac{opp.}{hyp.} = \dfrac{9}{15} = \dfrac{3}{5}$.

14. (D)

Difficulty: M

Category: Volume and Surface Area

Strategy: Let r = radius of cylinder A and h = height of cylinder A. Use the formula given to write an expression for the surface area of both cylinders. Compare the final expressions by dividing them. Alternatively, plug in numbers for the radius and height of the two cylinders and compare the surface areas.

Solution: If r = radius of cylinder A and h = height of cylinder A, then $3r$ = radius of cylinder B and $3h$ = height of cylinder B.

Surface area of cylinder A = $2\pi rh + 2\pi r^2$

Surface area of cylinder B = $2\pi(3r)(3h) + 2\pi(3r)^2 = 9(2\pi rh + 2\pi r^2)$.

Surface area of B: Surface area of A = 9:1. Thus, cylinder B has 9 times the surface area of cylinder A.

15. (B)

Difficulty: H

Category: Circles

Strategy: Plug in the y-coordinate of the endpoint given into the equation to determine the x-coordinate of the point. It may be useful to sketch the graph here. Determine the point that lies on the opposite endpoint of the diameter.

Solution: The equation $(x − 4)^2 + (y + 3)^2 = 16$ is in center-radius form, so the center must be at the point (4, −3) and the radius has length 4. Plug in y = 1 to the equation to find the x-coordinate of the diameter endpoint: $(x − 4)^2 + (1 + 3)^2 = 16$, which gives $(x − 4)^2 = 0$, or x = 4. Therefore, the endpoint of the diameter has coordinates (4, 1). Note that this point is 4 units directly above the center, and so the other endpoint of the circle must be 4 units directly below the center at (4, −3 − 4) = (4, −7).

16. (40)

Difficulty: H

Category: Angles

Strategy: Note that all 6 central angles must sum to 360°. Express the measures of the two angles not included in angle x in terms of angle z. Write an equation for the sum of all six angles in terms of z. Solve for z.

Solution: The two central angles not included in angle x are congruent to y and z (since they are vertical angles to angles y and z). The sum of angle x with those two angles must be 360°, since the central angles together form a circle. Therefore, $x + y + z$ = 360. Substitute the expressions given for x and y to find $6z + 2z + z$ = 360. Combine like terms to get $9z$ = 360. Solve to find z = 40.

17. (C)

Difficulty: H

Category: Triangles

Strategy: Use the Pythagorean Theorem to determine the value of x. Note that the smaller right triangles and the large triangle are all similar, since they share the same angles. Set up a proportion to solve for y.

Solution: $x^2 + (2\sqrt{11})^2 = 12^2$. This can be re-written as

$x^2 + 44 = 144$. Solve to find $x = 10$. Note that all of the right triangles in the figure are similar because they share the same angles. Therefore, their side lengths are all in proportion to one another. Set

up a proportion to solve y: $\dfrac{y}{12} = \dfrac{2\sqrt{11}}{10}$. Cross-multiply to get

$10y = 24\sqrt{11}$. Divide by 10 on both sides to find $y = 2.4\sqrt{11}$

18. (D)

Difficulty: H

Category: Complex Numbers

Strategy: Multiply the top and bottom of the fraction by the complex conjugate of the denominator. Simplify.

Solution: Multiply the numerator and denominator of the fraction by the complex conjugate of the denominator (the complex conjugate of $a + bi$ is $a - bi$):

$\dfrac{13 - 5i}{5 - 3i} \cdot \dfrac{5 + 3i}{5 + 3i} = \dfrac{65 + 39i - 25i - 15i^2}{25 - 9i^2}$. Since $i^2 = -1$, the fraction can

be simplified further:

$\dfrac{65 + 39i - 25i - 15i^2}{25 - 9i^2} = \dfrac{65 + 14i + 15}{25 + 9} = \dfrac{80 + 14i}{34}$. The numerator and

denominator have a common factor of 2 that can be canceled:

$\dfrac{80 + 14i}{34} = \dfrac{40}{17} + \dfrac{7}{17}i$.

Hence, $a = 40/17$ and $b = 7/17$, so $a - b = \dfrac{40}{17} - \dfrac{7}{17} = \dfrac{33}{17}$.

Additional Topics in Math – Angles – Pages 484-487

1. (B)

Difficulty: E

Category: Angles

Strategy: There are two transversal lines intersecting the parallel lines. Note which angles formed by these lines must be congruent or supplementary and note their measures. Once both angles adjacent to x are known, set up an equation to solve for x. Mark up the figure.

Solution: Same side interior angles on a transversal intersecting two parallel lines should always be supplementary. Mark those angles in the figure below:

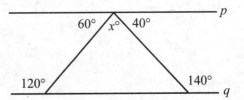

The top three angles just below line p must add up to 180°, so $60 + x + 40 = 180$. Solve to find $x = 80°$.

2. (C)

Difficulty: E

Category: Angles

Strategy: Mark up the figure with the known angles, congruent sides, and parallel sides. Note that triangle ACE is an isosceles triangle. Find the measure of its base angles. Know the relationship between angles formed by a transversal intersecting parallel line to find the measure of angle ABD.

Solution: Begin by marking up the figure with the values given in the problem.

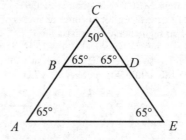

Since sides AC and CE of the larger triangle are congruent, then the angles opposite them are congruent. All angles in a triangle must sum to 180, so the two base angles must measure $(180 - 50)/2 = 65°$. Line segments BD and AE are parallel. Thus, angle CBD must measure 65 degrees, since it is a corresponding angle to angle A. Finally, angle ABD and CBD are supplementary and must add to 180. Hence, angle ABD must measure $180 - 65 = 115$ degrees.

3. (C)
Difficulty: E
Category: Angles
Strategy: Mark the figure with known angles. Know the relationship between vertical and supplementary angles.

Solution: Begin by marking up the figure with the values given in the problem. Since vertical angles are equal, mark the vertical angles of each known angle in the figure too:

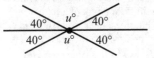

Notice that the three angles above the center line (and the three angles below) must sum up to 180. Therefore, $40 + u + 40 = 180$. Solve the equation to get $u = 100$.

4. (50)
Difficulty: E
Category: Angles
Strategy: Use the relationship between vertical and supplementary angles to find the measures of the other three angles in the quadrilateral. Use the sum of angles in a quadrilateral to solve for x.

Solution:

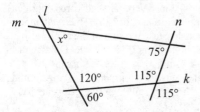

The angle opposite to x in the quadrilateral must be 115°, since vertical angles are equal. The angle marked 120° must have this value because it is supplementary to the 60° angle. Therefore, three of the angles in the quadrilateral are 75°, 115°, and 120°. The sum of the angles in a quadrilateral must add up to $(4 - 2) \cdot 180 = 360°$. Hence, $x + 75 + 115 + 120 = 180$. Solve to find $x = 50$.

5. (D)
Difficulty: E
Category: Angles
Strategy: Use the relationship between supplementary angles to find the measure of angle ACB and angle ECD. While you cannot find the values of the individual angles, it is possible to find the value of $x + y$ and of $z + w$, using the fact that the angles in a triangle must sum to 180°.

Solution: Angle ACB is supplementary to angle ACE, and so their measures must sum to 180. Since angle ACE is 140°, angle ACB must measure $180 - 140 = 40°$. Angle ECD must also measure 40°, since angles ACB and ECD are vertical angles. The three angles of a triangle must sum to 180°. Therefore, $x + y + 40 = 180$ and $z + w + 40 = 180$. While it is not possible to solve for the individual angles, it is possible to find $x + y = 140$ and $z + w = 140$. Therefore, $x + y + z + w = 140 + 140 = 280$.

6. (60)
Difficulty: M
Category: Angles
Strategy: Know the relationship between supplementary angles to find the measure of angle ACB. Determine the measure of angle y using the fact that the angles of a triangle must sum to 180°. Use the same reasoning to find the measure of angle x. Find the sum of the two values.

Solution: Angle ACB and its adjacent angle $BCD = 125$ degrees are supplementary. Therefore, angle $ACB = 180 - 125 = 55°$. The angles in triangle ABC must sum to 180. Therefore, $y + 90 + 55 = 180$. Solve to find $y = 35$. Since two angles in triangle BCD are known, the measure of angle x can be determined from the equation $30 + 125 + x = 180$. Solve to find $x = 25$. $x + y = 25 + 35 = 60$.

7. (D)
Difficulty: M
Category: Angles
Strategy: Draw two intersecting lines and label the 4 angles formed. Find which angles are supplementary and which are congruent, vertical angles. Write an equation relating the measure of angles A and B. Determine the measure of angle B.

Solution: Any intersection of two lines will form four angles with only two distinct measures (since two pairs of congruent vertical angles will be formed), and the two distinct measures will add up to 180° (as the two angles will form a straight line). Therefore, if angle B is four times the measure of angle A, they must be distinct and must add up to 180°. If $A + B = 180$, then $A + 4A = 180$. Solve to find $A = 36°$. Hence, $B = 4(36) = 144°$.

8. (C)
Difficulty: M
Category: Angles
Strategy: Mark the figure with all known angles and congruent angles. Use the fact that the three angles of a triangle must sum to 180° to find the measure of angles 2 and 3. Since angles 3 and 5 can be determined, find the measure of angle 4. Compare the measures of angle 4 and the angle 1 to determine if the lines m and n must be parallel. Determine which of the statements must be true.

Solution: $m(\angle 2) + m(\angle 3) + 110 = 180$. Since $m(\angle 2) = m(\angle 3)$, then the equation can be rewritten as $2m(\angle 2) = 70$. Divide by 2 on both sides to find $m(\angle 2) = m(\angle 3) = 35$. Since $m(\angle 4) + m(\angle 3) + m(\angle 5) = 180$, then $m(\angle 4) + 35 + 45 = 180$. Solve to find $m(\angle 4) = 100°$.

Statement I is false. The problem does not state that the lines are parallel, and you cannot assume so based on appearance. If the lines were parallel, then $m(\angle 4) = m(\angle 1)$, since alternating interior angles formed by a transversal line intersection parallel lines must be congruent. However, $100° \neq 110°$, and so lines m and n cannot be parallel.

Statement II is true, since the problem states that the measures of angles 2 and 3 are congruent. Therefore, the lengths of the sides opposite those angles must also be congruent. The resulting triangle must then be isosceles.

Statement III is true from the calculations above.

9. (D)

Difficulty: M

Category: Angles

Strategy: Draw parallelogram *ABCD*. Mark which angles must be congruent and which are supplementary. Use the relationship between angles *B* and *C* to determine the measures of both angles. Find the measure of angle *A*.

Solution:

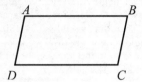

Since angles *B* and *C* are same-side interior angles formed by the transversal line segment *BC* intersecting parallel sides *AB* and *DC*, then they must be supplementary, and so $m(\angle B) + m(\angle C) = 180$. The problem also states that $m(\angle C) = 2.5m(\angle B)$. Substitute into the first equation to find $m(\angle B) + 2.5m(\angle B) = 180$. Solve to find $m(\angle B) \approx 51.4°$. Thus, $m(\angle C) \approx 2.5 \cdot 51.4° \approx 129°$. Opposite angles in a parallelogram are congruent (same side angles are supplementary), and so $m(\angle A) = m(\angle C) \approx 129°$.

10. (C)

Difficulty: M

Category: Angles

Strategy: Note all four central angles must sum to 360°. Use this and the congruence of vertical angles to write an equation concerning the sum of angle *AED* and of angle *BEC*. Substitute the expression for angle *AED* into the equation to solve for the measure of angle *BEC*.

Solution: The vertical angle theorem states that the included angle *BEC* and its opposite angle (the 4th central angle not included in $\angle AED$) must have equal measures. Let $m(\angle BEC) = x$. Since the four central angles must sum to 360, then $3x + 44 + x = 360$. Simplify to get $4x = 316$. Solve to find $x = 79°$.

11. (C)

Difficulty: M

Category: Angles

Strategy: Apply the formula given to evaluate the measure of an exterior angle of a regular heptagon and hexagon. Note that the sum of an exterior and interior angle must be 180 degrees. Use this fact to determine the measure of an interior angle of the hexagon. Alternatively, find the sum of the interior angles in a hexagon and divide by 6 to determine the measure of any interior angle in the polygon.

Solution: A heptagon has 7 sides and a hexagon has 6. The measure of an exterior angle of a regular heptagon is $360/7 \approx 51.43°$. The measure of the exterior angle of a regular hexagon is $360/6 = 60°$. Hence, the measure of an interior angle in the regular hexagon must be $180 - 60 = 120°$. $51.43° + 120° = 171.43°$.

12. (D)

Difficulty: M

Category: Angles

Strategy: Use the formula given and the formula for the sum of interior angles in an *n*-sided polygon to determine which statement must be true. If helpful, choose a number for *n* and evaluate the measure of an interior and exterior angle of the regular polygon.

Then, determine the sum of all interior angles and the sum of all exterior angles. Test what happens for a polygon with 2*n* sides.

Solution: The sum of interior angles in an *n*-sided polygon is $(n-2)180$. If *n* is doubled, then the new sum is $(2n-2)180 = 2(n-1)180 \neq 2(n-2)180$, so eliminate choice A.

The sum of exterior angles in an *n*-sided polygon must be *n* times the measure of a single exterior angle. Use the formula given to determine that the sum of exterior angles must always be $n \cdot (360/n) = 360°$. This value will stay constant for any value of *n*, so eliminate choice B. The measure of an interior angle of a regular *n*-sided polygon must be the sum of the interior angles divided by *n*, or $((n-2)180)/n$. For a regular polygon with 2*n* sides, the measure of a single interior angle would be $((2n-2)180)/(2n) = ((n-1)180)/n$, which is not half the value of $((n-2)180)/n$ for all values of *n*. Eliminate choice C. The measure of an exterior angle of an *n*-sided regular polygon is $360/n$, according to the equation given. The measure of an exterior angle of a 2*n*-sided regular polygon is $360/2n$, which is half of $360/n$. Thus, answer choice D must be correct.

13. (D)

Difficulty: M

Category: Angles

Strategy: Mark the figure with all known angles and note any congruent vertical angles. Use this information to determine which statements must be true.

Solution: If $a = 90$, then $d = 90$ (since vertical angles are congruent), and $b + c = 90$ (supplementary angles add to 180). Thus, statement I is true. Furthermore, $e + f = 90$ because the sum of the two is also supplementary with *a*. Thus, Statements II is also true. For statement III, $d = 90$, so the statement asks if $b + f = 90$. Since because $b + c = 90$ and $c = f$ (vertical angles are congruent), use substitution to prove that $b + f = 90 = d$. Therefore, all three statements are true.

14. (A)

Difficulty: H

Category: Angles

Strategy: Find the measure of the central angle that subtends arc *BC*. The measure of an inscribed angle is half the measure of the central angle that subtends the same arc. Alternatively, use estimation and process of elimination to determine which answer could be possible.

Solution: Let point *O* represent the center of the circle. Central angle *BOC* must measure $360/5 = 72°$. Angle *BXC* subtends the same arc, but since it is an inscribed angle, its measure must be half the measure of central angle *BOC*. Therefore, the measure of angle *BXC* must be $72/2 = 36°$.

15. (140)

Difficulty: H

Category: Angles

Strategy: Note that line segments *AC* and *AB* are congruent, since they are radii of the same circle. Use this fact to determine the measure of angle *ABC*. Solve for the measure of angle *ACB* by setting up an equation for the sum of the three angles in the triangular flag. Use the other information given to determine the measure of angle *ACD*.

Solution: Line segments *AC* and *AB* are congruent because they are radii of the same circle. Thus, the measures of angles *CBA* and angle *CAB* must be congruent, since they are opposite to congruent sides of an isosceles triangle. Therefore, $m(\angle CBA) = 65°$. Since the angles of a triangle must add up to 180°, the measure of *ACB* must be equal to $180 - 65 - 65 = 50°$. From the given information, the measure of *BCD* is 90°, and therefore the measure of *ACD* is $90° + 50° = 140°$.

Additional Topics in Math – Triangles – Pages 489-493

1. (B)

Difficulty: E

Category: Triangles

Strategy: Draw the triangles to note which sides/angles are corresponding. Use the relationship between angles in an isosceles triangle to determine the measures of each of the angles in triangle *MNO*. Corresponding angles between similar triangles are congruent, so use this fact to determine the measure of angle *R*.

Solution: Draw a quick sketch of the similar isosceles triangles and note the measures of any angles and relationships between sides given in the problem:

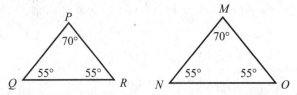

Because $\overline{MN} \cong \overline{MO}$, angles *N* and *O* must be congruent (opposite angles to congruent sides in an isosceles triangle must be congruent). Since the third angle is 70 degrees, and the sum of the degree measure of angles in a triangle is 180, then angles *N* and *O* must both have measure (180 – 70)/2 = 55°. Since triangles *MNO* and *PQR* are similar, then angle *R* must have the same measure as angle *O*. Thus, the measure of angle *R* must be 55°.

2. (B)

Difficulty: E

Category: Triangles

Strategy: Draw a quick sketch of the similar isosceles triangles and label corresponding sides *XY* and *UV* as *a* and *b*. Use the relationship between the sides to find the ratio of *a* and *b*. Then, set up a proportion to solve for the perimeter of *XYZ*. Alternatively, choose numbers for side lengths that work in the constraints given and solve.

Solution: Since $5XY = 2UV$, then $5a = 2b$. Rearrange to find $a/b = 2/5$. Note from your figure that sides *XY* and *UV* are corresponding sides of similar triangles, so the perimeters of the triangles (and all other corresponding pairs of sides) must be in the same proportion. Therefore, (perimeter of *XYZ*)/50 = 2/5. Cross multiply to get 5(perimeter of *XYZ*) = 100. Solve to find that the perimeter of *XYZ* must be 20.

3. (D)

Difficulty: E/M

Category: Triangles

Strategy: Mark up the figure with all of the information given in the problem. Know the sum of angles in a triangle to determine the measure of each angle in triangle *PQR*. Use this information to determine what type of special triangle *PQR* is, and then solve for its perimeter.

Solution: Since line segments *SQ* and *SR* have the same length, then *PS*, the bisector of angle *QPR*, must be a perpendicular bisector to base *QR*. Thus, triangle *PQR* must be isosceles, with congruent angles *PQR* and *PRQ*. The remaining angle in the triangle is angle *QPR*, which measures 60°. Thus, the other two angles must sum to 120° (sum of the measures of angles in a triangle is 180°). Since they are also congruent, then all angles of triangle *PQR* must measure 60°. Hence, triangle *PQR* is equilateral. A side length (line segment *QR*) of the triangle has length 8, so the perimeter must be 3 · 8 = 24.

4. (B)

Difficulty: M

Category: Triangles

Strategy: Mark up the figure with all of the information given in the problem. Determine which angles in the two triangles formed in the figure must be congruent. Determine the relationship between the triangles formed by the intersecting lines and line segments.

Solution: Angles *ABE* and *DBC* are congruent because they are a pair of vertical angles. Angles *E* and *C* must also be congruent since they are alternating interior angles formed by a transversal line intersecting two parallel lines. The same reasoning can be used to show angles *D* and *A* are congruent. Since the two triangles have congruent angles, conclude that triangles *ABE* and *DBC* are similar. Therefore, their sides should be proportional to one another. It may be useful to redraw one of the triangles, so that corresponding sides line up more intuitively. The problem asks which ratio of sides in the larger triangle is equal to the ratio of sides *DB* and *DC* of the smaller triangle. Side *AB* is the corresponding side to *DB*. Similarly, side *AE* is the corresponding larger triangle side to side *DC* of the smaller triangle. Therefore, $\dfrac{DB}{DC} = \dfrac{AB}{AE}$.

5. (C)

Difficulty: M

Category: Triangles

Strategy: Use the triangle inequality law to set up inequalities relating the sides of each potential triangle in the answers. Eliminate any choices that violate the rule.

Solution: The triangle inequality law states that the sum of any two sides of a triangle must be greater than the length of the third side. Answer choice A can be eliminated because 1 + 6 is not greater than 7, which means a triangle cannot be formed. Answer choice B can be eliminated because 2 + 9 is not greater than 12. Answer choice D can be eliminated because 4 + 7 is not greater than 13. However, answer choice C satisfies all three inequalities needed to confirm the inequality law: 3 < 12 + 14, 12 < 3 + 14, and 14 < 3 + 12. Therefore, C is the only choice that represents a set of possible lengths of a triangle.

6. (B)

Difficulty: (M)

Category: Triangles

Strategy: Use the Pythagorean Theorem to find the length of side *FG*. Find the area of the triangle using the legs as the base and height. Note that the degree measure of the largest angle in a right triangle is 90. Find what percent the area is of 90.

Solution: Let the length of $FG = x$. Thus, $x^2 + 13^2 = \left(\sqrt{218}\right)^2$.

Rewrite as $x^2 + 169 = 218$, or $x^2 = 49$. Thus, $x = 7$. The area of a triangle is $(1/2)bh$. Since the legs are perpendicular to each other, they can be used as the base and height of the triangle. Thus, the area of the triangle is $(1/2)\cdot13\cdot7 = 91/2 = 45.5$. The largest angle in a right triangle always has degree measure 90 (since the other two angles must sum to 90). Thus, the problem asks what percent of 90 is 45.5, which is $(45.5/90) \cdot 100\% \approx 51\%$.

7. (C)
Difficulty: M
Category: Triangles
Strategy: Label the right angle given and the congruent angles between the two triangles. Determine that the two triangles are similar. Find the ratio between corresponding sides. Use proportions to find the heights of both triangles (vertical legs), and express the lengths of the bases (horizontal legs) of both triangles in terms of k. Write an expression for the area of the larger triangle in terms of k.
Solution: The problem states that $\angle F \cong \angle B$. Furthermore, $\angle D = 90°$, and so $\angle D \cong \angle C$. Since two pairs of angles between triangles ADF and ACB are congruent, then the triangles must be similar, and the lengths of their corresponding sides must be proportional. D is the midpoint of line segment AC. If DC has length 4, then AD must also have length 4. Thus, the height of the smaller triangle (AD) is one half the height of the larger triangle (AC), which is 8. Hence, the lengths of the sides of the smaller triangle are one half the lengths of the corresponding sides of the larger triangle. Triangle ADF has a base of k. Thus, the base of larger triangle ABC must have length $2k$. Area of a triangle is $(1/2)bh$. Thus, the area of triangle ABC is $(1/2)(8)(2k) = 8k$.

You might also notice that triangle ADF is a special 3-4-5 right triangle. In this problem, that does not help, but technically, you can find the value of k, and from there determine the numerical value of the area. The problem does not ask for this however.

8. (6)
Difficulty: M
Category: Triangles
Strategy: Note that the water line is parallel to the base of the cross-section, and so the smaller triangle above the water line is similar to the larger triangle. Use the scale factor for the areas to determine the scale factor for the lengths of the sides of the smaller triangle. Determine the height of the iceberg that is above water, and then subtract this value from 9 to find the distance from the base.
Solution: Since the water line is parallel to the base of the cross-section of the iceberg, then the smaller triangle above the water line must be similar to the large triangle. Thus, the smaller triangle must have a height of $9a$ and a base of $15a$, where a is the scale factor between the triangles. The area of the larger triangle is $(1/2)bh = (1/2) \cdot 9 \cdot 15 = 67.5$. Thus, the area of the smaller triangle must be $(1/9) \cdot 67.5 = 7.5$. Therefore, $(1/2) \cdot 15a \cdot 9a = 7.5$. Simplify and rearrange the equation to find $a^2 = 1/9$. Thus, $a = 1/3$. Therefore, the height of the smaller triangle must be $9a = 9 \cdot (1/3) = 3$ m. Conclude that the water line must be $9 - 3 = 6$ m from the base of the iceberg.

9. (B)
Difficulty: M
Category: Triangles
Strategy: Compare the horizontal base lengths of areas II and III. Write an expression for the area of II and III in terms of each triangle's height and base and compare the areas to determine the ratio of their heights.
Solution: Since line segment AC bisects line segment BD, then DE must have the same length as line segment BE. Thus, the horizontal bases of triangles II and III are congruent. The areas of two triangles can be compared using the formula for the area of a triangle = $(1/2)bh$. Since their bases are the same length, the only thing that can account for their different areas is their heights (line segment AE for triangle II, and line segment EC for triangle III). Their heights must therefore be in the same ratio as their areas, and so the ratio of the heights must also be 4:7.

10. (C)
Difficulty: M
Category: Triangles
Strategy: Determine that the two congruent triangles are 30-60-90 triangles. Use the ratio of sides in a 30-60-90 triangle to determine the vertical height of each triangle, which is the length of the side of the square. Find the area of the square.
Solution: From the information provided, conclude that the triangles are 30-60-90 right triangles. The ratio of the sides of a 30-60-90 triangle are always in a $1 : \sqrt{3} : 2$ ratio. Since the length of the side opposite the 30° angle is 3, then the side opposite the 60° angle must be $3\sqrt{3}$. This is also the side length of the square. The area of a square is s^2, where s = length of a side of the square. Therefore, the area of the square must be $\left(3\sqrt{3}\right)^2 = 27$.

11. (A)
Difficulty: H
Category: Triangles
Strategy: Determine that triangles CDE and CAB are similar. Let the length of line segment $CD = x$. Set up a proportion that relates corresponding sides of the similar triangles and solve for x.
Solution: Triangles CDE and CAB are both right triangles and share angle C. Since they share two pairs of congruent angles, then they must be similar. Thus, the side lengths of corresponding sides in the triangle must be proportional. Let the length of line segment $CD = x$. Set up the following proportion:
$$\frac{AC}{CD} = \frac{BC}{CE} \rightarrow \frac{AD+CD}{CD} = \frac{BE+CE}{CE} \rightarrow \frac{3+x}{x} = \frac{5+(8+x)}{8+x}$$
Cross multiply to get $(3+x)(8+x) = x(13+x)$. Distribute the products on both sides to find $x^2 + 11x + 24 = x^2 + 13x$. Combine like terms to find $2x = 24$. Solve, to find $x = 12$.

12. (A)
Difficulty: H
Category: Triangles
Strategy: Label all congruent angles in the triangles and determine that triangles RSV and UTV are similar. Find the length of line segment SV from the information given. Determine the ratio of lengths of corresponding sides between the triangles. Use this information to set up an equation that relates the sum of lengths RV and VU.
Solution: The problem states that angles VUT and angle VRS are congruent. Furthermore, angles UVT and RVS must also be congruent because they are vertical angles. Therefore, triangles UTV and RSV must be similar because they share all of their angle measures. The length of SV is equal to $ST - VT$, or $18 - 12 = 6 = SV$. Thus, the ratio of corresponding sides between the triangles must be 6:12 = 1:2. Let RV have length x. UV must be twice as long, and should have length $2x$. Since $RV + UV = 15$, then $x + 2x = 15$. Solve to find $x = 5$.

13. (A)

Difficulty: H

Category: Triangles

Strategy: Find the unlabeled angle in the triangle (use the fact that the three angles of a triangle must sum to 180). Draw a height from the top vertex angle down to the 20 in. base. Use special triangle relationships to find the length of the height. Find the area using the triangle area formula.

Solution: First, subtract the known angles from 180° to find that the missing angle measures $180 - 103 - 47 = 30°$. Then, draw an altitude from the 20 in. side to the opposite vertex, which will form a 30-60-90 right triangle on the right of the altitude. The ratio of the sides of a 30-60-90 triangle are always in a $1 : \sqrt{3} : 2$ ratio. Thus, the altitude, which is opposite the 30° angle, must be half the length of the hypotenuse $= (1/2) \cdot 16 = 8$ inches. The area of the triangle is $(1/2)bh = (1/2)(20)(8) = 80$ square inches.

14. (A)

Difficulty: H

Category: Triangles

Strategy: Determine that triangles APC and CPB are similar. Note that the triangles also share a side, CP. Set up a proportion to solve for the length of CP. Use the Pythagorean Theorem to solve for the length of CB.

Solution: Triangles APC and CPB both have congruent angles. Thus, triangle APC must be similar to triangle CPB.

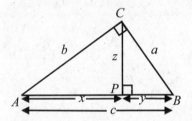

Set up a proportion to solve for z = length of CP, the side both triangles have in common.

$\frac{z}{y} = \frac{x}{z} \rightarrow \frac{z}{125} = \frac{720}{z} \rightarrow z^2 = 90000 \rightarrow z = 300$. Then, use the

Pythagorean Theorem on triangle CPB to solve for a:

$a^2 = y^2 + z^2 = 125^2 + 300^2 = 105,625$. Therefore, $a = 325$.

15. (D)

Difficulty: H

Category: Triangles

Strategy: View the front and top sides of the solid as a flat rectangle (imagine you were to fold up the top of the figure). The shortest distance would be the straight-line distance along the rectangle from point S to point B. Use the Pythagorean Theorem to find this value.

Solution:

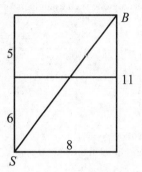

The shortest distance would be the straight-line path on the rectangle from S to B. Use the Pythagorean theorem to solve for the distance:

$SB = \sqrt{8^2 + 11^2} = \sqrt{64 + 121} = \sqrt{185}$.

16. (A)

Difficulty: H

Category: Triangles

Strategy: To form a triangle, length b must touch the base. Its minimum length would come from the formation of a 30-60-90 triangle, and so it must have a length at least half the length of a. If b is longer than this length, then consider if two different triangles could be formed. Consider each case and use process of elimination.

Solution: Case I. $b = 5.5$ equals ½ of $a = 11$. This is what would occur in a 30-60-90 triangle, and there is only one such triangle that can be formed:

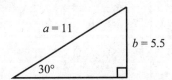

Case II. $b = 6$, which is less than 7 or ½ of $a = 14$

No triangle can be formed as b is too short to form the right triangle.

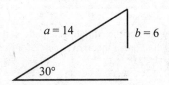

Case III. $b = 10$, which is greater than 8 or ½ of a, but less than $a = 18$, so two triangles can be formed.

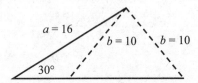

Case IV. $b = 18$ is greater than ½ of a, so 2 triangles can be formed.

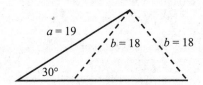

17. (26)

Difficulty: H

Category: Triangles

Strategy: Mark up the figure with all of the information given in the problem. Note any relationships between triangles in the figure.

Solution: Mark up the figure with the information given in the problem:

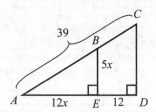

Note that triangle ADC is similar to triangle AEB since they both share angle A, and they both have a right angle.

Use the Pythagorean Theorem to find the length of line segment AB in terms of x: $(5x)^2 + (12x)^2 = (AB)^2$.

Expand to find $25x^2 + 144x^2 = 169x^2 = (AB)^2$. Take the square root of both sides to find $AB = 13x$. Note that triangle ABE must be a multiple of the 5-12-13 triangle. Now, set up a proportion between the triangles, relating corresponding sides:

$\frac{12x}{12x+12} = \frac{13x}{39}$. Cross-multiply to get $468x = 156x^2 + 156x$. Set the quadratic equation equal to zero to get $156x^2 - 312x = 0$. Factor to get $156x(x-2) = 0$. Setting each factor equal to zero, we find $x = 2$, which means that AB has length $2 \cdot 13 = 26$.

Additional Topics in Math – Circles – Pages 495-497

1. (C)
Difficulty: E
Category: Circles
Strategy: Set the formula for the area of a circle equal to the area given. Find the radius of the circle. Multiply by two to find the diameter.
Solution: Area of a circle = πr^2, where r is the radius of the circle. Thus, $16\pi = \pi r^2$. Divide both sides by π to find $16 = r^2$. Take the square root of both sides to find $r = 4$. Since the diameter is twice the length of the radius, then the diameter must have a length of 8.

2. (B)
Difficulty: M
Category: Circles
Strategy: Graph the points, and draw the circle described in the problem. The center is the midpoint of the two points, and the radius is half the distance between the two points. Determine these values and plug them into the center-radius equation of a circle.
Solution: Every diameter goes through the center of a circle, and the center should lie halfway along any diameter. The center can be determined by finding the midpoint of the two endpoints of the diameter given:

Center = $\left(\dfrac{-2+4}{2}, \dfrac{0+0}{2}\right) = (1, 0)$. The length of the diameter should be the distance between the two points listed. If drawn on a graph, notice that both points lie on the x-axis, and you can quickly determine that they are a distance 6 from each other. The radius is half this length, so the radius should have length 3. The Center-Radius equation for a circle is $(x - h)^2 + (y - k)^2 = r^2$, where the center is at (h, k) and r = radius. Therefore, the correct equation of the circle should be is $(x - 1)^2 + y^2 = 9$.

3. (C)
Difficulty: M
Category: Circles
Strategy: Set the formula for arc length equal to the length of the arc given. Solve for central angle x.
Solution: For a central angle x, arclength = $2\pi r\left(\dfrac{x}{360}\right)$. The circle has radius of length 9 and arclength 7π. Therefore,

$7\pi = 2\pi(9)\left(\dfrac{x}{360}\right)$. Simplifying the right side leads to the following

equation: $7\pi = 18\pi\dfrac{x}{360}$. Canceling common factors gives

$7\pi = \pi\dfrac{x}{20}$. Divide by π on both sides to get $7 = x/20$. Multiply by 20 on both sides to find $x = 140$.

4. (C)
Difficulty: M
Category: Circles
Strategy: Use the center-radius equation of the circle to find the center and radius of the circle given. Sketch the circle and the point. Draw a line through the points to find the other point where the line must intersect the circle.

Solution: The equation of the circle is given in center-radius form. From it, we can determine that the center of the circle is at $C(-2, 1)$ and the radius is 3. Below is a sketch of the circle and the point $S(-2, -2)$:

Note that S is located exactly three units down from the center. Therefore, to create a line segment that goes through the center, T must be located exactly three units above the center and should be at $(-2, 1 + 3) = (-2, 4)$.

5. (C)
Difficulty: M
Category: Circles
Strategy: Find the center of the circle by finding the midpoint of the points given. Find the diameter by finding the distance between the points. Divide this value by 2 to find the radius. Plug the center and radius into the center-radius form of the equation of the circle. Alternatively, plug the (x, y) endpoints into the equations. Endpoints of the diameter lie on the circle, so the (x, y) pairs will satisfy the correct circle equation.
Solution: Evaluate the midpoint of $(2, 5)$ and $(-4, -3)$ to find the center of the circle. Center = Midpoint = $((2 + -4)/2, (5 + -3)/2) = (-1, 1)$. The distance between the two points is equal to the length of the diameter = $\sqrt{(2 - -4)^2 + (5 - -3)^2} = \sqrt{36 + 64} = 10$. Thus, the radius must have length 5. The center-radius equation for a circle is $(x - h)^2 + (y - k)^2 = r^2$, where the center is at (h, k) and r = radius. Therefore, the correct equation of the circle should be is $(x + 1)^2 + (y - 1)^2 = 25$.

6. (C)
Difficulty: M
Category: Circles
Strategy: The radius is known and can be plugged into the center-radius form of the equation of the circle. Plug the point given into each equation in the answers to determine which circle contains the point. Use process of elimination.
Solution: The center-radius equation for a circle is $(x - h)^2 + (y - k)^2 = r^2$, where the center is at (h, k) and r = radius. While the center is not given in the problem, $r = 9$, so $r^2 = 81$. Eliminate choice A, which lists a circle with a radius of 3. A circle passes through a point (x, y) if x and y satisfy the circle equation. Plug in $x = -\sqrt{7}$ and $y = -\sqrt{2}$ into each equation to determine which circle passes through the point:

B: $\left(-\sqrt{7} + 3\sqrt{7}\right)^2 + \left(-\sqrt{2} - 2\sqrt{2}\right)^2 = 28 + 18 \neq 81$.

C: $\left(-\sqrt{7} + 4\sqrt{7}\right)^2 + \left(-\sqrt{2} - 2\sqrt{2}\right)^2 = 63 + 18 = 81$.

D: $\left(-\sqrt{7} + 4\sqrt{7}\right)^2 + \left(-\sqrt{2} - 3\sqrt{2}\right)^2 = 63 + 32 \neq 81$.

Only answer choice C describes an equation that contains the point.

7. (D)
Difficulty: M
Category: Circles
Strategy: Find the center of the circle by finding the midpoint of the points given. Find the diameter by finding the distance between the points. Divide this value by 2 to find the radius. Plug the center and radius into the center-radius form of the equation of the circle. Alternatively, plug the (x, y) endpoints into the equations. Endpoints of the diameter lie on the circle, so the (x, y) pairs will satisfy the correct circle equation.
Solution: The center is the midpoint of $(2, -3)$ and $(2, 11)$, which is $((2 + 2)/2, (-3 + 11)/2) = (2, 4)$. Find the radius by counting the difference in the y value between either of the two given points and the center. The radius is 7. The center-radius equation for a circle is $(x - h)^2 + (y - k)^2 = r^2$, where the center is at (h, k) and $r = $ radius. Therefore, the correct equation of the circle should be is $(x - 2)^2 + (y - 4)^2 = 49$.

8. (B)
Difficulty: M
Category: Circles
Strategy: Find the circumference of the circle. Divide by 6 to find the length of any of the congruent arcs.
Solution: The circumference of a circle $= 2\pi r$. Thus, the circle has circumference $2\pi(12) = 24\pi$ cm. If this circumference is divided into 6 congruent arcs, each will have a length of $(1/6) \cdot 24\pi = 4\pi$ cm.

9. (A)
Difficulty: (M)
Category: Circles
Strategy: Use the information given to determine the height of the equilateral triangle. Use the ratio of the sides of a 30-60-90 triangle to find the length of half of the base of the equilateral triangle. Determine the length of the base. Find the area of the triangle.
Solution: Given that the diameter of the circle is $20\sqrt{3}$, the radius of the circle must be $10\sqrt{3}$. Because vertex v of the triangle is at the midpoint of the radius, conclude that the height of the triangle directly along the segment of the radius shown is $5\sqrt{3}$. The radius of the circle as shown bisects the vertex angle v and the base of the equilateral triangle. Since all angles in the triangle are 60°, the radius of the circle cuts the equilateral triangle into two congruent 30-60-90 triangles. The ratio of the sides of a 30-60-90 triangle are always in a $1 : \sqrt{3} : 2$ ratio. Since the length of the side opposite the 60° angle is $5\sqrt{3}$, the side opposite the 30° angle (i.e. half the base of the equilateral triangle) must be 5. Thus, the length of the base of the triangle is 10. The area of a triangle is $(1/2)bh = (1/2) \cdot 10 \cdot 5\sqrt{3} \approx 43.30$.

10. (D)
Difficulty: M
Category: Circles
Strategy: Set the formula for the arclength equal to the length of arc AB. Solve for the length of the radius. Cube the value.
Solution: For a central angle x, arclength $= 2\pi r\left(\dfrac{x}{360}\right)$. Therefore, $2.7\pi = 2\pi r\left(\dfrac{36}{360}\right) = \dfrac{1}{5}\pi r$. Cancel π on both sides and solve to find $r = 13.5$. Cube the value to find $13.5^3 \approx 2460.375$.

11. (D)
Difficulty: M
Category: Circles
Strategy: A circle with radius r is tangent to both the x and y axes if its center is r units away from both axes. Note that the answers list equations in the center-radius form of the equation of a circle. It may be useful to quickly sketch each choice to determine which of the circles' centers will be 7 units away from both axes. Use process of elimination.
Solution: The standard formula for a circle is $(x - h)^2 + (y - k)^2 = r^2$, where the radius is r and the center of the circle is (h, k). Each circle shows the correct radius, so only the position of the center matters when choosing the correct answer. A circle with $r = 7$ that is tangent to both the x and y axes should have its center 7 units from each axis. Thus, $|h| = |k| = 7$. Only answer choice D shows a circle with these characteristics.

12. (D)
Difficulty: H
Category: Circles
Strategy: Use the information in the diagram to determine the measure of angle ACB. Subtract this value from 90 to find the measure of angle BCD. Use the formula for arc length to find the length of arc BD.
Solution: Note that triangle ACB is isosceles because line segments CB and CA are congruent radii of length 7. Therefore, angle CBA is congruent to angle CAB, which has measure 55°. Thus, the measure of angle ACB is $180 - 2(55) = 70°$ (You can also determine this fact by noting that angles FCE and ACB are congruent vertical angles). Subtract this from 90 to find the measure of angle $DCB = 90 - 70 = 20°$. For a central angle x, arclength $= 2\pi r\left(\dfrac{x}{360}\right)$. Therefore, length of arc $BD = 2\pi(7)\left(\dfrac{20}{360}\right) = 14\pi\left(\dfrac{1}{18}\right) = \dfrac{7\pi}{9}$.

13. (D)
Difficulty: H
Category: Circles
Strategy: Draw the line segment CO. Mark all other known lengths and angles in the figure. Determine the central angle. Use the formula for sector area.
Solution: Draw the line segment CO in the figure. Note that triangles OAC and OBC are congruent right triangles. They both have 90-degree angles since tangent lines to circles are always perpendicular to the radii drawn to the point of tangency. Both have an angle of $30/2 = 15°$. Therefore, the measures of angles AOC and BOC are both $180 - 90 - 15 = 75°$. Thus, central angle AOB is $2 \cdot 75° = 150°$. For a central angle x, sector area $= \pi r^2\left(\dfrac{x}{360}\right)$. Therefore, sector area $= \pi(6)^2\dfrac{150}{360} = 36\pi \cdot \dfrac{5}{12} = 15\pi$.

14. (B)
Difficulty: H
Category: Circles
Strategy: Complete the square twice (once for the terms with variable x and once for the terms with variable y) to find the center-radius form of the equation of the circle. Find the radius and multiply by 2.
Solution: $x^2 - 5x + y^2 + 10y = -100 + 75 = -25$.
$x^2 - 5x + (-5/2)^2 + y^2 + 10y + (10/2)^2 = -25 + (-5/2)^2 + (10/2)^2$.
Therefore, $(x - 2.5)^2 + (y + 5)^2 = 6.25$.
The equation is now in center-radius form. The radius is the square root of $6.25 = 2.5$. The diameter is twice this length, which is 5.

15. (D)
Difficulty: H
Category: Circles
Strategy: Determine the initial center and radius of the circle from the circle's equation. Determine how far the circle must move to the right if it completes three revolutions. Add this value to the x-coordinate of the initial center to determine the center of the circle's new position.
Solution: The circle starts with a center at $(-\pi, 1)$. Its radius is 1. One complete clockwise rotation of the circle moves the center a full circumference length to the right. The circumference of the circle is 2π. After three complete rotations, the x-coordinate of the center will be shifted 6π units to the right. Thus, the center of the circle at its final position will be $(-\pi + 6\pi, 1) = (5\pi, 1)$. It still has radius 1, so the center-radius equation of the circle at its final position should be $(x - 5\pi)^2 + (y - 1)^2 = 1$.

16. (B)
Difficulty: H
Category: Circles
Strategy: It may be useful to sketch a graph of the circles. Determine the centers and radii of the two circles. Find the distance between the centers. Then, subtract the radii of both circles to find the shortest distance between any two points on the figures.
Solution: The first circle has center at $(4, -2)$ and has a radius of length 9. The second circle has center at $(-16, -23)$ and has a radius of length 4. The shortest distance lies on the line segment that connects the centers of the two circles. First, calculate the length of the line segment using the distance formula:
$\sqrt{(4--16)^2 + (-2--23)^2} = \sqrt{20^2 + 21^2} = \sqrt{841} = 29$. The radii of the two circles are 9 and 4, a total of 13. The distance between the two circles is the distance between the two midpoints minus the lengths of their respective radii: $29 - 13 = 16$.

Additional Topics in Math – Volume & Surface Area – Pages 499-503

1. (C)
Difficulty: E
Category: Volume & Surface Area
Strategy: Set the formula for volume equal to the maximum capacity of the wastebasket and solve for s. Alternatively, work backwards through the problem and plug the answers into the formula given for volume.
Solution: Set the formula for volume equal to the maximum capacity, and solve for s: $(7/12) \cdot s^3 = 1008$. To eliminate the fraction, multiply both sides by 12 to get $7s^3 = 12096$. Divide by 7 on both sides to get $s^3 = 1728$. Take the cube root of both sides to find $s = 12$.

2. (A)
Difficulty: E/M
Category: Volume & Surface Area
Strategy: Use the formula for the volume of a cone given on the test form.
Solution: The volume of a cone is $(1/3) \cdot \pi r^2 h$, where r is the radius of the circular base, and h is the height of the cone. Note that this formula is listed at the beginning of every math section on the SAT test. The problem states that the diameter of the base is 10 in, and so the radius must have a length of 5 in. The height is 10 in. Plugging into the equation gives a total volume of $\frac{1}{3}\pi(5)^2 \cdot 10 = \frac{250\pi}{3}$ cubic inches.

3. (B)
Difficulty: E
Category: Volume & Surface Area
Strategy: Find the surface area of one corner cut and compare it to the surface area of the corner it is replacing. Alternatively, find the surface area of the figure after all cuts are made and compare it to the surface area of the original cube. Find the percent change. Note that this method is more time consuming.
Solution: Note that while the volume of the surface will change, the surface area will not. Since the cuts are all at right angles, the 3×3 faces of each cut can be shifted in a parallel direction to restore the original 9×9 cube faces. Thus, the surface areas of the original and notched cube are the same. The percent change in surface area is 0%.

4. (C)
Difficulty: M
Category: Volume & Surface Area
Strategy: Find the volume of the prism and the pyramid using the formulas given on the test form. Sum the values.
Solution: The volume of a rectangular right pyramid is $(1/3)lwh$, where lw is the area of the base of the pyramid, and h is the height of the pyramid. The base of the square right pyramid is congruent to the base of the prism, which has an area of 9 square inches (since it is a square base, you can infer that the side lengths of the square base have length 3 inches, but this information is not needed for the problem). The height of the pyramid is twice the height of the prism, so it must have a height of $2 \cdot 1.5 = 3$ inches. Therefore, the volume of the pyramid $= (1/3) \cdot 9 \cdot 3 = 9$ cubic inches. The volume of the prism is the area of the base times the height. Thus, the volume of the prism is $9 \cdot 1.5 = 13.5$ cubic inches. The total volume of the post cap is the sum of these two volumes, which is 22.5 cubic inches.

5. (D)

Difficulty: M

Category: Volume & Surface Area

Strategy: Evaluate the volume of the oil drum using the formula for the volume of a cylinder given on the test form. Then, use the density to convert the volume of the biodiesel to its weight in pounds.

Solution: The volume of a cylinder is $\pi r^2 h$, where r is the radius, and h is the height. Note that this formula is listed at the beginning of every math section on the SAT test. Since the oil drum will be completely filled, the volume of the biodiesel should equal the volume of the drum. Therefore, the volume of the biodiesel = $\pi(11.25)^2 \cdot 33.5 \approx 13,320$ in^3. The density of the biodiesel is .0316 lb/in^3. This value can be used to convert the volume measurement to the weight of the biodiesel in the drum:

$$13320 in^3 \cdot \frac{.0316 lb}{1 in^3} \approx 421 lb.$$

6. (A)

Difficulty: M

Category: Volume & Surface Area

Strategy: Find the volume of the cylindrical container using the formula for the volume of a cylinder. Find the volume of the three spherical tennis balls using the formula for the volume of a sphere. Find the difference.

Solution: The volume of the empty space surrounding the tennis balls should be the volume of the cylindrical container minus the volume of the three spherical balls. The volume of a cylinder is $\pi r^2 h$. The diameter of the cylindrical base is 6 cm, so the radius must be half this length, or 3 cm. The height of the container is equal to three times the diameters, so the height $h = 3 \cdot 8 = 18$ cm. Therefore, the volume of the cylindrical can is $\pi(3)^2(18) = 162\pi$. The volume of a sphere is $(4/3)\pi r^3$. The diameter of the spherical tennis ball is 6 cm, and so its radius must be 3 cm. Therefore, the volume of one of the spherical tennis balls is $(4/3)\pi(3)^3 = 36\pi$. There are three balls, each with the same volume, so the total volume of all three balls is $3 \cdot 36\pi = 108\pi$. The volume of the space surrounding the balls must then be $162\pi - 108\pi = 54\pi$.

7. (C)

Difficulty: M

Category: Volume & Surface Area

Strategy: Find the original volume using the formula for the volume of a rectangular prism. Find the length and width of the new crates, and then calculate the new total volume. Use the percent change formula to determine the percent increase in volume.

Solution: The volume of a rectangular prism is lwh, where l is the length, w is the width, and h is the height. The original crate used has a volume of $24 \cdot 36 \cdot 18 = 15,552$ in^3. The width of the new crate is 110% of the original width = $1.1 \cdot 36 = 39.6$ in. The new length is 115% of the original length = $1.15 \cdot 24 = 27.6$ in. The depth, or height, is unchanged, so depth = 18 in. The volume of the new crate is $39.6 \cdot 27.6 \cdot 18 = 19,673.28$ in^3. The percent change formula = (change/original) $\cdot$ 100%. Plug in to find the percent change in volume = $((19,673.28 - 15,552)/15,552) \cdot 100\% = 26.5\%$, which rounds to 27%.

8. (D)

Difficulty: M

Category: Volume & Surface Area

Strategy: Draw a sketch of the gas canister. Use the radius and length given to find the height of the cylinder. Evaluate the volume of the cylinder using the formula for the volume of a cylinder. The two hemispheres add up to one sphere, so find the volume of the hemispheres using the formula for the volume of a sphere. Add the volumes.

Solution: The height of the cylinder is the total length of the canister minus two times the radius of the hemispheres (the radius of the cylinder is equal to the radius of the two hemispheres, so both are 12 ft). Thus, $h = 104 - 2(12) = 104 - 24 = 80$. The volume of a cylinder is $\pi r^2 h = \pi(12)^2(80) = 11,520\pi$. The two hemispheres together form one sphere with a radius of 12 ft. The volume of a sphere is $(4/3)\pi r^3$. So, the volume of the two hemispheres = $(4/3)\pi(12)^3 = 2304\pi$. To find the volume of the gas canister, add the volume of the cylinder and sphere to get $11,520\pi + 2304\pi = 13,824\pi$.

9. (A)

Difficulty: M

Category: Volume & Surface Area

Strategy: Find the volume of the box using the formula for the volume of a rectangular prism. Set this value equal to the formula for the volume of a sphere. Solve for r.

Solution: The volume of the plastic box is $4 \cdot 3 \cdot 8 = 96$. The volume of a sphere is $(4/3)\pi r^3$. Thus, $96 = (4/3)\pi r^3$.

Multiply both sides by (3/4) to get $72 = \pi r^3$. Divide by π on both sides to find $r^3 \approx 22.92$. Take the cube root to find $r \approx 2.84$.

10. (A)

Difficulty: (M)

Category: Volume & Surface Area

Strategy: Find the total surface area that will be covered with snow (the area of the driveway – the area of the two cars + the area of the walkway). Convert the height of the snow into feet. Find the volume of snow that Zack will need to remove by multiplying the area by the height of the snow. Finally, use the rate of the snow removal to convert the volume into the number of hours it will take Zack to complete the job.

Solution: Zack must clear surfaces made up of the driveway – a large rectangle – minus two smaller rectangles, which are the vehicles. Add to that another rectangle that represents the walkway. The total area that he needs to clear is $(20 \cdot 70) + (4 \cdot 10) - (2 \cdot 6 \cdot 12) = 1400 + 40 - 144 = 1296$ square feet. 18 inches of snow has accumulated, but the measurement must first be converted to feet. 18 in. $\cdot$ (1ft/12in) = 1.5 ft. The total volume of snow Zack must remove is the area he needs to clear times the height of the snow = $1296 \cdot 1.5 = 1944$ cubic feet. He uses a snowblower which removes 400 cubic feet per hour, so the time it will take him to remove the snow is 1944 ft$^3 \cdot$ (1hr/400 ft^3) $\approx$ 4.9 hours.

11. (C)
Difficulty: (M)
Category: Volume & Surface Area
Strategy: Find the volume of the liquid by computing the volume of the cylinder. Find the volume of the cube into which Jake transferred the liquid. Compare the values. Use process of elimination.
Solution: The volume of a cylinder is $\pi r^2 h$. The diameter of the cylinder base is 6, so the radius must be half this length, or 3. The height of the container is equal to twice the diameter, so the height $h = 2 \cdot 6 = 12$. Thus, the volume of the liquid = volume of the cylinder = $\pi(3)^2(12) \approx 339.3$.

The volume of a cube with side length s is s^3. Therefore, the volume of the cube container into which the liquid is transferred is $7^3 = 343$. This volume is only slightly larger (but not equal) to the volume of the cylinder. Therefore, the cube will hold all of the liquid with just a little bit of room left to spare.

12. (B)
Difficulty: M
Category: Volume & Surface Area
Strategy: Convert the side length of the storage bin into feet. Find the total surface area of one of the storage bins in cubic feet. Multiply by 6 to determine the total surface area of all 6 storage containers. Multiply by 3 to find the total surface area of paint needed to cover all bins with three coats. Divide this quantity by 40, and round up to determine how many cans of paint will be required.
Solution: Each storage bin has a side length of 18 inches · 1ft/12in = 1.5 ft. The surface area of one side of the bin is $1.5 \cdot 1.5 = 2.25$ ft^2. The cube has 5 faces (one of the faces of the cube is missing to allow access), so the total surface area of each storage bin is $5 \cdot 2.25 = 11.25$ ft^2. There are 6 storage bins, so they have a total surface area of $6 \cdot 11.25 = 67.5$ ft^2. Each of the bins will be coated 3 times, so the total surface area of paint required is $3 \cdot 67.5 = 202.5$ ft^2. Each can of paint can cover 40 ft^2. Use this fact to convert the surface area of paint needed into cans of paint required: 202.5 ft^2 · (1 can/40 ft^2) = 5.0625 cans. 5 cans would not be quite enough, so the handyman will need 6 cans of paint to complete the job.

13. (C)
Difficulty: H
Category: Volume & Surface Area
Strategy: Convert 0.5 inches into centimeters. Find the volume of rain that will be collected using the formula for the volume of a cylinder. Set this equal to the formula for the volume of a cone. Find the relationship between r and h, and express r in terms of h for the inverted cone given. Solve for h.
Solution: First, convert 0.5 inches into centimeters: 0.5 in · (2.54 cm/in) = 1.27 cm of rain. The volume of rain that the cone will capture is equivalent to volume of a cylinder with the radius of the cone and a height of 0.5 in. The volume of a cylinder is $\pi r^2 h$. The diameter of the cylinder is the same as the diameter of the cone, which is 20 cm. The radius must be half this length, or 10 cm. The height of the cylinder of rain captured is equal to the inches of rainfall = 1.27 inches. Therefore, the volume of rain collected = $\pi(10)^2(1.27) = 127\pi$. A cross section of the empty cone in the problem is a triangle with a ratio of height : radius = $h{:}r = 20{:}10$ or 2:1. Therefore $r = 0.5h$. The formula for the volume of a cone is $(1/3)\pi r^2 h = (1/3)\pi(0.5h)^2 h = (1/12)\pi h^3$. Set this formula equal to the volume of the rainwater collected and solve for h (the water level in the cone):
$(1/12)\pi h^3 = 127\pi$. Divide both sides by π to get $(1/12)h^3 = 127$. Multiply both sides by 12 to find $h^3 = 1524$ cm^3. Take the cube root to find $h \approx 11.5$ cm.

14. (D)
Difficulty: H
Category: Volume & Surface Area
Strategy: Find the volume of 1.5 inch of rainfall that would be collected by evaluating the volume of a cylinder with the appropriate dimensions. Set this equal to the formula for the volume of a cone. Find the relationship between r and h for the inverted cone given, and express r in terms of h. Solve for h. Then, subtract your answer from question 16 to find the additional height.
Solution: First, convert 1.5 inches into centimeters: 1.5 in · (2.54 cm/in) = 3.81 cm of rain. The volume of rain that the cone will capture is equivalent to volume of a cylinder with the radius of the base of the cone and a height of 3.81 cm. The volume of a cylinder is $\pi r^2 h$. The diameter of the cylinder is the same as the diameter of the cone, which is 20 cm. The radius must be half this length, or 10 cm. The height of the cylinder of rain captured is equal to the inches of rainfall = 3.81 inches. Therefore, the volume of rain collected = $\pi(10)^2(3.81) = 381\pi$. A cross section of the empty cone in the problem is a triangle with a ratio of height : radius = $h{:}r = 20{:}10$ or 2:1. Therefore $r = 0.5h$. The formula for the volume of a cone is $(1/3)\pi r^2 h = (1/3)\pi(0.5h)^2 h = (1/12)\pi h^3$. Set this formula equal to the volume of the rainwater collected and solve for h (the water level in the cone): $(1/12)\pi h^3 = 381\pi$. Divide both sides by π to get $(1/12)h^3 = 381$. Multiply both sides by 12 to find $h^3 = 4572$ cm^3. Take the cube root to find $h \approx 16.6$ cm. Subtract the answer from the solution in problem 16 to find the additional height the rain takes up = $16.6 - 11.5 = 5.1$ cm.

15. (A)
Difficulty: H
Category: Volume & Surface Area
Strategy: Convert 287 cm into inches. Set this value equal to the circumference of a circle and solve for r, the radius of the sphere. Evaluate the volume of the ball using the formula for the volume of a sphere.
Solution: First, convert 287 cm into inches: 287 cm · (1 in/2.54 cm) $\approx$ 113 in. The circumference of a circle is $2\pi r$. So, $2\pi r = 113$ in. Solve for r to find $r \approx 17.98$ inches. The volume of a sphere is $(4/3)\pi r^3$. Thus, the volume of the beach ball is $(4/3)\pi(17.98)^3 \approx 24,361$ in^3. Rounded to the nearest thousand cubic inches, the value is 24,000.

16. (4)
Difficulty: H
Category: Volume & Surface Area
Strategy: Set the volume of water that Cone Inc. cones can hold equal to the volume of a right circular cone. Solve for h, the height of the cone. Find the volume of water that the competitor cones can hold. Find the height of their cones using the information in the problem. Set the new volume equal to the formula for the volume of a cone and find the radius of the competitor's cone. Multiply by 2 to find the diameter.
Solution: The original cone has a diameter of 2 cm, and so its radius must be 1 cm. The formula for the volume of a cone is $(1/3)\pi r^2 h$. Therefore, $2250\pi = (1/3)\pi(1)^2 h$. Divide both sides by $(1/3)\pi$ to find $h = 6750$ cm. The competitor's cone holds $4 \cdot 2250\pi = 9000\pi$ cubic centimeters of water, and its height is still 6750 cm. Thus,

$$9000\pi = \frac{1}{3}\pi r^2 (6750) \rightarrow r^2 = 4 \rightarrow r = 2 \rightarrow d = 4.$$

17. (D)

Difficulty: H

Category: Volume & Surface Area

Strategy: Use the given information to find all of the diameters and heights of the three cylindrical cups. Compute their volumes using the formula for the volume of a cylinder. Multiply the volume of cup A by 3, the volume of cup B by 2, and the volume of cup C by 3. Sum the three values to find the total volume of ingredients used.

Solution: From the given information, find that A has a diameter of 5 cm (half the diameter of C), which is a radius of 2.5 cm and a height of 8 cm. This means $V_A = \pi(2.5)^2(8) = 50\pi$ cm³. Cup B has twice the radius of A, so its radius must be 5 cm. It has the same height as A, so $h = 8$ cm. Therefore, $V_B = \pi(5.0)^2(8) = 200\pi$ cm³. Cup C has the same radius as B and half the height, so $V_C = \pi(5.0)^2(4) = 100\pi$ cm³. Three of cup A, two of cup B, and four of cup C would have a total volume of $3(50\pi) + 2(200\pi) + 4(100\pi) = 950\pi$ cm³ ≈ 3000 cm³.

18. (A)

Difficulty: H

Category: Volume & Surface Area

Strategy: Find the original surface area of the cube in terms of s. Find the new surface area after the cylindrical hole is drilled. You will need to subtract the area of the top and bottom faces of the cylinder and add the lateral surface area of the cylinder drilled. Determine the percent increase in surface area by using the percent change formula. Alternatively, pick a number for s and evaluate the percent change numerically.

Solution: The surface area of the cube is $6s^2$. Drilling a round hole increases the cube's surface area by the lateral surface area of a cylinder and reduces the cube's surface area by the area of two circles. The cylinder has a radius of $s/8$ and a height of s; The circular tops have a radius of $s/8$.

The new surface area $= 6s^2 + 2\pi rh - 2\pi r^2$. Substituting in $r = s/8$ and $h = s$, the new surface area $= 6s^2 + 2\pi(s/8)(s) - 2\pi(s/8)^2 = 6s^2 +$

$2\pi\dfrac{s}{8}s - 2\pi\left(\dfrac{s}{8}\right)^2 = 6s^2 + 2\pi\dfrac{7}{64}s^2 = 6s^2 + \dfrac{7\pi}{32}s^2$. Percent change $=$ (change/original) $\cdot$ 100%. So, the percent change $=$

$\dfrac{6s^2 + \dfrac{7\pi}{32}s^2 - 6s^2}{6s^2} \cdot 100\% = \dfrac{\dfrac{7\pi}{32}s^2}{6s^2} \cdot 100\% \approx 11.5\%$.

19. (D)

Difficulty: H

Category: Volume & Surface Area

Strategy: Find the linear scale factor by taking the cube root of the volume scale factor. Then square the result.

Solution: The scale factor of volume is k^3, where k is the linear scale factor (the area scale factor would be k^2). Since the ratio of the volumes is $5\sqrt{5}:1$, the linear ratio is $\sqrt[3]{5\sqrt{5}}:\sqrt[3]{1}$. This is simplified to $\sqrt{5}:1$. The area scale factor is this ratio squared, i.e. 5:1.

Additional Topics in Math – Trigonometry – Pages 505-508

1. (C)

Difficulty: E

Category: Trigonometry

Strategy: Convert from radians into degrees.

Solution: To convert from radians into degrees, multiply by $\dfrac{180°}{\pi}$:

$\dfrac{5\pi}{4} \cdot \dfrac{180°}{\pi} = 225°$.

2. (B)

Difficulty: E

Category: Trigonometry

Strategy: Label the length of the hypotenuse on the figure and use SOH CAH TOA to solve for the length of the line segment.

Solution: SOH CAH TOA states that the sine of an acute angle in a right triangle is equal to the opposite side length over the hypotenuse (SOH). The problem states that the length of the hypotenuse is 5. The opposite side to angle B is the line segment AC. Therefore, $\sin B = AC/5 = 0.85$. Multiply the equation through by 5 to solve for the length of line segment $AC = (.85) \cdot 5 = 4.25 \approx 4.3$.

3. (A)

Difficulty: E

Category: Trigonometry

Strategy: There is a trigonometry identity that may be used to solve this very quickly, but the problem can also be solved by drawing a triangle with the ratio listed and using SOH CAH TOA to find the trigonometric value asked for in the problem.

Solution: Since angles a and b are the acute angles of a right triangle, then they must be complementary, which means that they sum to 90°. In general, $\sin a° = \cos(90 - a°)$. Since $b° = 90° - a°$, then $\sin a = \cos b$. Conclude that $\cos b = 1/\sqrt{5}$.

4. (B)

Difficulty: E/M

Category: Trigonometry

Strategy: Draw a right triangle using vertices P and O, with a leg along the x-axis. Label the lengths of the sides of the triangle. Determine which special triangle is represented to determine the angle asked for in the problem. Then, convert the angle from degrees into radians.

Solution: From point P, draw a vertical line segment down toward the x-axis, and label the lengths of the two legs. Recognize that you have drawn an isosceles right triangle, i.e. the 45-45-90 special triangle. Thus, angle POQ measures 45 degrees. To convert from degrees into radians, multiply by $\pi/180$: $45 \cdot \pi/180 = \pi/4$.

5. (B)
Difficulty: M
Category: Trigonometry
Strategy: Conclude that triangles ABE and ACD are similar. Use the information given to find the length of line segment AC. Then find the length of AB. Use this value to set up a proportion to determine the length of BE.
Solution: SOH CAH TOA states that the sine of an acute angle in a right triangle is equal to the opposite side length over the hypotenuse (SOH). Therefore, $\sin A = CD/AC$. Plug in the information given to solve for the length of AC: $\frac{5}{13} = \frac{25}{AC}$. Cross-multiply and solve for AC to get line segment AC has length 65. Find the length of $AB = AC - BC = 65 - 39 = 26$. Note that ABE and ACD are similar (both share angle A and have a right angle). Set up a proportion to solve for the length of BE: $\frac{BE}{26} = \frac{25}{65}$. Cross-multiply and solve to find the length of BE is 10.

6. (C)
Difficulty: M
Category: Trigonometry
Strategy: Use SOH CAH TOA to find the base of the toy. Use SOH CAH TOA again with this length as the hypotenuse of the shadow. Don't round until the end of the question or you might get an incorrect answer
Solution: The base of the toy is the same length as the hypotenuse of the shadow. Find the length of the base first by using SOH CAH TOA: $\tan(56)$ = base/3. Multiply both sides by 3 to find base = $3\tan(56)$. Use SOH CAH TOA one more time to find the length of s in the shadow: $\cos(21) = s/(3\tan(56))$. Therefore, $s = \cos(21) \cdot 3\tan(56) \approx 4.152$.

7. (B)
Difficulty: M
Category: Trigonometry
Strategy: Draw the triangle and use SOH CAH TOA to write out possible lengths for the sides based on the values given in the problem. Use these lengths to determine which of the answer choices is correct. Use process of elimination.
Solution: Draw a sketch of the triangle, labeling all of the vertices. Since $\tan x = 3/4$, assume that two of the sides of the triangle are 3 and 4 (although they can be any multiple of these two values). SOH CAH TOA states that $\tan A$ = opposite/adjacent (TOA). Therefore, the side opposite to angle A can be labeled 3, and the side adjacent to angle A can be labeled 4. Use the Pythagorean theorem to find the hypotenuse has length 5. Check each answer to find which one is correct:

- $\sin x = \frac{opp}{hyp} = \frac{3}{5} \neq \frac{4}{5}$, so A is false.

- $\cos(90 - x) = \sin(x) = \frac{3}{5}$, so B is true.

- $\cos x = \frac{adj}{hyp} = \frac{4}{5} \neq \frac{3}{5}$, so C is false.

- $\sin(90 - x) = \cos x = \frac{4}{5} \neq \frac{3}{5}$, so D is false.

8. (C)
Difficulty: M
Category: Trigonometry
Strategy: Using SOH CAH TOA, label the triangle with possible lengths for the sides based on the values given in the problem. Use these lengths and SOH CAH TOA to determine the value of $\tan(p)$.
Solution: Since $\sin q = 12/13$, assume that two of the sides of the triangle are 12 and 13 (although they can be any multiple of these two values). SOH CAH TOA states that $\sin q$ = opposite/hypotenuse (SOH). Therefore, the side opposite to angle q can be labeled 12, and the hypotenuse can be labeled 13. Use the Pythagorean theorem to find the length of the other leg is 5 ($13^2 = 5^2 + 12^2$). The problem asks for the value of $\tan p$, which is the length of the side opposite to p divided by the side adjacent to angle p (TOA). Thus, $\tan p = 5/12$.

9. (A)
Difficulty: M
Category: Trigonometry
Strategy: Draw the triangle and use SOH CAH TOA to write out possible lengths for the sides based on the values given in the problem. Use these lengths and SOH CAH TOA to determine the value of $\cos D$.
Solution: Draw a sketch of the triangle, labeling all of the vertices. Since $\cos E = 15/17$, assume that two of the sides of the triangle are 15 and 17 (although they can be any multiple of these two values). SOH CAH TOA states that $\cos E$ = adjacent/hypotenuse (CAH). Therefore, the side adjacent to angle E can be labeled 15, and the hypotenuse can be labeled 17. Use the Pythagorean theorem to find the length of the other leg must be 8 ($8^2 + 15^2 = 17^2$). $\cos D$ = side adjacent to angle D/hypotenuse = 8/17.

10. (C)
Difficulty: M
Category: Trigonometry
Strategy: Substitute the value of x into the first equation, and solve for p. Substitute this value for p in the second equation. Solve for $\sin y$. Take the inverse sine to find a possible value for y.
Solution: Substitute $x = 90°$ into the first equation to find $16(1)/8 = 2 = 1/p$. Multiply by p on both sides to find $p = 0.5$. Plug this value in for p into the second equation to get $\frac{1}{2} = \frac{0.25\sqrt{2}}{\sin y}$. Cross multiply to find $\sin y = 0.5\sqrt{2}$. Take the inverse sine function to find a possible value for $y = \sin^{-1}(0.5\sqrt{2}) = 45°$.

11. (C)
Difficulty: M
Category: Trigonometry
Strategy: Sketch a diagram of a right triangle where one leg is the height of the lamppost, the other leg is the distance from Emily's feet to the base of the lamppost, and the hypotenuse is the distance from Emily's feet to the top of the lamppost (forming an angle of elevation of 48°). Use SOH CAH TOA to determine the height of the lamppost.
Solution: Let x = height of the lamppost. Based on the diagram, $\tan(48) = x/21$. Multiply both sides by 21 to find that $x = 21 \cdot \tan(48)$.

12. (B)
Difficulty: M
Category: Trigonometry
Strategy: Using SOH CAH TOA, label the triangle with lengths for the sides based on the values given in the problem. Use these lengths and the Pythagorean Theorem to determine a possible length of the hypotenuse.
Solution: The problem states that tan EFG = 2/7, which means that the side opposite to angle EFG must have length $2x$ and the side adjacent to angle EFG must have length $7x$. In order for these values to be integers, then x must be an integer. Use the Pythagorean theorem to determine the length of the hypotenuse in terms of x: $(2x)^2 + (7x)^2 = 53x^2 = $ hypotenuse^2. Therefore, the hypotenuse must have length $x\sqrt{53}$, where x is an integer. The only solution that takes this form is answer B.

13. (C)
Difficulty: M
Category: Trigonometry
Strategy: Use SOH CAH TOA to compute the length of line segment EZ. Then, use the Pythagorean Theorem to find the length of the missing leg.
Solution: The problem states that $\sin F = \dfrac{5}{\sqrt{32}}$. Use SOHCAHTOA to find that the length of line segment EZ must be 5. Use the Pythagorean Theorem to find the length of the missing leg: $EF^2 = \sqrt{32}^2 - 5^2 = 32 - 25 = 7$. Therefore, the length of $\overline{EF} = \sqrt{7}$.

14. (D)
Difficulty: M
Category: Trigonometry
Strategy: Convert the degree measurement into radians. Set this equal to $x\pi$ and solve for x.
Solution: To convert a degree measure from degrees to radians, multiply an angle's measurement in degrees by $\pi/180$. Therefore $1080° = 1080 \cdot \pi/180 = 6\pi$. If $6\pi = x\pi$, then $x = 6$.

15. (D)
Difficulty: H
Category: Trigonometry
Strategy: Use process of elimination. Rewrite each expression in the answer choices in terms of $\sin x$ and $\cos x$. Simplify to find the expression not equal to $\sin x$.
Solution: Choice A, tan $x \cdot \cos x$, can be rewritten as $\dfrac{\sin x}{\cos x} \cdot \cos x = \sin x$. Choice B, $\dfrac{1}{\csc x}$, can be rewritten as $\dfrac{1}{\dfrac{1}{\sin x}} = \sin x$. Choice C, $\sqrt{1 - \cos^2 x}$, is equal to $\sin x$ for all x defined, based on the fact that $\sin^2 x + \cos^2 x = 1$. Choice D, cot $x \cdot \sin x$, can be rewritten as $\dfrac{\cos x}{\sin x} \cdot \sin x = \cos x \neq \sin x$. Thus, D is correct.

16. (A)
Difficulty: H
Category: Trigonometry
Strategy: Use the identity $\sin^2 x + \cos^2 x = 1$ to find possible values for $\sin A$. Note which quadrant angle A is in to determine the correct sign of the value.

Solution: Substitute the known value into the trig identity $\sin^2 x + \cos^2 x = 1$ and solve for the unknown value. Note that the angle is in the third quadrant, because $\pi < m\angle A < \dfrac{3\pi}{2}$:
$\sin^2 A + 5/12 = 1$. Therefore, $\sin^2 A = 7/12$. Thus, $\sin A = \pm\sqrt{\dfrac{7}{12}} = \pm\dfrac{\sqrt{7}}{2\sqrt{3}} = \pm\dfrac{\sqrt{21}}{6}$. Since angle A is in the third quadrant, then $\sin A < 0$, and so $\sin A = -\dfrac{\sqrt{21}}{6}$.

17. (D)
Difficulty: H
Category: Trigonometry
Strategy: Draw the triangular cross-section of the cone that has a base equal to the length of the diameter and a height equal to the height of the cone. Draw an altitude from the angle to the base, splitting the isosceles triangle into equal halves. Use SOHCAHTOA to determine the length of the radius (the base of each half of the triangle). Multiply by 2 to find the diameter.
Solution: Draw the diagram described above. Note the altitude will split the isosceles triangle into two congruent triangles with vertex angle 12° (the altitude of an isosceles triangle is a bisector of the vertex angle and a perpendicular bisector of the base). Use SOHCAHTOA to determine the radius: tan (12) = radius/118. Solve to find radius = 118 tan (12°). Multiply by two to find the diameter = 236 tan(12°).

18. (C)
Difficulty: H
Category: Trigonometry
Strategy: Use rules of parallel lines to identify the values of x and $2x$. Use SOH CAH TOA to find the length of line segment FG.
Solution: Since $ABCH$ is a rectangle and line segments BH and CG are parallel, then $x = 19°$ (corresponding angles formed by a transversal intersecting parallel lines are congruent), and so $2x = 38°$. All the horizontal line segments in the diagram are 7 cm. In the triangle DFG, angle $FDG = 38°$, and $DG = 7$. Using SOH CAH TOA, conclude that tan (38) = FG/7. Thus, the length of line segment $FG = 7 \cdot$ tan (38) ≈ 5.47.

19. (C)
Difficulty: H
Category: Trigonometry
Strategy: Sum the angles and set them equal to 180 (the interior angles of a triangle must sum to 180). Determine the value of angle $a + b$. Then, check each answer choice and use process of elimination.
Solution: The sum of the angles in the triangle is $a + b + (a + b) = 2(a + b) = 180$. Therefore, $a + b = 90$. Since one of the angles in the triangle measures $(a + b)°$, or 90°, then the triangle must be a right triangle, and so Statement I is true. Additionally, in a right triangle, the sine of one of the non-right angles will always equal the cosine of the other, so statement III is also true. There is not enough information to either prove or disprove Statement II (since a does not necessarily have to equal b).

Additional Topics in Math – Complex Numbers – Pages 510-511

1. (C)

Difficulty: E

Category: Complex Numbers

Strategy: To add two complex numbers, sum the real parts together and sum the imaginary parts together.

Solution: To sum two complex numbers, just combine like terms: $5 + 6i + 2 - 2i = (5 + 2) + (6i - 2i) = 7 + 4i$.

2. (A)

Difficulty: E

Category: Complex Numbers

Strategy: Distribute the minus sign through the second parenthetical expression. Convert i^2 to its equivalent real number value. Combine all like terms.

Solution: Since $i = \sqrt{-1}$, $i^2 = -1$. Rewrite the expression: $(4 + 10i) - (4i^2 + 5i) = 4 + 10i - (-4 + 5i)$. Distribute the minus sign through to get $4 + 10i + 4 - 5i = 8 + 5i$.

3. (B)

Difficulty: E

Category: Complex Numbers

Strategy: To add two complex numbers, sum the real parts together and sum the imaginary parts together.

Solution: Eliminate the parentheses and combine like terms in the expression to simplify as a complex number of the form $a + bi$: $5 - 2i + 3i - 6 = -1 + i$.

4. (D)

Difficulty: E

Category: Complex Numbers

Strategy: Use the distributive property to expand the product. Convert i^2 to its equivalent real number value. Combine all like terms.

Solution: Begin by distributing the product: $-i(-2 + 6i) = 2i - 6i^2$. Since $i = \sqrt{-1}$, $i^2 = -1$. Therefore, $2i - 6i^2 = 6 + 2i$.

5. (D)

Difficulty: E

Category: Complex Numbers

Strategy: Expand the product by using the distributive property or FOIL. Convert i^2 to its equivalent real number value. Combine all like terms.

Solution: Use the distributive property to expand the product: $(2 + 3i)(1 - 2i) = 2 - 4i + 3i - 6i^2$. Since $i = \sqrt{-1}$, $i^2 = -1$. Substitute this value into the expression: $2 - 4i + 3i - 6i^2 = 2 - i + 6 = 8 - i$.

6. (C)

Difficulty: E/M

Category: Complex Numbers

Strategy: Multiply the top and bottom of the fraction by the complex conjugate of the denominator. Simplify.

Solution: Multiply the numerator and denominator of the fraction by the complex conjugate of the denominator (the complex conjugate of $a + bi$ is $a - bi$):

$$\frac{2 + 4i}{i} \cdot \frac{-i}{-i} = \frac{-2i - 4i^2}{-i^2}$$. Since $i^2 = -1$, the fraction can be simplified

further: $\frac{-2i - 4i^2}{-i^2} = \frac{-2i + 4}{1} = 4 - 2i$.

7. (C)

Difficulty: (M)

Category: Complex Numbers

Strategy: Rewrite the root as a product of the square root of –1 (or i) and the square root of 63. Then find if there are any square factors of 63 that can be taken out of the square root sign.

Solution: Since $i = \sqrt{-1}$, then $\sqrt{-63} = \sqrt{-1}\sqrt{63} = i\sqrt{7 \cdot 9}$

$= 3i\sqrt{7}$.

8. (D)

Difficulty: M

Category: Complex Numbers

Strategy: Multiply the top and bottom of the fraction by the complex conjugate of the denominator. Simplify.

Solution: Multiply the numerator and denominator of the fraction by the complex conjugate of the denominator (the complex conjugate of $a + bi$ is $a - bi$):

$\frac{13}{3+i} \cdot \frac{3-i}{3-i} = \frac{13(3-i)}{9-i^2} = \frac{39 - 13i}{9 - i^2}$. Since $i^2 = -1$, the fraction can be

simplified further: $\frac{39 - 13i}{9 - i^2} = \frac{39 - 13i}{9 + 1} = \frac{39 - 13i}{10}$.

9. (D)

Difficulty: M

Category: Complex numbers

Strategy: Note that the powers of i are periodic with a period of 4. Therefore, i raised to any power is the same as i raised to the remainder when the power is divided by 4. Use this fact to determine which answer choice is correct. If helpful, choose an integer value for k and evaluate the power of i.

Solution: The powers of i repeat with a period of four: $i^0 = 1$, $i^1 = i$, $i^2 = -1$, $i^3 = -i$. If you continue with consecutive higher powers, the cycle will begin to repeat this set of values. Since k is a positive integer, $12k$ must also be a positive integer that is divisible by 12 and thus also divisible by 4. Therefore, $i^{12k + 3} = i^{12k} \cdot i^3 = 1 \cdot i^3 = -i$.

10. (A)

Difficulty: M

Category: Complex Numbers

Strategy: Expand the product by using the distributive property or FOIL. Convert i^2 to its equivalent real number value. Combine all like terms.

Solution: $(3 + 2i)(3 + 2i) = 9 + 6i + 6i + 4i^2$. Since $i = \sqrt{-1}$, $i^2 = -1$. Substitute this value into the expression:
$9 + 6i + 6i + 4i^2 = 9 + 12i - 4 = 5 + 12i$.

11. (D)

Difficulty: H

Category: Complex Numbers

Strategy: Multiply the top and bottom of the fraction by the complex conjugate of the denominator. Simplify. Consider each statement and rewrite the expressions in the statements using the same procedure wherever needed. Use process of elimination.

Solution: Multiply the numerator and denominator of the fraction by the complex conjugate of the denominator (the complex conjugate of $a + bi$ is $a - bi$):

First, try re-expressing without i in the denominator:

$\dfrac{5+2i}{2+i} \cdot \dfrac{2-i}{2-i} = \dfrac{10-5i+4i-2i^2}{4-i^2} = \dfrac{10-i-2i^2}{4-i^2}$. Since $i^2 = -1$, the fraction can be simplified further:

$\dfrac{10-i-2i^2}{4-i^2} = \dfrac{10-i+2}{4+1} = \dfrac{12-i}{5} = \dfrac{12}{5} - \dfrac{i}{5}$.

Therefore, statement I must be true. Statement II must be false, since it shows a different complex number. Rewrite the expression in statement III using the same procedure used earlier:

$2 + \dfrac{1}{2+i} = 2 + \dfrac{1}{2+i}\left(\dfrac{2-i}{2-i}\right) = 2 + \dfrac{2-i}{5} = \dfrac{10}{5} + \dfrac{2-i}{5} = \dfrac{12-i}{5}$. This is

equivalent to the value of the original fraction, and so statement III is also true. Choice D is correct.

12. (C)

Difficulty: H

Category: Complex Numbers

Strategy: Multiply the top and bottom of the fraction by the complex conjugate of the denominator. Simplify.

Solution: Multiply the numerator and denominator of the fraction by the complex conjugate of the denominator (the complex conjugate of $a + bi$ is $a - bi$): $\dfrac{2+3i}{4-i} \cdot \dfrac{4+i}{4+i} = \dfrac{8+2i+12i+3i^2}{16-i^2} = \dfrac{8+14i+3i^2}{16-i^2}$.

Since $i^2 = -1$, the fraction can be simplified further:

$\dfrac{8+14i+3i^2}{16-i^2} = \dfrac{5+14i}{17}$.